Peasants, Lords, and State

The Northern World

NORTH EUROPE AND THE BALTIC C.400–1700 AD
PEOPLES, ECONOMIES AND CULTURES

VOLUME 89

The titles published in this series are listed at *brill.com/nw*

Peasants, Lords, and State

Comparing Peasant Conditions in Scandinavia and the Eastern Alpine Region, 1000–1750

Edited by

Tore Iversen
John Ragnar Myking
Stefan Sonderegger

BRILL

LEIDEN | BOSTON

Cover illustration: Miniature of three men scything grass, on a calendar page for June. (c) The British Library Board: Royal MS 2 B VII, ff 71r–83v: fol. 76v.

Library of Congress Cataloging-in-Publication Data

Names: Iversen, Tore, editor. | Myking, John Ragnar, editor. | Sonderegger, Stefan, editor.
Title: Peasants, lords, and state : comparing peasant conditions in Scandinavia and the Eastern Alpine region, 1000-1750 / edited by Tore Iversen, John Ragnar Myking, Stefan Sonderegger.
Other titles: Comparing peasant conditions in Scandinavia and the Eastern Alpine region, 1000-1750
Description: Leiden ; Boston : Brill, [2020] | Series: The Northern world, 1569-1462 ; vol.89 | Includes bibliographical references and index. |
Identifiers: LCCN 2020024555 (print) | LCCN 2020024556 (ebook) | ISBN 9789004429703 (hardback) | ISBN 9789004433458 (ebook)
Subjects: LCSH: Peasants--Scandinavia--History. | Peasants--Alps Region--History.
Classification: LCC HD1536.S29 P33 2020 (print) | LCC HD1536.S29 (ebook) | DDC 305.5/63309480902--dc23
LC record available at https://lccn.loc.gov/2020024555
LC ebook record available at https://lccn.loc.gov/2020024556

Typeface for the Latin, Greek, and Cyrillic scripts: "Brill". See and download: brill.com/brill-typeface.

ISSN 1569-1462
ISBN 978-90-04-42970-3 (hardback)
ISBN 978-90-04-43345-8 (e-book)

This book is printed on acid-free paper and produced in a sustainable manner.

Contents

PART 4
Appendix

Preface

Our project 'Peasants' control over land and resources from the High Middle Ages to the end of the early modern period – Norway, Scandinavia, and the eastern Alpine region 1000–1750' started in 2003 as a response to the tendency to isolate the study of agrarian societies within the framework of national or regional geographical limits. No matter how valuable and innovative such local and national studies may be, an unintended consequence may be that traits and developments common to a variety of countries or regions may be accentuated as features characteristic only of the country or region subject to the investigation. On the other hand, such studies may also overlook causes of national and regional development that can only be detected when highlighted by the historical development in other countries or regions.

Our primary aim with the project was to challenge a long-lasting perception that Scandinavian and especially Norwegian peasants had much greater self-determination then their European counterparts. Inspired by an unfinished project from the 1920s (see 'Introduction'), we have chosen the Alpine region as a suitable region for comparison with Scandinavia. In the Alpine region we have included Bavaria, which can serve as a suitable comparison to Scandinavian Denmark. To enable us to detect long-term changes, we have settled for a time span that covers the period from *c.* 1000 to around 1750.

The huge span of time and the multitude of available local, national, and regional studies have made our work challenging, and the sheer extent of the task may account for misreading and many misinterpretations of the work of outstanding colleges. Our hope is nevertheless that we have managed to accentuate traits that can explain similar, as well as different, developments in the two regions, thus creating a sound basis for evaluating the perception of a Scandinavian 'Sonderweg' when it comes to peasant self-determination.

Funding by the Norwegian Research Council in the period 2004–2007 enabled us to arrange three major seminars: Trondheim in 2004, Frauenchiemsee in 2005, and Bergen in 2007, in addition to three minor workshops in Copenhagen, Innsbruck, and Vienna in 2006. These sessions provided us with a wide network of contacts with Scandinavian- and German-speaking colleagues, which we have been fortunate to draw on in our project. We are greatly indebted to our colleges who contributed to these meetings. Some of their contributions are printed in this and our two previous publications (2005[1] and

1 Tore Iversen and John Ragnar Myking (eds), *Land, Lords and Peasants: Peasants' Right To Control Land in the Middle Ages and the Early Modern Period – Norway, Scandinavia and the Alpine Region*, Trondheim Studies in History, 52 (Trondheim: NTNU 2005).

2007[2]), along with articles written especially for these volumes. Our sincere thanks to everybody who participated in our project, either through papers or simply by taking part in the discussions.

Some colleagues have contributed to our project on a more regular basis than others. We are especially indebted to the late Gertrud Thoma (1956–2009), senior lecturer in medieval history at the University of Munich, who from the start acted as our German co-ordinator, organized our seminar in Frauenchiemsee, and enthusiastically introduced us to a well of German literature. She was also a co-editor of the second volume of our project. In our work, we also received great help from the late Professor Heinz Dopsch (1942–2014) at the University of Salzburg, whose comprehensive knowledge of Central European rural history made it easier for us to understand the complexity of the German historical tradition and its focus on the relationship between lordship and peasant society. Professor Stefan Sonderegger, Stadtarchiv St Gallen / University of Zurich, has been part of the project since 2007, greatly contributing to our understanding of the Alpine region with his insight into alpine rural history. After Dopsch's death in 2014, Sonderegger stepped in as co-editor of this final volume of the project.

Tore Iversen and John Ragnar Myking

2 Tore Iversen, John Ragnar Myking, and Gertrud Thoma (eds), *Bauern zwischen Herrschaft und Genossenschaft: Peasant Relations to Lords and Government. Scandinavia and the Alpine Region 1000–1750* (Trondheim: Tapir Akademisk Forlag, 2007).

Acknowledgements

This concluding volume to our project is long overdue. We would like to thank our contributors to the chapter on historiography, who delivered their contributions years ago, for their patience. A special thanks to Professor Michael Mitterauer and the late Professor Markus Cerman (1967–2015) who wrote their joint article on sub-peasant strata especially for this volume.
Thanks also to Maria Tranter for translating German texts into English, and to our copy-editor, Philadelphia Ricketts, who not only has secured a coherent and prudent English throughout the volume, but who has also called our attention to illogical reasoning and obscure formulations on our part.

Tore Iversen, John Ragnar Myking and Stefan Sonderegger

Figures

Notes on Contributors

Markus Cerman
(1967–2015) was professor of economic and social history at the University of Vienna. His publications include studies on European proto-industrialization and the development of agrarian institutions in late medieval and early modern Europe in a comparative perspective.

Tore Iversen
is professor emeritus in medieval history at the Norwegian University of Science and Technology. He has published monographs and articles on medieval slavery, property and land tenancy in a Scandinavian and European context.

Michael Mitterauer
is professor emeritus of social history at the University of Vienna. He has published numerous books and articles on social and economic history, including Why Europe? The Medieval Origins of Its Special Path.

John Ragnar Myking
is professor emeritus in medieval and early modern history at Western Norwegian University of Applied Sciences. He has published monographs and articles on local and regional history and land tenancy in a European context.

Josef Riedmann
is professor emeritus in medieval history at Leopold-Franzens-Universität-Innsbruck. He has published monographs and articles on the history of the Holy Roman Empire and Italy in the Middle Ages and on the history of the Tyrol.

Werner Rösener
is professor emeritus in medieval and modern history at the University of Giessen, Germany. He has published monographs and articles on agrarian history, the social and cultural history of European peasants as well as historiographical studies.

Helge Salvesen
is professor emeritus in medieval and early modern history and director of the Library at the University of Tromsø – The Arctic University of Norway. He has published monographs and articles on medieval and early modern economic and agrarian history, as well as sami history.

Stefan Sonderegger
is professor in medieval history at the University of Zurich and Head of the City Archive of St.Gallen, Switzerland. His research focus is on economic history and document edition.

PART 1

Introduction

CHAPTER 1

Historiographical and Methodological Reflections

Tore Iversen and John Ragnar Myking

This volume is the third and last publication from the research project titled 'Peasants' control over land and resources from the High Middle Ages to the end of the early modern period – Norway, Scandinavia, and the eastern Alpine region'.[1] The aim of the project is to render research-based knowledge about the degree of peasant control over land and resources in Scandinavia on the one hand, and the eastern Alpine region, including Bavaria, on the other. Furthermore, our ambition has been to gain a better understanding of the dynamic development of peasant control and influence in the intersection between local peasant communities and regional and national institutions, i.e., the church, the aristocracy, and territorial sovereigns. Our two first publications[2] dealt with regional studies related to central aspects of our project as a basis for further comparison, without aspiring to offer more than tentative attempts to draw comparative conclusions. In this volume, comparing different regions is our main methodology and our prime objective.

In our project, we have chosen the eastern Alpine region as a basis for a comparison with Scandinavia. Within Scandinavia, we have focused on Norway and Denmark as contrasting examples, with Sweden as a complementary object of our studies. Within the eastern Alpine region, we have focused on Bavaria and Tyrol, including South Tyrol, with excursions to Salzburg and the eastern part of Switzerland when an extended comparison seemed appropriate.

One of our aims has been to shed light on a widespread view, rooted in the historical thinking of the nineteenth century, that Scandinavian and especially Norwegian peasants experienced a special historical development compared to other European peasants north of the Alps.[3] According to this view, their

1 The project (2004–2007) was funded by the Norwegian Research Council.

2 Tore Iversen and John Ragnar Myking (eds), *Land, Lords and Peasants: Peasants' Right to Control Land in the Middle Ages and the Early Modern Period – Norway, Scandinavia and the Alpine Region*, Trondheim Studies in History, 52 (Trondheim: NTNU, 2005); Tore Iversen, John Ragnar Myking, and Gertrud Thoma (eds), *Bauern zwischen Herrschaft und Genossenschaft: Peasant Relations to Lords and Government. Scandinavia and the Alpine Region 1000–1750* (Trondheim: Tapir Akademinsk Forlag, 2007).

3 For an historiographical overview, see for exemple Bjørn Poulsen and Søren M. Sindbæk (eds), *Settlement and Lordship in Viking and Early Medieval Scandinavia* (Turnhout: Brepols, 2011), 4–5.

 | DOI:10.1163/9789004433458_002

special standing was characterized by 'peasant freedom', that is, much greater self-determination then their southern counterparts. The notion of 'peasant freedom' included the marginal existence of slaves and people with other kinds of unfree status, extensive control over land and agricultural products, widespread ownership of land, and comprehensive judicial influence through the institution of the *thing*. Some of the basis for this perception can be found in the Germanistic ideology of the nineteenth and early twentieth century.

One of the reasons for choosing Tyrol in the eastern Alpine region is its marked topographical resemblance to the mountainous parts of Scandinavia (Norway and the northern parts of Sweden). By including Bavaria, we can also contrast the fertile plains of Denmark and the southern parts of Sweden, until 1658 a part of Denmark, with the equally fertile plains of Bavaria. Topographical conditions play an important part in the development of agriculture and peasant conditions. Such factors have, therefore, traditionally been stressed by Norwegian agricultural historians in their comparison with continental countries. The mountainous areas of Norway and northern Sweden, and Tyrol in the eastern Alpine region, leave peasants with less land suited for cultivation but ample space for grazing and foresting. In Norway and northern Sweden, a northern or southern location, altitude, and, in part, the distance from the coastline determine conditions for agriculture, in much the same way as altitude does in the mountainous Alpine areas. On the other hand, the fertile plains with moraine soil in Bavaria, Denmark, and southern Sweden provide ample space for grain growing, securing a higher output of crops on limited land.[4]

The variation in topographic conditions is partly, but not entirely, responsible for a wide range of settlement patterns. Single farms are frequently found in parts of Norway, northern Sweden, and some of the Alpine areas, but we also find multiple settlements and villages in Scandinavia, as well as in the Alpine region.[5] Both regions are thus characterized by a complex topography and a wide range of settlement patterns, which may help us assess the influence of topography on the development of peasant conditions in the two regions, thus making it easier to evaluate the impact of other factors. Furthermore, except for the influence of the pan-European church organization, these two regions

4 Hansjörg Küster, *Geschichte der Landschaft in Mitteleuropa – von der Eiszeit bis zur Gegenwart* (Munich: Beck, 1996).

5 Werner Trossbach and Clemens Zimmermann, *Die Geschichte des Dorfes – von den Anfängen im Frankenreich zur bundesdeutschen Gegenwart* (Stuttgart: UTB, 2006); Bjørn Myhre and Ingvild Øye (eds), *Jorda blir levevei 4000 f.Kr. – 1350 e.Kr.*, i: Bjørn Myhre, Åsta Brenna, Ingvild Øye, and Reidar Almås (eds), *Norges landbrukshistorie* (Oslo: Samlaget, 2002), 286–94.

are sufficiently removed from each other to exclude extensive formative cultural contact.

We also have a historiographical motivation for comparing Scandinavia and the Alpine region. At the Norwegian Institute for Comparative Cultural Research (Institutt for sammenlignende kulturforskning), founded in Oslo in the 1920s, the historian Edvard Bull initiated a comparative research programme for the study of phases of development in peasant societies. In his work programme (1929), he pointed to the Alpine region as a region especially well suited for comparative studies with Norway and Sweden.[6] Bull maintained that the Austrian Alpine region especially had already been thoroughly studied when it came to peasant life and phases of development, and that a considerable amount of information thus was available for comparative research. This information could then make up the foundation for studies of an 'original conformity', similar to all peasant societies.[7] Strongly influenced by historic-materialistic thinking, Bull operated with a fundamental division between the economic *basis* of society and its *superstructure*. In this bipolar universe, the economic basis was the cardinal element in historical development.

Believing it possible to find valid laws of historical evolution, Bull's ambitious programme aimed at finding 'objective correlations' between different peasant societies. Knowledge should consequently be inductively structured from below.[8] The Second World War effectively stopped these comparative studies before they were properly established, and they were not resumed in

6 Edv. Bull, *Sammenlignende studier over bondesamfundets kulturforhold: Et arbeidsprogram*, Institutt for sammenlignende kulturforskning Serie C, 2.2 (Oslo: Institutt for sammenlignende kulturforskning, 1929).

7 Bull, *Sammenlignende studier*, 3–21. Bull managed to involve well-known historians, such as Marc Bloch and Alfons Dopsch in the project. Thus, Alfons Dopsch's renowned monography, *Die ältere Wirtschafts- und Sozial-geschichte der Bauern in den Alpenländern Österreichs*, Instituttet for sammenlignende kulturforskning Serie A, 11 (Oslo: Aschehoug, 1930) was published by the Norwegian Institute for Comparative Cultural Research. Other historians working within the same tradition include the renowned Tyrolean regional historian Otto Stolz. His monograph, *Die Schwaighöfe in Tirol. Ein Beitrag zur Siedlungs- und Wirtschaftsgeschichte der Hochalpentäler*, Deutscher und Österreichischer Alpenverein, Wissenschaftliche Veröfentlichungen, 5 (1930), inspired a similar study by the Norwegian historian Lars Reinton, published by the Norwegian Institute for Comparative Cultural Research: *Sæterbruket i Noreg i-iii* (Oslo: Institutt for sammenlignende kulturforskning, 1955, 1959, 1961).

8 The Norwegian Institute for Comparative Cultural Research's ambitious programme for comparing peasant societies aimed at finding a 'primordial homogeneousness' in human cultures, and furthermore discerning differences in cultural forms depending on 'external natural conditions, race, and historical development'. Based on a Marxist outlook from the 1920s, Bull maintained that comparative historical research in the future would be able to detect universal laws for historical development (Bull, *Sammenlignende studier*, 5 and 14f).

the post-war period.[9] Although our project may in one way be seen as a continuation of these planned comparative studies, our ambition is not to search for 'valid laws' or 'objective correlations'. It is, however, far easier to follow Bull's plan for *concrete* studies in which conspicuous parallels could outline conditions determining similarities and differences. Such studies may be aided by a substantial literature on agrarian history in Scandinavia and in the Alpine region.[10]

9 In a subsequently planned comparative project on landed property in ancient societies within the framework of the Institute for Comparative Cultural Research, the Norwegian agrarian historian Andreas Holmsen (1940) maintained that the Alpine countries were especially well suited to a comparison with Norway. (Application to the Institute for Comparative Cultural Researcnh (1940), enlarged on and printed as Andreas Holmsen, 'Problemer i norsk jordeiendomshistorie', in *Historisk tidsskrift (norsk)*, 34 (1946–48), 220–55.)

10 For Scandinavia, Helge Salvesen offers a survey of the Norwegian agrarian-historic tradition in 'The Strength of Tradition: A Historiographical Analysis of Research into Norwegian Agrarian History during the Late Middle Ages and the Early Modern Period', *Scandinavian Journal of History*, 7 (1982), 75–133, while the report Svend Gissel, Jørn Sandnes, and Eva Österberg (eds), *Desertion and Land Colonization in the Nordic Countries c. 1300–1600* (Stockholm: Almqvist and Wiksell, 1981), summarizes the findings of the 'Scandinavian Research Project on Deserted Farms and Villages' from the 1970s. From the end of the 1980s to the beginning of the first decade of the twenty-first century, national agrarian histories were published in several volumes in Denmark (1988–89), Sweden (1998–2001), and Norway (2002). One volume has been published in English for Sweden: Janken Myrdal and Mats Morell, *The Agrarian History of Sweden 4000 BC to AD 2000* (Lund: Nordic Academic Press, 2011) and one for Norway: Reidar Almås and Brynjulv Gjerdåker (eds), *Norwegian Agricultural History* (Trondheim: Tapir Academic Press, 2004). For Denmark, Nils Hybel and Bjørn Poulsen's *The Danish Resources c. 1000–1550: Growth and Recession*, The Northern World, 34 (Leiden: Brill, 2007) can be read as a substitute for an updated English version of the Danish agricultural history for the medieval period.
Since the 1980s, the rural societies of Germany, Austria, and especially Switzerland have been the object of comprehensive regional studies. For a historiography, see Julien Demade, 'The Medieval Countryside in German-language Historiography since the 1930s', in Isabel Alfonso Antón (ed.), *The Rural History of Medieval European Societies: Trends and Perspectives* (Turnhout: Brepols, 2007), 173–252. An excellent survey of German agrarian history can be found in the following contributions by Werner Rösener: 'Agrarwirtschaft, Agrarverfassung und ländliche Gesellschaft im Mittelalter', in Lothar Gall, et al. (eds), *Enzyklopädie deutsche Geschichte*, vol. 13 (Munich: Oldenbourg, 1992); 'Die Erforschung der Grundherrschaft', in Ruprecht Kurzrock (ed.), *Mittelalterforschung*, Forschung und Information, 29 (Berlin: Colloquium Verlag), 1981), 57–65. For a wider European setting, see Werner Rösener, *Bauern im Mittelalter* (Munich: C.H. Beck, 1985); Engl. trans. as *Peasants in the Middle Ages* (Cambridge: Polity Press, 1997). For Bavaria, see Philippe Dollinger, *Der bayerischen Bauernstand vom 9. bis zum 13.Jahrhundert* (Munich: C.H. Beck, 1982) and Helmut Rankl, *Landvolk und frümoderner Stat in Bayern 1400–1800*, Studien zur Bayerischen Verfassungs- und Sozialgeschichte, 17 (Munich: Kommision für Bayerische Landesgeschichte, 1999). Two Austrian regional histories, Josef Fontana, et al. (eds), *Geschichte des Landes Tirol*, i (Bozen / Vienna: Verlagsanstalt Athesia, 1985) and Heinz Dopsch's volumes

In our project, we have been interested in synchronic and diachronic 'case studies', in which agrarian structures interact with social structures, but our main objective has been to compare synchronic cross-sections of different societies rather than studying longitudinal development in one and the same society. Diachronic comparison will, however, turn out to be fruitful when comparing longitudinal studies of different societies. From a methodological point of view, our comparison of peasant control and influence are a type of 'contrasting contexts', an acknowledged methodological principle when comparing various phenomena.[11] By comparing complete 'case studies' we hope to be able to focus on the *unique connections* of each phenomenon. Our intention is less focused on seeking general historical patterns and more on asking one and the same question and expecting multiple answers. Comparative studies may thus supplement our understanding of phenomena within their context. Furthermore, such an approach may prove to be a solid basis for more detailed studies of determining causes within a certain context. In some cases, however, it may be of interest to substantiate a more general hypothesis, for example, concerning relations between the territorial sovereign, the aristocracy, and the peasantry.

In line with this way of comparative thinking, Marc Bloch has called attention to an important *heuristic* factor when it comes to the implementation of new sources as well as the selection of questions we put to well-known sources. As an example, Bloch highlights a contextual analysis of the confusing diversity of unfree statuses in European peasant societies in the Middle Ages. In this case, comparative analysis, for instance of varying judicial authority over unfree men, may lead to new insight. Comparing different contexts may also

---

in Heinz Dopsch and Hans Spatzenegger, *Geschicte Salzburs – Stadt und Land* (Salzburg: Universitätsverlag A. Pustet, 1981–1991) contain passages on rural society and references to research in agrarian history. In Switzerland, Professor Roger Sablonier and Professor Hans-Jörg Gilomen and their students have been involved in studies on *Grundherrschaft* and rural societies. A survey of the works by Sablonier can be found in Thomas Meier and Roger Sablonier (eds), *Wirtschaft und Herrschaft. Beiträge zur ländlichen Gesellschaft in der östlichen Schweiz (1200–1800)* (Zurich: Chronos Verlag, 1999). A bibliography of more recent literature on rural society in the German-speaking regions of Switzerland can be found in Katja Hürlimann and Stefan Sonderegger, 'Ländliche Gesellschaft im Mittelalter', *Traverse: Zeitschrift für Geschichte*, 18/1 (2011), 48–76.

11 See, for example, Theda Skocpol and Margaret Somers, 'The Uses of Comparative History in Macro-social Inquiry', *Comparative Studies in Society and History*, 22/1 (1980) 174–97; Daniel Chirot, 'The Social and Historical Landscape of Marc Bloch', in Theda Skocpol (ed.), *Vision and Method in Historical Sociology* (Cambridge: CUP, 1984), 22–46; Patrick J. Geary, 'Vergleichende Geschichte und sozialwissenschaftliche Theorie', in M. Borgolte (ed.), *Das europäische Mittelalter im Spannungsbogen des Vergleichs* (Berlin: Akademie Verlag, 2002), 29–39.

reveal that apparent similarities between two social phenomena may have dissimilar meaning and function when analysed in their respective contexts. Bloch, therefore, preferred some proximity in time and space for a meaningful *heuristic* comparison.[12] Our intention is to satisfy Bloch's conditions when it comes to the inherent *heuristic* function of comparison, for instance regarding the alleviation or total abolition of unfree statuses in Scandinavia or the eastern Alpine region and the power relations involved in the organization of the *thing* institution in Norway and Tyrol. Generally speaking, in studying only one society without comparing it to other societies one tends to lose sight of control mechanisms necessary to isolate specific causal connections. In doing so, we therefore run the risk of developing or intensifying national myths (see the section 'Peasants in National Historiography', below).

Very often, peasant control and influence has been formed through prescriptions from or compromises with controlling forces outside the peasant society itself. Concrete political interaction between peasant society and controlling forces often determines peasant influence over land and institutions. Studying such encounters, it is essential to bear in mind that the controlling forces were also undergoing change, as in the case of the struggle between the Tyrolean sovereign and his aristocracy from the middle of the thirteenth century (see below). A main objective for our research will therefore be to investigate peasant control and influence in interactions between peasants, aristocracy, and a territorial power.

Investigations into external and internal power relations in peasant societies call for a discussion of the meaning of phrases like *bóndi* or *gebur*, equivalents to the modern term 'peasant'. In medieval Germanic languages, such phrases represent a resident man living in a community and performing work. The Nordic *bóndi* (ON; modern Norwegian: sing. *bonde*, pl. *bønder*) is contrasted with the *þræll* (ON, slave), that is, he is a free man. As the head of a household, the '*bonde* / *Bauer*' (latter word, modern German: sing. *Bauer*, pl. *Bauern*) was integrated into a wider political-economic community. In Scandinavia and in the Alpine region, '*bønder* / *Bauern*' was formed as a social layer during the High Middle (see also chapters 'Slavery and Unfreedom', and 'Summary and Conclusion' in Part 2). In addition to the delimitation downwards towards

12 Marc Bloch, *Slavery and Serfdom in the Middle Ages: Selected Essays*, trans. William R. Beer (Berkeley: University of California Press, 1975). Another example from European agrarian history comprises the use of new sources to study an 'enclosure' movement in France comparable to the well-known English enclosure movement between 1400 and 1800: see Marc Bloch, 'A Contribution towards a Comparative History of European Society', in *Land and Work in Medieval Europe. Selected papers by Marc Bloch*, trans. J.E. Anderson (Berkely: University of California Press, 1967), 44–81.

dependent or unfree persons in the social hierarchy, the '*bønder / Bauern*' were increasingly delimited upwards towards the aristocracy. The concept of a '*bonde / Bauer*' as an agriculturalist was then added to the definition.[13] A reliable sign of such a novel formation of social estates can be seen in the fact that the ancient distinction between free and unfree was replaced by a new main distinction between peasants and the aristocracy, as we can observe by comparing the Norwegian *Frostathing Law*, written down in the twelfth century and last edited around 1260, and the *Norwegian Law of the Realm of 1274*.

From the High and late Middle Ages through the early modern period, a new and very complex social class beneath the actual peasantry emerged in both regions. This group was recruited from the peasant class and was socially and economically closely related to this class. In the Alpine region, they are called *Unterbäuerliche Schichten* (see Part 4 'Appendix'), in Scandinavia *husmenn.*[14]

1 Peasants in National Historiography

To incorporate our investigation into a broader perspective, four historians – Helge Salvesen, Josef Riedmann, Stefan Sonderegger, and Werner Rösener – have been reviewing the shifting historical presentations of the part played by peasants in the national history of Norway, Tyrol, Switzerland, and Germany, respectively (see Part 3, 'The Portrayal of Peasants').

The Norwegian historian Helge Salvesen calls our attention to the fact that, after the country gained independence in 1814, many Norwegian historians saw peasants as carriers of the ideal of freedom and liberty in the Middle Ages. Due to the lack of political and military manorial control, they held a unique

13 'Bonde' (articles for Danmark, Norge, Island, Sverige) in *Kulturhistorisk leksikon for nordisk middelalder* (hereafter KLNM), ii, 84–99; Arne Bø, 'Hauld', in KLNM, vi, 251–54; Heinrich Beck, 'Philologische Bemerkungen zu "Bauer" im Germanischen', in R. Wenskus, H. Jankuhn, K. Grinda (eds), *Wort und Begriff 'Bauer': Zusammenfassende Bericht über die Kolloquien der Kommision für die Altertumskunde Mittel- und Nordeuropas* (Göttingen: Abhandlungen der Akademie der Wissenschaften in Göttingen, 1975), 58–72; Tore Iversen, 'Die frühe norwegische Dinggenossenschaft zwischen Herrschaft und Genossenschaft', in *Bauern zwischen Herrschaft und Genossenschaft: Peasant Relation to Lords and Government. Scandinavia and the Alpine Region 100–1750*, in Tore Iversen, John Ragnar Myking, and Gertrud Thoma (eds) (Trondheim: Tapir Akademisk Forlag, 2007), 167–86, at pp. 171–73; 'Bauer, Bauerntum', in Robert-Henri Bautier,et al. (ed.), *Lexikon des Mittelalters* (hereafter LexMA), 9 vols (Munich and Zurich: Artemis [vols 1–6] and LexMA-Verlag [vols 7–9], 1977–1999), vol. i, 1563–70, 1574–76, (W. Rösener) 1586–89.

14 KLNM, vii, 143–49.

position compared to their peasant counterparts in continental Europe. A basic alliance between peasants and the crown also gave the king democratic legitimacy. After 1910, prominent Norwegian historians like Halvdan Koht and Edvard Bull (see above) were influenced by historical materialism. According to Salvesen, this shift was met with little resistance in Norway, because historians continued to emphasize the part played by peasants in Norwegian national history.

According to historians influenced by historical materialism, the basic contradiction (in Marxist terms) in the medieval period and during the union with Denmark was that between landowners and peasants, that is, the producers. Since land was the most important form of capital at the time, studying ownership to land and how land was distributed among different groups of owners was held to be of the utmost importance, even more so as a free and equal society of peasants was considered to be the first stage in the Marxist theory of social development. In this tradition, the king, as one of the largest landowners, was naturally held to side with other secular and ecclesiastical landowners. However, when the Norwegian upper classes were replaced by foreigners after the Reformation, peasants came to constitute the only national class in Norway. Still, it was not until the end of the eighteenth century that they developed consciousness as a class and started to fight for their interest within a national framework.[15]

The historical-materialistic research on medieval and early modern peasant society was not very dogmatic, and, especially after 1945, it was characterized by criticism of the sources and quantitative empirical research (Andreas Holmsen, Jørn Sandnes), as well as a recognition of new trends in international social science (Kåre Lunden). Even if recent Norwegian research on ancient peasant society has been inspired by international trends, it still usually lacks a comparative element, especially outside Scandinavia.

In his contribution, the Austrian historian Josef Riedmann aims at clarifying peasant participation in the government of Tyrol since the Middle Ages. Tyrol occupies a crucial geographical location in the Alpine region, as well as a leading political position. The principality was built up by a native family in the latter part of the thirteenth century. At this point, the influence of the aristocracy was curtailed, and the sovereign made the peasants his direct subjects. Serfdom was greatly reduced, hereditary tenures were introduced, and the land was divided into administrative districts and *Gemeinde* where peasants acquired a substantial degree of self-administration. From 1420, the

15 Halvdan Koht, *Norsk bondereising: Fyrebuing til bondepolitikken* (Oslo: Aschehoug, 1926), especially 1–6.

district courts (*Gerichte*) were amply represented in the legislative assembly (*Landtag*), where their representatives sided with the sovereign against the aristocracy. Most of the peasant representatives came from the local peasant elite. Following the introduction of absolutism, the *Landtag* lost its political influence.

In the first part of the twentieth century, new attention was drawn to the historical role played by the peasants in the Tyrolean *Landtag*, as exemplified by the works of internationally renowned historian like Hermann Wopfner and Otto Stolz. Their work was used by members of the Catholic conservative opposition to the centralized power in Vienna. According to Riedmann, their focus must not be associated with the totalitarian 'Blut und Boden' romanticism. Riedmann concludes that peasant co-determination in Tyrol was far greater than in most German territories, although recent historical research by others, including Peter Blickle, has concluded that peasant representation in constituent assemblies was not unusual in the transition from the Middle Ages to the early modern period.

The Swiss historian Stefan Sonderegger confronts the established state ideology of Switzerland's origin as a peasant state, founded by peasants of different cantons. According to Sonderegger, the old Swiss confederacy started as a confederation between towns and the surrounding rural districts with the towns as the strongest part. The peasant state ideology developed in the midst of nineteenth-century Swiss patriotic history writing, as exemplified by the works of the Swiss historian Johannes von Müller. It was backed by tales of mythical peasant heroes like William Tell, who rebelled against Habsburgian oppression, and by the European bourgeoisies' idealised concept of the Swiss alpine landscape. Sonderegger proffers the town of St Gallen and the surrounding Appenzeller rural district in eastern Switzerland as an example. He finds few traces of peasant control over Appenzeller communes. He concludes that, at best, peasant influence was vague in the late Middle Ages. A far more important power in this region was the Swabian urban confederation, into which four Appenzeller districts were incorporated in 1377 under the leadership of the town of St Gallen. Sonderegger sees a similar town-land pattern with a marked town dominance in the first inner-Swiss confederacy as well. The city of Zurich, with its long-distance trade, was a centre for distribution of commercial products from the neighbouring district of Glarus and from the Alpine cantons of Uri and Schwyz as well as grain from Swabia. Leading elites, among them some of the local aristocracy, established close ties with the ruling Habsburg dynasty before the wars of liberation in the fourteenth century.

In his contribution, the German historian Werner Rösener renders an overview of peasant ideologies in German historiography. Beginning in the nineteenth century, he distinguishes between a conservative and a liberal tradition. The conservative tradition founded by Wilhelm H. Riehl, who published an influential work in 1848 in which he portrayed the German peasants as a conservative-traditional force, but also as the future of the German nation. The real peasant was the embodiment of the archetypal German type of man. He had singular hereditary succession to the farm, the opposite of divided inheritance. Important causes for the decrease in the number of real peasants include the division of land, the rise of the combination of occupations, and the emergence of a monetary economy, as well as political and economic reforms from the beginning of the nineteenth century. Riehl developed the concept of *Grundherrschaft* (manorialism). According to Riehl, this meant that the lord gave his serfs bread and security, while his liberal opponents saw this arrangement as an obsolete remnant of feudal society. The extended household (*das ganze Haus*) was, according to Riehl, a fundamental part of the pre-industrial social order. Social inequalities within a household must therefore be considered natural.

In contrast to Riehl, a liberal tendency stressed ancient peasant autonomy. Georg F. von Maurer (1856) was an advocate of the theory of initial communal ownership of outfield resources (*Markgenossenschaftsthorie*) in the Germanic past. Free land and communal ownership originated in the time of the first land claim and was thus deeply connected with German economic and social history, as well as with the development of a German constitution. Villages and farms were later separated from the communal land. A theoretical-juridical basis for the *Markgenossenschaft* theory was established by the legal historian Otto von Gierke (1841–1921). He developed a theory of organic evolution of societies containing complex compositions of social groups (*Genossenschaften*). Gierke considered German development from an early paternalism to constitutionalism in the nineteenth century to be influenced from *Herrschaft* (dominion) as well as *Genossenschaft*. He saw peasant loss of influence in the Middle Ages as a result of the victory of manorial estates (*Gutherrschaft*). A core of peasant autonomy was still left, he maintained.

Interestingly, Friedrich Engels and Karl Marx studied Gierke's work, especially the theory of *Markgenossenschaft*. The revolutionary activities of German peasants in the peasant wars of the first part of the sixteenth century became the topic of studies by Wilhelm Zimmermann (1841–45) and Engels (1850). Following a period of peasant reforms in Germany (1750–1850), an idealizing of the past resulted in peasant society being portrayed as a contrast to contemporary bourgeois society (cf. Riehl). According to Rösener, most historians came to represent peasants as a homogeneous social group without any significant difference in economic strength or influence in society. The concept of a homogeneous peasant group also dominated German historical writings in the twentieth century.

From the 1930s, new concepts of lordship and state in the Middle Ages led to new perspectives on peasant society. Historians advocating these perspectives were Theodor Meyer, Günther Franz, Walter Schlesinger, Heinrich Dannenbauer, and Otto Brunner. According to them, control over households rather than control over land constituted the fundamental basis of social power in the Middle Ages. Aristocratic power emerging from the household contained public-juridical elements and this power did not have to be shared with any sovereign. The historians stressed that lordship in the Middle Ages was formed by a variety of rights and privileges, such as judicial power (*Gerichtsgewalt*), ownership to land (*Grundherrschaft*), corporal control (*Leibherrschaft*), and control over clients (*Gefolgsherrschaft*). Different forms of lordships could be combined. Under favourable conditions, such lordships could result in territorial control. Dannenbauer (1941) stressed the aristocratic lordship where peasants had to obey, work, and provide services without having any influence whatsoever. Brunner (1939), on the other hand, saw a lordship characterized by mutual fidelity. Rösener points out that this harmonious picture was criticized, especially by Marxist rural historians, for not taking into consideration rents, fees, and taxes, as well as other factors such as famines, rebellions, and the state of the market. According to them, the harmonious picture was in reality an illusion.

Rösener remarks that 1945 was not an essential dividing line in historical research on German agrarian history, even though two younger historians, Wilhelm Abel and Friedrich Lütge entered the scene around 1950, assisted by Günther Franz. Franz edited a three-volume work (1962–70) in which they addressed agrarian economy (Abel), changes in the agrarian structure (Lütge), and the history of the German peasant class (Franz) from the early Middle Ages to the middle of the nineteenth century. Even though these works represented important broad research studies, they have been criticized for lacking an integrated perspective and interaction between the basic subjects. Rösener maintains that Franz was, in essential aspects, reproducing Riehl's view that a homogeneous peasant class was a conservative bulwark against left-wing upheavals. Lütge is being criticized for a judicial point of view on the agrarian structure, only marginally touching on subjects like power structure and demographic, economic, and social issues. Gerhard Heitz (1977) has criticized all three for not highlighting peasant struggle for more freedom and influence, especially in the late Middle Ages. In spite of such fundamental criticism, these three historians lay part of the foundation for new tendencies and directions in agrarian history in the decades following the 1970s. An example is the concept of 'communalism' developed by Franz's assistant Peter Blickle.

We may add that Blickle himself (1998) emphasizes, in spite of his own objections, the importance of the German agrarian-historical tradition in an era dominated by historicism. He sees the three-volume work (1962–70) cited above as the end of an epoch. The contributions from Karl S. Bader have been fundamental to more recent research on villages, communes (*Gemeinde*), and neighbourhood communities (*Nachbarschaft, Talschaft*). Newer agrarian historians (Werner Rösener, Roger Sablonier, Heide Wunder, Peter Bierbrauer, and Peter Blickle) thus emphasize the peasant community to a greater extent than their predecessors. In the words of Heide Wunder, the shift from the Middle Ages to the early modern period represented a change from '*Herrschaft mit Bauern*' to '*Herrschaft über Bauern*'.[16]

As a whole, our four contributions (see Part 3, 'The Portrayal of Peasants') highlight the fact that an historical interest in the role played by the peasant class in the formation of medieval society was developing from the nineteenth century. Early historians in Scandinavia and in the Alpine region often painted an image of an initial peasant liberty of free and independent peasants living in Germanic societies where land was used communally. The ideology of an initial peasant liberty was given relevance in the national struggle for freedom and democracy (Norway, Switzerland, and Tyrol), as peasants were supposed to represent the people of the past, in spite of the fact that the sources to the history of ancient peasants were often ambiguous and open to interpretation. Today, however, it is clear that the concept of an initial democracy of free and equal peasants cannot be upheld for empirical reasons, either in the east Alpine region or in Scandinavia.

16 Karl Siegfried Bader, *Das mittelalterliche Dorf als Friedens- und und Rechtsbereich* (Weimar: Hermann Böhlaus Nachfolger, 1957); Karl Siegfried Bader, *Dorfgenossenschaft und Dorfgemeinde* (Weimar: Hermann Böhlaus Nachfolger, 1962); Karl Siegfried Bader, *Rechtsformen und Schichten der Liegeschaftsnutzung im mittelalterlichen Dorf* (Vienna: Böhlau, 1973); Roger Sablonier, 'Das Dorf im Übergang vom Hochmittelalter zum Spätmittelalter, Untersuchungen zum Wandel ländlicher Gemeinschaftsformen im ostschweizerischen Raum', in Lutz Fenske, Werner Rösener, and Thomas Zotz (eds), *Institutionen, Kultur und Gesellschaft im Mittelalter: Festschrift für Josef Fleckenstein* (Sigmaringen: Thorbecke, 1984), 120–34; Heide Wunder, *Die bäuerliche Gemeinde in Deutschland* (Göttingen: Vandenhoeck und Ruprecht, 1986); Peter Bierbrauer, *Freiheit und Gemeinde im Berner Oberland 1300–1700* (Bern: Historischer Verein des Kantons Bern, 1991); Peter Blickle, *Deutsche Untertanen: Ein Widerspruch* (Munich: Beck, 1981), 23–60; same author, 'Der Kommunalismus als Gestaltungsprinzip zwischen Mittelalter und Moderne', in Nicolai Bernard and Quirinius Reichen (eds), *Gesellschaft und Gesellschaften: Festschrift Ulrich Im Hof* (Bern: Wyss, 1982), 95–113.

To be sure, peasants acquired new specific rights at some point in the historical past, rights that can be validated by historical sources. In most cases, however, this enlarged influence was achieved through an alliance between peasants, usually the peasant elite, and a growing sovereign power, in the years following the end of the first millennium AD. Such alliances often emerged at the expense of an older aristocratic stratum. Enhanced liberty for peasants, in the sense of personal status, control over land, and judicial influence, did not emerge as a result of political alliances and peasant power alone, but was embedded in demographic and economic factors of development (see the section 'A Sketch of the Historical Background', below). The sovereign's interests were then often satisfied by taxes and the conscription of soldiers.

In Tyrol, this common interest was, according to Riedmann, established from the latter part of the thirteenth century. In Switzerland, the balance of power differed, first and foremost due to the strength of the towns. Sonderegger distances himself from the prevalent peasant national-democratic ideology that stressed peasant rebellion against a 'foreign' sovereign. Instead, he points to the forming of alliances between powerful towns and peasant elites in the surrounding rural districts, with the towns as the strongest party in the alliance against the sovereign power. In Switzerland and Norway, the peasant ideology had a national character. In Switzerland, peasants were held to be the main force in the shaping of the country as a peasant democracy. In Norway, they were supposedly the only national class during foreign dominance and thus were the sustaining element of a national democratic identity. In Tyrol as well, peasant ideology had a democratic aspect directed against the central authorities.

In pan-German historiography, a liberal trend concerning the historical role of the peasantry gained ground from the nineteenth century. The liberal point of view emphasized the influential, now abounded thesis based on the idea of an initial democracy of free and equal peasants. The legal historian Gierke stresses different forms of social affiliation and community. His use of the term *Genossenschaft* is associated with this liberal tradition. German agrarian historical research has lately again focused on villages and other peasant neighborhood associations (see chapter 'Peasant Participation' in Part 2). Such peasant communities and their share in decision making and administration may best be studied in combination with the complex power relations that the twentieth-century German agrarian historical tradition has sought to explain, such as judicial power (*Gerichtsgewalt*), control of land (*Grundherrschaft*), corporal control (*Leibherrschaft*), and control over clients (*Gefolgsherrschaft*). These terms of power also correspond to our three main themes in this volume, corresponding to our chapters 'Slavery and Unfreedom', 'Leashold and

Freehold' and 'Peasant Participation in Thing and Local Assemblies' in Part 2.[17]

We believe that agrarian history and the question of peasant control over land and other resources has to be related to general historical trends – demographic, economic, and political. Historians, especially in the Scandinavian agrarian tradition, have often treated historical peasant societies separately from the political development and changes in power relations of their time. Blinded by national ideologies regarding peasants' role in ancient societies, they have also seen these societies as too homogeneous in spite of obvious internal divisions. To address these difficulties, we will try to sketch some historical trends influencing peasant history in the two regions chosen for our study.

2 A Sketch of the Historical Background

2.1 *The Middle Ages until 1350*

Peasant control over land and resources from the beginning of the second millennium until the end of the early modern period was influenced by the changing power of aristocratic, ecclesiastical, and lay landowners on the one hand, and the emergence and growing influence of sovereign territorial power on the other.

Following the German tradition, the influence of these powers can be referred to as *Herrschaft*. Not only did the strength of these powers change over time, they also developed differently from region to region. Their growth and decline was modified by a variety of interdependent factors ranging from developments in agriculture, trade, and urban economy to changes in the structure of the population. The conditions for agriculture, defined by the natural conditions on the one side and changes in power relations on the other side, set the limitations within which peasant households could use the land they were allotted and take part in decisions vital to their interests.

17 Ownership of landed property has been the dominant focus when studying power relations in Norwegian agrarian history. However, in contrast to the modern concept of landed property, the concept of property before the thirteenth century had a far more vague and more comprehensive meaning. See, for example, Tore Iversen, 'Property and Land Tenancy in Norwegian Medieval Laws and the European Learned Law', in Per Andersen, Ditlev Tamm, and Helle Vogt (eds), *How Nordic Are the Nordic Medieval Laws? Proceedings from the First Carlsberg Conference on Medieval Legal History*. 2nd edn (Copenhagen: DJØF Publishing, 2011), 135–76; Gudmund Sandvik, *Prestegård og prestelønn* (Oslo: Universitetsforlaget, 1965), 87–99, et passim.

It must be underlined that these boundaries are not to be seen as absolutes, since the peasants could exercise considerable influence through their peasant communities, which, following the German tradition, may be referred to as *Genossenschaft*. In this introduction, we will try to outline some of the long-term socio-political changes in Scandinavia and the eastern Alpine region that may have influenced the degree of peasant control over resources and their partaking in vital decisions in their respective regions.

2.1.1 The Eastern Alpine Region

Peasant conditions in the eastern Alps are closely connected to structural changes in agriculture and rural society. To explain such structural changes, we have to study general economic, social, and political factors. The original Bavarian tribal duchy consisted of most of the east Alpine territory and was a part of the Carolingian-German kingdom. In this duchy, the social-political situation was as follows in the centuries before and after the end of the first millennium: peasant control over land and resources was changing significantly due to increasing public authority being transferred to the landowning aristocracy in Bavaria. Counts (*comes*), formerly prominent men in royal service, became independent landlords gaining judicial power and the right of succession to their land. Their former counties were turned into fiefs and divided into manors (*Villikationen*) with demesne land and dependent peasants. A central main farm was run by the landlord or his steward (*Meier*) and was worked by unfree farm labourers. The rest of the manor was rented to dependent peasants obliged to do corvée labour on the demesne (cf., below, the more loosely organized *multiple estates* in Scandinavia).[18]

Furthermore, feudal overlords profited, especially from around the year 1000, by becoming advocates (*Vogt*) for independent ecclesiastical institutions like bishoprics and monasteries, rendering them military and administrative services. Peasant influence was thus affected by obscure and fluctuating lordship and by the dwindling importance of peasant military service.[19] Even if binate manors dominated important areas in the eastern Alps until about the end of the twelfth century, other forms also existed, ranging from large farms deploying only an internal workforce to independent holdings paying rent, as

18 About *Villikation*, see Werner Rösener, in LexMA, viii, 1694–95. *Grundherrschaft* is used in a wider sense, including agricultural proceedings and social and legal aspects (Rösener, in LexMA, iv, 1739–40).

19 Dollinger, *Der bayerische Bauernstand*, 53–83; Pankraz Fried, 'Zur Geschichte der bayernischen Landgemeinde', in Theodor Mayer (ed.), *Die Anfänge der Landgemeinde und ihr Wesen*, 2 vols, Vorträge und Forschungen, 7 (Stuttgart: Jan Thorbecke, 1964), i, 79–106, at p. 94.

well as a substantial category of freeholders on allodial land.[20] As for judicial affiliation, peasants belonging to a binate manor were subject to a manorial court, while free-standing peasants were attached to public courts. Peasants were not totally derived of judicial participation, but the conditions for their participation varied according to their status.[21]

While scholars formerly held different views regarding the dissolution of the *Villikation* system, the prevailing view in the aftermath of Philippe Dollinger's study on Bavarian peasants before the thirteenth century (1982) holds this dissolution to be of great social and economic importance.[22] It meant that the manorial lord reduced or gave up his own demesne farming, parcelling out the demesne to his peasants or lending it to his bailiff. This did not, however, result in an immediate and complete transition to a rental-based exploitation of the land. Transitional forms, where the demesne continued to play an important role, still existed, especially in Bavaria.

The transition to scattered holdings and a land-rent system without corvée labour (*Rentengrundherrschaft*) implied that peasant farming became more autonomous. The disappearance, or comprehensive reduction, of corvée labour also improved the personal status of dependant persons. This transition from an integrated manorial system to a more diversified system did not take place at the same time or in the same way all over southern Germany. In the Bavarian region, the most intense period of transformation took place in the twelfth century.[23]

The transition to a land-rent system based on scattered holdings must be seen in connection with several interconnected economic and social factors, among them population increase, the clearing of new land, increasing trade,

20 Werner Rösener, *Grundherrschaft im Wandel i: Untersuchungen zur Entwicklung geistlicher Grundherrschaften im südwestdeutschen Raum vom 9. bis 14. Jahrhundert*, Veröffentlichungen des Max-Planck-Instituts für Geschichte, 102 (Göttingen: Vandenhoeck und Ruprecht, 1991), 559–60; Dollinger, *Der bayerische Bauernstand*, 137.

21 K. Schultz, 'Hofrecht', in LexMA, v, 77–78. Werner Rösener underlines the importance of the binate *Villikationen* by stressing that it was the material basis for king, church, and aristocracy in a long period from the ninth to the twelfth century: Rösener, *Grundherrschaft im Wandel*, 560.

22 Dollinger, *Der bayerische Bauernstand*, 121–23, cf. Rösener, *Agrarwirtschaft*, 81. Alfons Dopsch maintained that the dissolution was not a fundamental transformation: Alfons Dopsch, *Herrschaft und Bauer in der deutschen Kaiserzeit: Untersuchungen zur Agrar- und Sozialgeschichte des hohen Mittelalters mit besonderer Berücksichtigung des südostdeutschen Raumes* (Jena: Gustav Fischer, 1939), 135.

23 Dollinger, *Der bayerische Bauernstand*, 138–39. See also Werner Rösener (ed.), *Grundherrschaft und baüerliche Gesellschaft im Hochmittelalter* (Göttingen: Vendenhoeck und Ruprecht, 1995), 16–31, 116–62, 184–254, 443–60.

and the growth of towns. The following transformation from corvée labour to land-rent may then be seen as a consequence of an increasing supply of labour, leading to an evolution from slave to free or half-free status (for a more detailed discussion, see chapter 'Slavery and Unfreedom' in Part 2).

A turning point in medieval social and agrarian history, more or less coinciding with the dissolution of the *Villikation* system, was the evolution of compact village communities. Formerly, scholars understood these village communities as remnants of a collectivist settlement pattern (see Rösener on the theory of the *Markgenossenschaft* in Part 3, 'The Portrayal of Peasants' and above, p. 12).[24] Later studies tend to see the great increase in population as the fundamental cause for the formation of village communities in the High Middle Ages. We must, however, be aware of the fact that villages did not dominate the whole of the east Alpine area. Hamlets and single farms were also frequently found.

Structural changes in agrarian society were closely connected to the development of different estates during the High Middle Ages, that is, an ecclesiastical and secular aristocracy, a town-based class of merchants, and a peasant estate. The aristocracy was in the middle of a transformation from loosely connected families to aristocratic dynasties. These dynasties were now seeking more effective political and administrative power than the binate manorial system could offer. The ultimate goal was territorial sovereignty. Such a sovereignty (*Landesherrschaft*) could be built through strategic exploitation of existing lordships under the leadership of a few of the most influential aristocratic dynasties. In the vast and composite German Empire, no strong sovereign existed to control this evolution. From the twelfth century onwards, some of the aristocratic dynasties thus managed to become territorial sovereigns (*Landesfürsten*).[25]

As a whole, this period of slackened bonds between peasant and lords before the crisis of the late Middle Ages has been portrayed as 'a golden age for

---

24 A review of the older literature on the subject is given by K.S. Bader, *Das mittelalteliche Dorf*; cf. Rösener, *Bauern im Mittelalter*, 54–73; K.H. Schröder and G. Schwarz, *Die ländlichen Siedlungsformen in Mitteleuropa*, Forschung zur deutschen Landeskunde, 175 (Trier: Univeristy of Trier, 1978); Karl Kroeschell, 'Dorf' in Adalbert Erler, et al. (eds), *Handwörterbuch zur deutschen Rechtsgeschichte* (hereafter HRG), 5 vols (Berlin: Schmidt, 1964–1991), i, 51ff. For the theory of collectivistic village commons as remnants of a primodial collectivistic settlement pattern, see Uwe Meiners and Werner Rösener (eds), *Allmenden und Marken vom Mittelalter bis zum Neuzeit* (Cloppenburg: Schriften des Museumsdorfs Cloppenburg, 2004); Otto Stolz, *Rechtsgeschichte des Bauernstandes und der Landwirtschaft in Tirol und Voralberg* (Hildesheim: Georg Olms Verlag), 1949.

25 Rösener, *Bauern im Mittelalter*, 31–39.

the German peasant'.[26] As we will see, however, there are marked differences in the relationship between sovereign and peasants from principality to principality, that is, Bavaria and Tyrol. In Bavaria, the power of the prince relied to a large degree on compromise and an alliance with the secular and ecclesiastic aristocracy, although their peasants also had some influence (see chapter 'Peasant Participation' in Part 2). The house of *Wittelsbach*, which took over the new Bavarian duchy from 1180, began a slow building up of their territory. This development was also promoted by a statute issued by the German king, in which German princes were granted unlimited jurisdiction over their own territories. Reforms to the legal system in the thirteenth century marked the beginning of a development in which the Bavarian duke consolidated his own territory and brought the legal power of the clerical and secular nobility under control. While control over legal assemblies and legal authority over peasants had been part of the privileges of fief-holders until the thirteenth century, the Bavarian dukes gradually succeeded in acquiring many such rights for themselves.[27] The duke's main instrument in this development was the new territorial peace legislation inspired by the church.

Now, severe deeds of violence were understood to be crimes against the communal peace of society, a peace that the territorial prince was solely responsible for upholding. This new public view of punishment divided the jurisdiction into two clearly delimited categories: a *high jurisdiction* or 'blood jurisdiction' involving crimes against social peace, and a *lower jurisdiction*, relating to civil conflicts and ordinary finable offences. This crucial development for Bavaria started with Duke Otto III's written pledge of 1311. The term *Landgericht* is related to the transformation of the duke's jurisdictional power into territories of jurisdiction. *Hofmarken* were smaller territories covering one or several villages, but also single farms. Most *Hofmarken* belonged to the secular and clerical nobility and to monasteries, in which the lord of the Hofmark held the lower jurisdiction, but a good number of them also belonged to the duke. The *Hofmark* institution originated in the early medieval *Grundherrschaft*.

In mountainous Tyrol, with its valleys and mountain passes, the power of the prince emerged at about the same time as in Bavaria, but in Tyrol this power primarily relied on an alliance with peasants led by a peasant elite. The

26 Alfons Dopsch, *Herrschaft und Bauer*, 218; cf. H. Kellenbenz (ed.), *Handbuch der europäischen Wirtscahfts- und Sozialgeschichte*, ii: *Europäische Wirtschafts- und Sozialgeschichte im Mittelalter* (Stuttgart: Clett-Cotta, 1980), 112.

27 Sebastian Hiereth, *Die bayerische Gerichts- und Verwaltungsorganisation vom 13. bis 19. Jahrhundert*, Historischer Atlas von Bayern, Teil Altbayern, 1 (Munich: Komm. für Bayer, Landegeschichte, 1950), 6–7; Fried, 'Zur Geschichte der bayerischen Landgemeinde', 79–106.

background for this alliance has occupied Tyrolean historians for a long time. The historian Otto Stolz pointed to the high degree of freehold from the thirteenth to the fifteenth century, which in western Tyrol amounted to more than half of the land.[28]

From the eleventh century onwards, probably also in Tyrol, the peasant population lost much of the influence they had at the counts' assemblies of the past. Contemporary Tyrolean historians have thus found very little support for the older perception that popular participation in the prince's *things* later in the Middle Ages was rooted in the so-called *Markgenossenschaften,* ancient, originally communal managed areas going back to the Germanic Migration Period (see chapter 'Peasant Participation' in Part 2).[29] Recently, historians have emphasized contemporary political factors to a greater extent in the shaping of the peasant assemblies of the thirteenth century. In a process of concentration, several types of rights of dominion were combined and then made territorial. It is not the free-standing peasant assemblies rooted in ancient communal communities that was typical for the legal assemblies in Tyrol but, on the contrary, the early interventions of the territorial prince in the shaping of the assemblies.[30]

In his reign, Count Meinhard II (1258–95) curbed the power of the Tyrolean nobility by inheriting or ransoming their noble rights, or simply by driving them away from their territories. This could be accomplished because the aristocracy in Tyrol was in a weaker position then in the neighbouring regions. Part of the explanation for their weakness may have been of a topographical nature, that is, scarcity of continuous arable land. The strong position of the count of Tyrol was also due to Tyrol being a mountain pass state with transport and trade providing the prince financial and military superiority. In addition, substantial income came from mining industry, at first salt, then silver mining, both by princely monopoly. After Meinhard, the counts were members of the powerful Habsburg family. This may also have strengthened their position.

28 Otto Stolz, *Rechtsgeschichte*, 90–91.

29 Otto Stolz, *Geschichte der Gerichte Deutschtirol, Abhandlungen zum historischen Atlas der Österreichischen Alpenländer*, special print (Sonderdruck), Archiv für österreichische Geschichte, 102 (Vienna: Hölder, 1913), 198–214, 218f.; Stolz, *Rechtsgeschichte,* 304. As mentioned early in the introduction, the Tyrolean regional historical tradition seems to have been an important background for the Norwegian historian Edv. Bull's planned comparative project in the 1920s.

30 Franz Huter, 'Zur Frage der Gemeindebildung in Tirol', in Theodor Mayer (ed.), *Die Anfänge der Landgemeinde und ihr Wesen,* 2 vols, Vorträge und Forschungen, 7, (Stuttgart: Jan Thorbecke, 1964), i, 222–235.

2.1.2 Scandinavia

There are marked differences in historical sources in our two regions of comparison. In the eastern Alpine region, written sources appear by the early Middle Ages and are quite frequently found from the thirteenth century. On the other hand, Scandinavia almost completely lacks written sources before 1100. For Scandinavia, we therefore have to rely more heavily on interpretations of archaeological investigations and cultural-topographic knowledge for this period.

Inspired by the Germanistic nineteenth-century tradition, Scandinavian historians used to perceive the Nordic countries around 1000 as societies consisting of a majority of free, allodial Nordic peasants. This Nordic 'Sonderweg' contrasted with the Western European medieval manorial system.[31] Since the 1990s, the concept of a Nordic 'Sonderweg' has given way to a new dominant concept, most clearly formulated in Norway and Sweden. According to this view, magnates at the end of the Viking Age controlled a number of unfree persons (*thralls* and descendants of *thralls*), and had established strong bonds to a population of free peasants, from their bases on *multiple estates*.[32]

In the last few decades, archaeologists have documented the existence of estates in connection with magnate farms, for example, along the coast of Norway from the seventh century, in Östergötland in Sweden, and in Danish Scania, a part of Denmark until 1658.[33] In some cases, minor farms without burial

31 Poulsen and Sindbæk (eds), *Settlement and Lordship*, 4–28, esp. 4–14.

32 For Norway, see, for example, Tore Iversen, 'Fremveksten av det norske leiglendingsvesenet i middelaldren – en forklaringsskisse', *Heimen*, 32 (1995), 169–80 and subsequent contributions to the debate in the same journal by several Norwegian historians. For a comparison with continental conditions, see Frode Iversen, 'Den nyere norske forskningen om jordegods i vikingtid og tidlig middelalder: En sammenligning med undersøkelsene av manor- og Grundherrschaftsystemer i Vest-Europa', *Varia*, 71 (2009), 59–70, http://urn.nb.no/URN:NBN:no-30052 (permanent link). For the new approach in Sweden inspired by Iversen's contribution in Norway, see Mats Widgren, 'Hur drevs den vikingtida-medeltida storgården?: några frågor från Lägerbovada, Ydre' in Olof Karsvall and Kristofer Jupiter (eds), *Medeltida storgårdar: 15 uppsatser om ett tvärvetenskapligt forskningsproblem* (Uppsala: Gustav Adolfs akademien Acta Academiae Regiae Gustavi Adolphi, 2014), 59–72, at p. 69. For a discussion about *multiple estates*, see Granville R.J. Jones, 'Multiple Estates and Early Settlement', in P.H. Sawyer (ed.), *Medieval Settlement – Continuity and Change* (London: Edward Arnold Publishers, 1976), 15–40. For the relation between dependent tenants close to the estates and a more independent peasantry further away, see Rosamond Faith, *The English Peasantry and the Growth of Lordship* (London: Leichester University Press, 1997).

33 Myhre and Øye, *Norges landbrukshistorie*, 119–276; Olof Karsvall and Kristofer Jupiter, *Medeltida Storgårder: 15 uppsatser om ett tvärvetenskapligt forskningsproblem* (Uppsala: Gustav Adolfs akademien Acta Academiae Regiae Gustavi Adolphi, 2014), passim; Anne

mounds encircle a main farm with several burial mounds, interpreted as minor farms worked by unfree people.[34] In Northern Norway, some of the magnate farms can be directly linked to historically important known chieftain centres. Sites nearby these centres have been interpreted as *thing* sites for the local inhabitants.[35]

There are strong indications that these early Scandinavian estates may be characterized as *multiple estates*, that is, estates with a more diversified resource basis encircling the central settlement than was the case on the continental estates.[36] Compared to many continental estates, these multiple estates were made up of diversified resources, and the outlying parts of the estates covered vast areas. Such estates were characterized by *tributary* relations between patrons and clients. This included exchange in the form of gifts and repayments for gifts and benefits. Services and modest tributes were conceived of as gifts of honour rather than rent. Relations were personal and reciprocal, even though they depended on the status of the parties and even when the client appears to have been unfree, but not wholly of slave status.[37] The main farms of such multiple estates were probably worked by slaves or unfree persons, who, as a part of their manumission, were given the opportunity to clear new land within the area controlled by the magnate (for a fuller discussion, see chapter 'Slavery and Unfreedom' in Part 2).

We can observe similarities as well as differences in the socio-economic structures of the magnate estates in our two main regions. The binate manors of the eastern Alps were usually geographically concentrated, had clearly defined borders, and were more thoroughly organized than the Scandinavian multiple estates. Scandinavian multiple estates were more loosely organized, spanned a wider geographical area, had borders that were less clear and included a more diversified bundle of resources. Such estates were held together

---

Carlie, 'Magnate Estates along the Road: Viking Age Settlements, Communication and Contacts in South-West Scania, Sweden', *Acta Archaeologica*, 79 (2008), 110–744.

34 Frode Iversen, 'Eiendom, makt og statsdannelse: Kongsgårder og gods i Hordaland i yngre jernalder og middelalder', PhD thesis, University of Bergen, Bergen, 2004, 65–89, 380–90, passim; Svein Indrelid, *Strilesoga: Nord- og Midhordland gjennom tidene*, i: *Frå steinalder til vikingtid* (Oslo: Eide, 1997); Andreas Holmsen, *Nye studier i gammel historie* (Oslo: Universitetsforlaget, 1976), 75–81.

35 Inger Storli, *Hålogaland før rikssamlingen: Politiske prosesser i perioden 200–900 e.Kr.*, Institut for Sammenlignende Kulturforskning, Serie B, Skrifter, 123 (Oslo: Novus forlag, 2006), 39–75.

36 Jones, 'Multiple Estates', 15–40; Faith, *The English Peasantry*; Iversen, 'Den nyere norske forskning', 59–70.

37 Chris Wickham, *Farming the Early Middle Ages: Europe and the Mediterranean 400–800* (Oxford: Oxford University Press, 2005), passim.

to a great extent by bonds between patrons and clients and were thus, due to competition between chieftains, less stable than the continental binate estate system. Nevertheless, they could sustain Scandinavian magnates' dominion over land and people. Besides multiple estates, family-worked, nearly autonomous farms, many of them also holding slaves, were frequently found in Scandinavia in the Middle Ages, especially in northern Scandinavia.

From the seventh century, Scandinavia was hierarchically structured under a group of competing chieftains / aristocrats. A few of these managed to establish themselves as kings, eventually resulting in the formation of three separate kingdoms. At the end of the ninth century, a Norwegian chieftain managed to establish a kingdom from his base in western Norway, crushing some of his rivals and allying himself with other chieftains from the coastal Norwegian aristocracy. This aristocracy drew their power and wealth from control over fertile areas, strategic sea routes, maritime trade, and Viking raids. Some of them were lords over loosely organized territories with multiple estates.

Kings with fortunes won in Viking raids in England, like Olav Haraldsson (1015–30), continued the process of unifying the Norwegian territories. They strengthened their position further by introducing the Christian faith and establishing an administrative core of literate clergy. At the same time, Danish kings secured control over parts of England, thus establishing a North Sea kingdom that, for shorter periods due to shifting alliances with the remaining Norwegian aristocracy, came to include Norway.[38]

From the tenth century, a regional *thing* system was organized by the king in a growing alliance with the peasant elite. The purpose was to keep the peace and, initially, also to tame the old coastal aristocracy with their local strongholds and regional ambitions. Many of the legal proceedings among the peasants themselves was, however, settled through a presumably independent *dómr* (ad hoc committee) arrangement, that is, a panel of six or twelve members chosen by two parties for settlement or arbitration.[39] In this way, the peasant elite played a crucial role in settling disputes in their local communities.

After a period of relative stability, civil war (1130–1227) between different pretenders to the crown broke out in Norway. In the end, these wars resulted in a unified and strong royal power. During the civil war period, peasant society, as well as the aristocracy, underwent significant changes, but these changes were only slightly connected to the conflict itself. They can best be described

38 Cf. Birgit and Peter Sawyer, *Medieval Scandinavia: From Conversion to Reformation circa 800–1500* (Minneapolis: University of Minnesota Press, 1996), 49–80.

39 Eyvind Fjeld Halvorsen, 'Domr', in KLNM, iii, 214–18.

as a shift from control over people to control over land.[40] On multiple estates and in loosely organized chiefdoms, controlling people was the key to obtaining a surplus from agricultural production. When, from the twelfth century, multiple estates were largely given up in exchange for a system of land-rent paid by tenants (see chapter 'Leasehold and Freehold' in Part 2), controlling landed property became the most important issue.

From the tenth to the thirteenth century, relations between the elite and the people who worked the land developed in different directions in the three Scandinavian countries.[41] In Norway, qualitative changes in the structure of estates began to appear well into the twelfth century. Population increase and new settlement structures influenced the dissolution of multiple estates. Some multiple estates, which the king had confiscated from the aristocracy, became part of the foundations of ecclesiastical institutions. The aristocracy and the king scaled back their own farming, instead relying on land-rent just like the church. From the beginning of the thirteenth century, slavery and milder forms of unfreedom started to fade away in Norway. However, a formal dissolution of slavery in Scandinavia was only issued in Sweden, in the king's decree for Västergötland in 1335 (see chapter 'Slavery and Unfreedom' in Part 2).

From the end of the thirteenth century, a 'share-of-rent-ownership' system, in which individuals and institutions could own shares in a farm, was fully developed in Norway (see chapter 'Leasehold and Freehold' in Part 2). In this system they did not own a concrete part of the land, only a share of the land-rent. This system was well adapted to the multitude of dispersed farms and shares in farms transferred to ecclesiastical institutions from the crown, the aristocracy, and individual peasants. By this time, the regional laws had developed precise terms for concepts of landholding, and the concept of owning landed property was separated from the concept of having authority and control over people. By the thirteenth century, Norwegian landowners thus drew their incomes from landed property almost exclusively in the form of land-rent

40 The shift from control over people to control over land is thematized by Susan Reynolds in*Kingdoms and Communitiesin Western Europe, 900–1300*(Oxford: Clarendon Press, 1984), 108–16. When landed property became more important to landlords, the division between free and unfree people tended to be more obscure. The tendency to territorialization is stressed by Robert Davis Sack in his *Human Territoriality: Its Theory and History* (Cambridge: Cambridge University Press, 1986). Examples of how control over unfree people could be used to strengthen lords' territorial control can be found in Bavaria in the late Middle Ages (see Part 2, chapter Slavery and Unfreedom, page 79–80).

41 For a full discussion of this problem, see Tore Iversen and John Ragnar Myking, 'Changes in the Nordic Elites' Way of Extracting a Surplus from Landed Resources', in Bjørn Poulsen, Jon Vidar Sigurdsson and Helle Vogt (eds), *Nordic Elites in Transformation 1050–1250*, i: *Material Resources* (New York: Routledge, 2019).

from tenants. Their relationships with tenants were now purely contractual, and the landowners had no interest in interfering with their tenants' agricultural practices.

Unlike Denmark and parts of Sweden (see below), where demesne production based on corvée labour was reintroduced in the early modern period,[42] a new binate manorial system did not develop in Norway after the dissolution of the multiple estates in the twelfth century. Land-rent remained the basic income for the landholding classes. Compared to the vast landed properties belonging to ecclesiastical landlords and institutions, the amount of land belonging to the aristocracy was rather small, and they did not enjoy tax exemption for their landed possessions, apart from their residences. The material basis for the Norwegian aristocracy was therefore far weaker than for the Danish aristocracy. With the strengthening of royal power and the establishment of royal control in close cooperation with the church from the thirteenth century, the Norwegian nobility thus increasingly relied on serving the king.

In the thirteenth century, the Norwegian kings aimed at turning the regional assemblies into more professional institutions and controlling them through royal officials, especially the *lagmaðr* (lawman). He was a professional trained in written law and appointed by the king. The lawman's newly acquired ability to pass judgement made him an alternative to the local courts at the local assemblies. In cooperation with the king's officials, the lawman also had the power to censor local court decisions. Nevertheless, at the local level, peasant cooperation and self-administration was strengthened from the fourteenth century onwards, as witnessed by the many local charters signed by the local peasant elite (see chapter 'Peasant Participation' in Part 2).

The roots of royal power in Denmark went further back in time than in the other Nordic kingdoms.[43] Great fortifications, like the *Danevirke* from the seventh century on the border with Germanic tribes, and several so-called *trelleborgs*, circular fortifications from the tenth century, show an early state formation. Tribute, a periodical payment rendered by people for protection and a token of acknowledgement and submission to a patron, chieftain, or prince, seems to have been a very important factor underpinning the strength of the Danish elite, including the Danish crown.[44]

42 Carsten Porskrog Rasmussen, 'Manors and States: The Distribution and Structure of Private Manors in Early Modern Scandinavia and Their Relation to State Policies', *Scandinavian Economic History Review*, 66/2 (2018), 201–18.

43 Bjørn Poulsen, 'Den danske konges indtægter i middelalderen', in Sverre Bagge, et al. (eds), *Statsutvikling i Skandinavia i middelalderen* (Oslo: Dreyer, 2012), 55–61.

44 Poulsen, 'Den danske konges indtægter', 55–57.

By the end of the eleventh century, Viking raids from Scandinavia had come to an end. The Scandinavian elite therefore had to rely on incomes from resources in their own territories.[45] As in Norway, a close cooperation with the church strengthened the Danish crown, for example, the sacralization of King Knut (1101) and the creation of an archbishopric located in Lund (1003/1004). By the death of Valdemar the Great (1182), the Danish kingdom showed its strength at home and abroad, especially through its expansion into the territories of the heathen tribes along the Baltic coast. By the reign of Valdemar the Victorious (1202–41), the Danish realm reached its greatest extent, stretching from the Baltic Sea in the east to the river Elben in the west.

The Danish historian Bjørn Poulsen has drawn attention to the transition from tribute, compulsory contributions in exchange for protection and recognition, to regular land-rent.[46] For a long time, tribute seems to have constituted the most important portion of royal income from free peasants under the king's direct control. Furthermore, sources from the twelfth century prove that the king received tribute even from larger areas like Bornholm and Northern Frisia, areas well outside the crown's direct control.

In the beginning of the thirteenth century, the *Law of Scania*, probably due to ecclesiastical influence, indicates a more refined understanding of landed property, in accordance with the influence that high medieval learned law had in Denmark. This new concept of property visualized land-rent as a contractual form of contribution, detached from personal relations. This conforms well to a development from a loosely organized multiple estate system towards the strictly organized manorial system of the high medieval period.[47]

In Denmark, the old multiple estates from around 1200 were substituted by these more strictly organized 'classical' manors with rent-paying tenants.[48] In

45 See, for example, Thomas Lindkvist, 'Social and Political Power in Sweden 1000–1300: Predatory Incursions, Royal Taxation, and the Formation of a Feudal State', in Ross Samson (ed.), *Social Approaches to Viking Studies* (Glasgow: Cruithne Press, 1991), 137–45.

46 Bjørn Poulsen, 'A Classical Manor in Viking Age and Early Medieval Denmark?', in Yoshiki Morimoto, Jean-Pierre Devroey, and Alexis Wilkin (eds), *Autour de Yoshiki Morimoto: Les Structures Agricoles en Dehors du Monde Carolingien: Formes et genèse: Actes des journées d'études organisées à l'Université Libre de Bruxelles les 6, 7 et 8 mai 2010* (Brussels: Le Livre Timperman, 2012), 451–65.

47 Lars Jørgensen, 'From Tribute to the Estate System, 3th–12th Century: A Proposal for the Economic Development of the Magnate's Residence in Scandinavia Based on Settlement Structure from Gudme, Tissø and Lejre in Denmark', in B.Arrthenius (ed.), *Kingdoms and Regionality: Transactions from the 49th symposium 1998 in Uppsala* (Stockholm: Stockholm University, 2001), 73f.

48 Erik Ulsig, 'Peasants' Right To Control Land in Denmark' and Knut Helle 'Comments on the Presentations of Ulsig, Iversen and Myking', in Tore Iversen and John Ragnar Myking

contrast to Norway, however, a physical proximity between landlord and tenant was preserved. The thirteenth-century Danish manorial system consisted of demesnes run by bailiffs (*villici / bryder*) and holdings worked by dependent tenants. The *villici* were originally unfree men, but at this point in time they were fully free, although they were under the supervision of the lord as a part of his household. Some of the tenants probably also originated from unfree status. This 'classical' Danish manor can be seen as a regular continuation of the more loosely organized multiple estate system.[49]

The church was a leading institution in this development. Its landed property was increasing until about 1200, to a large degree at the expense of the king. The king tried to compensate his loss by transforming tributes, for example, gifts, service, and duties, into fixed taxes. This was done, for example, with naval service, which had lost its military importance and which the *Law of Jutland* (1241) affirmed had been converted to a tax. The king's greatest worry, however, was that his income did not suffice to pay for increased expenses.

In the fourteenth century, the crown experienced a crisis due to a sharp decrease in taxes. From the second part of the thirteenth century, the lay and ecclesiastical aristocracy increased its power. The archbishop and the bishop of Roskilde even attempted to create independent principalities after the German model. At the same time, landlords managed to ensure their dependent peasants were exempt from royal taxes. The Danish historian Erik Ulsig maintains that the appellation *villicus,* denoting a landlord's dependent servant, spread at the expense of the appellation *colonus*, who was a taxable royal subject. The transformation of *coloni* into *villici* meant that almost everybody working the landlords' estates came under the power and protection of his lord instead of the king.[50]

When King Erik Menved tried to compensate for decreasing royal income by raising extraordinary taxes, this led to a large rebellion from peasants, as well as aristocrats in Jutland (1313). Even though this rebellion was put down, from then on, the king had to finance his wars by mortgaging land and castles. Until the introduction of absolutism in 1660, Erik's successors had to sign charters (*håndfestinger*) confirming the aristocracy's rights and privileges in exchange for being elected king by the national council.[51]

(eds), *Land, Lords and Peasants: Peasants' Right To Control Land in the Middle Ages and the Early Modern Period – Norway, Scandinavia and the Alpine Region*, Trondheim Studies in History, 52 (Trondheim: NTNU, 2005), 29–45; Poulsen, 'A Classical Manor', 462–66.

49 Poulsen, 'A Classical Manor', 464.

50 Ulsig, in LexMA, iii, 528–30.

51 'Håndfesting', in KLNM, vii, 210–12.

A *thing* system also developed in Denmark, but its origin is obscure (see chapter 'Peasant Participation' in Part 2). The *herredsting* is believed to have been introduced in the eleventh century on the initiative of the king. The strong position of the aristocracy in Denmark in the thirteenth century resulted in a partially overlapping jurisdiction. The nobility came to hold the stronger standing in the *thing* system (*herredsting* and *landsting*), where landlords had a hold over their peasants, especially their tenants.

The king's *retterting*, usually without peasant representatives, competed with the ordinary *thing* system. The king also organized *birks*, areas under his special protection with their own *thing* assemblies. The standing of the different *thing* assemblies seemed to have been variable in the high and late medieval periods because of the ongoing struggle between the king and the nobility. In a Scandinavian setting, the peasant assemblies in Denmark may be used to contrast the Norwegian development. While in Norway the balance of power before 1350 developed over time in favour of the king in close cooperation with the peasants, in Denmark conflicts between the king and a strong aristocracy influenced peasant participation at the *things*.

2.2 *The Crisis in the Late Middle Ages*

In the late Middle Ages, most of Europe experienced a marked population decline resulting in deserted farms and villages. Most historians maintain that the main cause of this dramatic decline was the multiple outbreaks of plague from the middle of the fourteenth century onwards, although a deterioration of climate may have been a contributory factor.[52] This crisis hit Scandinavia and the Alpine region.[53] For Scandinavia, a settlement setback is well documented in the Scandinavian Research Project on Deserted Farms and Villages of the early 1970s. The majority of abandoned settlements were, as one would expect, found in areas with single farms and small hamlets, rather than in areas with village settlements. In large settlements, a decline in family units would not necessarily lead to total desertion of a whole village.[54]

52 Klaus Bergdolt, *Die Pest: Geschichte des Schwarzen Todes* (Munich: C.H. Beck, 2006), 46. Svend Gissel, et al. (eds), *Desertion and Land Colonization in the Nordic Countries c. 1300–1600* (Stockholm, Almquist and Wiksell International, 1982), 237–38. For the hundred years of famine before the plague, see William Chester Jordan, *The Great Famine: Northern Europe in the Early Fourteenth Century* (Princeton: Princeton University Press, 1996).

53 For the Alpine region, see a general overview in Jon Mathieu, *Die Alpen: Raum–Kultur–Geschichte* (Stuttgart: Reclam, 2015), 84–86.

54 Gissel, et al., *Desertion and Land Colonization*, 101–10.

A general overview of deserted settlements in Germany, based on older local studies, was published in the mid-1950s by Wilhelm Abel,[55] but detailed studies of deserted farms, hamlets, and villages are lacking for Alt-Bayern and Tyrol.[56] However, in the neighbouring regions of Salzburg and Franken and in the southwestern region of Germany local studies indicate a decline in settlements from the middle of the fourteenth century. This decline was especially marked in high altitude localities and in other marginal areas that were settled late during the settlement expansion before the middle of the fourteenth century.[57] It is therefore arguable that the whole Alpine region and Bavaria also experienced a settlement and population decline during the late Middle Ages, an assumption substantiated by the fact that Tyrolean decrees from 1352 and 1404 tried to stop peasants leaving their farms. This assumption is further supported by scattered accounts of deserted settlements in Bavaria and Tyrol, and by contemporary accounts of plagues in Tyrol, Salzburg, and Bavaria.[58]

In Scandinavia, recolonization of deserted settlements was under way in the sixteenth century, indicating a new population increase.[59] A marked population increase also took place in Tyrol in the same period, especially in the new, expanding mining districts in the mountains, where the population in some areas had reached a higher level by the beginning of the fifteenth century than existed in the first half of the fourteenth century.[60]

Inevitably, a fall in population leading to deserted farms and villages in the late Middle Ages must have affected the balance of power between landlords and their peasants. With fewer households to work the land, peasants were in a position to obtain better conditions in return for staying on their farms or renting vacant land. Landlords, on the other hand, had to choose between offering their peasants better conditions or restricting their ability to leave their

55 Wilhelm Abel, *Die Wüstungen des ausgehenden Mittelalters*, 2nd edn (Stuttgart: Gustav Fischer Verlag, 1955), 5–12.

56 Peter Rückert, 'Wüstungen (Spätmittelalter)', in *Historisches Lexikon Bayerns*. URL: http://www.historisches-lexikon-bayerns.de/artikel/artikel_45701 (accessed 28.01.2014); Josef Riedmann, Mittelalter, in Josef Fontana, et al. (eds), *Geschichte des Landes Tirol*, i, (Bozen / Vienna: Verlagsanstalt Athesia, 1985), 489.

57 Rückert, 'Wüstungen (Spätmittelalter)'; Herbert Klein, 'Das Grosse Sterben von 1348/49 und seine Auswirkung auf die Besiedlung der Ostalpenländer', in *Festschrift zum 65. Geburtstag von Herberg Klein*, Gesellschaft für Salzburger Landeskunde (Salzburg: Gesellschaft für Salzburger Landeskunde 1965), 33–113.

58 Klein, 'Das Grosse Sterben', 34–42, 104–13; Riedmann, 'Mittelalter', 487–89.

59 Gissel, et al. (eds), *Desertion and Land Colonization*, 33–35.

60 Riedmann, 'Middelalter', 489. Rudolf Palme, 'Frühe Neuzeit (1480–1665)', in Josef Fontana, et al. (eds), *Geschichte des Landes Tirol*, ii (Bozen / Vienna: Verlagsanstalt Athesia, 1986), 196.

land. Most landlords in Scandinavia and in the Alpine region chose the first option, offering their tenants reduced rent, consenting to secure or even hereditary tenures, or relieving their obligation to work on the demesne. (see chapter 'Leasehold and Freehold' in Part 2)

The centuries following the first plague in the middle of the fourteenth century saw a breakthrough for lower rents and more secure tenures and, in many places, also for the end of corvée labour. However, in both regions we also find scattered attempts to restrict peasants' ability to leave their farm and the estate. In Denmark, landlords imposed restrictions on the movement of their tenants on the eastern Danish isles in the last decade of the fifteenth century.[61] In southern Germany, including Bavaria, local monasteries and secular and ecclesiastical landlords tried to prevent their tenants from leaving their land. In this process, some monasteries exchanged *Eigenleute* (serfs / dependent peasants) with other monasteries in order to construct closed territories. Sheer force, though, was not enough to keep peasants from switching to other landlords or moving into nearby towns. Therefore, the same landlords also tried to make it more attractive to stay on their territories by introducing lifelong or hereditary tenures, reducing or stabilizing rents, and abstaining from excessive claims to the deceased tenant's estate.[62] Recent research in Germany and Switzerland indicates that relationships between peasants and their lords were characterized by permanent interaction, marked by conflicts as well as by cooperation.[63]

Restrictions on the free movement of tenants were not only introduced by ecclesiastical or lay landlords. As early as 1352, the Tyrolean prince, in agreement with the *Landstände* (estates), issued a decree prohibiting peasants from

61 John Ragnar Myking and Carsten Porskrog Rasmussen, 'Scandinaiva, 100–17050', in Bas J.P. van Bavel and Richard Hoyle, *Rural Econony and Society in North-Western Europe, 500–2000*, i: *Social Relations: Property and Power* (Turnhout: Brepols, 2010), 287–312, at p. 301.

62 Peter Blickle, *Von der Leibeigenschaft zu den Menschenrechten: Eine Geschichte der Freiheit in Deutschland* (Munich: C.H. Beck, 2003), 53–57.

63 Alfred Zangger, 'Alltagsbeziehungen zwischen Klosterherrschaft und Bauern am Beispiel des Prämonstratenserklosters Rüti im 15. Jahrhundert', in Thomas Meier and Roger Sablonier (eds), *Wirtschaft und Herrschaft. Beiträge zur ländlichen Gesellschaft in der östlichen Schweiz (1200–1800)*, (Zurich, 1999), 295–309; Sigrid Hirbodian, 'Ländliche Rechtsquellen und die politische Kultur in Spätmittelalter und Früher Neuzeit', in Carola Fey and Steffen Krieb (eds), *Adel und Bauern in der Gesellschaft des Mittelalters. Internationales Kolloquium zum 65. Geburtstag von Werner Rösener*, Studien und Texte zur Geistes- und Sozialgeschichte des Mittelalters, 6, (Korb, 2012), 165–76; Katherine Brun, *The Abbot and His Peasants: Territorial Formation in Salem from the Later Middle Ages to the Thirty Years War*, Quellen und Forschungen zur Agrargeschichte, 56 (Stuttgart: Lucius & Lucius , 2013). Stefan Sonderegger, *Aktive Grundherren und Bauern: Beziehungen zwischen Herren und Bauern im wirtschaftlichen Alltag im 14. bis 16. Jahrhundert*, forthcoming.

leaving their holdings without permission from their landlord.[64] This was repeated in the *Landesordnung* from 1404, which also stated that a tenant had to find a successor before leaving and that a landlord could order his *Eigenleute*, sitting on holdings belonging to other landlords, to take over one of his holdings.[65]

On the whole, in spite of attempts to restrict their free movement in some areas, the population crisis of the late Middle Ages, disregarding the horrible human sufferings of the plague period, meant better conditions for tenants. The power of landlords was weakened or transformed, and many tenants gained more secure control over the land they worked. With a few exceptions, the subsequent population increase did not result in a reversal of this trend. To a large degree, this lack of reversal resulted from the growth of territorial power.

2.3 *The Early Modern Period*

The early modern period in Europe was characterized by the strengthening of territorial states and the monopolization of political power in the hands of a king or a territorial prince.[66] These territorial states aimed at creating uniform confessional systems and expanding their judicial control within their territories, as well as funding a strong military power. They therefore tended to develop a centralized bureaucratic administration with a comprehensive system of taxation.[67] As the majority of taxable resources were still found in the countryside, where landlords controlled a great part of the surplus created by the peasant households, territorial states therefore sought to turn peasants into taxable subjects, liable to territorial courts, at the expense of seigneurial influence and control.[68] This process of transformation occurred at different speeds and at different points in time in Scandinavia and the Alpine region.

64 Riedmann, 'Mittelalter', 489; Blickle, *Von der Leibeigenschaft*, 50.

65 Klein, 'Das Grosse Sterben', 111–12.

66 Peter Blickle, 'Conclusion', in Peter Blickle (ed.), *Resistance, Representation and Community* (Oxford: Clarendon Press, 1997), 325.

67 Jan Glete, *War and the State in Early Modern Europe: Spain, The Dutch Republic and Sweden as Fiscal-military States 1500–1660* (Routledge: London, 2002); Steinar Imsen and Günter Vogler: 'Communal Autonomy and Peasant Resistance', in Peter Blickle (ed.), *Resistance, Representation and Community* (Oxford: Clarendon Press, 1997), 5–43, at p. 17.

68 Charles Tilly, 'Reflections on the History of European State-Making', in Charles Tilly (ed.), *The Formation of National States in Western Europe* (Princeton: Princeton University Press, 1975), 19–21.

2.3.1 The East Alpine Region

The Scandinavian kingdoms had already formed strong territorial states in the Middle Ages (see above). A corresponding process lasted longer in the Alpine region and neighbouring areas in southern Germany, where the transition from the Middle Ages to the early modern period was characterized by the development from *Landesherrschaften*, territories controlled by members of the secular or ecclesiastical aristocracy, monasteries, or even city councils, to territorial states. This late development of territorial states must be seen in connection with the gradual dissolution of the German empire from the thirteenth century.

Counts belonging to the Görz family, from the thirteenth century, and to the Habsburgian family, from 1364, secured their grip over the county of Tyrol at the expense of the aristocracy and ecclesiastical institutions.[69] In Bavaria, from the end of the late Middle Ages to the early modern period, the Wittelsbach family managed to create a strong duchy. Although it was repeatedly subdivided in the fourteenth and fifteenth centuries, it was again unified under one and the same branch of the Wittelsbach family by the beginning of the sixteenth century, and in 1623, it received the status of an electorate in the German Empire. Bavaria also included more or less independent *Landesherrschaften*, like the ecclesiastical principality of Freising, which continued to exist throughout the early modern period.

The Swiss territorial confederacy, formed at the end of the thirteenth century and in the following century enlarged with sizable city-states like Bern and Zurich, profited greatly from the difficult situation the aristocracy endured. The territorial expansion of the Swiss city-states was mainly a peaceful process in which the cities bought or acquired mortgaged territories and incorporated members of the aristocratic and ecclesiastical elites, as well as ordinary people, into their citizenship.[70] The city councils, represented through their bailiffs in the countryside, were now the new lords over the peasants in their territories.[71]

69 Josef Riedmann, *Geschichte Tirols* (Vienna: Verlag für Geschchte und Politikk, 1988).

70 Roger Sablonier, 'Schweizer Eidgenossenschaft im 15. Jahrhundert: Staatlichkeit, Politik und Selbstverständnis', in Josef Wiget (ed.), *Die Entstehung der Schweiz. Vom Bundesbrief 1291 zur nationalen Geschichtskultur des 20. Jahrhunderts* (Schwyz: Historischer Verein des Kantons Schwyz, 1999), 17f.

71 Regarding Zurich, see 'Zurich (Kanton)', in *Historisches Lexikon der Schweiz*, xiii (Basel, 2013), 848–56. Doris Klee, *Konflikte kommunizieren: Die Briefe des Grüninger Landvogts Jörg Berger an den Zürcher Rat (1514–1529)* (Zurich: Chronos, 2006). Regarding Bern, see 'Bern (Kanton)', in Marco Jorio (ed.), *Historisches Lexikon der Schweiz*, 13 vols (Basel: Schwabe, 2002–2014), ii, 258–66.

The Swiss confederation was characterized by a high degree of local, communal autonomy, as exemplified by one of the most important ecclesiastical *Landesherrschaften*, the monastery of St Gallen. With the help of village statutes and territorial regulations, the sovereign abbot secured his privileges at the same time as a partial co-determination was granted to the peasants, especially in economic matters, for example, when it came to the use of common outfield resources like forests and alpine pastures.[72]

Although this was a period that severed many of the remaining bonds between landlords and their tenants, remnants of unfree bonds were still found in Bavaria and the eastern Alpine region, with the exception of Tyrol, especially on ecclesiastical estates where such bonds could be used to consolidate geographical territories or to increase incomes.[73] The tendency to make peasants subject to the territorial state was also strongly felt in the eastern Alpine region, especially in Tyrol where, from the end of the thirteenth century, the territorial prince embarked on a practice that undermined aristocratic and ecclesiastical jurisdiction and these groups' control over their peasants. During the late Middle Ages, peasants became subjects of their territorial lord with no personal bonds to their landlords.[74] Aristocratic and ecclesiastical lords were stripped of their judicial and administrative authority, which was transferred to local *Gerichte* (district assemblies). The alliance between peasants and the territorial power became so close that a peasant elite representing these *Gerichte* were even represented in the Tyrolean *Landtag* (state assembly).[75]

2.3.2 Scandinavia

From 1397 until 1523 the three Scandinavian kingdoms were formally united under a common king in the Kalmar Union. Sweden left the union in 1523, while Norway, which had already entered into a personal union with Denmark in 1380, stayed with Denmark until 1814.

Until the 1530s, these unions were little more than loose confederations with a common king. Each country retained a sovereign council with aristocratic and ecclesiastical representatives. Although the royal government in

72 Philip Robinson, *Die Fürstabtei St. Gallen und ihr Territorium 1463–1529* (St Gallen: Staatsarchiv und Stiftsarchiv, 1995).

73 Dopsch, Heinz, 'Zur entwicklung des bäuerlichen Bestizrechts im Ostlpenraum' in Tore Iversen and John Ragnar Myking (eds), *Land, Lords and Peasants: Peasants' Right to Control Land in the Middle Ages and the Early Modern Period – Norway, Scandinavia and the Alpine Region*, Trondheim Studies in History, 52 (Trondheim: NTNU, 2005), 63–80, at pp. 78–79.

74 Riedmann, *Geschichte Tirols*, 56.

75 Riedmann, *Geschichte Tirols*, 83; Riedmann, 'Mittelalter', 452–54.

Copenhagen had the most influence, the king had to take the power of the sovereign councils into consideration, since they elected the king and dictated the conditions to which he had to consent. Each country kept its own laws, and the administration of each country was, with some adjustments, built on national tradition dating back to the Middle Ages.

The later union between Norway and Denmark from the time of the Reformation 1536/1537 had quite a different character. The relatively strong Norwegian Catholic church had provided the backbone of the Norwegian sovereign council. With the Reformation, its land was confiscated by the crown and the church was controlled from Copenhagen. At the same time, the sovereign council itself was abolished. From this point until 1814, Norway was ruled from Copenhagen, a fact that did not change after the introduction of absolutism in 1660.

Although the central government in Copenhagen controlled both countries, great topographical and socio-economic differences between the two kingdoms forced the Danish government to differentiate their policies in each country towards peasants and landowners. In Denmark, with its fertile plains and powerful aristocracy, landlords were pretty much left in charge of their tenants and in time came to be intermediaries between their peasants and the Danish state. From the sixteenth century, Danish landlords greatly expanded their demesnes, using corvée labour from their tenants,[76] and from the first half of the sixteenth century, the Danish aristocracy gained the right to prosecute their tenants and to collect fines from them.[77] Quite a few of them also obtained the right to appoint judges to their manorial courts (*birketing*).[78]

After the introduction of absolutism in 1660, Danish landlords' control over their peasants was furthered by the fact that they had to collect taxes on behalf of the government, and that they were held personally responsible for the sums their tenants were due to pay. When, from the beginning of the eighteenth century, they were also given the responsibility for the conscription of soldiers on their estates, for all practical purposes, Danish manorial lords took over full public authority over their peasants. For the state, the outsourcing of public tasks meant stable incomes and secure conscription. For peasants, it meant that they came even more under the power of their landlords than

76 Rasmussen, 'Manors and States', 210–12.
About 'hoveri', see: http://danmarkshistorien.dk/leksikon-og-kilder/vis/materiale/hoveri/. Last viewed 01 Feb 2016. See also Erik Ulsig, 'Hoveri', in KLNM, xxi, 199–201.

77 Myking and Rasmussen, 'Scandinavia', 301. URL: http://danmarkshistorien.dk/leksikon-og-kilder/vis/materiale/hals-og-haandsret-1400-1660/. Last viewed 23 Dec 2017.

78 http://danmarkshistorien.dk/leksikon-og-kilder/vis/materiale/det-verdslige-juridiske-system-foer-1660/. Last viewed 23 Dec 2017.

before. Even if the restrictions on leaving the estates on the eastern Danish islands (see above) were lifted by the beginning of the sixteenth century, new restrictions were introduced. From 1733, all adult men up to the age of thirty-six were obliged to remain on the estate where they were born. However, in contrast to the continental 'new' serfdom, this adscription did not impose restrictions on females and marriage.[79]

Conditions in Norway called for quite another approach from the central government in Copenhagen. From the Middle Ages, Norwegian peasants had been subject to their kings without any seigneurial jurisdictional control. The only exception came in the second half of the seventeenth century when two newly established counties and a barony, along with a few other scattered estates, were given *birkerett*, that is, the right to appoint judges and to collect fines.[80] As we have already seen, Norwegian tenants' relations with their landlords were, from the thirteenth century onwards, purely contractual without any personal bond. A majority of peasants were tenants, and with the dissolution of multiple farms from the twelfth century onwards, landlords, of which the church was the major one, drew their incomes almost exclusively from rent.

Following the Reformation in 1537, the crown controlled more than half of the landed property, the aristocracy probably less than 10 percent. Merchants, officials, and peasants owned the rest of the land. Due to the complicated share-of-rent-ownership system (*skyldpartsystem* – see above), by the 1660s less than 20 percent of the peasants themselves owned the land they and their family worked. Given these circumstances, by the first half of the sixteenth century, the Danish government chose to keep rents deliberately low to secure Norwegian peasants as viable taxpayers. This relatively peasant-friendly policy was carried further in the seventeenth century, when a new Norwegian peasant army was established.

Like Norwegian peasants, most Swedish peasants were subject only to the jurisdiction of the crown. However, from the second half of the sixteenth century, Swedish counts and barons gradually acquired judicial authority in their fiefs. These privileges were confirmed in 1634, but annulled by 1692.[81] Even

---

79 Birgit Løgstrup, *Jorddrot og offentlig administrator: Godsejerstyret inden for skatte- og udskrivningsvæsenet i det 18. århundrede.* (Copenhagen: Gad, 1983); Carsten Porskrog Rasmussen, 'Gård og gods', in John Erichsen and Mikkel Venborg Pedersen (eds), *Herregården: Menneske – samfund – landskab – bygninger* (Copenhagen: Nationalmuseet, 2004), 201–06.

80 'Birk' in *Norsk historisk leksikon*, Steinar Imsen and Harald Winge (eds), 2nd edn (Oslo: Cappelen, 2004).

81 Kenneth Johansson, 'Herrar og bönder: Om jurisdiktionen i några småländske friherrskap på 1600-talet', *Scandia*, 2 (1990), 161–82, at pp. 162–63. 'Borgrätt', in *Nordisk familjebok*, iii: *Bergsvalan-Brandstad*, 2nd edn (Stockholm, 1905), 1192–93.

though the Swedish crown thus secured nearly a complete monopoly of jurisdiction in much the same way as the Danish Crown did in Norway, it did not monopolize the collection of taxes in the early modern period, nor did it, as was the case from the second half of the seventeenth century in Denmark, use landowners to collect taxes for the crown.

Instead, noble landowners were allowed to use taxes for their own purposes, and in the early seventeenth century a considerable amount of crown land, with the right to collect rents and taxes, was transferred to a growing class of noblemen serving as officers and civil servants. At the end of the seventeenth century, *frälsebønder*, that is, peasants belonging to these aristocratic estates, worked a third of the total land in Sweden. Especially in the southern province of Scania, which was transferred from Denmark to Sweden in 1658, they were obliged to render heavy corvée labour. To a great extent, these tenants were controlled by the owners of the estates, some of them also belonging to noble jurisdiction until the end of the seventeenth century. Although some of the land given to noblemen in the early seventeenth century was recalled by the crown in the 1680s, taxes from this land still were designated to specific civil and military officials and officers.[82]

The consolidation of territorial states had fundamental consequences for peasants' relations with their landlords, as well as with their territorial lords. In some countries or territories, such as Norway and Tyrol, we can observe the territorial lord gaining complete jurisdiction and control over taxes by the Middle Ages, making every peasant a subject of the territorial lord without interference from an aristocratic or ecclesiastical elite. This was true also for Norway, even if the country came to be ruled from Copenhagen, the capital of the united kingdom of Denmark-Norway, from the late Middle Ages onwards. In Denmark, however, the same government allowed landlords a wide range of authority over their tenants, even to the point where landlords became intermediaries between the crown and their peasants regarding jurisdiction, tax collection, and conscription. In Bavaria, compromises regarding jurisdiction dating back to the Middle Ages continued well into the early modern period, allowing landlords substantial influence over their tenants in their closed territories (*Hofmarken*).

82 John Ragnar Myking, *Herre over andre si jord? Norske leiglendingsvilkår i europeisk lys 1500–1800* (Kristiansand: Høyskoleforlaget, 2005), 34–35.

PART 2

Comparing Scandinavia and the Eastern Alpine Region

CHAPTER 2

Slavery and Unfreedom from the Middle Ages to the Beginning of the Early Modern Period

Tore Iversen

Slavery in Scandinavia used to be perceived as quite short-lived, in contrast to conditions on the Continent. This assumption, based on the Viking raids as the prime source of recruiting slaves, was one of the arguments for the thesis of a Nordic *Sonderweg*. For the eastern Alpine region and continental Europe slavery is believed to have existed from the Germanic period, but gradually alleviated already in the Early Middle Ages (see 'Introduction').

Today slavery / unfreedom is held to be an important element in the rural societies in Scandinavia, as it has been for long time in the eastern Alpine region. I will therefore try to highlight the most important elements in the character and development of peasant unfreedom in these two regions. Comparing unfreedom in this way may also provide new insight into similarities and differences in other fields of rural society.

One of the great difficulties facing any attempt to compare different forms of unfreedom in the Middle Ages is the confusing multitude of terms that often occur without any contextual references.[1] To solve this problem, the terms *unfree* and *unfreedom* will be used in this article as comprehensive terms for a wide range of personal bonds to a lord or a master. At one end of this spectrum we find an almost complete subordination in the form of slavery and the existence of slaves (Norw: *þrældómr / þrælar – pl., þræll – sing.*; Lat: *servitus / servi – pl.; servus – sing.*), as in the eastern Alpine region in the early Middle Ages and in Scandinavia well into the High Middle Ages. These persons were considered to belong to their lord or master as a form of property. At the other end of this spectrum, unfreedom was diminished, for example, the unfree persons were increasingly given partially legalized personal rights. Still, these persons were considered as property. They were personally dependent and often had to obtain their master's permission before making important decisions. At this end of the spectrum, we find, among others, the *servi / Eigenleute* in the eastern

1 Marc Bloch, *Slavery and Serfdom in the Middle Ages: Selected Essays*, trans. William R. Beer (Berkeley: University of California Press, 1975), 19, 21, 22.

 | DOI:10.1163/9789004433458_003

Alpine region and different forms of freedmen in Scandinavia.[2] (see 'The Legal Portrayal of Slaves and Unfree Persons', below).

In my opinion, it is to no avail to operate with any fundamental distinction between slave and serf (*slave / Sklave – serf / Hörig*) in our period, because there are usually only gradual transitions over long periods of time. There is no clear difference between these two types of terms, and they are often intertwined and blurred. This is especially true for the eastern Alpine region, where a multitude of forms and terms for unfreedom is found. In Scandinavia, unfreedom became less uncompromising and absolute in the High Middle Ages, before it eventually disappeared. In the eastern Alpine region, unfreedom was also partially transformed. Yet in other periods of time, unfreedom grew harsher, as during the so-called second serfdom in Eastern Europe in the early modern period or during colonial slavery of the same period.[3] As a consequence, a doctrine implying a general and fundamental transition from a distinct 'slave society' based on exploitation of slaves to a 'feudal society' based on exploitation of serfs cannot be tenable. In my opinion, it is therefore better to apply a broad definition of unfree people in order to obtain insight into unfreedom in a variety of medieval and early modern European societies. In this way, unfreedom is not associated with one period only (see 'The Legal Portrayal of Slaves and Unfree Persons', below).

The development of unfreedom is closely connected to demographic changes, development in agricultural structures, and changes in the forms of *Herrschaft* (dominion). For Scandinavia, unfreedom will be analysed mainly on the basis of Norwegian studies, since historical sources to slavery and unfreedom are older and considerably more differentiated in this country than in Denmark and Sweden. Swedish slavery has a lot in common with Norwegian slavery (*þrældómr*). However, as the wave of releases to half or full freedom came later in Sweden, Swedish studies and sources can primarily throw light on the last stages of medieval slavery and bondage in Scandinavia. For Denmark, the

2 Within this group, we also find people who were not considered unfree, that is, minors and other incapacitated members of the family whose condition was temporary (Tore Iversen, *Trelldommen: Norsk slaveri i middelalderen*, Universitetet i Bergen Skrifter, 1 (Bergen: Historisk institutt, 1997), 37–54 [German edition: *Knechtschaft im mittelalterlichen Norwegen*, trans. Katharina Freche in collaboration with Angelika Landau, Abhandlungen zur rechtswissenschaftlichen Grundlagenforschung, 94 (Ebelsbach: Aktiv, 2004), 62–87].

3 Cf. Paul Freedman and Monique Bourin, 'Introduction', in Paul Freedman and Monique Bourin (eds), *Forms of Servitude in Northern and Central Europe: Decline, Resistance, and Expansion* (Turnhout: Brepols, 2005), 1–15.

lack of sources is even more problematic, and this country furthermore lacks thorough studies on slavery.[4]

In the eastern Alpine region, unfreedom lasted longer than in Scandinavia. Regarding the Alpine region, we are starting our study in the ancient tribal duchy of Bavaria with the early medieval *Lex Baiuvariorum*, probably written down gradually from the first part of the eighth century. This law remained existing law into the beginning of the high medieval period. For some local regions of the ancient duchy, especially Upper Bavaria and Tyrol, we must, however, scrutinize the historical development more deeply, since unfreedom in the eastern Alpine region, in contrast to Scandinavia, though less absolute, still existed in the early modern period.[5]

In contrast to Central Europe, where the scope of unfreedom has been little contested,[6] the scope of this phenomenon in medieval Scandinavia has been much debated among Scandinavian historians. Most Scandinavian medieval historians, especially until the beginning of the 1970s, held the opinion that slavery (*þrældómr*) played a marginal role. This opinion, based on their belief that slavery was insignificant, that slaves were few in number, and that they were rather quickly manumitted, was an important part of their ideology of an ancient Scandinavian peasant freedom. According to these historians, the end of the Viking raids and the influence of the Christian faith were the causes for the institution of slavery disappearing in the High Middle Ages. However, little effort was made to substantiate this belief.[7]

In the 1970s, a new debate on the scope and impact of medieval *þrældómr* was initiated by the historian Kåre Lunden (1971), who strongly argued for a re-evaluation of slavery. Jørn Sandnes (1979) assessed the number of unfree

---

4 Nils Skyum-Nielsen's *Kvinde og slave* (Copenhagen: Munksgaard, 1971) is an exception.

5 Because this study spans several centuries, as well as a wide geographical area, it has been necessary to rely heavily on a study of literature instead of original historical sources regarding the eastern Alpine region. However, I made an exception for legal sources, primarily the *Lex Baiuvariorum* and the *Schwabenspiegel*. The use of such sources thus means that the discussion of the concept of *servus* covers the whole of Germany east of the Rhine.

6 In Central Europe, the debate, as will later be demonstrated, has been concentrated instead on the question of the *character* of slavery and bondage, especially in the early medieval period.

7 An example of this ideology is Andreas Holmsen's assertion that our knowledge of early social development in Norway contradicts any suggestion that there a number of dependant people existed in peasant households (Andreas Holmsen, *Norges historie: Fra de eldste tider til eneveldes innførelse* (Oslo: Gyldendal, 1939, repr. 1961), 70–71, 184; see also Arne Odd Johnsen, *Fra ættesamfunn til statssamfunn* (Oslo: Aschehoug, 1948), 151–53. The Marxist historian Edvard Bull, *Det norske folks liv og historie*, ii (Oslo: Aschehoug, 1935), 15, also shared this opinion: see the introduction to this volume).

people to be 20 percent of the total population of Norway.[8] Inevitably, this also raised the question of the economic importance of a subjugated work force, which resulted in Swedish and Danish studies by Clara Nevéus (1974) and Thomas Lindkvist and Janken Myrdal (2003). This problem was also discussed by Ruth Mazo Karras (1988) and Tore Iversen (1997, 2004) in their studies on Norwegian and Scandinavian slavery.[9]

1 Sources for Slavery in Scandinavia

The regional laws are among the oldest sources for unfreedom in Scandinavia. The Norwegian *Gulathing Law* (G) is known in two editions. The first, dated to the end of the eleventh century, is only preserved in fragments. The second, dated to the 1160s, is quite complete. The *Frostathing Law* (F) is extant in several editions. At least two of them can be dated to the first half of the thirteenth century. References to slaves and other unfree persons occur quite frequently in these laws. In King Magnus the Lawmender's *Norwegian Law of the Realm of 1274* (L), unfree people are hardly mentioned at all.[10] Also, in Sweden and

8 Kåre Lunden, 'Om årsakene til den norske bondefridomen: Ein økonomisk-historisk forklåringsmåte', *Heimen*, 15 (1971), 213–22; Jørn Sandnes, 'Bondesamfunnet', in Nina Karin Monsen and Ingrid Semmingsen (eds), *Norges kulturhistorie*, i: *Vår fjerne fortid* (Oslo: Aschehoug, 1979), 50.

9 Clara Nevéus, *Trälarna i landskapslagarnas samhälle. Danmark och Sverige*, Studia historica Upsaliensia, 58, published dissertation, University of Uppsala, 1974 (Uppsala: Almkvist och Wiksell, 1974), 156 f.; Thomas Lindkvist and Janken Myrdal, *Trälar. Ofria i agrarsamhället från vikingatid till medeltid*, Skrifter om skog- och lantbrukshistoria, 17 (Stockholm: Nordiska museet, 2003); Ruth Mazo Karras, *Slavery and Society in Medieval Scandinavia*, (New Haven: Yale University Press, 1988), 80–91; Iversen, *Trelldommen*; Iversen *Knechtschaft*.

10 For dating of the Norwegian medieval laws: Knut Helle, *Norge blir en stat: 1130–1319*, Handbok i Norges historie, 3, 2nd edn (Oslo: Universitetsforlaget, 1974), 224–29; Absalon Taranger, 'De norske folkelovbøker', *Tidsskrift for Retsvidenskab*, 39, 41 (1926, 1928), 183–211, 1–68. We also find early Norwegian jurisdiction in the two east Norwegian Christian Laws, the *Eidsivathing Law* (E) and the *Borgarthing Law* (B) and in fragments from a town law for Trondheim (Bj). The Norwegian laws from the High Middle Ages are edited and published by Rudolf Keyser, P.A. Munch, Gustav Storm and Ebbe Hertzberg in: *Norges gamle Love* (hereafter NgL), 5 vols (Christiania: Chr. Grøndahl, 1846–95). English translations occur in: *The Earliest Norwegian Laws: Being the Gulathing law and the Frostathing Law*, ed. and trans L.M. Larson, Records of Civilizations, 20 (New York: Columbia University Press, 1935). German translations in: *Norwegisches Recht: Das Rechtsbuch des Gulathings*, ed. Rudolf Meissner, Germanenrechte, 6 (Weimar: Böhlau, 1935); *Norwegisches Recht: Das Rechtsbuch des Frostothings*, Germanenrechte, 4 (Weimar: Böhlau, 1939); *Landrecht des Königs Magnus Hakonarson*, trans. Rudolf Meissner (Weimar: Böhlau, 1941); *Danmarks*

Denmark, written laws are our main sources when studying unfreedom: the *Law of Scania* (SkL) from the beginning of the thirteenth century and the 'Law of the Thralls' from 1250 in *King Valdemar's Law for Zealand* (VL). In the *Law of Jutland* (JL) from 1241 there is, however, no significant trace of any unfreedom. The Swedish laws can mostly be dated to the end of the thirteenth century, and the *Law of Uppland* (UL) from 1296 shows the last stage of *þrældómr* in Scandinavia.[11] In addition to these laws, we have important documentary sources for unfreedom, especially for Sweden, with testaments from the period 1258–1310 concerning the release of slaves (see below).[12]

In the huge literary corpus covering the western Nordic region, including the Norwegian Kings' sagas and especially the Icelandic family sagas, we find a multitude of stories staging *þrælar* in the background. Even if most of these sagas were composed in Iceland, the family sagas often refer to conditions in Norway. The royal sagas were first written down around 1100, most of them dating from the end of the twelfth century onwards. From around 1130, these sagas are supported by contemporary eyewitness reports and written notes. The Icelandic sagas were mostly written in the thirteenth century. These sagas are important sources for living conditions in Norway and Iceland, as well as for the social and psychological conditions of the *þrælar*.[13]

---

gamle Love paa Nutidsdansk, ed. E. Kroman and S. Iuul, Danske Sprog- og Litteraturselskab, 3 vols (Copenhagen: G.E.C Gad, 1945–48); *Svenska landskapslagar, tolkade och forklarade för nutidens svenskar*, ed. and trans. Ake Holmbäck and Elias Wessén, 5 vols (Stockholm: Hugo Gebers, 1933–46).

As for the dating of these sources, I follow what in German is known as *schriftliche Rezeptionstheorie*, that is, that they were recorded on parchment after a deliberate political assessment. None of the essential parts of these laws could therefore be outdated at the time they were written down (Iversen, *Knechtschaft*, 62–66; Elsa Sjöholm, 'Rättshistorisk metod och teoribildning', *Scandia*, 44 (1978), 229–56); Elsa Sjöholm, 'Medeltids-lagarna som historiske källor', in Hedda Gunneng and Birgit Strand (eds), *Kvinnans ekonomiska ställning under Nordisk medeltid* (Upsatser framlagda vid ett kvinnohistorisk symposium i Kungälv 8.-12.oktober 1979), Kvinnohistoriskt arkiv, 19 (Stockholm: Kompendiet, Lindome, 1981), 74–81.

11 See Nevéus, *Trälarna*, 14–25.

12 Nevéus, *Trälarna*, 23–25.

13 Most important are: Snorri Sturluson's *Heimskringla* (hereafter Hkr), ed. Finnur Jónsson (Copenhagen: Gad, 1911); the Icelandic Family sagas: *Egils saga* (ed. Sigurður Nordal), *Borgfirðingar sögur* (ed. Guðni Jónsson), *Eyrbyggja saga* (ed. Einar Ól. Sveinsson), *Laxdæla saga* (ed. Einar Ól. Sveinsson), *Vestfirðinga sögur* (ed. Guðni Jónsson), *Grettis saga* (ed. Guðni Jónsson), *Vatnsdæla saga* (ed. Einar Ól. Sveinsson), *Ljósvetninga saga* (ed. Björn Sigfússon), *Brennu-Njáls saga* (ed. Einar Ól. Sveinsson), *Kjalnesinga saga* (ed. Jóhannes Halldórsson), Islenzk fornrit (hereafter ÍF) 2–8, 10, 12, and 14 (Reykjavík: Hið Íslenzka fornritafélag, 1933–59); *Landnámabók* (hereafter Lnb) in *Íslendingabók. Landnámabók*, ed. Jakob Benediktsson, ÍF, 1 (Reykjavík: Hið Íslenzka fornritafélag, 1968); *Sverris saga*

2 Eastern Alpine Sources

The sources throwing light on the existence and conditions of unfree people in the eastern Alpine region differ distinctly from the Norwegian and Nordic sources.[14] For the social history of Bavaria and the eastern Alpine region, '*Traditionsbücher*', belonging to monasteries and bishoprics, are the most important. These are collections of documents, in which the acquisition or exchange of land or persons is recorded. They often inform in relative detail about the social standing of the manorial subjects.[15] Another group of sources is comprised of leasing contracts, which increase greatly in number from the thirteenth century. To this we can add the cadastres (*Urbare*) that not only recorded the manorial land but also the work, the rent, and other dues that the manors' dependent people (*Eigenleuten*) were obliged to render to their manorial lord. From the late Middle Ages, the different forms of leaseholds by which peasants held their land were also recorded.[16]

For a long period, the *Lex Baiuvariorum*, recorded in writing around 743/48, was valid law in Bavaria and the eastern Alpine region.[17] It was enlarged

(hereafter Sv. s)*: etter cod.* AM *327 4to*, ed. Gustav Indrebø and Karl Jónsson (Kristiania: Dybwad, 1920).

14 I am indebted to the late Professor Heinz Dopsch for this survey.

15 Oswald Redlich, 'Ueber bairische Traditionsbücher und Traditionen', *Mitteilungen des Instituts für Österreichische Geschichtsforschung*, 5 (1884), 1–82; Theodor Bitterauf (ed.), *Die Traditionen des Hochstifts Freising (744–1284)*, 2 vols (Munich: Rieger, 1905–09).

16 Leaseholds are edited in several volumes of the *Monumenta Boica*, ed. Franz Lorenz Richter, Johann Paul Voetter, Johann Nepomuk Fritz and Anton Franz, Königliche Akademie der Wissenschaften, 18 vols (Munich: Monachii, Typis Academicis, 1763–1808), especially vols 4, 7, 8, 11 and 13. As *Urbare*, we can denote all lists and catalogues that give an overview of incomes and expenses; see Philippe Dollinger, *Der bayerische Bauernstand vom 9. Bis zum 13. Jahrhundert* (Munich: C.H. Beck, 1982), 24–29 for a survey of *Urbare* in the eastern Alpine region in the period 850–1300. For the late Middle Ages, especially concerning the difference between dues recorded in *Urbaren*, and the real rents and dues paid by peasants as they also were recorded in the *Urbaren*, see Stefan Sonderegger, 'Landwirtschaft auf dem Papier und in der Praxis', in Carola Fey and Steffen Krieb (eds), *Adel und Bauern in der Gesellschaft des Mittelalters. Internationales Kolloquium zum 65. Geburtstag von Werner Rösener*, Studien und Texte zur Geistes- und Sozialgeschichte des Mittelalters, 6 (Korb: Didymos, 2012), 249–70. A survey of sources is also provided in Katja Hürlimann and Stefan Sonderegger, 'Ländliche Gesellschaft im Mittelalter', *Traverse: Zeitschrift für Geschichte*,18/1 (2011), 48–76.

17 H. Siems, 'Lex Baiuvariorum', in Adalbert Erler, et al. (eds), *Handwörterbuch zur deutschen Rechtsgeschichte* (hereafter HRG), 5 vols (Berlin: Schmidt, 1964–1991), ii, 1887–1901; Franz Gutmann, *Die soziale Gliederung der Bayern zur Zeit des Volksrechtes* (Straßburg: K.J. Trübner, 1906), 13–15, 84f.; Theodore John Rivers, 'Seigneurial obligations and "Lex baiuvariorum" i.13', *Traditio*, 31 (1975), 336–43; Peter Landau, *Die Lex Baiuvariorum. Entstehungszeit,*

through *capitularien* issued by the Carolinian kings and emperors in the eighth and ninth centuries. From the beginning of the twelfth century, the Bavarian *Landesfrieden* (territorial agreements on peace), soon made into voluminous law, played an increasingly important role. Another law that we will focus on is the *Schwabenspiegel*. After the 'private' codification of this law in Augsburg in 1275, it was implemented as a text of law over a wide area from Schwaben to Switzerland and Bavaria.[18] The territorial law of the emperor Ludwig the Bavarian for the duchy of Upper Bavaria, issued in two different editions in 1335 and 1346, also had a great impact on jurisdiction. The *Hofrechte* (manorial provisions, especially for bishoprics and monasteries) from the eleventh century onwards, valid mainly for the subjects of a manorial lord also render valuable information about the rights and duties of unfree people. The oldest *Hofrechte* were later replaced with regional collections of customary law (*Weistümer*), institutional provisions (*Stiftrechte*), and village laws and regulations (*Dorfrechte*).[19]

We can thus observe significant divergence between sources for medieval unfreedom in Scandinavia and in the eastern Alpine region. For the eastern Alpine region, we have more comprehensive sources, especially relating to ecclesiastical institutions. Their early written recording was primarily due to the role of the church and its knowledge of writing, which impacted the whole of the ancient Bavarian settlement area. An increase in written sources can be observed in the eastern Alpine region as early as the middle of the twelfth century,[20] but this increase was not as dramatic as in Scandinavia, where literacy was established later. In the Central European region, a written tradition, in large part in the form of deeds, became even more common in the thirteenth

---

Entstehungsort und Charakter von Bayerns ältester Rechts- und Geschichtsquelle, Sitzungsberichte: Bayerische Akademie der Wissenschaften, Phil- Hist. Klasse, 3 (Munich: Beck, 2004).

18 K. Nehlsen-von Stryk, 'Schwabenspiegel', in Robert-Henri Bautier,et al. (ed). *Lexikon des Mittelalters* (hereafter LexMA), 9 vols (Munich and Zurich: Artemis [vols 1–6] and LexMA-Verlag [vols 7–9], 1977–1999), vii, 1603–05.

19 'Lex Baiuvariorum' (hereafter LBai), in Karl August Eckhardt (ed.), *Germanenrechte, Texte und Übersetzungen*, ii: *Die Gesetze des Karolingerreiches 714–911* (Weimar: H. Bohlau, 1934), 74–187; *Der Schwabenspiegel, übertragen in heutiges Deutsch mit Illustrationen aus alten Handschriften*, ed. Harald Rainer Derschka (Munich: Beck, 2002); Ludwig von Rockinger, *Kaiser Ludwigs erstes oberbaierisches Land- und Lehenrecht*, Abhandlungen der historischen Klasse der Königlich Bayerische Akademie der Wissenschaften, Phil- Hist. Klasse, 24/3 (Munich: Verlag der K.B. Akademie der Wissenschaften, 1909), 463–563; Knut Schultz, 'Hofrecht', in LexMA, v, 77–78; Dollinger, *Der bayerische Bauernstand*, 34–35.

20 Evaluation made by the late Professor Heinz Dopsch.

and fourteenth centuries. Increasingly, the driving force behind this development was the towns.[21]

3 The Legal Portrayal of Slaves and Unfree Persons

In my opinion, the best approach to establish criteria that can provide a comprehensive and systematic survey of the nature and development of slavery and unfreedom is to study provisions found in a selection of key laws regarding slaves and unfree persons in milder forms of bondage. This is true for Norway as well as for the rest of Scandinavia. If we study statements about unfree people in one and the same law, for example the *Gulathing Law*, we can establish a sort of collective presentation that is a normative *ideal image* of the lawmakers and their norms and intentions.[22] These ideal images of norms and intentions can then be compared with each other.[23]

This procedure will also tentatively be used to compare the ideal image of slavery / unfreedom in two regional laws in the eastern Alpine region. The choice of the early *Lex Baiuvariorum* and the late *Schwabenspiegel* offers an early normative image from the end of the early medieval period that can be compared with a much later ideal image from the beginning of the late medieval period. The representativeness of this comparison over such a large span of time is, however, uncertain. Hopefully, it can nevertheless give a certain insight into changes in the normative character of unfreedom over a long period of time in the eastern Alpine region and maybe also indicate differences and similarities with Scandinavia.[24]

---

21 Stefan Sonderegger, 'Vom Nutzen der Bearbeitung einer regionalen Urkundenedition. Dargestellt am Chartularium Sangallense', in Theo Kölzer, Willibald Rosner and Roman Zehetmayer (eds), *Regionale Urkundenbücher. Die Vorträge der 12. Tagung der Commission Internationale de Diplomatique* (St Pölten: Niederösterreichisches Institut für Landeskunde, 2010), 86–116, and see graphics p. 112.

22 Iversen, *Trelldommen*, 39–40; Iversen, *Knechtschaft*, 67–68. For the dating of these sources, I follow the theory that a redaction of the law was recorded on parchment after a deliberate political assessment: see about *schriftliche Rezeptionstheorie*, fn 10.

23 Partly, criteria for such a study can be found in modern international research on slavery; see, for example, Orlando Patterson's comprehensive worldwide study, *Slavery and Social Death: A Comparative Study* (Cambridge, MA: Harvard University Press, 1982).

24 The Nordic laws date to a relatively short span of time, around 150 years, and the circumstances under which they were made are relatively well known. In contrast to this, the circumstances regarding the two laws from the eastern Alpine region are less clear. The great distance in time and space also makes a comparison more hypothetical. Comparing the *Schwabenspiegel* with the Nordic laws of the thirteenth century is less problematic.

4 Scandinavia

In the Norwegian legal sources from the eleventh to the thirteenth century a broad concept of property appears as an important characteristic of unfreedom. In the *Gulathing Law* (G) and *Frostathing Law* (F) the *þræll* / slave emerges as his master's property, but in a similar way a free man also had a proprietary right to, amongst other things, his children, and his wife. Concerning the *þræll* / slave, a crucial factor was the master's ability to control the slave's free movement and to minimize his opportunity to escape. The slaves could also be sold or used as a means of payment. Their master was entitled to receive compensation in the same way as he was for damages to other forms of property.[25] The verb *eiga* (to own) or *eign* (property) are used to explain the master's relation to his slaves. But it is important to underline that *eiga* / *eign* has a broad meaning. A person could 'own' his wife, her husband, or their children, but he could also 'own' (*eiga*) authority, rights, and demands. In brief, the meaning of the medieval property relations is to explain the specific relations between slaves and masters.[26] The normative criteria of slavery in the Norwegian laws shows that a modern reifying proprietary perception of unfreedom is not a satisfactory approach for fully understanding its portrayal in the legal provisions in G and F. Medieval slavery and unfreedom can therefore hardly be properly explained and understood through a criterion of property alone.

A reifying or absolute concept of property, early phrased by the Norwegian legal historian Frederik Brandt, seems rather to obstruct a deeper understanding of the meaning in the provisions concerning slavery, primarily because such a concept lacks the personal aspect of the slave. Thus, in Brandt's concept the slave is not considered to be a contemplative social being. He is only described from the point of view of the slaveowner. Most importantly, with an absolute concept of property alone, slavery will appear socially as a by-product, not as a structural part of the general patterns of dependency in society.[27]

In fact, the slave *was* recognized as a human being, but placed on the lowest level in society. The lawmakers thus presumed that a slave-person, contrary to cattle, *could* act on his own but should be responsible to his master or in some

25 See Iversen, *Trelldommen*, 40–51; Tore Iversen, *Jordeie og jordleie – Eiendomsbegrepet i norske middelalderlover*, *Collegium Medievale*, 14 (2001), 79–114.

26 During the thirteenth century, there was a tendency to use a superior concept of property taken from the medieval Roman jurisprudence (Iversen, *Jordeie og jordleie*, 109).

27 Brandt: 'By property [also over slaves] we understand the universal dominion over a thing in its totality'. (Frederik Brandt, *Tingsretten, fremstillet efter den norske Lovgivning*, (Kristiania: Damm, 1878), 72).

cases to the authorities. In a behaviouristic way he could be given punishment and reward for his acts by his master. When it comes to punishment he was to be controlled in a field where he possessed some autonomy, that is, over his own body. Whipping was the normal type of punishment. In this way, by making him bodily responsible, could he be monitored socially. The lawmakers thus presumed that a slave-person, contrary to cattle, could act on his own and be responsible with his body. The slave's bodily responsibility thus indicates that the slave was *a person in negative sense.*[28]

The opposite way of monitoring the slave was to give him the opportunity to do extra services for his master. As a slave could act on his own will, he obviously also appears in some provisions as a person in a *positive sense*. As a person in a positive sense he was guaranteed rights that offered him some scope of action, like a limited right of movement or the right to have his own possessions. This scope of action is an integrated part of the same image of slavery / unfreedom, an image that also provided the master with an advantage. Positive rights are also essential to the image of a composite freedom, in so far as they, when they are examined, point to improved status, partial freedom, and even the possibility of manumission. Most laws take it for granted that such property primarily would be used to purchase their manumission.[29]

It must be stressed that a manumission process was incorporated into slavery as an institution, with few exceptions (slavery in the southern states of the USA was an exception). Such a manumission process could, however, slow down or stop altogether. Furthermore, a new partial unfreedom could be reintroduced into a society where slavery was abolished (see, for example vornedskab in Denmark below).

To summarize, a wide criterion based on property is important to understand forms of unfreedom, from pure slavery to milder forms, especially as slaves were fully acknowledged as a personal attachment to their masters. But the reifying proprietary perception of unfreedom is not a satisfactory approach to fully understanding slavery and milder forms of unfreedom. We have therefore added the concepts of the slave as a person in a *negative* or a *positive* sense in a behaviourist way. These concepts represent the master's and the society's reaction to the actions of slaves' and unfree persons. But the understanding of the slave as a person in a negative and especially in a positive sense also points

28 See Iversen, *Trelldommen*, 52–63; Iversen, *Knechtschaft*, 87–107. The German legal historian Hermann Nehlsen sees this as early elements of a public criminal law: Hermann Nehlsen, 'Entstehung des Strafrechts bei den germanischen Stämmen', in Karl Kroeschell (ed.), *Gerichtslauben-Vorträge. Freiburger Festkolloquium zum 75. Geburtstag von Hans Thieme* (Sigmaringen: Thorbecke, 1983), 7–12.

29 Iversen, *Knechtschaft*, 107–14.

to him as an active human being attempting to improve his and his closest kin's living conditions.

4.1 *The Recruitment of Slaves in Scandinavia*

The earliest written sources in Scandinavia suggest that slavery (*þrældómr*) had, by then, become a normal part of the social order. The old Norse Edda and skaldic poems substantiate that unfreedom was a stable social reality in the Viking Age (800–1050). Some farm names suggest, furthermore, that *þrældómr* must have existed much further back in time. Interestingly, the Norwegian regional law codes of G and F, the last one dating to after 1200, both differentiate between imported *þrælar* and *þrælar* who were raised in Norway. Several accounts provide information about Norwegian settlers in Iceland who took slaves in the region around the Irish Sea and brought them with them to Iceland.[30] In Viking towns like Dublin, the slave trade was at its peak in the eleventh century. Even though it is difficult to quantify the import of slaves to Norway, the volume must have been substantial between 800 and 1100.[31] Import of slaves from the Baltic region is possibly even older and, due to tribes like the Wends clinging to their ancient pagan belief, it may have lasted into the twelfth century.[32] Nevertheless, both regional law codes seem to hold domestic slaves to be the 'normal' slaves. By then, the family structure among unfree people must have been strengthened, as witnessed especially by F, thus leading to better conditions for reproduction (see above, persons in a positive sense).[33]

4.2 **Þrælar** *and Other Unfree Persons in Nordic Agriculture*

When we study the role played by *þrælar* in agriculture, it is important that we raise the question of who controlled the land. The sagas and cultural-topographic sources clearly indicate that a great number of *þrælar* were kept on and around the ancient seats of local chieftains, dating back to the Viking Age or earlier.[34] These agrarian structures, called *multiple estates*, have some

30 Iversen, *Knechtschaft*, 162–68. Interesting studies into Icelandic blood groups show similarities not only with Norwegian blood groups, but also with Irish ones (Peter H. Sawyer, *Medieval Settlement: Continuity and Change* (London: Edward Arnold, 1976), 238).

31 Barbara E. Crawford, *Scandinavian Scotland*, (Leicester: Leicester University Press, 1987), 43, 134–36; P. Holm, 'The Slave Trade of Dublin', *Peritia*, 5 (1986), [full page spread], at p. 317f.

32 Iversen, *Trelldommen*, 90–93; Iversen, *Knechtschaft*, 154–58; Nevéus, *Trälarna*, 33, 55, 137, 141.

33 Iversen, *Trelldommen*, 82–93; Iversen, *Knechtschaft*, 140–44, 148, 175–92.

34 Retrospective studies on concentrations of ancient landed property in the vicinity of chieftains' seats clearly indicate the *Herrschaft*-function of such centres. Andreas Holmsen, *Nye studier i gammel historie* (Oslo: Universitetsforlaget, 1976), 101–31; Per Sveaas

clear parallels in the structure of continental manors (see 'Introduction', section 'A Sketch of the Historical Background'). The main difference seems to be that the landholdings belonging to Norwegian multiple estates covered a wider area. While continental manors primarily consisted of fertile areas suitable for arable farming, Norwegian multiple estates were more differentiated and included a variety of resources, like outfield or alpine pastures, fishing, and hunting. Corvée labour on the main farm is hardly mentioned in Norwegian medieval sources. These multiple estates, more loosely organized than the continental manors, were dissolved from around 1100.[35]

We find accounts of the existence of unfree people on magnate farms belonging to chieftains (*hersir, lendrmenn*) in the Norse sagas. In *Egils saga*, written in the thirteenth century but referring to events taking place in the tenth and eleventh centuries, we find a story about the chieftain Torolv Kveldulvsson from Helgeland in Northern Norway. We learn about his large household, his extensive exploitation of resources, and his large attendance of servants, free and unfree.[36] The best-known account of a very large household in the highest social layer is *Heimskringla's* story about Erling Skjalgsson's household at Sola in southwestern Norway. This saga emphasizes Erling's power and wealth as a chieftain and continues: 'Erling always had thirty þrælar in his household, besides other servants'. The saga then goes on to relate how freedmen cleared new land and settlements.[37] (see below).

Regional laws give us the most systematic information about *þrælar* in Norwegian agriculture. From prescriptions about censuses that should serve as the basis for naval service, the *leiðangr*, we can glean a general understanding of how widespread the use of slaves was in the last part of the twelfth century. According to G 296, a man was responsible for reporting himself and his servants,

Andersen, *Samlingen av Norge og kristningen av landet 800–1130*, Handbok i Norges historie, 2 (Bergen: Universitetsforlaget, 1977), 215–20; Frode Iversen, 'Eiendom, makt og statsdannelse: Kongsgårder og gods i Hordaland i yngre jernalder og middelalder,' PhD thesis, University of Bergen, Bergen, 2004; Frode Iversen, *Var middelalderens lendmannsgårder kjerner i eldre godssamlinger*, Arkeologiske avhandlingar og rapporter frå Universitetet i Bergen, 4 (Bergen: Arkeologisk Institutt, 1999); Dagfinn Skre, *Herredømme, bosetning og besittelse på Romerike 200–1350 e. Kr.*, published PhD thesis, Acta humaniora 32 (Oslo: Universitetsforlaget, 1998).

35 Frode Iversen; 'Den nyere norske forskning om jordegods i vikingtid og tidlig middelalder. En sammenligning med undersøkelsene av manor- og Grundherrschaftsystemer i Vest-Europa', *Varia*, 71 (2009), 59–70; Iversen, *Var middelalderens lendmannsgårder*, 27–33; Iversen, *Knechtschaft*, 415–17; Andersen, *Samlingen*, 296–97; Halvard Bjørkvik, 'Det norske krongodset i mellomalderen', *Historisk Tidsskrift (norsk)*, 40 (1960/61), 201–31.

36 *Egil saga*, ÍF 2, 38–41, 51–58.

37 Hkr, 193–96.

free and unfree, when censuses were made. If he kept back information, he was to hand over a *þræll* to the royal bailiff, or the bailiff could pick one himself.[38] To keep *þrælar* was thus seen as an integrated part of the normal workforce in a household.[39] Normally the regional laws do not indicate the number of *þrælar* in each household. An exception is the provision in F IV 44, stating that a man who had been blinded should receive a peasant farm with twelve cows, two horses, and three *þrælar* as compensation.[40]

Most provisions concern normal peasant households (for example, F IV 44, F XV 16) rather than large households on magnate farms (for example, G 255).[41] We also get the impression that free labour was not more frequent on large farms than unfree labour. Our sources indicate that *þrælar* were occupied with hard work on or in the vicinity of the farm, thus enabling necessary surveillance.[42] Summing up, we can conclude that a variety of sources establish that *þrælar* were frequently found in various types of households in Norway and that they had a great impact on the economy by around 1100.

Information on the impact of *þrælar* in Danish agriculture is harder to come by due to the lack of sources. In Denmark, one or several villages and, in addition, some scattered possessions could belong to one and the same manor (*curia / mansion*). Corvée labour from tenants does not seem to have played an important role on Danish manors before the beginning of the fourteenth century, and then only on a very limited scale.[43] A considerable workforce was still needed to run the large manors. The character of this workforce, in contemporary sources sometimes termed *familia*, is hard to define, but it most probably consisted of a combination of servants and wage labourers, and before manumission also of slaves. Some Danish regional laws indicate that provisions

38 The more recent F VII 10 (*Frostatingsloven* (hereafter F), in NgL, i, 119–258.) states that a man was to pay the *leidang* tax for his *þræll* as well as for himself, but not for any free men of full age belonging to his household.

39 Even if households without slaves were also found (G 296: *Gulatingsloven* (hereafter G), in NgL, i, 1–118.), the regional laws refer to freed slaves who could possess unfree persons themselves (G 198, F IX 11). In addition to freeholders and tenants, persons who leased land on other contracts than those of ordinary tenants could also hold *þrælar* (F XIII 1–3).

40 The historian Jørn Sandnes has maintained that a peasant holding with twelve cows and two horses was a normal peasant holding in Trøndelag until the twentieth century: Jørn Sandnes, 'Tolv kyr, to hester ogtre træler', *Historisk Tidsskrift (norsk)*, 62 (1983), 79–82.

41 Iversen, *Trelldommen*, 113–19; Iversen, *Knechtschaft*, 193–205.

42 Iversen, *Trelldommen*, 120–25; Iversen, *Knechtschaft*, 206–14.

43 Nils Hybel, 'The Roman Catholic Institutions', in Bjørn Paulsen and Søren Michael Sindbæk (eds), *Settlement and Lordship in Viking and Early Medieval Scandinavia*, The Medieval Countryside, 9 (Turnhout: Brepols, 2011), 235.

about slavery existed until the thirteenth century.[44] The historian Saxo (early thirteenth century) also wrote a great deal about slavery.[45] It is therefore probable that *þrælar* also played an important part in Danish agriculture, especially on manors and magnate farms.

The Swedish regional laws from the second half of the thirteenth century and the beginning of the fourteenth century contain many provisions about unfree people. As mentioned, we also encounter a new group of sources that render an important insight into the last stage of the *þrældómr*: that is, testaments with provisions on manumission. A total of twenty-nine testaments have clauses on manumission between 1256 and 1310. In twenty-seven of these testaments, from one to twelve, or, in some cases, 'all' *þrælar*, were promised their freedom. Some cases concerned *þrælar* on main farms (*curiae*), others concerned *þrælar* on different types of holdings.[46] These testaments thus indicate that unfree people worked on magnate farms and on normal holdings in medieval Sweden.

4.3 *Manumission and Long-lasting Dependency – The Case of Norway*

We have already ascertained that the positive rights belonging to a *þræll* were an integrated part of the image of unfreedom. These rights also point towards manumission or some sort of half-free status. We have also mentioned that the *þrælar* had more positive rights in F than in G. G has its own designation, *orka,* like the *peculicum* in Roman law, for property belonging to a *þræll* and treats this form of property explicitly. As the later F lacks an explicit treatment of unfree people's property, such property was possibly treated as ordinary property. This assumption is backed by provisions in F, substantiating that a tenant farmer could give the *þrælar* belonging to him permission to cultivate a piece of land (*reit*) on his rented farm without asking the owner of the farm (F XIII 2). Interestingly, recent research has shown that existing farms ending with – *reit* (clearing) refer to small farms from the Middle Ages that belonged to larger and older farms before they became independent units.[47] It is also important to underline that, in cases between themselves, the *þrælar* in F (XI 21) were mutually entitled to one-third of the penalties pertaining to their lords.[48] Especially important is the fact that the *þræll,* according to F, in all probability had

44 Nevéus, *Trälarna*, 52.

45 See Skyum-Nielsen, *Kvinde og slave*, 175–80.

46 Nevéus, *Trälarna*, 132–38, 184–89; Mazo Karras, *Slavery and Society*, 90–92.

47 Jørn Sandnes, *Ødetid og gjenreisning. Trøndsk Busetningshistorie ca.1200–1660* (Oslo: Universitetsforlaget, 1971), 38–48.

48 Iversen, *Knechtschaft*, 107–14.

the right to marry freely (see F III 22), in contrast to the provisions in G, where the *þrælar* were excluded from ordinary marriage.[49]

Several Norwegian provisions presupposed that manumission was a gradual process, in which the freedmen (*leysingi*) jettisoned their *þræll*-like dependence step by step. Two stages in this process were characterized by symbolic rituals. The first stage was *gefa frelsi*, that is, 'to become their freedom'. The more important second stage, the drinking of beer together with their invited former master that symbolizing manumission (*frelsisol*), gave the freedman broad personal rights, especially a limited right to inheritance.[50]

A freedman was not truly free, even after manumission. The *þyrmslir* (obedience, Lat. *obsequium*) signified dependence in a general sense. In G, the freedman's dependence should last for two generations, in F even longer, for four generations. In the more recent F, this dependence is even more severe: the freedman had to ask permission from his master to enter into all forms of agreement and contract, except tenure contracts (XI 23) and presumably also marriage.[51] These ties of dependence were also transferred to every child from *mixed* marriages between free and unfree persons.[52] In time, the number of people with such ties of dependence to a master would then be multiplied. In F, the *þyrmslir* dependency was more severely interpreted and played a far more important role than in G.

Those who inherited from a freedman also had to accept that a part of the inheritance was due to the freedman's former master. These persons of both sexes that their former master's relatives could hope to inherit from were named *vánarmen*. *Vánarmen* were thus persons with a definite unfree stigma (Cf. German *Heimfallsrecht*). This arrangement was far more important in F than in the older G. In F, it reached downwards to the ninth generation for all descendants of mixed marriages. This would substantially have enlarged the number of people exposed to such restrictions.[53] For all practical purposes,

---

49 Iversen, *Knechtschaft*, 347–53. F III 22 states that women have the right to say no to marriage. This clause makes no exception for unfree women.

50 Iversen, *Trelldommen*, 213–5; F IX 12, cf. G 22.

51 Iversen, *Trelldommen*, 100–12, 196–209; Iversen, *Knechtschaft*, 170–92, 333–55. For the influence of the church concerning marriage and property of the unfree, and thereby the dating of the main redation of F to 1220s, see Tore Iversen, 'Landskapslovene og kanoniske rett', in Audun Dybdahl and Jørn Sandnes (eds), *Nordiske middelalderlover. Tekst og kontekst. Rapport fra seminar ved Senter for middelalderstudier 29.-30. nov 1996*, Skrifter fra Senter for middelalderstudier, 5 (Trondheim: Tapir, 1997), 69–84, especially p. 82.

52 This is the principle which in German is called the 'ärgeren Hand'.

53 For the relation between *frelsisol*, *þyrmslir*, and inheritance due to a former master on the one hand, and the lower strata of peasant society on the other hand, see Iversen, *Trelldommen*, 210–28; Iversen, *Knechtschaft*, 356–86.

this must have been part of an attempt to create a grey zone of mild dependency and unfreedom between free and unfree people.

4.4 *Accounts of Freedmen and the Clearing of Land – Norway*

Freedmen (*leysingi*) thus still had ties to their former master. In time they could, however, gradually free themselves completely from their dependence, primarily by compensation to their master in the form of money, goods, or work. It is possible to understand this process of emancipation, especially prolonged in the more recent law (F), as an expression of the interests of the former masters, a way to extract work and favours from persons they had promised their freedom. What *þrælar* and *leysingi* earned by working the land was thus primarily used to buy their freedom. This explains the interest *þræll* and master alike had in extra work.[54]

Some of the accounts in the Kings' sagas demonstrate how emancipation took place on the main farms of the chieftains. As an example, we can refer to the expressive account of the manumission process in the eleventh century on the main farm belonging to Erling Skjálgsson at Sola in southwestern Norway, where *þrælar* and *leysingi* worked their way to freedom. This presentation is found in the Kings' saga *Heimskringla* from the thirteenth century:

> Erlingr always also had thirty slaves in his establishment besides the rest of his household. He assigned day work to his slaves and gave them time after it and permission for each man who wanted to work for himself in the evening or at night, he gave them arable land to sow their own corn and to use the produce to enrich themselves. He set a price and redemption value on each of them. Many freed themselves in the first or second year, and all those that were any good freed themselves in three years. With the money thus gained Erlingr would buy himself other slaves, and some of his freedmen he put into herring fishing and some into other profitable occupations. Some cleared woodland and set up dwellings there. He enabled all of them to get on in some way.[55]

This account gives a nearly ideal-typical illustration of *þrældómr* as an institutional arrangement, leading to the planned clearing of new land, first in the vicinity of the main farm, later by the settlement of freedmen in fjords and coastal areas. As clients spread over a large region, these freedmen must have

54 See, for example, Iversen, *Trelldommen*, 54–56; Iversen, *Knechtschaft*, 92–94.

55 Snorri Sturluson, *Heimskringla*, ii, trans. Alison Finlay and Anthony Faulknes (n.p.: Viking society for Northern Research, 2014), chapter 23.

been an important element in Erling's economic enterprises, strengthening his role as a chieftain. Such an economic-social arrangement also fits well with the existence of *multiple estates* (see above, and 'Introduction', section 'A Sketch of the Historical Background'). In the sagas, we find additional accounts of unfree people belonging to or originating from a main farm of a chieftain who nevertheless worked for their own benefit.[56]

The regional laws, especially F, throw light on the emancipation process on normal holdings. F (XI 23) shows that the lawmaker in the thirteenth century presupposed that the lowest strata of freedmen, who had not yet celebrated their *frelsisol*, should also obtain a special allowance for clearing new land. Only in one case did the freedman not need the permission of his master, that is, when renting land and buying seed corn in connection with this. The F (XIII 1–3) states that a peasant, who himself is a tenant, could allow his own *þrælar* to cultivate a *reit*, that is, a stretch of the holding's arable land, for himself.[57]

Our sources substantiate that freedmen who had not yet celebrated their *frelsisol*, perhaps together with a number of *þrælar*, merged into a group of personal dependent agriculturist on holdings on the outskirts or in the vicinity of farms belonging to their former master. Place names show quite clearly that unfree persons' settlements were often found on marginal soil.[58] This accords well with the *þrælar's* desire to free themselves through work. This assumption

56 We have previously referred to the account in the thirteenth century *Egils saga* about the chieftain Torolv, who lived in Helgeland, Northern Norway, in the tenth century (see above). Torolv had two main farms (Sandnes, Torgar). He settled his freed persons in fishing villages and hamlets where they were engaged in hunting. At the same time, he brought new, unfree persons into his own household. The saga describes in detail his son, Skallagrim's, colonization of Iceland. Skallagrim's household consisted of family members, as well as free and unfree, dependent people. Such colonized areas served as a resource pool for different chieftains. (*Egil saga*, ÍF 2, 28, 72–80; Lnb, ÍF 1, 88.) Furthermnore, in Lnb several unfree persons, at least sixteen, are listed in connection with the clearing of new land, see Iversen, *Trelldommen*, 258–63; Iversen, *Knechtschaft*, 438–43.

57 There he could establish his own small household – not unlike the *Häusel* or *Keusche* in the Alpine region (Information from the late Professor Heinz Dopsch, Salzburg). Another provision, F IX 12, shows that, in this way, *þrælar* could work their way to their *frelsisol*. According to the agricultural historian Jørn Sandnes, holdings with names ending by -*reit* in Trøndelag (mid-Norway) are situated amid ancient farms in the region's central agrarian settlements: Jørn Sandnes, 'Reitar. En namegruppe som agrarhistorisk kilde', *Heimen*, 14 (1968), 388–95.

58 Names of these medieval settlements contained words like*ruð, brenna, buð, gerði, hagi, holt, hús, svið* and *kot*. We find *kot* (insignificant hut) used as a noun or adjective in a demeaning sense in written sources, pointing to small settlements on the outskirts of larger farms. (Sandnes, *Ødetid og gjenreisning*, 38–48; Iversen, *Trelldommen*, 128–31, 240–55; Iversen, *Knechtschaft*, 220–25, 408–28).

can be substantiated in a quantitative way by counting deserted medieval farms where only the names of the farms have survived to this day.[59]

Norwegian historians have pointed to a general increase in population as the main reason for the clearing of new land, as well as for other structural changes in the medieval period. For my part, I will also underline the process of manumission as an important element in the clearing of new land and the establishment of new settlements. This argument enhances, rather than contradicts, the influence of population increase. There is also good reason to believe that unfree people played an important role in the medieval leaseholding system in Norway.[60]

4.5 *The End of Unfreedom in Scandinavia*

When it comes to the final stage of unfreedom, the laws, especially the Norwegian ones, are our best sources for dating its cessation. The *Gulathing Law* (G), the *Frostathing Law* (F), and the King Magnus the Lawmender's *Norwegian Law of the Realm* (1274) each represents different stages of unfreedom in Norway and may thus help us to discern an evolution. The Danish, and especially the Swedish laws, the *Older and Younger Law of Västergötland, the Law of Östergötland* and the *Law of Uppland*, primarily represent the last stages of unfreedom in their respective countries.

We have previously stated that the master's responsibility for his *þræll* was reduced in F relative to G, and that unfree people had thus been furnished with different positive rights. On the other hand, longer lasting *þræll*-like bondage, *þyrmslir* (obedience), was introduced in F following manumission. These bonds were to be transferred to their successors, but the successors could gradually free themselves from them through their purchase. The *Norwegian Law of the Realm* (1274) paints a completely different picture. This law does not contain any direct provisions about unfreedom at all.[61] The question is therefore

59 Iversen, *Trelldommen*, 240–55; Iversen, *Knechtschaft*, 398–428.

60 A corresponding theory states that the Norwegian leaseholding system (Rentengrundherrschaft), in the last part of the twelfth century based on rental incomes from scattered possessions, for the most part succeeded an older system based on dependent leaseholders, unfree as well as increasingly also free persons and with personal ties to the landlord, who settled in the vicinity of a magnate farms. Jørn Sandnes has named this system a 'primitive leasehold system' (Sandnes, 'Tolv kyr', 82; Iversen, *Trelldommen*, 235–58, esp. p. 245; Iversen, *Knechtschaft*, 398–433, esp. pp. 415–17; Tore Iversen, 'Fremveksten av det norske leilendingsvesen i middelalderen: en forklaringsskisse', *Heimen*, 32 (1995), 169–80.

61 However, it contains several hints about unfreedom, and in some provisions, *friáls* (free) are mentioned in new contexts where *friáls* obviously contrasts unfreedom. It is possible

why every mention of the institution of unfreedom was omitted from the *Norwegian Law of the Realm* (see below).

In Denmark, manumission is mentioned only in the *Law of Scania* (Skl) and *the Law of Zealand* (VL) from the first half of the thirteenth century. The *ättledning* ('admission to the family') in the Danish and especially the later Swedish *Older and Younger Västgöta Law* and the *Östgöta Law* (VgL I and II, ÖgL) and the *Law of Uppland* (UL) relieved the former masters of any binding responsibility stemming from unfreedom. In Denmark, these provisions could reflect the judicial situation in the first half of the thirteenth century, at the end of the period characterized by unfreedom. The *þræll* could either receive his freedom from his master, or he could free himself.[62] Afterwards, he could be taken into the family of another free person (*takæ i æt / ætteledning*). The unfree persons had, at this late point in time, relatives who were personally free or relatives who were in the process of manumission. The *ättledning* is most likely an expression of a new attitude towards unfreedom and marks a later stage of this development than the Norwegian *Frostathing Law*.

In the two versions of the Swedish *Law of Västergötland*, one from 1220 and the other from the end of the thirteenth century, freedmen are divided in three categories: *frælsgivi*, *fostre* (provided for) and *ätleðe* (admitted into the family). Even though they were freed, their former masters were, nevertheless, to inherit from them. Such people had the right to marry free persons, and their children were then born free.[63] These positive rights were of the utmost importance. A *fostre* was doubtless a *þræll* who had been given land to cultivate by his master. He was still his master's property and probably could not enter into economic agreements on his own. But if the peasant wanted to sell his *fostre*, he had to do that in exchange for landed property.[64] In the later Swedish *Law of Uppland* (UL) (1297), some provisions show a stage of complete dissolution of unfreedom: a *þræll* should gain his freedom if he were to be sold by his

that the lawmaker reckoned that there were still some unfree persons in the country (L III 4, IV 10, and compare IV 3.1 [*The Law of the Realm 1274* (hereafter L), in NgL, ii, 7–178]). In some cases, any mentioning of unfree persons was deleted in provisions that were phrased in almost the same way as in F (F XIII 2/L VII 18.2, F IV 4/L IV 3, F XIII 15/L VII 20).

62 Nevéus, *Trälarna*, 46–52; Mazo Karras, *Slavery and Society*; Iversen, *Knechtschaft*, 443 f.; Iversen, *Trelldommen*, 263 f.

63 Nevéus, *Trälarna*, 83–86, 106; Iversen, *Knechtschaft*, 333–53, 469–72; Iversen, *Trelldommen*, 196–209.

64 Nevéus, *Trälarna*, 105–12; Thomas Lindkvist, *Landborna i Norden under äldre medeltid*, published thesis, Studia Historica Upsaliensia, 110 (Uppsala: Almkvist & Wiksell, 1979), 117–19; Mazo Karras, *Slavery and Society*, 93–95.

master. If a child was born into an unfree marriage, he was still to have his freedom. If his mother was unfree, the mother and the child were to be free.[65] That King Valdemar's *Law of Jutland* (1241) hardly mentions unfreedom, and that the *Norwegian Law of the Realm* (1274) only indirectly hints at its existence, are signs indicating that the time for unfreedom in Scandinavia was coming to an end. Nevertheless, a formal royal decree on the dissolution of unfreedom was only proclaimed in Sweden, that being King Magnus Eriksson's decree for Västergötland (1335).[66]

4.6 *Causes for the Dissolution of Unfreedom in Scandinavia*

The causes for the dissolution of slavery and the milder forms of unfreedom in Scandinavia must be assessed from a variety of perspectives. The increase in population was obviously a basic contributing factor. So were the changes in and the expansion of settlements, which, as elsewhere throughout Europe, resulted in reduced disparity between the economic and social statuses of free and unfree people.

The clearing of new land and the changes in social and economic agrarian structure also played an important part in the dissolution of unfreedom. Several sources indicate that unfree people were an especially flexible element in the clearing of new land. Norwegian sources demonstrate that the efforts of unfree people were welcome in this respect, and that they were especially involved in the clearing of new land in marginal areas. In Norway, the sagas inform us of the planned clearing of new land by unfree people from central farms belonging to chieftains (see above).

Unfree settlements also originated from large peasant farms. The number of freed slaves (*þrælar*) from these agrarian units must have been great. Usually, such unfree people settled in the vicinity of the farm they were released from and then gradually spread from there. The unfree people who settled in this manner soon lost their bonds to their former masters. We must assume that such bonds were most easily dissolved where unfree people, coming from small or normal-sized holdings, began clearing remotely situated land.[67] Most

65 Nevéus, *Trälarna*, 128–31; *Lex Uplandiae: Upplandslagen, E codice membr. Bibli. Univ. Upsal. Xii* (hereafter UL), ed. Dag Strömbäck, Corpus codicum Suecicorum medii aevi Hafniae, 15 (Hafniae: Munksgaard, 1960), Km 3; Ä 19.

66 *Diplomatarium Suecanum* (hereafter DS), ed. Johan Gustaf Liljegren, Emil Hildebrand, et al., utgivet av Kungl. Vitterhets historie och antikvitetsakademien och Riksarkivet, 11 vols (Stockholm: Nordstedt, 1842-[2014]), vol. iv, no. 3106; Mazo Karras, *Slavery and Society*, 138–40.

67 As indicated by F XI 23.

likely, unfree people played an important role in the development of a leasehold system in Norway.[68]

In Denmark, a manor-like system with demesnes and dependent peasant holdings seems to have developed from the end of the twelfth century into a more complex system with demesnes, large farms managed by *villici*, and smaller holdings worked by tenants (*coloni*). The existence of unfree people must have played a part in these changes, as a portion of the smaller holdings were settled by unfree persons, as witnessed by legal sources.[69] In Sweden, middle-sized main farms situated in central areas played an important part in agriculture.[70] Smaller dependent tenant and crofter holdings were found in their vicinity. From the thirteenth century, these structures were changing. Most of the demesnes and main farms were split up. Only a few kept their original size or were even enlarged. The great landowners were increasingly dependent on incomes from scattered tenant farms.[71] Examples also exist of collective new settlements of unfree people established on the initiative of aristocratic lords.[72] For Sweden, there seem to be a connection between unfreedom ending late and the prolonged process of new settlements.

In Denmark, the power of the aristocracy was also stronger than in the other Scandinavian countries (see below). The aristocracy was in constant conflict with the crown. From the Middle Ages, its members had great power over the peasants, not least in the context of the *things*. From the end of the fifteenth

68 Iversen, *Trelldommen*, 235–59; Iversen, *Knechtschaft*, 398–436.

69 For instance, in the quite elaborate 'Law of the Thralls', see 'Valdemars sjællandske lov: Eldre og yngre redaktion samt sjællandske kirkelov', in Erik Kroman (ed.), Danmarks gamle Landskabslove med Kirkelovene, viii: *Valdemars sjællandske lov* (Copenhagen 1941), 86j.

70 Erik Ulsig, 'Peasants' Right To Control Land in Denmark' and Knut Helle, 'Comments on the Presentations of Ulsig, Iversen and Myking', both in Tore Iversen and John Ragnar Myking (eds), *Land, Lords and Peasants: Peasants' Right To Control Land in the Middle Ages and the Early Modern Period – Norway, Scandinavia and the Alpine Region*, Trondheim Studies in History, 52 (Trondheim: NTNU, 2005), 29–37, 39–45; Iversen, *Trelldommen*, 263–65; Iversen, *Knechtschaft*, 443–45.
Lindkvist, *Landborna i Norden*, 39–50; Mazo Karras, *Slavery and Society*, 150–53; Janken Myrdal and Clas Tollin, 'Brytar och tidigmedeltida huvudgårdar', in Thomas Lindkvist and Janken Myrdal (eds), *Trälar. Ofria i agrarsamhället från vikingatid till medeltid*, Skrifter om skog- och lantbrukshistoria, 17 (Stockholm: Nordiska museet, 2003), 133–69.

71 Lindkvist, *Landborna i Norden*, 39–45; Mazo Karras, *Slavery and Society*, 150–53; Myrdal and Tollin, 'Brytar', 133–68.

72 Stefan Brink, 'Slavery in Scandinavia, as reflected in Names, Runes and Sagas', in Per O. Hernæs and Tore Iversen (eds), *Slavery Across Time and Space: Studies in Slavery in Medieval Europe and Africa*, Trondheim Studies in History, 38 (Trondheim: Norwegian University of Science and Technology, 2002), 107–29.

century, the great landowners on the fertile island of Sjælland managed to establish a new system of protection (*vornedeskab*) on the island, with a ban on peasants leaving the manor they belonged to. The *vornedeskab* lasted until the beginning of the eighteenth century.[73] (To the south of the border of the kingdom of Denmark, the duchies of Schleswig and Holstein were governed by the Danish king. In these duchies, the 'second serfdom' of the eastern German type was developed.)[74]

In summary, the increase in population and the consequent clearing of new land played an important role in the dissolution of unfreedom in Scandinavia. The large agrarian entities (multiple estates), where unfree people worked on the main farm or in their vicinity, had changed dramatically. Most of them were divided or dissolved. In Norway, these large, manor-like but loosely organized complexes were completely dissolved from the beginning of the twelfth century onwards. In Sweden, some of the main farms continued as before. This was the case also in Denmark, where some magnate farms became more structurally organized and even enlarged. The diverse development in these three countries is mostly connected to agrarian-topographical conditions. Danish land was well suited for large units depending on arable agriculture. These demesnes could as easily be worked by labour from surrounding tenant smallholdings.

Even though the end of unfreedom is not as thoroughly studied in Denmark as in Norway and Sweden, it looks like the *þrælar* and different groups of freedmen disappeared from the medieval sources in the same period in all three countries, with complete manumission coming last to Sweden. Population increase and changes in the agrarian structure alone can only provide a partial explanation for the dissolution of unfreedom. The decisive factor in the removal of legal provisions regarding *þrælar* and freedmen in the *Norwegian Law of the Realm of 1274* could be due to the development of *public authority* in Norway, partly at the expense of the aristocracy. Following the increase of royal power, a comprehensive judicial organization was established, and a general tax was introduced. Comparing the two laws G and F and taking the judicial

---

73 Jeppe Büchert Netterstrøm, 'Freud, Protection, and Serfdom in Late Medieval and Early modern Denmark (c.1400–1600)', in Paul H. Freedman and Monique Bourin (eds), *Forms of Servitude in Northern and Central Europe: Decline, Resistance, and Expansion*, Medieval Texts and Cultures of Northern Europe, 9 (Turnhout: Brepols, 2005), 370–84. Netterstrøm sees here the *vornedeskab*-institution as the Danish variant of the new serfdom of late medieval and early modern Europe.

74 Michael H. Gelting, 'Legal Reforms and Development of Peasant Dependence' in *Forms of Servitude in Northern and Central Europe: Decline, Resistance, and Expansion*, Medieval Texts and Cultures of Northern Europe, 9 (Turnhout: Brepols, 2005), 343–67.

circumstances in the twelfth and thirteenth centuries into consideration may provide us with a deeper insight into these developments. The growing royal influence on the *familia* of magnate farmers can be observed through the establishment of the royal tax (*leiðangr*) and especially through the provisions concerning penalties to the king (G 296, F VII 10).[75]

Behind this development, we can discern a royal intention to increase income and strengthen royal jurisdiction. Positive rights for the *þrælar* were also beneficial to royal income.[76] The provisions regarding slavery thus show a distinct development from G to F. In accordance with the importance of *þrælar* as a part of the household (*familia*), the oldest law, G, contains a ban on fines to the king for *þrælar* breaking the law (G 204).[77] This ban also indicates that the king tried to acquire additional income in this way. Against this, the lack of a corresponding provision in F underlines the king's newly acquired opportunity to enlarge his income in this way.[78] Both laws give the impression that unfree people in peasant households were quite common.

That the crown played a crucial role in the dissolution of unfreedom in Scandinavia is especially obvious in Norway and Sweden. We can observe growing royal influence on the relations between *þræll* and master already in G, in provisions concerning taxation, and jurisdiction relating to unfree people. As we have previously shown, a formal royal decree on manumission was only issued in Sweden (King Magnus Eriksson's decree for Västergötland of 1335).

75 Regarding the establishing of the royal tax, the older G (296) states that the owner of a farm was responsible for himself and his servants (*hiún*: family members, free dependant persons, and unfree servants), including those who had been given their freedom, in accordance with the total number of persons on his farm. Correspondingly, F (VII 10) states that a master of a household was only responsible for people under age and for his *þrælar*, and accordingly, not as before, for people to whom he had grated their freedom.

76 G 198 concerns a *þræll* who is attacked while a part of his master's retinue at 'public places': the *thing*, a church, or a beer house. The unfree person was himself entitled to one-twelfth of the belonging to his master, and a fine was also due to the king according to G 198. Provisions in the younger F (IV 61, see also 58) presuppose that *þrælar* who follow their master to these three places should receive the *same* judicial protection as free people (IV 58). The king was entitled to a fine twice as high as in the older G (198). Other examples, see Iversen, *Trelldommen*, 281–84; Iversen, *Knechtschaft*, 472–79.

77 If a *þræll* hits a free man, this man must reach a settlement with the owner of the *þræll*. The provision also added that the king should not get anything from this settlement.

78 A provision in F (XI 21) states that a *þræll* was entitled to a personal penalty in disputes between them, and that their *masters* were not entitled to anything. On the other hand, because the *king* is not mentioned in this connection, he is probably entitled to a monetary penalty.

The jurisdiction initiated by the Norwegian and Swedish kings, backed by strong criminal penalties, aimed at making freedmen and their successors free persons dependent on casual jobs. In the *Norwegian Law of the Realm* (1274) and in the Swedish *Law of Uppland*, corporal punishment, customary for unfree persons, also became more common for free people.[79] All in all, the consequences of the main factors behind manumission seem to be much the same in Norway and Sweden, even though we also find discrepancies. Even though the Danish king sought to increase his power, the Danish aristocracy occupied a stronger position in the thirteenth century than in Sweden and especially in Norway. From about 1300, the Danish aristocracy could therefore reinforce their power over their tenants. In legal cases, aristocratic witnesses had priority where property was concerned.[80]

5 The Eastern Alpine Region

To compare Nordic unfreedom, from slavery to milder forms, with unfreedom in the eastern Alpine region, it is of the utmost importance that we clarify and define our understanding of the different terms we meet in continental sources. Only then is it possible to describe to what extent divergences existed in the development and function of unfreedom in Scandinavia and the eastern Alpine region. The next step would then be to explain such differences.

The most important terms for unfree people in the early Middle Ages were *servus, mancipia, ancilla*, and from the High Middle Ages *Eigenmann / Eigenleute, Zensuale*. How these terms should be construed is closely connected to the historiography of Central European unfreedom in the Middle Ages and the early modern period.

5.1 *Historiographical Concepts of the Term* Servus

In contrast to most French medieval historians, most German historians maintained that the judicial position of *servi* in the ancient Germanic laws differed from that of the slaves known as *servi* to the Romans. In the Germanic laws, they argued, *servi* had to be translated with milder terms like *Unfreie, Hörige*, or

79 Iversen, *Trelldommen*, 60–63, 75–79, 258–60; Iversen, *Knechtschaft*, 101–106, 129–34; 433–38; Nevéus, *Trälarna*, 166–78.

80 Jeppe Büchert Netterstrøm, *At forsvare til rette. Værneforholdets og bøndernes retslige stilling i Danmarks senmiddelalder 1400–1513* (Kerteminde: Landbohistorisk Selskab, 2003); Friedlev Skrubbeltrang, 'Bonde', in John Granlund (ed.), *Kulturhistoriskt lexikon för nordisk medeltid – från vikingatid till reformationstid*, 22 vols (Malmö: Allhem, 1956–78), ii, 87.

Leibeigene.[81] Friedrich Lütge (1963) thus argued that Germanic unfree people were not in any real sense a 'thing' (*res*) like the Roman slaves, but a *persona*;[82] in the same way, Hans K. Schulze (1981) characterized Carolingian *servi* as unfree, but not slaves.[83]

The legal historian Hermann Nehlsen has argued against this position in his studies. The *servi* must be understood as a 'thing', not only in the ancient laws of the Teutonic tribal realms, but also in the Carolingian period, for example in the Bavarian, Saxonian, and Alemannian *leges* from the eighth, ninth, and tenth centuries. Nehlsen is of the opinion that the term 'slave' is the right one in these cases and that these *servi* legally and socially were even worse off than their predecessors from Late Antiquity.[84] In this context, the studies of the Belgian historian Charles Verlinden are important. His comprehensive studies of the original sources have shown unambiguously that there were many slaves in the Carolingian period, and, further, that an extensive slave trade between Eastern and Western Europe existed.[85] On the other hand, Hans-Werner Goetz

81 W. Rösener, 'Vom Sklaven zum Bauern. Zur Stellung der Hörigen in der frühmittelalterlichen Grund-herrschaft', in Brigite Kasten and Dieter Hägermann (eds), *Tätigkeitsfelder und Erfahrungshorizonte des ländlichen Menschen der frühmittelalterlichen Grundherrschaft* (Stuttgart: Steiner, 2006), 71f.

82 Friedrich Lütge, *Geschichte der deutschen Agrarverfassung vom frühen Mittelalter bis zum 19. Jahrhundert* (Stuttgart, 1963), 14f.

83 Hans Kurt Schulze, *Grundstrukturen der Verfassung im Mittelalter*, i (Stuttgart: Kohlhammer, 1985), 140–43. Obviously, Tacitus's interpretations from the first century of *servi* as independent economic subjects had a great impact on German historians. Tacitus describes in his *Germania* Germanic society, stressing the natural differences between Roman and Germanic slavery. The Teutons employed their slaves in agriculture and animal husbandry; the slaves lived in their own huts and delivered products to their masters (Tacitus, *Germania*, ed. Alfons Dopsch, et al. (Leipzig: Teubner, 1930), xxiv. 4, xxv. 1–2). Allowing slaves, a certain independence in this way, for example in economic affairs, was also recognized by the Romans (William Warwick Buckland, *The Roman Law of Slavery* (Cambridge: CUP, 1908), 131–238).

84 Hermann Nehlsen, 'Die servi, ancillae und mancipia der Lex Baiuvariorum. Ein Beitrag zur Geschichte der Sklaverei in Bayern', in Heinz Bellen and Heinz Heinen (eds), *Fünfzig Jahre Forschungen zur antiken Sklaverei an der Mainzer Akademie 1950–2000* (Stuttgart: Steiner, 2001), 505–21; Hermann Nehlsen, *Sklavenrecht zwischen Antike und Mittelalter*, i: *Ostgoten, Westgoten, Franken, Langobarden: Germanisches und römisches Recht in den germanischen Rechtsaufzeichnungen*, Göttinger Studien zur Rechtsgeschichte, 7 (Göttingen: Musterschmidt, 1972), 58; Hermann Nehlsen, 'Mancipia', in, iii, 219–30; Hermann Nehlsen, 'Unfreie', in HRG, iv, 464–75. Also, Philippe Dollinger sees the *servi* of the ninth century as property, hardly as persons. Nevertheless, he will not describe them as slaves. (Dollinger, *Der bayerische Bauernstand*, 196).

85 Charles Verlinden, 'Medieval Slavery in Europe and Colonial Slavery in America', in *The Beginnings of Modern Colonization: Eleven Essays with an Introduction* (Ithaca: Cornell University Press, 1970), 36; Charles Verlinden, 'Wo und warum gab es einen Großhandel

adhered to the older understanding when he maintained that the *servi* in the Bavarian and Alemanian *leges* had obtained a position comparable with *Hörigen* people (serfs), because they delivered fixed dues to their master and owed corvée labour to them.[86]

Comparing new studies on unfreedom in our two regions reveals a coherent development: in Scandinavia and in Central Europe, including the eastern Alpine region, we observe a general tendency to re-evaluate the older understanding of unfreedom primarily seen as slavery. In Norway, but also in Sweden over the last thirty to forty years, there has also been a tendency to upgrade the number of unfree people and their impact on the agrarian economy in the Middle Ages (see above). Such a general re-evaluation of unfreedom for the eastern Alpine region has not been as widespread or influential for German historians, even if a tendency to see early medieval unfreedom not as a milder form of unfreedom, but as pure slavery, has been fronted, primarily by the legal historian Nehlsen.[87]

5.2 *The* Servi *in the Early Middle Ages*

Lex Baiuvariorum (LBai) was valid law for a long time in the eastern Alpine region and is thus of great interest to our understanding of the social standing of unfree people before the year 1000. As mentioned above, Hermann Nehlsen (2001) argues that the *servi / mancipia* in LBai must be understood as slaves.[88] This position has also been taken by Carl I. Hammer, who maintains that the

mit Sklaven im Mittelalter', *Vierteljahrschrift für Sozial- und Wirtschaftsgeschichte*, 66 (1979), 153–73. In ancient Bavaria, then including the whole eastern Alpine region, the Hungarian attacks before 955 had a rather favourable influence on the slave trade. In the following period, such attacks occurred less frequently, and they ceased completely in the twelfth century (see Dollinger, *Der bayerische Bauernstand*, 30, 245, 255).

86 Thus, according to Goetz, slavery had changed its character and had become an integrated part of the manorial system (*Grundherrschaft*). See Hans-Werner Goetz, 'Serfdom and the Beginnings of a "Seigneurial System" in the Carolingian Period: A Survey and the Evidence', *Early Medieval Europe*, 2/1 (1993), 29–51, at pp. 35, 46.

87 The more recent points of view on unfreedom in Scandinavia and the eastern Alpine region can be seen as confrontations with former prevailing perceptions of a 'Nordic peasant freedom' or a wider 'Germanistic ideology'. The 'Germanistic ideology' draws on Tacitus's text on Germanic unfreedom. In contrast to the 'absolute' Roman slavery, 'Teutonic slavery' is seen as a 'social' unfreedom with background in a 'Germanistic perception of property'. A critical survey of the 'Germanistic perceptions of property' can be found in Karl Kroeschell, 'Zur Lehre vom "germanischen Eigentumsbegriff"', in Hans Thieme, *Rechtshistorische Studien. Hans Thieme zum 70. Geburtstag zugeeignet von seinen Schülern* (Cologne: Böhlau, 1977), 34–71.

88 Nehlsen, 'Die servi, ancillae und mancipia', 505–21.

existence of *servi / mancipia* was widespread in Bavaria.[89] Some of the *servi / mancipia* were born into slavery, while some were recruited through warfare and/or debt (LBai XVI 11, 14). They were placed on equal terms with cattle and could be sold or given away, used as payment, or to settle penalties.[90] As their master's property, they were protected, even if the fine for the manslaughter of a slave did not exceed a corresponding private legal compensation. This fine was invariably owed to the master.[91] The catalogue of fines indicates unambiguously that the master was responsible for his *servus*, including when the misdeed of his *servus* affected free men.[92]

On the other hand, this law also contains provisions that imposed on the master a solemn responsibility for the corporal punishment of his *servus* as a '*person in a negative sense*', in contrast to the mere proprietary aspect of cattle. For theft, the slave was to be whipped; for arson, he was to lose both eyes and hands. If weapons and military equipment were stolen, he lost both hands. Robbery and other violence required the death penalty. A *servus* who started a fight at the court of the duke should lose both hands, without any opportunity to absolve himself of this punishment.[93] In these cases, his master was to compensate for all damages.

Judging from provisions in this law, it seems to have been self-evident that, in certain circumstances, the slaves could also enjoy positive rights under their master's responsibility. The juridical distinction between the slave's standing as a person in a 'negative' or 'positive' sense derived, as we have already seen, from the distinction between punishment and remuneration as a way of control. LBai presupposes a form of *peculium* (a limited right of disposal / *Untereigentum*) that could be almost freely at the disposal of the *servi / mancipia*. A *servus* could thus have his own house, and, to a certain degree, lifelong relations were also acknowledged.[94] An interesting provision in LBai concerns every *coloni / servi ecclesiae* who belonged to an ecclesiastical manor and had

89 Carl I. Hammer, *A Large-Scale Slave Society of the Early Middle Ages: Slaves and Their Families in Early Medieval Bavaria* (Aldershot: Ashgate, 2002), 67–71 and passim; Carl I. Hammer, 'Family and Familia in Early Medieval Bavaria', in Richard Wall, Jean Robin and Peter Laslett (eds), *Family Forms in Historic Europe* (Cambridge: CUP, 1983), 217–49.

90 LBai I 1; XVI 9; I 9; XVI 9.

91 LBai VI 1–11; VI 12; VIII 12, cf. VI 12.

92 LBai IV 1–31. Nehlsen maintains the master had the opportunity to release the *servus* from his custody by handing him over (Nehlsen, 'Die servi, ancillae und mancipia', 515). For the discussion of the definition of slave / unfree, see the section 'The Legal Portrayal of Slaves and Unfree Persons', above, in this chapter.

93 LBai IX 6; I 6; II 6; II 5; II 10.

94 LBai XVI 3, 6, 7; VIII 12; X 1. See Hammer, 'Family and Familia', 217–49, and Hammer, *Large-Scale Slave Society*, 21–34.

to render duties (*tributa*) and services (*servitia*).[95] The *coloni / servi* should render a fixed rent and other specified duties, but he also had to perform specified services at the demesne, for example, ploughing, sowing, digging, and transport. At the end of these provisions, it states that the *servi* was to work three days a week at the manor and three days a week for himself.

As for the legal distribution of the workdays between the lord and the *servus* the days the *servus* could work for himself must be taken as a positive right in the sense defined above.[96] But these provisions can also be an admonition to certain lords not to neglect agriculture deriving holdings close to the manor worked by *servi*. In the name of the common interest, the same type of regulation can be observed in the regulation of punishment against the *servus* as a 'person in a negative sense' mentioned above, for example, the prescriptions to carve out both eyes and cut off both hands.[97] The positive rights belonging to the *servi*, as a contrast to the corvée labour stipulated in LBai I 13, can therefore easily be reconciled with the two other abovementioned characteristic aspects of slavery – the slave as property and the slave as a 'person in a negative sense'. The basis for the unfree leaseholder's right to use the land and their 'positive' right to their own crop lay most certainly in their *peculium*, their limited right of disposal / *Untereigentum*. If the lord possessed the final right of disposal over the *peculium* belonging to his *servi*, the positive rights in LBai I 13 can be combined with the *servi* being the lord's property. The slaves' lifelong alternation between corvée labour in their master's inner zone (demesne) and their work on their 'own' holdings in the outer zone also contains an element of social control.[98]

In my opinion, it is not necessary to place the *servi* in the *Lex Baiuvariorum* and the *servi* in the sources from the following period into two contradictory domains: on the one hand, a *legal* domain, which develops quite slowly and where the *servus* is characterized as a slave, and on the other hand, a more practical, *socially* formed domain, in which a *servus* is a manorial leaseholder who can be characterized as a serf (*Höriger, Leibeigener*).[99] We achieve a more accurate picture when we try to understand these two sides – legal and social – as a whole. To the lord's sovereignty, *Leibeigenschaft* over his *servi*, originating

95 LBai I 13.

96 LBai I.

97 Provisions that overrule the master's proprietorial right to punish their slaves are known from most medieval laws, e.g., G 259.

98 The importance of the tightness of social control by the exchange of labour between demesnes and small peasant farms in the lifetime of the *servi*; see Hammer, 'Family and Familia', 217–49; Hammer, *Large-Scale Slave Society*, 21.

99 Goetz, 'Serfdom', 34–39, 46f.

in his claim to them as his property, we must add the positive and negative legal aspects of the slaves as persons as a way for the lord to exercise social control over them.[100] The provisions concerning slaves in the *Lex Baiuvariorum* thus contain a marked protection of their right to farm their own land for their own benefit at the same time as the provisions aim to control them through draconian penal provisions. Incorporated custom seems to lay behind the division of the slave's days of labour on the lord's demesne and the time he could spend for himself and his family at his hut nearby. We find the same division in the sources in England from the same period.[101] This seems to be a fairly common European organization of forced labour. I do not see any sound reason for not using the term slave for all aspects of the *servi* in the *Lex Baiuvariorum* even though they could work for themselves and their family some days in the week.[102]

5.3 Servi *and the Manorial System* (Grundherrschaft / Villikation)

The development of unfreedom is closely connected to the development of the manorial system that formed the basic economic and social relations in medieval agrarian society.[103] Although terms like 'manorial system' or

100 According to Goetz, everyone who continues to use the term 'slave' to denote the early medieval *servi* must concede that slavery had changed since Antiquity. Goetz seems here to view the Roman *servus* as a model for the real slave. We must consider as well that the Roman slave in Roman law also had substantial positive rights, particularly the right to *peculium*. Even though a slave could not possess any 'pure' property, slaves were widely entitled to administer and enlarge their *peculium*. The slave could also determine what to do regarding parts of his *peculium*. Slaves played an important role in social life. Thus, the Roman slave emerges more as a legally liable person in contrast to the impression given by the law where corporal punishment held a prominent place. A master's responsibility for his slaves was less prominent than in the *Lex Baiuvariorum* (cf. Buckland, *Roman Law of Slavery*, 131–238).

101 'By the time of King Alfred [last part of the ninth century], on larger and stable manors, customs regulating the hours of work of slaves probably evolved in the same way as customs prescribing their food rations' (David A.E. Pelteret, *Slavery in Early Medieval England* (Woodbridge: Boydell, 1995), 242–43). This was probably also the background for dividing the workdays between the demense and the *servi's* 'own' farming in England, as well as in Bavaria.

102 Slavery in LBai is, in other words, primarily different from classical Roman slavery. The provisions about *peculium* and the positive economic rights in LBai are concentrated within the agrarian sphere and probably point to the development of a binate manorial system where unfree people only had limited independence.

103 F. Lütge has given a classical definistion of *Grundherrschaft*, which in English may be translated as: 'Dominion over people who live on a defined rural property (*Grund und Boden*) and thus are affected by this dominion'. ('Herrschaft über Menschen, die auf einem bestimmten Grund und Boden ... ansässig sind und die darum von der Herrschaft

'*Grundherrschaft*' / '*Villikation*' are modern constructions,[104] LBai indicates that an early form of this agrarian system was already widespread in the eastern Alpine region in the early Middle Ages. This manorial system (*Villikationen*) consisted of a central farm (demesne / *Fronhof*) and smaller holdings of varying distance to the farm that delivered dues and performed corvée labour at the central farm. In this context, it is important to note that *servi*, as well as free people, were employed on both parts of this binate system.[105] Because of their closer ties to their masters, most *servi* / *mancipia* tended to work on the central farm and on smaller holdings in the vicinity of this farm.

As substantiated by more recent studies, the basic elements of this binate system existed in various forms in the Middle Ages.[106] Studies on the early medieval manors (*Grundherrschaften*) in the eastern Alpine region have shown that the fundamental structures were only concurrent with the ideal concept of *Grundherrschaft* to a certain degree and that they differed to a surprising extent in size. Beside binate manors (*Villikationsverfassungen*), other forms of agrarian systems were also found in the early medieval period, such as *Gutwirtschaft*, agrarian production on a demesne (*Fron* / *Zentralhofbetrieb*), and *Abgabengrundherrschaft*, in which central farms were collection points for the delivery of dues in various forms.

Unfree people were employed in every one of these agrarian systems.[107] Until the thirteenth century, we can divide the unfree people (*servi*) of the eastern Alpine region into three different groups. The first group lived on their master's farm (*domus*) and were totally subjugated to him when it came to working the land or performing other duties. The second group were unfree leaseholders on the manor and had to deliver services and dues. A third group,

---

erfasst werden'); cf.Werner Rösener, 'Agrarwitschaft, Agrarverfassung und ländliche Gesellschaft im Mittelalter', in Lothar Gall, et al. (eds), *Enzyklopädie deutsche Geschichte*, xiii (Munich: R. Oldenbourg, 1992), 7.

104 Rösener, 'Agrarwitschaft', 7.

105 Dollinger, *Der bayerische Bauernstand*, 245–52. His book, published in French in 1949, is still held to be a remarkable study on the Bavarian peasantry in the Middle Ages.

106 Hans-Werner Goetz, 'Frühmittelalterliche Grundherrschaften und ihre Erforschung im europäischen Vergleich', in Michael Borgolte (ed.), *Das europäische Mittelalter im Spannungsbogen des Vergleichs* (Berlin: Akademie Verlag, 2001), 75–87.

107 Wilhelm Störmer, 'Frümittelalterliche Grundherrschaft bayerischer Kirchen (8. – 10. Jahrhundert)', in Werner Rösener (ed.), *Strukturen der Grundherrschaft im frühen Mittelalter* (Göttingen: Vandenhoeck und Ruprecht, 1993), 377–88. Störmer lists six types. In the same volume, see also: Adrian Verhulst, 'Die Grundherrschaftsentwicklung im ostfränkischen Raum vom 8. Bis 10. Jahrhundert. Grundzüge und Fragen aus westfränkischer Sicht', pp. 29–47, and Werner Goetz, 'Zur Grundherrschaftsentwicklung der Abtei St.Gallen', especially pp. 217–31.

the *ministeriales*, for the most part originated from the two other groups and, from the eleventh century, rose to a higher social standing performing important military and administrative functions.[108] A special group in the eastern Alpine region, situated between free and unfree persons, was the *Zensualen* (see below). They were obliged to render dues mostly derived from their position in the manorial *familia* and were only loosely connected to a manorial lord.[109]

The day labourers on their master's farm could be sold or given away, and they could not marry outside the manorial estate (*Grundherrschaft*). Still, they could possess their own property. As for jurisdiction, the day labourers were the direct subjects of their masters, in contrast to the manorial leaseholders on holdings of their own, who had to appear at the master's annual court. From the High Middle Ages on, the *servi*, living on manorial holdings, constituted the greater part of the agrarian workforce in Bavaria.[110] Nevertheless, the difference in their economic standing was great. Those leasing initially unfree holdings had to deliver heavy corvée labour, while new leaseholder on free holdings (*Freihufen*) did not have to perform corvée labour at all. Unfree leaseholders were counted as part of the inventory of the holding and could be sold together with the holding itself. They were not granted the right to live on the holding throughout their lives, but at the same time they were not allowed to move away of their own will, even if many unfree people fled. The increase in population gradually changed the manorial lord's attitude to this problem. Many manorial lords were satisfied with an annual personal fee (*Kopfzins*) from their *zensualen* settling outside the manorial land (*Grundherrschaft*).[111]

From the beginning of the High Middle Ages, the question of the stability of the manorial units seems to be important. From this point on, we find evidence of hereditary transmission of some ecclesiastical holdings. This tendency did not last, as the manorial lords succeeded in excluding any claims to inherit such holdings in the thirteenth century. The manorial lord preferred to transfer a holding to an unfree person, due to such a person being more dependent. The general increase in population, including the unfree portion of the population, made this possible. That a direct manumission within the manorial system was relatively infrequent was, according to Dollinger, connected to the discontinuation of the praxis of heavy corvée labour. This development was accelerated to a certain extent by the general dissolution of the binate

108 Dollinger, *Der bayerische Bauernstand*, 245–85.

109 Knut Schultz, 'Zensualen, Zinsleute, Zensualität', in LexMA, ix, 530–33; Dollinger, *Der bayerische Bauernstand*, 304–44.

110 In the sources, they are simply named *servi* and *mancipia* instead of being given special denotations like other groups (Dollinger, *Der bayerische Bauernstand*, 259).

111 Dollinger, *Der bayerische Bauernstand*, 261.

manorial system (*Villikationsverfassung*). The unfree leaseholder differed increasingly less from his free counterpart.[112]

6 The Dissolution of the Binate Manorial System (*Villikation*) and the Creation of a Peasant Estate

As early as the beginning of the High Middle Ages, a certain convergence between the two groups of peasants, the free and the *servi*, can be observed within the confines of the manorial system to the east of the River Rhine. We can witness a socio-economic elevation of the *servi* at the same time as the workload of the two groups tended to become more equal. This development is connected to a fundamental change in the manorial organization in the High Middle Ages. Historians have explained the scope and the dating of these changes in different ways.[113] What is still clear is that a development from an 'ancient', binate manorial system (*Villikation, Fronhofverfassung*) to a 'younger', rental-based manorial system (*Rentengrundherrschaft*) was occurring. The question remains whether this change can be seen as a 'revolution' in the twelfth century, as Phillipp Dollinger maintained, or as process of evolution, spanning a couple of centuries in the high medieval period, as Werner Rösener assumes.[114] According to Rösener, detailed studies indicate that the process of dissolution of the ancient system in some areas, such as Lotharingia, began as early as the eleventh century, increased during the twelfth century, and was completed by the end of the thirteenth century. In some Bavarian and Austrian areas, this process was completed as late as the fourteenth century.

In this process of dissolution, the demesnes were dissolved and parcelled out in the form of new peasant holdings. Many of these holdings were the size of a normal tenant holding (*mansus*) and were given to *servi* and peasants;

---

112 Dollinger, *Der bayerische Bauernstand*, 259–64, 282–85.

113 This economic change in the High Middle Ages has been accepted by most historians, but not by Alphons Dopsch: A. Dopsch, *Herrschaft und Bauer in der deutschen Kaiserzeit: Untersuchungen zur Agrar- und Sozialgeschichte des hohen Mittelalters mit besonderer Berücksichtigung des südostdeutschen Raumes* (Jena: Gustav Fischer, 1939), especially chapters 8 and 12.

114 Ph. Dollinger, *Der bayerische Bauernstand*, 123; Werner Rösener, *Grundherrschaft im Wandel: Untersuchungen zur Entwicklung geistlicher Grundherrschaften im südwestdeutschen Raum vom 9. bis 14. Jahrhundert*, Veröffentlichungen des Max-Planck-Instituts für Geschichte, 102 (Göttingen: Vandenhoeck and Ruprecht, 1991), 557–66.

only a few served as main farms and hubs for collecting dues for the manorial lord (*Meierhöfe*). Corvée labour was now mostly redundant due to the reduction in the manorial production on the demesne itself. The duty to perform corvée labour was mostly transformed into monetary fees during the shift to a rental-based manorial system (*Rentengrundherrschaft*). Nevertheless, Rösener points out that the change in the manorial system in the High Middle Ages by no means meant that any kind of agrarian production on the demesnes was given up, as exemplified by the granges belonging to the Cistercian Order. In Germany, the expansion of princely, ecclesiastical, and aristocratic administrative organizations, as well as the social elevation of the *ministeriales*, led to the establishment of several smaller manorial estates (*Grundherrschaften*).[115]

The general decline of corvée labour and the subsequent softening of the connection between main farms and dependent peasant holdings also led to looser ties of dependency between unfree people and their lords. The dominant distinction between *liberi* and *servi* gradually gave way to a peasant estate, although a markedly differentiated one. The waning of unfree people's personal dependency within the framework of the manorial system has been characterized by some historians as a 'high medieval peasant liberation'.[116] The ancient unfreedom, including remnants of pure slavery, was clearly losing ground, and the personal status of the unfree gave way to 'factual', i.e forms of obligations, especially fees and dues. The vast majority of rural people gained greater freedom: for example, long-term security of tenure, greater opportunity to work the land in the way they saw fit, and last but not the least, the freedom to leave, even if many had to render a fee to do so.[117]

Rösener highlights the changes in the manorial system in the long period from the eleventh to the fourteenth century as perhaps the most important period of upheaval in medieval agrarian history.[118] The most important driving force behind this transformation was the strong increase in population, resulting in the extensive clearing of new land and in the intensification of agrarian

115 Rösener, *Grundherrschaft im Wandel*, 557–66 and passim; Werner Rösener, 'Grundherrschaft', in LexMA, iv, 1746f.; Ludolf Kuchenbuch, 'Potestas und Utilitas', *Historische Zeitschrift*, 265/1 (1997), 117–46; Hans Kurt Schulze, '*Grundherrschaft*', in HRG, especially pp. 1824–42.

116 Hermann Kellenbenz, et al. (eds), *Handbuch der europäischen Wirtschafts- und Sozialgeschichte*, ii: *Europäische Wirtschafts- und Sozialgeschichte im Mittelalter* (Stuttgart: Klett-Cotta, 1980), 112.

117 Rösener, 'Grundherrschaft', in LexMA, 1746; Rösener, *Grundherrschaft im Wandel*, 531; Rösener, *Bauern in Mittelalter* (Munich: C.H. Beck, 1985), 225–27; Kuchenbuch, 'Potestas und Utilitas', 123.

118 Rösener, *Grundherrschaft im Wandel*, 557–66; Werner Rösener, *Grundherrschaft und bäuerliche Gesellschaft im Hochmittelalter* (Göttingen, Vandenhoeck und Ruprecht, 1995), 10.

production, as witnessed by a stronger emphasis on the production of grain and by specialization, for example, of livestock in mountainous regions and the production of wine in the vicinity of towns.[119] As Stefan Sonderegger has demonstrated in his study of St Gallen, urban landowners, such as hospitals and merchants, were active in the agrarian production in areas surrounding the towns.[120] They took over fiefs from the ancient monastery of St Gallen and leased this land to peasant families. Thus, urban players managed to link agrarian production to their commercial interests. Consequently, relations between manorial lords and peasants changed in the direction of legal to economic relations.[121]

Increasing trade between towns and countryside replacing the former division of work in the binate manorial system (*Villikationssystem*) had consequences for the dissolution of the binate manorial system, for the production on the demesnes, and therefore also for the social position of unfree people.[122] The development of towns was slower in the eastern Alpine region than in the southwestern parts of the German-speaking areas.[123] In connection with this slow development, we can highlight the many new settlements, in which unfree people in the high medieval period still played an essential part. This internal colonization, if there was new land to clear in the midst of Europe, was driven by the dissolution of the demesne system and by a greater mobility. In the High Middle Ages, internal colonization and the densification of settlements were,

119 See, for example, the Swiss regional study by Stefan Sonderegger, 'Landwirtschaftliche Spezialisierung in der spätmittelalterlichen Nordostschweiz', in Markus Cerman and Erich Landsteiner (eds), *Zwischen Land und Stadt. Wirtschaftsverflechtungen von ländlichen und städtischen Räumen in Europa 1300–1600*, Jahrbuch für Geschichte des ländlichen Raumes, 2009 (Innsbruck: Studien Verlag, 2010), 139–60.

120 Stefan Sonderegger, 'The Financing Strategy of a Major Urban Hospital in the Late Middle Ages (St Gallen 15th Century)', in Francesco Ammannati (ed.), *Assistenza e solidarietà in Europa Secc. XIII–XVIII / Social Assistance and Solidarity in Europe from the 13th to the 18th Centuries: atti della 'Quarantaquattresima Settimana di Studi', 22–26 aprile 2012*, Atti delle Settimane di Studi e altri Convegni, 44 (Florence: Florence University Press, 2013), 209–26.

121 Stefan Sonderegger, 'Getreide, Fleisch und Geld gegen Wein. Stadt-Umland-Beziehungen im spätmittel-alterlichen St Gallen', in Frank Konersmann andKlaus-Joachim Lorenzen-Schmidt (eds), *Bauern als Händler. Ökonomische Diversifizierung und soziale Differenzierung bäuerlicher Agrarproduzenten (15.–19. Jahr-hundert)*, Quellen und Forschungen zur Agrargeschichte, 52 (Stuttgart: Lucius & Lucius, 2011), 17–33. Stefan Sonderegger, 'Bauernfamilien und ihre Landwirtschaft im Spätmittelalter. Beispiele aus Untersuchungen zur ländlichen Gesellschaft der Nordschweiz', *Zeitschrift für Agrargeschichte und Agrarsoziologie*, 60/2 (2012), 35–57.

122 Rösener, *Grundherrschaft im Wandel*, 373–86.

123 Dollinger, *Der bayerische Bauernstand*, 438.

in contrast to in the early Middle Ages, driven by the planned and organized clearance of new land.[124]

In the eastern Alpine region from the twelfth century, settlements ending in –*reuth* converge with the present limits of the forest in the Bavarian highland. Monasteries and bishoprics were especially active in this transformation. Further to the east, colonization came later and reached its peak in the thirteenth century.[125] The famous German formulation '*Rodung macht Frei*' has been criticized for implying an automatic progression from the clearing of new land and the foundation of new settlements to a general dissolution of unfree statuses. Surviving settlement and tenure contracts from the twelfth century clearly show that everybody who participated in this movement was provided with new 'liberties', for example, economic advantages and better forms of tenure.[126]

6.1 *Unfree People* (Eigenleute) *in the* Schwabenspiegel

As a comprehensive legal codification from the year 1275, the *Schwabenspiegel* (S) can indicate the legal status of unfree people in the eastern Alpine region by the end of the High Middle Ages. This 'unofficial' book of law was very widely distributed and served as a model for the Bavarian and Austrian territorial laws.[127] If we use the same criteria as delineated earlier, the unfree as his master's property and persons with negative or positive rights, we find radical changes to the older LBai.

In LBai, the *servus* is described as a slave. In S: unfree people were still the property of their masters (only free men and ecclesiastical institutions could possess *Eigenleute*) (68c); children were accorded the same right and status as their mother (68b); property that the *Eigenmann* himself had acquired belonged to his master (374 I); *Eigenleute* could be used as dowry; a destitute father could sell his child as property (357); and *Eigenleute* were prohibited from fleeing (356).

The changes are more obvious when it comes to the corporal punishment of unfree people. Such punishment was no longer restricted to unfree men, but

124 Werner Rösener, 'Landesausbau und Kolonisation', in LexMA, v, 1643–45.

125 Dollinger, *Der bayerische Bauernstand*, 84–86.

126 Ludwig Schmugge, 'Mobilität und Freiheit im Mittelalter', in Johannes Fried (ed.), *Die abendländische Freiheit vom 10. bis zum 14. Jahrhundert*, Vorträge und Forschunge: Konstanzer Arbeitskreis für mittelalterliche Geschichte, 49 (Sigmaringen: Jan Thorbecke, 1991), 312–14.

127 Edition used for this article: *Der Schwabenspiegel*, Derschka (ed.). The *Schwabenspiegel* is a civil law text composed in Augsburg 1275/76 for the south German area and presents itself as an imperial book of law. See K. Nehlsen-von Stryk, 'Schwabenspiegel', 1603–05.

was extended to all free men who were unable to pay their monetary fines (see, for example, §174).[128] The positive rights of unfree people were also markedly extended in S: he who took the life of his *Knecht* (unfree servant) had to pay a fine to the judge (73a) or lose his life himself (201a). If the master hit his *Eigenmann* so he lost his eye (201b) or prevented him from getting necessary help when he needed such (71), the unfree man was to get his freedom. Property that the unfree man inherited or received as a gift belonged to him and not to his master (374, see also 259). However, an unfree person could not marry a free person (319 I).

Some provisions in the law code concerning the commitment to stay on the manor (*Schollengebundenheit*) and concerning marriage restrictions show signs of a milder unfreedom. To this, we may add other tokens of a milder unfreedom, such as *Leibzins,* that is, a lifelong fee to be paid for *Eigenleute* who lived outside the manorial estate (see *Zensualen*), and *Todfallabgabe,* that is, the manorial lord's right to a fraction of the property or livestock in case of the leaseholder's death.[129] We may then conclude that the *Eigenleute* in the *Schwabenspiegel* enjoyed rights and a status that fell between those of slaves and free people, even if these rights and status often approached a free status.

6.2 *Comparing Unfree People in the* Schwabenspiegel *and the Nordic Laws*

It is difficult to compare the 'civil / private' law of the *Schwabenspiegel* (S) with the royally initiated Nordic laws. However, their nearly synchronous proximity in time makes it worthwhile. In the Norwegian laws G and F from the twelfth and the first part of the thirteenth century, respectively, the *þrælar* were the property of their masters. They could be bought and sold and could be used as a means of payment. In S, the *Eigenleutes*' bondage to their masters, their master's partial control over their property, their inability to freely leave the manor, and the restrictions on their right to marry are evident. However, the general purchase and sale of *Eigenleute* is not mentioned. Corporal punishment, in G and F mainly prescribed for unfree people, is not restricted to *Eigenleute* as a group in S but is extended to every lower category in the social order. The positive rights in S are markedly extended compared to G and F. In the *Schwabenspiegel,* they are even extended to the point where *Eigenleute* could receive property through inheritance or bequest. They could also obtain better personal protection or even obtain freedom if their master harmed them severely.

128 See Dollinger, *Der bayerische Bauernstand,* 210f.

129 Alfred Wretschko, 'Über Eigenleute und Eigenleuteteilungen in Tirol', *Zeitschrift der Savigny-Stiftung für Rechtsgeschichte: Germanistische Abteilung,* 46 (1926), 366–74.

The Swedish *Law of Uppland* (UL) from 1296 displays some similarities to these provisions, in the *Schwabenspiegel* in so far as a *þræll* received his freedom if he was sold by his master. The evolving manumission is, however, far more evident in UL than in S, as a mother and a child also gained their freedom when she married.

6.3 *Unfreedom in the Eastern Alpine Region from the High Middle Ages to the End of the Late Middle Ages*

The high medieval development makes it evident that milder forms of unfreedom, although with great regional differences, existed in the eastern Alpine region. Heinz Dopsch has maintained that the concept of 'freedom' in this period had become very diversified and unclear. An important aspect of this concept was freedom from obligations to do corporal work (*opus servile*) and the freedom of movement. In the eastern Alpine region, the *Zensualen* were a numerous group in between freedom and unfreedom (see also above). Their increase came primarily from the transformation of unfree people to the status of *Zensualen*, especially from the twelfth century and primarily on the manorial estates of ecclesiastical institutions. When they obtained the status of *Zensualen*, they were freed from almost every mark of serfdom (*servitus* / *Leibeigenschaft*).

The transformation to *zensual* status is referred to as 'becoming the freedom' from their masters, but free persons also entered *zensual* status through their own will. The personal freedom of the *Zensualen* was, though, in no way unlimited. They were obliged to render an annual personal fee (*Kopfzins*) and were entitled in return to the protection of their master as members of his *familia*. In addition to the annual personal fee, their successors had to hand over a part of the estate of the deceased person (*Todfallabgaben*), and certain restrictions also existed in their ability to freely marry. If they failed to pay their *Kopfzins* for three consecutive years, they lost their *Zensualrecht* (right to *zensual* status) and were downgraded into the group of unfree people (*servi*).

At the end of the twelfth century, the *Zensualen* constituted the second largest social stratum on the ecclesiastical manorial estates in the duchy of Bavaria. The dissolution of serfdom (*Leibeigenschaft* / *servitus*) and the transition to the status of *Zensualen* did more than simply promote the transformation of the manorial system. From the thirteenth century, *Zensualen* coming from rural areas also played an important part in the dynamic transformation of towns, in the foundation of a bourgeoisie, and in the clearing of new land in mountainous areas; the *Zensualen* gradually disappeared as a closed group, as many of them had their occupation in the towns or became *Ministerialen*.

Some free people entered into *zensual* status by their own will as late as the second half of the fifteenth century.[130] The *Freisassen* in the territory of Salzburg constituted a parallel group.[131]

In the territory of Tyrol, unfree peasants also appear in the documents of the thirteenth and fourteenth centuries. Over the course of the thirteenth century, terms like *servi / mancipia* were replaced with the term *Eigenleute*. Around the middle of the thirteenth century, *Eigenleute* constituted a minority in the peasant population. *Eigenleute* could not belong to the free peasantry; they were the property of the Tyrolean territorial princes, the aristocracy and ecclesiastical institutions. The manorial estates in Tyrol were not large, geographically closed manors. They were usually dispersed over scattered possessions in the eastern Alpine region.[132] From the middle of the thirteenth century, the power of the territorial prince increased markedly. This increase was due to his cooperation with the peasant elite, represented at the local courts and at the territorial assemblies of the fifteenth century, against the aristocracy and the ecclesiastical lords and institutions. The territorial prince secured the

---

130 Heinz Dopsch, 'Neue Leibeigenschaft oder alte Hörigkeit? Zu den Beschwerden und Forderungen aufständischer Bauern im Ostalpenraum an der Wende zur Neuzeit', in Paul Freedman and Monique Bourin (eds), *Forms of Servitude in Northern and Central Europe* (Turnhout: Brepols, 2005), 313–40; Dollinger, *Der bayerische Bauernstand*, 304–46; Schulz, 'Zensualen, Zinsleute, Zensualität', 530–33; Rösener, *Grundherrschaft im Wandel*, 532f.

131 The *Freisassen* were the archbishop of Salzburg's unfree people (*Eigenleute / homines proprii*). They had once cleared and settled on land belonging to other manorial estates but were now considered to be the archbishop's serfs (*Leibeigene*). Because of the great decline in population during the plague of 1348/50, it was now possible for their *Leibherr*, the archbishop, to revive their old dependency. He could therefore remove the *Freisassen* from other manorial lords' estates and settle them on his own estates. In such cases, the *Freisassens*' ties of bondage to the archbishop as *Leibherr* outweighed their ties to their manorial lords within the limitations of the *Grundherrschaft* (Dopsch, 'Neue Leibeigenschaft', 322–24; Herbert Klein, 'Die Salzburger Freisassen', in *Beiträge zur Siedlungs-, Verfassungs- und Wirtschaftsgeschichte von Salzburg: Festschrift zum 65. Geburtstag von Herbert Klein*, Mitteilungen der Gesellschaft für Salzburger Landeskunde, Ergänzungsband, 5 (Salzburg: Selbstverlag der Gesellscahft für Salzburger Landeskunde, 1965), 253f.).

132 Otto Stolz, *Rechtsgeschichte des Bauernstandes und der Landwirtschaft in Tirol und Voralberg* (Bozen: Ferrari-Auer, 1949), 47, 92f. The Norwegian research project, 'Peasant Control over Land and Resources – Scandinavia and the Eastern Alpine Region 1000–1750' organized a workshop 22–23 May 2006 in Innsbruck regarding Tyrol in the Middle Ages, with partipication from the following historians: W. Beimrohr, M. Bitschnau, H. Dopsch, T. Fornwager, C. Haidacher, L.I. Hansen, T. Iversen, J. Myking, H. Noflatscher, J. Riedmann, H. Salvesen, and G. Thoma. The following paragraphs draws heavily on the debate at this workshop.

peasants favourable free hereditary tenures (*Erbzinsrecht*), the dominant form of tenure from then on in Tyrol.[133] (see also chapter 'Leasehold and Freehold')

The territorial princes also merged their subjects into a homogeneous federation of subjects with uniform contributions in the form of a general tax and military conscription. For example, the prince issued a tax for 'everyone who belongs to us', including their *Eigenleute*.[134] For the territorial prince, other lords' *Eigenleute* presented a serious obstacle to his aspiration to create a homogeneous confederation of subjects. From the late-fourteenth century, the unfree peasant population (*Eigenleute*) declined, and over the course of the fifteenth century, it was turned into a marginal phenomenon.[135] At this point of time, however, no official abolition of serfdom was proclaimed in Tyrol or in any of the other Habsburgian territories.

A variety of factors contributed to the gradual decline of unfreedom in Tyrol, for example, the agrarian forms of production in this mountainous region, and the relationship between peasants, aristocracy, and the territorial prince who aimed at creating a homogeneous confederation of subjects. In addition, the demographic reductions due to plagues since the middle of the fourteenth century may also have been a contributing factor.[136]

6.4 *Unfreedom as a Means of Securing Territorial Control*

By the thirteenth century, the restructuring and dissolution of manors (*Grundherrschaft*) had resulted in the division of ownership of land and ownership of unfree people working the land (see *Zensuales*, above). Some manorial lords then entered into legal agreements to overcome the difficulties of divided

---

133 In this context, Heinz Dopsh highlights the importance of not confusing personal freedom with political co-determination and favourable forms of tenure such as 'freieigener Besitz, freie Erbleihe' (Dopsch, 'Neue Leibeigenschaft', 317).

134 In the year 1406, the representatives of the territorial aristocracy had to promise that their *Zins-* and *Eigenleuten* were unconditionally obliged to render tax and military duty to the prince and the territory of Tyrol, at the request of the territorial prince or by the free will of their manorial lords. A survey of subjects from 1447 lists everyone who was obliged to render tax, military duty, or was subject to the prince's legal authority (Stolz, *Rechtsgeschichte*, 98–102,128).

135 Wilfried Beimrohr, 'Bäuerliche Besitzrechte und die ländliche Gemeinde in Tirol', in Tor Iversen, John Ragnar Myking and Gertrud Thoma (eds), *Bauern zwischen Herrschaft und Genossenschaft: Peasant Relations to Lords and Government. Scandinavia and the Alpine Region 1000–1750* (Trondheim: Tapir Akademisk Forlag, 2007), 85–108, at pp. 88–91. According to Josef Riedmann, serfdom (*Leibeigenschaft*) lost ground by the High Middle Ages: Josef Riedmann, 'Tirol', in LexMA, viii, 803.

136 Heinz Dopsch, at the workshop on 22–23 May 2006 at Innsbruck.

ownership of land and people.[137] To begin with, this new instrumentalization of unfreedom was influenced by the church's novel teaching about unfree people's right to engage in marriage (see the *Frostathing Law* in Norway). Two great neighbouring monasteries, Benediktbeuren and Tegnersee, thus allowed marriage between their unfree people as early as 1217 and, at the same time, entered into an agreement concerning how the children from these marriages should be divided between the two monasteries. The reason why these large monasteries were especially interested in binding unfree people to themselves was not, first and foremost, their need for labour, but the fact that unfree people were easier to control than a free workforce.

The two monasteries' legal control over their unfree people (*Leibeigene*) was then used systematically to gain independence from the Bavarian duke's authority (see chapter 'Peasant Participation'). Even the duke himself used unfreedom to enlarge his own power in western Bavaria, where he possessed little land.[138] In these circumstances, unfreedom became an instrument in gaining territorial control, a role usually played by control over land (*Grundherrschaft*) or judicial authority (*Gerichtsherrschaft*).[139] In the southwestern part of Germany, we find several examples of successful territorial expansions through control over unfree persons, in which a unified group of subjects (*Untertanenverband*) developed and the oath of the serf later became the general oath of the subjects in the territory.[140]

In Bavaria, unfreedom generally diminished in the period before 1500. The difference in status between free and unfree now formally consisted of the lack of free movement (*Freizügigkeit*) and less personal authority (*Mindermündigkeit*). Public rights and duties were the same for free and unfree persons. Still, unfreedom (*Leibeigenschaft*) was not formally abolished until 1808.[141]

137 Roberto Fröhlich, 'Die Eigenleute des Johanniterhauses Bubikon. Eigenschaft und Leibherrschaft im Herrschaftsbereich der Johanniterkomturei Bubikon 1192–1789', dissertation, University of Zurich, Zurich, 1993, 145–53.

138 Before 1500, the duke managed to make children of mixed marriage, in which one of the marriage partners belonged to the duke, his possession. In addition, he succeeded in gaining ownership of land worked by these unfree people. (Monika Ofer, 'Leibeigenschaft am westbayerischen Alpenrand', unpublished paper, 2005).

139 cf. Philip Robinson, *Die Fürstabtei St.Gallen und ihr Territorium 1463–1529: eine Studie zur Entwicklung territorialer Staatlichkeit*, St Galler Kultur und Geschichte, 24 (St Gallen: Staatsarchiv und Stiftsarchiv, 1995), 127–40.

140 Fröhlich, 'Die Eigenleute, 182'.

141 Ofer, 'Leibeigenschaft am westbayerischen Alpenrand'.

7 Comparing Unfreedom in Scandinavia and the Eastern Alpine Region – A Summary

An important basis for this study has been the use of the concept of *unfreedom* as a description for a wide spectrum, ranging from milder forms of unfreedom to pure slavery in Scandinavia and the eastern Alpine region. Furthermore, unfreedom is comprehended as a concept consisting of three characteristics: first, unfree persons as property, that is, as a possession of their masters; and the second and third, as persons in a negative sense and in a positive sense, that is, unilateral punishment and reward. A widening of the positive rights led to a milder form of unfreedom and finally to its total abolition. This tripartite design, with the aim of analysing unfreedom in a synchronic, and to a lesser and more insecure extent, in a diachronic structural connection, has led to some definite conclusions that we will now try to summarize.

A comparison of the development of unfreedom in Scandinavia and the eastern Alpine region from the early Middle Ages until the end of the thirteenth century indicates distinct parallels, as well as some differences. First, an unfreedom of the type found from the first part of the medieval period until the end of the twelfth century in the medieval legal sources must be characterized as a pure form of slavery. Furthermore, it seems to have lasted about as long in both regions in the same high medieval period. Pure slavery is clearly mitigated in the *Schwabenspiegel* (1275), and to a certain point also in the somewhat older *Frostathing Law*. The issue of *matrimonium* seem to have played a more important role in the Frostathing Law than in the laws of the eastern Alpine region.

The *þrældómr* in the oldest Nordic laws, the *Gulathing Law* (an edition from the end of the eleventh century is only extent in a fragmentary form, while an almost completely preserved edition dates to the 1160s) must be perceived as a type of pure slavery. The important features of the unfreedom described in the *Lex Baiuvariorum* of the eighth century must be understood as another type of pure slavery as well. This law was valid for several centuries to come.

A closer look at unfreedom in the two regions conveys the following impression: the masters' stronger responsibility in LBai than in G for the misdoings of their *servi* may be taken as a sign of the strong position of a large *familia* in the manorial system in early medieval Bavaria. Legally prescribed corporal punishment for the *servi* played a part in LBai, especially punishment that incapacitated slaves so that they were unable to work, such as losing hands or eyes. This is the flip side of the *servi's* positive rights in the same law. The positive rights included the *servi's* relative independence within the framework of an early manorial system where, in addition to their obligation to perform corvée labour on the demesne, they were also entrusted with land they could work for their own benefit. In the Norwegian *Gulathing Law*, the *þræll's* corporal punishment, especially flogging, seems to have played an important role. In some cases, the king's bailiffs were accordingly given an important position in executing such punishments.

The binate structure of the classical manorial system in the eastern Alpine region was the same for free (*coloni*) and unfree (*servi*), although *coloni* had to render less corvée labour. Heavy corvée labour thus became an attribute of unfreedom in the eastern Alps. Many of the *servi* simultaneously also belonged to smaller holdings near the domus of the manor. The Norse sagas and cultural-topographic sources frequently refer to *þrælar* at the ancient seats of chieftains, and on and in the vicinity of main farms. This way of organizing agriculture displays some similarities to the continental manorial system. The most important difference is that, due to the topography of this sparsely populated country, the Norwegian manor-like units were spread over a wider area and had less cultivated acreage. Corvée labour is rarely mentioned. This form of system, also named *multiple estates* (see 'Introduction', section 'A Sketch of the Historical Background'), was more loosely organized than its counterpart on the Continent, and it was dissolved from around 1100. According to the *Gulathing Law* and other legal sources, *þrælar* and other unfree people were employed in a variety of households in Norway, large as well as smaller ones.

In the eastern Alpine region, the further development of unfreedom was closely connected to changes in the manorial system. The manorial system as an economic and social arrangement was much differentiated. However, some central lines of development from the eleventh (southwest Germany) to the end of the thirteenth century (southeast Germany) can be clearly discerned: primarily the transformation from a manorial system with demesnes (*Villikationen*) to a rental-based system (*Rentengrundherrschaft*). The general decline of corvée labour on the demesnes led to looser ties between unfree people and their manorial lords. Consequently, the status of *servi* started to approach the status of free people, and the original sharp division between these groups became blurred. The main forces behind this social transformation were the marked increase in population, evident in the widespread clearing of new land and in the intensification and specialization of agricultural production. The growth of towns also played a part in this process.

According to Dollinger, slavery or harsh unfreedom in the eastern Alpine region was diminished from the last part of the twelfth century.[142] Scandinavian sources present a somewhat different picture. The last version of the *Gulathing Law* (1160s) portrays *þrældómr* as pure slavery, while the Danish *Law of*

142 Dollinger, *Der bayerische Bauernstand*, 195–218, 242–44.

Scania from the beginning of the thirteenth century presents the *þræl* as enjoying very few positive rights. The same is the case in the Swedish *Law of Västergötland* from the end of the thirteenth century. As for the increase in population, there were still plenty of opportunities for clearing new land in Norway and Sweden in the twelfth and thirteenth centuries. Peasant freeholders and tenants on large farms could employ their *þrælar* in extensive clearing of new land to widen their acreages and remain in control of these newly acquired resources for a period of time. A possible factor, especially for Sweden, could have been that the import of slaves from the Baltic area lasted longer. Although the *Gulathing Law* distinguishes between native and foreign *þrælar*, internal recruitment was nevertheless the normal way of supplying additional unfree labour.

In the first part of the thirteenth century, the Norwegian *Frostathing Law* shows clear signs of a milder form of *þrældómr*, in which the *þrælar* had gained several positive rights, for example, the right to be entitled to receive fines from each other and perhaps also a normal right to marry. Most important are the provisions about the *þrælar's* agrarian opportunities, especially concerning the clearing of new land, in the process of which they were settled on smallholdings on the outskirts of the farms belonging to their former masters. There, they could improve their conditions until they were finally free. According to the *Frostathing Law*, the only contracts that freedmen of the lowest status could enter into without the consent of their master were leasehold contracts.[143] Other sources show that unfree men in time settled on more infertile soil in rather remote areas, far from the central farms.

The process of manumission, also influenced by the general increase in population, was evidently a driving force for the clearing of new land, and the clearing of new land stimulated manumission. Unfree people also played a part in the development of a leasehold system in Norway from the late-twelfth century, based on scattered possessions and rental incomes. In Sweden from the thirteenth century, most demesnes were divided. The owners' income was subsequently based on rent from scattered leaseholdings and new settlements. According to the manumission testaments, several *þrælar* worked their own land even before they received their final freedom. Therefore, freedmen in Sweden also played an important part in the clearing of new land.

143 F probably also granted the unfree the right to free marriages, because this theme is not mentioned at all in F. In the older G, on the other hand, these marriages were thoroughly schematized, but free marriage is only for the manumitted. About the important question of the church's teaching of right marriage for unfree people in the twelfth and thirteenth centuries, see Tore Iversen, *Trelldommen*, 196–208 and Iversen, *Knechtschaft*, 315–53.

Evidently, from the second half of the twelfth century and continuing throughout the thirteenth, the eastern Alpine region experienced a diminution of unfreedom. Unfree people in this region came to enjoy more positive rights, as indicated in the *Schwabenspiegel*. Their counterparts in Scandinavia followed suit, as the *Frostathing Law* indicates. The boundaries between free and unfree thus became even more blurred, but in F these boundaries are still clearly visible; people in the process of manumission were still held to be unfree or stained with unfree attributes for several generations. As a former mark of unfreedom, the regulations of corporal punishment in the *Schwabenspiegel* can be taken as a sign of the general deterioration of this boundary between free and unfree and the increasing importance of other marks of social standing. In this book of law (S), in contrast to the provisions in F, such punishment was not only reserved for unfree people, but for people belonging to all lower social strata.

The numerous groups of *Zensualen* in the eastern Alpine region illustrate this social transition. Admission to the *Zensualität* meant relief from *servitus* (corvée labour), and as a member of the *familia* it included a hereditary Zensual-recht. The *Zensualen* had to pay an annual personal tax (*Kopfzins*) and mortuary fees (*Todfallabgaben*), and their right to free marriage was restricted. This group displays some similarity to the Scandinavian group of unfree people on their way to complete manumission for whom this transition could last for four generations, if the unfree person was unable to buy his full freedom at once. In addition, his former master and his successors could claim inheritance (see above). The main difference between the Nordic freedmen and the *Zensualen* in the eastern Alpine region is that the *Zensualen*, especially those belonging to ecclesiastical institutions, enjoyed their lords' protection. In F, freedmen enjoyed only a time-limited, decreasing protection from their original masters and their successors. More importantly, royal legislation in Norway and Sweden strove to include all subjects within royal jurisdiction, including freedmen who had severed their ties to their former masters. The prince of Tyrol followed the same strategy.

On the other hand, in Norway we may possibly be witnessing an attempt to create a new social group with stigmatizing dependence in the wake of the prolonged process of manumission. An indication of this is the provision in F that allows the master and his successors to claim inheritance for eight generations, four generations more than the four generations needed to reach full manumission. However, this new, diminished unfreedom was deleted from the *Law of the Realm of 1274*. In the last phase of unfreedom in Scandinavia, legislation in Denmark and especially in Sweden in the late-thirteenth century seemed to aim, in contrast to the *Frostathing Law*, to *free* the former masters from any binding responsibility. This is probably a reflection of the increase in population that had led to an abundant supply of labour.

That unfreedom is only indirectly referred to in the *Norwegian Law of the Realm of 1274* is a token of its final abolition. In the year 1335, King Magnus Eriksson's decree about the abolition of unfreedom in one area of Sweden was issued. Within a period of around a hundred years, Scandinavia thus went from having a *þrældómr* class perhaps more absolute and uncompromising than in the eastern Alpine region to complete abolition. This full emancipation contrasts the development in the eastern Alpine region, where personal dependency was only diminished.

The development in the late Middle Ages did not follow the same lines in the whole of the eastern Alpine region. In the territory of Tyrol, only the aristocracy, the ecclesiastical institutions, and the territorial prince could possess unfree people (*Eigenleuten*). Peasants could not. Aided by the peasant elite, from the middle of the thirteenth century the territorial princes started to enlarge their power by issuing a general territorial tax and by conscription. The Tyrolean princes saw other lords' ability to possess *Eigenleute* as a threat to their attempts to create their own confederation of territorial subjects. From the late-fourteenth century, unfreedom in Tyrol declined, and over the course of the fifteenth century, had become a totally marginal phenomenon.

8 Main Factors Explaining the Development of Unfreedom

A comparative presentation of the main factors explaining the development of rural unfreedom in Scandinavia and in the eastern Alpine region from the early until the late Middle Ages can be summarized in the following way: topographic conditions played an important role in the development of agrarian systems. Fertile areas were thus generally best suited for closed agrarian units dependent on an unfree workforce, and mountainous areas were less suited. In our period, the general *increase in population* was, however, the main driving force, a force that also influenced the evolution of agrarian systems. In both regions, the increase in population positively influenced the statuses of unfree people. This impact, by which *servi* and *þrælar* gained considerably more positive rights, can be observed from around the end of the eleventh century in the eastern Alpine region, and in Scandinavia probably not until around 1200.

The agrarian systems were of great importance for the development of unfreedom. The transformation of the manorial system (*Grundherrschaft*) in the eastern Alpine region from widespread use of corvée labour on manorial demesnes to a rental-based leasehold system (*Rentengrundherrschaft*) diminished unfreedom. Still, unfreedom survived for a long period, especially in the large *familia* units. In Scandinavia, *þrælar* were found within a broader range of households than in the eastern Alpine region, even though the large, manor-like estates with a great number of unfree people were partly dissolved in the twelfth century. It was perhaps easier to preserve some form of diminished unfreedom in the large *familae* of the reformed, geographically closed manorial estates (*Grundherrschaften*) in the eastern Alpine region. As a rule, these large estates, such as those in Bavaria, had been provided with jurisdictional privileges, while in Scandinavia, especially in Norway and Sweden, jurisdiction was monopolized by the king in cooperation with the church during the high medieval period. Royal legislation encouraged unfree people to clear new land in order to buy themselves positive rights and thus become free.

In Scandinavia, the strengthening of royal power, especially in the thirteenth century and the first half of the fourteenth century, contributed considerably to the final abolition of unfreedom. This expansion of power often carried with it conflicts as well as compromises with the aristocracy. The strength of the aristocracy is evidently a factor that could have obstructed or delayed the abolition of unfreedom. On the other hand, the crown tried, by way of the introduction of general jurisdiction and taxation, to make every inhabitant their territorial subject. The omission of any direct provisions concerning unfreedom in the *Norwegian Law of the Realm of 1274* and the abolition of unfreedom in one area of Sweden (1335) can be interpreted because of royal monopolization in these fields. While the members of the aristocracy were associated with a local region in the previous period and drew their incomes from this region, they increasingly became, above all in Norway, an aristocracy serving the king.

In the eastern Alpine region, princely power developed in a somewhat different direction. In the duchy of Bavaria, the territorial princes indeed strove to curtail the power of the ecclesiastical and secular manorial lords, but they had to make a great number of concessions. The ecclesiastical manorial estates especially enjoyed wide privileges in their *Hofmarken* (see chapter 'Peasant Participation'). From the end of the High Middle Ages, the legal status of free and unfree people converged, even though the unfree status still endured. Only in the county of Tyrol and in the neighbouring principality of Salzburg, belonging to the archbishop of Salzburg, did the territorial princes managed to obtain full jurisdiction in the fourteenth century and thus secure territorial control. In these territories, unfreedom had lost all significance by then.

In the two regions that have been the subject of our comparison, *social mobility* played an important role in the diminution of unfree statuses and in their final abolition, as well as in the *restructuring* of high medieval society. This restructuring included a great expansion of settlement, the transformation of the agrarian system, and the creation of a relative homogeneous peasant estate as one of several social estates the thirteenth century. We can also include the expansion of territorial power and the forming of a confederation of territorial subjects within the framework of the territorial states. In this case, unfree people as persons in a negative sense, expressed through punishment of *servi* and *þrælar*, played a part, as these forms of punishment also constituted the basis for disciplining of the lower social groups in the federation of territorial subjects.

Acknowledgements

I am indebted to the late professor Heinz Dopsch for comments and suggestions to the section titled: 'Unfreedom in the Eastern Alpine Region from the High Middle Ages to the End of the Late Middle Ages'.

CHAPTER 3

Leasehold and Freehold *c.* 1200–1750

John Ragnar Myking

From the High Middle Ages to the end of the early modern period, the peasant population's ability to control land and resources was greatly affected by changing power relations between peasants on the one hand, and an elite of secular and ecclesiastical aristocrats and institutions, including territorial sovereigns, on the other. These power relations affected the conditions under which a majority of peasants rented their land and the ability of some peasant households to remain or become independent freeholders. However, to understand the development of tenures and peasant ownership, we must begin with a discussion of the conditions under which an elite extracted a surplus from land at the end of the early Middle Ages and the beginning of the High Middle Ages.

By this point in time, continental Europe was dominated by binate manors (*Villikationen*). A central main farm was run by the landlord or his steward (*Meier*) and worked by unfree farm labourers. The rest of the manor was divided into holdings on which free tenants (*coloni*) or unfree men (*servi casati*) were obliged to render products to the main farm or perform corvée labour on the demesne.[1] (see also chapter 'Slavery and Unfreedom') Even though binate manors dominated important areas in the eastern Alps, other forms also existed, ranging from large farms deploying only an internal workforce to independent holdings paying rent, as well as a substantial category of freeholders on allodial land.[2]

From the twelfth until the thirteenth century, the manorial systems of continental Europe underwent a radical transformation. From relying on a combination of demesne farming and dependent smaller units, manorial lords increasingly divided their land into independent holdings cultivated by tenants

1 On *Villikationen*, see Werner Rösener, 'Villikationen', in Robert-Henri Bautier, et al. (ed.), *Lexikon des Mittelalters*, 9 vols (Munich and Zurich: Artemis [vols 1–6] and LexMA-Verlag [vols 7–9], 1977–1999), viii, 1694–95.

2 Werner Rösener, *Grundherrschaft im Wandel: Untersuchungen zur Entwicklung geistlicher Grundherrschaften im südwestdeutschen Raum vom 9. bis 14. Jahrhundert*, Veröffentlichungen des Max-Planck-Instituts für Geschichte, 102 (Göttingen: Vandenhoeck und Ruprecht, 1991), 559–60; Philippe Dollinger, *Der bayerische Bauernstand vom 9. Bis zum 13. Jahrhundert* (Munich: C.H. Beck, 1982), 137.

 | DOI:10.1163/9789004433458_004

with fewer strict personal bonds to their lord. This transformation came in many forms. In some cases, most of the demesne was divided into smaller holdings; in other cases, the landlord kept some of it as a collection point for goods and rents. In yet other cases, the demesne continued to be farmed under the direction of the lord or a reliable administrator.

The general trend, however, was a development in the direction of what, following the German terminology, has been called a *Rentengrundherrschaft*, where labour services were replaced by rents. This transformation of the classical manorial system gave peasants greater control over resources and extended personal freedom, even though in many regions personal bonds lingered on for centuries to come.[3] The dissolution of the binate manorial system took place at different times in different regions of continental Europe. Philippe Dollinger thus claims that the binate manorial system (*Villikation*) lasted well into the twelfth century in Bavaria, which, at the time, comprised most of the eastern Alpine area.[4]

Only after the dissolution of the old manorial systems, with its widespread use of unfree labour, is it possible to discern a separate group of people definable as 'peasants' (*Bauern*), inhabiting identifiable holdings and working the land for their family's own sustenance. These peasants could be freeholders without any landlord claiming rent, or, as was most frequently the case, tenants, who paid rents to a landlord. Irrespective of the conditions by which they held their land, they could be either free men or be bound to a lord by personal bonds (see also chapter 'Slavery and Unfreedom').

Until some decades ago, there used to be a gap between the continental portrayals of the classical binate manorial system and the Scandinavian perception of a kin-based society of free and equal peasants, rooted in nineteenth-century Germanistic tradition. Today, this perception has been abandoned in

3 Heinz Dopsch, 'Zwischen Herrschaft und Genossenschaft – Grundstrukturen bäuerlichen Lebens im Ostalmpenraum', in Tore Iversen, John Ragnar Myking, and Gertrud Thoma (eds), *Bauern zwischen Herrschaft und Genossenschaft: Peasant relations to Lords and Government. Scandinavia and the Alpine Region 1000–1750* (Trondheim: Tapir Akademinsk Forlag, 2007), 65–72; Werner Rösener, *Peasants in the Middle Ages* (Cambridge: Polity Press, 1992), 27–28; Rösener, *Grundherrschaft im Wandel*; Werner Rösener, 'Das Verfügungsrecht der Bauern über Land im südwestlichen Deutschland', in Tore Iversen and John Ragnar Myking (eds), *Land, Lords and Peasants: Peasants' Right to Control Land in the Middle Ages and the Early Modern Period – Norway, Scandinavia and the Alpine Region*, Trondheim Studies in History, 52 (Trondheim: NTNU, 2005), 47–62; Adrian Verhulst, 'Aspekte der Grundherrschaftsentwicklung des Hochmittelalters aus westeuropäischer Perspektiv', in Werner Rösener (ed.), *Grundherrschaft und bäuerliche Gesellsahft im Hochmittelalter* (Göttingen: Vandenhoeck und Ruprecht, 1995), 16–30.

4 Dollinger, *Das bayerische Bauernstand*, 138–39.

favour of a view that magnates at the end of the Viking Age and the beginning of the Middle Ages controlled a number of unfree persons (*thralls* and descendants of *thralls*), as well as a population of dependent free peasants, from their bases on *multiple estates*. Relations between magnates and peasants may be characterized as tributary relations between patron and clients. The existence of a considerable number of allodial peasants, documented in all Nordic countries, can thus easily be incorporated into such a system (for a fuller discussion of Scandinavian *multiple estates*, see 'Introduction', section 'A Sketch of the Historical Background').

From the end of the twelfth century, royal legislation began regulating land-rent in Norway. An investigation into the land-rent clauses in the oldest regional Norwegian law, the *Gulathing Law*, from the twelfth century, reveals that a developed land-rent system had not yet been implemented.[5] This law does not appear to operate with any clear separation of terminology between having the right *to rule* and having the right *to own*. In contrast, the law codes of the thirteenth century have precise terms for landed property and land leasing. The church was probably the initiator of this important change, followed by the king, during the thirteenth century.[6] Land leasing contracts were legally protected in the thirteenth-century king's laws. Land-rent was paid in kind and, before 1300, a fixed land-rent value was in the process of being established on every farm in the kingdom. The king took the initiative in this development because all tenants and freeholders were to pay their royal taxes according to the value of the land-rent.[7]

In Norway in this period, a share-of-rent-ownership system (*skyldpartsystem*) was also developing (see also 'Introduction'). This system was based on the value of each holding. The value of the holding could therefore be divided into ideal parts without physically dividing the holding itself. Thus, the running of the holding was little influenced by the ownership of the land. In the

5 The *Gulathing Law* has two editions: the Olav text, which is the oldest, refers to an edition of law in a codex that was probably written down at the end of the eleventh century for King Olav Kyrre (1067–97). The new redaction of the law was recorded during the rule of King Magnus Erlingsson (1161–84). (See Tore Iversen, 'Property and Land Tenancy in Norwegian Medieval Laws and the European Learned Law', in Per Andersen, Ditlev Tamm, and Helle Vogt (eds), *How Nordic Are the Nordic Medieval Laws? Proceedings from the First Carlsberg Conference on Medieval Legal History*, 2nd edn (Copenhagen: University of Copenhagen, 2011), 135–76, esp. pp. 136–39).

6 Iversen, 'Property and Land Tenancy', 171–72.

7 King Magnus the Lawmender's *Law of the Realm 1274*, in Rudolf Keyser, P.A. Munch, Gustav Storm and Ebbe Hertzberg (eds), *Norges gamle Love indtil 1387*, 5 vols (Christiania: Chr. Grøndahl, 1846–95), vol. 2, pp. 7–178: iii, 6 and vii, 7.3; Iversen, 'Property and Land Tenancy', 168–70.

share-of-rent-ownership system, a tenant could rent his holding from several landlords. He could also own an ideal part himself.[8]

In parts of Sweden, the transition from multiple estates and territorial dominion to a largely rental-based tenant system lasted longer than in Norway and involved a transitional phase with extensive demesne farming. In the period from around 1100 to 1300, magnate farms worked by *thralls* and day labourers were replaced by demesne farming and corvée labour from tenants who also paid land-rent. Only in the late Middle Ages were manors fully dissolved and replaced by a purely rental-based tenant system.[9]

In Denmark, demesne farming seems to have predominated over tenancy as late as the twelfth century. In contrast to Sweden, demesnes seem to have been run through wage labour, not through corvée labour from surrounding tenants. From the end of the twelfth century, the Danish elite farmed most of their manors, thus increasingly relying on rental incomes instead of having their property managed by bailiffs.[10] In order to raise the land-rent or collect taxes themselves, landlords in the thirteenth century formally turned a number of their taxpaying *landboer* (*coloni*) into *bryder* (*villici*), a term originally used for bailiffs. The *bryder* were supposed to be in the service of the landlord and were thus exempted from taxes. This meant that landlords could burden them with additional fees.[11]

By the thirteenth and fourteenth century, then, the vast majority of peasants in the eastern Alpine region and in Scandinavia held their land by leasehold. The terms of their leaseholds differed greatly over time, as well as between countries and regions. In addition, Denmark and parts of Sweden experienced a reintroduction of demesne faring in the early modern period. A number of

8 Andreas Holmsen, 'Det norske "skyldeie"', in Jørn Sandnes, Arnfinn Kjelland, and Claus Krag (eds), *Norske historikere i utvalg*, v: *Nye middelalderstudier* (Oslo: Universitetsforlaget, 1981), 178–181, at p. 178; Tore Iversen, 'Property and Land Tenancy', 163–76.

9 Johan Berg, *Gods och Landskap: Jordägand, begyggelse och samhälle i Östergötland 1000–1562* (Stockholm: Kulturgeografiska institutionen, Stockholms universitet, 2003), 231–51.

10 Niels Hybel, 'The Rise and Fall of Leasehold in Denmark c. 1100–1550', in Bas J.P. van Bavel and Phillipp R. Schofield (eds), *The Development of Leasehold in Northwestern Europe c. 1200–1600*, Comparative Rural History of the North Sea Area, 10 (Turnhout: Brepols, 2008), 99–111, at pp. 100–02.

11 Erik Ulsig, 'Landboer og bryder, skat og landgilde', in Karsten Fledelius, Niels Lund, and Herluf Nielsen (eds), *Middelalder, Metode og medier: Festskrift til Niels Skyum-Nielsen* (Copenhagen: Museum Tusculanum, 1981), 149–50, 154–56.
For a more detailed discussion of the transition to a rental-based tenant system in Scandinavia, see Tore Iversen and John Ragnar Myking, 'Changes in the Nordic Elites' Way of Extracting a Surplus from Landed Resources', in Bjørn Poulsen, Jon Vidar Sigurdsson, and Helle Vogt (eds), *Nordic Elites in Transformation 1050–1250*, i, *Material Resources*, (New York: Routledge, 2019), 32–59.

peasant farms were turned into demesnes and tenants were burdened with corvée labour, ranging from around 100 working days on manors in southern Sweden (Skåne) to 200–300 days on manors in eastern Denmark. Nevertheless, the overwhelming majority of Norwegian tenants, and most Swedish ones, still only paid land-rent and were not obliged to render any labour service.[12]

As for leases, many Scandinavian tenants, especially in the first centuries after their introduction, had to be content with short-term leases with a low degree of security for themselves and their descendants.[13] However, in time, an increasing number came to enjoy formal or de facto hereditary tenures, and some even gained full ownership of the land they worked. As for resources, some controlled every available resource on their holding, others had to be content with using resources needed for the viability of their household.

The development of such a variety of conditions has to be seen in connection with differences and similarities within the two regions, as well as within each region, bearing in mind the diversity of topography and power relations. As for topography, we will be comparing the mountainous Alpine region, well suited for animal husbandry, with similar regions in Norway, while the grain-growing plains of Upper Bavaria and parts of Tyrol lend themselves to a comparison with the lowland regions of Denmark and parts of Sweden. As for power relations, we will have to take into account that landlords in the Alpine region and Bavaria exercised power over their peasants in a far more intricate way than their Scandinavian counterparts. Besides their authority as mere landlords, either with some sort of demesne system (*Grundherrschaft*) or relying merely on rent income from their tenants (*Rentengrundherrschaft*), many of them also exercise judicial authority (*Gerichtsherrschaft*) and even some sort of personal control over their peasants (*Leibherrschaft*).[14] Such a grouping of dominion over their tenants was not enjoyed by most Scandinavian landlords, the notable exceptions being the judicial authority of some Danish landlords from the late Middle Ages until the end of the early modern period and the adscription of their tenants on some major Danish island in the same period (See chapter 'Peasant Participation'). Very important for power relations

12 Carsten Porskrog Rasmussen, 'Manors and States: The Distribution and Structure of Private Manors in Early Modern Scandinavia and Their Relation to State Policies', *Scandinavian Economic History Review*, 66/2 (2018), 201–18, at pp. 210–15.

13 Iversen, 'Property and Land Tenancy', 128–68, esp. pp. 146–49.

14 See, for example, Heinz Dopsch, 'Zur entwicklung des bäuerlichen Bestizrechts im Ost-Alpenraum' in Tore Iversen and John Ragnar Myking (eds), *Land, Lords and Peasants: Peasants' Right to Control Land in the Middle Ages and the Early Modern Period – Norway, Scandinavia and the Alpine Region*, Trondheim Studies in History, 52 (Trondheim: NTNU, 2005), 63–80.

between landlords and tenants was the strength of the respective territorial lords, who, in some cases, as in Norway and Tyrol, established robust ties to their subject peasants at the expense of the lay and ecclesiastical nobility.

1 Tenures

For the majority of peasants in Scandinavia and the Alpine region who were tenants, secure tenures were important. With the introduction of the learned law at the end of the twelfth century, the concept of a divided property developed in which the landlord kept the *dominium directum* (*Obereigentum*), while the tenant possessed the *dominium utile* (*Nutzeigentum*). This concept was incorporated into the common European judicial tradition, the *Ius Commune*.[15]

From the Middle Ages and throughout the early modern period, tenures tended to be granted for longer periods, thus becoming more secure. This was true for the Alpine region and for Scandinavia. The most frequent forms of tenure in the Alpine area were tenancy at will (*Freistift*), lifelong tenure (*Leibrecht*), and hereditary tenure (*Erbrecht*). *Freistift* lasted formally for only one year, but it was renewable. Lifelong tenures (*Leibrecht*) and hereditary tenures (*Erbrecht*) allowed their holder the opportunity to sell or pledge their holdings with the consent of their landlord, an opportunity not open to the *Freistift* tenant, who, according to the contemporary concept of property, possessed no *dominium utile*.[16]

From a variety of tenures in the Middle Ages, some of them rather short but renewable, others granted for one or even several lives, lifelong tenures were

15 Helmut Coing, *Europäisches Privatrecht*, i: *Älteres Gemeines Recht (1500 bis 1800)* (Munich: C.H. Beck, 1985), 4, 33–36, 293; Hans-Rudolf Hagemann, 'Eigentum' in Adalbert Erler, et al. (eds), *Handwörterbuch zur Deutschen Rechtsgeschichte*, 5 vols (Berlin: Schmidt, 1964–1991), vol. 1.

16 Wilfred Beimrohr, 'Bäuerliche Besitzrechte und die ländliche Gemeinde in Tirol', in Tore Iversen, John Ragnar Myking, and Gertrud Thoma (eds), *Bauern zwischen Herrschaft und Genossenschaft: Peasant Relations to Lords and Government. Scandinavia and the Alpine Region 1000–1750* (Trondheim: Tapir Akademisk Forlag, 2007), 85–108, at pp. 91–95; Dopsch, 'Zur entwicklung des bäuerlichen Bestizrechts', 69–73; Helmut Rankl, *Landvolk und Frühmoderner Staat in Bayern 1400–1800*, Studien zur Bayerischen Verfassungs- und Sozialgeschichte, 17, i-ii (Munich: Kommision für Bayerische Landesgeschichte, 1999), 308–41; Gertrud Thoma, 'Klosterbauern in Bayern und Tirol im Spätmittelalter', in Tore Iversen and John Ragnar Myking (eds), *Land, Lords and Peasants: Peasants' Right to Control Land in the Middle Ages and the Early Modern Period – Norway, Scandinavia and the Alpine Region*, Trondheim Studies in History, 52 (Trondheim: NTNU, 2005) 25–39, at pp. 110–13.

formally introduced in Scandinavia at the beginning of the late medieval period and the beginning of the early modern period. This introduction, at least in Norway and on some categories of landed property in Sweden, also implied that tenants acquired a *dominium utile* to their land. They could then sell or hand over the right to the tenure. As in the Alpine area, the tenant needed the approval of his landlord.

What then were the exact conditions for tenants according to these different forms of tenures and why did tenures develop in different directions within as well as between our regions of investigation?

1.1 *The Alpine Region and Bavaria*

Freistift was the original form of tenure throughout the Alpine region. Originally, it did not comprise a proprietary right. Although such tenures were often renewed, a holding granted on the basis of pure *Freistift* could be withdrawn at the yearly manorial court meeting, the so called *Bauding* or *Stifttaiding*, and be granted to someone else. *Freistift* was not regulated by law, and the tenant did not have a contract.[17] Consequently, peasants did not have an incentive to invest in their holding. Therefore, over the course of the late Middle Ages, in Salzburg and Bavaria, this form of tenure tended to develop into *Veranleitete Freistift*. Every new tenant then had to pay an entrance fee, an *Anleit*, for the lord's renouncement of yearly renewal, which the lord would have to pay back if he withdrew the holding. In this way, such tenants also secured a *dominium utile* in the property.[18]

Territorial lords, who relied more on taxes and military service than on land-rents, were the most willing to grant better tenures. In central areas of Tyrol, hereditary tenures were spreading from the twelfth and thirteenth century, especially in the wine-producing regions on the south side of the Alps, where landlords wanted tenants to have a long-term interest in the land.[19] In their struggle to secure their control over territory and jurisdiction against lay and ecclesiastical lords, the territorial lords of Tyrol played a decisive role in securing hereditary tenures. In 1404, with the consent of the Tyrolean diet, the count of Tyrol issued a statute (*Landesordnung*) which secured the position of the peasants against their landlords and established in law the *Erbbau* peasants'

17 Beimrohr, 'Bäuerliche Besitzrechte', 92–94; Dopsch, 'Zur entwicklung des bäuerlichen Bestizrechts', 69–70; Rankl, *Landvolk*, 327.

18 Rankl, *Landvolk*, 329–30.

19 Beimrohr, 'Bäuerliche Besitzrechte', 91; Josef Riedmann, *Geschichte Tirols* (Vienna: Verlag für Geschichte und Politikk, 1988), 47.

hereditary rights, including their right to alienate their holding.[20] This helped the further spreading of hereditary tenures. By the end of the late Middle Ages, *Freistift* was only found in those parts of Tyrol that were included after 1500, like the Lower Inn Valley, formerly belonging to Bavaria, and contemporary Osttiroll, which had been a part of Kärnten.[21] However, this type of tenure on land belonging to the few landlords still practicing *Freistift* was gradually changing into a sort of lifelong tenure which even secured the tenure for the tenants' descendants.[22]

Therefore, from the twelfth and thirteenth century, an increasing number of Tyrolean peasants enjoyed the hereditary tenure of *Erbbaurecht*, which, at the beginning of the early modern period became the dominant form of tenure in Tyrol. This Tyrolean form of hereditary tenure was set down in legal form in consecutive *Landesordnungen* from the beginning of the fifteenth to the beginning of the sixteenth century. Even though the hereditary rights and the right to sell or pledge land were legalized, the landlord had to give his consent or buy the holding himself. If the property was transferred outside of a closely defined part of the family, the landlord was entitled to an entrance fine and a departure fine.[23] Nevertheless, as several Tyrolean historians have pointed out, *Erbbaurecht* tenants came close to a de facto ownership.[24] Tenures were secure, but could be retracted if the tenant owed rents or other debts.[25] The rent from the holding was fixed and usually paid in cash, which tended to give peasants an advantage, as the value of money deteriorated in the early modern period. To avoid this, rents were often registered in crops and goods that kept their value but were paid in cash. Rents were usually lower on land held by *Erbbaurecht* than by *Freistift*.[26]

The dominant force behind the shift to this form of secure hereditary tenure in Tyrol was clearly the Tyrolean territorial lords (*Landesfürsten*). Their goal was to increase their power at the expense of the lay and ecclesiastical

20 Beimrohr, 'Bäuerliche Besitzrechte', 92; Köfler, Werner: *Land, Landschsft, Landtag: Geschichte der Tiroler Landtage von den Anfängen bis 1808*. Veröffentlichungen des Tiroler Landesarchivs, 3 (Innsbruck: Universitätsverlag Wagner, 1985), 46, 83; Riedmann, *Geschichte Tirols*, 67.

21 Beimrohr, 'Bäuerliche Besitzrechte', 95; Riedmann, *Geschichte Tirols*, 131.

22 Beimrohr, 'Bäuerliche Besitzrechte', 94, Riedmann, *Geschichte Tirols*, 131.

23 Beimrohr, 'Bäuerliche Besitzrechte', 92.

24 Riedmann, *Geschichte Tirols*, 131, Beimrohr, 'Bäuerliche Besitzrechte', 92, with reference to Hermann Wopfner, *Bergbauernbuch: von arbeit und leben des Tiroler Bergbauern in Vergangenheit und Gegenwart*, ed. Nikolaus Grass, Tiroler Wirtschaftsstudien, 47–49, 3 vols (Innsbruck, 1995–97), i, 469f.

25 Beimrohr, 'Bäuerliche Besitzrechte', 93.

26 Beimrohr, 'Bäuerliche Besitzrechte', 93, Riedmann, *Geschichte Tirols*, 131.

aristocracy. They did this by reducing tenants' judicial (see chapter 'Peasant Participation') and tenurial dependence on their lords. Dependent tenants were thus converted into loyal tax-paying subjects who could be relied on to perform military service. As loyal subjects, they were then given representation by their local *Gerichtsgemeinden* in the Tyrolean diet, there serving as a possible counterweight to aristocratic or ecclesiastical interests. The reason the Tyrolean territorial lords succeeded in achieving their goal where others, like the Bavarian territorial lords, failed may be due in part to the weakness of the Tyrolean aristocracy. The bulk of the Tyrolean aristocracy did not possess much landed property and their property was often scattered over large areas. Therefore, many of them relied on receiving fiefs or offices from their territorial lord. Furthermore, urban and ecclesiastical institutions, as well as merchants and even peasants who owned landed property, were more interested in a secure rental income than in establishing a common opposition to their territorial lord.[27]

The influence from a territorial lord cannot, however, explain the similar development of strong hereditary tenures in the inner Alpine regions of Switzerland (Graubünden and Wallis). This development must rather be seen in connection with the growth of communal movements and a lack of powerful lordships. In this region, many peasants, from the fifteenth and sixteenth centuries, were even allowed to buy out *Herrschaftsrechte* belonging to local lay and ecclesiastical lords. Such buyouts could include tithe and jurisdiction and were often funded by a peasant collective. This favourable development for the inner Alpine Swiss peasants has been explained by the varying impact of landlord control, which was strong in territories dominated by Swiss cities but much weaker in rural areas where peasant communal movements were strong.[28]

What then were the reasons for a majority of Bavarian peasants not gaining hereditary tenures? After all, such tenures were widespread in the neighbouring territories of Salzburg and Tyrol, in Tyrol even becoming totally dominant.[29] On the other hand, in Bavaria, it has been estimated that less than 20 percent of the holdings were granted with *Erbrecht*, less than 10 percent with *Leibrecht* and over 60 percent with *Freistift* (the rest, up to 10 percent, being

27 Beimrohr, 'Bäuerliche Besitzrechte', 95–97, Riedmann, *Geschichte Tirols*, 67–72.

28 Jon Mathieu, *Eine Agrargeschichte der inneren Alpen. Graubünden, Tessin, Wallis 1500–1800* (Zurich: Chronos Verlag, 1992), 82–87.

29 Beimrohr, 'Bäuerliche Besitzrechte', 94–95. Heinz Dopsch and Hans Spatzenegger, *Geschichte Salzburg: Stadt und Land*, 2 vols (Salzburg: Universitätsverlag A. Pustet, 1981), i, 416; Riedmann, *Geschichte Tirols*, 83.

Freieigen and *Bauernlehen*, which came close to freehold status) at the beginning of the early modern period.[30]

Two main explanations may help shed light on this problem. Firstly, power relations between the Bavarian dukes and the aristocracy were not as much to the advantage of the territorial lord as they were in Tyrol. It took centuries for the Wittelsbacher line in Bavaria to enjoy anything like the territorial control established by the Habsburg line in Tyrol during the Middle Ages. In Bavaria, secular and ecclesiastical lords and institutions managed to exercise dominion (*Herrschaft*), including jurisdiction in minor cases (*Niedere Gerichtbarkeit*) and often also unfree personal bonds (*Leibeigenschaft*), over their tenants on their manorial territories (*Hofmarken*) well into the early modern period (see chapter 'Peasant Participation') far beyond anything their Tyrolean counterparts could dream of.[31] Secondly, *Freistift* did not endow the tenant with a *dominium utile* in the property. Thus, according to Bavarian law and customs, only the movable objects were subject to territorial taxation, not the property itself.

Seen from the point of view of the landlord, *Freistift* thus minimized competition from taxation as a means to confiscate surplus from their tenants. Against this, they had to consider that the selling of hereditary rights brought greater sums of cash, which some lords needed to cope with financial shortcomings, and that, in the case of transformation into *Veranleitete Freistift* and *Leibrecht*, they could reckon with the *Anleit* that was due with every change of occupier. Nevertheless, ecclesiastical lords in particular persisted in granting their tenants pure *Freistift*, although it was often de facto renewed every year and handled like hereditary tenures.[32]

Freistift tenants seeking better tenures had on their part to consider the cost of gaining such tenures. In the case of hereditary tenures, this included the cost of buying hereditary rights and, which was also the case when obtaining *Leibrecht* or *Veranleiteted Freistift*, to pay taxes for their *dominium utile* in the property, expenses pure *Freistift* tenants did not have. In the cases of *Leibrecht* and *Vernanleiteted Freistift*, a new tenant also had to pay an *Anleit*. The fear of increased taxes was therefore a common denominator that motivated tenants as well as landlords to avoid transforming *Freistift* into *Erbrecht*.[33] Even the territorial lord could, in some cases, benefit from keeping land in *Freistift* tenure, as this made transactions of land from ecclesiastical institutions to nobles more difficult. During the sixteenth century, in their capacity as ecclesiastical

30 Rankl, *Landvolk*, 326.
31 Rankl, *Landvolk*, 339.
32 Rankl, *Landvolk*, 329–41.
33 Rankl, *Landvolk*, 333–34.

supervisors (*Kirchenhoheit*), they therefore imposed a status quo on tenures granted by ecclesiastical lordships, thus obstructing any further transition to hereditary tenures in order to avoid farms being obtained by nobles.[34]

What then was the content of Bavarian tenures, and how did they develop? In Lower Bavaria, hereditary tenures were granted on the holdings belonging to the territorial lord in the fifteenth century. In Upper Bavaria, hereditary tenures were not widespread at all, due to the strong position of ecclesiastical and lay lords.[35] *Erbrecht* and *Leibrecht* in Bavaria were secured by contracts and gave their holders the opportunity to sell or pledge their holdings with consent of their lords. *Leibrecht* often worked like *Erbrecht*, as the holding could be sold or passed on to an heir during a tenant's lifetime with the consent of the lord. When the holding was given to a new holder, an entrance fee had to be paid. These *Laudemien* (fees) were often the reason for peasant protests and appeals to the territorial lord against their *Hofmarksherren*, alongside undue demands for work and assistance (*Scharwerk*).[36] Frequent increase of these fees worsened the better tenure rights in Bavaria.

Tenures were on the whole fairly secure, even though they were granted on the basis of *Freistift*; a widow was allowed to stay on the holding after her husband's death and was usually granted the tenure, perhaps after having paid a mortuary fee (*Todfall*) in the case of the deceased being a bondsman (*Leibeigen*). Tenures could be withdrawn, if the tenant neglected the holding, if he did not pay his dues for three years, if he sold or pledged it or part of it without the consent of the lord, or if he took more timber out of the woods than necessary for running his holding (*Hausnotdurft*). In the sixteenth century, Bavarian territorial law strengthened the lord's position in these cases, and the widespread use of *Freistift* and *Leibrecht* allowed lords to increase demands for fees and labour service, both of which reached a comparatively high level in Bavaria.[37]

Whatever hope Bavarian peasants might have entertained for better rights than *Freistift* was finally extinguished in the territorial law of 1616, which, however, also restricted lordly demands for extensive *Scharwerk*.[38] Territorial lordship had gained control in the whole of Bavaria from around 1600, but the nobility was still very strong and was able to prevent an improved situation for

34 Rankl, *Landvolk*, 325.

35 Rankl, *Landvolk*, 308–12.

36 Renate Blickle, 'Agrarische Konflikte und Eigentumsordnung in Altbayern 1400–1800', in Winfred Schulze (ed.), *Aufstände, Revolten, Prozesse: Beiträge zu bäuerlichen Widerstandsbewegungen im frühneuzeitlichen Europa*, Geschichte und Gesellschaft: Buchumer Historische Studien, 27 (Stuttgart: Clett-Cotta, 1983), 166–87, at pp. 169–74.

37 Rankl, *Landvolk*, 315, 321, 339.

38 Rankl, *Landvolk*, 632–33.

peasants and those of the lower rural strata (*unterbäuerlicher Schichten*).[39] State (taxes) and landlords (rents) competed for yields of the peasants' work, the latter probably being the more repressive.[40] On the whole, the position of peasants who held the better tenure rights that had spread during the late Middle Ages was diminished, while the position of the those who originally held poorer rights improved, thus to a certain extent equaling the rights belonging to different tenures.[41]

1.2 *Scandinavia*

As we have seen, the dissolution of multiple estates advanced the development of a tenant system in Scandinavia. The chronology and content of this process varied between the Scandinavian countries, but by the twelfth to thirteenth century, tenants were established as a large social group in all three countries.[42]

In high medieval Denmark and some regions of Sweden, there was a clear distinction between *villici* (*bryder*) and *coloni*. The *colonus* (*landbo*) rented his land from the landowner on short-term leases, while the *villicus* entered the service of the landowner. The *villicus* was a supervisor of thralls before the end of the twelfth century. Later, he was often a sharecropper, working land the landlord could not manage himself. In Denmark, his attachment to the landlord was underlined by the fact that he, in contrast to the *colonus*, was free from *expedition* (war service and tax) and that the fine of three marks to the king would go to the king's men whom he served.[43] In order to obtain the same privileges for their peasants, many landlords turned their holdings formerly rented to *landboer* (*coloni*) into *brydegårder* (farms run by *villici*), or simply named them *brydegårde* instead of *landbogårde*. Thus, landlords were able to increase their income, either by collecting and keeping some of these taxes themselves or by raising the land-rent, as their peasants now did not have to

39 Rankl, *Landvolk*, 629, 809.

40 Rankl, *Landvolk*, 1071–72.

41 Rankl, *Landvolk*, 325–26, 1080–81.

42 Iversen and Myking, 'Changes in the Nordic Elites' Way'. See also Introduction in this volume.

43 Erik Ulsig, 'Peasants' Right to Control Land in Denmark', in Tore Iversen and John Ragnar Myking (eds), *Land, Lords and Peasants: Peasants' Right to Control Land in the Middle Ages and the Early Modern Period – Norway, Scandinavia and the Alpine Region*, Trondheim Studies in History, 52 (Trondheim: NTNU, 2005), 29–37, at p. 31. John Ragnar Myking and Carsten Porskrog Rasmussen, 'Scandinavia, 1000–1750', in Bas J.P. van Bavel and Richard W. Hoyle (eds), *Social Relations. Property and Power*, Rural Economy and Society in North-western Europe, 500–2000, 1 (Turnhout: Brepols 2010), 287–314, at pp. 293–94.

put aside some of their surplus production to pay their taxes.[44] During the course of the fourteenth and fifteenth centuries, the categories of *bryde* and *landbo* amalgamated into a uniform class of tenants.[45] By then, what may have existed of larger estates with dependent peasants had long ago given way to impersonal landlord-tenant relations all over Scandinavia. A majority of Scandinavian peasants were now tenants, but unlike many of their Alpine and Bavarian counterparts, they were free men without any forms of bondage. The exception was some Danish tenants who, from the end of the fifteenth century, were legally restricted from leaving the estates on which they were born (see below).

In the wake of the dissolution of *multiple estates*, tenures started to be recorded in Scandinavian regional and national laws. The one-year lease mentioned in the oldest Norwegian regional law, the *Gulathing Law* from the 1160s, indicates that a form of *Freistift* may have existed in parts of Norway before *c.* 1200. A fully developed tenant system was, however, not completed by this time, as indicated by the lack of a formal term for 'tenant' in this regional law.[46] Tenures recorded in the many Scandinavian regional and national laws in the thirteenth and the fourteenth centuries, at a time when a fully developed tenant system was in place, were also formally of rather short duration. These short and rather insecure forms of tenure were, as was the case in the Alpine region, replaced by somewhat longer tenures during the following centuries. The *Frostathing Law* of the first half of the thirteenth century and the *Norwegian Law of the Realm* from 1274 stated a minimum tenure of three years, while regional Swedish laws from the end of the High Middle Ages prescribed from six to eight years.[47]

However, this legal framework referred only to minimum contract terms; it did not restrict the landlord from signing longer contracts.[48] No contracts are extant for Denmark and Sweden, but Norwegian contracts from before the middle of the fourteenth century indicate that actual tenures could be extended far beyond the minimum term. Twenty-three contracts issued between 1289

44 Ulsig, 'Landboer og bryder', 150, 154–56.

45 Ulsig, 'Peasants' Right', 31. Myking and Rasmussen, 'Scandinavia', 293–94.

46 Iversen, 'Property and Land Tenancy', 144–46.

47 Lars-Arne Norborg, 'Landbo', in John Granlund (ed.), *Kulturhistoriskt lexikon för nordisk medeltid – från vikingatid till reformationstid* [hereafter KLNM], 22 vols (Malmö: Allhem, 1956–78), x, 202. Thomas Lindkvist, *Landborna i Norden under äldre medeltid*, Studia Historica Upsaliensia, 110 (Uppsala: 1979), 87–93.

48 Iversen, 'Property and Land Tenancy', 149.

and 1348 cover a wide variety of lengths.[49] Only one of them, from 1348, prescribes a term of one year.[50] Five contracts were issued for the length of three years each,[51] while an additional four contracts were issued for specified periods of time, spanning six to twelve years.[52] Among the remaining fourteen contracts, four were issued for the life of the tenant,[53] another three gave the tenant the right to an eternal tenure,[54] while seven specifically offer his descendants the right to take over the tenure.[55] These contracts thus reveal a variety of tenures from quite short ones resembling forms of *Freistift* to a majority stating lifelong and even hereditary tenures.

In clear contrast to the policy followed by ecclesiastical institutions in Bavaria, Scandinavian ecclesiastical institutions in particular seem to have been willing to offer lifelong or hereditary tenures. The different strategies can probably be ascribed to differences in taxation. Formal *Freistift* minimized competition from territorial taxation in Bavaria, whereas tax exemption did not play a role in Norway (see above). Ensuring tenants took care of their landed property and securing long-term income was probably more important for Norwegian ecclesiastical institutions. Although the Norwegian contracts cannot be used to substantiate the length of tenures in Sweden and Denmark, they at least indicate that the legal framework only prescribed minimum tenures.

Tenures were obviously determined after negotiations between tenants and landlords and were influenced by the number of available holdings. The population crises from the middle of the fourteenth century struck Scandinavia

49 Harald Unneland Dyngen, 'Leilendingenes vilkår i Norge – økonomisk og rettslig fram til ca. 1350', Master's thesis, University of Bergen, Bergen, 1986.

50 *Diplomatarium Norvegicum: Oldbreve til Kundskab om Norges indre og ydre Forhold, Sprog, Slægter, sæder, Lovgivning og Rettergang i Middelalderen* [hereafter DN], Chr. C.A. Lange, C.R. Unger, et al. (eds), 23 vols (Christiania: P.T. Mallings Forlagshandel, 1847–2011), iv, no. 331 (1348). Dyngen, 'Leilendingenes vilkår', 65–66. Unneland Dyngen argues that the reason for this short length of time, especially when the owner was a clerical institution, who usually rented out their land for longer periods, may have been that the institution in this particular case was concerned about the reliability of the tenant and thus may have issued a trial contract.

51 DN iii, no. 156 (1330), DN x, no. 27 (1337), DN x, no. 27 (1337), DN iv, no. 270 (1343), DN iv, no. 297 (1346), cf. Dyngen, 'Leilendingenes vilkår', 64–65.

52 DN xii, no. 18 (1293), DN iv, no. 204 (1333), DN xii, no. 44 (1309), DN i, no. 152 (1317), cf. Dyngen, 'Leilendingenes vilkår', 66–67.

53 DN xviii, no. 12 (1331), DN xxi, no. 60 (1341), DN iii, no. 175 (1333), DN ii, no. 20 (1289).

54 DN iii, no. 211 (1342), DN v, no. 134 (1340), DN v, no. 156 (1341).

55 DN iii, no. 178 (1334), DN iii, no. 195 (1338), DN x, no. 34 (1339), DN xii, no. 16 (1293), DN xii, no. 91 (1340), DN ii, no. 124 (1316), DN i, no. 178 (1324).

quite heavily and resulted in many deserted farms and vacant holdings.[56] Under such circumstances, long-term or hereditary tenant contracts must have been even more advantageous to landlords than before. It is therefore not surprising that twenty of twenty-nine Norwegian contracts from the late Middle Ages were issued for minimum the life of the tenant, and half of them were also hereditary tenures.[57] We may also assume that there was a distinct possibility that such a lengthening of contracts also took place in Sweden and Denmark.

In contrast to the Alpine region, further development towards legalized hereditary tenures did not take place in Scandinavia. In Denmark and Norway, lifelong tenures were established as a legal norm by the middle of the sixteenth century.[58] In Sweden, however, the length of contracts depended on which category of landholders the land belonged to. Tenants on *frälsejord* (whose landlords were nobles) enjoyed short contract periods, while tenants on land belonging to the crown were given long-term leases.

However, lifelong tenures did not prevent the development of a de facto hereditary right for tenants' descendants in parts of Scandinavia. By the seventeenth century, Norwegian tenants had acquired the prerogative to appoint their successor when giving up their lifelong tenure, and they were even allowed to sell or transfer their right to the tenure. The landlord was entitled to approve their choice of successor but could not freely appoint a new tenant of his own choosing.[59] In Sweden, where tenures depended on the category of landed property, tenants on Swedish crown land were able to enjoy hereditary tenures from the end of the seventeenth century, while their counterparts on land belonging to the aristocracy still had to be content with less than lifelong tenures.[60] As in Norway, hereditary tenures on crown land implied the right to

56 Svend Gissel, et al. (eds), *Desertion and Land Colonization in the Nordic Countries c. 1300–1600* (Stockholm: Almquist and Wiksell, 1982).

57 John Ragnar Myking, *Herre over andre si jord? Norske leiglendingar i europeisk lys 1500–1800*, Studia Humanitatis Bergensia, 21 (Kristiansand: Høyskoleforlaget, 2005), 64–66.

58 Myking, '*Herre over andre si jord?*', 70; Friedlev Skrubbeltrang, *Det danske landbosamfund 1500–1800* (Odense: Den danske historiske forening, 1978), 20–21, 78.

59 Myking, '*Herre over andre si jord?*', 128–47.

60 Christer Lundh and Mats Olsson, 'Tenancy Contracts in Scania from the Middle Ages to the Nineteenth Century', in Bas J.P. van Bavel and Phillipp Schofield (eds), *The Development of Leasehold in Northwestern Europe, c. 1200–1600*, Comparative Rural History of the North Sea Area, 10 (Turnhout: Brepols, 2008), 113–37, at p. 126. Formal heritable tenures were only granted on land rented to crown tenants who paid rents within the military allotment system (*rusthall*), but the six-year tenancy periods were routinely renewed, even in the case of transmission between generations.

sell the lease or to transfer it to their children by means of a retirement contract.[61]

In Schleswig, too, tenures differed according to whom the land belonged to, but also depending on whether demesne farming or rent was the most important source of income for the landlords. As in Norway and Denmark, most tenants seem to have enjoyed lifelong tenures by the middle of the sixteenth century. During the following centuries, tenures in Schleswig developed in three different directions: hereditary tenures, life tenure, and tenures at will, with the most secure tenures being most frequent on crown land and land where rents were the most important income for the landlord.[62]

In Denmark, tendencies similar to those that shaped peasant rights in Norway can be found in areas where tenants owned the buildings, as in southwestern Jutland and on some minor islands, but in most parts of Denmark landlords controlled succession to holdings, thus preventing any de facto hereditary right to evolve. This can also be observed on manors belonging to the Swedish aristocracy, many of them in the region of Scania, which Denmark lost to Sweden in 1658, and can most likely be ascribed to the extensive control landlords exercised over their tenants in that area.

Restricting tenants' relocation had been one of the landlords' main strategies to counteract the effects of the crisis of the late Middle Ages. In 1377, the Danish Council of the Realm curbed attempts from landlords to restrict tenants' free movement, and even to interfere with the wedding of tenants' daughters.[63] However, from the end of fifteenth century, tenants on the island of Zealand and some surrounding islands were legally restricted from departing from the estates where they were born, thus eliminating any attempts to bargain better conditions by moving to the estates of another landlord.[64] Camouflaged as an opportunity to be protected (Dan: *værnet*) by their landlord, this *vornedskab* on the eastern islands became a major instrument for landlords to control their tenants. Although these restrictions were modified by the turn to the eighteenth century, new restrictions for adult males connected to military conscription were introduced in 1733.[65]

61 Lundh and Olsson, 'Tenancy Contracts', 119.

62 Carsten Porskrog Rasmussen, *Rentegods og hovedgårsdrift: Godsstruktur og godsøkonomi i hertugdømmet Slesvig 1524–1770*, 2 vols (Aabenraa: Institut for grænseregionsforskning, 2003), i, 530–35.

63 Ulsig, 'Peasants' Right', 34.

64 Frank Pedersen, *Vornedskabets gennemførelse*, (Odense: Landbohistorisk selskab, 1984).

65 'Stavnsbånd 1733–1800', in Danmarkshistoriendk. URL: http://danmarkshistorien.dk/leksikon-og-kilder/vis/materiale/stavnsbaand-1733–1800. Last accessed 30 January 2017.

In Denmark, the landlords' authority over their peasants was further strengthened by the fact that some of them obtained extensive judicial powers. By the early fourteenth century, Danish noble and ecclesiastical landlords acquired the right to collect almost all fines from their peasants, and from 1523, they definitively held the so-called 'right of neck and hand', that is, the right to prosecute their tenants for crimes committed and to execute punishment. This 'right of neck and hand' did not comprise the right to render verdicts,[66] but from the end of the late Middle Ages an increasing number of noble landlords gained the right to have their own manorial courts where they appointed the judge (see chapter 'Peasant Participation'). In the fifteenth century, the Swedish aristocracy also sought to restrict tenants' ability to relocate, but these attempts failed.[67] So did largely their efforts to obtain judicial power over their tenants.

The introduction of absolutism in 1660 curbed the influence of the Danish aristocracy at the national level, but it left them with considerable influence at the local level, including a set of new assignments. Danish landlords were now given the task of collecting taxes according to a national cadastre and of administering military conscription on their estates. In this way, Danish society was built on a feudal system of authority without, however, reducing the income for the state in a substantial way. This conglomerate of authority gave landlords considerable power over their tenants, although peasants could appeal to royal district governors.[68] New, non-noble, landlords were not given the 'right of neck and hand', but did gain access to the other forms of landlord authority.

In Denmark, arrears of taxes may have added to tenants' debts to their landlords and may therefore partly explain the very high number of forfeitures that can be observed on some estates in the seventeenth and eighteenth centuries.[69] A comparable squeeze may have been experienced by tenants on the *frälsejord*, land belonging to the aristocracy in Sweden, whose landlords could collect the taxes for their own support in addition to ordinary rents or corvée labour. On these estates, contracts were also issued for shorter periods than life, and there was a constant risk that tenant holdings could be added to the demesne of their landlord. Such risks also existed in parts of Schleswig.

66 Carsten Porskrog Rasmussen, et al. (eds), *Det danske godssystem – udvikling og afvikling 1500–1919* (Århus: Historia, 1987), 11. Ulsig, 'Peasants' Right', 35.

67 Janken Myrdal, *Jordbruket under feodalismen 1000–1700*, Det svenska jordbrukets historia, 2 (Borås: Natur og Kultur/LTs förlag, 2000), 153.

68 Birgit Løgstrup, 'Den bortforpagtede statsmagt: Godsejeren som offentlig administrator i det 18. århundrede', *Bol og by: Landbohistorisk Tidsskrift*, 1 (1985), 21–58.

69 Skrubbeltrang, *Det danske landbosamfund.*

Denmark, and partly also Sweden, saw a reintroduction of demesne farming from the beginning of the early modern period (see 'Introduction', section 'A Sketch of the Historical Background'). In Denmark, demesne land doubled from the end of the Middle Ages to the last decades of the seventeenth century, comprising 9 percent of the land by 1682, but further expansion was then largely obstructed.[70] Private manors centred around demesnes comprised most of the private estates of Denmark and the 'noble' estates of Sweden. Such estates covered up to two-thirds of all land in Denmark, but less than one-third in Sweden. They were the dominant form of landownership in most Danish regions, largely irrespective of natural conditions, but only in certain parts of Sweden, mainly located on the central plains. On these manors, rents were mixed, comprising taxes in money, rents in money and kind, and also a rather substantial labour rent.[71]

The majority of Scandinavian tenures, in the same way as in the Alpine region, seem to have been fairly secure, as long as tenants did not neglect their holding, paid their rents without serious delay, and did not take more timber than necessary for the running of the holding. In Norway and Denmark, a tenant's widow was allowed to stay on the holding without paying a new entrance fee, as long as she did not remarry.[72] A widow of a Norwegian tenant also had the same right that her former husband had to transfer or sell her tenure. A new husband automatically gained the right to the leasehold, which made tenants' widows attractive marriage partners.[73]

1.3 *Trans-Regional Comparison*

Like their peasant counterparts in the Alpine region and Bavaria, Scandinavian tenants on the whole enjoyed improved tenures from the Middle Ages to the early modern period. The Scandinavian development, however, was not as clear-cut as in Tyrol and Switzerland, where an early and comprehensive transition from short-term (*Freistift*) to hereditary tenures (*Erbleihe*) took place. Scandinavian tenants were still better off than the majority of tenants

70 Gunnar Olsen, *Hovedgård og bondegård: Studier over stordriftens udvikling i Danmark i tiden 1525–1774*, Landbohistoriske skrifter, 1 (Copenhagen: Landbohistorisk Selskab, 1975), esp. 15–175; Erland Porsmose, 'Middelalder O. 1000–1536', in Claus Bjørn, et al. (eds), *Det danske landbrugs historie*, i: *Oldtid og middelalder* (Odense: Landbohistorisk Selskab, 1988).

71 Myking and Rasmussen, 'Scandinavia', 296.

72 Myking, *'Herre over andre si jord?'*, 72–73; Skrubbeltrang, *Det danske landbosamfund*, 78.

73 John Ragnar Myking, 'Attractive Marriage Partners? Tenant Widows and Remarriages in Western Norway in the Seventeenth and Eighteenth Century', *Scandinavian Journal of History*, 24 (2004), 225–39.

in Bavaria, where most tenures were still based on the concept of *Freistift* (although this could be granted successively for the life of a tenant).

How then can we explain the general development, on the one hand, towards longer and more secure tenures in both regions, and, on the other, the obvious differences?

We can isolate at least three main factors that may have influenced tenures:

1. The influence of the territorial lord
2. *Herrschaftsrechte* (dominion) belonging to manorial lords (jurisdictional power, personal bonds)
3. The balance between *Rentengrundherrschaft* and demesne farming.

We have already emphasized the importance of the territorial lord in Tyrol for the development of hereditary tenures. He had a clear interest in diminishing the lay and ecclesiastical lords' influence over their tenants, as manorial power in the Alpine region, like most of the surrounding areas in the medieval period, also included jurisdictional power and a form of bondage / unfreedom (*Leibherrschaft*).

Such a combination of *Herrschaftsrechte* was a potential threat to the territorial unity of Tyrol and therefore also to the power of the territorial lord. More secure tenures, abolition of manorial jurisdiction, and unfreedom (*Leibherrschaft*) were thus measures by which the Tyrolean territorial lords managed to secure their monopoly of power by the late Middle Ages. In this struggle to ensure peasants were reliable taxpaying subjects, promoting hereditary tenures was only one of several options followed by the Tyrolean count.

In Bavaria, the territorial lords may have had the same interest in curbing the influence of landlords, but not the same opportunity. They were in no position to diminish the lay and ecclesiastical lords' influence over their tenants, nor were they able to legally regulate the length and content of tenures. Tenures were thus left, for the most part, to the balance between landlords and their tenants. With the ultimate goal of avoiding territorial taxation, lay and ecclesiastical lords seem to have preferred a kind of *Freistift* (see above), while the territorial lords, depending mostly on taxes for their income, were more inclined to grant longer and more secure tenures, like *Erbrecht*.

Scandinavian kings were established as territorial lords when the transition to a contractual tenant system was completed in the thirteenth century. After the dissolution of the *multiple estate* system in Scandinavia (see 'Introduction', section 'A Sketch of the Historical Background'), manorial lords did not have access to a package of rights over their tenants comparable to their Alpine and Bavarian counterparts. Although some of the former patron-client relations between peasants and the local nobility may have lasted into the period when the contractual tenant system was established, the nobility did not exercise jurisdictional power. Nor were tenants bound to their landlords through any kind of unfreedom, except for freed slaves, who, according to a Norwegian regional law from the early thirteenth century, had to ask permission from their former masters when entering into contracts and agreements, except tenure contracts (see chapter 'Slavery and Unfreedom'). The lack of such *Herrschaftsrechte* meant that kings did not have to fear that bonds between landlords and their tenants should result in diminishing royal authority. Therefore, at the time, an urgent need to interfere with the form and content of tenures by passing legislation did not exist.

From relying on tributes in the first centuries of the High Middle Ages, Scandinavian kingdoms largely drew their incomes from fines, taxes, and landed property from the thirteenth century, the latter being enhanced as a consequence of the Protestant Reformation of the early sixteenth century. However, this was not enough to satisfy the increased demand for revenue due to the escalating rivalry between Denmark-Norway and Sweden. The next two centuries saw a continuous struggle for hegemony in Scandinavia and the Baltic area, resulting in both countries turning into military states with a growing demand for funds. In their efforts to subsidize their respective military machines, they chose different strategies, each one with long-term consequences for their subject peasants.

One of these strategies was to secure peasants as loyal taxpaying subjects by curbing excessive landlord demands. The legal introduction of lifelong tenures in Denmark and Norway from the sixteenth century, as well as restrictions on rents and revenues, may be seen from this long-term perspective. In Norway, with very few aristocratic landowners and the extensive lands of the former Catholic Church confiscated by the crown, this form of protection took its clearest form. The rise in annual rents was curbed from the 1520s by making any increase subject to approval by local commissions manned by fellow peasants, as well as setting a limit on the entrance fee in the 1680s.[74]

A similar strategy was not as easily enforced in Denmark, as the aristocracy was still considered the backbone of the state's military force. From the late Middle Ages, using their position in the royal council where a new king had to be approved, they had succeeded in acquiring *Herrschaftsrechte* over their tenants in a manner in which none of their class fellows had in other parts of Scandinavia, including jurisdiction and, on some of the Danish islands, a ban on relocation. The restrictions for peasants on some of the islands on leaving the estates they were born on (*vornedskab*), introduced by the end of the

74 Myking, '*Herre over andre si jord?*', 92, 100–04.

fifteenth century, were not lifted until about 1700.[75] Moreover, the crown did not tamper with the rights of jurisdiction, including the right of 'neck and hand' acquired in the early sixteenth century. Measures resembling the Norwegian restrictions were only introduced on royal land, where increasing rent had to be approved by a panel of older, well-renowned peasants in many cases, in order not to overburden the tenants.[76] Rents on private estates were not regulated, but any increase was not welcomed. Danish landlords therefore found raising rents above the traditional levels difficult, leaving the entrance fee and corvée labour better options for increasing the exploitation of peasants.[77]

After the introduction of absolutism in 1660, the need to secure taxes was met in Denmark, as we have already seen, by giving landlords the responsibility for the payment of all peasant taxes.[78] The need to interfere in landlord-tenants relations thus decreased, leaving the problem of viable households able to pay rents and fines, as well as taxes, entirely up to the landlords. This probably contributed to the curbing of any development of de facto hereditary tenures, like the ones found in Norway.

In Sweden, funding the military state was done partly by extracting taxes from peasant households, partly by transferring landed property and the right to taxes to an aristocracy with military functions. Three classes of property can be distinguished: (1) tax land, where freeholders in the form of owner-occupiers paid taxes to the crown, (2) crown land, where tenants paid rents and taxes to the crown, and (3) *frälsejord*, tax-exempted land where tenants paid rents and taxes to their landlord.

This led the crown to adopt different strategies towards their subject peasants according to the character of the land. On *frälsejord*, tenants were, for the most part, left on their own to meet the demands from their landowner, having rather short and insecure tenures. Some of them experienced increased corvée labour, while others were threatened with confiscation in order to increase the demesne land.[79] However, by the mid-seventeenth century, dwindling taxes,

75 'Vornedskab', *Den store danske*: Gyldendals åbne encyklopædi, http://www.denstoredanske.dk/Danmarks_geografi_og_historie/Danmarks_historie/Landbohistorie/vornedskab. Last accessed 19 August 2010.

76 Skrubbeltrang, *Det danske landbosamfund*, 84.

77 Skrubbeltrang, *Det danske landbosamfund*, 70, with reference to the works of Johs. Steenstrup.

78 Løgstrup 'Den bortforpagtede statsmagt', 21–58.

79 Mats Olsson, *Skatta dig lycklig: Jordränta och jordbruk i Skåne 1660–1900* (Södertälje: Gidlunds förlag, 2005), 147–48. Mats Olsson, *Storgodsdrift: Godsekonomi och arbetsorganisation i Skåne från dansk tid till mitten av 1800-talet* (Lund: Almquist & Wiksell International, 2002), 294–96.

caused by a massive transfer of crown land and tax land to the aristocracy, threatened the Swedish state with bankruptcy, at the same time as the shortcoming of the same aristocracy as a military force became obvious. In the 1680s, this resulted in a comprehensive transmission of *frälsejord* back to the crown, making the three classes of property approximately equal in size.[80]

Only on land owned by the crown did royal initiatives interfere with the length and content of tenures, providing tenants with secure lifelong and even hereditary tenures from the end of the seventeenth century, while on land allotted to the aristocracy, tenures continued to be rather short and insecure with constant risk of increasing corvée labour or tenant holdings being added to the demesne.[81]

The Swedish experience therefore underscores the importance of taxation policy for the conditions of Scandinavian tenants. In cases where tenants were shielded by the crown for taxation purposes, as in Norway and on crown land in Sweden, tenures were relatively secure and tended to become hereditary. When this was not the case, as on *frälsejord* in Sweden, tenures tended to be short term and insecure as tenant holdings could be added to the demesnes.

Herrschaftsrechte could play an influential part in preventing tenants from obtaining the most desired tenures, but these rights were themselves influenced by external forces. They could be subject to limitations by territorial lords, if those lords had the inclination or the strength to enforce restrictions. In Denmark, with the development of *Herrschaftsrechte* for the aristocracy from the late Middle Ages, the crown used much the same strategy for shielding its own tenants for taxation purposes as in Norway. The aristocracy's tenants were, however, left in a more insecure position, especially after the landlords were given the task of collecting taxes, although they also enjoyed a formal lifelong tenure. The Danish *Herrschaftsrechte,* at least as long as the crown recognized the leading military and political role of the aristocracy in the country, therefore seem to have modified whatever intentions the crown may have had of making all tenants viable taxpayers. In Bavaria, such *Herrschaftsrechte* proved an insurmountable obstacle to the dukes' attempts to establish direct bonds with all their subjects, while the relative strength of the Tyrolean counts made them succeed where their Bavarian counterparts failed.

Concerning our third point, the balance between *Rentengrundherrschaft* and demesne farming, the best conditions for tenants were clearly found in areas where *Rentengrundherrschaft* dominated, for example, in Tyrol, Norway, and most of Sweden, whereas in areas where demesne farming was reintroduced

80 Myrdal, *Jordbruket under feodalismen*, 334–39.

81 Olsson, *Skatta dig lycklig*, 148–49.

in the early modern period, as in most of Denmark and Scania in the south of Sweden, tenures tended to be more insecure. In Schleswig, there also seems to have been a close correlation between the way estates were run and tenures in the early modern period. This does not mean, however, that the form of farming and surplus extraction was the decisive factor in forming tenant conditions. In Bavaria, for example, where demesne farming played a negligible role by the Middle Ages, tenants of lay and ecclesiastical lords enjoyed less favourable tenures, even though they were part of a *Rentengrundherrschaft* system. In this case, the importance of the *Herrschaftsrechte* counteracted the benefits that the rent system could offer them.

2 Peasant Ownership

Most peasants in the Alpine region and Bavaria, as well as in Scandinavia, were tenants in the Middle Ages and the early modern period. However, in all regions some peasants themselves owned the land they worked. They were freeholders, in the sense that they did not pay any rent or other dues to a landlord for using the land.

Freeholders in Scandinavia were usually personally free. Their counterparts in Tyrol and Bavaria, in contrast, did not necessarily enjoy personal freedom. On the contrary, in the Middle Ages they were usually *Eigenleute*, with unfree bonds to an ecclesiastical or lay lord.[82] Later, as personal bonds were gradually severed, freeholders and tenants became personally independent. In Tyrol, *Eigenleute* constituted a minority by the second half of the thirteenth century, and they had all but vanished by the beginning of the sixteenth century.[83] In Bavaria and other east Alpine areas, such bonds lasted well into the early modern period, in Berchtesgaden until 1807 and in Bayern until 1808, although the bonds increasingly turned into formal recognition without any significant implications for the persons involved.[84]

2.1 *The Origins of Freehold*

The origin and scale of medieval freehold is obscure and has been widely disputed in Scandinavia, the Alpine region, and Bavaria. Scandinavian historians

82 Dopsch, 'Zur entwicklung des bäuerlichen Bestizrechts', 74–75; Ernst Klebel, 'Freies Eigen und Beutellehen in Ober- und Niederbayern', *Zeitschrift für Bayerische Landesgeschichte*, 11 (1938), 45–85, at pp. 65–67; Rankl, *Landvolk*, 286.

83 Beimrohr, 'Bäuerliche Besitzrechte', 87, 89–90.

84 Dopsch, 'Zur entwicklung des bäuerlichen Bestizrechts', 76–79, Rankl, *Landvolk*, 235.

used to portray the Norse communities in the transition from the Viking Age to the Middle Ages as kin-based societies where the family or individual households owned the great majority of land. A more recent view maintains that big men or chieftains with multiple estates also controlled surrounding tributary peasant households.[85] (see the introduction to this chapter, and the main introduction, section 'A Sketch of the Historical Background'). According to the first view, freehold would have been substantial in the first centuries after year 1000 AD. Later, many of these freeholders became tenants under the aristocracy, the church, or the crown. The more recent view stresses a continuation of landholding structures in which peasants originally dependent on big men or chieftains became tenants in the later impersonal tenant system that can be observed by the thirteenth century. In both scenarios, a majority of peasants were by then tenants, although a substantial minority were freeholders.

In the Alpine area and Bavaria, the development of freehold has been ascribed to two main factors: the clearing of new land and the need to secure frontiers. As most of late medieval or early modern *Freies Eigen* (allodial holdings) in Bavaria were situated in regions with single farms going back to colonization during the High Middle Ages, they are supposed to have had their origin in the clearing of new land, which seems to have provided some peasants (who were personally unfree) with the opportunity to gain possession of the land they had cleared.[86] However, it is highly disputed whether these freeholders also had military functions.[87] Such military functions are more likely to be the background for the medieval freeholders along the frontiers in Kärnten, Steiermark, and Krain.[88]

A link to military and fiscal functions may also be found in Tyrol, although not in the form of personal bonds. In this area, from the thirteenth to the fifteenth century, *Freileute*, free peasants, were obliged to pay taxes and render military service to their territorial lord. Later, these were duties levied on all Tyrolean peasants, both freeholders and tenants. These *Freileute* were especially abundant in western Tyrol, and many of them had allodial possession of their holding.[89] It was also possible for tenants to buy the land they worked. In the seventeenth and eighteenth centuries, the need for cash led some landlords in

85 Tore Iversen, 'Fremveksten av det norske leiglendingsvesenet i middelaldren – en forklaringsskisse', *Heimen*, 32 (1995), 169–80, at pp. 169–171, 174–76.

86 Klebel, 'Freies Eigen und Beutellehen', 53–57; Rankl, *Landvolk*, 287.

87 Rankl, *Landvolk*, 286.

88 Dopsch, 'Zur entwicklung des bäuerlichen Bestizrechts', 75–76.

89 Beimrohr, 'Bäuerliche Besitzrechte', 88–89.

the East Alpine region to offer their tenants the opportunity to become freeholders for quite considerable sums of money.[90]

2.2 *The Alpine Region and Bavaria*

As long as personal bonds were important, territorial lords (*Landesherren*) seem to have tolerated peasants' ownership more often than did mere landlords (*Grundherren*), because they had an opportunity to extract money from the peasants by means of fines and taxes instead of land-rent. Freeholders were also obliged to do military service and to render different forms of labour service (*Scharwerk*) to the lord exercising judicial authority over them (*Gerichtsherr*).[91] In late medieval and early modern Bavaria, we thus find freeholders mainly in regions controlled by the territorial lord, and hardly any in regions where an ecclesiastical or lay lord occupied a strong position.[92]

In Tyrol, the power of the territorial lords expanded over the course of the high medieval period. Tyrol, incidentally, also differs from other Alpine and Bavarian regions by the fact that freehold seems to have been more widespread. At the end of the Middle Ages, freeholders in Bavaria comprised more than 5 percent to 20 percent of the holdings in most regions and their number diminished in the early modern period. In the sixteenth century, *Freieigen* and *Bauernlehen* together may have been reduced to one-tenth, or even less.[93] On the other hand, in Tyrol, peasant ownership by the last quarter of the eighteenth century amounted to almost one-quarter of all holdings, and in the western parts of this region even the majority of holdings.[94] In contrast to Tyrol, where peasant freehold may have been stimulated by the efforts of the territorial lord to make all peasants his subjects, peasant freehold in Switzerland was under constant pressure from lay and ecclesiastical landlords and small-scale territorial lords in the Middle Ages. Freeholders could nevertheless still be found in the fifteenth century in some regions, such as the Neuenburger Juras, Aargaus, Thurgaus, und Appenzellerland.[95]

Freeholdings had a tendency to become very small, especially in regions where hereditary customs allowed division of land among heirs, as in the

90 Dopsch, 'Zur entwicklung des bäuerlichen Bestizrechts', 76.

91 Rankl, *Landvolk*, 286; Klebel, 'Freies Eigen und Beutellehen', 56–58, 60–62, 66.

92 Rankl, *Landvolk*, 287–88, 293.

93 Rankl, *Landvolk*, 290, 326.

94 Beimrohr, 'Bäuerliche Besitzrechte', 87–88.

95 Peter Walliser, 'Allod', *Historisches Lexikon der Schweitz*, https://hls-dhs-dss.ch/de/articles/008978/2002-06-04/. Last accessed 10 August 2009.

western parts of Tyrol.[96] Thus, freeholdings did not guarantee peasants more suitable conditions than larger tenant holdings. In regions where tenant holdings dominated, as in Bavaria from the late Middle Ages, they could also be amalgamated with tenant land. Thus, many freeholdings became subject to manorial rule (*Grundherrschaft*) over the course of time, especially in regions where small units could not survive.[97]

A form of possession very similar to peasant ownership was the *Beutellehen* or *Zinslehen*, which occurred in the Alpine region in the late Middle Ages. In such arrangements, peasants were invested with former feudal tenures (fiefs). Only the personal status of their holder and the obligations arising out of the tenure distinguished these tenures from *Ritterlehen* (fiefs) whose noble holders were obliged to do military service. Similar to freehold, these tenancies could be passed on to heirs, sold, and divided. The holders of *Beutellehen* were not obliged to pay rents, but they had to pay a mortuary fee when either the vassal or the lord died (*Mannfall* or *Herrenfall*). Over the course of the early modern period, *Beutellehen* were often granted as hereditary tenures.[98]

2.3 *Scandinavia*

Freehold in Scandinavia differed from the Alpine region in scale as well as in substance. So did the character and conditions of freehold within Scandinavia itself. Freeholders in Denmark and Sweden, like their Alpine and Bavarian counterparts, were mainly owner-occupiers. So were also many Norwegian freeholders, although they, as well as ordinary Norwegian tenants, were allowed to own land let out to other peasants as well.

In Denmark and Sweden, the crown claimed superior ownership to all freehold land from the fifteenth century.[99] By doing this, the crown not only could claim the right to regular taxes and dues from this category of land, but it could also prevent such land from being transferred into tax-free ownership. This

96 Riedmann, *Geschichte Tirols*, 131–32; Georg Jäger, 'Siedlungsausbau und soziale Differenzierung der ländlichen Bevölkerung in Nordtirol wärend der frühen Neuzeit', *Tiroler Heimat*, 60 (1996), 87–88, 95–100. In western Tyrol, farms with hereditary tenures (*Erbbaurecht*) were also extensively divided.

97 Rankl, *Landvolk*, 295–96.

98 Rankl, *Landvolk*, 297–308; Dopsch, 'Zur entwicklung des bäuerlichen Bestizrechts', 73–74; Klebel, 'Freies Eigen und Beutellehen', 67–82; Beimrohr, 'Bäuerliche Besitzrechte', 90–91; Herbert Klein, 'Ritterlehen und Beutellehen in Salzburg', in *Beitrage zur Siedlungs-Verfassungs- und Wirtschaftsgeschicte von Salzburg: Festschrift zum 65. von Herbert Klein.* Mitteilungen der Gescellschaft für Salzburger Landeskunde, Ergänzungsband, 5 (Salzburg: Gesellschaft für Salzburger Landeskunde, 1965), 325–65.

99 Skrubbeltrang, *Det danske landbosamfund*, 57, 172–74; Myrdal, *Jordbruket under feodalismen*, 334; Myking and Rasmussen, 'Scandinavia', 287–314.

was important, as lay and ecclesiastical landlords in Denmark and Sweden during the late thirteenth and early fourteenth century managed to have their lands and tenants exempt from taxes and dues.[100] By claiming superior ownership, any transition of property from freehold status in Sweden and Denmark had to be approved by the crown.

In Norway, on the other hand, every peasant had to pay taxes, regardless of who owned the land. This made ownership of little relevance to the crown, thus freely allowing ecclesiastical institutions and members of the aristocracy, as well as other peasants, to acquire freehold land. In contrast to freeholders in the two other Scandinavian kingdoms, Norwegian freeholders thus retained full ownership, without any superior ownership being imposed on them by the crown.[101] An exception to this general rule was land cleared in some remote commons to which the king claimed a superior property right.[102]

Due to a lack of sources, the scale of freehold in Scandinavia is very difficult to measure before the beginning of the early modern period. Clearly, most peasants were tenants. Former freeholders and their descendants were also added to their numbers through gifts of freehold land to ecclesiastical institutions. Nevertheless, freehold is thought to have played an important part in all three Scandinavian countries in the Middle Ages. While freehold still played a prominent part in all Scandinavian countries by the end of the late Middle Ages, in the early modern period freehold in Denmark dwindled to almost nothing as the crown alienated its superior ownership of a substantial amount of freehold land and allowed the new owners to purchase full property rights over former freehold land. Tentative estimates in the first decades of the sixteenth century suggest that 15 percent of all land in Denmark were freehold land. At the end of the seventeenth century, this amount had reduced to only 2 percent.[103] By the early sixteenth century, around half of the land in Sweden was freehold land, formally categorized as tax land, that is, land owned by peasants paying taxes only to the crown. As the overlordship to a fair amount of this land, including the right to taxes, was transferred from the crown to nobles and newly ennobled civil and military servants between *c.* 1620 and

100 Niels Hybel and Bjørn Poulsen, *The Danish Resources c. 1000–1550: Growth and Recession*, The Northern World, 34 (Leiden: Brill, 2007), 308; Myrdal, *Jordbruket under feodalismen*, 104.

101 Myking and Rasmussen, 'Scandinavia', 289.

102 Jon Solem, 'Den norske almenningsinstitusjonen i middelalderen', *Heimen*, 4 (2003), 243–65.

103 Hybel and Poulsen, *Danish Resources*, 400; Skrubbeltrang, *Det danske landbosamfund*, 172; Myking and Rasmussen, 'Scandinavia', 290.

1660, owner-occupiers on freehold land have been calculated as constituting about one-third of all land by the late-seventeenth century.[104]

It has been estimated that one-third of the land-rent in Norway was owned by peasants by the 1660s, but this does not mean that these peasants were owner-occupiers.[105] A complicated *share-of-rent ownership system* (see above) allowed peasants to own shares of the holdings they lived on or of land rented to others.[106] By around 1660, then, only one-fifth of the land, measured in land-rent, was owned and worked by owner-occupiers.[107] By the turn of the next century, the number of owner-occupiers was rapidly increasing. Since 1660, town merchants and officials had received a substantial amount of crown land to compensate for losses on loans to cover Danish warfare, mainly against Sweden, loans the crown was unable to repay. Together with other landholdings, these possessions were offered to tenants in the following decades, as merchants and officials found more rewarding opportunities for investment than renting out land. By 1800, then, as much as 57 percent of the land, measured in land-rent (*landskyld*), was owned by peasants working their own holdings – compared to 20 percent 140 years earlier.

Even though peasant freehold was more widespread in Norway and Sweden than in Denmark, we find some interesting regional patterns across the Scandinavian borders. As in the Alpine area, some regions show a significantly higher percentage of freehold land than others. In Sweden, this was true for the entire northern part of the country, where owner-occupiers owned a vast majority of the land by the beginning of the eighteenth century, and for certain other forested regions further south.[108] In Norway, freehold dominated part of the inland districts of southern Norway, where owner-occupiers held from one-third to more than two-thirds of the land in some valley districts by 1661.[109]

104 Myking and Rasmussen, 'Scandinavia', 290.

105 Ståle Dyrvik, 'Overgangen til sjølveige i Norge: Nokre nye data for 1700-talet', *Historisk tidsskrift*, 56 (1977), 1–18, at p. 3.

106 Lars Ivar Hansen, 'Peasants, Land and Inheritance: Peasant Property and Rent Ownership in the Parish of Fyresdal, Southern Norway', in Tore Iversen and John Ragnar Myking (eds), *Land, Lords and Peasants: Peasants' Right to Control Land in the Middle Ages and the Early Modern Period – Norway, Scandinavia and the Alpine Region*, Trondheim Studies in History, 52 (Trondheim: NTNU, 2005), 181–98. Knut Dørum, *Oppløsningen av skyldeiesystemet: En studie av eiendomsformer og eierinteresser knyttet til jord i Norge ca. 1600–1800* (Oslo: Tingbokprosjektet, 1996).

107 Dyrvik, 'Overgangen til sjølveige', 3, 6.

108 Carl-Johan Gadd, *Den agrara revolutionen 1700–1870*, Det svenska jordbrukets historia, 3 (Borås: Natur og Kultur/LTs förlag, 2000), 43–44; Myrdal, *Jordbruket under feodalismen*, 334.

109 Dyrvik, 'Overgangen til sjølveige'.

Freehold in Sweden and Norway from the Middle Ages thus seems to have been strongest in regions furthest removed from the medieval royal, aristocratic, and ecclesiastical centres. This arguably supports the hypothesis that these regions were not dominated by chieftains or big men at the end of the Viking Age and the beginning of the Middle Ages, as personally dependent peasants later must have become tenants. In most of Denmark, except for a couple of minor provinces in the east, freehold domination could only be found at parish level, not at a regional level.[110] In the duchy of Schleswig, with no clear centre, freeholders dominated the western part and were numerous on land belonging to the territorial lord, whereas the southeastern parts were dominated by manors and tenant land.[111]

An owner-occupier's right to exploit resources on freehold land differed between the Scandinavian countries. In Norway, owner-occupiers had full ownership of their land. Their use of resources was only regulated by the common use of infield or outfield resources with neighbouring peasants, and they could freely make use of timber resources. Through their *odelsrett* (allodial right), pre-emption and redemption were limited to relatives, and the crown could not interfere in land transactions.[112] In contrast, Swedish freeholders, over whom the crown held overlordship, were restricted from exploiting their forest and timber resources freely, nor had they the right to use burn and slash cultivation in their own forests without the consent of the crown. The Swedish *bördsrett* may be compared with the Norwegian *odelsrett*, but the Swedish crown held the right of pre-emption to freehold land sold to non-relatives, and three years of tax arrears led to the forfeiture of the land to the crown. In theory, although not always in practice, they were even subjected to visitation by crown officials every third year in order to inspect the state of the holding.[113]

The few freeholders who remained in Denmark were subject to even more severe restrictions than their Swedish counterparts. They had to pay recognition to their overlord, normally the crown, and they could be called upon to perform corvée labour, although on a smaller scale than tenants.[114] It has

110 Myking and Rasmussen, 'Scandinavia', 291.

111 Rasmussen, *Rentegods og hovedgårdsdrift*, i, 553–54.

112 Per G. Norseng, 'Odelsrett – The Norwegian retrait lignager', in Tore Iversen and John Ragnar Myking (eds), *Land, Lords and Peasants: Peasants' Right to Control Land in the Middle Ages and the Early Modern Period – Norway, Scandinavia and the Alpine Region*, Trondheim Studies in History, 52 (Trondheim: NTNU, 2005), 201–27.

113 Gadd, *Den agrara revolutionen*, 71–72.

114 Skrubbeltrang, *Det danske landbosamfund*, 172–74.

therefore been suggested that these peasants, at least in the early modern period, had more in common with European hereditary tenants than Norwegian freeholders.

3 Trans-Regional Comparison

Even though the origins of freehold are obscure in both the Alpine region and in Scandinavia, we have indications of quite different patterns of evolution in the two regions. In Bavaria and the Alpine region, clearing of new land by dependent peasants may have contributed to the development of freeholdings. So may have the need for military service. In Scandinavia, none of these factors seem to have had any impact on the development of freehold. On the contrary, clearing of new land by freed slaves or dependent peasants resulted in new tenant farms and holdings (see chapter 'Slavery and Unfreedom'),[115] and there seems to have been no need to supply peasants with freehold land in order to guard frontiers. A reasonable deduction may therefore be that a number of freeholders already existed in Scandinavia in the first centuries after the year 1000 AD, probably with strong ties to a local chieftain. This amount of freehold land may well have been reduced by gifts to ecclesiastical institutions before the Reformation, but it is believed to have been quite substantial in all three Scandinavian kingdoms in the medieval period.

While manorial ambitions in clearing land and territorial objectives of securing frontiers may have been essential factors in the early development of freehold in Bavaria and the Alpine region, the further development of freehold in this region, as well as in Scandinavia, seems to be closely connected to the question of taxation. In Bavaria, the domination of secular and ecclesiastical landlords prevented any large-scale transformation to freehold. These landlords were furthermore inclined to lease their land on the formal basis of short-term tenures without any *dominium utile*, the *Freistift*, as this form of tenure did not give their tenants a taxable form of property right in their holding. The territorial lords, on the other hand, tolerated the existence of freehold on the grounds of this yielding them taxes and provided them with military service and labour (*Scharwerk*).

115 Tore Iversen, *Knechtschaft im mittelalterlichen Norwegen*, trans. Katharina Freche in collaboration with Angelika Landau, Münchener Universitätsschriften, Juristische Fakultät, Abhandlungen zur Rechtswissenschaftlichen Grundlagenforschung, 94 (Ebelsbach: Aktiv, 2004), 398–433.

This inclination to further, or at least tolerate, freehold seems to be common for most territorial lords, in the Alpine region as well as in Scandinavia. While freehold in the easternmost part of the Alps, such as Kärnten, lost its importance by the beginning of the early modern period, freehold in Tyrol gained momentum through support from the territorial lord. In Scandinavia, royal interest in taxing freeholders may explain difference in the conditions for freehold. As all Norwegian peasants, tenants, and freeholders alike paid taxes from the Middle Ages, freeholders were treated as ordinary landowners. The crown saw no reasons to introduce any superior ownership, and freeholders could use every available resource on their land, including the forest, without interference.

This was not so in Denmark and Sweden. In these countries, the crown claimed a superior ownership of freehold land from the beginning of the fifteenth century. This measure was introduced in order to avoid any more of this type of land being transferred into the category of tax-free aristocratic land. This goal was, however, willingly laid aside in Denmark from the latter half of the sixteenth century as part of the effort to concentrate the crown's landed property through property exchanges with the aristocracy. The subsequent transfer of superior ownership of freehold land to the aristocracy almost led to the total disappearance of this category of land in Denmark by the mid-seventeenth century. In Sweden, freehold land was protected as a separate category and a secure base of taxation by restrictions on owner-occupiers on their free transfer of land. The crown's claim to superior ownership was furthermore used to secure the collection of taxes and to benefit from available forest resources on freehold land.[116]

The differences between hereditary tenures and freehold, with the exception of Norwegian freeholders' control over forests and timber, lay mainly in the form and extent of the expropriation of a surplus from farming, not in any qualitatively better freehold control over resources. Tenants' control over transfer of land was, however, more open than at least that of the Scandinavian freeholders, where descendants and relatives could claim pre-emption and redemption for a varying length of time. For Norwegian freeholders, the *åseterett* even designated the oldest son as the one to take over the entire holding. As the majority of tenants in both regions then were in control of most resources and even controlled succession on their holding, the level of expropriation, be it by rent, corvée labour, or taxation, may have been the most marked difference.

116 Myrdal, *Jordbruket under feodalismen*, 334; Gadd, *Den agrara revolutionen*, 71–72.

4 Conclusion

Over time, Scandinavian and Alpine peasants held their land under a wide range of conditions. At one end, there were tenants with short-term leases without any form of property rights in the land at all, such as the medieval Alpine and Bavarian *Freistift* and the Norwegian one-year lease prescribed in the regional *Gulathing Law* from the twelfth century. At the other end, we find peasants with full property ownership, like the Norwegian freeholder, or, as in the Alpine area and in Denmark and Sweden, freehold modified by the territorial lord's superior ownership. In between, constituting the great majority of landholding in both regions at the beginning of the early modern period, we find long-term and even hereditary leases with a secure share in the property. Even though considerable local divergences can be discerned, the general trend from the Middle Ages until the end of the early modern period seems to have been a development in the direction of longer and more secure tenures in both regions, at the same time as freehold expanded at the expense of tenures in some territories, especially in Tyrol and Norway.

Long-term and hereditary tenures meant greater security and an added ability for tenants to handle transfer of holdings without interference from their landlord. This did not, however, greatly widen their control over resources. In both regions, even with short-term leases, the tenant household already controlled most of the necessary resources needed for the viability of the household. What they could not exploit fully was supplementary resources not necessary in the ordinary running of the holding, like timber and some other forest products. These were normally controlled by the landlord or, in the case of freeholders, the territorial lord. In Tyrol, the territorial lord claimed a superior property right to commons and forests,[117] and in Bavaria, successive rulers from the late Middle Ages tried to restrict peasants' exploitation of the forest to the needs of the household.[118] The only exception in this respect seems to have been the Norwegian freeholder, over whom not even the king held a superior ownership. On the other hand, in the Alpine region and Bavaria, as well as in Scandinavia, the exploitation of metal resources was completely controlled by the territorial lord, regardless of any superior or inferior property right in the land itself.

As for factors explaining the general development of tenures and control over resources, the strength of the territorial lords and their relation to manorial lords and other landlords in their realm seems crucial. Where the territorial

117 Beimrohr, 'Bäuerliche Besitzrechte', 101–02.

118 Rankl, *Landvolk*, 63–67.

lord was strong, he promoted long-term leases, a moderate increase in rent, and even transition to freehold, often against the manorial lords' interests, in order to establish peasants as viable subjects able to pay taxes. This goal was, however, played down if the aristocracy held important military or political positions, as in Denmark and Sweden from the end of the late Middle Ages until the last part of the seventeenth century and in Bavaria from the High Middle Ages. The contrasting development in Norway and Denmark, united under the same king and administered from Denmark from the late medieval period, underlines this argument. The Swedish experience, on the other hand, shows a territorial lord able to balance the benefit of having an aristocracy with important military and political assignments with the advantage of creating viable conditions for the crown's own tenants and keeping a strong element of freeholders in the form of owner-occupiers.

Manorial power, on which military and political influence was founded, was closely connected to topography and manorial structures. The easily controlled plains of Bavaria, Denmark, and parts of southern Sweden, well suited for grain growing and effective control over relatively concentrated manors, offered a solid basis for manorial power. The more mountainous regions of Tyrol and Norway, where a weaker aristocracy offered less resistance to the territorial lords' efforts to establish direct links to his subjects, did not. In these regions, manorial *Herrschaftsrechte* were either underdeveloped, as in Norway, or gradually repealed, as in Tyrol, thus limiting the manorial lords' ability to control their tenants. This may explain why Tyrolean and Norwegian peasants as taxable royal subjects enjoyed some of the best tenures, while at the same time these territories also exhibited a considerable number of freeholders, especially in areas farthest removed from medieval centres of power.

Acknowledgements

I am greatly indebted to the late Gertrud Thoma for an early draft regarding conditions in Bavaria, a draft that has been enlarged on and included in this chapter.

CHAPTER 4

Peasant Participation in *Thing* and Local Assemblies *c.* 1000–1750

Tore Iversen and John Ragnar Myking

1 Introduction

Long before the beginning of the second millennium, peasants in Scandinavia and in the Eastern Alpine region participated in a variety of assemblies on a local and regional level.[1] Such assemblies were meeting places for a broad range of collective social actions and activities, where agreements were reached and decisions made. They were arenas for playing out interests and launching demands from within or from outside the society of peasants. The assemblies made decisions concerning internal matters for the peasant society, as well as in matters originating from external authorities. Two ideal type of concepts from German historiography, *Herrschaft* (dominion) and *Genossenschaft* (community), may be of help to us to adhere to the intertwined connection between peasant communities and outside power factors, even though these concepts is rooted in nineteenth-century historiography.[2]

Genossenschaft represents forms of communities organized on a horizontal level, like the peasant assemblies in villages and neighbourhoods. This kind of community defines itself by engaging in collective activities. They were less controlled by formal regulations than by shared values and norms, especially in the early part of our period.[3] *Herrschaft* (dominion) represents the vertical

1 About popular assemblies as a global phenomenon with ancient roots, see R. Wenskus, 'Ding', in Johannes Hoops and Heinreich Beck (eds), *Real-enzyklopädie der germanischen Altertumskunde* (Berlin, 1973–2015) v, 443–55.

2 Regarding the concepts in German historiography, see Tore Iversen, John Ragnar Myking and Gertrud Thoma (eds), *Bauern zwischen Herrschaft und Genossenschaft: Peasant Relations to Lords and Government. Scandinavia and the Alpine Region 1000–1750* (Trondheim: Tapir Akademisk Farlag, 2007), esp. the article by Werner Rösener ('Bauern zwischen Herrschaft und Genossenschaft in Deutschland – Ein Überblick', 9–24). See also Tore Iversen, 'Bauern zwischen Herrschaft uns Genossenschaft – Einleitung', in Tore Iversen, John Ragnar Myking and Gertrud Thoma (eds), *Bauern zwischen Herrschaft und Genossenschaft: Peasant Relations to Lords and Government. Scandinavia and the Alpine Region 1000–1750* (Trondheim: Tapir Akademisk Forlag, 2007), 1–9.

3 See Susan Reynolds, *Kingdoms and Communities in Western Europe 900–1300* (Oxford: Clarendon Press, 1997), 2.

 | DOI:10.1163/9789004433458_005

influence of authorities outside the peasant community. The concept of *Herrschaft* comprised kings', territorial princes', and in many cases also clerical and secular landlords' political-judicial power over peasants (*Gerichtsgewalt*). These lords also exercised power over peasants through their proprietary rights over peasant-cultivated land (*Grundherrschaft*) and in some cases also over people themselves living and working on this land (*Leibherrschaft*) (see 'Introduction', section 'Historical and Methodological Reflections'). Both communities and lordship must thus be taken as constituent elements in medieval and early modern society.[4]

In some peasant communities, outside power factors like manorial or territorial lords had minimal influence while in other communities such factors would be quite dominating. The use of the concepts *Herrschaft* and *Genossenschaft* should, first and foremost, help us avoid a tendency to view peasants as passive objects for manorial and territorial lords or to look at peasant communities as independent worlds of their own. Because of the magnitude and fundamental importance of the peasantry, manorial or territorial authorities always had to take peasants and their communities into account in some way or another. On the other hand, in their cooperation with external powers, peasant communities and peasant assemblies clearly accepted inequality and subordination.[5] Such acceptance also applied internally in peasant communities and peasant assemblies, as peasant elites normally exercised considerable influence in the assemblies.

A closer outline of the diverse tasks and activities of assemblies in which peasants participated marks out the distribution and administration of agricultural resources, the rotation of crops, and the use of commons, as well as the regulation of everyday life as a main concern for the peasant community. These tasks and activities are primarily associated with village or neighbourhood assemblies. Such matters were regulated by village or customary law laid down by local village assemblies or other local institutions, in some cases in cooperation with their landlord or some local authority. Assemblies with such local agricultural and social tasks were especially frequent in regions dominated by open field agricultural systems and village settlement, as in Bavaria and Denmark, but were also found in the mountainous areas of Bavaria and

4 In fact, elements of vertical power, *Herrschaft*, also existed within the peasant communities, exercised by the peasant elite, and elements of community, *Genossenschaft*, also existed within the upper strata, for example, in the nobility, especially in the later part of our period.

5 Reynolds, *Kingdoms and Communities*, 332.

Tyrol, where village settlements were intertwined with hamlets and single farm settlements.

Two other fields of activity are primarily associated with local or regional *thing* institutions or courts. The administration of justice was an initial field of concern for many assemblies in Scandinavia and in the eastern Alpine region. The law and order aspect of these assemblies was crucial for maintaining local peace and settling disputes. The second field comprises the violation of law and civil litigation, and the execution of sentences rapidly became a matter for the manorial or territorial lord. Over the course of the medieval period, territorial lords gained ever more control over the administration of justice at the expense of the peasant community, a control that was fortified in the early modern period. Manorial control was also significantly weakened, although manorial lords managed to retain some of their influence in Bavaria and even gain new influence in Denmark during the early modern period. Some regional assemblies, like the regional *things* (*lögthing* = lawthing) in Norway, also possessed some legislative power, but such power was significantly reduced from the thirteenth century.

A third and more loosely defined field of activity could be labelled administrative-legal, signifying that the administrative actions were linked to customary and written law with economic consequences for peasants, as well as for manorial and territorial lords. Administrative-legal supervision within the peasants' society, for example, the transfer of landed resources, was entrusted to assemblies under the auspices of a territorial or a manorial lord, as was the administration of rent, taxes, and corvée labour due to manorial or territorial lords. In Norway and Tyrol, such assemblies were held responsible for military duties and conscription, including the inspection of weapons and boats. These three fields of activity (agricultural / social, judicial, and administrative) do not necessarily correspond to the actual construction of peasant assemblies in our two main regions. Our two last points merely indicate that the administration of justice and other administrative-economic purposes were at the core of the activity in many assemblies, while our first point indicates activities crucial to peasant everyday work and social life. In assemblies most concerned with the first type of activity, the *Genossenschaft* side of our dichotomy dominated, although *Herrschaft* may also have played a part. In the two last types, the *Herrschaft* activities tended to play an ever-increasing part over the course of the centuries, reflecting the development of a more professional legal and administrative policy from the top of society.[6]

6 Reynolds, *Kingdoms and Communities*, 332; Iversen, 'Bauern zwischen Herrschaft uns Genossenschaft', 180.

In our period, however, there are shifting forms of peasant influence within and between different forms of assemblies and institutions, from genuine peasant self-administration found in many village and neighbourhood assemblies via co-determination typical of some forms of *thing* institutions to mere passive attendance as witnesses in some kinds of local territorial or manorial courts. The difficulties of estimating the degree of peasant influence are however considerable, not only due to the lack of sources from the earlier period, but also because inequality and subordination were values internalized in different ways than in modern democracies.

We will start our analysis with Scandinavia before turning to the eastern Alpine region. Even though the different fields of activity are intertwined and elements of *Herrschaft* and *Genossenschaft* can be found in all of them, we have found it useful for a clearer presentation to differentiate between *thing* institutions and legal and administrative assemblies on the one hand[7] and village and neighbourhood assemblies on the other.

2 Scandinavia

2.1 *The Earliest* Things *in Northern Scandinavia*

Recent archeological excavations and research, often in combination with other types of evidence, have thrown light on the *thing* as an arena for peasant self-management and cooperation in the early Middle Ages. This research confirms that Scandinavia was a stratified society at the time and emphasizes the importance of chieftains for the organization of the early Scandinavian *thing*. Places believed to be 'court sites' have been found along the Norwegian coast as late as from the eleventh century in Northern Norway and in middle Sweden into the twelfth century. It is generally agreed that these sites were not permanent settlements but meeting places where the *thing* most likely convened. The majority of the north Norwegian sites had been in use for a shorter or longer period from the late Roman period until AD 600. Only two of them, in addition to a more recently established one, were still in use after 1000.[8]

7 The old term for such assemblies in both regions is *thing* / *Ding*, a term that in most places in the eastern Alpine region was replaced by other denominations during the Middle Ages, see Jürgen Weitzel, 'Gericht', in Robert-Henri Bautier, et al. (ed). *Lexikon des Mittelalters* [hereafter LexMA], 9 vols (Munich and Zurich: Artemis [vols 1–6] and LexMA-Verlag [vols 7–9], 1977–1999), iii, 1058.

8 A survey of such archaeological investigations in Northern Norway is given in Inger Storli, *Hålogaland før rikssamlingen. Politiske prosesser i perioden 200–900 e.Kr.*, Institut for sammenlignende kulturforskning, Serie B, Skrifter, 123 (Oslo: Novus forlag, 2006), 39–75; Inger

Although many sites were situated in the vicinity of centres of power, the oldest sites were found in-between such centres. There are nevertheless indications of a sort of interdependence between the *thing* and the centres of power, possibly due to competition among chieftains in recruiting local peasant followers. The wealth of the northern chieftains was based on trade of arctic hunting products.[9] From about 600, the power struggle between chiefdoms led to some of the chieftaincies being able to expand their sphere of influence into regional supremacy. The three *thing* sites still in use after 1000 can be linked to important sites for Northern Norwegian chieftains, according to later Norse sagas.[10]

The outlying portion of the early Scandinavian multiple estates (See 'Introduction', section 'A Sketch of the Historical Background') covered far greater areas compared to the central farm than was the case on eastern Alpine manors, and the boundaries between the estates were more loosely defined. As mentioned earlier, social relations on these vast estates can be characterized as tributary relations between patrons and clients, that is, they were personal and reciprocal. The court sites may have functioned as assembly places for meetings and negotiations between the peasants of the outer districts, and between them and the chieftain in the centre. The ninth- and tenth-century emigrants to Iceland, led by their chieftains, resumed the forms of organization they knew from coastal Norway. The rich descriptions of the Icelandic *things* in Icelandic medieval literature may therefore throw some light on the early

---

Storli, '"Barbarians" of the North: Reflections on the Establishment of Courtyard Sites in North Norway', *Norwegian Archaeological Review*, 33/2 (2000), 98–100; Alexandra Sanmark, 'Administrative Organisation and State Formation: A Case Study of Assembly Sites in Södermanland, Sweden', *Medieval Archaeology*, 53 (2009), 205–40. Recently, Asle Buen Olsen gave a presentation of two court sites from a west Norwegian fjord district in use to end of the ninth century: A. Buen Olsen, 'Courtyard Sites in Western Norway: Central Assembly Places and Juridical Institutions in the Late Iron Age', in Marianne Hem Eriksen, Unn Pedersen, Bert Rundberget, Irmelin Axelsen and Heidi Lund Berg (eds), *Viking Worlds: Things, Spaces and Movement*, (Oxford: Oxbow, 2015), 43–55.

9 An account of this trade is found in the North Norwegian chief Ottar's account of his journey to the Anglo-Saxon king Alfred around AD 890; see Janet Bately and Anton Englert (eds), *Ohthere's Voyages: A Late 9th Century Account of Voyages along the Coasts of Norway and Denmark and its Cultural Context* (Roskilde: Viking Ship Museum, 2007).

10 In *Heimskringla* (Snorri Sturluson's Kings' saga), these places are mentioned as sites of chieftains, especially when it comes to two of them. About the northern centres, for example, *Bjarkøy and Tjøtta*, see, from the thirteenth century, Snorri Sturluson, *Heimskringla: Nóregs konunga sögur* (hereafter Hkr), ed. Finnur Jónsson (Copenhagen: Gad, 1911) (Þiotta: pp. 148, 156–58, 276, 281, 328, 350–98, 403, 428; Bjarkey: pp. 61, 102, 311–12, 326–28, 519); English translation: Snorri Sturluson, *Heimskringla: History of the Kings of Norway*, trans. Lee M. Hollander (Austin: University of Texas Press, 1964).

development of the Norwegian *thing*.[11] According to the historian Jón Viðar Sigurðsson, chieftains first established chieftaincies with affiliated peasants on a basis of property and personal qualities. The chieftains then competed in associating peasants to the local *things* and the *Althing*, from 930 the common *thing* for the whole of Iceland, which also functioned as a main political arena.[12]

When the number of chieftaincies was reduced, limited regional realms were established and the competition for followers decreased. The *thing* then lost its political function, and some chieftains obtained nearly full control over their *things*. The Icelandic power struggles did not end until all Iceland recognized the Norwegian king as their overlord at the *Althing* in 1264.[13] The *Althing* subsequently changed from being an independent legislative and judicial institution to a court of law, while the smallest local peasant assemblies, the *hreppr*, acquired a greater independence and significance. The *hepprs*' tasks included poor relief, some regulations on farming, and the collection of the new tax to the king.[14]

For the Swedish province of *Södermanland*, the archaeologist Alexandra Sanmark has carried out a multidisciplinary case study of local *thing* assembly sites from the beginning of the Viking Age (*c*. 800) to the mid-thirteenth century, using monument records (rune-stones), documentary evidence, and place names. As opposed to earlier studies stressing the long-term continuity of the *thing* sites, this study found that continuity was not a general pattern. Due to changes in the balance of power, new assembly sites may have emerged frequently within a local entity in the ninth to eleventh centuries. Sanmark suggests that the relocation of assembly sites within a locality and the enhancement of such sites with rune-stones, especially in the eleventh

11 The sagas claim that the central *Althing* (the *thing* for the whole of Iceland) was founded in 930 on the model of the west Norwegian *Gulathing*, see Ari Þorgilsson, *Íslendingsbók*, ed. Anne Holtsmark, Nordisk filologi: Teskster og Lærebøker til universitetsbruk, Serie A, 5 (Oslo: Dreyer, 1967). *Íslendingsbók* dates to the twelfth century. The two mentioned court sites from west Norway seem to have been abandoned at the beginning of the settlement of Iceland. These court sites were situated in the same district where the first settler, Ingólfr Arnarson came from, according to the Icelandic thirteenth-century *Landnámabok*; see Olsen, 'Courtyard Sites', 51–53.

12 Jón Viðar Sigurðsson, 'Goder og maktforhold på Island i fristattiden', PhD thesis, University of Bergen, Bergen, 1993, 94–168.

13 Jón Viðar Sigurðsson, 'Goder og maktforhold', 276–93; Storli, *Hålogaland før rikssamlingen*, 137–49.

14 Jón Viðar Sigurðsson, 'The Icelandic Aristocracy after the Fall of the Free State', *Scandinavian Journal of History*, 3 (1995), 153–66; Magnús Már Lárusson, 'Hreppr', in *Kulturhistorisk leksikon for nordisk middelalder*, 22 vols (Malmö: Allhem, 1956–78) [hereafter KLNM], vii, 18–22; Jakob Benediktsson, 'Thing, Island', in KLNM, xviii, 359–60.

century, were power statements by local chieftain families in response to the growing central power of the Svea kingdom. In the long run, the old local chieftains nevertheless inevitably lost influence.[15]

The evidence from Northern Norway, Iceland, and Sweden thus suggests that, as long as local chieftains competed for followers, the *thing* seem to have existed with a degree of interdependence with local power centres. Many of the early *things* disappeared, and some were newly created in accordance with changes in power relations and political strategies. By the time of a transition to larger realms ruled by regional chieftains, the *things* seem to be more closely connected to centres of power (chieftaincies).

Following the establishment of strong royal power, the chieftains' tight grip on the *thing* peasants slackened. In the following, we will therefore focus on the *thing* assemblies as political arenas for conflicts and cooperation between the crown, the aristocracy, and a peasantry headed by the peasant elite. Regarding Norway, we will concentrate on the development of two regional *things*: the *Frostathing* in Trøndelag and the *Gulathing* in western Norway, with law codes of their own, before turning to development of a uniform legal system for the entire kingdom from the beginning of the thirteenth century.

2.2 *Norway – The* Thing *in the Establishment of Royal Power*

Historians believe that a regional law community was established in Trøndelag (mid-Norway) by the ninth or during the tenth century, following the gradual creation of eight minor provinces, *fylker*, in the region.[16] The *fylker* of Trøndelag were ruled by a group of chieftains.[17] The *things* of these provinces are

15 In one example (*Kjula ås*), a rune stone from the eleventh century at the *thing* site indicated that a person and his family created the site or had taken possession of it. In another example (*Aspa thing*), a rune stone from the eleventh century possibly shows two families fighting for power over or sharing the *thing* site: Sanmark, 'Administrative Organisation', 211–19, 225–27, 230–35; cf. Mats G. Larsson, *Från stormannagård till bondby. En studie av mellansvensk bebyggelseutveckling från äldre järnårder till medeltid*, Acta Archaeologica Lundensia, series 8, 26 (Stockholm: Almqvist and Wiksell, 1997), esp. 181–85.

16 The name of the fertile northern region, *Tröndelag* (*Þrændalog*), means 'the law community of the *tröndr*': see Jørn Sandnes, 'Trøndelags eldste politiske historie', in Claus Krag and Jørn Sandnes (eds), *Nye middelalderstudier – Kongedømme, kirke, stat.* Norske historikere i utvalg, 6 (Oslo: Universitetsforlaget, 1983), 39–50. Within the territory of a *fylke*, archaeologists have found a central area, not far from the sea, consisting of large farms and power symbols, such as large burial mounds and sometimes large boathouses: see Erna Stene, 'Økonomi og samfunn i Inntrøndelag i jernalderen, Storgårder og kirkesteder', *Årbok for Nord-Trøndelag Historielag*, (1992), 23, 30.

17 Olav Skevik, *Folk og fylker i fjerne tider. Inntrøndelags historie før 1600* (Stjørdal: Nord-Trøndelag fylkeskommune, 1997), 143–60. The rule of these chieftains is stated in the later Kings' saga of Snorri Sturluson: Hkr, 44–47.

found nearby the power centres.[18] This leads us to believe that these *thing* arenas were hubs in more or less loosely organized multiple estates of the type we have discussed above. In the tenth century, one of the chieftains, the earl of Lade, intermittently both ally and enemy of the up-and-coming superior kings emerging from western Norway, achieved supremacy, and his *thing* at *Frosta* became the main *thing* in Trøndelag in the tenth century.[19] Although the chieftains seemed to have secured the loyalty of the peasants, their power lasted only into the middle of the eleventh century.[20]

By the beginning of the eleventh century, the king, as a means of establishing his own power, organized a new *thing* in Trøndelag, the *Eyrathing*, in his recently founded city of Nidaros (Trondheim). The *Frostathing* and the *Eyrathing* came to have different functions, and the latter one became a *thing* for the hailing of new kings.[21] By the thirteenth century, the king instructed the peasants in *Trøndelag* to attend the assemblies at a new type of local *thing* at the *skipreiða* instead of going to the traditional and larger *things* of the *fylke*.[22] The history of the *thing* organization in Trøndelag thus illustrates how changes in power relations in a society could result in the foundation of new *things* and *thing* sites, in a way similar to that in the early phase in Sweden and in the prehistoric period in Northern Norway.

In western Norway, unlike in *Trøndelag*, a regional *thing* system was established by the king in a growing alliance with the peasant elite. The purpose was to keep the peace and initially also to tame the old costal aristocracy. In this region, the scene was at first dominated by an aristocracy who drew their power and wealth from control over some fertile areas, strategic sea routes, and

18 Lars F. Stenvik, 'Skei – et maktsenter fram fra skyggen', VITARK, 2 (Trondheim: Vitenskapmuseet, NTNU, 2001) 23–27, 66–70.

19 Merete Røskaft, *Maktens landskap. Sentralgårder i Trøndelag ca. 800–1200*, Skriftserie fra Historisk institutt, 39 (Trondheim: Norges teknisk-naturvitenskapelige universitet, 2003), 111.

20 Saga literature from the thirteenth century refers to the loyalty of the peasants to their chieftain *Einarr* before the middle of eleventh century (for example, Hkr, 472–74).

21 Per Sveaas Andersen and Knut Mykland, *Samlingen av Norge og kristningen av landet 800–1130* (Bergen: Universitetsforlaget, 1977), 58–62.

22 The *skipreiða* (from before about 1000 a unit that was to equip ships and crew) was turned into an administrative / legal unit for the entire kingdom in about 1200. The introduction to the *Frostathing Law* indicates that the *skipreiða thing* was a novel unit in Trøndelag (F I 23: *Frostatingsloven*, in Rudolf Keyser, P.A. Munch, Gustav Storm and Ebbe Hertzberg (eds), *Norges gamle Love indtil 1387* [hereafter NgL], 5 vols (Christiania: Chr. Grøndahl, 1846–95), i, 119–258, and *Frostatingslova*, trans. Jørn Sandnes and Jan Ragnar Hagland (Oslo: Det norske samlaget, 1994), both at I, 23). All references given relate to the number of the provision, e.g., F, I, 23, and thus can be found in any version of the law.

maritime trade. Some of them were lords over loosely organized territories with multiple estates, that is, manor-like centres.[23]

After about 900, King Harold established his realm in western Norway and installed his bailiffs at central manor-like farms. A regional *thing*, the *Gulathing*, was organized by the king, presumably before 930.[24] The *Gulathing* became a *thing* of representatives where a fixed number of selected peasants met at the regular assemblies. The *lendmaðr* (a descendant of the old chieftains, that is, with his own inherited land and additionally royal fiefs) and the *ármaðr* (bailiff / king's service man of low and partly unfree status) were to select the representatives (see G 3). Our main source for the organization of the *thing* is the *Gulathing Law* (G) in a preserved redaction from the 1160s with fragments of another version from the end of the eleventh century.[25] The linking of the local *thing* (*skipreiðaþing*) and the king's naval *leiðang* became crucial for the organization of both of them and also very important for a long-lasting alliance of interests between king and peasants, headed by the peasant elite.[26]

This alliance also aimed at keeping the local and regional nobility in check, as demonstrated by a regulation that forbids peasant freeholders at the *thing* from transferring their land under a *lendmaðr* for protection. This regulation can be seen as a legal protection of peasant family ownership (*óðal*) against

23 Cf. some assemblies in multiple estates, or manor-like systems, may be dated to the period before 900, for example, at the centre of the island of Åmøy. A court site for people gathering at the local *thing* is found on this island: Bjørn Myhre, 'Boathouses as Indicators of Political Organization', *Norwegian Archaeological Review*, 18 (1985), 37–60; Bjørn Myhre, 'Boathouses and Naval Organization', in Anne Nørgård Jørgensen and Birthe L. Clausen (eds), *Military Aspects of Scandinavian society in a European perspective*, AD *1–1300*, (Copenhagen: The National Museum, 1997), 169–83.

24 Year 930 is *terminus ante quem* for this institution, because the Icelandic *Althing* was organised around 930 after the model of the *Gulathing* (see, among others, Knut Helle, *Gulatinget og Gulatingslova* (Leikanger: Skald, 2001), 23–30).

25 Helle, *Gulatinget*, 20–23. The *Gulathing Law* is the oldest extant law in Scandinavia. For English translation: *The Older Law of the Gulathing*, in Laurence M. Larson (ed. and trans.), *The Earliest Norwegian Laws: Being the Gulathing Law and the Frostathing law*, Records of Civilization, 20 (New York: Columbia University Press, 1935), 35–213. For German translation: *Norwegisches Recht: Das Rechtsbuch des Gulathing*, ed. Rudolf Meissner, Germanenrechte 6, (Weimar: Böhlau, 1935). For Norwegian translations: *Gulatingsloven*, in NgL, i, 1–118, and *Gulatingslovi. Umsett frå gamalnorsk av Knut Robberstad*, trans Knut Robberstad, Norrøne bokverk 33, 3rd end (Oslo: Det norske samlaget, 1969). All references given relate to the number of the provision, e.g., G 3, and thus can be found in any version of the law.

26 Historians have calculated a fixed connection in the law between the numbers of peasant representatives to the *Gulathing* and the numbers of rowers on the *leiðang* ships (see Asgaut Steinnes, 'Kor gammal er den norske leidangsskipnaden?', *Syn og Segn*, 35 (1929), 49–65; Halvard Bjørkvik, 'Skipreide', in KLNM, xv, 546–51; Helle, *Gulatinget*, 32–33).

the local *lendmaðr*'s patronage.[27] The *Gulathing Law* furthermore states that if a *lendmaðr* misbehaves or neglects his duties as the king's man, his fine should be divided between the king and the collective body of the *thing* peasants (G71, 152, 253).

The law's curtailment of the power of the king's most important servant at the *thing*, the *ármaðr*, shows that there was a limit to the king's influence, too. Thus, the peasants at the *thing* had a legal right to react against the *ármaðr*'s abuse of power, and they were collectively entitled to receive the entire fine he was to pay for the abuse. The *thing* peasants, perceived as a collective body, also had a good deal of executive power in cooperation with the king's *ármaðr*.[28] On the other hand, this collective setting also included communal liability and punishment, for example, if quarrel and murder took place in alehouses. The people present were obliged to find the guilty parties. If not, they should collectively pay compensation to the victim's kinsmen and to the king.[29]

A good deal of the legal proceedings among the peasants themselves were settled through a presumably independent *dómr* arrangement.[30] The *dómr* was a panel of six or twelve members chosen by two parties for settlement or arbitration. In this way, the peasant elite played a crucial role in settling disputes in their local communities. Their sentences concerned only the compensations between the parties, not the fines to the king. The *dómr* also functioned as a real court of justice in the local society, first and foremost in cases concerning property in the broadest sense. A *dómr* sentence had to be respected by both parties; if not, the king's service man (the *ármaðr*) or the *thing* assembly

27 G 267. The prohibition on transferring land to a *lendmaðr* for protection is stated in a context where the topic at the *thing* concerns a relative of the actual peasant possessor who lays claim to the allodial right to the possessor's land (*leysa óðal*). The fact that G 267 is not repeated in the younger thirteenth-century laws could indicate that there was now less fear of transfer of peasant land to the local *lendmaðr*. This may have been a result of the change in the system of landowning in the direction of scattered land property systems from the twelfth century onwards, at the expense of manor-like systems, such as multiple estates.

28 G 35, 37, 77, 162. Required assistance from *thing* peasants also occurs also in later laws (F IV 10, L IV 9).

29 G 187, cf. 157; Alexandra Sanmark, 'The Communal Nature of the Judicial Systems in Early Medieval Norway', *Collegium Medievale*, 19 (2006), 31–64.

30 In G 37, both the *lendmaðr* and the king's *ármaðr* are forbidden to be present at the *dómr* in a dispute case. Still, the *dómr* meeting place seems to have been the same as that of the local *thing*.

would be involved. In the thirteenth century, the *dómr* came under stricter control of the king's men (see below).[31]

All in all, the *Gulathing Law* (G) demonstrate cooperation between the peasants at the *thing* and the king, and it expresses the wish of the king to preserve a harmonious relationship with the *thing* peasants, especially their elite. Furthermore, the law underlines the limits of the king's power. According to G, the peasants had a considerable degree of self-government and a certain degree of self-determination vis-á-vis the king.[32]

2.3 *The* Thing *in the Strong Kingdom of Norway*

The strengthening of royal power and the creation of a strong Norwegian state from about 1200 created a nobility in the service of the king. At the higher political-administrative level, the influence of *thing* assemblies was reduced, but they continued to play an important part on a local level. At this level, we can still observe some sort of peasant self-administration under the king's control. The civil war (1130–1224) was the crucial transformation period. In this period, a typical Norwegian land tenancy system based on dispersed farms gained ground at the expense of the former concentrated estates on the one hand, and smaller, new peasant landowners on the other (see chapter 'Leasehold and Freehold').[33] At the same time, the *lendmenn,* during their involvement in the internal fight between pretenders to the throne, changed from being regional headmen with their own power bases to members of a high-status group of men serving the king.

31 Eyvind Fjell Halvorsen, 'Dómr', in KLNM, iii, 214–18; Knut Helle, *Norge blir en stat: 1130–1319*, 2nd edn, Handbok i Norges historie, 3 (Oslo: Universitetsforlaget, 1974), 180–81; NgL, v, 134–46.

32 As background to the power concessions to the *thing* peasants, a different type of sources, the Kings' sagas from the thirteenth century, render several stories about conflicts of interest at the *thing* arena in the eleventh and twelfth centuries. The antagonists in these quite violent conflicts are kings and powerful representatives of the local and regional nobility. (*Heimskringla*, 472–74 and *Fagrskinna*, 261–63, *Morkinskinna*, 136–42, 170–74, 228–32). (Editions of the sagas: Hkr; English trans: Hollander, *History of the Kings of Norway*; *Ágrip af Nóregskonunga sögum. Fargskinna, Nóregs konunga tal*, ed. Bjarni Einarsson. Íslenzk fornrit, 29 (Reykjavík: Hið Íslenzka fornritafélag, 1985); *Morkinskinna*, ed. C.R. Unger (Christiania, 1867)).

33 Andreas Holmsen, 'Det norske "skyldeie"', in Jørn Sandnes, Arnfinn Kjelland, and Claus Krag (eds), *Norske historikere i utvalg*, v: *Nye middelalderstudier* (Oslo: Universitetsforlaget, 1981), 178–181, at p. 178; Tore Iversen, 'Property and Land Tenancy in Norwegian Medieval Laws and the European Learned Law', Ditlev Tamm and Helle Vogt (eds), in *How Nordic are the Nordic Medieval Laws?* (Copenhagen: University of Copenhagen Press, 2005), 135–76, at pp. 163–68.

At the level of the local *thing*, the king's new noble officials (*sýslumenn*) replaced both the old noble *lendmenn* and the partially unfree *ármenn.*[34] In contemporary sagas, peasants more clearly appear as a broad, but distinct social group, represented by the peasant elite.[35] This seems to conform to the development in the laws. While the *Gulathing Law* (G) and the *Frostathing Law* (F)[36] operate with many layers of free and half-free status above the slaves (thralls), King Magnus's *Law of the Realm* (1274) has omitted the regulations about slaves or half-free status (see chapter 'Slavery and Unfreedom').

In the thirteenth century, the kings aimed at turning the peasant assemblies into stricter legal institutions and, to a certain degree, also strengthening them on the local level. A novelty was the establishment of assemblies of the best men in the realm, an arrangement which reached its peak in the thirteenth century. These assemblies, which included representatives from the ecclesiastical and secular nobility as well as members of the peasant elite, took charge of the formal sanction of new kings and the approval of new laws. Even though they filled an important function in the strong thirteenth-century Norwegian kingdom, these assemblies were never formally institutionalized.[37]

The establishment of a panel of thirty-six men, the *lagrétta,* drawn from the peasant representatives at the regional *things*, was also part of the process aiming at making *thing* assemblies stricter legal institutions.[38] The reduction of

34 The *sýslumaðr* seems to combine the high status of the *lendmaðr* with the *ármaðr's* intimate bonds to the king (Helle, *Norge blir en stat*, 207); KLNM.

35 For Sverris saga: *Sverris saga. Böglunga sögur*, in Gudni Jónsson (ed.), *Konunga sögur II* (Reykjavík: Íslendingasagnaútgáfan, 1957), 32, 130–33, 152, 177, 304–18; for Böglunga sögur: *Böglunga sögur* in *Fornmanna sögur*, 10 (Copenhagen, 1835), 203–05. Concerning peasant leaders, see *Baglarsoger*, trans. Gunnar Pedersen, in Halvdan Koht, Gunnar Pedersen and Karl Jónsson (eds), *Kongesoger*, Den norrøne litteraturen, 4 (Oslo: Det norske samlaget, 1962), 201–86, at pp. 278–86.

36 A special feature in the *Frostathing Law*, representative of the period from the end of the twelfth century and most of the first part of the thirteenth, is the so-called resistance paragraphs (F IV 50–53), where the peasants generally are given the right to rise up against assaults from a king, earl, and *lendmaðr*. The F IV 50–53 paragraphs are not unique to Norway; they are also found, for example, in the *Sachsenspiegel* (Ldr.III 78 §2); see G. Dilcher, 'Widerstandsrecht', in Adalbert Erler, et al. (eds), *Handwörterbuch zur deutschen Rechtsgeschichte*, 5 vols (Berlin: Schmidt, 1964–1991), v, 1351–64; Th. Brückner, 'Widerstandsrecht', in LexMA, ix, 64–66.

37 Knut Helle, 'Riksmøter', in KLNM, xiv, 252–57; Knut Helle, *Konge og gode menn i norsk riksstyring ca. 1150–1319*. (Oslo: Universitetsforlaget, 1972), 247–54, 309; Helle, *Norge blir en stat*, 216–24.

38 Mentioned in the *Law of the Realm 1274*, in NgL, ii, 7–178, at i, 3 and 3. All references given relate to the number of the provision and thus can be found in any version of the law. There are some indications (F I 2) of an older age of the *lagrétta*; see Arne Bø, 'Lagting', in KLNM, x, 178–84; Helle, *Norge blir en stat*, 182–84.

the numbers of peasant representatives at the regional *things* (1274) and the king's efforts to make peasants attend the local *thing* instead of larger *things* (1260) could be seen in the same light.[39] A side effect of this policy was reinforced control of these institutions through royal officials, especially through the *lögmaðr* (lawman). This legally trained man was now appointed by the king. From the thirteenth century, the *lagrettemenn* (peasant representatives) were reduced to court witnesses when the king's lawman passed sentences at the regional *lagting* (law *thing*). His newly acquired ability to pass sentences made him an alternative to the local courts at the local assemblies. In cooperation with the *sýslumaðr*, the lawman also had power to censor local court decisions. Only the king himself could alter the lawman's decision. After 1300, an increasingly large source group, local charters from nearly all over the kingdom, gives descriptive insight into peasant assemblies and how they functioned locally.[40] These charters demonstrate above all the peasant communities' self-administration and cooperation with the king's men within the framework of local assemblies and ad hoc committees (*dómr*).

The middleman between the local peasantry and the authorities was the *lensmaðr*, a new office from the end of the thirteenth century, recruited from the local peasant elite.[41] In Norway, the local *thing* assemblies and ad hoc committees (*dómr*) were mostly concerned with judicial, administrative, and military matters. The purpose of the *thing* assemblies and the *dómr* was to keep the peace locally in a broad sense, including settling disputes, and they searched for consensus, not majority decisions. Ongoing agricultural tasks were not part of their agenda. This belonged to the sphere of the household. Another characteristic was that the nobility and the church did not enjoy any immunity at the local *thing* assemblies or in the *dómr* committees. In this regard, it still must be emphasized that the peasant assemblies and committees accepted inequality and subordination in their cooperation with external, high-standing men.[42]

In summing up concerning peasant assemblies until 1350, it can be argued that the development of the *thing* organization from the eleventh to the middle of the fourteenth century emphasizes the alliance between the growing

39 The number of the regional *things* was increased, though the numbers of peasant representatives were reduced, see Helle, *Norge blir en stat*, 182; Helle, *Konge og gode menn*, 93.

40 Steiner Imsen, *Norsk bondekommunalisme fra Magnus Lagabøte til Kristian Kvart*, i: *Middelalderen* (Trondheim: Tapir, 1990), 15–21, 41–119. Imsen has investigated about 600 charters from the period 1320–50. Most of the letters concern conflicts and aim at keeping the peace locally.

41 Imsen, *Norsk bondekommunalisme: Middelalderen*, 41–121, 193–203, esp. pp. 200, 210; Rolf Fladby, 'Lensmann', in KLNM, X, 505–06.

42 Reynolds, *Kingdoms and Communities*, 332.

power of the king and the peasant elite, beginning with the king organizing a new *thing* system before the middle of the eleventh century linked to the existing naval organization. This alliance also aimed at taming the power of the old coastal aristocracy. In the cooperation between the *thing* assembly and the king, some limits on the king's power vis-à-vis the *thing* assembly are demonstrated in the *Gulathing Law*. After 1200, political development reduced the influence of the peasants at a higher judicial level, through the undermining of the influence of peasant members of the *lagrétta*, and the lawman (*lögmaðr*) started to judge according to written law (F I 2). However, peasant cooperation and self-administration was strengthened on the local level, as documented from about 1300 onwards by the many local charters. The kings thus aimed at strengthening the local *thing* institutions at the same time as they aimed at controlling them through their royal officials and making them a part of the royal administration.

The king's attitude towards the peasants in the strong medieval Norwegian kingdom thus had a protective, paternalistic character, as he and his men could intervene if they thought it necessary. The change of attitude is reflected in the laws from the twelfth century onwards. The older *Gulathing Law* is concerned with the *thing* peasants' right to compensation for the *ármaðr*'s (the king's servant's) illegal behaviour, and they were even given the right to punish him physically.[43] The *Law of the Realm* (1274) and later amendments focus on the control of the peasants at the local *thing*s, correcting their potentially illegal decisions and actions through re-examination and censorship by the king's noble official, the *lögmaðr*. At the same time, the royal government aimed at creating a more uniform stratum of taxpaying peasant subjects. An aspect of this policy, emerging in the thirteenth century, was to make the unfree layers of peasant society legal subjects of the king (see chapter 'Slavery and Unfreedom').

2.4 *Norway – The Late Middle Ages and the Early Modern Period*

In 1380, Norway joined a union with Denmark that lasted until 1814.[44] Although, initially, this union was only based on a common king and Norway retained its

43 The partially unfree personal status of the *ármaðr* in the *Gulathing Law* is therefore not incidental (see Tore Iversen, *Trelldommen: norsk slaveri i middelalderen*, Universitetet i Bergen Skrifter, 1 (Bergen: Historisk institutt, 1997), 174–79; Tore Iversen, *Knechtschaft im mittelalterlichen Norwegen*, trans. Katharina Freche in collaboration with Angelika Landau, Münchener Universitätsschriften, Juristische Fakultät, Abhandlungen zur rechtswissenschaftlichen Grundlagenforschung, 94 (Ebelsbach: Aktiv, 2004), 286–308).

44 The following subchapter is a revised and abridged version of my article: John Ragnar Myking, 'Peasant Participation in Local Thing and Conflict Handling Institutions in

own laws and legal system, royal power and administration was gradually transferred to Copenhagen. What impact then did this union have on peasant participation at the local *thing* and other conflict-handling institutions? For a long time, Norwegian historians maintained that the distant Danish ruling power left local administration of conflicts more to the localities, thereby strengthening the local *thing* and the commissions.[45] Against this, the Norwegian historian Steinar Imsen maintains that the local *thing* and commissions already occupied a strong position before the Black Death, as well as in the mid-fifteenth century.

From the first half of the fifteenth century, the members of ad hoc committees (*dómr*) (see above) were increasingly *lagrettemenn*, sworn in by the *lagmann* to serve as co-witnesses at the *lagting*. Their main duty, however, seems to have been to serve in local commissions (*dómr*), dealing with a variety of cases.[46] These committees handled transactions of property, disputes over *odel* and boundaries between farms, inheritance and divisions of estates, and disputes about pastures and roads. They seldom issued any sentences regarding such conflicts. Instead, they set up witness letters in which witnesses from the neighbourhood stated how outfield resources and alpine pastures used to be distributed or how boundaries had been drawn from ancient times, thus aiming at a general consensus in the disputed case. The members of these ad hoc committees usually owned a seal of their own, a prerequisite for making the witness letters a legal charter. In the fifteenth and sixteenth centuries, such committees were institutionalized in a local *lagrett* where such men served.[47]

From 1590, the *lagrett* at the local *thing*, usually consisting of six *lagrettemenn*, became the court of first resort in a new hierarchic judicial system. At the local level, two new government officials came into existence, the *fut* (*fogd*) and the *sorenskrivar*, both serving on circuits consisting of several local *thing* districts. The *fut*, formerly the servant of the *lensherre*, became a royal *bailiff*, mainly handling prosecution and tax collection.[48] In 1591, the *sorenskrivar* (literally, a sworn-in writer) was appointed to help the *lagrette* at the local

Norway', in Tore Iversen, John Ragnar Myking and Gertrud Thoma (eds), *Bauern zwischen Herrschaft und Genossenschaft: Peasant Relations to Lords and Government. Scandinavia and the Alpine Region 1000–1750* (Trondheim: Tapir Akademisk Forlag, 2007), 187–203.

45 Imsen, *Norsk bondekommunalisme: Middelalderen*, 121–22, with references to works by Jens Arup Seip, Andreas Holmsen, and Ole Jørgen Benedictow.

46 Imsen *Norsk bondekommunalisme: Middelalderen*, 143, 146–48.

47 Myking, 'Peasant Participation', 187–203.

48 Rolf Fladby, *Fra lensmannstjener til Kongelig Majestets Foged* (Oslo: Universitetsforlaget, 1963).

thing.[49] The appointment of sworn-in writers was probably made in response to problems facing the *lagrettemenn* at the local *thing*. The *lagrette* was now obliged to render sentences at the *thing*, and they were made financially responsible for their verdicts. Danish language, which by then had replaced Old Norwegian in official writing, made writing more difficult for the peasant elite in the *lagrette*. This task was now delegated to the sworn-in writer.

From being a helper, and probably also an adviser, the *sorenskrivar* rapidly became a co-judge together with the *lagrette* from 1634. Following the new legislation in the *Norwegian Code of 1687*, he even became the sole judge in most cases, and the *lagrettemenn* were reduced to witnesses. There were, however, important exceptions to this new arrangement. The *lagrettemenn* still rendered verdicts together with the *sorenskrivar* in cases involving life, property, and honour, even after 1687.[50] The importance of these exceptions should not be underestimated. Life, property, and honour were some of the most important issues in peasant society.

What real influence did the *lagrettemenn* have then in the seventeenth and eighteenth centuries? As a rule, the verdict rendered at the *thing* was unanimous. However, sometimes (although not very often) the *lagrettemenn* intervened when they considered the *sorenskrivar's* verdict to be unjust or unreasonable.[51] The *lagrette* might even leave the *thing* to obstruct a verdict.[52] It should, however, be underlined that cases like these were rare. The *lagrettemenn* might obstruct a verdict at local level but they could not stand in the way of an appeal to a higher court. We may therefore suppose that in many cases they rather chose to influence the *sorenskrivar* and then join a unanimous verdict that they did not hugely disagree with. Their voices were still heard, however, as witnessed by occasional references to the fact that a judge had consulted the *lagrettemenn* before passing sentence. This was true, even after the majority of judges had received formal Danish juridical university education – introduced in 1736 – by the second half of the eighteenth century. In a few

49 'Sorenskriver', in Rolf Fladby, Steinar Imsen and Harald Winge (eds), *Norsk Historisk Leksikon* (Oslo: Cappelen, 1974), 312–15.

50 Ditlev Tamm, et al., 'The Law and the Judicial System', in Eva Österberg and Sølvi Bauge Sogner (eds), *People Meet the Law: Control and Conflict-handling in the Courts* (Oslo: Universitetsforlaget 2000), 27–56, at pp. 45–46.

51 John Ragnar Myking, *Herre over andre si jord? Norske leiglendingsvilkår i europeisk lys 1500–1800*, Studia Humanitatis Bergensia, 21 (Kristiansand: Høyskoleforlaget, 2005), 73–75; John Ragnar Myking, 'Lagrettemenn og bygdeelite ca. 1650–1750', *Heimen*, 33 (1996), 159–83, at p. 182.

52 Bergen State Archive, Sorenskrivaren i Nordhordland, tingbok 20, 1681, folio 24a.

cases, it is also evident that these laymen perceived the cases brought before the court in ways other than the *sorenskrivar* did.[53]

The more streamlined judicial system of the seventeenth and eighteenth centuries thus did not altogether do away with peasant influence. How important a part they played is evident from many local *thing* districts, when experienced *lagrettemenn* returned to the *lagrette* again and again, constituting a body of the 'best men' in the local community, even after this *ombud* (commission) was supposed to rotate among all peasants according to the *Norwegian Code of 1687*. Furthermore, when the government tried to introduce a mandatory school system and a new poor relief system in the mid-eighteenth century, government officials still called on the 'best men' in the local communities, men from well-known *lagrette* families to make foundations, create funds, and regulate taxation. Only in this way could they be sure that the rest of the peasant community would accept the outcome.[54]

Norwegian tenants were also allowed to use the legal system against their landlords. When landowners attempted to raise land-rent again after the dramatic reduction in the late Middle Ages,[55] the Danish-Norwegian state intervened, probably because the crown wanted to build up tenants as viable taxpayers. From 1539, well before the reorganization of the *thing* in 1590, all claims to raise the annual land-rent, the *landskyld*, had to be approved by a commission of six men.[56] This gave the local community, represented by the elite of *lagrettemenn*, the power to stall such claims.

Other disagreements between peasants and landlords regularly seem to have appeared before the local *thing*. These involved, among other cases, attempts by landlords to evict their tenants on grounds of failing to pay rents and fees or neglecting buildings or farmland. In these cases, the local *thing*

53 Jørn Øyrehagen Sunde, '"Fornuft og Erfarenhed". Framveksten av metodisk medvit i dansknorsk rett på 1700-talet', Dr. juris. dissertation, University of Bergen, Bergen, 2006, 269–89.

54 Myking, 'Lagrettemenn', 159–83. John Ragnar Myking, 'Førebuing til 1814? Bøndene si deltaking i formelle lokale institusjonar før 1814', in Anne Hilde Nagel and Ståle Dyrvik (eds), *Folkestyre? Kritisk lys på 1814-demokratiet* (Bergen: Bodoni forlag, 2014), 13–22.

55 By the early sixteenth century, land-rent in Norway was reduced to between one-fourth and one-fifth of the usual value prior to the mid-fourteenth century; see Helge Salvesen and Jørn Sandnes, *Ødegårdstid i Norge. Det nordiske ødegårdsprosjekts norske undersøkelser* (Oslo: Universitetsforlaget, 1978), pp. 109–41.

56 Truid Ulfstands and Claus Billes recess 24 June 1539 Oslo, 20.08 Bergen (paragraph 9), later accentuated in *rettartingsrecess* 18 January 1557 Bergen (paragraph 5), Jørgen Lykkes, Bjørn Andersøns and Kristoffer Valkendorfs recess 13 March 1568 Bergen and 04 April 1568 Trondheim (paragraph 19).

generally ruled in accordance with the law, which gave tenants a high degree of security of tenure (see chapter 'Leasehold and Freehold').[57]

The *thing* could also handle conflicts between local communities and the crown. The congregation at the *thing* was not expected to comment on royal decrees and tax regulations that were announced there. In some cases, however, the local *thing* might have become a forum for negotiations between the crown and the peasant community concerning the application of decrees and regulations. Such negotiations may have been especially frequent at the beginning of the seventeenth century.[58] However, examples are not confined to the seventeenth century. When a heavy tax was levied to fund the crown's expenses in the Great Nordic War at the beginning of the eighteenth century, payment was obstructed in many regions of Norway. In Nordhordland, near Bergen, in 1713 peasants at every one of the eleven local autumn *things* refused to even serve on the twelve-man commissions appointed to levy the tax locally.[59] In periods with lower levels of confrontation, however, such commissions could be implemented more easily to resolve problems.[60]

Along with complaints and even peasant rebellions, the largest and best known being the regional risings of 1765 and 1786–87 against taxes and abuses by royal officials, such occurrences may be interpreted as an ongoing discourse between the crown and its subjects. This discourse can be traced from the Middle Ages to the end of the early modern period, and it changed continually in character and intensity.[61] Sometimes the *thing* might have been used as an

57 Myking, *Herre over andre si jord?*, 113–22.

58 Some cases in the oldest preserved *thing* protocols from the early seventeenth century point in this direction, for example, when the crown requested a new fleet of small naval vessels to be built and manned in 1618. A regional *thing* in Ryfylke then demanded two weeks to present their written response to this claim, and taxes to fund the fleet were obstructed. See Steinar Imsen, *Norsk bondekommunalisme fra Magnus Lagabøte til Kristian Kvart*, ii: *Lydriketiden*, Skriftserie fra Historisk institutt, 7 (Trondheim: Tapir forlag, 1994), 151–53.

59 Bergen State Archive, *thing* protocol for Nordhordland No. 33, 1712–15, folios 67a, 68b, 70b, 71a-b, 72b, 74a, 75b, 76b, 77a-b, 79b, 80a.

60 In 1755, the decision of a twelve-man commission of *lagrettemenn*, concerning the organization of transport for government officials, was published at a local *thing* near Bergen. This was in response to many years of peasant complaints. The basis for the plan seems to have been laid by the members of the commissions, but only after they had secured the advice of the *fut* (regional bailiff). (Atle Døssland, *Strilesoga. Nord- og Midhordland gjennom tidene*, iii: *Frå 1650 til 1800* (Bergen: Eide, 1998), 89).

61 For a general introduction to peasant resistance in Scandinavia, see: Kimmo Katjala, *Northern Revolts: Medieval and Early Modern Peasant Unrest in the Nordic Countries*, Studia Fennica, Historica, 8 (Helsinki: Finnish Literature Society, 2004). And especially on Norway: Magne Njåstad, 'Resistance in the Name of the Law', in Kimmo Katjala, *Northern*

arena for such discourse, sometimes confrontations and negotiations were conducted outside this institution.

The majority of cases at the local early modern *thing* only involved members of the local communities. Some were criminal cases initiated by the *fut* or the local *lensmann*, but peasants and their family members, including women, often saw fit to elevate conflicts involving honour, violence, and even theft into the public sphere. Only in this way could they cleanse their good names and reputations and regain their positions in local society.[62]

2.5 *Solving Conflicts over Boundaries and Resources*

In the Norwegian infield – outfield form of agriculture, which was also found in large parts of Sweden, the use of resources was a prominent source of conflict within local communities. Boundaries between farms were quite often fixed before the Middle Ages, as was the use of many alpine pastures. Still, conflicts over boundaries between farms and disputes over the right to use forests and pastures were frequent. To prevent grazing cattle from ruining the harvest, adequate fencing between meadows and fields on the one hand, and pastures on the other, were of utmost importance, and negligence furthered conflicts between neighbours.

Thus, the *Law of the Realm of 1274* instructed neighbours on farms with two or more holdings to hold a meeting, a *Grannestemne*, in the midst of May to approve the work done on fences that could keep cattle from grazing on the infields from the beginning of May until the middle of October. This clause was repeated in the next comprehensive Norwegian legislative codes from 1604 and 1687.[63] Meadows and fields were not enclosed, and fields and meadows were increasingly divided among households belonging to each farm, especially along the Norwegian coast. As in the village districts on the Continent, this further increased cooperation between neighbours. Along the Norwegian coast, some of the large nucleated settlements approaching the size of villages are even known to have developed informal institutions resembling the village

Revolts: Medieval and Early Modern Peasant Unrest in the Nordic Countries, Studia Fennica, Historica, 8 (Helsinki: Finnish Literature Society, 2004), 90–117.

62 An introduction to the functioning of the local *thing* in early modern Scandinavia and the cases raised there can be found in Eva Österberg and Sølvi Bauge Sogner (eds), *People Meet the Law: Control and Conflict-handling in the Courts* (Oslo: Universitetsforlaget 2000).

63 The *Law of the Realm 1274*, in NgL, vol. ii, at vii, ch. 30; King Christian IV, *Kong Christian den Fjerdes norske Lovbog af 1604*, ed. and trans. Frederik Hallager and Frederik Peter Brandt (Christiania: Feilberg and Landmark, 1855; repr. Oslo: Norsk historisk kjeldeskrift-institutt, Den rettshistoriske kommisjon, 1981), vi, ch. 28; King Christian V, *Christian V's Norske Lov 1687*, ed. Otto Mejlænder (Christiania: P.T. Malling, 1883; repr. 1892), 3-12-17.

assemblies of Denmark and Sweden in the early modern period (see below), but without the formal *by* laws found in these countries.[64]

Some of the conflicts between peasants on the same farm or between neighbouring farms were solved by informal agreements. If amicable settlements could not be reached, peasants were left with two options. Until the beginning of the early modern period, they could try their case before a commission (*dómr*) or reach for a verdict at the local *thing* (see above). From the seventeenth century, such cases were still dealt with out of court as a rule, in special commissions, although proofs, witnesses, agreements, or verdicts were later incorporated into the official *thing* protocol.

Even in the seventeenth and eighteenth century, such on-the-spot cases (*åstadsaker*) had much the same appearance as similar cases at the end of the High Middle Ages. Usually six or more men were appointed to an *åstadrett*, resembling the medieval six-men commissions (see above). During the early modern period, however, procedures were more strongly supported by the legal bureaucracy. Members of the commission, in most cases described as sworn-in *lagrettemenn*, were appointed by the *fut*, not by the parties involved. They no longer had to describe their decisions in writing themselves or make the outcome public by using their seals. In the early modern period, this was left to the *sorenskrivar*, who entered the proceedings into his *thing* protocol. Still, the decisions made by the commission were entirely made by the members of the committee themselves.

In the case of tenant farms, it seems that disputes over borders and grazing rights were advanced mostly by tenants, not by landlords. The tenants were the only ones who knew how resources were usually divided and used, by which stream or valley the border was to be drawn, or how many cows the holding should be allowed to keep on the pastures in summer. They also had a strong interest in securing these resources for their own use.

Drawing and securing borders was a serious business. Even when appointing new *lagrettemenn* had become common practice each year a few decades into the eighteenth century, there still seems to have been a core of *lagrettemenn* serving in such cases out in the field year after year. They had the experience – and the necessary authority – that randomly appointed men

64 Bjørg Seland, *Gardtinget. En norsk landsbyorganisasjon*, ADH-serien, 75 (Kristiansand: Agder distriktshøgskole, 1994). For a comparison between conflict-handling institutions in Norway and the rest of Scandinavia, see John Ragnar Myking and Carsten Porskog Rasmussen, 'Scandinavia, 1000–1750', in Bas J.P. van Bavel and Richard W. Hoyle (eds), *Social Relations: Property and Power*, Rural Economy and Society in North-Western Europe, 500–200, 1 (Turnhout: Brepols, 2010), 287–314, at pp. 302–05.

did not have. The local community could not have managed without their service.[65]

2.6 *Norway after 1350 – Summing Up*

How then may we sum up the characteristics of Norwegian peasant participation at *thing* or other conflict-handling institutions at the local level from the medieval to the early modern period? On the one hand, there were no legal institutions controlled by landlords in Norway, except for a few estates being granted the right to appoint judges (*birkerett*) at the end of the sixteenth century. These courts, nevertheless, had to operate according to the national law, having no statues or customs of the manor of their own, unlike the German *Weistümer* or *Hofrechte*, or the customary law at the Danish *birketings* (see below).[66] The dominant institutions in the Norwegian legal system at the local level from the Middle Ages until the end of the early modern period were the *thing* and the commissions. On the whole, the dualism of local peasant participation in these institutions and the legal framework provided by the state and administered by crown officials seems to have served the interests of the state and the peasant community, from the High Middle Ages to the end of the early modern period, although the system underwent changes over time.

Peasant participation, to some degree delegated to representatives of a local elite, seems to have been strong and continuous, even when the Danish-Norwegian state restricted lay influence in the seventeenth century, allowing the *sorenskrivar* to pass most sentences alone. From the end of the seventeenth century, peasants, represented at the local *thing* by *lagrettemenn*, were reduced to court witnesses, except in cases involving life, property, and honour. As such matters were some of the most important ones to the local communities, peasants still had considerable influence in local courts. This was especially true when it came to conflicts regarding boundaries and the use of resources, which frequently seem to have been handled in special *åstad* commissions. In such cases, peasants, by virtue of their local knowledge, were still in full control,

---

65 Aud Mikkelsen Tretvik, '"… med mig tiltagne 2de edsvorne Lagrettemænd…". Om bønders deltakelse i lokalforvaltningen på 1700-tallet', *Heimen*, 33 (1996), 189–200, at 198–200.

66 For references to *Hofrechte* and *Weistümer*, see articles by Rösener ('Bauern zwischen Herrschaft und Genossenschaft') and Gertrud Thoma ('Klosterbauern zwischen Herrschaft und Genossenschaft – Die Hofmarkordnung von Seebruck auf dem Hintergrund der Gemeindeentwicklung in Bayern im Spätmittelalter'), in Tore Iversen, John Ragnar Myking and Gertrud Thoma (eds), *Bauern zwischen Herrschaft und Genossenschaft: Peasant Relations to Lords and Government. Scandinavia and the Alpine Region 1000–1750* (Trondheim: Tapir Akademisk Forlag, 2007).

leaving the *sorenskrivar* to be the administrator and writer he was originally intended to be.

Thus, there was an important peasant influence from the High Middle Ages to the end of the early modern period in matters most important to the peasant community, an influence that in many cases was delegated to a peasant elite.

2.7 Thing *Organization in Denmark – The Medieval Period*

In a Scandinavian setting, Denmark may be used to contrast the Norwegian development. While in Norway the positions over time steadily developed in favour of the king, in Denmark positions and conflicts between the king and a strong aristocracy had a more variable and recurrent character. Peasants at the *thing* in Denmark did not play a central role in the predominant conflict between the king and the nobility.

Although Danish historians consider the *thing* institution to be of considerable age and of great importance to peasant society, the early development of this institution has been little discussed. Presumably, one of the reasons for this has been the long-lived high standing of the Germanistic doctrine, with its focus on a free and to a certain degree egalitarian peasantry.[67] In Denmark, as in the rest of Scandinavia, the discussion has recently shifted to emphasizing the hierarchical character of Viking society and to highlighting the significance of rural lordship for social power.[68] As we have seen in the Norwegian discussion, this newly acquired understanding must have consequences for the interpretation of the influence peasants may have had at the *thing*.[69]

Two types of *thing* assemblies are frequently recorded in medieval sources, the local *herredsting* (county *thing*) and the regional *landsting* (regional *thing*). In between these two, a *sysselting* (*thing* for a smaller region) is also mentioned

67 Cf. Aksel E. Christensen, in Inge Skovgaard-Petersen, Aksel E. Christensen and Helge Paludan (eds), *Danmarks historie*, v, part 1, (Copenhagen: Gyldendal, 1977), 102–03, 106–08; Aksel E. Christensen, *Ret og magt i dansk middelalder: forelæsinger* (Copenhagen: Gyldendal, 1978), passim. According to Aksel E. Christensen, there was no exploitative class in the Viking period and few slaves. The nobility first gained significance from the eleventh century onwards. Some of the Norwegian historian Andreas Holmsen's points of view and arguments are similar; see Andreas Holmsen, *Norges historie fra de eldste tider til 1660*, 3rd edn (Oslo: Universitetsforlaget, 1961).

68 Bjørn Poulsen and Søren Michael Sindbæk (eds), *Settlement and Lordship in Viking and Early Medieval Scandinavia* (Turnhout: Brepols, 2011), 1–28.

69 Lars Jørgensen, 'Manor, Cult and Markets at Lake Tissø', in Stefan Brink and Neil Price (eds), *The Viking World* (London: Routledge, 2008), 77–82. Archaeological material from large manors excavated at Tissø dated to the Viking Age could indicate periodic gathering of people in assembly meetings.

in Jutland.[70] Because the *herred* unities comprised the smaller and much more regular *skiben* units of the naval *leding*, historians formerly believed them to have a military origin, dating back to the Viking period.[71] The *sysselting* was held to be an even older organization. The regional provinces *land* and *landskab* and the institution of the *landsting* were considered to originate far back in time, since they were assumed to be remnants of old tribal provinces in Denmark, in spite of the fact that the names of provinces and their *things* were first mentioned in sources from the eleventh and twelfth centuries.[72]

Danish historians now seem to have left the dating of the three types of *thing* to an obscure past in favor of dating them as political institutions in a historical setting. Per Andersen has argued for a dating of the secular *sysselting* outside northern Jutland as late as the end of the twelfth century.[73] Regarding the entity of *herred* and the institution of the *herredsting*, it is now generally recognized that they were probably introduced in the eleventh century on the initiative of the king.[74] The connection between the *herredsting* and the smaller sea military *skiben* units remains uncertain.[75] The word for the naval military organization '*leding*' turns up in the twelfth century in Denmark. Niels Lund has proposed a theory claiming that the earliest naval military organization was organized by local chieftains and their warrior retinues and placed at the king's disposal. Not until the Danish regional laws, the oldest dating back to the end of the twelfth century, does the organization of the naval military *leding* appear as an arrangement between the kings and the peasants.[76]

70 Troels Dahlerup, 'Syssel', in KLNM, xvii, 649–50.

71 Poul Rasmussen, 'Herred', in KLNM, vi, 488–91; Svend Aakjær, 'Om det olddanske Herred og Sogn', in P. Nørlund (ed.), *Festskrift til Kristian Erslev: den 28. Decbr. 1927 fra danske historikere* (Copenhagen: H. Hagerups boghandel, 1927), 1–30.

72 Herluf Nielsen, 'Landskap', in KLNM, x, 235–36.

73 Per Andersen, *Rex imperator in regno suo, Dansk Kongemagt og rigslovgivning i 1200-tallets Europa* (Odense: Syddansk universitetsforlag, 2005), p.73f.

74 The *herred* is first mentioned in St Knud's *Gavebrev 1086*. Complete division of the kingdom into *herred* is known from King Valdemar's cadastre from 1231. See Kaj Hørby, 'Middelalderen', in *Samfundet i vikingetid og middelalder 800–1500*, Dansk social historie, 2 (Copenhagen: Gyldendal, 1980), 77–314; Anders Andrén, 'Städer och kungemakt – en studie i Danmarks politiske geografi före 1230', *Scandia*, 49/1 (1983), 31–76.

75 Cf. Jens Ulf Jørgensen, 'Herred', in Jørn Lund (ed.), *Den store danske encyklopædi* (Copenhagen: Danmarks Nationalleksikon, 1994–2002), vol. 8. Concerning the military origin of the local *thing*, see the Norwegian discussion mentioned above. See also Niels Lund, *Lið, leding og landeværn, Hær og samfund i Danmark i ældre middelalder* (Roskilde: Vikingeskibshallen, 1996), 295.

76 Lund, *Lið, leding og landeværn*, 1–26, 245–301. According to Lund, the sea military alliance between the king and peasants should have an older dating in Norway than in Denmark; see above, under west Norway.

In the period of the Danish provincial laws, from the end of the twelfth and into the thirteenth century, the sources offer more detailed information about social groups connected to the different types of *things*. Although there was no clear hierarchy between them, except for some serious crimes, the *landsting* had greater authority because more prominent men were present there.[77] Those attending such *things* were local or regional aristocrats, members of the peasant elite, and ordinary peasants. The aristocrats, although at this time not a homogeneous group, had great economic, political, and social power. They often possessed manor-like estates and could own an abundance of farms. From the beginning of the thirteenth century, they were the backbone of the king's civil and military organization, especially in his standing army. To be a peasant (*bonde*) in connection with the *thing* meant to be a freeholder who owned enough property to be able to pay a fine of three marks. At the *thing*, tenants (*landbo, coloni*) and bailiffs (*bryti, villici*) were under the guardianship of their landlord in cases related to their rented land. In personal matters they had, nevertheless, full legal capacity, even though they were clients in client-patron relationships with landowners and owed fidelity in return for protection. Increasingly, some of the king's privileges were furthermore transferred to the landlords, among them the right to collect fines from their peasants and to keep some of these themselves.[78]

By the middle of the thirteenth century, there were three, partly overlapping jurisdictions in the Danish kingdom: that of the *thing* (*herredsting* and *landsting*), that of the king, and that of the church. Due to solidarity among noble families, their local power, and the evolution of a more formal way of treating evidence, the secular nobility enjoyed a higher standing in the *thing* system.[79] The king, on his part, developed his own courts, the king's *retterting,* from the end of the thirteenth century. These courts functioned independently and in competition with the local and regional *herredsting* and *landsting*, and judges were dispatched to every part of the country on the king's behalf. This became an effective way of bringing cases to court and carrying out the sentences, and

77 Per Andersen, *Studier i dansk processhistorie. Tiden indtil Danske Lov 1683* (Copenhagen: Jurist- og Økonomforbundets forlag, 2010), 14–18.

78 Jeppe Büchert Netterstrøm, *At forsvare til rette. Værnsforholdet og bøndernes retslige stilling i Danmarks senmiddelalder 1400–1513* (Århus: Landbohistorisk selskab, 2003), 87–125; Per Andersen, *Studier i dansk processhistorie*, 18–20; Thomas Riis, 'Villici og coloni indtil 1340. Et forsøk på en begrepsanalyse', in Svend Gissel (ed.), *Landbrugshistoriske studier tilegnede Fridlev Skrubbeltrang på halvfjerdsårsdagen,* Landbohistorisk Selskab, 4 (Copenhagen, 1970), 1–20.

79 Anders Bøgh, 'Magten i middelalderen. En skitse af statsmagtens etablering og udviklingen af dommer-funksjoner', in *Individ, slægt og magt i dansk middelalder,* Den Jyske historiker, 42 (Aarhus: Aarhus Universitetsforlag, 1987); Riis, 'Villici og coloni'.

the arrangement was thus institutionalized. As the king's courts were founded on the revived understanding of the king's higher sovereignty and judicial power, no assembly of peasants or nobility was needed. The nobles strongly opposed this expansion of the king's power and were able to enforce written promises from new kings (*håndfæstninger*) to secure their judicial position in the period before the royal power temporally collapsed in 1320.[80]

Another institution organized by the king was the *birk*, an ancient, separate area of jurisdiction, especially for towns and marketplaces under the king's protection.[81] In Denmark, *birk* areas also comprised a great number of the king's manors from the beginning, which gave peasants on these manors extra royal protection. The *birker* had their own *things*. A central feature of this institution was that those belonging to a *birk* had the right to be summoned only there, not at the *herredsting*. Clerical *birker* were almost as old as those of the king, and some monasteries received the privilege to hold them in the thirteenth century. Some *birker* belonging to the nobility date back to the late medieval period, but the great majority of the noble *birker* were established as late as the sixteenth century.[82]

2.8 *The Late Middle Ages and the Early Modern Period*

The *thing* system evolving in the High Middle Ages continued into the late Middle Ages and the early modern period, although it underwent significant changes. While the king's *retterting* in the Middle Ages primarily dealt with cases concerning property, from 1536/37 it turned into a superior court in a new appeal system. Cases from the *herredsting* and the *birketing* could now be appealed to the *landsting* and finally to the king's *rettarting*, although the *retterting* remained the first port of call for every case pertaining to the life and honour of the aristocracy.[83] From 1660, it was replaced by the *Høyesteret* as the superior court.

80 Henrik Lerdam, *Kongen og tinget. Det senmiddelalderlige retsvæsen 1340–1448* (Copenhagen: Museum Tusculanums Forlag, 2001), 9–21, 257–62; Lars Hamre, 'Rettarting', in KLNM, xiv, 101–08; Herlof Nielsen, 'Justitiar', in KLNM, viii, 47–49.

81 The notion of *birk* has been mush discussed, but the term cannot explain the origin of the institution. The most likely explanation of the word, which always appears in the folk language, is that it has similarity with the Icelandic *bjarga*, meaning an enclosed peace protected area (see next fn).

82 Henrik Lerdam, *Birk Lov og Ret. Birkeretens historie i Danmark indtil 1600*, (Copenhagen: Museum Tusculanums Forlag, 2004), 10–23, 93–98, and passim; Poul Meyer, 'Landbirker', in KLNM, i, 659–61.

83 Michael Nobel Jakobsen, 'Det verdslige juridiske system før 1660' (edited 28 May 2014), in *Danmarkshistoriken.dk* http://danmarkshistorien.dk/leksikon-og-kilder/vis/materiale/det-verdslige-juridiske-system-foer-1660/, last accessed 01 August 2016.

The Reformation in Denmark in 1536 saw the transition of the former Catholic Church into a Protestant state church. In the wake of this upheaval, some of the former ecclesiastical *birketing* were merged with existing royal *birketings*, while others were transferred to members of the aristocracy.[84] Although a few aristocratic *birketings* were founded in the fifteenth century, the decades following the Reformation saw a marked increase in such institutions in Denmark. A major increase in aristocratic *birketings* followed in the seventeenth century. To obtain such privileges, aristocratic landowners had to reallocate their scattered possession, a transformation which coincided with the shift from a primarily *Rentengrundherrschaft* based on income from tenants peasants, to a combined *Gutherrschaft* based partly on demesne land worked by tenants rendering corvée labour, and partly on rents from tenants.[85]

In the medieval period, committees (Norw: *dómr / nemnd*, Sw: *nämnd*, Dan: *nævn*) were appointed to resolve differences and pass verdicts at or outside the *thing* in all Scandinavian countries (see sections on Norway, above).[86] In Denmark, many of the medieval permanent or ad hoc committees known from the regional laws gradually lost their authority to pass judgement. From the fifteenth century, this capacity was instead transferred to a *foged* (bailiff), who, at first, was introduced as a leader of the *thing* and who, in time, also became a co-judge. In the sixteenth century, the *herredsfoged* became the only judge. According to the *Danish Code of 1683*, the judge (*herredsfoged / birkefoged*) should pass sentences alone in all cases, except homicide and witchcraft.[87] Except for the *foged*, who for a long time was recruited from the peasant elite (see below), the influence of common peasants was thus increasingly reduced at the *herredsting* as well as the *birketing*. Still, a certain number of men (*stokkemænd*) should witness the proceedings, and from the mid-sixteenth century, the *herredsfoged* had to take co-judges (*sandemænd*) in cases that could involve the death penalty. In cases of theft, men appointed by the assembly (*rannævinger*) should decide if the accused party was guilty, even as late as the sixteenth and seventeenth century.[88]

The *foged* at a *herredsting* was appointed by the king, at a *birketing* by the person or institution the *birketing* privilege belonged to. Until 1660, the *foged* at a *herredsting* and at a *retterting* was usually appointed from among one of

84 Lerdam, *Birk Lov og Ret*, 56.
85 Lerdam, *Birk Lov og Ret*, 58–61.
86 Articles on 'Dómr', 'Næmd', 'Ting', and 'Herredsting' in KLNM.
87 Jakobsen, 'Det verdslige juridiske system'; P.J. Jørgensen, 'Herredsfoged', in Isac Salmonsen, *Salmonsens Konversationsleksikon*, 11, ed. Christian Blangstrup (Copenhagen: Schultz, 1921); Tamm, et al., 'The Law and the Judicial System', 40–41.
88 Jakobsen, 'Det verdslige juridiske system'.

the peasants belonging to the *thing*.[89] Later, the office of *herredsfoged* could be given to anyone who the government found had a suitable knowledge of law. This person was then given a farm to live on. After judicial education was introduced at the University of Copenhagen in 1736, the *herredfoged* were increasingly drawn from the juridical ranks.[90]

The proceedings at the *herredsting* and the king's *retterting* were based on regional and later on national laws, whereas proceedings at the ecclesiastical and aristocratic *retterting*, when a national *birkerett* was codified, were based on customary law until 1623.[91]

An important aspect of the Danish judicial system was the aristocracy's '*hals- og håndsret*', that is, their privilege to impeach their tenants at the *herredsting* or their own *retterting* and to carry out the verdicts or cash in the penalties of their tenants' sentences. Some individual aristocrats obtained such privileges by the fifteenth century, and these privileges were extended to the whole aristocracy by 1536.[92] On the other hand, the *birkerett* (the right to separate courts of justice and the right to appoint judges at these courts) were only given to aristocratic landlords with large estates.[93] These combined rights gave landlords additional influence over their peasants, not so much in the concrete verdicts as in their ability to reduce penalties and thus show a degree of mercy that strengthened peasants' bonds to their lordships.[94]

In summing up *thing* organization in Denmark, it can be said that, while Danish historians used to be preoccupied with dating the institution of the *thing* back to a distant past, recently they have been inclined to see the *thing* system in light of political evolution in a fixed historical period. Thus, the *herredsting* is now believed to have been introduced in the eleventh century on the initiative of the king. The strong position of the nobility in Denmark in the thirteenth century resulted in a partially overlapping jurisdiction. The nobility came to hold a stronger standing in the *thing* system (*herredsting* and *landsting*) where landlords had control over their peasants, especially the tenants.

89 Lerdam, *Birk Lov og Ret*, 77; Tamm, et al., 'The Law and the Judicial System', 40.

90 Jakobsen, 'Det verdslige juridiske system', Jørgensen, 'Herredsfoged'.

91 Lerdam, *Birk Lov og Ret*, 80.

92 Jeppe Büchert Netterstrøm and Michael Nobel Jakobsen, 'Hals og håndsret 1400–1660', in *Danmarkshistorien.dk*, http://danmarkshistorien.dk/leksikon-og-kilder/vis/materiale/hals-og-haandsret-1400-1660/?no_cache=1, last edited 06.072012, last accessed 03 August 2016.

93 Dorte Kook Lyngholm, *Godsejerens ret. Adelens retshåndhævelse i 1700-tallet – lov og praksis ved Clausholm birkeret* (Auning: Dansk Center for Herregårdsforskning og Landbohistorisk Selskab, 2013), 14–15.

94 Lyngholm, *Godsejerens ret*, 252–53.

The king's *retterting*, usually without peasant representatives, competed with the *thing* system dominated by the aristocracy. The king also organized *birker* areas under his special protection with their own *thing* assemblies. The standing of the different *thing* assemblies seems to have been diffuse in the high and late medieval periods due to the ongoing struggle between the king and the nobility, and, in contrast to Norway, there is no trace of a general alliance between the *thing* peasants and the king.

From the late medieval to the early modern period, corresponding with growing royal power, a hierarchical judicial system developed in which cases from the *herredsting* and the *birketing* could be appealed to a higher court. Nevertheless, the aristocracy retained a strong hold over their tenants through their 'hals- og håndsret', their privilege to impeach their tenants, and carry out the verdicts or collect the penalties. An increasing number of aristocratic landlords were also allowed to establish their own *birketings* for their tenants. Peasant influence at the *herredstings* and at the *birketings* was gradually reduced in favour of appointed judges, although, from the end of the seventeenth century, peasants were still appointed assessors in cases related to life or witchcraft. After customary law had been replaced by national law at the *birketings* by the early seventeenth century, proceedings at all *things* were based on national law.

2.9 *Denmark – Village Organization*

In pre-medieval Denmark and parts of Sweden, settlements were relocated within the village area from time to time. Due to demographic growth and a subsequent growing emphasis on arable farming in an open field system, most Danish villages stabilized into permanent settlements by the eleventh and twelfth centuries.[95] Each villager had common right to the fields, and the provincial laws from the thirteenth and fourteenth centuries also considered commons, woodland, and other waste as common land. As in the eastern Alpine region, this necessitated some sort of collective organization to deal with the rotation of crops, the reaping of harvests, and the enclosure of fields, as well as grazing and other use of outfield resources. Nevertheless, little is known about the actual communal organization of these medieval villages. Provincial laws from the thirteenth century describe a village meeting (*gadestævne*) where minor controversies between villagers could be settled, and the statute of Funen from 1492 decreed that decisions made at a village meeting should not be

95 Poulsen and Sindbæk (eds), *Settlement and Lordship*, 6–7. Nils Hybel and Bjørn Poulsen, *The Danish Resources c. 1000–1550: Growth and Recession*, The Northern World, 34 (Leiden: Brill, 2007), 146–54.

violated by members of the community.[96] Thus, some sort of village organization must have already existed in the Middle Ages.

A more detailed picture of the communal organization of Danish villages can be constructed from village statutes, the *by-laws*, the oldest extant ones dating back to the sixteenth century. Village meetings were usually held at fixed intervals, frequently on Sundays, or summoned at the request of village officials.[97] The head of every peasant household, including widows, had the right and duty to attend these meetings. Other women could appear if their husband was not able to. In many villages, cotters also had the right to attend, but they had no say in decisions made at the village meeting.[98]

The village meeting appointed an *oldermand*, usually for one year at the time. In most villages, this commission circulated among the heads of the peasant households, but he could also be elected or, in exceptional cases, appointed by the manorial lord. The *oldermand* had many responsibilities. He was to see to that his fellow villagers observed the obligations laid down in the village *by-laws* and that sentences were passed according to it. He was also responsible for the economic affairs of the village, including fines for violating the village statutes or other regulations set down at the village meeting. He also represented the village in legal conflicts or in negotiations with other villages, and he was a spokesman for the village in relation to their manorial lord. In addition to the *oldermand*, the attendees of the village meeting also hired a shepherd and appointed men to oversee the building and preservation of hedges.[99]

The attendees of the village meeting, or men appointed at the village meeting, were given the right to fix the time for tilling, sowing, and harvesting. Village statutes or decisions taken at the village meeting regulated fencing and herding and often also fixed the number of cattle that each peasant household or cotters were permitted to graze on the commons and the fallow. In short, village statutes and other decisions made at the village meeting aimed at securing a smooth exploitation of common resources and preventing conflicts between the households inhabiting the village.[100] Some statutes also contained clauses aimed at some sort of social security within the village, like

96 Poulsen and Hybel, *Danish Resources*, 144–46.

97 Poul Meyer, *Danske bylag* (Copenhagen: Nyt nordisk forlag, 1949), 100–04.

98 Meyer, *Danske bylag*, 93–95.

99 Meyer, *Danske bylag*, 106–20.

100 Meyer, *Danske bylag*, 124–77.

providing help to neighbours who had been taken ill or who had lost their draught animals.[101]

When statutes were adopted by a majority of the peasant households, every head of such households had to consent to the content of the statutes by signing or putting his seal to the statute. The village statutes were then automatically also binding for any newly arrived household.[102] Fines to the village community were often fixed in barrels of beer, which the villagers could then assemble to drink, a form of fine which strengthened the bonds between villagers at the same time as adequately warning the culprit of the consequences of breaking the norms laid down in the village statutes.

At first, most village statutes were adopted by the village assembly without any form of approval from any other authority, including the manorial lord, even though fines in some cases were divided between the village community and the manorial lord. However, during the seventeenth century, this changed. Now statutes, or changes to statutes, were usually presented to the manorial lord for approval, and in the eighteenth century, the manorial lords' bailiffs increasingly supervised the affairs of the village.[103]

2.10 *Inter-Village Cooperation*

Due to extensive exploitation of potential arable land in southern Scandinavia from the Middle Ages, the fields of many villages bordered the fields of neighbouring villages, and some villages were even separated from local outfields and pastures by land belonging to other villages. These problems called for inter-village solutions in the form of *vanglag*, an institution that, at least on the Danish island of Zealand, can be traced back to the regional *Law of Zealand* from the thirteenth century. The peasants of the villages involved congregated to work out a system of field rotation that each year ensured the fallow field on one village bordered the fallow field of the next village. They thus created a common grazing area for their cattle and at the same time minimized the work need for maintaining fences in between the arable land of the villages involved.

Such systems, as exemplified by conditions on the island Møn at the end of the seventeenth century, could also establish corridors for grazing cattle, so that villages that did not border on the common outfields could also have access to their part of the common outfield grazing resources.

101 Meyer, *Danske bylag*, 49.
102 Meyer, *Danske bylag*, 88–89.
103 Meyer, *Danske bylag*, 52, 54, 82–83.

To organize such systems, it was necessary for the peasants of the villages involved to meet for discussions. Then they also had to decide how many cattle each village was permitted to graze on the fallows and the common land, and whether they should appoint a common shepherd. Furthermore, they had to agree on the exploitation of other resources in the outfields, such as the gathering of fodder and the taking of turf, the latter being an important resource in a landscape with few forests. To make such agreements work, the village representatives involved had to elect a common supervisor.[104]

2.11 *Conflict-handling Institutions and Village Organization – An Excursion to Sweden*

In Scania, which belonged to Denmark until 1658, we find the same communal village system as in the rest of Denmark, but manorial influence, which characterized the rest of Denmark from the second half of the seventeenth century, did not manifest itself in Scania. Instead, as in the rest of Sweden, village assemblies in Scania felt an increasing influence from local government, aimed at demarcating the authority of the village community from that of governmental administration and legal institutions.[105]

In Sweden outside Scania and some of the western plains of Sweden, villages were often small. The parish community (*sockenstämma*), initially created to deal with administrative and religious matters within the parish, therefore often became an arena for resolving conflicts.[106] The institution of the *sockenstämma* was also found in Denmark in the Middle Ages, but its influence in this country was limited to religious matters from the early sixteenth century onwards.[107] Even though the *sockenstämma* retained its importance as a conflict-resolving institution in Sweden in the early modern period, more or less formal village assemblies were also found there. From the first part of the eighteenth century, the Swedish government, in an attempt to regulate rural society, put great effort into forcing every village to set up their own statutes. A draft prepared by the government in 1742 was thus, with local adjustments, adopted in most villages. Very often, this was done at the local *sockenstämma*, a sign of the importance of this institution as a communal forum for local peasants.[108]

---

104 Karl-Erik Frandsen, *Vang og tægt. Studier over dyrkningssystemer og agrarstrukturer i Danmarks landsbyer 1682–83* (Esbjerg: Bygd, 1983).

105 Meyer, *Danske bylag*, 69–75, 82.

106 Janken Myrdal, *Jordbruket under feodalismen 1000–1700*, Det svenska jorbrukets historia, 2 (Stockholm: Natur och Kultur, 1999), 199; Meyer, *Danske bylag*, 60–69.

107 Meyer, *Danske bylag*, 51.

108 Meyer, *Danske bylag*, 75–78.

2.12 *Denmark – Summing Up*

The medieval division between three competing *thing* institutions in Denmark, the *herredsting*, often influenced by the aristocracy, on the one hand, and the kings's *retterting* and *birketing* on the other (see above), continued in modified form into the late Middle Ages. From the fifteenth century, a new division between aristocratic *birketing* on the one hand and the royal *herredsting* on the other came into being. This development was accelerated by the Reformation of 1536, when a large proportion of former ecclesiastical *birketing* were transferred to the aristocracy, a shift that gathered momentum in the next century.

In sharp contrast to Norway, Denmark thus experienced a division of jurisdiction between the crown and the aristocracy by the early modern period, not unlike conditions in Bavaria. However, this division occurred much later in Denmark than in Bavaria, where it dates back to the Middle Ages (see below). Unlike the *sorenskrivar* at the Norwegian local *thing*, the *herredsfoged* (judges) were usually appointed from among the peasants until 1660. Like the *sorenskrivar* in Norway, the *herredsfoged* became the sole judge at the *herredsting* by the end of the seventeenth century, although peasants were still court witnesses and participated in rendering judgement in vital cases involving a possible death sentence.

Even at the *birketing* belonging to the aristocracy, judges were appointed from among the peasants until the beginning of the eighteenth century. We must, however, bear in mind that the landlord, by virtue of his capacity to appoint judges and his ability to moderate sentences, may have used this court for his own benefit. Over the course of the early modern period, peasant influence at the local Danish *things*, like in Norway, seems to have been gradually reduced, although not completely eliminated. In both countries, this was primarily due to a deliberate professionalizing of the legal system at the local level.

Village organization in Denmark, at least until the late-seventeenth century, seems to have been fairly independent of manorial influence. This is all the more striking, as Danish landlords had a firm grip on their tenants when it came to administration of justice, collection of taxes, and, from the middle of the eighteenth century, conscription of soldiers (See Introduction, Section 'A Sketch of the Historical Background'). This paradox may, however, be explained by the fact that the main interest of the manorial lords lay increasingly in exploiting the work force of their tenants in demesne farming on their manors, not in supervising the way their tenants conducted their own farming or organized their activities in the village. Besides, while some villages belonged to one and the same landlord, others were divided between several owners, thus making landlord intervention in village affairs more difficult.

3 The Eastern Alpine Region

3.1 *The Early Medieval Period*

Tacitus (AD 55–*c*.120) gives us the first known account of the Germanic *thing*.[109] For the early medieval Bavarian tribal dukedom, that is, the entire eastern Alpine region, the *Lex Baiuvariorum* (740–88) provides us information about *thing* assemblies. The dukedom was subdivided into entities under counts belonging to aristocratic families. These entities could comprise several *things*. In 788, the dukedom was loosely incorporated into the realm of Charles the Great. According to the *Lex Baiuvariorum*, every free man, including the vassals of the king and the duke if staying in the region, should be obliged to meet at fixed *thing* assemblies dealing with matters of the peace, under the supervision of the *iudex*. This figure may have been a judge, but most likely he prepared and presented sentences, a kind of co-judge.[110] If so, he had a function similar to the *Schöffen*, a group of advisory judges also known later in Bavaria.[111] The king's envoy (*missus*) was to elect and supervise these *Schöffen*, together with the count and the *thing* assembly. The most respected men of the community, often well-to-do peasants, were usually elected as *Schöffen*.

Thus, in the Carolingian period, several social groups are mentioned in connection with the count's *thing*: free men (peasants), well-to-do peasants, and representatives of the tribal duke and the Carolingian king. The intention of introducing *Schöffen* has been deemed to be the Carolinian and later the German king's desire to create a unified jurisdiction at the *things*, while at the same time curtail the influence from the count and other aristocrat families.[112]

---

109 Tacitus, *Germania*, ed. Alfons Dopsch, et al. (Leipzig: Teubner, 1930), 11–12. According to Tacitus, free members of a tribe met in an assembly to secure peace and resolve controversial issues. In the assembly, the leading men of the tribe (called *principes*) passed sentences according to the advice of the tribe's most respected members (G. von Olberg, 'Gerichtsverfassung', in Johannes Hoops and Heinreich Beck (eds), *Real-enzyklopädie der germanischen Altertumskunde* (Berlin, 1973–2015), xi, 171–81).

110 Eugen Wohlhaupter, *Hoch- und Niedergerichts in der mittelalterlichen Gerichtsverfassung Bayerns*, Deutschrechtliche Beiträge, 12/2 (Heidelberg: C. Winter, 1929), 154–63; Jürgen Weitzel, 'Iudex', in LexMA, v, 793–94.

111 Wohlhaupter, *Hoch- und Niedergerichts*, 163–64; Philippe Dollinger, *Der bayerische Bauernstand vom 9. Bis zum 13. Jahrhundert* (Munich: C.H. Beck, 1982), 61.

112 Jürgen Weitzel, *Dinggenossenschaft und Recht*, i: *Untersuchungen zum Rechtsverständnis im fränkisch-deutschen Mittelalter* (Cologne: Böhlau Verlag, 1985), 575–605; Jürgen Weitzel, 'Schöffen', in Johannes Hoops and Heinreich Beck (eds), *Real-enzyklopädie der germanischen Altertumskunde* (Berlin, 1973–2015), xxvii, 233–36; Jürgen Weitzel 'Schöffe, -ngericht, -nbank', in LexMA, vii, 1514–16; F. Battenberg, 'Schöffen, Schöffengericht', in Adalbert Erler, et al. (eds), *Handwörterbuch zur deutschen Rechtsgeschichte*, 5 vols (Berlin: Schmidt, 1964–1991), iv, 1436–69.

Even though the king, with some sort of cooperation from the peasants at the *things*, theoretically was the supreme lord of jurisdiction, his superior jurisdiction was only partly implemented in the early medieval empire. The king in fact began outsourcing part of his power of jurisdiction at the same time as the aristocracy further developed their own jurisdiction and the church systematically expanded its own jurisdiction. Gradually, clerical and secular immunity spread to groups and territories where the king's jurisdiction had no access.

In spite of periods of great display of power under Ottonian rule in the tenth century, the political division of the German kingdom increased.[113] Nevertheless, the Bavarian tribal dukedom continued to be a relatively unified and independent principality until the end of the eleventh century. The original territories belonging to the count, however, developed into hereditary fiefs or *Grundherrschaft* (manor) systems, where jurisdiction was transferred from the territories formerly belonging to the count.[114] These new fief-holders could also become bailiffs (*Vogt*) for clerical institutions, and thus enjoy large incomes from carrying out secular fiscal, judicial, or military tasks. Although it is difficult to get a clear picture of the distribution of fiefs and jurisdictional entities from the end of the eleventh century in the eastern Alpine region, it is obvious that the peasantry had lost the former contact and influence enjoyed at the *things* of the counts in the early medieval period. This loss of influence may partly be due to confusing power relations between the count, the aristocracy, and the clerical institutions, but may also be traced back to the dwindling military importance of the peasantry.[115] Nevertheless, the peasantry probably retained some of its influence on an agrarian level by attending the local manorial assemblies.

3.2 *The Eastern Alpine Region from the High Middle Ages – Bavaria*

Towards the end of the twelfth century, the tribal dukedom of Bavaria was divided into five principalities: the new duchies of Bavaria, Austria, Styria (*Steiermark*), Carinthia (*Kärnten*), and the county of Tyrol.[116] In the following, we will

113 H. Drüppel, 'Gericht, Gerichtbarkeit', in LexMA, iv, 1322–24; C. Schott and H. Romer, 'Immunität', in LexMA, v, 390–92.

114 Families of counts expanding from the eleventh century onwards included Andechs, Falkenstein, and Wittelsbach (Dollinger, *Der bayerische Bauernstand*, 54–56).

115 Dollinger, *Der bayerische Bauernstand*, 53–83; Pankraz Fried, 'Zur Geschichte der bayerischen Landgemeinde', in Theodor Mayer (ed.), *Die Anfänge der Landgemeinde und ihr Wesen*, 2 vols, Vorträge und Forschungen, 7, (Stuttgart: Jan Thorbecke, 1964), i, 79–106 at p. 94.

116 Max Spindler, 'Die Auseinandersetzungen mit Landeladel, Epiropat und Königtum unter den drei ersten wittelsbachischen Herzögen (1180–1253)', in Max Spindler (ed.), *Handbuch*

concentrate on assemblies in the first and the last of these principalities. Reforms of the legal system in the thirteenth century initiated a development in which the Bavarian duke tried to consolidate his own territory and bring the legal power of the clerical and secular nobility under control. While control over legal assemblies and legal authority over peasants had been incorporated into the privileges of fief-holders until the thirteenth century, the dukes of *Wittelsbach* gradually succeeded in acquiring many such rights for themselves in Bavaria. Miscellaneous legal authority originating in privileges belonging to former counts and bailiffs (*Vogt*) were now combined within new offices with territorially defined applicability.[117]

The duke's main instrument in this development was the new territorial peace legislation inspired by the church. With this legislation, a new and 'public' view of breaking social peace was created. Severe violence had formerly been perceived as harm to the injured party, which consequently was to be compensated for according to his status and the nature of the offence. Now severe deeds of violence were understood to be crimes against the communal peace of society, a peace that the territorial prince was solely responsible for upholding.[118] Via this new public view of punishment, it became possible to divide jurisdiction into two clearly delimited categories: a *high jurisdiction* or 'blood jurisdiction' involving crimes against social peace, and a *lower jurisdiction*, relating to civil conflicts and ordinary finable offences. This development started in 1311. Financial need compelled the duke to grant lower jurisdiction over peasants to nobility and monasteries in their consolidated territories, while reserving for himself the monopoly of higher jurisdiction, regardless of who possessed lower jurisdiction. On his own landed property, lower jurisdiction was his as well.[119]

---

der bayerischen Geschichte (Munich: C.H. Beck), ii, 11–72; Hubert Glaser (ed.), *Wittelsbach und Bayern*, i: *Die Zeit der frühen Herzöge – von Otto I. zu Ludwig dem Bayern* (Munich: Hirmer, 1980); Heinz Lieberich, 'Zur Feudalisierung der Gerichtsbarkeit in Bayern', *Zeitschrift der Savigny-Stiftung für Rechtsgeschichte germ. Abt.* (1954), 304.

117 Sebastian Hiereth, *Die bayerische Gerichts- und Verwaltungsorganisation vom 13. Bis 19. Jahrhundert*, Historischer Atlas von Bayern, Teil Altbayern, 1 (Munich: Komm. für Bayer, Landegeschichte, 1950), 6–7; Fried, 'Zur Geschichte der bayerischen Landgemeinde', 79–106.

118 Wohlhaupter, *Hoch- und Niedergerichts*, 180.

119 Dollinger, *Der bayerische Bauernstand*, 67f.; Maria Rita Sagestetter, *Hoch- und Niedergerichtsbarkeit im Spätmittelalterlichen Herzogtum Bayern* (Munich: Beck'sche Verlagsbuchhandlung, 2000), 568–71; Lieberich, 'Zur Feudalisierung', 335–38; Wohlhaupter, *Hoch- und Niedergerichts*, 169–85.

3.3 Landgerichte *and* Hofmarken

The term *Landgericht* is related to the transformation of the duke's personal jurisdictional power into territories of jurisdiction. As early as 1204, the office of *Wiztum* (*vicedominus*) is mentioned, a deputy performing all types of jurisdiction on behalf of the duke. A distinction between administration and jurisdiction under a *Pfleger* (local territorial administrator) and a judge (*iudex*), respectively, was also introduced into the *Landgericht* districts. Since *Schöffen* (see above) were abolished in Bavaria in the thirteenth century, a judge appointed jury members from the *thing* assembly. These co-judges belonged to the group of the most highly esteemed men in the assembly district. The responsibility for requesting the death penalty according to the territorial peace legislation was soon transferred to *Schergen*, a new civil servant office. He was, for example, to summon the assembly meeting, arrest criminals, hold them in custody, and arrange for their execution.[120] In sum, these measures, aimed at professionalizing jurisdiction, were soon to put peasant influence at the *Landgericht* at risk.

Hofmarken were smaller territories covering one or several villages, but also single farms. Most *Hofmarken* belonged to the secular and clerical nobility and to monasteries. The *Hofmark* institution originated in the early medieval *Grundherrschaft*, but contained elements stemming from immunities granted to ecclesiastical institutions from the tenth to the twelfth century as well. Where noble landowners had appropriated continuous territory, they also made efforts to introduce their own jurisdiction into the territory. In this way, the *Hofmarken* came to represent legal territories where the aristocracy and the monasteries exercised lower jurisdiction in the fourteenth century. The duke nevertheless exercised lower jurisdiction over approximately half of all landed property in Bavaria in the fourteenth century, even though he himself owned only 20 percent of the land.[121]

Each *Hofmark* was closely linked with the peasant communities within its territory. Regulations concerning agriculture and the use of resources within the *Hofmark* were resolved at the *Bautaiding*, a *thing* assembly where tenants, as well as the landlord, who had the responsibility of confirming and

120 Wohlhaupter, *Hoch- und Niedergerichts*, 173–76; cf. H. Drüppel, 'Landgericht', in LexdMA, v, 1660–61; Wolfgang Schnelbögl, *Die innere Entwicklung der bayerischen Landfrieden des 13.Jahrhunderts*, Deutschrechtliche Beiträge, 13/ 2 (Heidelberg: C. Winter, 1932), 193–201; Dollinger, *Der bayerische Bauernstand*, 61–64.

121 Thoma, 'Klosterbauern zwischen Herrschaft und Genossenschaft', 28; Pankraz Fried, 'Grundherrschaft und Dorfgericht im spätmittelalterlichen Herzogtum Bayern', in Hans Patze (ed.), *Grundherrschaft im späten Mittelalter*, 2 vols, Vorträge und Forschungen, 27 (Sigmaringen: Thorbecke, 1983), ii, 277–312.

proclaiming the regulations, were present (see below). The *Hofmark* tenants usually elected an *Ammann* or a collective body called *Vierer*, an election that later was to be confirmed by the lord of the *Hofmark*. Even though the variations were great between different *Hofmarken*, these officials may be regarded as intermediaries between the lord of the *Hofmark* and the peasants of the peasant community. At the legal assemblies of the *Hofmark*, headed by a *Richter* (judge), peasants functioned as 'finders of law' and co-judges.[122] Not all peasants belonging to a *Hofmark* lived within the borders of a closed *Hofmark*. Many villages had several landlords. In such cases, every household in the village was subject to the local territorial court (*Landgericht* – see below), even though they belonged to the *Hofmark* of an ecclesiastical or aristocratic landlord.[123]

After the middle of the thirteenth century, a few village institutions, *Dorfgerichte* (*iudicum villae*), appear in some sources. These institutions managed police tasks and looked after the interest of the community, and in some cases they also managed to acquire lower jurisdiction. Taking everything into account, one may claim that the peasants in Bavaria at the end of the thirteenth century possessed quite a few 'liberties' through their rights of co-determination and self-administration. These 'liberties' were not, as the older historical doctrine assumed, surviving leftovers from old liberties originating in early Germanic societies. On the contrary, contemporary historians believe that these liberties came into being during the High Middle Ages.[124]

It has been maintained that in the case of *Hofmarken*, the relationship between the lord (*Herrschaft*) and the peasants (*Genossenschaft*) was a reciprocal one. Peasants participated in decisions concerning agrarian and minor legal issues at the annual *Ehafttaiding*, which thus can be characterized as a 'tight' arrangement where agrarian and legal issues were intimately linked. Peasants also had a say in electing *Hofmark* officials.[125] However, an opportunity for complete peasant self-management did not exist in the *Hofmarken*.

In the considerably larger ducal *Landgericht* territories, peasants' rights of co-determination within the judicial field were clearly declining after the

122 Thoma, 'Klosterbauern zwischen Herrschaft und Genossenschaft', 25–39; Hiereth, *Die bayerische Gerichts-*, 8–16; Sagestetter, *Hoch- und Niedergerichtsbarkeit*, 322–468.

123 Monika Ofer, 'Nachbarschaft und Gemeinde – Zur dörflichen Selbstverwaltung im westlichen Oberbayern im 16. und beginnenden 17. Jahrhundert', in Tore Iversen, John Ragnar Myking and Gertrud Thoma (eds), *Bauern zwischen Herrschaft und Genossenschaft: Peasant Relations to Lords and Government. Scandinavia and the Alpine Region 1000–1750* (Trondheim: Tapir Akademisk Forlag, 2007), 41–57, at pp. 44–45.

124 Dollinger, *Der bayerische Bauernstand*, 375–78.

125 Fried, 'Zur Geschichte der bayerischen Landgemeinde', 98–106.

thirteenth century. Their co-determination disappeared after the Upper Bavarian *Landrecht* was introduced in 1346, as its *Buchsage* pushed aside the peasants' role of 'finding the law'. In the *Landgericht* territories, the activity of the village communities was primarily concentrated on agrarian conditions (see below). In this area, the peasants of the village community, having been liberated from the *Grundherrschaft* arrangement, had extended self-management. The ducal *Landgericht* also secured their self-management against intrusion from the nobility. It was not until the fifteenth century that the *Landgericht's* supervision of the peasants' self-management came into play.

3.4 *Upper Bavaria – Village Organization and* Hofmarken

While the scattered settlements of Tyrol were most often organized on an inter-settlement basis (see below), village organization dominated Bavaria. The dissolution of the classical manorial system, with its combination of demesne farming and dependent smaller units, in the couple of centuries leading up to the fourteenth century, is often held by German historians to be a prerequisite for the establishment of villages and village assemblies.[126] This classical manorial system was most widespread in Bavaria,[127] whereas its possible existence in Tyrol is heavily debated.[128] With the dissolution of this system, decisions on farming, formerly issued by the manorial lord or his assistants, were now left to the peasant communities, creating a need for formal institutions, either on village level or embracing several settlements.

The local Bavarian expression *Gmain* denotes an association of inhabitants holding a plot of land in a village with the right to use common land belonging to this village.[129] Although some sort of village organization may have replaced the crumbling manorial system in Bavaria before fourteenth century, and protection of common village land was included in the Bavarian law of 1346, it is not until centuries later that we are able to study the exact organization of these village communities. In Upper, that is, southern Bavaria, written village statutes have survived from the turn of the sixteenth century.[130]

126 Rösener, 'Bauern zwischen Herrschaft und Genossenschaft', 13; Heide Wunder, *Die bäuerliche Gemeinde in Deutschland* (Göttingen: Vandenhoeck und Ruprecht, 1986), 33.

127 Wilhelm Störmer, 'Grundherrschaften frühmittelalterlicher Klöster und Stifte im Wandel des Hochmittelalter', in Werner Rösener (ed.), *Grundherrschaft und bäuerliche Gesellschaft im Hochmittelalter* (Göttingen: Vandenhoeck und Ruprech, 1995), 184–214.

128 Workshop in Innsbruck with Austrian and Norwegian historians, 22–23 May 2006. Unpublished summary.

129 Ofer, 'Nachbarschaft und Gemeinde', 41.

130 Ofer, 'Nachbarschaft und Gemeinde', 46 and 50.

These statutes show that, as in other regions with open fields, the main tasks for the village community included planning crop rotation and regulating access to common resources like pastures, commons, timber, and firewood. The community also organized common tasks like the maintenance of roads, water supply, and other vital installations, and it saw to the proper enclosure of fields and the herding of cattle. Hygienic matters could also be a concern for the *Gmain*. Thus, dung heaps in the village itself were not tolerated, nor were pigs allowed to wander freely around the village. In some villages, lodgers also had to be approved by the *Gmain*. In order to finance a shepherd, a common bath, a blacksmith's workshop, or any other common expenses, the *Gmain* had to collect fees from its members, usually in the form of money or grain.[131]

Village statutes and other regulations were adopted by village assemblies in which every household with a house and a plot of land in the village was represented, but it is unclear whether these assemblies appointed the village officials who were to administer village regulations and finances. Apparently, such assignments might also circulate among the village households. A typical *Gmain* usually had from three to five officials, a bit illogical, called *Vierer* (literary four men). Some villages, though, only had one *Dorfmeister*. These officials had to account to the village assembly for all income and expenses, and they also represented the *Gmain* in court. Usually, such officials were recruited among peasants with the largest holdings in the village. Some of the smallest settlements, however, did not have any officials at all and were thus represented by the village assembly in full. Others, even in larger villages, left the administration of their statutes and regulations to territorial officials.[132]

The Bavarian *Gmain* was closely connected to the local territorial administration (*Landgericht*), or in some cases, a manorial administration (*Hofmark*).[133] In villages under the authority of a territorial administration, village assignments were sometimes even merged with territorial administrative offices, as when village officials combined their duties with the duties of minor local officials, *Obleute*, like the *Hauptmann*. Most importantly, village statutes and other decisions made by the village assembly had to be approved by the local territorial administrator (*Pfleger*) to be legally binding, and fines for breaking village statutes and regulations were due to the authorities.[134] Even though Bavarian villages exercised a considerable degree of self-administration under

131 Ofer, 'Nachbarschaft und Gemeinde', 51–53.

132 Ofer, 'Nachbarschaft und Gemeinde', 54–56; Helmut Rankl, *Landvolk und Frühmoderner Staat in Bayern 1400–1800*, Studien zur Bayerischen Verfassungs- und Sozialgeschichte, 17 (Munich: Kommision für Bayerische Landesgeschichte, 1999), 56, 74.

133 Ofer, 'Nachbarschaft und Gemeinde', 44–45.

134 Ofer, 'Nachbarschaft und Gemeinde', 55–57.

the auspices of the local territorial administration, they were thus not autonomous associations. In 1616, village assemblies belonging to a territorial administration were even forbidden to congregate without the consent of the authorities.[135]

While peasants in villages subjected to the territorial courts organized agriculture and social matters on a village level, most peasants belonging to *Hofmarken* had their corresponding needs and institutions regulated on an inter-settlement level within the borders of the *Hofmark*. Peasants in these *Hofmarken* also had officials like the *Amman* or *Vierer* found in the villages belonging to territorial courts (see above), but unlike their counterparts in these villages, these officials also played a part in the administration of justice (see above). In much the same way as the officials of the *Gmain* were appointed by the village community and approved by the territorial administrator, *Hofmark* officials were elected by the *Hofmark* community and approved by the manorial lord. Unlike most village officials in the territorial *Gmain*, these *Hofmark* officials performed duties for the lord of the *Hofmark* at the same time as they represented and took care of the interest of the peasants of the *Hofmark*.[136] The scope of their duties depended on whether they primarily were exercising duties for the manorial lord or whether they primarily concentrated on tasks vital to the peasants belonging to the *Hofmark*.[137]

The statutes of Bavarian *Hofmarken* addressed many of the same problems as the Bavarian village statutes. They were concerned with the administration of common land, access to limited resources, and the organization connected with field rotation. The most striking difference is that, in contrast to the village statutes laid down according to communal agreement and ancient usage and which only had to be approved by a representative of the territorial power, the statutes of the *Hofmarken* were usually worked out in close cooperation between the manorial lord and the peasants. It may therefore be assumed that manorial influence characterized these statutes in a way landlords were not in the position to do when village statues were compiled. Still, the range of manorial influence differed quite widely. Some statutes indicate a strong manorial influence, especially in *Hofmarken* where an aristocratic lord resided inside the *Hofmark*. Others reveal a high degree of peasant involvement, almost to the point of full autonomy in the compilation of statutes.[138]

135 Ofer, 'Nachbarschaft und Gemeinde', 43.

136 Thoma, 'Klosterbauern zwischen Herrschaft und Genossenschaft', 27–28, 34.

137 Rankl, *Landvolk*, 56.

138 Thoma, 'Klosterbauern zwischen Herrschaft und Genossenschaft', 27.

While all peasants using land in Upper Bavarian villages were included as full members of the village assembly, we have less information about communal participation of the inhabitants of the *Hofmarken*. At least one of the *Hofmark* statutes, from Seebruck from 1391/98, makes a clear distinction between community members with full rights to resources and others with lesser rights, but we do not know if this had any implication for their participation in the communal assembly or for their potential participation in elections of communal commissions.[139] What we do know is that fines were paid to the manorial lord, thus paralleling procedures in villages belonging to the manorial courts, where fines were paid to the authorities.[140]

We may then conclude that in at least some of the Bavarian *Hofmarken*, peasants enjoyed much the same autonomy when it came to regulating access to limited resources and the relations between the inhabitants as did their fellow peasants in territorial villages. The degree of autonomy, however, varied to a greater degree in *Hofmarken* than in territorial villages, with the presence of an aristocratic lord imposing the most restrictions. Moreover, the commissions and officials in these communities more often served the need of the manorial lord and the community at the same time. They played a role both in administering justice at the *Gerichtsding* (in Bavaria called *Ehafttaiding*) and participated in resolving agricultural issues at the *Bautaiding*. The presence of the manorial lord may have been felt in both circumstances. We must not forget that the manorial lords in their *Hofmarken* combined landownership, jurisdiction, and very often personal bondage over their *Hofmark* peasants, a combination that necessarily must have limited these peasants' autonomy more than was experienced by peasants in territorial villages where landownership, jurisdiction, and personal bondage often belonged to different lords.

Sometimes peasants could organize themselves into short-lived associations spanning several existing administrative districts, *Landgerichte* as well as *Hofmarken*. Examples of such a type of organization are found in the Alpine area of Bavaria. To secure their common rights to timber and alpine pastures, peasants of the *Landgericht* Tölz and the *Hofmark* Hohenburg-Lengrie, on the border with Tyrol, addressed themselves as the '*Untertanen der Talgemeinschaft*', that is, the subjects in the valley community, in a conflict with the territorial power in 1479. The following year, the neighbouring '*Talgemeinde*' of Jachenau managed to secure its right to wood and timber against the manorial lord, the monastery of Benediktbeuern.[141] In Bavaria, such peasant associations,

139 Thoma, 'Klosterbauern zwischen Herrschaft und Genossenschaft', 36–37.
140 Thoma, 'Klosterbauern zwischen Herrschaft und Genossenschaft', 37.
141 Rankl, *Landvolk*, 52, 81–83.

spanning areas larger than a village or a *Hofmark*, seem to be ad hoc associations established to protect common resources from intrusions from a territorial or manorial power. In contrast, in neighbouring Tyrol (see below), such multi-settlement organization, in the form of *Nachbarschaften*, was a normal way of administering resources and regulating peasant everyday life.

3.5 Talschaften – *Switzerland*

In Switzerland, inter-settlement communities in the form of *Talschaften* were quite common. They clearly had many more functions and a far more complex organization than the *Talschaften* found in the Alpine parts of Bavaria near the border with Tyrol. Like their Tyrolean equivalents, the *Nachbarschaften*, they could have administrative functions, and like the Tyrolean *Gerichte*, they were also courts of laws. Most of these *Talschaften* were under the authority of some manorial or territorial power, but some of them succeeded in acquiring the much-sought-after *Reichsfreiheit*. Then, they were under the direct authority of the Holy Roman Emperor and the Imperial diet, without any intermediary manorial or territorial control. In Graubünden and Wallis, *Talschaften* merged to form confederations joining the greater confederations of the Swiss *Eidgenossenschaft*.[142] The geographical scale and the magnitude of tasks far beyond the administration of common resources led *Talschaften* to develop an organization much more complex than was needed for the mere administration of common resources (see below). The members elected officials and a commission, with the consent of the authorities if they did not possess the *Reichsfreiheit*.[143] The administration of common resources was clearly still a very important task for these *Talschaften*.

3.6 *Tyrol*

To a greater degree than the neighboring regions, Tyrol was marked by a homogeneous peasant estate in the fourteenth and fifteenth centuries. Heritable land tenure was widespread, and peasants enjoyed a considerable degree of self-management with its basis in local assemblies (*Nachbarschaften*) and courts (*Gerichte*). These assemblies had furthermore acquired a certain political influence through their delegates at the count of Tyrol's territorial diet

142 Hans Stadler, 'Talschaft', in *Historischen Lexikon der Schweitz*. http://www.hls-dhs-dss.ch/textes/d/D26442.php. Last accessed 13 September 2011.

143 Peter Bierbrauer, 'Ländliche Gemeinde in oberdeutschen-schweizerischen Raum', in Peter Blickle (ed.), *Landgemeinde und Stadtgemeinde in Mitteleuropa. Ein struktureller Vergleich*, Historische Zeitschrift, 13 (Munich, 1991), 169–90.

(*Landtag*).[144] What then was the background for this strong peasant standing from the end of the fourteenth century? According to an older point of view, held by Tyrolean regional historians headed by the well-known historian Otto Stolz, the *thing* assemblies could be traced back to Carolingian period. The popular participation in the counts' *things* at that time was, according to Stolz, rooted in the *Markgenossenschaften,* ancient areas originally communally managed going back to Germanic Migration Period.[145] The doctrine of the *Markgenossenschaft* was based on retrospective conclusions deriving from communally managed outfield resources that were seen as leftovers from what was originally communal property.[146]

The retrospective conclusions embedded in the doctrine of the *Markgenossenschaft* have now been left behind (see 'Introduction', section 'Historiography and Methodological Reflections'). In Tyrol, Franz Huter, Ernst Bruckmüller, and lately also Wilfried Beimrohr, have found very little support for this interpretation in the very sources used by Stolz.[147] The count's jurisdiction crumbled in the High Middle Ages, mainly because the German king offered immunities, including jurisdiction, to ecclesiastical institutions which then

144 Wilfried Beimrohr, 'Bäuerliche Besitzrechte und die ländliche Gemeinde in Tirol', in Tore Iversen, John Ragnar Myking and Gertrud Thoma (eds), *Bauern zwischen Herrschaft und Genossenschaft: Peasant Relations to Lords and Government. Scandinavia and the Alpine Region 1000–1750* (Trondheim: Tapir Akademisk Forlag, 2007), 85–108, at pp. 95–97; Josef Riedmann, 'Mittelalter', in Josef Fontana, et al. (eds), *Geschichte des Landes Tirol* (Bozen / Vienna: Verlagsanstalt Athesia, 1985), 291–698, at pp. 529–32.

145 Otto Stolz, *Geschichte der Gerichte Deutschtirol, Abhandlungen zum historischen Atlas der Österreichischen Alpenländer*, special print (Sonderdruck), Archiv für österreichische Geschichte, 102 (Vienna: A. Höldner, 1913), 214, 218f.; Otto Stolz, *Rechtsgeschichte des Bauernstandes und der Landwirtschaft in Tirol und Voralberg* (Bozen: Ferrari-Auer, 1949; repr. Hildesheim: Georg Olms Verlag, 1985), 304. As mentioned in the 'Introduction', the regional Tyrolean historical tradition seemed to serve as an important background to the Norwegian historian Edvard Bull's planned comparative project in the 1920s.

146 Werner Rösener, 'Die Entstehung der Markgenossenschaften des Mittelalters in Theorie und Realität', in Uwe Meiners and Werner Rösener (eds), *Allmenden und Marken vom Mittelalter bis zur Neuzeit* (Cloppenburg: Schriften des Museumsdorfs Cloppenburg, 2004), 17–19.

147 Wilfred Beimrohr, *Mit Brief und Siegel. Die Gerichte Tirols und ihr älteres Schriftgut im Tiroler Landesarchiv*, Tiroler Geschichtsquellen, 34 (Innsbruck: Tiroler Landesarchiv, 1994), 34–38; Franz Huter, 'Zur Frage der Gemeindebildung in Tirol', in Theodor Mayer (ed.), *Die Anfänge der Landgemeinde und ihr Wesen*, 2 vols, Vorträge und Forschungen, 7 (Stuttgart: Jan Thorbecke, 1964), i, 223–25; Rösener, 'Die Entstehung der Markgenossenschaften', 19–20; Ernst Bruckmüller, 'Täler und Gerichte', in Ernst Bruckmüller, Helmuth Stradal and Michael Mitterauer (eds), *Herrschaftsstruktur und Ständebildung. Beiträge zur Typologie der österreichischen Länder aus ihren mittelalterlichen Grundlagen*, 3 (Munich: De Gruyter Oldenbourg, 1973), 30–31.

installed secular bailiffs (*Vögte*).[148] The critiques also found that influence from some sort of manorial system (*Grundherrschaft*) had a greater impact on these assemblies then Stolz had assumed.[149] Further, from the eleventh century onwards, the peasant population in Tyrol probably lost much of the influence it had at the older county assemblies. The critiques thus concluded that the former jurisdiction of the count either had disappeared altogether by the beginning of the High Middle Ages or was too diffuse for the later *Landgericht* institution to have been derived from this jurisdiction.[150]

Recently, historians have therefore emphasized contemporary political factors to a much greater extent in the shaping of the Tyrolean *Landgericht* in the late Middle Ages. In a process of concentration, several types of rights of dominion were combined and applied to a delimited territorial region. Huter has used the *Landgericht* of Kastellbell from the end of the thirteenth century as an example of such a process of concentration. Dominion over serfs (*Eigenleute*) on a number of manors (*Grundherrschaft*) was combined with *Vogt* (bailiff) rights over several ecclesiastical estates and one parish. These territories were then formed into a newly organized *Gerichtsgemeinde* with a sort of unified administration.[151] Huter underlines that these territories of jurisdiction were formed gradually; they were made up by a variety of elements, differing from territory to territory according to traditions and natural conditions. He sums up his evidence in the following way: it is not the free-standing *Gerichtsgemeinde* rooted in ancient communal communities that was typical for the legal assembly in Tyrol, but, on the contrary, the early interventions of the territorial prince in the shaping of an assembly of peasants.[152]

It was the first princes of the family Tirol-Görz, especially Meinhard II (1258–95), who began the concentration process and the Habsburgian prince Friedrich (1411–39) 'with the empty purse' who completed it. During his reign, Meinhard II nearly extinguished the Tyrolean nobility by inheriting or ransoming their noble rights, or simply by driving them away from their territories. This could be accomplished because the aristocracy in Tyrol was in a weaker position then in the neighboring regions, with Vorarlberg as an exception. A part of the explanation for their weakness may have been of a topographical nature, that is, scarcity of continuous arable land. On the other hand,

148 Nikolaus Grass, 'Aus der Frühzeit des ländlichen Gemeinde in Deutschtirol', in Alois Stadler (ed.), *Die ländliche Gemeinde: Historietagung in Bad Ragaz* (Bozen: Athesia, 1988), 127; Beimrohr, *Mit Brief und Siegel*, 34–37.

149 Huter, 'Zur Frage der Gemeindebildung', 235.

150 Beimrohr, *Mit Brief und Siegel*, 35–36.

151 Huter, 'Zur Frage der Gemeindebildung', 231–35.

152 Huter, 'Zur Frage der Gemeindebildung', 235.

the territories of the ecclesiastical institutions were particularly strong in Tyrol because the German king had endowed these institutions with rich donations in the early Middle Ages in order to secure reliable sites of support in the mountain passes to Italy. The territorial prince later succeeded in getting hold of the *Vogt's* (bailiff) right over the most important ecclesiastical territories, the diocese of Brixen and Trient (1210).

The strong position of the count of Tyrol was also due to the fact that Tyrol was a mountain pass state, with transport and trade providing the prince financial and military superiority. Substantial income also came from the mining industry, at first salt, then silver mining, both by princely monopoly. The fact that Tyrol became a legal unity under the territorial prince in 1282 was also of great significance. Following the rule of Meinard II, the determined efforts to consolidate the peasant court assemblies also aimed at consolidating territory and increasing the princes' power at the expense of the power of the nobility. The goal of the Tyrolean counts was to establish a direct relationship between the ruler and his subject for the entire population of the county. Ernst Bruckmüller thus characterizes Tyrol as a 'modern' state formation at the end of the Middle Ages. Even if a certain 're-feudalization' took place in Tyrol in the fourteenth century, the new fiefs, many of them previously confiscated from the old aristocracy, were given to a nobility serving the territorial prince.[153]

The final territorializing of the Tyrolean court assemblies came when the *Gericht / Gerichtgemeinde* (court/court assembly) were connected to the *Nachbarschaft / Gemeinde* (neighbourhood/neighbourhood assembly) (see below). The latter entities were communal neighbourhood institutions (*Gemain*) containing one or several villages, as well as single farms. Each *Nachbarschaft / Gemeinde* had a *Gemeinde* assembly where every household working a piece of land had the right to attend. The main tasks of the *Gemeinde* assembly were of an agrarian nature, such as administering the use of the commons and field rotation (see below). Heading the *Gemeinde* was a *Dorfmeister* chosen by and responsible to the assembly. From c. 1300, a *Nachbarschaft / Gemeinde* was normally congruent with the court assembly, led by an appointed judge (*Richter*) normally presiding over a selection of twelve sworn men from the *Gerichtsgemeinde*. The *Gerichtsgemeinde* could also establish their own commissions (*Gerichtsausschüsse*) on different occasions.

In Tyrol, every *Gericht* achieved lower jurisdiction, in the sense that they passed sentences through their representatives. The same applied to the police

153 Riedmann, 'Mittelalter', 399–410; Bruckmüller, 'Täler und Gerichte', 14–15; Ernst Bruckmüller, *Sozialgeschichte Österreichs* (Vienna: Herold-Verlold, 1985), 113–14; Grass, 'Aus der Frühzeit', 134–36.

authorities. From the beginning of the fifteenth century, the *Gericht* assemblies also selected peasant representatives for the count of Tyrol's territorial diet (*Landtag*).[154] The local judges (*Richter*) were appointed by the territorial prince, and the sworn-in men could not handle cases involving high jurisdiction (*Hoch- / Blutsgerichtsbarkeit*). Such cases were handled in special assemblies, named *Landgerichte.* Collecting taxes were, however, the responsibility of the *Gericht,* but the actual collecting was delegated to the *Gemeinde* assembly. This assembly was also given the responsibility for enlisting soldiers. These assignments contributed to linking the popular assemblies closer to the territorial prince.[155]

3.7 Nachbarschaften – *Tyrol*

In Bavaria, monasteries and nobles were able to gain and maintain minor jurisdiction; in Tyrol, the territorial lord seized control of both major and minor jurisdiction in most regions. There were thus very few ecclesiastical *Hofmarken* left by the fifteenth century, and they too lost their authority in the next century. While the territorial lord in this process monopolized jurisdiction (see above), Tyrolean peasant society was pretty much left to organize other duties and responsibilities as they themselves saw fit. This they did within the framework of their local communities, so called *Nachbarschaften*, organized either on village or inter-settlement level depending on the structure of the settlements in the area. A *Nachbarschaft* could thus consist of settlements spanning from a single densely populated village to a cluster of scattered, sparsely populated single farms.[156]

These communities and their organization had two main functions: on the one hand, oversee communal tasks that the peasant society itself deemed necessary to resolve, and on the other hand, perform responsibilities that the territorial power laid upon the local community to address. Communal tasks involved the administration and regulation of common land belonging to one or

154 Adelina Wallnöfer, 'Die Bauern in der tiroler "Landschaft" vor 1500. Politische Aktivität der Gerichte und deren Repräsentanten auf den Landtagen', PhD dissertation, University of Innsbruck, Innsbruck, 1984. Most of the peasants' representatives came from the local assemblies the well off and average strata.

155 Riedmann, 'Mittelalter', 529–33; Bruckmüller, *Österreichische Sozialgeschichte*, 113–14; Beimrohr, 'Bäuerliche Besitzrechte', 95–108; Martin P. Schennach, *Gesetze und Herrschaft. Die Entstehung des Gesetzgebungsstaates am Beispiel Tirols*, Forschung zur deutschen Rechtsgeschichte, 28 (Cologne: Böhlau, 2010), 76–89, 335–41, 711–15.

156 Wilfred Beimrohr, 'Die ländliche Gemeinde in Tirol aus rechtsgeschichtlicher Perspektive', *Tiroler Heimat. Jahrbuch für Geschichte und Volkskunde Nord-, Ost- und Südtirols*, 72 (2008), 161–78, at p. 174.

several settlements, the regulation of field rotation, and the need for providing necessary infrastructure in villages and other densely populated settlements. Tasks laid upon them by the authorities were the compilation of tax rolls, the collection of land taxes, and the mustering of soldiers.[157]

One of the most important functions of the neighbourhood was to regulate access to common land, the *Gemain*. The *Gemain* included every type of land that was used communally by the neighbourhood, mainly forests, alpine pastures, and outfield commons. As a rule, a *Gemain* belonged to only one neighbourhood, but in the case of some forested areas or alpine pastures, the forest could be controlled jointly by two neighbourhoods.[158] In addition to being involved in the administration of the *Gemain*, more densely populated settlements had to resolve problems relating to the open field structure and common tasks like the construction and maintenance of roads, bridges, wells, artificial watering systems, and fire protection.[159] The tax community (*Steuergemeinde*), which also had military functions, was usually, but not always, concurrent with the *Gemain*. In northeastern Tyrol, several *Nachbarschaften* were thus merged into one tax community.[160]

Every *Nachbarschaft* or community (*Gemeinde*) had an assembly that met at least once every year. This assembly, which every head of household with its own house and holding had the right to attend, decided on the use and regulation of common resources and other important questions for the community, and compiled village laws (*Dorfordnungen*).[161] To implement such decisions, the community needed community officials. In 1573, each *Nachbarschaft* was instructed by the authorities to elect or appoint four, six, or eight 'sensible' men in every quarter section of the community, in order to supervise the tasks laid upon the community by the authorities, who should also confirm the elections or appointments. Otherwise, these communities were pretty much left to organize themselves in a way they themselves saw fit.[162] Usually, they elected a *Dorfmeister* or, if several localities should be represented, a corporate body of two to four men. Such commissions could, however, also rotate between the holdings belonging to the community.[163]

157 Beimrohr, 'Bauerliche Besitzrechte', 99–104.

158 Beimrohr, 'Bäuerliche Besitzrechte', 100–01; Beimrohr, 'Die ländliche Gemeinde in Tirol', 170.

159 Beimrohr, 'Bäuerliche Besitzrechte', 103–04.

160 Beimrohr, 'Bäuerliche Besitzrechte', 103.

161 Beimrohr, 'Die ländliche Gemeinde in Tirol', 174.

162 Land Tirol – Archivglossar – G: 'Gemeinde'. http://www.tirol.gv.at/themen/kultur/landesarchiv/glossar/archivglossar-g/. Last accessed 12 September 2011.

163 Beimrohr, 'Die ländliche Gemeinde in Tirol', 174.

Although the neighbourhoods had great autonomy when it came to administering the use of their *Gemain*, they also experienced some restrictions. The Tyrolean territorial lord claimed in principle a superior ownership to all outfield resources, included in the *Gemain*. To him, the forests were the most important. Tyrol is one of the oldest mining regions in Europe, and the neighbourhood's use of the forests was restricted in order to provide timber and firewood for the mines. The territorial administration also monitored closely every change from collective to individual use of the *Gemain*, like the turning of forest or pastures into enclosed fields or meadows.[164] On the other hand, from the end of the late Middle Ages, the authorities also protected the *Gemain* from any manorial intrusion.[165]

As a consequence of the rise in population in the early modern period, neighbourhoods were presented with multiple new problems. One of them was the pressure from peasant households to convert collective land, especially forests, to individual use, thus shielding their portion from the ever-growing strain on resources.[166] Another was the rise of a new class of smaller peasants and cotters wanting a share in the *Gemain* (see Part 4, Appendix, '*Sub-peasant Strata*'). Many held only a tiny amount of land, their main livelihood coming from mining or other occupations. If, and to what extent, these households were to obtain a portion of the common resources of the *Gemain*, was left to the members of the *Gemain*, peasants with a house and a holding, to decide.[167]

3.8 *The Eastern Alpine Region – Summing Up*

While the Scandinavian kingdoms reinforced themselves and their kings actively reorganized or created new *thing* assemblies, the eastern Alpine region developed in the opposite direction from the early medieval period, as legal, military, and political power was increasingly divided and parcelled out to ecclesiastical institutions and lay aristocracy, thus feudalizing the authority of the assemblies. Dwindling peasant influence was reflected in the declining importance of the counts' regional *things*, although peasant influence on the agrarian level probably was maintained at local manorial assemblies. Part of this development had its foundation in the weakening and decay of the vast medieval empire on both sides of the Alps. After this fragmentation of political-juridical authority, the new duke of Bavaria started a slow reconstruction from

164 Beimrohr, 'Bäuerliche Besitzrechte', 100–01.
165 Beimrohr, 'Die ländliche Gemeinde in Tirol', 170.
166 Beimrohr, 'Bäuerliche Besitzrechte', 101–02.
167 Beimrohr, 'Bäuerliche Besitzrechte', 100.

the middle of the thirteenth century. In Tyrol, the count simultaneously began a somewhat faster reconstruction.

The new *thing* organization in Bavaria was based on a compromise between the aristocracy and the prince, reflected in a division of high and low jurisdiction. Lower jurisdiction became the responsibility of the aristocracy in their *Hofmarken*, where their tenants had the right of *co-determination* at the manorial peasant assemblies. Through his territorial courts, the *Landgerichte*, the prince held higher jurisdiction over the whole dukedom. He also held lower jurisdiction over around half of all landed property. The Bavarian compromise between prince and nobility lasted for a long time, and there was thus no room for an alliance between the prince and the peasantry. The stabilizing influence of this compromise can be contrasted with the development in Denmark where the king and a strong aristocracy competed for influence over *thing* peasants in the thirteenth century. In Bavarian villages subject to the territorial courts, peasant exercised a considerable degree of *self-administration* in agricultural and social matters through their village communities. Their degree of self-determination was, however, closely monitored by the local territorial administration, even to the degree that, from the early seventeenth century, village assemblies were forbidden to congregate without the consent of the authorities.

The manorial agricultural system was never as strong in Tyrol as in Bavaria. Relying on income from mountain pass trade and later from mining, the Tyrolean prince had the power to oust the aristocracy from their former judicial positions. By the late Middle Ages, most nobles had been reduced to be mere landowners. At the same time, the territorial power's concentration of jurisdictions was followed by a consolidation of court assemblies into territorialized entities. In this process, an alliance was formed between the sovereign and the *thing* peasants as taxpayers and soldiers. The tasks of most local assemblies (*Nachbarschaft / Gemeinde*) were of an agrarian kind, but as the assemblies were often congruent with the court assemblies (*Gericht*), they also possessed lower jurisdiction. The *thing* peasants thus enjoyed self-administration in agrarian matters through their *Nachbarschaft/Gemeinde*, and co-determination in courts and in matters relating to taxes and military conscription. In the regional *Landgerichte*, the judge appointed by the territorial prince had high jurisdictional power assisted by sworn peasants.

4 Integrated Conclusions

Our objective has been to study the development of peasant influence in a variety of assemblies and courts in the cross-section between the interests of lords (territorial and manorial) on the one hand (*Herrschaft*), and the interests of peasants on the other (*Genossenschaft*). We have described the development of such institutions chronologically within each region and country (Norway, Denmark, Bavaria, and Tyrol), but for practical and analytical purposes, we have also distinguished between *thing* assemblies and courts on the one hand and neighbourhood institutions dealing with the allocation of resources and daily agricultural problems on the other. We are, however, well aware of the fact that both *Herrschaft* and *Genossenschaft* played an important part in almost every one of these institutions and that legal and agricultural aspects are often difficult to discern. In this final section, we will therefore try to turn our dual investigation into an integrated conclusion on peasant influence and degree of self-determination, co-administration, or self-administration in various assemblies and institutions.

The distance alone between Scandinavia and the Alpine region should indicate that each of these regions would generally display distinctive features contrasting with the other region. Despite this, the wide range of topography within each of our regions might also reveal internal differences, and these differences may lay the foundation for similarities across the two regions. On the other hand, the influence of the Roman church created a common ecclesiastic and secular aristocratic culture in which large segments of the European aristocracy were integrated. This furthered similarities in legal institutions and relations between lords and peasants. In order to compare and explain the long-term development in our two regions, we have analysed the differences and similarities along two main lines, one being topography, the other the general socio-political development.

We will begin our summing up with analysing the development of *thing* assemblies; next, we will turn to institutions primarily dealing with the allocation of resources and daily agricultural problems, before summarizing these developments along socio-political and topographical lines.

In the eastern Alpine region, the early medieval count was a noble in the service of the German king / emperor. Representatives from important sections of society should be present at the *count's things* until well into the eleventh century. The participants represented the German king, the tribal duke, the count of the district, ecclesiastical and lay aristocrats, and free peasants. Even though different levels of society were thus present, they belonged to or were associated with households or families with varying degrees of wealth and power. In this way, free men were gathered according to their status. The most important dividing line in society was drawn between free and unfree men. Unfree men were excluded from participating at the *thing* in the eastern Alpine region, as well as in Scandinavia.

The early Scandinavian *things*, at least in Norway and Sweden, seem to have some sort of connection to local centres of power as hubs in more or less organized multiple estates. Competition among chieftains for peasant loyalty may subsequently have led to regional centralization of the *things*. At the Norwegian regional *things* (*lawthings*), many of them first organized by the emerging royal power, peasant representatives, probably from about 1000, met together with aristocrats and royal and ecclesiastical representatives. By the thirteenth century, these *lawthings* were turned into ordinary courts under the control of the king and his lawman (*lögmaðr*), and the peasant representatives were reduced to court witnesses. Similar meetings of free peasants and chieftains also took place at the Icelandic *Althing* (common *thing*) from 930 to the thirteenth century, when this institution also came under the Norwegian king's control.

From the eleventh century to the twelfth, socio-political development in the eastern Alpine region took a different direction than in Scandinavia, marked by a feudal fragmentation of jurisdiction. The German king / emperor endowed large monasteries in the Alpine valleys with jurisdiction, and lay aristocrats managed to obtain the same privileges in other regions. The German kings themselves did not, however, establish direct contact with peasant assemblies. The fragmentation of jurisdiction led to diminishing influence for peasants, who now increasingly belonged to manorial courts.

A similar development did not take place in Norway because the king allied himself with the peasant elite from the eleventh and twelfth century. From the end of the twelfth century, the king controlled the *things*, especially the *skipreiða thing* at the local level and the regional *thing* at the higher regional level. At the same time, the secular nobility increasingly entered into royal service. The coastal topography of Norway was a central element in the creation of a strong royal power. This topography also furthered peasant influence at the *things*, an influence that largely evolved from their participation in the naval defence, the *leidang*.

In Denmark, royal power had long been based on naval power and tributes, but in the twelfth and thirteenth centuries, the power of the aristocracy was, in contrast to Norway, increasing. This had consequences for jurisdiction. The secular nobility in general enjoyed a higher standing in the *thing* system, while the king established his own courts. By the middle of the thirteenth century, there were three, partly overlapping jurisdictions in the Danish kingdom: that of the *thing*, that of the king, and that of the church. The king's *retterting* and the church's *things* functioned without peasant representation. In this way, the king and the noble estate shared jurisdiction over Danish peasants. A similar division of jurisdiction did not take place in Norway, where regional *thing* meetings with selected peasant representatives continued into the thirteenth century.

In the eastern Alpine region, the establishment of separate principalities after the de facto dissolution of the German empire led to far-reaching jurisdictional reforms from the end of the thirteenth century. However, Bavaria and Tyrol developed in quite different directions. A compromise between the duke and the Bavarian nobility (1311) restored and transformed peasant influence in Bavaria into a new bipolar estate-based jurisdiction. By this compromise, which lasted into the eighteenth century, the duke monopolized higher jurisdiction in the most severe cases ('blood cases'). On this level, he also established local / regional courts (*Landgerichte*), where peasant influence gradually disappeared in favour of judicial experts appointed by the duke. In time, these judges passed verdicts 'according to written law' (*Buchsage*). The ecclesiastical and lay nobility were allowed to establish their own courts with lower jurisdiction (*Hofmarken*). In these *Hofmarken*, peasants retained their influence well into the early modern period.

In Tyrol, the territorial lord, the count, managed to circumscribe the power of lay and ecclesiastical lords from the thirteenth century onwards. The strong position of the count of Tyrol was also due to the fact that Tyrol was a mountain pass state with trade providing the prince financial and military superiority. Substantial income also came from the mining industry (first salt and then silver) by princely monopoly. A whole new *thing* system was created by way of combining the functions of former assemblies. From the second part of the thirteenth century, the old nobility was excluded from participation at the *thing* assemblies. As in Norway, the nobility in Tyrol was transformed into a landowning aristocracy in the service of the count.

By the late Middle Ages, the counts of Tyrol succeeded in making all peasants subjects to the territorial lord, severing whatever legal bonds they had to their manorial lords. Jurisdiction was now largely monopolized within the framework of the emerging territorial state. The peasants became militarily important. At the local level, *Gerichte* (courts and administrative units) were normally congruent with the traditional neighbourhood associations, the *Nachbarschaften*, from the fourteenth century. The local courts were headed by an appointed judge (*Richter*), but peasants participated as co-judges in giving verdicts. Unlike in Norway, Denmark, and Bavaria, these administrative and judicial institutions also elected representatives, very often peasants, to the territorial assembly of Tyrol.

Although Norway and Denmark were united into one kingdom in the late Middle Ages, their judicial systems did not converge even in the early modern period. The most marked difference was that many Danish manorial lords gained jurisdiction over their tenants. In Norway, the *lagrette* at the *thing*, a panel of the best peasants sworn in by the king's lawman, was turned into a local *thing* court in a nationwide appeal hierarchy from the turn of the seventeenth century. At the same time, peasants serving as co-judges and court witnesses gradually came under the influence of an appointed judge (*sorenskrivar*). Still, the local Norwegian peasant elite had a high degree of self-determination when it came to resolving disputes concerning landed resources, through the local *thing* and ad hoc committees in the Middle Ages, and through the *thing* and special committees in the early modern period.

Even though manorial power was extensive in Denmark, peasants played a role at the local level in Denmark, too. Peasants were active participants in a variety of cases in the medieval *things*, and a jury of peasants was still participating in handing down verdicts by the beginning of the early modern period. Even in the manorial courts (*birketing*), there was some peasant participation. However, from the beginning of the seventeenth century, peasants belonging to these courts, as well as to ordinary *herredsting*, were reduced to court witnesses and excluded from verdicts, except in cases that could involve the death penalty. Until 1660, the *foged* (judge and administrator) was usually appointed from among one of the peasants attached to the *thing*. Only by the end of the early modern period was this office exclusively given to trained jurists. We can, therefore, discern peasant influence on a local level in Danish *things* and the succeeding courts that replaced them, but, as in Norway, this influence was waning during the early modern period. The aristocracy's increasing control over their tenants in legal and administrative matters also circumscribed Danish peasants' influence.

We may thus conclude that the development of *thing* assemblies in the eastern Alpine region and in Scandinavia had similar, as well as dissimilar features. Before the beginning of the second millennium, free peasants and powerful chieftains or nobles met at regional *thing* assemblies. From the eleventh century, feudal division of jurisdiction and land made such general assemblies obsolete in the eastern Alpine region. Following the development of an estate-based state, a bipolar jurisdiction over peasants emerged from the fourteenth century in Bavaria, divided between the king on the one hand and ecclesiastical and lay lords on the other. We may trace a similar development in Denmark, where aristocratic landlords were allowed to establish their own courts, *birketings* in the early modern period.

In Tyrol, on the other hand, a new *thing* arrangement was established in close cooperation with the peasant elite. This resembles the development in Norway, with the important exception that Norway, lacking the feudal period found in Tyrol in the first centuries of the new millennium, displays a continuous development of an alliance between the king and the peasant elite. The strengthening of Norwegian royal power in the High Middle Ages, however, led to a paternalistic turn in the relationship between the king and the peasants, a turn that was carried further in the union with Denmark.

In the early modern period, the central power's transformation of *thing* assemblies into legal courts and administrative institutions led to diminishing peasant influence in the eastern Alpine region and in Scandinavia, especially at a territorial or regional level, while their influence lasted longer at the local level. Tyrol, with its strong peasant influence, was a marked exception to this general trend.

Peasant self-determination and self-administration were stronger in institutions dealing with the allocation of resources and daily agricultural problems than in *thing* institutions. Peasant influence was also better preserved from the Middle Ages to the end of the early modern period in such institutions. However, the extent of peasant influence and the channels in which they could exercise such influence differed greatly between Scandinavia and the Alpine region, as well as within each of these regions.

Norway lacked formal institutions dedicated to agricultural matters. On multiple farms, peasants resolved problems between themselves at the annual *grannestemne* or at informal village meetings on larger hamlets in coastal Norway. The lack of specialized institutions at farm and hamlet level may be due to the dispersed character of Norwegian settlement, where farms very seldom contained more than a handful of holdings and most daily agricultural activities could be resolved by each individual peasant household. Only severe disputes were elevated to the legal sphere of the local *thing*. Problems between neighbouring farms and hamlets were resolved within the framework of the local *thing* or ad hoc commissions, where an influential and trustworthy peasant elite contributed to reaching agreements in matters involving boundaries and outfield resources. These institutions were already formed in the Middle Ages, and their functions were transformed into the more formalized legal system of the early modern Danish-Norwegian monarchy.

In marked contrast to Norway, Denmark, with its fertile plains and field rotation systems, was characterized by villages with formal village institutions. Peasants in these village assemblies had almost full self-determination when it came to agricultural and social matters within the village and in matters pertaining to the use of common resources with neighbouring villages. Village laws were laid down at village meetings and an *oldermann* and other officials were elected. The degree of self-determination at these meetings is remarkable, considering the growing manorial power exercised by the Danish aristocracy from the end of the late Middle Ages, a power that included manorial courts, the right to impeach their tenants, execute sentences, and collect fines. From the middle of the seventeenth century, manorial lords even became middlemen between the state and their own tenants when it came to collecting taxes and conscripting soldiers. Nevertheless, they were satisfied with leaving their peasants within the framework of the village communities to cope with everyday agricultural problems. The reason for this was probably that they concentrated on the running of their demesnes at the same time as they secured the control of their tenants by other means. Nor did the Danish state interfere in village affairs, as it gradually left more control over peasants to the nobility.

As for topography and settlement, in many respects Bavaria can be compared to Denmark. Still, there was a huge difference between villages belonging to territorial administration, and villages and holdings belonging to *Hofmarken*. The difference between the territorial villages and the *Hofmarken* can be traced back to the compromise between the Bavarian territorial lord and the lay and ecclesiastical nobility in the thirteenth century, where the nobility retained control over some of their tenants in their closed territories. A characteristic of the *Hofmarken* was the close integration of judicial and agricultural issues. Regulations concerning agriculture and the use of common resources, issues that elsewhere were resolved by village assemblies (Bavaria, Denmark) or neighbourhood institutions (Tyrol), were resolved at the *Bautaiding* in Bavarian *Hofmarken*. In this assembly, the manorial tenants, as well as the landlord, who had the authority to confirm and proclaim decisions and statutes (*Weistümer*), were present. The executive body of most *Hofmarken* was either a peasant (*Amman*) or a collective body of peasants (*Vierer*), elected by the *Hofmark* assembly and confirmed by the lord of the *Hofmark*. This body dealt with practical agricultural issues within the *Hofmark*, while a court, headed by a judge (*Richter*) and assisted by *Hofmark* peasants as 'finders of law' and co-judges, dealt with judicial issues according to customary law.

However, the majority of Bavarian peasants organized themselves in village communities dealing with agricultural problems, allocation of resources, and control of social life along much the same lines as in Denmark. A marked difference from Denmark was the territorial / princely lord's efforts to control village assemblies and their affairs. Village statutes and other decisions had to be approved by the local princely administrator and fines were due to the authorities, not the village community.

In Tyrol, matters relating to agriculture and the use of resources were resolved within the framework of neighbourhood associations, *Nachbarschaften*. These neighbourhood associations, usually consisting of one or several villages, hamlets, or single farms, regulated the use of common resources and social life in much the same way as village assemblies did in Denmark and Bavaria, and *Hofmark* assemblies in Bavaria. From the early sixteenth century, they were also given the task of collecting taxes and overseeing conscription of soldiers. The officials elected by the *Nachbarschaften* had, from that point of time, to be confirmed by the authorities. Apart from this, these associations and their officials had a wide range of self-determination in local matters, except for the use of forests, which the territorial lord, claiming a superior ownership to all outfield resources, reserved to himself in case they could be useful for his mining activities.

Social-political evolution was a crucial factor in the development of peasant assemblies in our two regions of comparison, the eastern Alpine region and Scandinavia. From a type of general *thing* institution where free men from every status group were represented, chieftains as well as peasants, this institution developed in more specific directions during the High and late Middle Ages. This development was basically connected to the formation of estates and the development of sovereign power that anticipated the early modern state. From the High Middle Ages, 'peasant' came to denote a man who worked the land, and thus a separate peasant estate was forming. Below the prince, a nobility of powerful families was formed. In Bavaria, this led to a dual *thing* organization with separate *thing* institutions for peasants belonging to the nobility. In Tyrol, where the nobility was weaker, they were excluded from the peasant assemblies, which became arenas for the prince and the peasants. In Denmark, where the nobility was strong, it managed to dominate ordinary *thing* institutions, thus compelling the king to establish alternative *things*. In Norway, as in Tyrol, the nobility was weak and the *thing* institutions became arenas for the king and the peasants.

Comparing Scandinavia with the territories of the eastern Alpine region, we must conclude that topography and other geographical conditions, together with noble or princely power, influenced peasant self-determination in agrarian affairs and set limits on their participation in the social-legal sphere. Norway and Tyrol are marked by a rugged topography with fragmented agricultural areas linked by fjords and sea (Norway) and valleys and mountain passes (Tyrol). This topography seems to have favoured the creation of strong territorial states with close ties between the territorial power and its subject peasants at the expense of aristocratic influence over their tenants. In both regions, peasants participated in regional and local assemblies. As the medieval assemblies were turned into courts of justice, the influence of Norwegian peasants was reduced, first at the regional level, and later, in the early modern period, at the local level. In Tyrol, peasant influence continued longer, and they were even represented at territorial estate assemblies from the late Middle Ages.

Even though there were some similarities in topography between Norway and Tyrol, the way common resources were managed and conflicts between peasant holdings were resolved was quite different. In Norway, such problems were primarily dealt with within the framework of a legal system created in the medieval period, involving the *thing* and ad hoc committees, while in Tyrol, where a uniform legal system came into being at a later point in time, neighbourhood associations dealt with the same problems. In both regions, peasants had a high degree of self-determination in matters involving agrarian problems and the allocation of common resources.

Topography and field rotation systems favoured village associations in Denmark and in Bavaria. In Denmark, these institutions, in spite of the aristocracy's growing power over their tenants, were pretty much left to peasants themselves to organize and administer, while manorial and territorial influence set limits on peasants self-determination in Bavaria. Still, Bavarian peasants had substantial influence over daily agricultural proceedings and the allocation of common resources, especially in villages not belonging to a *Hofmark*, As for their influence in the courts, Bavarian princely peasants were excluded from participating in giving verdicts in the late medieval period, whereas *Hofmark* peasants continued to be co-judges for a long time. This was clearly connected to the use of customary law in the *Hofmarken,* where peasants were still kept as 'finders of law', whereas in the territorial courts, written law excluded peasants from this function from the fourteenth century onwards.

We must therefore conclude that topographical factors influenced peasant conflict-handling institutions and neighbourhood associations in Scandinavia and in the eastern Alpine region. The way these institutions were formed and the degree of peasant self-determination was, however, highly influenced by territorial and manorial power factors. A common development in both regions seems to be the central power's transformation of primordial *thing* assemblies into legal courts and administrative institutions, a transformation that in many cases led to diminishing peasant influence, especially at a territorial or regional level, while their influence lasted longer at the local level. The close ties between the territorial prince and the Tyrolean peasants enabled an exception to this general trend, as peasants came to be represented in the territorial estate assembly from the late Middle Ages. Peasants in both regions maintained their influence in institutions dealing with the allocation of resources and daily agricultural problems, but their actual influence and the structure of these institutions were formed by topographical and socio-political factors.

CHAPTER 5

Summary and Conclusion

Tore Iversen and John Ragnar Myking

The aim of our project has been to assess the degree of peasant control over land and resources in two different European regions, Scandinavia and the eastern Alpine region from around 1000 to 1750. Our ambition has also been to gain a better understanding of the development of peasant control and influence in institutions dealing with social and agrarian issues in rural society, as well as of conflicts within peasant society, in these two regions.

We found our initial inspiration for selecting Scandinavia and the eastern Alpine region in the programme of the Norwegian Institute for Comparative Cultural Research, founded in 1920. In 1929, the renowned Norwegian historian, Edvard Bull, initiated a comparative study of peasant societies in the Alpine region and Scandinavia, aimed at finding 'valid laws' and 'objective correlations' of the development of peasant societies in the two regions. This project was never completed, due to the political development of the next decades. Today, any attempt to find objective historical laws have long been considered futile, but we are still inspired by the concrete studies carried out in the framework of the institute in our attempt to compare peasant control over land and resources in the two regions.

The eastern Alpine region has a marked topographical resemblance to Scandinavia. In the mountainous areas of Norway, northern Scandinavia and the eastern Alpine region, less land is suited to cultivation, while there is ample space for grazing and foresting. Particularly in Norway, a long and protected coastline allows for a combination of agriculture and fisheries, while mining was important in Tyrol. On the other hand, in Bavaria, Denmark, and southern Sweden, we find wide, fertile valleys and large, continuous plains with moraine soil. This variation in topography offers an opportunity to analyze the effect of topographical factors on peasant control over land and resources, without, however, neglecting the impact of hierarchical power structures involving ecclesiastical and aristocratic landlords, territorial lords, and emerging territorial states.

We have concentrated our research on three topics, resulting in three main chapters in Part 2 in this volume: 'Slavery and Unfreedom', 'Leasehold and Freehold', and 'Peasant Participation in *Thing* and Local Assemblies'. These three topics correlate with three different types of dominion over peasants in ancient European societies. In German, Austrian, and Swiss historiography, these

 | DOI:10.1163/9789004433458_006

types of dominion are labelled *Leibherrschaft* (dominion over body and person), *Grundherrschaft* (dominion over land) and *Gerichtsherrschaft* (legal dominion). These three forms of dominion were not clearly separated from each other, especially not in the beginning of the period we investigate. In sum, they indicate that peasant control over land and resources was circumscribed by hierarchical structures, although depending to a varying degree on the historical development of the different regions and countries.

In our fist main chapter in Part 2 ('Slavery and Unfreedom'), we have been occupied primarily with defining and characterizing unfreedom. We have also discussed the function and impact of slavery in Scandinavia and the eastern Alpine region, as well as its diminution from the first centuries of the second millennium, which contributed to the establishment of a concept of a uniform peasant estate in the two regions. In the next chapter ('Leasehold and Freehold'), we have highlighted tenants' security of tenure and degree of control over available resources, comparing their control over succession and resources to that of freeholders. In our final chapter ('Peasant Participation'), we have concentrated on peasant influence in conflict-handling assemblies, like local *things*, and village and manorial assemblies. In this summary, we will present our findings in each of these chapters in a chronological order, before we proceed to an overall discussion of the development of peasant control over land and resources against the background of topography and power relations in our two designated regions.

In our research, we have concentrated on Bavaria and Tyrol in the eastern Alpine region and Norway and Denmark in Scandinavia, as these territories have turned out to be the most rewarding when contrasting topography and territorial and manorial dominion. These territories will therefore also be highlighted in this summary. Other territories, like Sweden in Scandinavia and Switzerland in the eastern Alpine region, will only be commented on briefly, as far as they can shed additional light on similarities and differences between the eastern Alpine region and Scandinavia.

Peasants, and their degree of control over land and resources and their participation in rural institutions, are the object of our investigations. However, it must first be asked: at what point in time can we discern a specific group of rural people that we may characterize as 'peasants'? As for the earliest period, until well into the twelfth century, we maintain, in accordance with recent research, that there was a close connection between dominion over land and dominion over people. As pointed out, these forms of dominion were linked and cannot be clearly separated from each other. A main cause for the entanglement of dominion over land and people may be found in the correlation between the size of the population and the amount of available land for cultivation. Before the massive population increase beginning in the last half of the eleventh century, there was a shortage of labour in agriculture in Scandinavia and in the Alpine region, thus making it advantageous for the elite to establish and maintain domination over people they could use to exploit landed resources.

By the turn of the eleventh century, the *Grundherrschaft / Villikations* system was well established in the eastern Alpine region. In this system, free and unfree persons worked the area surrounding a central farm (*domus*). Unfree persons (*servi*) were subject to their lord's control and rendered labour on the central farm. Nevertheless, quite a few of them were also given land to cultivate in the vicinity of the main farm. Largely free men worked their own well-defined holdings. They were less personally dependent, although many of them belonged to the lord's manorial court.

In Scandinavia, power and resources were, to a certain degree, centred around what we, inspired by English historiography, have termed *multiple estates*. Compared to the continental and Alpine manorial system, these multiple estates covered a wider geographical area and exploited a complex variety of resources in addition to agriculture. These more loosely organized estates, to which free peasants were also attached, were to a great extent held together by *tributary* relations between patrons and clients. These relations included exchange in the form of gifts and repayment for gifts and benefits. Tribute was a recognition of the chief's or lord's supremacy, which gave him a partial dominion over the inhabitants. The labour of unfree people (*þrælar*) played an important role on these multiple estates, and in the course of their manumission, they were used to clear new land, maintaining close bonds to their lords for generations.

During the twelfth and thirteenth centuries, an increase in population, growth in trade, and expanding towns led to decreasing personal bonds, better legal conditions, and more favourable tenures in the Alpine region. The manorial system (*Villikationen*) was largely dissolved. Landlords now drew their incomes primarily from rents paid by their tenants (*Rentengrundherrrschaft*). Nearly all claims for corvée labour were abandoned, and the main farm was turned over to a steward (*Meier*) or parcelled out to peasants. In Scandinavia, furthered by the increase in population, former tributary relations between patron and clients gave way to contractual relations between tenants and their landlords.

1 The Emergence of a Peasant Estate

Only at this point, where dominion over people began to give way to more contractual relations between landlords and the people working the land, can we discern the gradual emergence of a peasant estate, clearly defined from other estates like the clergy, the aristocracy, and a town-dwelling class of merchants and craftsmen. Before this point in time, the crucial division in rural society was drawn between free and unfree people (see chapter 'Slavery and Unfreedom'). Only as this division was waning, a uniform concept of 'peasants', in the sense of farmers working the land, emerged in both regions, and only from this point in time will it be worthwhile to discuss peasant control over land and resources.

The German historian Werner Rösener raises the question of why the concept of a peasant estate distinguishable from other social estates emerged in the High Middle Ages and not earlier.[1] He maintains that one crucial factor was the emergence of a class of warriors replacing peasant military contributions, another being the intensification of agriculture requiring the peasant's constant presence. More generally, we may point to changes in the way manors were run and the rise of towns and commerce, but also to changes in warfare and territorial dominion. The concept of a society of estates may thus be an attempt to structure diverging traits of development in order to secure the power of the territorial lord. In the medieval period, this concept was, however, more deeply rooted in the thinking of the continental elites than in the ideology of their Scandinavian counterparts. The *Rigsþula*, a Norse work of poetry most likely dated to the thirteenth century, nevertheless divides society into three layers: slaves, free peasants, and aristocrats. This indicates that a breeding ground for an ideology based on estates was also found in Scandinavia at the time.[2] We are able to discern, at least in Denmark, such a way of thinking in the thirteenth and fourteenth centuries.

The development of the concept of a peasant estate is reflected in the evolution of concepts denoting people working the land. Before the eleventh century, the term *gebure* (Bauer) in German-speaking regions denoted an occupant of a house (*Bur*) belonging to a neighbourhood (*Burschap, Nachbur*). When sources in the early Middle Ages describe larger social groups within rural society, they use concepts such as *liberi* (free) *or servi* (slaves, unfree).[3] As the *Villikation* system from the twelfth century was disintegrating, it became increasingly difficult to distinguish between free and unfree status.[4]

1 Werner Rösener, *Peasants in the Middle Ages* (Cambridge: Polity Press, 1992), 11–14.

2 See, for example, Rudolf Simek and Hermann Pálsson, *Lexikon der altnordischen Literatur: die mittelateriche Literatur Norwegens und Islands* (Stuttgart: Alfred Kröner Verlag, 2007), 294–95.

3 See Part 2, chapter 'Slavery and Unfreedom', and Rösener, *Peasants in the Middle Ages*, 12.

4 Phillippe Dollinger, *Der bayerische Bauernstand vom 9. bis zum 13. Jahrhundert* (Munich: C.H. Beck, 1982), 432.

Also, in Scandinavia the distinction between free and unfree persons (*prælar* / slaves) was the main social distinction in rural society until the twelfth century. In Norway, the term *bonde* denoted a free man who, in contrast to unfree or half-free men, could own unfree persons. As unfreedom was waning by the thirteenth century, *bonde* came to denote a peasant working the land, and *bønder* came to denote a separate estate, distinguishable from the clergy, the aristocracy, and the royal house (see 'Introduction', section 'Historiographical and Methodological Reflections'). Regulations about slaves and persons with half-free status were omitted in the Norwegian *Law of the Realm* from 1274, and the distinction between free and unfree status also became obsolete in Denmark at the turn of the fourteenth century.

Even though a peasant estate was gradually forming in the Alpine region and in Scandinavia by the twelfth to the thirteenth century, members of this estate endured a variety of conditions when it came to personal freedom, control over resources, secure possession of land, and participation in conflict-handling assemblies. In the following, we will summarize our main findings in these three fields, beginning with personal unfreedom, before returning to a general discussion on possible explanations for the diversified development of peasant control and influence in our two regions.

2 Unfreedom

Slavery was widespread in the eastern Alpine region and in Scandinavia in the early Middle Ages and into our period of investigation. A rather sharp division between free and unfree persons remained the most important social dividing line well into the High Middle Ages, although this division lasted somewhat longer in Scandinavia than in the eastern Alpine region. Slaves were primarily born into slavery, but they were also a valuable commodity from wars and raids, such as the Scandinavian Viking raids. Often, they were traded in a market. In addition, persons could also be sentenced to slavery as a form of punishment.

Because slavery / unfreedom, ideological as well as in practice, was in integrated part of medieval society, we have used a broad definition that includes pure slavery as well as milder forms of unfreedom.[5] That the slave / unfree person was his master's property is an important part of this definition. But he was also a contemplative person who could act consciously and be punished or rewarded. In other words, he was a person in a negative or in a positive

5 All slaves are part of a broader unfree group, but an unfree person is not necessarily a slave.

sense. In the first case, he was punished corporeally, often by whipping, which is a characteristic element of all pure slavery all over the globe. On the other hand, he could also be rewarded, and in time be granted improved conditions, leading from strict slavery to milder unfreedom and eventually to full freedom. The road to freedom was a prolonged development which the masters of the unfree could take advantage of in several ways, including disciplining their slaves and developing their own property. Thus, the clearing of new land in Norway and Sweden was an important task for unfree people in the thirteenth century, which in Sweden lasted into the fourteenth century.

In Scandinavia, Norway and Iceland have the richest written sources concerning slavery and milder forms of unfreedom. The Nordic sagas contain accounts of extensive slavery on the estates of chieftains and magnates and the systematic settlement of unfree persons on the outskirts of their main farms. In many cases, this occurs within the framework of a *multiple estate* arrangement, but several clauses in the regional laws point to the fact that ordinary peasants also owned slaves.

Manumission clauses in the Norwegian *Gulathing Law* from the twelfth century standardize a strict slavery with a span of two generations before the descendants of slaves could obtain full freedom. Influenced by the church, the *Frostathing Law* from the first part of the thirteenth century delineates a much milder form of slavery. Yet this law prescribes several more generations before the descendants of slaves could obtain their full freedom. During the first part of this prolonged manumission process they also enjoyed less freedom than in the older *Gulathing Law*. The intent may have been to prescribe a type of stigma or unfreedom / half-freedom known from the Continent. However, in King Magnus the Lawmender's *Law of the Realm* from 1274, all clauses concerning slavery / unfreedom were removed.

The *Lex Baiuvariorum* from the early medieval period, which was current law in the eastern Alpine region for a long time, also prescribed a strict slavery. However, after the dissolution of manors (*Villikationen*), a milder form of unfreedom (*Servitium / Leibeigenschaft*) gained ground. Previously, the lord controlled persons and the land they lived on. When this dual control was divided, manorial lords still retained control over persons who lived on or were born on the estate, often referred to as *Eigenleute* (literally 'owned people'). These *Eigenleute* could not freely marry anyone belonging to another lord or leave the holding without the consent of their lord. In this way, a lord was able to keep a reserve workforce or secure the cultivation of vacant holdings. Leaving the estate was nevertheless possible, either by escaping or by paying a fee.

Although *Eigenleute* in Bavaria could marry freely from the beginning of the sixteenth century, children from marriages between persons originating on different estates were divided between these estates according to rules laid down in Bavarian law. Many ecclesiastical and aristocratic lords kept track of their *Eigenleute* for generations. Their unfree status was marked by a small annual fee (*Leibzins*) and fees to be paid on their death, but these fees normally did not amount to large sums.

During the population crisis in the wake of the plagues in the late Middle Ages, *Leibeigenschaft* turned out to be a tool for resettling vacant holdings in parts of Bavaria. Although this milder form of unfreedom was not directly recognized as unfreedom in Denmark, restrictions on tenants' free movement was introduced on the eastern islands of Denmark from the second part of the fifteenth century, thus eliminating any attempts to bargain for better condition by moving to the estate of another landlord. As with the *Leibeigenschaft* in the eastern Alpine region, this was camouflaged as a way of protecting their tenants.

In Bavaria, *Leibherrschaft* became a tool for aristocratic lords and ecclesiastical institutions to secure administrative and legal control over peasants on their estates. The Bavarian duke took this one step further as he managed to transfer the dependence of his *Eigenleute* from their persons to the land they were working, thus furthering his territorial control. *Leibeigenschaft* lasted in Bavaria until it was officially abolished in 1808, although many *Eigenleute* had bought their complete freedom earlier than this, and being bound to their lord had become a mere formality. In Tyrol, *Leibeigenschaft* was dramatically reduced by 1300 as a part of the territorial lords' efforts to make every peasant their territorial subject, and by the beginning of the sixteenth century, it was for all practical purposes eradicated.

At the beginning of the early modern period, then, only some peasants in Bavaria, mainly belonging to ecclesiastical and aristocratic estates, endured restrictions on movement and rendered fees marking their personal dependence to a lord. Restrictions on movement were shared by some tenants in Denmark, although they did not pay fees marking any personal dependence to their landlords. Thus, restrictions on movement lasted longer in areas where a landlord's influence was strongest, as in Bavaria and Denmark, while the efforts of territorial rulers to establish close ties to peasants as their territorial subjects, as in Tyrol and Norway, furthered personal freedom for peasants.

3 Leasehold and Freehold

When it comes to control over land and resources, we must underline that we have primarily studied peasants with full holdings, not crofters and other groups on the outskirts of peasant society. In the eastern Alpine region, and in Scandinavia, peasants could either be tenants or freeholders. In both regions, a majority of peasants were tenants from the High Middle Ages until the end of the early modern period.

The dissolution of the manorial system (*Villikationen*) in the eastern Alpine region and of the *multiple estates* of Scandinavia furthered the development of a rental-based tenant system. An exception was marked by the introduction of demesne farming on estates in Denmark and part of Sweden in the early modern period, where tenants rendered corvée labour as well as rent. From the twelfth to the thirteenth century, tenants became the dominant group of peasants in the eastern Alpine region and in Scandinavia. At first, many tenants were allotted their land on very short leases, like the one-year *Freistift* in the eastern Alpine region or the one-year lease resembling *Freistift* recorded in the Norwegian *Gulathing Law* from the twelfth century. Although in practice renewable every year, these short-term leases left tenants in an insecure position vis-à-vis their landlord, because a number of them were unfree persons at the outset. There was, however, a clear tendency toward longer and more secure tenures in the eastern Alpine region and in Scandinavia, even involving lifelong and hereditary tenure.

In the early modern period, lifelong tenures became the usual form of tenure in Norway and in Denmark, while the length of Swedish tenures depended on the category of landed property, with lifelong tenures on Swedish crown land from the end of the seventeenth century and shorter tenures on estates belonging to the aristocracy. In Tyrol, hereditary tenures (*Erbbaurecht / Erblehen*) were spreading from the twelfth and thirteenth centuries. On the other hand, in Bavaria, hereditary tenures were granted on the estates of the territorial lord in Upper (southern) Bavaria from the fifteenth century but were not widespread at all in Lower (northern) Bavaria. There, *Freistift* remained the dominant form of tenure well into the early modern period.

The tendency to assign longer tenures included a transformation to stronger tenant influence over landed property, especially in Tyrol, Switzerland, and Norway. While the landlord retained the *dominium directum*, the tenant gained a *dominium utile* in the property. Tenants with hereditary tenures (*Erbbaurecht*) in Tyrol gained the right to sell and pledge their land, but had to obtain the consent of the landowner to do so. In Norway, tenants in the early modern period could sell or transfer their land to whomever they liked, even without the consent of the landlord. These tenants thus came close to a de facto ownership of their holdings, even though the landlord retained a *dominium directum*.

This development was closely linked to the territorial power's ambition of making peasants reliable and taxable subjects on the one hand, and to the degree of a landlord's interest in controlling their tenants on the other. In Tyrol and Norway, territorial lords managed to establish direct bonds with the peasants by the Middle Ages, and landlords were content with extracting a surplus rent from the land they rented out to their tenants. As long as this rent was secure, they did not interfere with the use of the land, except for keeping for themselves certain resources, such as exploitation of timber exceeding the needs of the tenant household.

In regions where *Leibeigenschaft* still was common, as in parts of Bavaria, or where demesne farming was reintroduced, as in Denmark in the early modern period, landlords kept tighter control over their tenants. The character of tenures and tenants' control over landed property thus depended on their landlords' ability and willingness to make use of their power of dominion (*Herrschaftsrecht*) and the ability and willingness of the authorities to let them do so.

Freeholders generally had a higher degree of self-determination over their possessions than tenants. There were, however, restrictions on freeholders in some regions, as most governments claimed a superior ownership to freehold land. In Tyrol and Sweden, the crown claimed a superior ownership that restricted the exploitation of forests. In Sweden and Denmark, such superior ownership was also designed to control the transfer of land to other landowners, although, in fact, the government also used their superior ownership during the early modern period to enlarge the landholdings of the aristocracy. In Denmark, freeholders had to pay a recognition fee to the crown, and they could even be called upon to do corvée labour, although on a smaller scale than tenants. The freeholders' free transfer of land was also circumscribed in Norway and Sweden by a pre-emption and redemption for descendants and relatives, stretching over several generations.

From the Middle Ages until the early modern period, freehold expanded in some regions at the expense of tenure, while it declined in other regions. By the last quarter of the eighteenth century, peasant ownership amounted to almost one-quarter of all holdings in Tyrol. In Norway, one-fifth of the land was owned and worked by peasants themselves by the middle of the seventeenth century. This ratio increased to more than one-half of the land by the end of the eighteenth century.

On the other hand, in Bavaria, where freehold accounted to from 5 to 20 percent of the holdings in some regions at the end of the Middle Ages, their number diminished over the course of the early modern period. The most dramatic reduction was found in Denmark, where freehold land was reduced from around 15 percent of all land by the first decades of the sixteenth century to a mere 2 percent by the end of the seventeenth century. In Sweden, freehold was also reduced, from about one-half of the land by the early sixteenth century to one-third by the late seventeenth century.

In Tyrol and in Norway, the change to freehold was, if not directly furthered, then at least tolerated by the authorities, and, at least in Norway, aided by the decreasing interest shown by merchants and officials in investing in landed property run by tenants. In contrast, the government in Denmark and Sweden actively supported the reduction of freehold by transferring their claim to superior ownership to new landlords.

Comparing tenants with freeholders, some tenants, mainly in Tyrol and Norway, enjoyed control over land and resources that can be compared to that of freeholders. On the other hand, some freeholders, like those in Denmark in the early modern period, had more in common with the eastern Alpine tenants with hereditary tenure (*Erblehen*) than, for example, Norwegian or Tyrolean freeholders. A clear-cut division between freeholders with full control over their landed property, security of succession, and unlimited access to resources on the one hand, and tenants with insecure tenures, limited possession of land, and restricted access to resources on the other hand, is therefore hard to find, either between our two regions of comparison or within each of them.

Instead of looking for an explanation along regional lines, we must therefore seek the causes for the differences in security of possession and access to resources in the interest of the territorial lords and landlords. Where the territorial government was strong, it backed long-term leases, a moderate land-rent, and even a transition to freehold, often against the interest of manorial lords, in order to establish peasants as viable subjects able to pay taxes. On the other hand, where the aristocracy filled important administrative or military functions, as in early modern Denmark, this goal was minimized. Where the ecclesiastical and lay aristocracy possessed vital *Herrschaftsrechte* (dominion), as in Bavaria, they were able to keep tighter control over their tenants and thus delay the development of more favourable tenures and even full personal freedom.

4 Participation in Local Agrarian and Conflict-handling Institutions

In Scandinavia and in the eastern Alpine region, peasants participated in a wide range of institutions vital to their agricultural and social interests, ranging from village and neighbourhood assemblies dealing with everyday agricultural issues to larger *thing* assemblies with conflict-handling and legal tasks. Their degree of influence in such institutions ranged from complete self-administration, mostly found in institutions dealing with agrarian issues, to mere formal attendance without any co-determination at all, as was the case in some courts where they served as court witnesses.

The oldest form of participation from people working the land goes back to before the formation of a separate peasant estate, a period when the crucial dividing line was drawn between free and unfree people. According to the *Lex Baiuvariorum* (740–88), covering Bavaria and Tyrol, free men were to meet at fixed *thing* meetings administrated by the king's count. These free men belonged to various levels of society, and their influence was linked to the strength and power of the different households or families they belonged to.

From the eleventh century, feudal division led to, among other things, a fragmentation of legal power in the eastern Alpine region, as monasteries and some aristocrats managed to obtain jurisdiction on their estates. From the end of the thirteenth century, however, jurisdiction in Bavaria and Tyrol developed in separate directions. In Bavaria, the duke monopolized higher jurisdiction, that is jurisdiction in severe cases ('blood cases') concerning crimes against the social peace, from the beginning of the fourteenth century. To this end, he established regional courts (*Landgerichte*), which also handled lower jurisdiction as long as this did not belong to the manorial courts, *Hofmarken.* The duke thus exercised lower jurisdiction over approximately one-half of all landed property in Bavaria in the fourteenth century, even if he himself owned only 20 percent of the land.

The ecclesiastical and lay nobility could establish their own courts with lower jurisdiction in their *Hofmarken.* In these *Hofmarken,* which prevailed into the eighteenth century, peasants functioned as 'finders of law' and co-judges. Peasant judicial influence lasted longer in *Hofmarken* than in territorial courts, where peasant co-determination rapidly dwindled. Nevertheless, one must bear in mind that, in *Hofmarken,* we find all three forms of dominion (*Herrschaft*): dominion over land (*Grundherrschaft*), dominion over people (*Leibherrschaft*), and legal dominion (*Gerichtsherrschaft*). Ecclesiastical and aristocratic lords were thus in a position to keep a closer watch on their tenants in their *Hofmarken*, which in many cases also were their *Eigenleute*.

In Tyrol, jurisdiction and peasant participation in courts developed in quite another direction. Following a period of feudal division of jurisdiction, the territorial princes, in an alliance with the peasants, managed to secure complete jurisdictional control. In this process, which was completed by the fifteenth century, they used a variety of tools, including administrative control over ecclesiastical estates and dominion over serfs on several manors. The outcome was a homogeneous administration and jurisdiction based on local courts (*Gerichtsgemeinde*) with administrative and judicial tasks. In these local courts, an appointed administrator and judge passed sentences together with sworn-in peasant co-judges.

Peasant influence in courts thus developed in quite different directions from the Middle Ages to the early modern period in the eastern Alpine region. In Bavaria, peasants lost their influence in territorial courts, while peasants belonging to *Hofmarken* retained their participation, even if they must have felt the shadow of their lords hanging over them to varying degrees. In Tyrol, on the other hand, from the fifteenth century, peasants enjoyed real participation in local judicial affairs.

Moreover, in Scandinavia, only free men could meet at the earliest *things*. These *things*, at least in Norway and Sweden, seem to have some sort of connection to local centres of power, as hubs in more or less organized multiple estates. Later, competition among chieftains for peasant loyalty led to regional centralization of *things*. Peasant influence at these *things* was closely connected with their bonds to different chieftains, but from the eleventh century, an alliance between peasants and the king began to take shape at the expense of the local and regional aristocracy. In Norway, the first royal servant at the *thing* was the king's unfree servant, the *ármaðr*.

By the thirteenth century, the former Norwegian regional *things* where local representatives had met were replaced by regional courts of law where a royal lawman (*lögmaðr*) passed sentences with sworn-in peasant representatives as witnesses. While the king had a near-exclusive legal monopoly at the regional level, a peasant elite still participated at *things* and ad hoc committees (*domr*) on a local level. Members of this peasant elite passed sentences and reached agreements between conflicting parties for several centuries, sometimes also with the help of the legally trained *lögmaðr*.

By the end of the sixteenth century, the use of ad hoc committees came to an end and local *things* were turned into courts. A judge, the *sorenskrivar* (literary, 'sworn-in writer') was introduced, first as a helper for the peasants serving as *lagrettemenn* (peasants sworn in by the *lagmann*) at the local thing, then as a co-judge. From the end of the seventeenth century, he became the sole judge in most cases, except in the most important ones for the peasantry, cases relating to life, property, and honour where the *lagrettemenn* were still co-judges.

In Denmark, the early *thing* organization is more obscure than in Norway. Originally the *herredsting* was a meeting place for all free peasants living in the area. As in the rest of Scandinavia, conflicts were also resolved in ad hoc committees. The nobility came to have the higher standing at the *herredsting*, so the king established his own royal *retterting*, where members of *riksrådet* (the royal council) assisted in verdicts. The *retterting* became a court of appeal in the early modern period.

From the fifteenth century, the qualification to pass judgement and reach agreements was gradually transferred to a *foged* (bailiff), appointed from among the peasants, who at first was a leader of the *thing*, then became a co-judge. By the end of the seventeenth century, the *foged* became the only judge, peasants serving only as witnesses, except in cases involving the death penalty and witchcraft where they were still needed as assessors. Furthermore, they were to continue to decide if the accused was guilty or not in cases of theft. The fact that judges were usually appointed from among one of the peasants until 1660 was also a remnant of peasant influence.

In the early modern period, lords on aristocratic manors received the right to establish their own manorial courts, *birketings*. Peasant participation on these manorial courts did not differ much from peasant participation at the *herredstings,* and the judge (*foged*) at the *birketing* was also drawn from the ranks of the manorial peasants.

While the territorial power restricted peasant influence in many instances in the judicial system over the course of the early modern period, it had less interest in regulating institutions relating to peasants agricultural and social interest at the local level. Such institutions were therefore initiated by and operated according to the interests of the peasantry to a high degree, even though the territorial power and landlords set limits on peasant self-administration in some regions.

In regions well adapted to arable farming in an open field system, such as southern Scandinavia, Bavaria, and northern Switzerland, village organization with formal village institutions was the rule. In Bavaria, Denmark, and parts of Sweden, a village meeting where every peasant household could meet laid down village statues, elected officials, and decided vital matters relating to the rotation of crops, the maintenance of fences, and access to outfield resources.

The extent of village organization is difficult to trace in the early centuries of the High Middle Ages, but at least in Bavaria organization on a village level probably followed in the wake of the dissolution of the manorial system (*Villikationen*). From then on, peasants in southern Scandinavia and Bavaria resolved their agricultural problems and regulated social life within the framework of the village organization.

Peasant self-administration was greater in Denmark than in Bavaria. Except for some landlords who insisted on approving village statutes, Danish landlords did not interfere with village organization. A plausible reason for this was that they, over the course of the early modern period, controlled their tenants in other ways. They used them as a labour force on their demesnes, they had the right to impeach them for offences and execute penalties, and, from the middle of the seventeenth century, they acted as middlemen between their tenants and the Danish state in collecting taxes and conscripting soldiers.

A special form of peasant organization was found in the Bavarian *Hofmarken.* There, peasants were organized on an estate level, but the way of organizing agricultural and social affairs was much the same as in villages with village institutions. Nevertheless, landlord influence must have been more clearly felt because the lords of the *Hofmarken* often exercised several forms of dominion over their tenants, including legal dominion (*Gerichtsherrschaft*) and dominion over people (*Leibherrschaft*). In Bavarian villages belonging to the territorial administration, landlords did not interfere with village organization, but villages were heavily monitored by the territorial administration. Fines were due to the authorities, not to the village itself as in Denmark, and from the beginning of the seventeenth century, villagers were even forbidden to congregate without the consent of the authorities.

While peasant organization relating to agricultural issues in regions with arable farming with crop rotation was concentrated within villages or, as in parts of Bavaria, closed estates (*Hofmarken*), corresponding institutions in more mountainous regions where outfield resources and animal husbandry were more important appear to have been more diverse. In parts of coastal Norway where agrarian settlements with a complex distribution of arable land could approach the size of small villages or hamlets, some sort of peasant cooperation was vital when it came to the use of the complex distribution of arable land, fencing, and the use of outfield resources. Nevertheless, such cooperation was usually carried out without the establishment of formal institution, as in southern Scandinavia and Bavaria.

Beside this informal approach, conflict-handling between Norwegian neighbours relating to the use of resources was usually resolved within the framework of the judicial system created in the Middle Ages, either at the local *thing* or in ad hoc committees (*domr*) consisting of members of the peasant elite. As proceedings at the local thing were increasingly formalized in the early modern period and peasant influence was restricted, such conflicts were still dealt with at the local *thing* with peasant co-judges or in special commissions consisting of respected peasants and the local judge (*sorenskrivar*).

In Tyrol, conflicts over the allocation of resources were handled within the framework of the neighbourhood (*Nachbarschaft*). Each *Nachbarschaft* had an assembly that met at least once a year. This assembly decided on the use of common resources on the *Gemain,* that is, the common land, and it compiled village laws in densely populated settlements where problems relating to the open field structure also had to be resolved (*Dorfordnungen / Weistümer*).

Every household with its own house and holding could meet at the assembly, which also elected officials who implemented the decisions taken by the assembly. In this way, the Tyrolean arrangement resembled the village institution in Denmark and Bavaria, but unlike these institutions, they usually covered a wider area, which could include several villages, hamlets, and single farms. In its wider geographical scope, they could therefore resemble the Bavarian *Hofmarken*, which might also include several villages and settlements.

In addition to handling problems relating to the allocation and use of common resources, the Tyrolean authorities also assigned the *Nachbarschaften* tasks connected with the compilation of tax registers, the collection of land taxes, and the mustering of soldiers. In their capacity as a tax community, several *Nachbarschaften* could be merged into one tax community. The emergence of *Nachbarschaften* seems to have been closely connected to the creation of a uniform judicial system in Tyrol, which had replaced what was left of former manorial control and *Hofmarken* by the fifteenth century.

5 Conclusion

When we started our investigations, we expected two factors to have a profound impact on the degree of peasant control over land and resources, as well as on peasant influence in institutions dealing with social and agrarian issues. The first factor is topography, the other one territorial and manorial dominion. This expectation has been realized, although the relation between topography and territorial and manorial dominion over peasants has proven to be more complex than we originally anticipated.

Generally, there is a significant correlation between a high degree of peasant control over land and resources and areas with a rugged topography better suited for grazing and foresting than cultivation of grain. This is true for Norway and for Tyrol. Both regions display an early and permanent dissolution of unfreedom, a significant and increasing amount of freeholders, increasingly better tenures and control over succession on tenant holdings, and a high degree of peasant control over resources.

On the other hand, peasants in regions with fertile plains well suited for open field cultivation of grain, like Bavaria and Denmark, enjoyed more insecure tenures, and they were subject to a greater extent to some form of limitation on their personal freedom. However, when it came to self-administration and self-determination in agrarian and social affairs, they did not come second to their fellow peasants in more mountainous regions.

Generally, there is also a marked connection between topography and dominion. Agriculture on fertile plains usually aggregated a higher surplus than barren mountainous land, a surplus that landlords could appropriate, given the right circumstances. Such a topography, leading to dense settlements in villages, also made it easier to control the households that worked the land, either by using them as a labour force (Denmark) or by restricting their freedom of movement (Denmark and Bavaria). A rugged topography, with scattered, often rather small settlements, made control of tenants more difficult, resulting in landlords settling for pure rental incomes without any forms of control over persons.

Beneath this general and very superficial topographical pattern, a more complex structure involving manorial and territorial dominion is revealed. At the beginning of our period, manor-like agrarian units with an unfree and a free workforce existed in both our regions of research. These units, in the eastern Alpine region organized in *Villikationen*, in Scandinavia in more loosely connected *multiple estates*, were gradually displaced during the eleventh to the twelfth centuries by a *Rentengrundherrschaft* in which the elites derived their main income from rent paid by tenant households. During the same period, unfree people gradually gained their freedom in Scandinavia, although some peasants in Denmark experienced restrictions on movement for a quite long period. In the eastern Alpine region, strict unfreedom was replaced by milder forms in Bavaria and, by the early modern period, had become as good as extinct in Tyrol.

Behind these changes in the form of dominion, we can discern an increase in population, the clearing of new land, intensification of agriculture, and the growth of towns and trade, changes that made strict slavery obsolete and a restructuring of manors in the direction of *Rentengrundherrschaft* a better option for the secular and ecclesiastical elites. At the same time, the rise of territorial power initiated conflicts, as well as cooperation, between, on the one hand, lords trying to establish territorial dominion and, on the other, ecclesiastical and aristocratic landlords trying to shield their dominion over the peasant population and protect their control over the surplus from landed resources.

By the High Middle Ages, changes in the forms of dominion and the rise of a territorial power had a marked impact on peasant control over resources and their participation in institutions dealing with social and agrarian issues. Tenures were regulated, and peasants participated in *thing* institutions under the auspices of either a territorial power or a manorial lord. In fertile areas with dense population, this period saw the beginning of village organization and self-determination in agrarian and social affairs within the village community or the manor.

The demographic crisis of the late Middle Ages accelerated the movement towards better tenures, although in Denmark and Bavaria this was counteracted to some extent by measures to prevent peasants from leaving manors. The early modern period consolidated the movement towards secure tenures, especially in Tyrol and Norway, but also saw a return to stronger manorial dominion in some areas, especially in Denmark. This period was also marked by the territorial powers' professionalization of local courts, which, with the notable exception of Tyrol, led to less peasant participation in legal decisions. Peasants nevertheless retained their participation in other local conflict-handling institutions dealing with agrarian and social issues, like village assemblies or neighbourhood institutions.

We can discern many common elements in this development from the High Middle Ages to the early modern period across our two regions of study, but we can also observe some distinct differences. Interestingly, these common elements and distinct differences do not run between our two regions of study. Instead Bavaria and Denmark, each with strong manorial influence, have some common traits resembling each other, while Tyrol and Norway, where the territorial power was consolidated at quite an early phase (Norway from the first part of twelfth century onwards and Tyrol from the middle of the thirteenth century) display more common traits with each other than with the other areas in the regions.

This corresponds with differences and similarities in topography, but topography alone is not a sufficient explanation. We therefore also have to take a closer look at socio-economic factors to explain why Bavaria and Tyrol in the eastern Alpine region developed differently, and why peasants in Norway and Denmark experienced widely different conditions in spite of being subjects to the same king and government from the late Middle Ages to the end of the early modern period.[6]

We will start with a comparison between Bavaria and Tyrol before moving on to Norway and Denmark. Leaning on the idea of a territorial peace legislation inspired by the church, the Bavarian duke managed to gain high jurisdiction in the Bavarian dukedom, while financial need impelled him to grant lower jurisdiction over peasants belonging to nobility and monasteries in their consolidated territories (*Hofmarken*) by the early fourteenth century. The duke

6 That a central government developed quite different policies towards their population in regions with different socio-economic conditions is not particular to the early modern kingdom of Denmark-Norway, as shown by the ruling Habsburg family's government of Tyrol and Bohemia.

nevertheless retained lower jurisdiction over the majority of Bavarian peasants who were subject to his territorial courts (*Landgerichte*).

This compromise was clearly a token of the economic and political strength of the lay and ecclesiastical Bavarian aristocracy, a strength that was made possible by the surplus extracted from their estates, and it had a fundamental impact on peasant participation in local legal and agrarian institutions on these estates. Although peasants belonging to *Hofmarken* participated in such institutions within the *Hofmark*, their lords' combined dominion over land (*Grundherrschaft*), bodily control over people (*Leibherrschaft*), and jurisdictional control (*Gerichtsherrschaft*) must have cast a shadow over their self-determination and self-administration.

Despite monopolizing high jurisdiction and exercising jurisdiction over peasants subject to the local territorial courts, the territorial authorities in Bavaria never managed to restrain all aspects of lay and ecclesiastical landlords' dominion over their peasants. For the rest of the Middle Ages and the early modern period, this included the control over landed property (*Grundherrschaft*) and in some cases also bodily control over people (*Leibherrschaft*). During the late Middle Ages, secular and ecclesiastical landlords could use their right to restrict the movement of their *Eigenleute* in order to run vacant holdings, but during the early modern period, their dominion over *Eigenleute* came close to a mere monetary income, drawn from people, not land.

While the remnants of personal unfreedom vanished in Tyrol and Norway during the Middle Ages as a result of the territorial power's active policy for making every peasant their subject, the Bavarian authorities did not interfere with the remainder of this unfreedom. This may partly have been the result of their incapacity to abolish such bonds. Instead of attacking the aristocracy's personal bonds to their tenants, they transferred their dominion over their own *Eigenleute* also to the land these *Eigenleute* were working. Especially in western Bavaria, they used their dominion over people in this way to strengthen their territorial power.

In contrast to Denmark and Norway, where the length of tenures in the early modern period was fixed by law, the Bavarian territorial authorities did not issue any legislation on tenures. Instead, it was left to different landlords to choose a type of tenure that suited their interests best. The key to explain the diverse development of tenures in Bavaria seems to have been taxation. As tenants with short tenures (*Freistift*) did not possess a property right (*dominium utile*) in their landed holdings according to Bavarian law and customs, these landed holdings could not be subject to territorial taxation. By not granting longer or hereditary tenures, Bavarian ecclesiastical and aristocratic landlords were thus avoiding competition from the territorial power in extracting a surplus from peasants. This problem did not exist for the territorial lord, who was willing to grant hereditary tenures to a much greater extent. That a majority of tenants still held their land by short tenures well into the early modern period was due to the fact that ecclesiastical and aristocratic landlords owned a majority of estates, especially in Lower (northern) Bavaria. This account for the comparable insecure position of a majority of Bavarian tenants.

The strong position of Bavarian ecclesiastical and aristocratic lords and their competition with the territorial lord for the surplus from landed possession thus accounts for some of the variety of tenant control over land and resources in this region. The extensive self-administration and self-determination in agrarian affairs in Bavarian villages may have been a part of the same effort to maximize the extraction of a surplus for landed property. When the transition to a rental-based method of running estates was completed in the Middle Ages, they left their tenants to find the best way of working the land they rented.

In contrast to Bavaria, the balance of power in Tyrol tipped quite early in favour of the territorial lords, whose clear aim was to make the Tyrolean peasants their loyal taxpaying subjects. Due to the rugged Tyrolean topography that made it more difficult to extract a large surplus from landed properties, the aristocracy was rather weak. The Tyrolean territorial lords, on the other hand, received incomes from traffic through the mountain passes and from the mining industry – first salt and later silver.

From the thirteenth century, the Tyrolean territorial lords, through a combination of sheer force and acquisition of noble rights, managed to strip ecclesiastical institutions and the aristocracy of their legal and administrative dominion over their peasants. Instead, they created a uniform system in the form of local administrative institutions / courts (*Gerichte*), with a judge (*Richter*) appointed by the territorial lord and participating peasants. The Tyrolean dukes used their newly acquired power to further the transformation to hereditary tenures. The rights of tenants holding such tenures were established by law, including their right to alienate their holdings.

The territorial princes also counteracted what was left of personal bonds in the form of *Eigenleute*, as such bonds were an obstacle to their ambition of creating loyal subjects. Serfdom was never abolished by law, but by the fifteenth century it had become a marginal phenomenon. Together with wide self-determination over resources and social life in their neighbourhood institutions (*Nachbarschaften*), which were often congruent with the local courts (*Gerichte*), the Tyrolean peasants thus enjoyed a high degree of control over land and resources, self-determination in their agrarian and social activities within their communities, and co-determination in judicial affairs.

In their struggle against the nobility and ecclesiastical lords and institutions, the Tyrolean rulers enlisted the support of the Tyrolean peasantry. Besides their active participation in local jurisdiction and administration, this is most clearly demonstrated by the fact that, from the fifteenth century, the local courts (*Gerichte*) elected representatives, mostly from the peasant elite, to the Tyrolean diet. From the middle of the thirteenth to the fifteenth century, Tyrol thus developed in the opposite direction than Bavaria, resulting in a direct relationship between the territorial sovereign and the peasantry, without ecclesiastical and aristocratic lords exercising any dominion over their tenants, with the exception of their rental income.

In the two regions we have studied, Scandinavia and the eastern Alpine region, only Norway displays a correspondingly long-lasting link between a territorial sovereign and every peasant within his reign. The rugged Norwegian topography, with its long coastline, scattered settlements, and scarcity of arable land, may have been a contributing factor in the rise of royal power at the expense of a local or regional aristocracy. Its long coastline made communication and military regrouping relatively easy for the king, while the scattered arable land made consolidation of estates more difficult for the aristocracy.

In Norway, as in the rest of Scandinavia at the beginning of our period, chieftains on their multiple estates extracted a surplus from a variety of resources through their control over people, including slaves (*þrælar*), freed slaves, and peasants with a client-patron relationship to their chieftains. From the basis of such multiple estates, local *things* and possibly also some of the regional *things* were organized in the centuries leading up to the second millennium.

From the tenth century, a royal power, in shifting alliances with powerful chieftains, gradually gained territorial control over Norway, allying itself with the peasantry, especially the peasant elite. Early on, the newly established royal power also managed to establish a new system of regional *things*. The economic power and social influence of local and regional magnates still rested on control over people, but over the course of the civil wars of the twelfth and the beginning of the thirteenth centuries, they increasingly had to rely on royal service as a means of economic and social power and prestige. As slavery was gradually abolished during the thirteenth century and royal power increased, direct control over people became less significant. The church in particular, with its scattered landed possessions, then relied on rental income from tenants.

Over the course of the thirteenth century, then, we can observe a complete shift in the direction of a rental-based tenant system in Norway. In the course of this development, the Norwegian aristocracy was gradually deprived of their influence over the regional *things*, at the same time as their patron-client relationship with the peasantry was replaced by a purely contractual relationship with their tenants. To keep up their standing, the aristocracy became increasingly dependent instead on incomes form royal service. The crown, in an alliance with the church, thus managed to turn the emerging class of Norwegian peasants, freeholders as well as tenants, into taxable royal subjects, turning their ancient duty of serving in the naval *leidang* into a yearly tax.

From a period of transition with formally short tenures, most tenants were granted lifelong or even hereditary tenures, at least from the end of the thirteenth century. From the sixteenth century, tenures were issued for life, with a de facto right for the tenant to appoint their successor. While tenants endured more secure control over their holdings, peasant participation in the *thing* system at a regional level declined. In the thirteenth century, peasant participation at the regional *things* was reduced to mere attendance as court witnesses, but they still had real influence in local conflict-handling institutions within the framework drawn up by the thirteenth century. Even though this influence was reduced during the early modern period, Norwegian peasants enjoyed a high degree of control over land and resources with negligible influence from their landlords. They also had the opportunity to resolve a great number of their conflicts over resources themselves, either within the legal framework laid down by the authorities or through informal meetings between neighbours.

The Danish kingdom goes further back in time than the Norwegian one. At first, royal income consisted mainly of tributes from the outskirts of the kingdom and 'gifts' collected more irregularly from the central parts. As in Bavaria, Danish topography made control over land and persons easier than in mountainous regions like Tyrol and Norway. From a starting point not very different from the Norwegian magnates, the Danish lay and ecclesiastical aristocracy consolidated their estates, creating a strong economic basis for their conflicts with the Danish crown. When unfreedom was fading during the High Middle Ages, these manors were partly run or farmed out to bailiffs (*villici*) with a hired workforce, and partly by tenants (*coloni*) paying a yearly rent. In contrast to Norway and Tyrol, Danish peasants, like their Bavarian counterparts, played an unimportant role in the struggle between the crown and the aristocracy, and the aristocracy had much influence within the judicial system.

Tenants (*coloni*) had to pay taxes to the crown while bailiffs (*villici*) did not, probably because they were asserted to be of unfree status belonging to the household. Landlords therefore nominally turned many of their tenants into bailiffs by the thirteenth century, thus making it possible for them to expropriate a larger portion of the surplus from the land. Eventually, the difference between bailiffs (*villici*) and tenants (*coloni*) was waning, resulting in a relatively uniform peasant class, mostly consisting of tenants (*landboer*) with long tenures, and a minority of freeholders.

As in the Bavarian *Hofmarken*, over time, Danish landlords acquired a greater influence over their tenants, starting with prohibition on leaving the estate for tenants on the eastern Danish islands in the middle of the fifteenth century. However, strict manorial dominion was delayed in Denmark until the early modern period. It was then closely connected to the establishment of consolidated estates with demesne farming where tenants delivered corvée labour. Aristocratic landlords were granted the opportunity of creating manorial courts (*birkethings*), but, as in Bavaria, with substantial peasant influence. As the duty to collect taxes and conscript soldiers was transferred to the landlords from the middle of the seventeenth century, Danish landlords kept tight control over their tenants. As the number of freeholders dwindled to almost nothing due to official policy, the great majority of Danish peasants were subject to manorial rule by the end of the early modern period, rather than being subject to the Danish crown. In local agrarian and social affairs, however, Danish landlords were quite content to leave their tenants to settle their daily affairs and social life at the village assemblies themselves.

A general trend in the Alpine region, as well as in Scandinavia, is that peasant attendance and influence in *thing* assemblies and courts was affected from the High Middle Ages by the balance between the growing territorial power on the one hand and the influence of aristocratic power on the other. Only where aristocratic power was substantial, as in Bavaria and Denmark, the aristocracy managed to establish independent judicial institutions on some of their estates. The development of peasant influence in non-manorial *thing* assemblies and courts was a result of the territorial power's willingness and interest in maintaining peasants as active participants in judicial affairs. The decline of peasant influence in local courts in Denmark and Norway from the end of the seventeenth century can be taken as a token of a professionalization of the judicial system, where appointed officials and finally trained lawyers replaced the peasant elite as judges. Such a development occurred at an earlier point in Bavaria, while active peasant participation seems to have been strong all through the early modern period in Tyrol.

Denmark and Norway provide an interesting example of the impact of topography on peasant control and influence, but also on the strategy of growing territorial power. Although united under the same king and ruled by a common central government in Copenhagen, the Danish-Norwegian government's policy took quite different directions in the two countries in the early modern period. In Norway, where after the Reformation the crown controlled more of the landed property than the nobility and other private landowners, the government curbed any attempt to increase rents and other fees, in order to make Norwegian tenants viable taxpayers and a reliable base for conscripted soldiers. In Denmark, on the other hand, the same government allowed the strong Danish aristocracy to tighten its grip on their tenants, partly by allowing them to expand their demesnes using their tenants for corvée labour, and partly by giving them extended judicial authority and administrative tasks.

At this point, we may return to one of the initial aims of our project (see 'Introduction', section 'Historiographical and Methodological Reflections'), that is, to shed light on a widespread view, rooted in the historical thinking of the nineteenth century, that Norwegian and in part other Scandinavian peasants experienced a special historical development compared to other European peasants. According to this view, it has been maintained that Norwegian and in part other Scandinavian peasants enjoyed a special 'peasant freedom'. This 'peasant freedom' included a great deal more self-determination than their southern counterparts, the marginal existence of slaves and people with other kinds of unfree status, extensive control over land and agricultural products, widespread ownership of land, and comprehensive judicial influence through the institution of the *thing*.

Our investigation has shown that some of the characteristics relating to any such exclusive 'peasant freedom' may be found in any of our four investigated territories, not only in Norway. Unfreedom is found in every one of our selected areas of study in the first centuries of the High Middle Ages. It was as severe and widespread in Norway as in any other of our areas of investigation, and its early abolition may be compared to that of Tyrol. Subsequent dominion over people, such as restriction of movement in Bavaria and Denmark, was never introduced in Norway, but neither was it introduced in Tyrol. As for control over land, Norway had a substantial and increasing number of freeholders, but so had Tyrol. Norwegian tenants gained favourable tenures and a strong *dominium utile* in their holdings, but so had Tyrolean tenants. Norwegian peasants participated in *things* and other conflict-handling institutions, like their counterparts in the eastern Alpine region and in the rest of Scandinavia. As for participation in courts, their influence, as in most other places, was greatest at the local level and clearly declining during the early modern period, while their influence in resolving conflicts regarding the allocation of agrarian resources was retained. And, we may add, peasant self-administration in agrarian affairs is as evident in areas where other aspects of manorial influence was greater than in Norway.

We may thus conclude that any such exclusive Norwegian or Scandinavian 'peasant freedom' did not exist, either in the Middle Ages or in the early modern period. On the contrary, Norway, and indeed the rest of Scandinavia, exhibit characteristics that are clearly recognizable in Tyrol and Bavaria. The dividing line does not seem to run between Norway and our other areas of investigation, but rather between Norway and Tyrol on the one hand, and Denmark and Bavaria on the other. In other words, topography, and territorial and manorial power constructed on the basis of topography, led to a somewhat comparable development in Bavaria and Denmark, a development that is contrasted by the development in Tyrol and Norway. In this picture, Norway finds its place as an example of a topography well suited for the development of a strong royal power at the expense of an influential lay and ecclesiastical aristocracy.

PART 3

The Portrayal of Peasants in National Historiography

CHAPTER 6

The Historian as Architect of Nations: A Historiographical Analysis of the Norwegian Peasantry as Carrier of National Ideology and Identity in the Medieval and Early Modern Period

Helge Salvesen

The Norwegian constitution of 1814, facilitated by the fall of Napoleon, declares with naive optimism that Norway is a free and independent nation. It is, in other words, a true child of the French Revolution and the American *Declaration of Independence*. After Sweden's surrender of Finland to Russia in the wake of the Napoleonic wars, Norway was treated as a form of compensation and forced into a union with Sweden that lasted until 1905. Nevertheless, 1814 was the starting point for a nation-building process that initially, in the nineteenth and early twentieth century, championed a romantic national cult of freedom, and was later driven by a fascination for that most inhospitable area of the world, the polar region, and the glory to be gained by exploring it. We may regard these explorations in the nineteenth and early twentieth century as a national claim to independence.[1]

Many different actors participated in the construction of this idealistic-romantic undertaking: artists, poets, composers and musicians, engineers, adventurers, an aspiring economic and educated middle class, and, last but not least, researchers and teachers at the first Norwegian university, *Det Kongelige Frederiks Universitet* (the Royal Frederik's University) in Christiania (Oslo).[2] Strong Norwegian pressure had hastened the university's founding in 1811. As in other parts of Europe, however, the middle class was too small and exclusive to provide an ideological basis for national identity. Instead, the roots of that identity, which could be traced back to the proud history of the Vikings and the Middle Ages, were found in the peasantry. Peasants thus played a leading role

1 In the second half of the nineteenth century, the focus was less on discovering a new polar country than on undertaking geophysical studies, as the polar regions were suspected of holding the key to understanding meteorological and oceanographical conditions in the mid-latitudes (including and especially Norway). The scientific contribution at the international level at the same time contributed to Norway's renown.

2 Rune Slagstad, *De nasjonale strateger* (Oslo: Pax, 1998), 11–90.

 | DOI:10.1163/9789004433458_007

in the nation-building process, embodying ideals such as freedom, democracy, and resistance to foreign, and especially Danish influence.

Historians of the time adopted diachronic comparison – a method frequently employed to explain social questions. This also applied to their efforts to legitimize and create an identity for the fledgling Norwegian nation. For Norwegian historians in the early nineteenth century – a period characterized by a drive for national independence – Norway's growth and prosperity in the High Middle Ages were central themes of interest. Its subsequent 'decline' in the late Middle Ages served primarily to articulate a contrast between the earlier age of autonomy and the later period of subjugation. For as long as the focus rested chiefly on the political dimension of the problem, it was difficult to find a convincing explanation for the seeming paradox of this Norwegian decline.

However, Norway's late medieval development became significant for the discourse of nationhood in at least one respect: since the end of the twelfth century, or the first half of the thirteenth at the latest, peasants in Norway enjoyed legal status as freemen.[3] In contrast with many other countries in Europe, they retained this free status throughout the late Middle Ages. This placed Norway in an exceptional position. One explanation may be that the Norwegian feudal lords lacked the political and military agency to deprive peasants of their freedom, bind them with force to the land and its owner, or prevent them from offering their labour on the free market. Whatever the reason, this tradition of freedom fed into a historical narrative, one in which the Norwegian peasantry harboured a unique drive for independence. Scrutiny of Norway's late medieval history also reflected an interest among historians who, having observed the recent dissolution of Norway's union with Denmark in 1814 and now driven by an emerging spirit of nationalism, sought to explain the political decline that preceded unification and ultimately deprived them of independence. As the poorest country in Scandinavia, Norway was forced to assume the role of bystander, or perhaps of cautious participant, whilst struggles for supremacy in the North played out in the late Middle Ages.

An analysis of the Norwegian Middle Ages reveals that historians of the nineteenth and twentieth centuries had different views regarding, in particular,

3 The most comprehensive account of the development, function, and abolition of serfdom in Norway with comparative references to the situation in the rest of Europe is given by Tore Iversen, 'Trelldommen: norsk slaveri i middelalderen', dr.art. thesis, University of Bergen, 1994; in German translation, Tore Iversen, *Knechtschaft im mittelslterlichen Norwegen*, trans. Katharina Freche in collaboration with Angelika Landau, Abhandlungen zur rechtswissenschaftlichen Grundlagenforschung, 94 (Ebelsbach: Aktiv, 2004).

the role of the four social actors: the monarchy, the secular aristocracy, the clergy, and the peasantry.[4]

Historians of the nineteenth century saw a clash between the monarchy on one side, and the aristocracy and clergy on the other. Peasants were regarded as adherents and allies of kingship, who through alliance provided the monarchy a kind of democratic legitimacy. P.A. Munch (1810–63) and Ernst Sars (1835–1917) were especially representative of this view. Their views were motivated largely by the fact that Snorri Sturluson (*c.* 1178–1241) had already established this line of thinking. At the same time, however – and this is crucial – this perspective coincided with historians' own contemporary ideals, which were anti-aristocratic, anti-Catholic, and nationalistic. The anti-aristocratic attitudes of the nineteenth century corresponded to their observations of the late Middle Ages, when the secular aristocracy, who were royal officials of the monarchy, often had Danish or possibly Swedish origins. This aristocracy was regarded as a tool for peasant exploitation during the period of unification during the Kalmar Union (and later Norway's union with Denmark), and it was natural to judge the secular aristocracy of the High Middle Ages in a similar fashion, particularly as this mirrored the view espoused by the greatest historian of his age, Snorri Sturluson. Furthermore, a hostile attitude toward the medieval church was easily compatible with the modern Protestant state, which in the 1814 constitution explicitly forbade the entry of Jesuits, those standard-bearers of the Counter-Reformation. Since the Danish (or Swedish) king was, as monarch of the union, also king in Norway from 1319 to 1905, it was essential to stress that the monarchy in high-medieval Norway had fostered a kind of democratic alliance with the populace, e.g., the free Norwegian peasantry, in order to gain legitimacy. Snorri Sturluson was readily perceived as advancing a notion of kingship in the Viking Age and High Middle Ages in which rulers were only successful when acting in the best interest of the people.

Sverris Saga, a contemporary biography of King Sverrir Sigurðarson (around 1151–1202), may have been the role model for Snorri Sturluson's *Heimskringla* (Norway's Kings' sagas). The former presents a heroic national king, legitimized directly by God and in opposition to bishops and the clergy, who recruited followers from amongst the poor and dependent and identified himself with those who brought him glory. The saga also emphasizes that Sverrir consistently sought the advice of adherents when making important political decisions or devising strategies of war. This suggests that he represented an

4 The depiction of the Norwegian scholarship of the High Middle Ages as given by Helle is generally accepted. Knut Helle, *Norge blir en stat: 1130–1319*, Handbok i Norges historie, 3, 2nd edn (Oslo: Universitetsforlaget, 1974), 27–36.

expressed democratic ideal, insofar as it is possible to conceive of such an ideal in a medieval society. Snorri's concept of history is easily interpreted in light of such an ideal.

One principle of the 1814 constitution appears to support this nineteenth-century perception of history – this principle being a notion, rooted in the ideals of the Enlightenment, that Norwegian independence was derived from the sovereignty of the people. All legitimate state authority should originate with the people. Enriched by the romantic concept of a folkish creative spirit, this notion developed into the ideological drive in the nation-building process. The fruits of this national creative power were to show that Norwegians were indeed a nation of their own, with a unique, inspired, and free spirit. By referencing this principle of sovereignty, it was possible to legitimize the autonomy of the nation's government. Snorri's interpretation of Norway's past as that of *one* kingdom could provide strong argument for independence. Historians of the nineteenth century contributed to the documentation of this conception of history. However, the metaphysics of nationalism obscures the fact that state authority is not the manifestation of nationhood. The nation itself develops gradually through the interaction of different elements under a common political regime.

The period between c. 1910 and 1920 witnessed the emergence of a new perspective on the Norwegian Middle Ages, represented chiefly by Halvdan Koht (1873–1965) and Edvard Bull the elder (1881–1931). In 1913, Koht held a lecture with the title 'Sagaernes opfatning av vor gamle historie' ('The Sagas' View of Our Old History').[5] Koht's main theme was Snorri Sturluson's view of history in *Heimskringla*. He argued that Snorri's understanding of past events was coloured by his views on contemporary history, and that his skill as a historian lay in his ability to place his own views into a wider historical context. At the same time, Koht maintained that Snorri's views were not entirely correct. By arguing against the prevailing opinion, he paved the way for a new approach.

Snorri – in Koht's view – believed that the period from around 900 to 1200 was defined by a struggle between the monarch and the aristocracy. Koht believed, however, that these parties cooperated with one another. While Snorri assumed a struggle between King Sverrir and the aristocracy, Koht saw a struggle between the propertied classes and those without – in the way that one interpretation of the Industrial Revolution could also present these oppositions.

5 The lecture is published in Halvdan Koht, 'Sagaernes opfatning av vor gamle historie', *Historisk tidsskrift (norsk)*, 5th ser., 2 (1914), 379–96.

Koht's point of view went largely uncontested until about 1940,[6] and is still of current interest in Norwegian historiography. One of his principal arguments is that a natural solidarity existed between the monarchy, the aristocracy, and the church, as these actors shared the interests of landowners. It is interesting to ask how this opinion could establish itself so thoroughly. No new sources had been discovered, nor could one demonstrate that individual sources had been interpreted incorrectly. Rather, the reason was a new insight, based on studies of politically radical historians inspired by the German philosopher Karl Marx. Following the Marxist analysis of society and the abstraction of conflict, or rather the opposition of productive forces and conditions of production, as a moving force of historical events, one can see in the Norwegian Middle Ages an obvious conflict between the owners of the instruments of production, the landowners, and those who have to rent the land.

The way in which the materialistic view of history established itself between 1910 and 1920 amongst Norwegian historians revealed a comprehensive, ideologically justified model that offered new premises for further studies. Norwegian medievalists were introduced to a novel way of asking questions. Who owned the capital and how was it distributed across the different groups in society? Since agricultural land was the most important capital of pre-industrial times, it was important to know who owned the land and how the individual groups divided up the land amongst themselves. Next to the question of ownership, scholarship also concentrated to a large extent on the conditions of the peasantry. A particular focus of interest was the crisis that landowners and agrarian production were subject to in the late Middle Ages. Main points here were the extent of the crisis, its duration, and the impact on both those who lived off the work of others and the peasants themselves.

There are several reasons for the relative lack of opposition to the materialist view of history in Norway. First, it did not reduce, but rather amplified the attention paid to the peasantry. Free Norwegian peasants did not turn into extras on the societal stage; rather, the fortune of the whole state was reliant on their productivity. Another reason is that the politically orientated scholarship was no stranger to materialist reasoning. 'The material requirements' for the loss of independence in the late Middle Ages were first emphasized by representatives of the historical conservative school of thought, T.H. Aschehoug

6 In a programmatic article, Jen Arup Seip does not distance himself from a materialistic interpretation, but intends to modify the assumption that only general forces and structures direct developments. He is keen to emphasize that individuals, especially strong leading personages, are also able to influence the path of history. Jens Arup Seip, 'Problemer og metode i norsk middelalderforskning', *Historisk tidsskrift* (*norsk*), 32 (1940), 49–131.

(1822–1909) and Yngvar Nielsen (1843–1916), in the 1860s.[7] The late Middle Ages grew continually more interesting for historians towards the end of the nineteenth century. In the main, this can be seen as the result of social Darwinist evolutionary theories that emphasized continuity – the slow and gradual process of evolution, a development practically following a set pattern through historical stages of culture. The assumption of a causal, genetic continuity encourages the study of the long 'middle period', the Norwegian Middle Ages.

For conservative historians, it was typical to defend the transmitted political and cultural values and forms and to show that there was reason to value them, independent of whether they were originally Norwegian or Danish. Similar to what P.A. Munch and Rudolf Keyser (1803–64) had earlier argued, Aschehoug and Nielsen explained the decline through the diminution of the aristocracy, the class underpinning the interests of the state. However, they also pointed out that the reason for this diminution was a weakening of the economic basis of the aristocracy, and that this was more effective in Norway than in Sweden and Denmark. Aschehoug explained this weakening in Norway as being due to the 'specific nature of the country',[8] meaning the unfavourable natural conditions, while Nielsen underlined its cause as due to the 'long economic downfall'.[9]

It was natural to continue this economic line of thought regarding the peasantry, due to the ideological basis of the materialist view of history. The quantitative side of the economic decline was presented by a historian of agriculture at the Norwegian agricultural college, Sigvald Hasund (1868–1959), in 1920.[10] Hasund explored various avenues in his research: he claimed firstly that the reason for decline, including political decline, was an economic crisis in agriculture, and secondly cited the plague that had hit Norway in 1349–50 as a direct cause. With this, Hasund steered the discussion concerning Norway's decline in the late Middle Ages in a direction where the focus was on finding economic consequences of the crisis for agrarian society, and asking questions about the scope, and the direct social and economic consequences for landowners and tenants.

---

7 Ottar Dahl, *Norsk historieforskning i 19. og 20. århundre* (Oslo: Universitetsforlaget, 1970), 120.

8 T.H. Aschehoug, *Statsforfatningen i Norge og Danmark indtil 1814*, Norges offentlig ret (Christiania: i commission hos Feilberg & Landmark, 1886), 346: 'landets eiendommelige Beskaffenhed'.

9 Yngvar Nielsen, *Af Norges Historie* (Stockholm, Ljus, 1904), 44: 'en lang nedadgaaende økonomisk Bevægelse'.

10 Sigvald Hasund, *Ikring mannedauden: Ei liti sogestudie* (Kristiania, 1920).

Later historians studying Norway's decline in the late Middle Ages repeated Hasund's theses and merely elaborated on the question and the method. One focus was on settlement history and especially its agriculture. Following the work of two historians, Asgaut Steinnes (1892–1973) and Andreas Holmsen (1906–1989), who took the lead in continuing Hasund's theories, scholarship concentrated on the material consequences of the crisis for peasant society. Retrospective methods and techniques were developed in order to conduct studies of several centuries of peasant society. Such methods and techniques enabled the historian to discern long lines of development and to ascertain stable structures as well as changes that only become visible through investigations that cover a number of centuries. Causal relations were sought mainly when it came to events and conditions such as the plague, climate deterioration, overpopulation, and the like – that is, conditions outside the control of the individual.

The high point of this line of research was achieved with a project that, in the 1970s, studied deserted farmsteads in all the Nordic countries (*Det nordiske ødegårdsprojekt*). Some aspects of this research essential to Norwegian scholars could not convince Danish and Swedish scholars of their merit, especially in relation to the possibility of retrospectively drawing conclusions from younger sources for the settlements in older and less-well-documented periods.

For Norwegian historians who were inspired by a materialist view of history, it seemed natural to use the retrospective method as well as other structural analyst methods – such as the existence of tacit knowledge – in order to study society more thoroughly than possible through a mere analysis of everyday occurrences. This enabled a type of source criticism that was not only interested in the analysis of the preserved sources but also wanted an answer to the question of what the reality, about which the sources were silent, looked like – and why the sources were silent. The 'why' and 'what' of ignorance became just as important as a historical theory in the form of a bundle of hypotheses based on the data that the historian had extracted from the sources.

This view of history was developed in Norway partly before and partly alongside Marc Bloch (1886–1944), Lucien Febvre (1878–1956), and the theories of other members of the Annales School in France. Both Marc Bloch[11] and the

11 Marc Bloch's lecture series was published in the series of the Institute for Comparative Cultural Research in Human Culture in Oslo: Bloch, *Les caractères originaux de l'histoire rurale francaise*, Instituttet for sammenlignende kulturforskning Serie B, 19 (Oslo: Ascheoug, 1931). His work was newly edited in Paris 1952; in 1956 a supplementary volume was published: Bloch, *Les caractères originaux de l'histoire rurale francaise*, vol. 2: *Supplément établi daprès de l'auteur (1931–1944)*, ed. Robert Dauvergne (Paris: A. Colin, 1952–56). A Russian translation was published in 1957 and an English one in 1966.

Viennese historian Alfons Dopsch[12] (1868–1953) were invited to Oslo to give lectures on the old peasant societies in France and in the Alpine countries. Following these invitations, the Institute for Comparative Cultural Research Institute for Comparative Research in Human Culture (*Instituttet for sammenlignende kulturforskning*) in Oslo laid plans for a comprehensive comparative study of the settlement, economy, and legal position of the peasants in Norway and the Alpine regions.[13] The plan was never carried out in full, but one could say that the project of which this conference is one part has taken on some of the ideas that were presented in 1930.[14]

Due to this direction of research, Norwegian agricultural historians in the 1950s assumed that the distribution of property, that is, the economic power base, immediately prior to the great loss of inhabitants in 1349–50 could be deemed roughly as: the church owned 41 percent of all land, the aristocracy 15 percent, the crown 4 percent, while the rest – 40 percent – belonged to the peasantry, the middle classes, and the administrative class.[15] On the basis of these numbers, it is possible to argue that the aristocracy, the church and the king, who together owned 60 percent of all land, had common interests that outweighed all antagonisms.

But who was leading this aristocratic triumvirate? The crown was seen as an instrument of the nobility and the clergy. In this context, one speaks of an instrumentalized crown. The central tension in society was between the landowners and the tenant farmers. The crown became the instrument of exploitation. But there was little room for the personal power of the king; it was the general powers of society that ruled. By focusing on exploitation, the idea of the freedom of the peasantry faded into the background. The question now became: were the Norwegian peasants exploited more under Danish rule during the 400 years of union than they would have been had Norway been an independent country? Norwegian historians answered this in the affirmative for

12 Alfons Dopsch's lectures were also published by the Institute: Dopsch, *Die ältere Wirtschafts- und Sozialgeschichte der Bauern in den Alpenländern Österreichs*, Instituttet for sammenlignende kulturforskning Serie A, 11 (Oslo: Aschehoug, 1930).

13 Edvard Bull, *Sammenlignende studier over bondesamfundets kulturforhold: Et arbeidsprogram*, Institutt for sammenlignende kulturforskning Serie C, 2.2 (Oslo: Institutt for sammenlignende kulturforskning, 1929).

14 The project has been financed by the Norwegian Research Council 2004–2007 and has the title 'Bønders råderett over jord og gårdsdrift fra høymiddelalder til slutten av tidlig moderne tid – Norge og Europa'.

15 Halvard Bjørkvik, 'Jordejendom – Norge', in John Granlund, ed., *Kulturhistoriskt lexikon för nordisk medeltid – från vikingatid till reformationstid*, vii (Malmö: Allhem, 1962), 667.

a long time, but since the 1970s the answer has become more nuanced. It was argued that the Norwegian peasants would have had to produce more in order to keep an independent Norwegian state functional in the late Middle Ages than they were obliged to hand over to the Danish state.

Halvdan Koht was most influential in amalgamating the materialist and national perspectives. While developing the materialist view on conflicts of interest in medieval Norway, he also fashioned the theory that class struggle and national union were integrated features of the historical process.[16] While economic and social struggles in medieval Norway played out between the crown, aristocracy, and clergy, on one side, and the lower classes, represented by the peasantry, on the other, there was also a parallel conflict between the native peasantry and the upper classes of foreign origin. This occasioned a national alliance between the domestic king and domestic peasantry. Koht viewed class difference, with its inherent national contradiction, as the common theme throughout Norwegian history. Norway's earliest period of consolidation in the Viking period and the High Middle Ages was, according to Koht, a merging of the upper classes. It was the landowners who joined forces. The indigenous secular aristocracy assumed governance of the state and fostered a national culture. The monarchy was the political expression of this union and administered it through the recruitment of officials from the old Norwegian landed gentry. In addition to the national aristocracy, the church also established a new administrative class. With the founding of an independent archdiocese in Nidaros (Trondheim) in 1152/3, the church carved out a foothold in Norwegian society as one of the most prominent landowning institutions.

That national life rested so heavily on this union of the upper classes was, according to Koht, manifest in the aristocracy's denationalization in the late Middle Ages, as class interests transcended national boundaries and enveloped social groups in Denmark and Sweden.

This precipitated a national decline that in the course of a century cost Norway its independence and caused the country's stagnation in ensuing centuries, as it lacked both national leadership and cohesiveness that took precedence over all other factions.

Koht perceived a rebirth of nationalism in the formation of a new economic middle class. Beginning in the sixteenth century, this class gained increasing social authority and acted collectively in the pursuit of national interests. The monarchy and the royal administration became an instrument of the urban

16 These ideas were developed in the years between 1905 and 1926, demonstrated most clearly in Halvdan Koht, *Norsk bondereising: Fyrebuing til bondepolitikken* (Oslo: Aschehoug, 1926).

class. Although these were initially influenced more by the Danish state and culture than the Norwegian – naturally, since the Norwegian state was weakened and Norwegian culture was the domain of the lower classes – Koht still saw the emergence of an upper class, rooted both economically and culturally in the country, as a national advantage.

However, Koht did not see this economic middle class as a sufficient bearer of national identity. In his writings, the peasantry had no part in either power or nationalist thought. Economic conditions had driven the peasantry further into class struggle, first against the landowners and then against the middle class and bureaucracy. From the eighteenth century onwards, however, peasants developed class-consciousness that increasingly bound the peasantry and the middle classes together in a collective economic, political, and spiritual struggle. In a hard and bitter conflict, as Koht presented it, peasants gradually prevailed over the other classes. From this perspective, it was the traditional lower class that achieved supremacy and national victory. Koht saw this as the greatest achievement in Norwegian history, both because the class uniting and obtaining power was numerically the largest, and because this class had its entire economic and spiritual basis in Norway's indigenous traditions.

A new class, the working class, began to dominate in the twentieth century. However, Koht argued for a continuous democratic development. He saw growing democracy as national progress: whenever a new and powerful class emerged, the nation as a whole grew in scope and prosperity. Koht's view of history presented the Norwegian people's identity as the product of class development and struggle.

Koht attempted to formulate his theory in a manner that combined class oppositions with national contradictions – a foreign upper class against a domestic lower one. He thus promoted an overarching theory that appeared to confirm historical developments in America,[17] Germany, and other European countries.[18]

This theory is considered Koht's most original contribution to Norwegian historiography. But unlike the materialist view of history in Norway, Koht's theory on the historical development of nationhood did not have as great an impact on research. If there ever was a confrontation with the national idea in Norwegian historiography, then it occurred in the years following the Second World War. The renunciation of National Socialism prompted broad scepticism

17 Halvdan Koht, *Den amerikanske nasjonen i upphav og reising* (Kristiania: Aschehoug, 1920).

18 Halvdan Koht, 'The Dawn of Nationalism in Europe', *The American Historical Review*, 52 (1947), 265–80.

toward idealism, dark emotions, organic society, nationalism, and its corresponding historiography. This led to a 'demythologizing' of the years 1814 and 1905.[19] However, there was no concerted reappraisal of the older nationalist perspective in Norwegian scholarship. The influence of nationalist views combined with materialist approaches is remarkably patent in Andreas Holmsen's (1906–89) survey of Norwegian history from the earliest times to 1660,[20] a book that was used as the main introductory text for all students of Norwegian history from the close of the Second World War until the 1990s. Historians continued to consult Holmsen's survey until very recently. However, Jens Arup Seip[21] (1905–92), Knut Helle[22] (1930–2015), and others published thematically focused studies that eventually proved more influential than the overarching historical narratives and commentaries on the social function of history. A confrontation with the nationalist idea became unnecessary, as the question simply no longer applied.

More recently, Kåre Lunden (1930–2013) revived the question of medieval nationalism in Norwegian scholarship. Applying social anthropological and other theories from the social sciences, he questioned whether a specific national identity existed in the pre-modern era. His answer is affirmative for the following reason.[23]

Saga literature, he argues, is full of hints that a Norwegian identity was already in existence in the High Middle Ages. Lunden refers especially to the Kings' sagas, which he maintained demonstrate consciousness of a united Norway. In other parts of Europe, for instance, the terminology of kingship was emphasized. Shortly after gaining the throne in 1180, Philip Augustus changed his title from '*rex Francorum*' ('king of the French') to '*rex Franciae*' ('king of France'). Similarly, in England, King John ceased to style himself as '*rex Anglorum*', replacing that title with '*rex Angliae*' around 1200. This signalled an elevation from small tribal kings to that of king over an entire country. Erik Gunnes (1924–99) asserted that this development was facilitated by an awakening

19 Sverre Bagge, 'Fantes det en norsk nasjonal identitet i middelalderen?', in May-Brith Ohman Nielsen (ed.), *Nasjonal identitet og nasjonalisme: Innlegg på HiFo-seminaret i Farsund* (Oslo: Den norske historiske forening, 1994), 7.

20 Andreas Holmsen, *Norges historie fra de eldste tider til 1660* (Oslo: Gyldendal, 1939), and various later editions.

21 Seip, 'Problemer og metode', 49–131.

22 Knut Helle, 'Tendenser i nyere norsk høymiddelalderforskning', in *Nytt fra norsk middelalder*, 2 (Oslo: Cappelen, 1970), 384–410.

23 Kåre Lunden has published repeatedly on this theory, in Lunden (1992, 1993, 1994), among others. I refer mainly to Kåre Lunden, 'Fanst det ein norsk nasjonal identitet i mellomalderen?', in May-Brith Ohman Nielsen (ed.), *Nasjonal identitet og nasjonalisme: Innlegg på HiFo-seminaret i Farsund* (Oslo: Den norske historiske forening, 1994), 22–39.

nationalism amongst medieval learned lawyers.[24] The concept of fatherland, of *patria*, had Roman heritage. In the twelfth century, however, this fused with a kind of primitive tribal pride being fostered in all Germanic countries. From this point onward, one can perceive a true sense of national identity, bound to a specific region.

Lunden based his argument on excerpts from the Kings' sagas, *Ágrip, Fagrskinna, Heimskringla*, and *Orknøyinga saga* from the late-twelfth and early thirteenth centuries. These employ the term '*Noregskonungr*' ('king of Norway'), and never that of '*Normannakonungr*' ('king of the Norwegians'). Lunden's obvious conclusion is that if this terminological shift signalled the development of national identity and unity in other regions of Europe, then it must have been the same in Norway. But he went a step further. These sagas never refer to '*Danmarkskonungr*' and '*Svitjodskonungr*' or '*Svearikeskonungr*', ('king of Denmark'; 'king of Sweden'). However, they often mention '*Danakonungr*' and '*Sviakonungr*' ('king of the Danes'; 'king of the Swedes'). Lunden highlighted parallels with European material and concluded that, in the High Middle Ages, perceptions of the Danish and Swedish king were rooted in primitive, tribal notions of kingship, whereas in Norway, a concept of kingship bound to a territory and, accordingly, a more highly developed sense of 'nationalism' existed. We must, however, acknowledge that saga authors were from Norway and regarded 'others' as unequal. This may explain why Danes and Swedes were not portrayed with the same national and stately terminology.

Lunden also addressed the prologue to the Kings' sagas. He noted that the author explicitly defined his objective: to explain, through narration, the existence and evolution of the author's own society, one in which kings were central and exceptionally successful individuals. The sagas thus legitimize the authors' society and facilitate the creation of collective identity. According to Lunden, the notion that positive functions of royal power passed from the leading figures in society to the peasantry reflects the Marxian concept of 'ideological dominance': peasants adopt the reality of the elite in matters of society, culture, and politics. In the context of Norway, ideas of positive royal function passed from the formerly elite groups to the peasantry, thus enabling peasants to adopt conditions in which a subjective Norwegian national identity could form. The abundance of historical literature on Norwegian kingship produced in the late-twelfth and thirteenth centuries – this is Lunden's main argument – demonstrates a social reality in which a group of people perceived themselves as 'Norwegians', in opposition to outsiders, and lived collectively in

24 Erik Gunnes, *Kongens ære: kongemakt og kirke i 'En tale mot biskopene'* (Oslo: Gyldendal, 1971), 232.

an integrated political society, a state personified by the king. This view is supported in Knut Helle's authoritative survey *Norge blir en stat, 1130–1319* (*Norway Becomes a State, 1130–1319*),[25] which encompasses a wider array of sources and previous scholarship.

In their emergence, societies need a narrative, traditional institutions, and traditional cultural material that matches the process of finding a national identity, a view that accords with social anthropologists' recent descriptions of different societies. Lunden compares the ideological patriotism of the sagas, which bask in the heroism and superior strength of Norwegians vis-à-vis neighbouring societies, with the patriotism espoused so ardently by Norwegian historians since the late-eighteenth century, a patriotism that continued to saturate scholarship into the nineteenth century. These generations of historians had a common motive: the narrative of history was both a facet and consequence of the growth of national identity and state formation. In articulating this parallel, Lunden supported the argument that Norwegian nationhood was not a construct of the nineteenth century, but rather an expression of a national consciousness with roots in the High Middle Ages.

Lunden thus demonstrated that the composition of sagas around 1200 played the same role in shaping the identity of Norway's fledgling nation – later revived with the formation of national identity in the nineteenth century – as that of modern approaches to nation-state development the world over. We may observe parallels with the role of epic poetry in the formation of national identity in Finland, the general function of history in the rebuilding of states long isolated, such as Albania, or the appropriation of history in the propaganda of the Third Reich. Rarely do old and well-established states reach for history to legitimize their national character with the same fervour as minority groups or states in the developing world.

In the Nordic countries, for instance, we may observe the importance of history for the cultivation of a Sámi national identity. Here we can recognize the same motifs and arguments for nationhood as those underpinning the medieval narratives and historical research of the nineteenth century.

The fact that Norway lacked a socially independent, educated middle class to advance the process of nation-building makes it something of an exception in the wider European context. However, Norwegian historians of the nineteenth and twentieth centuries embodied the same values as those of a self-conscious, independent, and educated middle class: in this analogy, the free peasant was styled as the icon of the fully-fledged and independent political subject. Norway's unique candour was rooted in the freedom of peasants and

25 Helle, *Norge blir en stat* (1964, 1974 and later editions).

expressed through counter-cultural movements that promoted the local church, abstinence, and the retention of traditional Norwegian language forms, as well the material and cultural independence of the 'little guy'. This is not the product of elite culture. A society born of small, independent peasants fosters the kind of individual that withstands intimidation and resists outside control. There was of course always a possibility, indeed a threat, that these independent people might devolve into a dependant proletariat. This tension between strength and weakness, between freedom and dependency, was perceived as the driving force in Norwegian history throughout the period of nation-building.

CHAPTER 7

The Participation of the Tyrolean Peasantry in the Government of the Country: Theory – Reality – Ideology

Josef Riedmann

It may well have been one of the most extraordinary scenes of European parliamentary life: in the second half of the twentieth century a delegate in the plenary takes out original charters from the first half of the fourteenth century in order to use them to reinforce his argument on the august duties of parliament. This remarkable scene occurred in 1961 in Innsbruck at the opening session of the *Tiroler Landtag*, the state assembly of representatives voted by the people of the Austrian state of Tyrol. On this occasion the father of the House, Dr Hans Gamper, a member of the Christian Conservative Tyrolean People's Party (*Christlich-konservative Tiroler Volkspartei*)[1] presented his colleagues with two original pieces of parchment complete with seals, from the year 1342, which he called the *beginning of the Tyrolean Constitution*.[2] With the help of these documents now displayed in the Tyrolean State Archives in Innsbruck (*Tiroler Landesarchiv*), one issued over 600 years ago by the then-governing Tyrolean territorial ruler, the margrave Louis of the House of Wittelsbach, and the other an analogous endorsement by his father, the emperor Louis IV the Bavarian, Dr Gamper tried to demonstrate that in Tyrol it had been the tradition since time immemorial to let the people as a whole participate to a certain degree in the political events of the day. For in those two documents old and new rights were affirmed for all the inhabitants of Tyrol, not just for the aristocracy, for the clergy, the urban middle classes, but for everyone, *rich and poor*, as it is stated. Participation in politics or a democratic disposition in general was

1 A newer recognition of Hans Gamper does not exist, even though he played a major role in Tyrolean politics over many decades. He was especially active in cultural activities between 1945 and 1965. See the many references in the contributions of various authors in the collection: Michael Gehler (ed.), *Tirol. 'Land im Gebirge': Zwischen Tradition und Moderne*, Geschichte der österreichischen Bundesländer seit 1945, 3 and Schriftenreihe des Forschungsinstituts für politisch-historische Studien der Dr.-Wilfried-Haslauer-Bibliothek, 6 (Vienna: Böhlau, 1999).

2 See Deutsche Nationalbibliothek, Leipzig and Frankfurt am Main, *Stenographische Berichte des Tiroler Landtages*. V. Periode, 1. Tagung am 7. November 1961, p. 1.

 | DOI:10.1163/9789004433458_008

thus, according to this Tyrolean politician, not only customary in Tyrol after 1945, after the end of the National Socialist dictatorship, but had already been common practice centuries ago – quite a different practice from the centralist habits of which Dr Gamper and his party colleagues accused the main government in Vienna, which at that time was made up of a coalition between the Christian Conservatives and the Social Democrats.

Dr Gamper's performance in 1961 was by no means an isolated occurrence. Fifteen years earlier, in November 1947, Dr Gamper had brought an application of urgency to the *Tiroler Landtag*, petitioning that in order to safeguard the federal character of Austria one should take up arms against the ever-increasing encroachments of centralism and other factors and call on the other states of Austria to take part in this fight for the freedom and autonomy of the states. Dr Gamper was concerned about 'safeguarding old legal traditions and a democracy that is in accordance with Austrian nature as well as safeguarding the valuable, rooted folk culture of the federal states'.[3] The basis for the following intense discussion in parliament was a long assessment commissioned by the president of the *Landtag* composed by the 'doyen of the Tyrolean historians, Prof Wopfner', who had prepared an 'overview of the historical development of our state and how it belongs to Austria'. The main argument of this exposé that was read out at length in the *Landtag* lay in sentences such as: 'At that time (1363), the Tyrolean *Landtag* already constituted a proper representation of the people according to the old democratic constitution',[4] and 'especially the peasantry in all the states is the enemy of centralism'.[5] At this point, it is beyond the scope of this section to detail the background of the ensuing debate, which arose from a number of prevailing circumstances.[6]

3 *Protocols of the Tiroler Landtag*, 1. Period, 10th day, 3rd session, 14th November (hectographically multiplied, deposited in the Tiroler Landesarchiv Innsbruck, Signature 6579), p. 330.

4 Protocols of the Tiroler Landtag, 331.

5 Protocols of the Tiroler Landtag, 336.

6 It was mainly about the repeatedly discussed question of the autonomous rights and historical claims of the federal states to the state of Austria. The points of contention included both some very specific and also quite heterogenous things, such as the expansion of the electricity industry, or the objects of art that been removed from Tyrol to Vienna centuries ago; see Eberhard Lang, 'Der Landtag in der Zweiten Republik (1945–1982)', in Richard Schober, *Geschichte des Tiroler Landtags im 19. und 20. Jahrhundert*, Veröffentlichungen des Tiroler Landesarchivs, 4 (Innsbruck: Universitätsverlag Wagner, 1984), 473–506, esp. p. 499, and briefly Martin Achrainer and Niko Hofinger, 'Politik nach "Tiroler Art – ein Dreiklang aus Fleiß, Tüchtigkeit und Zukunftsglauben". Anmerkungen, Anekdoten und Analysen zum politischen System Tirols 1945–1999', in Gehler, *Tirol*, 27–136, esp. p. 46. In all these sometimes very polemical and populist discussions, the antagonism between Catholic-Conservatives (the popular party dominated in Tyrol by the Bauernbund) and Socialists (Social Democrats)

An observation concerning certain historians of Tyrol is arguably highly important: that is, the most eminent historians of Tyrol in the first half of the twentieth century, who were partly also well-known in international circles, such as Hermann Wopfner or Otto Stolz, did not exclusively address the subject of the far-reaching tradition of democracy in Tyrolean public life, meaning primarily the peasantry's significant participation in public affairs, in academic publications. They also propagated their views again and again in political councils and at lectures given to schools and at other educational events throughout Tyrol.[7] These ideas, sometimes recounted in even more simplified terms, resonated widely and, until recently, were upheld in particular by the leading political powers in Tyrol, who belonged predominantly to the Catholic-conservative-agricultural class. The most frequent and pithy statements connected to these views were, for instance:

> The Tyrol is the oldest continental democracy, and its foundation was the Magna Carta of 1342, also called the Great Tyrolean Letter of Liberties. Or similarly the statement that there were at that time (1342) only two other letters of a similar nature: the Magna Carta, the great English letter of liberties, and the 'Golden Bull' of the Hungarians. A fourth did not exist. Other peoples still lived in deeply unfree circumstances. Their fields were worked by unfree serfs, bound to the land. This Tyrolean letter of liberties gave the whole populace, including the peasants, the three most important rights of sovereignty: the right to approve taxation, the right of legislative participation, and the right to control government.

played a central role. These discussions were also encumbered by the massive confrontations between these two camps in the so-called Austrian corporative state of the 1930s.

7 Compare the comments in Josef Riedmann, 'Geschichtsschreibung und Geschichtsbewußtsein in Tirol, vornehmlich in der 1. Hälfte des 20. Jahrhunderts', *Tiroler Heimat*, 57 (1993), 291–304, esp. 295. For example, the title of a widely read publication by Hermann Wopfner, *Von der Ehre und Freiheit des Tiroler Bauernstandes*, i: *Von der Freiheit des Landes Tirol* (Innsbruck, 1934). A planned second volume was never published since the author, even though he was the uncle of the first minister Kurt Schuschnigg, did not agree with the politics of the state. Soon after 1945, Hermann Wopfner's brochure for a wider popular audience was published, beginning with the programmatic statement: 'The Tyrolian peasant may be proud of his estate and his glorious history: first, due to the economic efficiency that his estate has proven; second, due to his freedom, both personal and political, which he had long since earned and kept; and third, due to his true Christianity, which has made him strong of character'. Hermann Wopfner, *Tiroler Bauer und Tiroler Landesfreiheit*, Tiroler Heimatschriften, 1 (Innsbruck, n.d.). See also, ibid. p. 47: 'The old democratic tradition that our Tyrolean peasant has is one of the most important safeguards against the widespread political lack of character of the last decades'.

This is another statement made by Dr Gamper in the Tyrolean *Landtag* of 1961.[8]

The idea of the high degree of participation documented in the charters, even of the *political equality* of the peasants, was even more important in combination with the *freedom* it was assumed the rural populace of Tyrol enjoyed to a much higher degree than that of the comparable neighbouring regions. Besides equality and freedom, a third criterion was the idea that the people who lived in those mountainous regions were highly capable of, as well as ready and willing to defend themselves, something which could be shown throughout the centuries. The battles for freedom in 1809 under Andreas Hofer against Napoleon and his allies as well as the resistance to the Italian attacks on the southern border in 1915 and 1918 were the most widespread testaments to this capacity for self-defence. Today, eminent politicians are less likely to utter pronouncements of such a kind, but they are still sometimes heard at so-called patriotic celebrations, especially in the sphere of the traditional memorial groupings (*Traditionsverbände*).

But how do younger generations of historians, usually less emotional and more prosaic, judge these issues, especially the role of the so-called '*Landstandschaft*' of the peasants in the Tyrolean *Landtag* which has been the representative of that part of the population since medieval times? The starting point for a new appreciation of the phenomenon was, first, the international comparison, which meant studying how far the situation in Tyrol was truly unique. We have mainly Peter Blickle and his circle to thank for having established that in quite a few larger and smaller territories of the Holy Roman Empire, there were representatives of lower social classes who were able to establish themselves at least temporarily in those institutions of the estates that were developing nearly everywhere in the later Middle Ages – not to mention the development in the regions of the Swiss Confederacy and the Graubünden that were geographically very close to Tyrol.[9]

Taking a wider look at the situation across the border led to a new appraisal of diverse statements in what were indeed sometimes decidedly important political documents, especially in the fourteenth century. In these, it appears that

8 See footnote 26.

9 See paradigmatically Peter Blickle, 'Friede und Verfassung. Voraussetzungen und Folgen der Eidgenossenschaft von 1291', in *Innerschweiz und frühe Eidgenossenschaft. Jubiläumsschrift 700 Jahre Eidgenossenschaft*, i: *Verfassung-Kirche-Kunst* (Olten: Walter, 1990), 15–202, or the contributions by Florian Hitz, 'Gesellschaft und Wirtschaft im Spätmittelalter (Mitte 14. bis Ende 15. Jahrhundert)' and Roger Sablonier, 'Politik und Staatlichkeit im spätmittelalterlichen Rätien', in *Handbuch der Bündner Geschichte*, i: *Frühzeit bis Mittelalter* (Chur, 2000), 215–43; 245–94.

the recipients of new rights were, more or less verbatim, not only aristocracy, clergy, towns, and marketplaces, but also those meant by such dual wording as *rich and poor, noble and common,* and the inhabitants of *täler und gerichte* (different administrative districts). What had long been thought of as obvious proof in Tyrol for the explicit inclusion of the lower classes in high politics was no longer so exceptional, due to the numerous parallels in other territories at the same time, for instance in the Duchy of Bavaria.[10]

A high point of disillusionment in this field was reached in 1983, when the Tyrolean state archivist, Sebastian Hölzl, argued convincingly that there were two copies of the lauded 1342 'Magna Charta' of Tyrol mentioned above – of which five copies have survived in total – that probably never even reached Tyrol, but were kept back by those issuing them, the emperor Louis the Bavarian and his son of the same name.[11] And of all the copies, it is these two, and practically only these two, in which the lower classes are specifically named as recipients of said rights and privileges.

It is perhaps necessary at this point to provide some information about the historical context for the year 1342:[12] the County of Tyrol, due to its geographic location between mid-Europe and Italy, was of the highest political importance and very profitable for its territorial rulers, the counts of Tyrol, not least because of the customs revenue on the main traffic routes between northern Italy and southern Germany. From 1330 onwards, it had become a bone of contention between the most powerful royal dynasties of the Holy Roman Empire at the time, the Bavarian Wittelsbacher, the Bohemian Luxemburger, and the Austrian Habsburg families. Marriage to the last member of the Tyrolean

10 See Sebastian Hölzl, 'Die Freiheitsbriefe der Wittelsbacher für Tirol (1342). Eine kritische Untersuchung der 'Magna Charta Tirols'. Mit einem Exkurs: Zur Kanzlei- und Archivgeschichte der Tiroler Freiheitsbriefe vom 28. Januar 1342 von Peter Moser', *Tiroler Heimat*, 46/47 (1982/83), 5–52, esp. 30ff.

11 Hölzl, 'Freiheitsbriefe'. In this groundbreaking study, Hölzl not only gives the background to the development of these charters but also an excellent overview of the critical appraisal of the documents in previous literature.

12 See the following in a wider context in: Josef Riedmann, 'Mittelalter', in Josef Fontana, et al. (eds), *Geschichte des Landes Tirol*, i, 2nd edn (Bozen: Athesia), 1990, 291–698, esp. 426ff.; the various contributions in the exhibition catalogue: Josef Riedmann and Giuseppe Albertoni (eds), *Eines Fürsten Traum. Meinhard II. – Das Werden Tirols. Tiroler Landesausstellung 1995*, Schloss Tirol, *Stift Stams* (Dorf Tirol: Südtiroler Landesmuseum Schloß Tirol, 1995); and recently the exhibition catalogue: Leo Andergassen and Julia Hörmann-Thurn und Taxis (eds), *Margarete Gräfin von Tirol – Margareta contessa del Tirolo* (Innsbruck: Studienverlag, 2007); as well as the essays in: Julia Hörmann-Thurn und Taxis (ed.), *Margarete 'Maultasch'. Zur Lebenswelt einer Landesfürstin und anderer Tiroler Frauen des Mittelalters*, Schlern-Schriften, 339 (Innsbruck: Universitätsverlag Wagner, 2007). This relevant publication from 2007 includes references to earlier specialist literature.

dynasty, Countess Margaret, later given the memorable but still not completely explained nickname 'Maultasch', served to legitimize pretensions.[13] First married to a member of the Luxemburg dynasty, Margaret sent her husband away in 1341 and married a second time – without a divorce from her first husband – the son of the emperor Louis of Bavaria, the margrave Louis of Brandenburg. The emperor looked on this marriage with great goodwill – control over the County of Tyrol suited his political ambitions in Italy perfectly, quite apart from the southern extension of the Wittelsbach territory that it brought. It was against this background that the emperor and his son granted and confirmed with understandable lavishness old and new rights for the new Tyrolean subjects, recorded in the five surviving charters. Specially mentioned recipients both in a charter of the margrave and one of the emperor were stated explicitly as 'alle leute, edel und unedel, reiche und arme, wie sie geheißen seien oder wo die gelegen oder gesessen sind in der Grafschaft Tirol' (all people, noble and non-noble, wealthy and poor, however they are named or wherever they live in the County of Tyrol).[14] But what was for a long time seen as essential proof of the substantial inclusion of the lower classes into the political process cannot be relied upon as evidence, as two of the charters with these recipients were obviously never distributed.[15] Only two copies reached Tyrol, in both of which only the clergy and the nobility were named as recipients, in addition to an imperial confirmation of the 'liberties' granted by the emperor's son. In this charter, there is mention of people who resided in the County of Tyrol, religious or secular, noble and common, citizens 'rich and poor, as they are called'.[16] But this original was also probably soon rescinded by the Wittelsbacher family. According to Sebastian Hölzl, we can summarize that, on the authority of current scholarship, the so-called Magna Charta of 1342 must be discarded as a basis for the institutional participation of the peasantry in the government of the state. But this means that there is no foundation left for the interpretation of similar quotations in documentation from the fourteenth century.[17] Incidentally, this is true in general for the assumption of more or less functioning state assemblies in this century. It is also true that, in this period, there were

13 For Margaret, Countess of Tyrol, as well as the development connected to her person, see the recent publication Hörmann-Thurn und Taxis (ed.), *Margarete 'Maultasch'*, as well as the exhibition catalogue Andergassen and Hörmann-Thurn und Taxis (eds), *Margarete Gräfin von Tirol*.

14 Hölzl, 'Freiheitsbriefe', 7f. (No. A and B) – translation of the Middle High German into New High German.

15 Hölzl, 'Freiheitsbriefe', 27.

16 Hölzl, 'Freiheitsbriefe' (No. C).

17 See Hölzl, 'Freiheitsbriefe', 30f.

various special occasions in which leading political powers of the state came forth successfully and with special initiatives. This was the case in particular when it came to change in the territorial dynasty. On this occasion, the new presumptive territorial lord needed to secure for himself the favour of the aristocracy, the clergy, and the towns that began to gain strength from 1360 onwards. The entirety of all subjects was not, however, included in this process – not even in the form of individual representatives of the numerically dominant peasantry. That only changed at the beginning of the fifteenth century under specific outside influences.[18]

In 1363, after the death of both her husband Margrave Louis and her son Meinhard III, Margaret 'Maultasch' transferred her right to Tyrol to her closest relatives, the Habsburg dukes of Austria. This arrangement would prove to have long-lasting consequences, including the County of Tyrol in a complex of territories no longer orientated north-south but east-west. Soon the dukes of Habsburg divided their rule. The government of the branch of the family that had its centre in Tyrol after 1400 is characterized by various adverse factors: further dispute within the family; external threat to the country, especially through the Swiss confederates who were gaining strength; difficult financial situations internally following the pawning of considerable territorial revenue to parts of the aristocracy, who in turn strove to gain more independence, in extreme cases even imperial immediacy. In these straightened circumstances, intensified by a dramatic conflict with King Sigismund of Luxemburg, Duke Frederick (who reigned in Tyrol at that time and later was given the epithet 'with empty pockets') sought and found assistance with the towns and marketplaces, as well as – and this was apparently a new approach, at least in such a direct form –with his subjects of lower social standing.

There had already been close ties between the Tyrolean territorial rulers and the mass of the peasantry in the days of Meinhard II, founder of the County of Tyrol in the second half of the thirteenth century. Meinhard's successful policy was focused on, among other things, limiting the reach of other powerful noble families and bringing their villeins under his direct control.[19] Sure

18 Compare the overview by Werner Köfler, *Land-Landschaft-Landtag. Geschichte der Tiroler Landtage von den Anfängen bis zur Aufhebung der landständischen Verfassung 1808*, Veröffentlichungen des Tiroler Landesarchivs, 3 (Innsbruck: Universitätsverlag Wagner, 1985). In this study (pp. 36–41), Hölzl's new insights into the evaluation of the 'great Tyrolean Charter of Liberties' were only received with caution.

19 For Meinhard II, see the publication by Hermann Wiesflecker, *Meinhard der Zweite. Tirol, Kärnten und ihre Nachbarländer am Ende des 13. Jahrhunderts*, Schlern-Schriften, 124 (Innsbruck: Wagner, 1955 [reprint 1995]), and the contributions to the exhibition catalogue: Riedmann and Albertoni (eds), *Eines Fürsten Traum.*

enough, around 1300 most of the inhabitants of the heartland of the County of Tyrol would have been direct subjects of the territorial ruler and not of noble or clerical lords. Villeinage had not been abolished, but it had receded over the course of general developments and the peasants were able to rent land on good conditions that was still held in ownership by the count or other secular or clerical landowners. If peasants who felt themselves treated unfairly by their noble or clerical lords turned to the count with their complaints, it proves that he was seen as a sort of superordinate means of protection.

Since the days of Meinhard II, the entire county – apart from the towns – was organized into individual administrative districts called '*Gerichte*', although the judge appointed by the territorial ruler mainly had administrative and not juridical responsibilities. These districts were the geographical superstructure for the individual peasant communities in which we see clear evidence from the twelfth and thirteenth centuries onwards for the incipient stages of self-government.[20] For instance, the regulations for problems concerning common pasture, common use of water and the forest, or measures put in place against flooding were in the hands of the village institutions, such as the *Dorfmeister*. This *Dorfmeister* was chosen by the leading members of the village and not by the feudal authorities. In this way, prominent individuals with standing in the village could distinguish themselves at this level. It is also worth mentioning that towards the end of the fourteenth century some of the districts provided the territorial ruler with sizeable sums of money in order for him to pay for their manumission by their feudal lords. Apparently, for most of the peasantry the count was a more congenial overlord than the local nobles. It was also often stated that the decisive military assistance that the subject peasants were at times expected to give their lord was proof of a closer link between count and populace in Tyrol. This was believed to have promoted participation in politics. However, recent scholarship has mostly departed from that view.[21]

---

20 More generally, for these and the following issues: Heinz Dopsch, 'Zwischen Herrschaft und Genossenschaft. Grundstrukturen bäuerlichen Lebens im Ostalpenraum' and Wilfried Beimrohr, 'Bäuerliches Besitzrecht und Abhängigkeitsverhältnisse in Tirol', in Tore Iversen, John Ragnar Myking, and Gertrud Thoma (eds), *Bauern zwischen Herrschaft und Genossenschaft: Peasant Relations to Lords and Government. Scandinavia and the Alpine Region 1000–1750* (Trondheim: Tapir Akademisk Forlag, 2007), 85–108. Both contributions were originally presented at the conference in Bergen 2007.

21 Compare the extensive introductory chapter in the book by Martin P. Schennach, *Ritter, Landsknecht, Aufgebot. Quellen zum Tiroler Kriegswesen. 14.–17. Jahrhundert*, Tiroler Geschichtsquellen, 49 (Innsbruck: Tiroler Landesarchiv, 2004), 14–108. The comparative approach (58ff.) especially puts the particularity of the Tyrolean situation into perspective.

The problems already briefly mentioned that confronted the Tyrolean count, the Habsburg Frederick IV (r. 1406–39), in the first decades of the fifteenth century, appear as a predominant reason for representatives of the *Gerichte* to have been continuously included in important political decisions from 1410.[22] And in a further phase, from about 1420, representatives were present at the now regularly convening *Tiroler Landtag*.[23] These representatives, together with those of the towns, consistently took the side of the territorial ruler against the strong noble opposition. This support for the position of the territorial ruler from the lower strata of society is not to be underrated.

Even though there are no procedural rules recorded from the Tyrolean *Landtag*, which convened more or less regularly from 1420 – there were probably never any written rules in the medieval period – it is still possible to reconstruct the commonly practiced procedure: in the case of a *Ständeversammlung* (assembly of estates) being convened, the *Gerichte* were also called upon to send messengers with letters of authority. The number of messengers varies, it is usually two per *Gericht*.[24] We do not know the exact procedure in which they were chosen by the community, and not all districts complied with the invitation. As far as the individual messengers can be situated in their social surroundings, they appear to be the owners of larger farms or innkeepers, as well as men who had also distinguished themselves as functionaries on the lowest level, as dispensers of justice or as church provost, managing the church funds. Around 70 percent of the messengers we can identify can be seen as belonging to the upper strata of peasant society. In addition, we can also find occasional tradesmen or judges installed by the territorial ruler himself. These and the following observations are based on the detailed studies conducted by Adelina Wallnöfer in 1984.[25]

The representatives of the *Gerichte* obviously had a voice in all matters that were debated in the *Landtag*. They first conferred with the representatives of the towns and marketplaces – similarly the nobles and the clergy first spoke to

22 See Köfler, *Landtag*, esp. 46ff. These developments are also extensively discussed in the sadly unpublished dissertation of Adelina Wallnöfer, 'Die Bauern in der Tiroler "Landschaft" vor 1500. Politische Aktivität der Gerichte und deren Repräsentanten auf den Landtagen', PhD dissertation, University of Innsbruck, Innsbruck 1984, although the dissertation is now published in a very expanded form: Adelina Wallnöfer, *Die politische Repräsentation des gemeinen Mannes in Tirol. Die Gerichte und ihre Vertreter auf den Landtagen vor 1500*, Veröffentlichungen des Südtiroler Landesarchivs – Pubblicazioni dell'Archivio provinciale di Bolzano, 41 (Innsbruck: Universitätsverlag Wagner, 2017).

23 See Wallnöfer, 'Bauern', 93ff.

24 For more detail, Wallnöfer, 'Bauern', 109ff.

25 Wallnöfer, 'Bauern', esp. 175ff.

each other. Subsequently, all representatives met for collective discussion and decision making, wherein each *Gericht* had one vote, whereas prelates and nobles had one vote per head. One example to illustrate the ratio: at the *Landtag* in 1474, there were four representatives of the bishops (Trient and Brixen), thirteenth prelates (mostly abbots) in attendance, and 123 nobles, as well as the deputies of eight towns and marketplaces and the representatives of fifty-nine *Gerichte*.[26] As seems clear, the representatives of the *Gerichte* did not play a marginal role. In addition, they were part of the committees that were growing ever more important, and from time to time were also part of delegations and acted as councillors elected by the *Landtag* for the count. However, the actual farmers rather receded into the background in relation to these functions.

The importance of the representatives of the *Gerichte* in the Tyrolean territorial estates is most evident when it comes to the affixing of seals to important documents. For example, when the then Tyrolean territorial ruler, the archduke Sigismund, renounced the government of Tyrol and further regions in favour of his Habsburg relative King Maximilian I, he had a ceremonial charter drawn up. The seals still hanging from the original are not only those of the king and the archduke, but also that of the abbot of Wilten as representative of the prelates, of the noble Nicolas of Firmian, the mayor of Innsbruck, and that of Martin Strauß from Latsch in the Vinschgau 'als von der gerichts wegen' (as representative of the *Gerichte*).[27] His seal is in no way smaller than that of the mayor of Innsbruck, and only marginally less ostentatious than those of the members of the high nobility.[28]

There can thus be no doubt that in the fifteenth century in Tyrol a small part of the upper class peasantry – though in no way the peasantry as an entire estate – was participating in political events, and to a decidedly higher degree than in most other German territories, although this occurred to a lesser degree than in the immediate neighbouring regions of the Graubünden or the Swiss confederacy. By the time of King Maximilian I around 1500, nobles and clergy were gaining strength, even though after the failure of the revolutionary peasant movement of 1525/6, when the lower classes tried to stake a claim to leadership in the country and failed, the representatives still remained in the

26 Wallnöfer, 'Bauern', 168.

27 For the charter, see Ernst Freiherr von Schwind and Alfons Dopsch, *Ausgewählte Urkunden zur Verfassungsgeschichte der deutsch-österreichischen Erblande im Mittelalter* (Innsbruck: Wagner, 1894), 418–43, no. 227.

28 Compare the depiction in Riedmann, 'Mittelalter', 507. Martin Strauß was regularly present as the representative of the district Schlanders at the Tyrolean *Landtag*; compare Wallnöfer, 'Bauern'. 273. His gravestone from 1518, decorated with his crest, is still extant in the parish church of Latsch (Vinschgau-Südtirol).

Landtag. However, this institution subsequently lost much of its relevance in the face of aristocratic absolutism – in Tyrol even more rapidly than in other Habsburg countries.

If the memory of the representation of the Tyrolean peasantry at the *Landtag* received excessive revitalization in the first half of the twentieth century, this was mainly due to the political situation towards the end of the nineteenth and at the beginning of the twentieth century – especially regarding the contrast of the conservative-catholic Tyrolean crown land to Viennese liberal centralism. And the increasingly self-confident and highly-organized peasantry of Tyrol managed to instrumentalize the real and supposedly glorious past for a long time as a supporting argument for their own interests.[29] A general romantic glorification of the original peasantry, as well as a focus on supposed or actual democratic traditions as a reaction to the dictatorships in the time before 1945, can be given as further reason for such a development. These endeavours doubtlessly reach back into the period before National Socialism and other fascisms,[30] and were not simply part of the 'Blood and Soil' romanticism of this totalitarian movement. Only in recent decades, with the general economic and social changes taking effect, a change in this attitude can be seen. That this change is also connected to new insights and evaluations in the field of medieval history is probably to be judged as more of a coincidence.

This contribution is equivalent without alterations to the text delivered in the year 2007 at the conference in Bergen.

---

29 See here the description by Benedikt Erhard, *Bauernstand und Politik. Zur Geschichte des Tiroler Bauernbundes*, Schriftenreihe der Michael Gaismair Gesellschaft, 1 (Vienna: Jugen und Volk, 1981).

30 In this context, see Wopfner, *Ehre und Freiheit* and Wopfner, *Tiroler Bauer*.

CHAPTER 8

Peasant Ideology in German Historiography

Werner Rösener

Adel und Bauern im deutschen Staat des Mittelalters (*Aristocracy and Peasants in the Medieval German State*) is the title of a collected volume published by Theodor Mayer, the director of the renowned *Reichsinstitut für ältere deutsche Geschichtskunde* (*Monumenta Germaniae Historica*), in the year 1943.[1] This volume contains twelve contributions discussing the theme of 'aristocracy and peasants' from the perspective of the aristocracy and its position in the German imperial constitution, as well as from that of the peasants within the framework of the medieval state. Geographical focus is on the high medieval empire, but some contributors also looked at neighbouring regions, especially at the conditions of the peasantry in the Scandinavian area. The editor programmatically formulated the starting point for the volume:

> The development of fixed stately forms and institutions, the incorporation of the entire population into the state and its subjection under state power, and lastly the acquisition of the German *lebensraum* through and for the state and the people – these processes with their enormous dynamic occupied the internal history of the German Middle Ages.[2]

The questions posed were about the methods and measures with which the medieval state was established and had developed within the conflicting priorities of king, nobles, and peasantry. 'They were not all the same, but manifold; they were dependent on numerous factors and thus the results show a great diversity that has been the hallmark of German state structure over centuries and that should not be supressed or neglected in any depiction'.[3]

Gerd Tellenbach, who had dealt with the development of the German empire in the early tenth century in a relevant study in 1939, studied the process of the transformation of the aristocracy in his contribution, from Carolingian

1 Theodor Mayer, *Adel und Bauern im deutschen Staat des Mittelalters* (Leipzig: Koehler and Amelang, 1943 [reprint, Darmstadt: Wissenschaftliche Buchgesellschaft, 1976]).
2 Mayer, *Adel und Bauern*, 1.
3 Mayer, *Adel und Bauern*, 2.

 | DOI:10.1163/9789004433458_009

imperial nobility to German principality.[4] The high nobility originally appeared as assistants and commissionaires to the king and they had earned their merits with the development of stately structures, but they subsequently became independent and concentrated all their power on territorial expansion. In 1950, Karl Bosl presented his great work on the *Reichsministerialität*,[5] in which he studied the role of the *Ministerialen* in the time of the Salier and Staufer rulers. The *Reichsministerialen* were energetic representatives of the royal politics of state and decidedly influenced the politics of the empire for a long time.

The position of the peasantry seems to have been most interesting in the High Middle Ages. Mayer says: 'Their relationship with the state was in general a passive one, but in certain circumstances they could also be active participants in the development of a state'.[6] The legal position of the peasants and the question of freedom and serfdom was important in these circumstances. According to Mayer, of decisive importance for the peasants was the issue of woodland clearing, which turned many into *Rodungsfreie* (free peasants working deforested land); their relationship with public authority, the king, or the territorial ruler, was crucial in maintaining the special rights of the free peasants. In more than one contribution of the collection, prominent authors therefore analysed settlement advances and the spread of free peasants. Karl-Hans Ganahl studied the position of the free peasants in the charters of St Gallen, Otto Stolz the special relationship between peasant and territorial ruler in Tyrol, and Rudolf Kötzschke the relationship between state and peasantry in the Thuringian-Saxonian region, whereas Erich Molitor concentrated his studies on the free peasants in the north of Germany and the spread of the *Hägerrecht* (the sets of privileges frequently given to peasants working deforested ground). The contribution of Claudius Freiherr of Schwerin, who dealt with the situation of the peasantry in the Scandinavian region, (Norway, Sweden, Denmark) was also of importance. The full picture resulting from these studies in the different regions was not uniform and no common denominator could be found, due to the various approaches and regional differences.

Apart from Mayer, German nationalist historiography of the peasantry was represented at that time mainly by Günther Franz, who in his well-known study *Der deutsche Bauernkrieg* (The German Peasants' War) (1933), accentuated the

4 Gerd Tellenbach, Königtum und Stämme in der Werdezeit des Deutschen Reiches (Weimar, 1939).

5 Karl Bosl, *Die Reichsministerialität der Salier und Staufer 1–2*, Schriften der Monumenta Germaniae Historica, 10, 1–2 (Stuttgart: Hiersemann, 1950/51).

6 Mayer, *Adel und Bauern*, 21.

political role of the German peasants.[7] For Franz, the German Peasants' War of 1525 was mainly a political revolution of the peasant estate that could be numbered among a series of other peasant revolts of the fourteenth and fifteenth centuries. 'The Peasants' War is only understandable when seen in the context of these precursors, as last link in a chain of revolutionary uprisings'.[8] Both Franz and Mayer saw the peasants as a relatively uniform class, whose internal differences were not studied in any depth. The economic and social situation of the peasants was not the main point of interest and was not to be studied in detail. Franz even believed that there were no definitive statements to be made about the economic situation of the peasants towards the end of the Middle Ages.

> Too many facts are today hardly or not at all verifiable (levels of debt, agricultural yield, the market situation, minimal existence levels, etc.). Knowing the tax burden alone does not solve the question; the psychological questions would appear to be much more relevant. The important thing is whether the peasant himself found his situation to be tolerable or not.[9]

Where did German scholarship's focus on a peasant class seen as uniform and the legal-political aspects of the peasantry come from? What are the roots of the ideology of the German peasant in the nineteenth century?

1 The German Peasantry as Seen in the Nineteenth Century

One strong influence on the concept of the German peasant and the assessment of the peasants in German societal development was doubtlessly Wilhelm Heinrich Riehl (1823–97).[10] Born in Hessen-Nassau, he was highly regarded as a cultural historian and social critic by a majority of his contemporaries, but only barely accepted by the developing academic cultural historiography of the nineteenth century. Though he completed his studies in theology and history with a theology exam, he then turned predominantly to

---

7 Günther Franz, *Der deutsche Bauernkrieg*, (Munich: Oldenbourg, 1933 [reprint, Darmstadt: Wissenschaftliche Buchgesellschaft, 1984]).

8 Franz, *Der deutsche Bauernkrieg*, ix.

9 Franz, *Der deutsche Bauernkrieg*, x.

10 Wilhelm Heinrich Riehl, *Die bürgerliche Gesellschaft*, Peter Steinbach (ed.) (Frankfurt: Ullstein, 1976), 7–52; W.H. Riehls, *Naturgeschichte des deutschen Volkes*, Gunther Ipsen (ed.) (Leipzig: Kröner, 1935).

political journalism. In Frankfurt he worked for the liberal-conservative *Oberpostamtszeitung* from 1845 to 1847, then from 1847 onwards as a member of the editorial staff of a newspaper in Karlsruhe. A turning point in Riehl's life was undoubtedly the 1848 revolution, which influenced him strongly. With the outbreak of revolution, Riehl left Karlsruhe for Wiesbaden, one of the small state centres of the revolutionary movement, and established the *Nassauische Allgemeine Zeitung*.

In this phase of his life, he developed a conservative understanding of politics, bound up in terms such as social order, estates, and social envy; he tried to suit every social group and every political party. The co-management of the royal theatre in Wiesbaden caused him to notably distance himself from politics, leading to his retirement from the editorial position in 1850. During this time, he began researching bourgeois society. In 1851, the first edition of his work (*Die bürgerliche Gesellschaft*) (*The Bourgeois Society*) was published, to great public interest. In the following years he expanded his research and short studies to a four-volume *Naturgeschichte des Volkes* (*Natural History of the People*). Three years after *Die bürgerliche Gesellschaft*, he published *Land und Leute* (*Land and People*), a study containing folkloristically and geographically interesting observations about peasant life. Riehl's basic conservative attitude and his *biedermeier*-style depiction of 'land and people' impressed the then king Maximilian II, who made him a member of the 'Literary Cabinet' at his court. He received academic honours with an honorary professorship from Munich University, which was tied to giving lectures on political sciences, economics, and cultural history. Soon, he was also a member of the royal table of illustrious scholars and was in contact with eminent academics. In 1859, he received the chair for cultural history in Munich, became member of the historical class of the Bavarian Academy of Sciences and Humanities, and then in 1862 he became a senator of the University.

The oeuvre that is most interesting for us is *Die bürgerliche Gesellschaft*, published only a few years after the revolution of 1848. It gives both a social-psychological depiction of the various societal classes and an interpretation of society with a restorative aim. Amongst the conservative powers of society (*Mächte des Beharrens*), which are best able to resist the floodwaters of the revolution, the peasants, according to Riehl, take pole position.

> There lies an insurmountable conservative power in the German nation, a strong centre in the midst of all change – our peasants. They are the true original core, the like of which no other nation has. The learned may be conservative based on reason but the peasant is conservative through the strength of his morals. He has played a greater part in the social struggles

> of our days than most people guess, because he was the natural barrier against the overflowing of French revolutionary doctrines into the lower strata of society. Only the dogged resistance of the peasants saved the German thrones in March 1848.[11]

Looking at the future of the German nation, Riehl also assigns an important role to the peasants: 'The peasant has political importance in our country as in very few other countries of Europe; the peasant is the future of the German nation'.[12]

When it comes to the entirety of the German peasantry, Riehl differentiates according to two categories: on one side the good peasant (*Bauer von guter Art*), and on the other the degenerate peasant (*der entartete Bauer*). The true German peasant embodies the 'historical type of the German race' (*der historische Typus des deutschen Menschenschlags*) which is not the case for the urban citizen. He who wants to be able to judge medieval people correctly must seek his model from among the peasants. The peasant values tradition and clings to all its forms, even when it would be sensible to give up these traditional elements.[13] According to Riehl, this concerns traditional forms of language, dress, architecture, and other areas of peasant life. With respect to the traditions of inheritance, Riehl prefers the *Anerbenrecht,* leaving the entire smallholding to one heir. 'The true peasant cannot understand the soft-hearted modern inheritance law, that gives all children everything, so that in the end none owns much of anything'.[14] Prime examples of the German peasantry could be found amongst the Westphalian peasantry, who had the greatest freedom in the Middle Ages.

> They were like free patrician citizens amongst the other peasant, had free constitutions according to age-old traditional rules, had their own judiciary, paid only a low amount of taxes. And these peasants who had long been free now appear as the most conservative, the archetype of the historical German peasant.[15]

The Westphalian peasants are a striking contrast to the peasantry in the small southwestern German territories, where the oppressed peasant is prevalent.

11 Riehl, *Die bürgerliche Gesellschaft*, 57.
12 Riehl, *Die bürgerliche Gesellschaft*, 57.
13 Riehl, *Die bürgerliche Gesellschaft*, 61.
14 Riehl, *Die bürgerliche Gesellschaft*, 66f.
15 Riehl, *Die bürgerliche Gesellschaft*, 66.

One main reason for the development of an unhealthy peasantry according to Riehl is the structure of smallholdings being divided up, which occurred especially in those parts of southwestern Germany where partible inheritance was common; the moral ruin of the peasantry usually coincided with economic factors. Such factors that contributed to the decline of the true peasantry were, apart from the partition of properties, mainly part-time work in agriculture, the influences of the monetary economy, and the intense participation in the market economy, subverting the original nature of the peasants. Those villages close to larger towns were especially in danger of this. 'Added to the moral deterioration, you have the direct influence of urban worthlessness... The proletariat of such villages is the most dangerous, for they were in no way second to the lowlife in town but surpassed it in brutality'.[16] According to Riehl, the deterioration of the true peasantry was especially advanced in the first half of the nineteenth century. For this decline, the modern state was foremost to blame, with its political, legal, and economic reforms, because, in the course of the territorial changes after the Napoleonic period, the political structure of Germany changed thoroughly, and the peasants were hurt deeply in their traditional loyalty by the frequent changes in rulership. This concerns mainly the territorially fractured regions in mid- and southwestern Germany, according to Riehl, where the historical tradition of the peasantry was the most thoroughly broken and a marked desire for rebellion developed during the course of the 1848 rebellion.

According to Riehl, the total overthrow of society during the revolution of 1848 is due solely to the peasants. Therefore, the peasant of the traditional type needs to be supported, as only through a healthy peasant class can the threat of socialism be stopped. It is in this sense that the German ideas about the true peasantry were strongly influenced by Riehl: from ancient Germanic times to the present, steeled by medieval bondage, the peasant was supposed to embody the raw, unadulterated core of German nature, through which national life could constantly rejuvenate itself. Riehl apparently conceived of this peasant ideology in order to stave off democratic advances and to solve the social question to his satisfaction.[17] The peasantry was supposed to be the saviour of the traditional order in the struggles with revolutionary movements and become the guarantee for the agrarian-conservative system. With this frame of

16 Riehl, *Die bürgerliche Gesellschaft*, 79.

17 See Christof Dipper, 'Bauern als Gegenstand der Sozialgeschichte', in Wolfgang Schieder and Volker Sellin (eds), *Sozialgeschichte in Deutschland. Entwicklungen und Perspektiven im internationalen Zusammenhang*, iv: *Soziale Gruppen in der Geschichte* (Göttingen: Vandenhoeck und Ruprecht, 1987), 9–33, esp. 13.

reference, Riehl also presented two historical interpretations that were widely distributed in the following academic context. The term *Grundherrschaft* (manorialism), previously mainly *Tendenzbegriff* in order to identify historical injustice,[18] was reinterpreted by Riehl to mean a modern form of public service (*Daseinsvorsorge*), as the bondsman in medieval times was always guaranteed the surety of a meal from his lord. 'The old bondage, which in a country largely still to be colonized and with a dispersed population was a true blessing, did much to stop the peasant from turning vagabond and to give him that dogged tenacity which was passed on to future generations, who might have more easily strayed'.[19] However, with the term *Grundherrschaft*, the liberal bourgeoisie had, since the eighteenth century, characterized the basis of the feudal system as an outmoded, obsolete social order. In the historic-political thought of the early nineteenth century, this term simultaneously fulfils the function of explanatory model and of a guide of how to act. 'Those who used it mainly did it to make the implementation of a free market und civil society evident as a historical necessity'.[20]

Riehl was also responsible for introducing the notion of the 'whole house' ('*ganzes Haus*') into the vocabulary of socio-historical research. Riehl saw the 'whole house', or household, which developed as a social structure particularly in the peasant sphere, as a basic element of pre-industrial society, whose social inequality was seen as natural and was offset against the comfort of conflict-free family.[21] According to Otto Brunner, the doctrine of economics in the bourgeois sense, of the 'whole house', was the original form of all peasant cultures: the household with its economic activities was the basic social structure for many peasants and nobles. 'The peasantry made up the foundation of the social structure of Europe from the Neolithic Age to the nineteenth century and in these millennia has hardly been touched in its substance by changes in the political structure of the upper classes'.[22] In the highly developed modern transaction economy, he said, the peasant economy, as opposed to all other

18 Klaus Schreiner, '"Grundherrschaft". Entstehung und Bedeutungswandel eines geschichtswissenschaftlichen Ordnungs- und Erklärungsbegriffs', in Hans Patze (ed.), *Die Grundherrschaft im späten Mittelalter*, 1, Vorträge und Forschungen, 27/1 (Sigmaringen: Thorbecke, 1983), 72; See Werner Rösener, *Grundherrschaft im Wandel. Untersuchungen zur Entwicklung geistlicher Grundherrschaften im südwestdeutschen Raum vom 9. bis 14. Jahrhundert*, (Göttingen: Vandenhoeck and Ruprecht, 1991), 14f.

19 Riehl, *Die bürgerliche Gesellschaft*, 65.

20 Schreiner, 'Grundherrschaft', 65f.

21 See Dipper, 'Bauern', 13.

22 Otto Brunner, 'Das "ganze Haus" und die alteuropäische "Ökonomik"', in *Neue Wege der Verfassungs- und Sozialgeschichte* (Göttingen: Vandenhoeck und Ruprecht, 1968), 103–27, esp. p. 107.

types, was able to withdraw itself as far as possible from market interdependences and concentrate on self-sufficiency. This view of the 'whole house' has brought out a plethora of conservative positions and discussions in German research to this day.[23] At any rate, Riehl's notion of a peasant economy and the peasant way of life found favour with the public, clearly visible in the great many editions of his books available.

Riehl's conservative idea of history and society was opposed in the nineteenth century by a liberal trend, whose representatives emphasized the characteristic liberties of the German peasantry. Georg Friedrich Maurer should be mentioned first, a defining proponent of the theory of the '*Markgenossenschaft*', who assumed a primeval freedom of the peasantry in Germanic time.[24] Free marches (*Marken*) and peasants *Markgenossenschaften* made up the basis of the German economic, social, and state constitution. Villages and smallholdings are entities separated from the old free communities (*Gemeinmark*) and eventually undermining the older *Grossmark*, confining it to the fringes and undistributed common forests. In his history of the *Markenverfassung* in Germany from 1856, Maurer writes: 'The *Markgenossenschaften* are connected to the early cultivation of the land. They go back to the first settlements in Germany, mostly back to prehistoric times, and probably were thus originally common throughout Germany'.[25]

Otto von Gierke (1841–1921) achieved the legal-dogmatic foundation of the doctrine of the *Markgenossenschaft* in legal history.[26] His acumen, his extraordinary authority in jurisprudence, and his political engagement helped to disseminate his doctrine of the '*altfreie Markgenossenschaft*'. Gierke's interest in legal history was focused especially on the organic development of society as a complex structure of group formations. His main work, the legal history of the German cooperative society, uses a broad range of sources in order to trace the development from Germanic patriarchalism to the constitutionalism of the nineteenth century between the conflicting priorities of lordship

23 See Claudia Opitz, 'Neue Wege der Sozialgeschichte? Ein kritischer Blick auf Otto Brunners Konzept des "ganzen Hauses"', *Geschichte und Gesellschaft*, 20 (1994), 88–98.

24 Georg Ludwig von Maurer, *Geschichte der Markenverfassung in Deutschland* (Erlangen: F. Enke, 1856); Georg Ludwig von Maurer, *Einleitung zur Geschichte der Mark-, Hof-, Dorf- und Stadtverfassung und der öffentlichen Gewalt*, 3rd edn (Aalen: Scientia Verlag, 1966); See Werner Rösener, 'Die Entstehung der Markgenossenschaften des Mittelalters in Theorie und Realität', in Uwe Meiners and Werner Rösener (eds), *Allmenden und Marken vom Mittelalter bis zur Neuzeit* (Cloppenburg: Museumsdorf, 2004), 17–30.

25 Maurer, *Geschichte der Markenverfassung*, 1.

26 See Hans Boldt, 'Otto von Gierke', in Hans-Ulrich Wehler (ed.), *Deutsche Historiker*, 8 (Göttingen: Vandenhoeck und Ruprecht, 1982), 7–23.

and cooperation.[27] He traces the loss of political participatory rights for the peasant cooperatives back to the triumph of manorialism in the High Middle Ages, though he did see the seeds of a libertarian structure preserved. Thus, in the course of the abolition of serfdom in the nineteenth century, the peasants gained the possibility of participation in the liberal social and constitutional state. The free *Markgenossenschaft's* ideas of original common property, the cooperative organization of the *Fronhofverband*, and the village and urban communities formed the view of many legal historians and economists.[28] This wide distribution of the doctrine of the *Markgenossenschaft* explains the great interest that Friedrich Engels and Karl Marx had in Maurer's work. In his text 'Die Mark', published in 1883, Friedrich Engels pointed to Maurer's findings that village communities with communal property were the archetypal form of all German tribal societies.[29] Through a 'rebirth of the *Mark*' in rejuvenated form and through a renewal of the land communities, there could be a new future guaranteed for German peasants.

The revolutionary concept of the peasant that occurs in Marx and Engels appeared in the first half of the nineteenth century in some historians' memorials to the German Peasants' War of 1525. Next to Friedrich Engels's text *Der deutsche Bauernkrieg* (*The German Peasants' War*) (1850), of special note is the splendid work of Wilhelm Zimmermann *Allgemeine Geschichte des großen Bauernkrieges* (*A General History of the Great Peasants' War*) (1841/44). Zimmermann shows the revolutionary activity of the German peasants in the war of 1525 in all its aspects and regional particularities, and his version of events conferred great popularity on them. In the course of the July revolution of 1830 and especially the February revolution of 1848, there were attempts in various places to include the peasants in the revolutionary and democratic movements, but this participation of the peasants abated relatively quickly in most German regions once the peasants' demands for agrarian reform had been fulfilled.[30] In the conflict between revolution and restoration during the period of the emancipation of the serfs between 1789 and 1850, a concept of the peasant established itself that may have included postulations of the reformers, but was devoid of revolutionary connotations due to the emphasis on their estate. The concept of the peasant was seen as referring to an idealized past and was

27 Otto von Gierke, Das deutsche Genossenschaftsrecht 1, Berlin 1868.

28 See Karl Siegfried Bader, *Dorfgenossenschaft und Dorfgemeinde*, Studien zur Rechtsgeschichte des mittelalterlichen Dorfes, 2 (Weimar: H. Böhlaus, 1962), 130ff.

29 Friedrich Engels, 'Die Mark', in Ludolf Kuchenbuch and Bernd Michael (eds), *Feudalismus: Materialien zur Theorie und Geschichte* (Frankfurt a.M.: Ullstein, 1977), 319–33.

30 See Christof Dipper, *Die Bauernbefreiung in Deutschland 1790–1850* (Stuttgart: Kohlhammer, 1980), 92f.

in opposition to an extreme liberalization, rationalization, and general levelling of bourgeois society. With the concept of a unified peasantry, the differences were eradicated between the various social strata, as well as between the social demarcation of actual peasants with plenty of arable land and the *Kleinstellenbesitzer* and groups with very small portions of land in the agrarian society.[31]

2 German Peasant Ideology in the Twentieth Century

The idea of a unified peasantry is also dominant in many historical texts of the twentieth century studying the history of the peasants. The idea of the peasantry as the healthy core of the German people, as presented by Riehl, was continued and added to after the First World War. In a time in which, in the face of advancing industrialization, the proportion of the peasants in the overall population grew steadily smaller,[32] the idea was established in scholarship and journalism that the renewal of the German people was possible through the vitality of the peasantry alone; industry and trade were thus reliant on the offspring of the peasantry. For instance, Gunther Ipsen, who taught at the University of Leipzig, understood his research on the sociology of the peasantry as a contribution to the history of the German nation.[33] He saw Riehl, whom he understood as having correctly predicted the decline of order and the denaturing of human life in the age of industry, as the main authority for the necessity of an academic examination of contemporary problems. But the subsistence of the German nation seemed to him not only to be threatened by the results of accelerated societal development, but also by the question of space.

Ipsen believed the people at the borders of the empire to be threatened after the loss of the war. In this crisis, sociology seemed to him to have a duty to search for new forms of political existence which would satisfy the needs of both ethnic and spatial issues.[34] Ipsen relied mainly on the traditionally minded peasant bound to the soil as a guardian of enduring forms of society, in

31 See Werner Conze, 'Bauern, Bauernstand und Bauerntum', in *Geschichtliche Grundbegriffe* (Stuttgart: Klett-Cotta 1972), i, 407–39, esp. 422.

32 See Werner Rösener, *Die Bauern in der europäischen Geschichte* (Munich: Beck, 1993), 242–252.

33 Gunther Ipsen, 'Das Dorf in der deutschen Gegenwart', *Archiv für angewandte Soziologie*, 2 (1930), 172–184, 228–41; Gunther Ipsen, *Das Landvolk: ein soziologischer Versuch* (Hamburg: Hanseatische Verlagsanstalt, 1933).

34 See Willi Oberkrome, Volksgeschichte. Methodische Innovation und völkische Ideologisierung in der deutschen Geschichtswissenschaft 1918–1945, Göttingen 1993, 116–122.

which the peasant figured as the fulfiller of an eternal, natural-religious mission. He thus interpreted the peasantry as guarantor of a true national ethnicity, and beyond that, the peasant family as the last bastion against the power-craving of the calculating economic society. In his opinion, urban society was the breeding ground of revolution, the industrial system a dehumanized tyrant, supplying uncontrolled power. On the other hand, he saw the traditional peasant as nurturer and a guarantor of the power of the nation, which is why he was emphatic in his welcome of the *Reichserbhofgesetz* (State Hereditary Farm Law) of 1933 as a core element of a new national order.

In the Third Reich, the concept of the peasant as profession and the peasant as the healthy foundation of national character and race ('Blood and Soil') was firmly connected.[35] Richard Walther Darré, who strongly influenced the National Socialist agrarian politics by means of propaganda in the last years before the Second World War, saw the peasantry 'as the source of life (*Lebensquell*) of the Nordic race': it was the task of the peasantry not only to safeguard the provision of the people but also to support the 'Norsification' (*Aufnordung*) of the German people.[36] The slogan 'Blood and Soil', which contained all the ingredients of a peasant ideology, was firmly entwined with National Socialist agricultural politics. Darré is legitimately credited with having invented the slogan; as organizer of the political machinery of the NSDAP in control of agriculture between 1930 and 1933, he strove to collect protest-voters from the peasantry. Many peasants saw themselves as being taken seriously again politically for the first time after centuries of discrimination, appreciated societally, and shown a possible better economic future. When he reached the very top of the agricultural organization in Germany as *Reichsbauernführer* and succeeded Hugenberg as *Reichsminister* for food and agriculture towards the end of 1933, he immediately began to incorporate his plans – motivated by racial ideology – into agricultural legislation. However, after early successes, it was personal failings and the conflict between necessary short-time measures and the long-term visions of his peasant ideology that led to his ultimate failure.[37]

Referring to the Scandinavian '*óðal*' (allodial rights), which provided a superior position only to the owners of an *Erbhof*, Darré wanted the peasant concept only to apply to those owners of a farm protected from divestment and encumbrance by the *Reichserbhofgesetz*. The title of peasant, '*Bauer*', should be

35 See Gustavo Corni and Horst Gies, *'Blut und Boden'. Rassenideologie und Agrarpolitik im Staat Hitlers* (Idstein: Schulz-Kirchner, 1994).

36 Richard Walther Darré, *Das Bauerntum als Lebensquell der Nordischen Rasse* (Munich, 1928). See also Hans F.K. Günther, *Das Bauerntum als Lebens- und Gemeinschaftsform* (Leipzig: B.G. Teubner, 1939).

37 See Corni and Gies, *'Blut und Boden'*, 24.

one of honour, devoid of all disparaging and discriminating connotation. In decidedly anti-liberal form, Darré connected the term '*Landwirt*', which since the eighteenth century had increasingly been used for the farmer versed in the streamlined economic system, with profit-mongering capitalism, and he thus deliberately used it in a pejorative manner.[38] However, the *Reichserbhofgesetz* did not entirely follow this pejoration, since *Landwirt* was used for those whose property was bigger or larger than just that reserved for the *Bauer* – an *Erbhof* of at least 7.5 ha to 125 ha of arable land. Thus, the word *Bauer* was largely separated from that of the smallholding and reserved for the middle freeholders.

The *Reichserbhofgesetz* introduced the *Anerbenrecht*, the impartible inheritance of land, as a mandatory legal norm. It applied to regions like Westphalia, where the *Anerbenrecht* was predominant, as well as to regions like Württemberg, where partible inheritance was predominant and irrespective of the wishes of the landowner, who was supposed to see his property as a 'fief of the people' in the service of his kin (*Sippe*). Different from under the Prussian *Erhbhofgesetz*, here the testator could neither restrict nor override the laws of inheritance. Even selling an *Erbhof* that was unprofitable in order to build up a different professional existence was principally ruled out. Thus, the programmatic statement in the preamble of the *Reichserbhofgesetz*:

> The Reich's government wants to safeguard the peasantry as a source of blood for the German people by saving the old German practice of inheritance. The farms shall be protected from over-indebtedness and fragmented succession, in order for them to remain permanently as inheritance of the kin in the possession of free peasants. We shall work towards a healthy distribution of agricultural property sizes, since a large quantity of viable small and middle-sized holdings distributed as far as possible over the whole country are the best guarantee of the continued health of people and state.[39]

This law specifically excluded the conjugal community of property and the community of heirs commonly practised in southern Germany. Women were clearly discriminated against in the succession as a result, since daughters were subordinated to sons, and there was no question of the wife inheriting at all. For those not in the direct line of succession, no rights existed to any kind

38 See Conze, 'Bauern', 438.

39 Corni and Gies, *'Blut und Boden'*, 104f.

of compensation, or to a dowry, which excluded an equivalent for any hitherto performed labours.[40]

In medieval historiography since the 1930s, new ideas of governance and state in the Middle Ages had emerged that changed the perception of the peasantry and rural society. Next to those historians already mentioned, Theodor Mayer and Günther Franz, we must also speak of Otto Brunner, Walter Schlesinger, and Heinrich Dannenbauer, who presented new concepts about basic forms of medieval governance.[41] The decisive element of medieval constitutional history was not seen in the dominion over land and property but in the authority of a nobility grown out of the household. This aristocratic *Herrengewalt* contained elements that, according to the new understanding, might be of a public-jurisdictional nature, but did not require special bestowal by the king. Medieval authority thus included a complex net of rights of government, forms of fealty, of bondage, manorialism, and jurisdiction. According to Schlesinger, the *Herrengewalt* of the nobility over land and people grew out of household authority and authority over the entourage, gradually extending under benevolent conditions in the course of the Middle Ages into territorial rulership.[42] In an essay published in 1941, Heinrich Dannenbauer mainly focused on the aristocracy and saw its roots in Germanic times.[43] 'The world of the Middle Ages is an aristocratic world. State and church and society are ruled by the aristocracy. A number of large, interrelated families, distinguished by noble birth and extended property, rule over land and people'.[44] The position of the peasants was a different one: 'The people of the countryside are to a large extent dependent, unfree in many different gradations. They are to be obedient, to work, to pay duties. They have no voice'.[45]

Otto Brunner's *Land and Lordship*, published 1939, had a great influence on medieval studies of his time and later.[46] According to Brunner, manorialism was at the centre of the relationship between lords and peasants. It was a case of 'rulership over land and property and over peasant, meaning over those

40 Corni and Gies, *'Blut und Boden'*, 36.

41 Hellmut Kämpf (ed.), *Herrschaft und Staat im Mittelalter* (Darmstadt: Wissenschaftliche Buchgesellschaft, 1964).

42 Walter Schlesinger, 'Herrschaft und Gefolgschaft in der germanisch-deutschen Verfassungsgeschichte', in Hellmut Kämpf (ed.), *Herrschaft und Staat im Mittelalter* (Darmstadt: Wissenschaftliche Buchgesellschaft, 1964), 135–90.

43 Heinrich Dannenbauer, 'Adel, Burg und Herrschaft bei den Germanen', in Hellmut Kämpf (ed.), *Herrschaft und Staat im Mittelalter* (Darmstadt: Wissenschaftliche Buchgesellschaft, 1964), 66–134.

44 Dannenbauer, 'Adel', 66.

45 Dannenbauer, 'Adel', 67.

46 Otto Brunner, *Land und Herrschaft*, 5th edn (Vienna: Rohrer, 1965).

people who hold the land and work it'.[47] The relationship between lord and vassal is one bound by reciprocity and loyalty; the lord gives the peasant house and land, while he is obliged to pay service and duties to his lord. This system of protection seen as harmonious was criticized especially harshly in Marxist historiography, since it did not take the class struggle between lords and peasants into account. In addition, Brunner does not refer much to the social differences in the peasant class, to the complete sum of feudal duties to be paid, monetary and in kind, to conflicts and peasant revolts, to agrarian economy and famines. Added to that, it is an illusion that medieval manorialism was in the main a system free of conflict, characterized by loyalty, favour, protection, and aid.[48] Brunner retained his view of the world of the peasant as a harmonious one without grave conflicts between lord and peasant in his work on the aristocratic country life around Wolf Helmhard of Hohberg, which was published in 1949, four years after the end of the war.[49]

The basic trends in the German history of agriculture already at the forefront in the period from 1930 to 1945 continued between 1945 and 1970. This applied to some research questions and overall concepts, and related to the work of the three main proponents of agricultural history, Abel, Lütge, and Franz, who were spearheading West German scholarship from 1949 to about 1970.[50] Their cooperation is most visible in the *Deutsche Agrargeschichte*, the middle part of which – early Middle Ages to the abolition of serfdom – was made up of separate volumes by the three authors. Willhelm Abel wrote the history of agricultural economy, Friedrich Lütge the development of the agricultural system, and Günther Franz the history of the German peasantry.[51] Which guidelines and questions lay at the centre of this complete overview? Which concept of the peasantry?

In the prologue to his history of the peasantry from 1970, Günther Franz, the initiator of the undertaking, talked about the difficulties involved: 'It is a risk to

47 Brunner, *Land und Herrschaft*, 242.

48 See Rösener, *Grundherrschaft im Wandel*, 22.

49 Otto Brunner, *Adeliges Landleben und europäischer Geist. Leben und Werk Wolf Helmhards von Hohberg 1612–1688* (Salzburg: O. Müller, 1949).

50 See Werner Rösener, 'Agrargeschichte an den deutschen Universitäten', *Zeitschrift für Agrargeschichte und Agrarsoziologie*, 47 (1999), 111–22; Andreas Dornheim, 'Die deutsche Agrargeschichte in der NS-Zeit und die Lehrstuhl-Berufungen nach 1945 in Westdeutschland', *Zeitschrift für Agrargeschichte und Agrarsoziologie*, 53/2 (2005), 39–55.

51 Wilhelm Abel, *Geschichte der deutschen Landwirtschaft vom frühen Mittelalter bis zum 19. Jahrhundert* (Stuttgart: E. Ulmer, 1962); Friedrich Lütge, *Geschichte der deutschen Agrarverfassung vom frühen Mittelalter bis zum 19. Jahrhundert* (Stuttgart, 1963); Günther Franz, *Geschichte des deutschen Bauernstandes vom frühen Mittelalter bis zum 19. Jahrhundert* (Stuttgart: E. Ulmer, 1970).

delineate in what is more of a lengthy essay than an outline the position of the peasantry in political life and to show which part it has taken, actively and suffering, in the history of our people'.[52] He thanks Peter Blickle, his assistant over many years, for his assistance and for the chapter 'Bäuerliche Landschaft und Landstandschaft', which was added to the volume. He continued to see the Peasants' War of 1525 mainly as a 'political revolution of the German peasantry' in which economic or religious motivations did not play a major role.[53] Franz conforms to the concept of a uniform peasantry whose political history he wants to depict during its various phases. He explicitly refers to Riehl and his depiction of bourgeois society and the peasant as the centre of the nation, thus adopting significant concepts of the German peasantry already discernible in Riehl.[54] When, in 1952, he answered the question of why one should study the history of the peasants at all with the suggestion that it could show 'what significance a strong peasantry has for a healthy society', he was adopting Riehl's perspective just as definitively as with his statement that 'the peasantry ... today, even more than in 1848, is a bulwark against the social revolution of Bolshevism'.[55] In his other academic work, Franz also often adhered to the paradigm of the nineteenth century. His main interest lay in the conflicts between lordship and community, the legal and political aspects of agricultural history, although the traditional *Hofbauerntum* with its role in the national superstructure was at the centre of his interest.

The classification that is often made in German agricultural history, of a history of the agricultural economy, the agricultural system, and rural society, was retained in the history of agriculture edited by Franz, which engaged with the difficulty of overall coherence. The separate depictions of these three domains meant that each of the three authors conceived his part according to his own criteria and that there was much overlap between them. This lack of coherence shows that there was no general concept worked out for the entire work and meant that the interdependencies between economic, legal, and social factors in the agricultural historical processes were not accentuated enough. Hans Rosenberg heavily criticized this overview of German agricultural history, based on the volume written by Lütge.[56] According to Lütge, the constitutional

52 Franz, *Geschichte des Bauernstandes*, 7.

53 Franz, *Geschichte des Bauernstandes*, 144.

54 Franz, *Geschichte des Bauernstandes*, 7.

55 Günther Franz, 'Wozu Bauerngeschichte?', *Übersicht. Monatsschrift für das deutsche Landvolk*, 3 (1952), 12–14; quoted after Dipper, 'Bauern', 14.

56 Hans Rosenberg, 'Deutsche Agrargeschichte in alter und neuer Sicht', in *Machteliten und Wirtschaftskonjunkturen. Studien zur neueren deutschen Sozial- und Wirtschaftsgeschichte* (Göttingen: Vandenhoeck und Ruprecht, 1978), 118–219.

history of agriculture mainly encompassed the depiction of the legal content of rural constitutions. The history of the agricultural structure was thus reduced to the clarification of jurisdictional points of rural rulership and institutional authorities, while the contributing political factors, power struggles, and shifts in the real balance of power were only touched upon; the tension-filled relationship between the theoretical legal position and reality remained largely unmentioned. From the perspective of social history, though, it was absolutely necessary to consider far more seriously the demographic, economic, and social factors when depicting agricultural history. Christoph Dipper found fault with the volumes of the *Deutsche Agrargeschichte* mainly because of the division of the central topic into an economic, legal, and political history of the pre-industrial agricultural conditions.[57] When it came to social conditions, Franz would simply speak of peasants without differentiating between the individual social groupings in detail.

From the Marxist perspective of GDR agricultural historiography, Gerhard Heitz commented on the volumes of the *Deutsche Agrargeschichte* in 1977.[58] Heitz felt the absence of a consciousness of class struggle and the achievements of the peasantry in the feudal period. Their striving for greater freedom in the High Middle Ages was above all 'a striving resulting from class-antagonism and reaching towards greater power of control over personal labour, over land and property, and the products of their own labour. It comes from the specifics of the feudal system of production and the dialectics of property and ownership'.[59] On the whole, Heitz said, the question one must ask oneself when reading these volumes is what the authors actually meant by the terms 'peasant', 'peasantry', and 'peasant estate' (*Bauer*, *Bauerntum*, and *Bauernstand*), since both from the perspective of economic history and from that of political history, it was shown that it was 'the man himself, organized in classes and estates, working and organizing, who was the actual object of historical research'.[60] According to Heitz, the differentiated depiction of agricultural conditions would have demanded a clear positioning of the authors regarding the problem of the peasants as class or estate. The result, however, he declared to be hardly satisfactory, since it lacked a coordinated common viewpoint of the authors and there was thus an imprecise use of terminology

57 Dipper, 'Bauern', 21f.
58 Gerhard Heitz, 'Landwirtschaft – Agrarverfassung – Bauernstand. Überlegungen zu fünf Bänden', *Jahrbuch für Wirtschaftsgeschichte*, 1 (1977), 183–207.
59 Heitz, 'Landwirtschaft', 183–207.
60 Heitz, 'Landwirtschaft', 196.

within the individual volumes. Heitz rightly pointed out the unclear terminology of the peasantry, still orientated along traditional criteria.

The three authors Abel, Lütge, and Franz were undoubtedly those most responsible for stimulating and carrying out agricultural history in West Germany for over two decades. Despite their different backgrounds in their specific fields of research and their focus on a traditional concept of the peasantry, they managed to achieve important results for German agricultural historiography up to the early 1970s. In the decades following, new trends and new scholars made an appearance, emphasizing different points and orientating themselves in relation to a different concept of the development of rural society. The themes of this new historiography were only partially a further development of the old core themes; often, they were the result of applying new methods and incorporating new trends of historical research in and outside Germany. It proved advantageous for agricultural history that nearly all the new focus points of the discipline, from social history to micro-history and the anthropologically focused cultural history, orientated themselves along the problems of rural society and opened up new perspectives.[61]

In his studies on agricultural history, Peter Blickle focused mainly on peasant revolts in pre-industrial society[62] and the many facets of the German peasantry in rulership, community, and the territorial assemblies, propagating the thesis of communalism in the context of early modern societal change.[63] Referring to the peasants in the late Middle Ages and the early modern period, he aimed to show 'what their history can add to the structural depiction of the system of society and its changes'.[64] The author of this current contribution added a number of studies on the active role of the peasants during the Middle Ages and the early modern period.[65] It was not the political and societal status of the peasants but the everyday life in family, neighbourhood, and village that were the focus of this contributor's research, in which peasants appeared as actors. The main aspect of the living conditions of the rural community was

61 See Peter Blickle, 'Deutsche Agrargeschichte in der zweiten Hälfte des 20. Jahrhunderts', in Werner Troßbach and Clemens Zimmermann (eds), *Agrargeschichte. Positionen und Perspektiven* (Stuttgart: Lucius und Lucius, 1998), 7–32.

62 Peter Blickle, *Die Revolution von 1525* (Munich: Oldenbourg, 1977); Peter Blickle (ed.), *Revolte und Revolution in Europa* (Munich: Oldenbourg, 1975); Peter Blickle, et al. (ed.), *Aufruhr und Empörung? Studien zum bäuerlichen Widerstand im Alten Reich* (Munich: Beck, 1980).

63 Peter Blickle, *Studien zur geschichtlichen Bedeutung des deutschen Bauernstandes* (Stuttgart, New York: de Gruyter, 1989).

64 Blickle, *Studien zur geschichtlichen Bedeutung*, ix.

65 Werner Rösener, *Bauern im Mittelalter* (Munich: Beck, 1985); Werner Rösener, *Die Bauern in der europäischen Geschichte*; Werner Rösener, *Grundherrschaft im Wandel*.

examined from various perspectives, focusing on an analyses of the economic, social, and cultural conditions of the peasant's existence.[66] In 1994, the *Arbeitskreis für Agrargeschichte* was founded in Göttingen, in which younger academics from different disciplines and institutions in particular came together to discuss methods and new paths for German agricultural history.[67] In the cultural-historical studies about agrarian society, the participants of this circle saw a chance to newly position German agricultural history in changed historiographical surroundings, to motivate innovative research, conduct international conferences, and cooperate with foreign researchers.[68]

66 Rösener, *Bauern im Mittelalter*, 17.

67 A bi-annual newsletter has been informing about the activities and projects of the 'Arbeitskreis für Agrargeschichte' since 1997.

68 Homepage of the 'Arbeitskreis für Agrargeschichte' since 2002: *Gesellschaft für Agrargeschichte*, www.agrargeschichte.de.

CHAPTER 9

Switzerland – A 'Peasant State'?

Stefan Sonderegger

It is hardly possible to better describe the ground on which Swiss historical tradition is built than with this history painting from the nineteenth century. One hugely determined and fearless man – Uli Rotach – fights alone against vastly superior numbers of well-armoured warriors. He is wearing peasant dress from the nineteenth century,[1] symbolizing the confederate peasants who, according to the national historiography of the nineteenth century, were supposed to have liberated themselves in glorious battles during the Middle Ages from the yoke of aristocratic oppression.

Peasant heroes like William Tell and the depicted Uli Rotach contribute to medieval Switzerland often being seen as an exemplar of a 'peasant state'. For instance, under the heading 'peasant states' in the *Lexikon des Mittelalters* (*Encyclopaedia of the Middle Ages*), you can read that the lack of a centralized ducal power in particular in the southwest of the Empire in the thirteenth century had led to the unfolding of the confederate peasant movement. The alliance of the Swiss cantons of the valleys in 1291 had been a direct result, behind which the free peasants, encouraged by the local aristocracy, were the prime moving force.[2] Both from a Swiss perspective and in the perception from across the borders, there is a noticeable tendency to glorify the history of the Confederacy, combining it sweepingly with concepts of peasants and freedom and seeing Switzerland as representing 'a lucky case' in Europe.[3] The Old Swiss Confederacy is equated with 'peasant associations' and a 'peasant state', as well as a 'peasant populace' or 'mountain people', and the inhabitants of the Swiss *Länderorte* (Uri, Schwyz, Ob- and Nidwalden, Glarus, and Appenzell) are called 'self-governing rural producers'.[4] The national historiography in

1 Heinrich Thommen, 'Uli Rotach im Kampf gegen zwölf Feinde. Ludwig Vogels Historiengemälde von 1829', *Appenzellische Jahrbücher* (2004), 59–75.

2 See 'Bauernstaaten' in Robert-Henri Bautier,et al. (ed). *Lexikon des Mittelalters*, 9 vols (Munich and Zurich: Artemis [vols 1–6] and LexMA-Verlag [vols 7–9], 1977–1999), i, 1622f.

3 Richard Wolfram, *Studien zur älteren Schweizer Volkskultur – Mythos, Sozialordnung, Brauchbewusstsein*, Österreichische Akademie der Wissenschaften, Philos.-hist. Klasse 362, (Vienna: Verlag der Akademie, 1980), 7–8.

4 Thomas Brady, *Turning Swiss. Cities and Empire, 1450–1550*, Cambridge Studies in Early Modern History, (Cambridge: Cambridge University Press, 1985), 6.

 | DOI:10.1163/9789004433458_010

FIGURE 9.1 Uli Rotach in battle with twelve enemies, 1829. Rotach is depicted wearing peasant dress, referring to the role that was ascribed to the peasants in the nineteenth-century history of liberation.
OIL PAINTING BY LUDWIG VOGEL, KANTONSBIBLIOTHEK APPENZELL A. RH., TROGEN

Switzerland also claims the term 'peasant state' for the late medieval Confederacy, in order to point out the singularity of Swiss statehood. In this, the basic assumption is that of a general peasant mindset that supposedly had existed since early times:

> In the traditional national historiography there is [...] general agreement that the Confederacy could be traced back to the foundation of a peasant state, that the peasant elements were a part of the nature of medieval confederations, and that the national consciousness that apparently emerged in the fifteenth century was to have shown a tendency to be influenced by the peasant population.[5]

5 Roger Sablonier and Matthias Weishaupt, *Die alte Schweiz als 'Bauernstaat'*, Reihe Kurzfassungen der Projekte (Basel: Nationales Forschungsprogramm 21: Kulturelle Vielfalt und nationale Identität, 1991), 2.

Considering the still scanty knowledge of the peasant population in modern Switzerland, it is surprising to read with what certainty the history of the medieval Confederacy is associated with assumed character traits of the peasants. It has been the achievement of a research project led by Roger Sablonier at the University of Zurich in 1991 to fundamentally question labels of this kind.[6] Using examples from recent scholarship about the economic, political, and social situation in the late Middle Ages, this contribution shows that the idea of Switzerland as a 'peasant state' is simply not tenable.

In 2006, the so-called *Bundesbrief* of 1291, the Letter of Alliance documenting the union of the three founding cantons, travelled to the US in order to be exhibited and – this was probably the main intention – to promote Switzerland. The fact that this icon of Swiss history was going to leave the country stirred the minds of many Swiss people.[7] Even though scholarship had some time earlier been able to prove convincingly that this letter was simply a standard thirteenth century document produced in connection with the securing of the general peace, wide circles still see it as the one document that cements the foundation of Switzerland. This point of view is based on the stories concerning the oath made by three proud peasants on the Rütli – a meadow by Lake Lucerne – in 1291; about William Tell – heroic freedom fighter; and about the battle of peasants and cowherds against the Habsburg authority.[8] Roger Sablonier sums up this foundation history succinctly and ironically:

> freedom-loving Alpine peasants successfully battle against oppression and exploitation, come together in solidarity amongst equals in 1291 and oblige each other with mutual aid and loyalty, chase the aristocracy and the reeves out of the country, start the foundation of the independent Swiss state, and defend their fatherland as a united people at the battle of

6 In that year, the 700th anniversary of the foundation of the Confederacy was celebrated with great extravagance. For the culture of this kind of celebration, see Georg Kreis, Jubiläen und Schlachtgedenken. Zivile Überlegungen zur militärischen Erinnerungskultur der Schweiz, in: *Appenzellische Jahrbücher* 2004, 13–27.

7 Political liberals and the political right especially exhibited outrage at this journey, as is visible in the media coverage and countless letters to the editors of Swiss newspapers. Numerous politicians of the Swiss People's Party wanted to buy the *Bundesbrief* in order to stop it leaving the country.

8 See, for example, Matthias Weishaupt, 'Hirten, "Bauern & Bürger" und Bauernsoldaten. Die ideologische Vereinnahmung der mittelalterlichen Bauern in der nationalen Geschichtsschreibung der Schweiz', in Albert Tanner and Anne-Lise Head-König (eds), *Die Bauern in der Geschichte der Schweiz*, Schweizerische Gesellschaft für Wirtschafts- und Sozialgeschichte, 10 (Zurich: Chronos, 1992), 23–39.

> Morgarten in 1315 against the overly powerful Habsburg lords, the foreign oppressor...[9]

That much of this and what is supposed to have happened just before and after 1300 in central Switzerland is not historically verifiable did not stop the creation of a Swiss 'peasant-state foundation-history' by cleverly arranging stories in the tradition of nineteenth century national historiography. Most remarkable is the role of the German author who did not know the Confederacy through his own experience but still made arguably the greatest contribution towards promoting and entrenching the tale. Friedrich Schiller's drama *Willhelm Tell* (premiered in 1804) became the greatest promoter of the old liberation narrative.[10] Unlike historians, a dramatist does not need to check the sources. Looking at the so-called foundation document of 1291, one would be hard pressed to find any indication that peasants had had a part in its creation; it is more likely that local gentry were the main initiators. The situation at the time suggests such elite involvement: the document could have been created shortly after the death of King Rudolf of Habsburg. As count and king, Rudolf had strengthened his power base in Switzerland, and his death meant juridical uncertainty. This is the background against which the alliance of 1291 must be understood. Representatives of the local authorities took over the task of keeping the peace, explicitly in recognition of the authoritative circumstances, as is noted in the document: every man should serve his lord according to his status. Peasants as the founders of a 'state' are in any case not visible.[11]

1 Free Swiss Mountain People

The authors who made a substantial contribution to the national historiography of the nineteenth century saw the earlier circumstances quite differently.

---

9 Roger Sablonier, *Gründungszeit ohne Eidgenossen. Politik und Gesellschaft in der Innerschweiz um 1300*, 2nd edn (Baden: Hier & Jetzt, 2008), 17.

10 Georg Kreis, Geschichten zur Gründungsgeschichte, in Erika Hebeisen, Pia Schubiger and Denise Tonella (eds), *Entstehung Schweiz. Unterwegs vom 12. ins 14. Jahrhundert* (Baden: Hier & Jetzt, 2011), 170–75, esp. at p. 175.

11 Compare for instance Werner Meyer and Heinz Dieter Finck, *1291 – Die Geschichte: die Anfänge der Eidgenossenschaft*, 4th edn (Zurich: Silva-Verlag, 1991), esp. 168ff. Further, 'Landfrieden' in Marco Jorio (ed.), *Historisches Lexikon der Schweiz*, 13 vols (Basel: Schwabe, 2002–2014), http://www.hls-dhs-dss.ch/textes/d/D8951.php (accessed 25.11.2011). A discussion of the *Bundesbrief* is also in Sablonier, *Gründungszeit ohne Eidgenossen*, esp. 163–78.

For Johannes von Müller, who wrote a monumental work of history in the 1820s, it was absolutely clear that the first Confederates had been peasants; he concludes his depiction of the so-called *Rütlischwur* with the comment: 'at the time everyone went to their huts, was silent, and overwintered their livestock'.[12] This quote from Müller leads us to a discussion of the role of the cowherd, which has also been a significant part of the national historiography until present. Müller will have been thinking predominantly of cowherds as he wrote, as it was he who was responsible for bringing the term 'herdsman country' to prominence for the pre- and northern Alpine regions between the Appenzell and the Gruyère district.[13]

The figure of the herdsman had a special relevance in the assessment of the national Swiss historiography that was focused on the peasant. Towards the end of the eighteenth and the beginning of the nineteenth century, the European bourgeoisie began viewing the Swiss Alps in a highly idealised manner, and it followed that the inhabitants of the Alps, with the cowherds seen as their main representatives, were also idealized.[14] In the *Schweizerhirte* (*Swiss herdsman*), travellers – often townspeople tired of civilization – found their saving ideal. The Frankfurt professor Johann Gottfried Ebel, author of the book *Schilderung der Gebirgsvölker der Schweitz* (*Depictions of the Swiss Mountain people*), travelled to Glarus and the Appenzell and admired in the 'herdsmen of the Appenzell [...] the traits of a healthy mind and proper feeling [...] of these uncrippled sons of nature [...]' and believed to be able to find in them '[...] what seemed so hard to combine: simple customs, true humanity of unaffected nature, healthy intelligence, directness of character, rectitude of the soul, and simple trustworthiness'.[15] But the travel writers found not only Arcadia in the Alps, but also a stronghold of liberty, as shown by the following quote from Ebel:

> That form of government that is called democracy, or the pure rule of the people, and of which we read so much in the history of Greece, is now

12 Johannes von Müller, Der Geschichten Schweizerischer Eidgenossenschaft, neue verbesserte und vermehrte Auflage, erster Theil – vierter Theil, Leipzig 1825/26, 644.

13 Von Müller translated Carl Victor von Bonstetten's Briefe über ein schweizerisches Hirtenland, 1782 from French into German and introduced the term 'Hirtenland' into the German language; see Matthias Weishaupt, *Bauern, Hirten und 'frume edle puren'. Bauern und Bauernstaatsideologie in der spätmittelalterlichen Eidgenossenschaft und der nationalen Geschichtsschreibung der Schweiz* (Basel, Frankfurt am Main: Helbing & Lichtenhahn, 1992), 25, see Chapter 7, footnote 3.

14 Weishaupt, *Bauern, Hirten und 'frume edle puren'*, 17–33.

15 Johann Gottfried Ebel, *Schilderung der Gebirgsvölker der Schweitz*, vol. i (Leipzig 1798), 69 u. 102.

> nowhere in existence but in Switzerland. The range of the Swiss Alps is inhabited by many small peoples who have lived for the last four to five hundred years in a pure democratic constitution, and seem happy. Here though are the herdsmen, reduced in their desires, simple, uneducated, and rough like the mountains that surround them. How exceedingly beneficial were by contrast the conditions with which the Greeks were favoured.[16]

2 Democracy of the Cantonal Assembly (*Landsgemeinde*)?

Ebel's enthusiasm was fed by, amongst other things, his visit to an assembly of the Appenzell (*Landsgemeinde*), the yearly gathering of the male *Landleute* (*fellow countrymen*) eligible to vote.[17] The assembly will have cemented his notion of the 'pure democratic constitution' of the mountain people. In this, he misjudged the real situation, since Ebel's depiction differs widely from the actual political and social circumstances of eighteenth-century Appenzell. Early information about the cantonal assembly is scarce, not very informative, and above all not contemporary. In the introduction to the older *Landbuch* of the Appenzell, a cantonal register from the second quarter of the sixteenth century, the process of legislation is set out and legitimized.[18] According to this entry, in 1409 – shortly after the Appenzell wars – an unnamed *Landamman* (the chief magistrate) and the *Landleute* had come together to consult (*zu Rate gekommen*).[19] This can be seen as a collective of eligible voters under the leadership of the magistrate, so something akin to an assembly, called *Landsgemeinde,* functioning as a legislative power. However, towards the end of the sixteenth century, the legislative competency had obviously moved away from the assembly to the council.[20] This loss of meaning as a legislative authority for a certain type of assembly can also be seen in the fewer by-laws (*Satzungen*) made out by the assembly itself. In the so-called *Older Landbuch* from the second quarter of the sixteenth century, the number of decrees published by the assembly and those by the council members were about equal. Since the 1570s,

16 Ebel, *Schilderung der Gebirgsvölker*, 78–79.

17 See 'Landsgemeinde' in *Historischen Lexikon der Schweiz* (accessed 25. 11. 2011).

18 Nathalie Büsser and Margrit Meyer Kälin (eds), *Die Rechtsquellen der Kantone Appenzell*, i: *Appenzeller Landbücher*, Sammlung Schweizerischer Rechtsquellen, Abt. 13 (Basel: Schwabe, 2009), xxxiv.

19 Büsser, *Appenzeller Landbücher*, 1.

20 Philipp Dubach, *Gesetz und Verfassung. Die Anfänge der territorialen Gesetzgebung im Allgäu und im Appenzell im 15. und 16. Jahrhundert*, Oberschwaben – Geschichte und Kultur, 6 (Tübingen: Bibliotheca Academica, 2001), 103 and 130.

however, there is no sign in the sources that the assembly still had anything to do with legislation.[21] The right of co-determination the *Landleute* held was thus at best slim in the seventeenth and eighteenth century. For instance, the assembly of Appenzell Ausserrhoden did not have the right of discussion. Had the *Landleute* had a general right of determination, the *Landsgemeine* would have decided on all daily business, as was the case in the twentieth century until the assembly of the canton Ausserrhoden was abolished in 1997. This would mean that the assembly decided over war and peace, published new laws, elected the government, conferred citizenship, and swore in members. In actual fact, however, only three of these issues were continuing concerns of the whole assembly: the election of the council members with the magistrate at their head, all conferring of citizenship until the nineteenth century, and the swearing-in. Everything else was addressed by the council members, the so-called *gnädige Herren*.[22]

Of the democracy of the assembly as Ebel described it in the nineteenth century, there was in actual fact only very little in existence. What he saw on his travels resembled an 'aristocracy of the *Landsgemeinde*' far more. In Ausserrhoden, many political functions remained in the hands of a small leading group for generations, whose members were not peasants or herdsmen but belonged to the social and cultural elite. For over 200 years, the two branches of the textile trading families Zellweger from Trogen supplied provisions to a council member 193 times. Over the course of seventy-four years, a Zellweger sat in the so-called chair, on the platform erected for members of the government at the assembly, and thus held the position of uncrowned cantonal king.[23]

---

21 According to Nathalie Büsser at the book launch of the *Appenzeller Landbücher* in 2009. Her speech is available to the author of this contribution in manuscript form.

22 For example, Dubach, *Gesetz und Verfassung*, 103ff. For the eighteenth century, Fabian Brändle, *Demokratie und Charisma. Fünf Landsgemeindekonflikte im 18. Jahrhundert*, published dissertation, University of Basel, 2002 (Zurich: Chronos, 2005), 45–110. Brändle cites the two Bernese brothers, Vinzenz Bernhard and Niklaus Emmanuel von Tscharner, who visited the Glarner *Landsgemeinde* in 1749, and afterwards stated: 'if I am to tell you the truth it seemed to me that this *Landsgemeinde* which they are so proud of is simply plays game with freedom and is basically a show to please the people. They have a council of 100 members who decides over war and peace, on the law, and has highly aristocratic powers'. For the lack of modern democratic principles in the democracy of the *Landsgemeinde*, see Andreas Sutter, 'Die Genese der direkten Demokratie – Aktuelle Debatten und wissenschaftliche Ergebnisse (part 1)', *Schweizerische Zeitschrift für Geschichte*, 62/3 (2012), 456–73, esp. 462–63.

23 Walter Schläpfer, 'Demokratie und Aristokratie in der Appenzellergeschichte des 17. und 18. Jahrhunderts', *Appenzellische Jahrbücher* (1948), 3–26, esp. p. 20, and Albert Tanner,

Politically important families such as the Zellweger from Trogen or the Wetter from Herisau were also at the top of the economy. Appenzell Ausserrhoden was one of the most highly industrialized regions of Europe in the eighteenth century. Industries in linen and then cotton-weaving had existed there since the late Middle Ages. In the eighteenth century, the so-called *Verlagswesen* was common: the weaver families received the raw material from the traders, processed it into textile for pay, and in turn left the Europe-wide trade to the merchants. The Zellwegers were one of the most important of these; they visibly expressed their wealth and power by surrounding the assembly place in Trogen with stone palaces.[24] This strongly contradicts the idealized and idyllized peasant and cowherd picture of Ebel and others. The lauded assembly democracy of the 'mountain people' of the Appenzell was in reality an aristocratic system governed by textile barons, rather than by herdsmen and peasants.

What do we know about the political structures and the development of communes? How can the participation of the peasants in the government be characterized for the Middle Ages? Was their role really as great as is frequently written?

If it is already unclear for the early stages of the Confederacy in 1300 whether peasants took part as 'founders of the state', in the fifteenth century the situation becomes even more opaque. That the Confederacy grew like a seed that was planted 1291 in central Switzerland is a widespread topos. Until the fifteenth century, hardly any overriding, para-state structures existed. The particular interests of the towns and states that kept allying themselves in new and different constellations were predominant.[25] The other notion, also built on the glorified view of the eighteenth and nineteenth century, that the federal states provided a model for the constitutional development of the Confederacy – as was proposed in the earlier quoted example of the travel writer Johann Gottfried Ebel – is also false. In actual fact, the role of the towns was probably much more important, as the examples of St Gallen and the state of Appenzell demonstrate.

Spulen – Weben – Sticken. Die Industrialisierung in Appenzell Ausserrhoden (Zurich: Juris Druck, 1982), esp. 405.

24 See, in more detail Andreas F.A. Morel, Andreas Moosbrugger and Peter Anton Moosbrugger, *Zur Stuckdekoration des Rokoko in der Schweiz*, Beiträge zur Kunstgeschichte der Schweiz, 2 (Bern: Gesellschaft für schweizerische Kunstgeschichte, 1973), 91ff.

25 Bernhard Stettler, *Die Eidgenossenschaft im 15. Jahrhundert. Die Suche nach einem gemeinsamen Nenner* (Zurich: Widmar-Dean, 2004), 13–18.

3 Urban Constitutions as Role Model

The Appenzell is a model case for showing that the towns impacted rural constitutional development. In this case, it was the southwestern imperial cities – in the fourteenth century allied in the Swabian League of Cities – with their close relationship between the town of St Gallen as regional centre and regions of the Appenzell as part of the economic catchment area that played an important part. In the late Middle Ages, St Gallen was connected to the most important towns around Lake Constance. The active policy of alliances within the framework of the Swabian League of Cities, of which included more than thirty imperial cities in the 1380s, was the main medium. On 26 September 1377, the inhabitants of the Appenzell, Hundwil, Urnäsch, Gais, and Teufen allied with fifteen Swabian imperial cities, including St Gallen.[26] These Appenzell '*Ländlein*' (*little countries,* as they were called) were the first and only non-cities to be admitted to the League. The nearby town of St Gallen and the town Konstanz, by Lake Constance, stood as sponsors. The reason for this lies in the mutual interests of the Appenzell and the town of St Gallen, mainly that of detaching themselves from the authority of the abbey, and to assist each other in that goal. In joining the League, they expected the imperial cities to assist them in their process of emancipation. The conditions for admission, set out in a later document of 22 May 1378, are enlightening: they show the beginnings of constitutional power moving in the direction of a *Land* (country) Appenzell. St Gallen and Konstanz were to aid the four *Ländlein* and represent them at the assemblies. The people of the Appenzell were thus put under the care of St Gallen and Konstanz. Konstanz and St Gallen were given comprehensive rights to act in the name of the League and were established as a protective power (*Schutzmächte*).[27]

The following is important in connection with the question of how the development of the constitution proceeded in the countryside: for the time before the acceptance of the Appenzeller *Ländlein* into the Swabian League, hardly any traces exist of a '*Land*' Appenzell with secure institutions of a political and legal constitution.[28] Contact with the town of St Gallen, whose constitution had been developing since the fourteenth century and was partly

26 *Chartularium Sangallense*, Otto P. Clavadetscher and Stefan Sonderegger (eds), 13 vols (St Gallen: Herausgeber- und Verlags- Gemeinschaft Chartularium Sangallense / Thorbecke, 1983-), ix (1373–1381), no. 5613.

27 *Chartularium Sangallense*, ix, no. 5646.

28 Stefan Sonderegger, 'Die Aufnahme der Appenzeller "lendlin" in den Schwäbischen Städtebund', in Peter Blickle and Peter Witschi (eds), *Appenzell-Oberschwaben* (Konstanz: Konstanzer Universitätsverlag, 1997), 33–64, esp. 49.

FIGURE 9.2 The Swabian league of cities around 1380, when the Appenzell was the only *Land* to be admitted into the League

already firmly established,[29] was stimulating. The acceptance into the League of Cities now started a new development: the towns demanded that the *Land* Appenzell institute a body of thirteen men who were to have the capacity to act and take decisions relating to the outside – in contact with the towns – and within.[30] In the towns, these tasks were attended to by the councils. What we can see here are the beginnings of the development of an Appenzell constitution, set in motion by the town of St Gallen and the Swabian League of Cities. There is hardly any sign of a communal movement emerging from the peasantry towards a peasant-influenced democracy of the assembly.

The strong urban influence on the constitutional development of the country is confirmed through a physical seal: attached to the documents of the alliance formed on 4 July 1379 between the thirty-two imperial cities, amongst them St Gallen, and the Appenzell, with the Dukes of Bavaria, the count

29 See ‘St Gallen (Gemeinde)’ in Marco Jorio (ed.), *Historisches Lexikon der Schweiz*, 13 vols (Basel: Schwabe, 2002–2014), http://www.hls-dhs-dss.ch/textes/d/D1321.php (accessed 25.11.2011).

30 Sonderegger, ‘Die Aufnahme’, 52.

FIGURE 9.3 Left is the seal of the city of St Gallen (Chartularium Sangallense, Bd. V, S. 546, Nr. 153), and right the first Appenzell state seal of 1379, with its likeness to that of St Gallen. (Chartularium Sangallense, Bd. IX, S. 586, Nr. 545)

palatinate of the Rhine, and the Margrave of Baden, is the oldest seal of the Appenzell, bearing the inscription S(IGILLUM) COMUNITATIS IN ABBATISCELLA.[31] Seals were used for authentication, just like present-day signatures. As a rule, those who had a seal commanded a degree of legal agency. The charter from 1377 however, from two years earlier, when the people of the Appenzell joined the League of Cities, has the private seals of the Appenzell magistrates (*Ammänner*) attached to it. It is therefore safe to assume that at that time there was no cantonal seal as yet in existence. But as a new member of the League, the Appenzell needed one, in order for them to identify themselves as a politically active authority like the cities. They obviously procured one in those two years. That this first state seal of the Appenzell is attached to the charter of the League of Cities is not a coincidence. Sealing as a community was taken over by the cities; as an ally, it was necessary for the state to possess a legally binding mode of authentication, just like the towns. The first Appenzell state seal is less an expression of a communal movement from the inside or from below, as it is viewed within the regional historiography still attached to the communalism theory,[32] than the result of a constitutional development

31 Otto P. Clavadetscher, 'Die ältesten Appenzeller Siegel als Quellen zur Verfassungsgeschichte', *Archiv für Diplomatik, Schriftgeschichte, Siegel- und Wappenkunde*, 54 (2008), 85–98, esp. 86.

32 Peter Blickle, 'Bäuerliche Rebellion im Fürststift St. Gallen', in Peter Blickle (ed.), *Aufruhr und Empörung? Studien zum bäuerlichen Widerstand im Alten Reich* (Munich: Beck, 1980), 215–95.

furthered mainly by the city of St Gallen, and therefore, from the outside. The leading role of St Gallen is obvious, as the imagery of the newly created Appenzell state seal is closely modelled on that of the city of St Gallen.

The written and illustrated depictions of the Appenzell wars at the beginning of the fifteenth century are in a line with the tradition of the national historiography. The wars are seen as a 'movement of the people' ('*Volksbewegung*'),[33] a 'peasant rebellion',[34] as a battle between the peasants and the regional rulers – the Abbey of St Gall. The Appenzell wars, often called the 'Appenzell wars of liberation', are thus presented as an exemplar of communalism emerging from the peasant population.

The historiography of the Appenzell reads like a smaller version of the early history of the Swiss Confederacy. Both for the Appenzell and for central Switzerland, similar constitutional developments – the 'state formation from below' – have been promoted. In both cases, the topos of the cantonal assembly-herdsman democracy (*Landsgemeinde-Hirtendemokratie*) is common. Both – the people of central Switzerland in the wars for freedom in the fourteenth century and the people of the Appenzell in the battles of Vögelinsegg in 1403 and by the Stoss in 1405 – had apparently heroically fought to rescue themselves from territorial rule. A quote from the book entitled *Schweizerschlachten* (*Swiss Battles*) by Hans Rudolf Kurz exemplifies this:

> The hot pursuit of freedom from the power of the aristocracy in order to independently control their fate that in the fourteenth century ruled the thoughts and actions of the states and towns of the eight confederate localities and that forced a violent decision through the wars of liberation also led to bloody controversies between the *Ländchen* and the Abbey of Saint Gall [...]. In the same spirit, the victories won at Morgarten, Sempach, and Näfels gave enormous stimulus to the striving for freedom of the people of Appenzell [...]. In a surprising inner and outer similarity in both battles of the Appenzell, the battle for freedom of the forest cantons (*Waldstätten*) and the Glarus repeated itself. In both cases, a people filled with the aspiration of freedom rises against its oppressors and rather chooses death in battle than the continuation of an unbearable rule.[35]

33 See 'Appenzeller Kriege' in Marco Jorio (ed.), *Historisches Lexikon der Schweiz*, 13 vols (Basel: Schwabe, 2002–2014), www.hls-dhs-dss.ch/textes/d/D8874.php (accessed 25.11.2011).

34 Blickle, et al., *Aufruhr und Empörung*, 215.

35 Hans Rudolf Kurz, *Schweizerschlachten* (Bern: Francke, 1977), 58.

FIGURE 9.4
Tell (in the left pillar) and Uli Rotach (in the right pillar). Frontispiece to the collection of all magistrates of the canton of Appenzell A. Rh., Edited by M. Steiner (1835). The combined depiction of the 'freedom heroes' of the Appenzell and Confederacy emblematizes the parallel drawn in the historiography between the liberation myths of the Confederacy and the Appenzell.

The parallels drawn by Kurz are striking. Both the people from the Appenzell and those from central Switzerland are seen as being unafraid, courageous, freedom-loving peasants. William Tell, the confederate figure of battle and freedom, is opposite the equally legendary figure of Uli Rotach who, as the picture at the start of this contribution showed, is to have given his life in heroic battle, with his back to the wall in a hut set on fire by his enemies. As the most important detail of the legend, it is recorded that he chose – after killing some of his enemies – to give up his life in the flames rather than allow himself to be taken.

The common name '*Appenzeller Freiheitskriege*' points to the widespread idea that it had been a fight limited to rural society against territorial rulers. This view is false and indebted to the local patriotic viewpoint of the Appenzell. The so-called Appenzell liberation wars are in fact a perfect example of town and country acting in conjunction against their rulers.

The urban contribution is especially obvious when you ask the question of who actually fought in the so-called Appenzell wars. The battle of the Stoss on

17 June 1405 is seen as the culmination of the wars and as an exemplar of how the peasant fighters defeated an army comprised of nobles and townspeople. The not wholly historically verifiable figure of Uli Rotach symbolizes the courage, the power, and the willingness to sacrifice oneself of the Appenzell people. The sources tend to argue against a real existence; however, due to numerous paintings and prints, Uli Rotach took on an ever more real appearance in the nineteenth and twentieth century. One decisive contribution undermining the existence of this 'symbol of the Appenzell struggle for liberation'[36] came in 1936. At the behest of the Appenzell Innerrhoden government, a so-called *Fahrtbrief* (*pilgrimage letter*) had been created for the yearly pilgrimage to the place of the battle, the Stoss. The text written by the *Landschreiber* (*head clerk of the chancery*) was to, '[…] on the basis of irreproachable historical facts, impressively show why the procession to Stoss was being undertaken'.[37] This rather late testimony was justified by the fact that it was: 'what actually would have been expected from our ancestors when they took the pilgrimage oath'.[38]

In 1939, the *Fahrtbrief* was looked at by a conservator from the Swiss National Museum, and the text was translated into understandable High German. 'Finally, the *Fahrtbrief* was given a "proper charter-like appearance" and the state seal attached. With this pseudo-medieval document, a state-sanctioned conception of history including Uli Rotach was constructed that – due to the religious context of the pilgrimage – ultimately eludes any critical discussion […]'[39] – but could easily be used for the *geistige Landesverteidigung* (the moral defence of the nation during and after the Second World War).

Peasant state ideology and facts could hardly lie further apart than in this case. There are hardly any reliable sources for the battle of the Stoss, and even archaeological finds are lacking. This is quite different from the second military operation on the same day in front of the gates of the town of St Gallen. One part of the attacking army under Austrian command had not moved towards the Stoss, but beleaguered the town St Gallen, as an ally of the people of Appenzell. In front of the town – and thus not at the Stoss – was the Duke of Austria. From one contemporary entry in the oldest necrology of the St Gall church of St Laurence, it is evident that thirty members of the ducal army and two St Gall citizens ('*de nostris*') fell in battle and that, to commemorate them,

36 Agathe Nisple, *Appenzell. Ein Dorf- und Kulturführer* (Herisau: Appenzeller Verlag, 2001), 33.

37 Quoted from Matthias Weishaupt, 'Uli Rotach. Faktum oder Fiktion?', in Peter Niederhäuser and Alois Niederstätter (eds), *Die Appenzellerkriege – eine Krisenzeit am Bodensee?*, Forschungen zur Geschichte Vorarlbergs, Neue Folge, 7 (Konstanz: UVK Verlagsgesellschaft, 2006), 175–79, esp. p. 178.

38 Weishaupt, 'Uli Rotach', 178.

39 Weishaupt, 'Uli Rotach', 178.

a procession was led into a chapel near the town.[40] This written evidence is supplemented by the archaeological. In the autumn of 1913, during the building of a water pipe at the place where this chapel used to be, a mass grave was excavated, containing thirty skeletons and, according to the experts called in, they must be the remnants of the victims of the battle outside the town of St Gallen.[41]

The number of victims and the description of the battles indicate that there had been no large open battle before the gates of the town with large armies clashing into each other. Rather, there were smaller skirmishes. It is a plausible assumption that the citizens of St Gallen were playing for time, pre-arranged with the people of the Appenzell, and disturbed the Austrian division with repeated attacks. In this way, they could keep the enemy near the town, into which they themselves could retreat. They thus aided or even enabled the victory of the Appenzell forces at the Stoss. The skeleton finds of 1913 were widely publicised at the time, but soon forgotten again: urban citizens did not accord with the idea of the confederacy as a 'peasant state'.

4 Economic Spread of the Town to the Surrounding Countryside

The facts presented here show clearly how strongly the idea of Switzerland as a 'peasant state' distorts the view of the facts. In the Middle Ages, the towns were the economic centres with strong ties to the countryside; this is the case for Switzerland as a whole, and also for the eastern part of it. St Gallen was the largest and most important town in the region. The food supply of grain, meat, dairy products, and meat stock was based in large part on the delivery from the surrounding countryside.[42] Conversely, the rural population bought commodities at the town market. Added to that, many estates in the countryside were the possessions of townspeople and urban institutions.[43] This enabled the town to directly influence the rural economy and enforce commercial interests.

40 Stefan Sonderegger, 'Ein beinahe vergessener Beitrag der St. Galler zu den Appenzellerkriegen', in Peter Niederhäuser and Alois Niederstätter (eds), *Die Appenzellerkriege – eine Krisenzeit am Bodensee?*, Forschungen zur Geschichte Vorarlbergs, Neue Folge, 7 (Konstanz: UVK Verlagsgesellschaft, 2006), 117–28, esp. 123–24.

41 Sonderegger, 'Ein beinahe vergessener Beitrag', 123–24.

42 In more detail, see Stefan Sonderegger, *Landwirtschaftliche Entwicklung in der Nordostschweiz. Eine Untersuchung ausgehend von den wirtschaftlichen Aktivitäten des Heiliggeist-Spitals St. Gallen*, St Galler Kultur und Geschichte, 22, published dissertation, University of Zurich, 1993 (St Gallen: Buchhandlung am Rösslitor, 1994).

43 Rezia Krauer, 'Der Erwerb von Besitzrechten im Umland der Stadt St. Gallen durch St. Galler Bürger von 1370 bis 1389', Licentiate Phil., University of Zurich, Zurich, 2010.

One result was the specialization of the agriculture of livestock and viticulture in certain zones of the surrounding countryside. This meant that the rural population became dependent on a supply of grain and other daily commodities to a certain extent. Within this economic regionalization, urban actors organized – with the exception of the urban market – the exchange of goods across the region and loaned money to the peasants in exchange for agricultural products. In addition, they advanced large mortgaged credit to livestock farmers from the Appenzell. Urban supply of foodstuffs and other goods to the countryside, as well as money loaned from the town, bound parts of the rural population enduringly to the town.

These economic dependencies between the town of St Gallen and the Appenzell in the fourteenth and fifteenth century can explain the mutual assistance of town and countryside in the emancipation from their shared ruler, the Abbey of Saint Gall. The relationship between the town of St Gallen and the Appenzell at the time of the Appenzell wars in 1405 was so tightly knit that there can be no distinguishing of urban and rural interests. It is literally nonsensical against the backdrop of this history to see the conflict as a purely peasant rebellion.[44] Both rural *and* urban parties were involved.

Our results correspond with other regional studies in Switzerland. How much the urban and rural economy, as well as the politics of the towns and cantons of the Confederacy of the fourteenth and fifteenth century, were intertwined can be exemplified by the Glarus: '[...] as Swiss history en miniature, as Glarus's path into the heart of the Confederacy and as parallel history to that of the history of the Uri, Schwyz, or Unterwalden'.[45] The aspiration of the people of Glarus was always seen to be freedom from Habsburg rule. The battle of Näfels on 9 April 1388 has traditionally been depicted in this light: with this battle, the people of Glarus freed themselves from the rule of the Habsburgs and became a part of the Swiss Confederacy – the same pattern as in the case of the Appenzell wars. However, the most recent studies show that, in opposition to the traditional view, the leading groups in power in Glarus before 1380 had close connections to the Habsburg rulers. They were in part local aristocrats or had inherited their positions. It is decisive that many of the leading Glarus elite were part of long-distance trade, which is the reason they often lived in Zurich. One could call them commuters between the town of Zurich and the *Land* Glarus.

---

44 Peter Blickle, *Aufruhr und Empörung*, 215.

45 Rolf Kamm, 'Die Schlacht bei Näfels 1388 – Kampf gegen den Erzfeind?', in Hans Rudolf Fuhrer (ed.), *Geschichte der Schweiz. Fenster in die Vergangenheit* i, Publikationen der Schweizerischen Gesellschaft für Militärhistorische Studienreisen, 32 (Wettingen: Schweizerischen Gesellschaft für Militärhistorische Studienreisen GMS, 2011), 61–69, esp. p. 63.

After 1390, significant changes are noticeable with the emergence of social climbers in the fourteenth century. Many of these came from the *hinterland* of Glarus, some of which violently enforced their economic interests, which were focused on export. Similar to the northeastern part of Switzerland, where a strong influence of the town of St Gallen on the countryside is perceptible, in Glarus you can see the influence of Zurich. The economic interests of this centre were what played the most important part, something that can be demonstrated very well by the animal husbandry and Alpine economy. The beginning of commercialization of the Alpine economy, at first with foreign livestock, became the most influential economic system in Glarus, and this lasted until the mid-fifteenth century. The loans for the capital-intensive trade in animals mainly came from Zurich; the commuters mentioned above, between Glarus and Zurich, functioned as 'door-openers'. As in the case of St Gallen and the Appenzell, in the case of the intertwined economy of Zurich and Glarus, hardly any distinctions can be made between urban and rural interests. The dependency of the town manifests in yet another aspect: it was not only Glarus's exports that tied the *Land* to the town, the imports did, too. Glarus imported massive amounts of grain, with Zurich playing an important part as the place of acquisition.[46] We can assume that this grain came from southwestern Germany in the Middle Ages; Zurich was effectively the regional distribution centre. This dependency of Glarus on the transport of foodstuffs is connected to the intensification of the export-orientated Alpine and pasture economy. Here, too, there are parallels to eastern Switzerland: the specializing in livestock farming in the pre-Alpine Appenzell backed by the town of St Gallen and the dependency on Swabian grain imports.[47]

Economic interests were a strong reason to intensify political relations. In eastern Switzerland, one can draw attention to the Swabian League of Cities discussed above, where the town of St Gallen urged the Swabian cities to accept Appenzell from own economic interests in its surroundings. Later, during the Appenzell wars at the beginning of the fifteenth century, the town of St Gallen again formed alliances with surrounding communities. Here, too, we can see parallels between the region of St Gallen / Appenzell on the one hand, and the town of Zurich and parts of its surrounding countryside on the other: in 1408, Zurich entered into an alliance with Glarus, although one that was strongly tailored to the interests of Zurich.[48] Glarus represents only one of the places Zurich was reaching out to in relation to economic and political issues.

46 Rolf Kamm, *Glarus zwischen Habsburg und Zurich. Die Entstehung des Landes im Spätmittelalter*, published dissertation, University of Zurich, 2009, (Baden: Hier & Jetzt, 2010), 184.

47 Sonderegger, *Landwirtschaftliche Entwicklung*, 207ff. and 241ff.

48 Kamm, 'Die Schlacht bei Näfels', 67.

The region of Schwyz also presented a natural *hinterland*, and in a slightly less pronounced way this was also the case for Uri.[49] Over a long period of time, the influence of the towns was primarily tied up with the activities of the towns' citizens. What Roger Sablonier has observed concerning Zurich and central Switzerland agrees with our observations of eastern Switzerland: he starts with the premise that the political influence of the towns was already greater in the fourteenth century than previously assumed. He also believes that: '[…] the written constitutionalism of central Switzerland as we see it in alliances and royal documents may well have occurred due to stimulus from the town. The interest of the towns to organize the *hinterland* is shown in the inclusion of the *Länder* in the League of Cities in 1327'.[50]

The circumstances depicted here show the role played by the towns in the late Middle Ages: in the fourteenth century, the towns grew more and more important, generally and also within the Swiss Confederacy. They were not only economically, but also politically setting the tone and reaching out to the countryside.

5 Instead of Peasant Myths

Concluding, we can say that the assumption that the late medieval Confederacy had been a 'peasant state' cannot be upheld. Regional studies, based on the evaluation of archival sources, show that in late medieval Switzerland the towns grew increasingly prominent. It has become clearer and clearer that the towns, rather than the *Länderorte*, were the most influential in the politics and economy of the Old Confederacy. The examples mentioned above of the town-countryside relations in eastern Switzerland in the fourteenth and fifteenth centuries underline this. Images of Switzerland as a peasant state have no basis in academic historical research and need to be explained through the political discourse that ultimately in Switzerland still exists to this day. In a political study of the early 1990s, it was shown that although only 4 percent of the Swiss population are farmers, 40 percent of Swiss people still identify strongly with agriculture and the rural farming population.[51]

Much more important than celebrating myths surrounding the peasant is the study of the living conditions of real peasants. This means that the discussion

49 Sablonier, *Gründungszeit ohne Eidgenossen*, 90. See also Thomas Maissen, *Geschichte der Schweiz* (Baden: Hier & Jetzt, 2010), 24–25.

50 Sablonier, *Gründungszeit ohne Eidgenossen*,189–90.

51 See Urs Paul Engeler, 'Der Tanz ums Kalb. Hirte, Held und Heimatschützer – der Schweizer bleibt in seinem Herzen, was er nie war: ein Bauer aus dem Bilderbuch', *Bauern, was nun? NZZ Folio*, (9/1994), 40–45, esp. 42.

should be guided again towards the study of rural society – by far the greatest part of the population until far into the early modern period. It is to be remembered that there were close links between town and countryside – cooperation and dependencies.[52] Swiss historiography has already much innovative research to offer, but the archives still contain many sources that have not yet been studied. The challenge of the future will be to make sure the rich tradition of economic and social historical research is not abandoned. To achieve this, the combined effort of many different institutions is needed, above all that of universities and archives. How fruitful the cooperation between teaching, research, and archival study can be is shown by such long-term projects as that on historical demographics[53] led by Markus Mattmüller (University of Basel) or that of Roger Sablonier (University of Zurich) on rural society.[54] These have led to countless MA theses and doctoral studies on different Swiss regions that have significantly broadened the current state of research on the economic, social, and cultural history of the Middle Ages and the early modern period, and that have also found their way into international discussion.[55]

---

52 Stefan Sonderegger, 'Getreide, Fleisch und Geld gegen Wein. Stadt-Umland-Beziehungen im spätmittelalterlichen St. Gallen', in Frank Konersmann and Klaus-Joachim Lorenzen-Schmidt (eds), *Bauern als Händler. Ökonomische Diversifizierung und soziale Differenzierung bäuerlicher Agrarproduzenten (15.-19. Jahrhundert)*, Quellen und Forschungen zur Agrargeschichte, 52 (Stuttgart: Lucius & Lucius, 2011), 17–33.

53 Bernhard Degen, Fridolin Kurmann, André Schluchter, et al. (eds), *Fenster zur Geschichte. 20 Quellen, 20 Interpretationen. Festschrift für Markus Mattmüller* (Basel, Frankfurt a.M.: Helbing und Lichtenhahn, 1992); Markus Mattmüller, Fridolin Kurmann and André Schluchter, *Bevölkerungsgeschichte der Schweiz*, Basler Beiträge zur Geschichtswissenschaft, 154, 2 vols (Basel: Helbing und Lichtenhahn, 1987).

54 See Thomas Meier and Roger Sablonier (eds), *Wirtschaft und Herrschaft, Beiträge zur ländlichen Gesellschaft in der östlichen Schweiz (1200–1800)* (Zurich: Chronos, 1999); See also the evaluation of Roger Sablonier's contribution to regional history in Thomas Meier and Regula Schmid, 'Roger Sablonier, 16. April 1941 – 8. Juni 2010', *Schweizerische Zeitschrift für Geschichte*, 60 (2010), 494–97; see further Hans-Jörg Gilomen, 'Sozial- und Wirtschaftsgeschichte der Schweiz im Spätmittelalter', *Schweizerische Zeitschrift für Geschichte*, 41 (1991), 41–66; Katja Hürlimann and Stefan Sonderegger, 'Ländliche Gesellschaft im Mittelalter', *Traverse. Zeitschrift für Geschichte/Revue d'histoire*, 18/1 (2011), 48–76. See also the homepage of the Schweizerische Gesellschaft für ländliche Geschichte: http://www.ruralhistory.ch/sglg/.

55 Stefan Brakensiek, 'Regionalgeschichte als Sozialgeschichte. Studien zur ländlichen Gesellschaft im deutschsprachigen Raum', in Stefan Brakensiek and Alex Flügel (eds), *Regionalgeschichte in Europa. Methoden und Erträge der Forschung zum 16. bis 19. Jahrhundert*, Forschungen zur Regionalgeschichte, 34, (Paderborn: Schöningh, 2000), 197–251; Julien Demade, 'The Medieval Countryside in German-Language Historiography since the 1930s', in Isabel Alfonso Antón (ed.), *The Rural History of Medieval European Societies: Trends and Perspectives* (Turnhuot: Brepols, 2007), 173–252 points to the innovative nature of Swiss research on rural society; Gilomen, 'Sozial- und Wirtschaftsgeschichte', 41–66.

PART 4

Appendix

The Sub-peasant Strata in the Late Medieval and Early Modern Eastern Alpine Region

Markus Cerman and Michael Mitterauer

In the past twenty to thirty years, the interest shown by German-speaking historians in the lower strata, or rather, the sub-peasant strata of early modern rural societies has grown. The criticism, which used to be fair, that agricultural history especially was only concerned with the history of the peasants, must now be modified. It is still true, though, that for certain periods, for example, the late Middle Ages, there is an obvious lack of research. One of the difficulties continues to be how to clearly distinguish between the rural lower classes. These social groups evade easy definitions. Depending on the region, even the terms for those belonging to the peasant and sub-peasant strata are different. Whilst in the region of Lower Austria, and similarly in neighbouring Czech lands, as a rule landless households or households with only small land ownership were called '*Häusler*', in Carinthia (Kärnten) and Styria (Steiermark) the term is '*Keuschler*', whereas in Salzburg and Tyrol '*Sölleute*', '*Söllhäusler*', or '*Söldner*' ('*Söldgüter*') is used.[1] Regionally, farmland of vastly different size could be indicated with these terms, from nearly landless households (house and gardens) to *Viertelhöfe* (one fourth of a farm). In the Middle Ages, non-peasant properties in rural areas were often called *Hofstätte* (area).[2] For

1 Michael Mitterauer, 'Lebensformen und Lebensverhältnisse ländlicher Unterschichten', in Herbert Matis (ed.), *Von der Glückseligkeit des Staates* (Berlin: Dunker and Humblot, 1981), 315–38, at p. 316. For the terms used in Austrian *Weisthümer*, see Hermann Wießner, *Beiträge zur Geschichte des Dorfes und der Dorfgemeinde in Österreich*, (Klagenfurt: Kleinmyr, 1946), 64.

2 Cf. with examples from Moravia and Lower Austria in Berthold Bretholz (ed.), Das Urbar der Liechtensteinischen Herrschaften Nikolsburg, Dürnholz, Lundenburg, Falkenstein, Feldsberg, Rabensburg, Mistelbach, Hagenberg und Gnadendorf aus dem Jahre 1414, Sudetendeutsche Geschichtsquellen, 3 (Liberec/Chomutov, 1930), xxxviii–xxxix; Alfons Dopsch (ed.), Die landesfürstlichen Urbare Nieder- und Oberösterreichs aus dem 13. und 14. Jahrhundert, Österreichische Urbare Abt. 1, 1 (Vienna: W. Bramüller, 1904), cxiv–cxv; Roman Zehetmayer, Das Urbar des Grafen Burkhard III. von Maidburg-Hardegg aus dem Jahre 1363, Fontes rerum Austriacarum, Abteilung 3, Fontes iuris 15 (Vienna: Böhlau, 2001), 116–17; about Styria, see Fritz Posch, 'Die sozialen, rechtlichen und wirtschaftlichen Grundlagen der neuzeitlichen bäuerlichen Siedlung und die Entstehung des Kleinbauerntums', in Hanns Leo Mikoletzky

 | DOI:10.1163/9789004433458_011

landless co-habitants in peasant and sub-peasant households who were not servants, we find terms such as '*Inleute*', '*Inwohner*', or '*Herberger*'.[3]

There has been some thought on how to differentiate the sub-peasant strata, the rural lower classes[4] in the eastern Alpine region in the early modern period, which it is eminently fitting to make use of for the late medieval conditions we will also be considering. The social status of rural lower classes will have to be judged differently from region to region, depending on whether there are whole settlements that need to be taken into account – such as in the Alpine regions in the case of the forestry business –or when there were no longer a significant number of peasant groups with substantial property, for example, after continuous partitioning of inheritance, as was the case in western Tyrol or Vorarlberg.[5] Also not to be overlooked is that diverse relations existed between peasant and sub-peasant groups. If one wishes to consider *Inwohner* (co-habitants) as well as *Kleinhäusler* as a separate group from peasants with sufficient property, one needs to be aware of the fact that a tight net of familial relationships created social connections right across supposed demarcations.[6] This applied especially to the peasants living on a pension (*bäuerliche Altenteiler*), if they are grouped with the *Inwohner.* When it came to social status, the handing over of the farm must surely have meant a lessening of prestige,[7] as well as a worsening as a rule of one's objective economic circumstances. Nevertheless, due to our modern idea of possession and property, it is difficult to imagine retired peasant couples with an annuity (*Altbauern im*

(ed.), Bericht über den 3. österreichischen Historikertag, Veröffentlichungen des Verbandes österreichischer Geschichtsvereine 4 (Vienna, 1954), 71–75; Fritz Posch, 'Bauer und Keuschler', in Fritz Posch (ed.), Das Bauerntum in der Steiermark, Zeitschrift des historischen Vereins für Steiermark, Sonderband 7 (Graz, 1963), 68–72, esp. pp. 68, 71, where the medieval 'Hofstatt' and the 'Keuschlergüter' are defined. For early modern Lower Austria, 'Hofstatt' is also a term for sub-peasant property; see Helmuth Feigl, 'Zur Rechtslage der unterbäuerlichen Schichten im 15., 16. und 17. Jahrhundert', in Herbert Knittler (ed.), Wirtschafts- und sozialhistorische Beiträge. Festschrift für Alfred Hoffmann (Vienna: Verlag für Geschichte und Politik, 1979), 247–71, at p. 250.

3 Cf. also the overview in Wießner, *Beiträge*, 44.

4 Mitterauer, 'Lebensformen', 316–23.

5 Mitterauer, 'Lebensformen', 317. Compare, for example, the case of Axam, where properties called a fief (*Lehen*) in 1175 had a mean size of only about 3.27 ha.; Franz Mathis, 'Wirtschaft im Wandel der Zeit', in Klemens Betz, Heinz Moser and Anton Zimmermann (eds), *Axams*, (Axams, 2005), 87–124, at p. 89.

6 See Markus Cerman, 'Unterbäuerliche Schichten in ländlichen Gesellschaften des spätmittelalterlichen östlichen Mitteleuropa', *Bohemia. Zeitschrift für Geschichte und Kultur der Böhmischen Länder*, 46 (2005), 373–401; Feigl, 'Zur Rechtslage', 270.

7 Compare the detailed discussion in Dana Štefanová, *Erbschaftspraxis, Besitz und Handlungsspielräume von Untertanen in der Gutsherrschaft* (Vienna: Oldenbourg, 2009), 167–218.

Ausgedinge) as belonging to a different stratum than the peasants themselves. On the whole, the argument here is in favour of a certain age group. In comparison to the overall population, both old people and women or widows were greatly over-represented amongst the *Inwohner*.

Often farmhands and maids were considered as part of the rural lower class. But for the peasant farmhands (*Gesinde*), the issue of membership of the family weighed much more heavily than with the *Inwohner*. Often after a farm had been handed over, the sons and daughters who did not inherit remained there to work as farmhands.[8] Foster-children are called farmhands from a certain age in the sources, and this phenomenon can be found sometimes even with step-children. Yet another argument is even stronger than familial ties and the childlike status of the farm hands: in most regions of what is now considered Austria, the job of farmhand in the period being examined is not a job for life but an age-dependent transitory stage. This fact distinguishes farmhands and maids quite decidedly from the *Inwohner*, whose social position was, as a rule, fixed. If we accept this premise, the farmhands belonged to a class determined by age rather than a class that was understood socially. As an age-dependent position, the job of farmhand was of course much more common among the younger generation of the rural lower class than amongst children of propertied peasants.

This overview shows that, on the one hand, not all groups recorded in the state or lordship sources as landless or belonging to those with little land necessarily belonged to these groups. This is particularly the case for some retired peasants or some of the farmhands. On the other hand, it becomes clear that sub-peasant groups and rural lower classes are nuanced in themselves. This becomes especially apparent in the differentiation of property including a house, and the ownership of smaller areas of land such as gardens or fields of entirely unpropertied *Inwohner*.[9] The differentiation between the sub-groups of rural lower classes appears similarly problematic. In the sources, we often find '*Inleute*', '*Anlieger*', or '*Herbergsleute*' if the holders of small houses only hold these in rent.[10] According to their economic and social situation, these *Inwohner* were closer to the *Häusler* (those in possession of a house) than to

8 Reinhard Sieder and Michael Mitterauer, 'The Reconstruction of the Family Life Course: Theoretical Problems and Empirical Results', in Richard Wall, Jean Robin and Peter Laslett (eds), *Family Forms in Historic Europe* (Cambridge: Cambridge University Press, 1983), 309–45.

9 For the differentiation according to the *Weisthümer*, see Karl F. Helleiner, 'Ländliches Mindervolk in niederösterreichischen Weisthümern', *Zeitschrift für Agrargeschichte und Agrarsoziologie*, 25 (1977), 12–34, esp. p. 21.

10 See, for instance, Helleiner, 'Mindervolk', 21.

other *Inwohner.* Of course, it was also possible for *Inwohner* without their own house to independently farm land. Daily workers were often given rights to independently farm a small piece of the arable land as remuneration for their labour.[11] The example of independently farmed plots by *Inwohner* shows that there are fluent transitions between those with little and those with no land. It is also important to point out that not all people with little or no land were necessarily part of the rural lower classes. Though that was as a rule the case, there are examples of rural artisans who did not own a substantial amount of land but due to their income were actually economically equal to landowning peasants or even surpassed them.[12]

1 The Development and Status of the Sub-peasant Strata in the Eastern Alpine Region

In German agricultural history, different inheritance laws, especially the difference between *Anerbenrecht* (entail) and *Erbteilung* (partible inheritance), have often been used to explain differences in the development of rural social structures. This is not the place for a detailed discussion of this assumption;[13] however, we should mention that there were various practices of inheritance in the eastern Alpine region, while the high frequency of rural lower classes was a general phenomenon. Added to that, even in regions with partible inheritance, such as western Tyrol, manorial (and later stately) institutions could influence the practice of inheritance.[14] Inheritance rulings also changed over time,[15] so that a classification of regions according to this feature would be a great oversimplification of the situation. The observed regional differences help call into question the postulated influence of the authoritative ruling: 'The juxtaposition of different manifestations hardly implies aristocratic directives'.[16]

11 See Hermann Wopfner, *Bergbauernbuch: von arbeit und leben des Tiroler Bergbauern in Vergangenheit und Gegenwart*, ed. Nikolaus Grass, 3 vols, Tiroler Wirtschaftsstudien, 47–49 (Innsbruck, 1995–97), i, 319.

12 Feigl, 'Zur Rechtslage', 251. Examples can also be found in Mathis, 'Wirtschaft', 95.

13 Compare Markus Cerman, 'Mittelalterliche Ursprünge der unterbäuerlichen Schichten', in Markus Cerman and Robert Luft (eds), *Untertanen, Herrschaft und Staat in Böhmen und im 'Alten Reich'*, Sozialgeschichtliche Perspektiven (Munich: Oldenburg, 2005), 323–50.

14 Wopfner, *Bergbauernbuch*, i, 133, 137f., 154f., 157, 187f.; for territorial rulings, Wopfner, *Bergbauernbuch*, i, 258.

15 For Tyrol, see Wopfner, *Bergbauernbuch*, i, 189.

16 Gerald Gänser, 'Zur mittelalterlichen Siedlungs- und Bevölkerungsentwicklung im Bezirk Voitsberg', in Gerhard Pferschy (ed.), *Siedlung, Macht und Wirtschaft. Festschrift Fritz Posch zum 70. Geburtstag* (Graz: Steiermärchicher Landesarchiv, 1981), 117–27, esp. p. 120.

Partition, especially in the Alpine region, was accompanied by a simultaneous acquisition of land through deforestation and processes of intensification, such as extending agricultural activity to the *Schwaighöfe* (farms focused on animal husbandry). Still, that could not prevent the long-term decline of average landownership per household. Thus, the dimensions of farms in Pfafflar, a community in the high-mountainous Lechtal, indicate that the size of shared lands (*Teilgüter*) at times did not exceed that of sub-peasant land. Until the sixteenth century, we can find single farms already divided into up to eight *Teilgüter*, and from then until the eighteenth century, it was up to twenty-nine. This creation of *Söllgüter* (the small agricultural plots thus created) is visible in the mills or workshops then emerging on such *Teilgüter*.

How far such mechanisms aided the establishment of sub-peasant classes in the eastern Alpine region still needs to be studied in more detail in a closer inquiry. Sub-peasant households with or without some associated land occurred in regions with partible inheritance, as well as in regions where entail existed.[17] Normative rulings suggest that landowners and village communities sometimes tried to limit the creation of new households or to stop new *Inwohner* being taken in, or at least make it dependent on the approval of the community.[18] This is the reason, for example, that the division of houses was employed in western Tyrol in the early modern period, so that *Weisthümer* (historic legal texts for villages) in the Tyrolean Vintschgau contain restrictions in this regard.[19] In the localities of the district Landeck (*Gericht Landeck*), there were 430 undivided houses in 1627/28 and 143 divided houses.[20] For the land property size of the sub-peasant *Keuschen* (small farmhouses), the main

For examples of manorial restraint on partition in Tyrol, see Konrad Linder, 'Beiträge zur Geschichte der Klostergrundherrschaft Stams unter besonderer Berücksichtigung der Leiheformen', in Nikolaus Grass (ed.), *Beiträge zur Wirtschafts- und Kulturgeschichte des Zisterzienserstiftes Stams in Tirol* (Innsbruck: Wagner, 1959), 1–199, esp. pp. 112–19.

17 Wopfner, *Bergbauernbuch*, i, 134f., 145f., 148f. For the partitioning in the context of inheritance laws, see Kurt Klein, *Daten zur Siedlungsgeschichte der österreichischen Länder bis zum 16. Jahrhunder* (Vienna, 1980), 104; Wießner, *Beiträge*, 49; Wopfner, *Bergbauernbuch*, i, 152f.

18 Wießner, *Beiträge*, 61, 64; Wopfner, *Bergbauernbuch*, i, 209f., 257.

19 A house might not have more than three fireplaces ('*denn drei Feuerstätt*'); see Ignaz V. Zingerle and K. Theodor von Inama-Sternegg (eds), *Die Tirolischen Weisthümer*, iii: *Vinstgau*, Österreichische Weisthümer, 4 (Vienna: Braumueller, 1880), 205, Zl. 21. About restrictions concerning sub-peasant households in late medieval Bavaria, see Pankraz Fried, *Herrschaftsgeschichte der altbayerischen Landgerichte Dachau und Kranzberg im Hoch- und Spätmittelalter sowie in der frühen Neuzeit* (Munich: Kommision für Byerisches Landesgeschichte 1962), 197.

20 Wopfner, *Bergbauernbuch*, i, 210; cf. for higher values, see Wopfner, *Bergbauernbuch*, i, 213f.

sources are plots of land and common land partitioned off from an original farmhouse.[21] Phases in which new households were founded alternate with phases in which partitioned land was consolidated again, that is, a phase of concentrated ownership. In this way, so-called '*Zugüter*' (additional land)[22] were created from previously independent households in the Alpine region, expansion of properties that could be used flexibly for the establishment of partly independent households, if the need arose (for instance, for retirees or married offspring). Every now and then a *Schwaighof* occurs as property expansion of a farm.[23]

Taking into account the division of property weakens another argument of traditional interpretation, according to which the development of sub-peasant classes was a modern phenomenon.[24] The wealth of evidence for division in the Alpine region in the course of the late medieval period documents the process of the emerging sub-peasant strata in this period.[25] In the expansion of the division, which continued throughout the early modern period, one can of course see clear regional differences.[26] Inner- and Außer-Villgraten, two communities in eastern Tyrol, are examples of this. In Inner-Villgraten, numerous divisions were carried out, down to a ninety-sixth of a farm. If they were not combined into peasant enterprises, 'they turned into small settlements that could not yield enough to secure the upkeep of a family'. In Außer-Villgraten, this was much less common.[27] Next to the numerous documented divisions, independent households of *Sölleute* were also not uncommon in the late medieval communities of Tyrol, and testify to the fact that it is possible to place the emergence of the sub-peasant strata in Tyrol, respectively in the Alpine regions in the late medieval period, as scholars like Wilfried Beimrohr and Franz Mathis recently have done.[28]

---

21 For Carinthia, see Karl Dinklage, *Geschichte der Kärntner Landwirtschaft* (Klagenfurt: Heyn, 1966), 69, 128; for Styria, see Posch, 'Grundlagen', 71f.

22 Wopfner, *Bergbauernbuch*, i, 190.

23 A corresponding use of *Schwaighöfe* for Lanis given by Wopfner, *Bergbauernbuch*, iii, 403.

24 See Posch, 'Grundlagen'; Walther Fresacher, *Der Bauer in Kärnten*, i: *Die persönliche Stellung des Bauers in Kärnten* (Klagenfurt, 1950), 48, 125.

25 Cf. Wopfner, *Bergbauernbuch*, i, 142, 145, 189; Mitterauer, *Lebensformen*, 324f.

26 Wopfner, *Bergbauernbuch*, i, 145–47.

27 Wopfner, *Bergbauernbuch*, i, 147ff.

28 Wilfried Beimrohr, 'Bäuerliche Besitzrechte und ländliche Gemeinde in Tirol', in Tore Iversen, John Ragnar Myking, and Gertrud Thoma (eds), *Bauern zwischen Herrschaft und Genossenschaf* (Trondheim: NTNU, 2007), 85–108, esp. p. 100; Franz Mathis, 'Bauern – Bergbau – Industrie. Die Absamer Wirtschaft vom Mittelalter bis zur Gegenwart', in Michael Laimgruber, Heinz Moser and Peter Steindl (eds), *Absam*, (Absam, 2008), 97–138, at p. 94. Contrasting however is Wopfner, *Bergbauernbuch*, i, 149f.

In the later abandoned village of Seding at the monastery of Rein in Styria, for instance, there were 16.5 *Hufen* (measurement of landholding) in 1396, distributed over fifteen farms, and thirteen large and fifteen smaller farmsteads which had previously been divided among two farms and ten estates comprised of only one to four farmsteads. Over the course of the late Middle Ages, the farmsteads were gradually merged into the farms and ceased to exist as independent property. This development is seen as being due not to demographics or political crises but to the relatively high payments that the farmsteads needed to make to be freed from previous socage (*Robotdienste* – the so-called '*Gaber*', '*Mader*', and '*Hauer*' *Pfennige*). Apparently, the farmsteads of Seding were originally linked to the manor's own production. During the agrarian crisis in the late Middle Ages, it must have become steadily more difficult for the sub-peasant economies to produce the surplus required for the rent, which is why they were abandoned for economic reasons.[29] This *Vereinödung* (turning farmland or settlements into wasteland) during the late Middle Ages could be one of the reasons why scholars within the field of traditional agricultural history assumed that sub-peasant estates had only ever emerged in the early modern period. There simply had not been enough research conducted on late medieval conditions.

The assumption that the sub-peasant strata emerged in the late Middle Ages is supported by the developments in neighbouring territories such as Swabia[30] or Bavaria.[31] On the basis of a regional study of the *Landkreise* Dachau and Kranzberg, Pankraz Fried has been able to prove that around 1500, roughly half of all rural estates belonged to the sub-peasant strata (*Sölden*), so that their settlement there must reach back far into the Middle Ages. In the early modern period, the *Sölden* continued to increase in larger localities[32] and in *Hofmarken* (territories with manorial jurisdiction) with demesnes where there was a higher demand for a rural workforce. In smaller villages and dispersed settlements with single farms, however, growth remained marginal. An

29 Othmar Pickl, 'Das Dorf "Sedin" des Klosters Reun. Ein Beitrag zur Wüstungsforschung', in *Blätter für Heimatkunde*, 32 (1958), 111–23. Gänser considers the diminishing of many small settlements in the Styrian territory of Piber due to economic reasons in the fifteenth century. They generally merged with larger estates; see Gänser, 'Siedlungs- und Bevölkerungsentwicklung', 121f., and Gerald Gänser, 'Strukturveränderungen im agrarischen Bereich während des 15. Jahrhunderts', *Zeitschrift des historischen Vereins für Steiermark*, 75 (1984), 23–30, esp. p. 25.

30 Hermann Grees, *Ländliche Unterschichten und ländliche Siedlung in Ostschwaben*, Tübinger geographische Studien, 58 (Tübingen, 1975).

31 Fried, *Herrschaftsgeschichte*, esp. pp. 186ff.

32 Similarly, for Carinthia, see Dinklage, *Geschichte*, 108.

extraordinary amount of new *Sölden* are visible on communal and church land in those villages where the villagers took part in the church administration. The settlement apparently helped raise the revenues of the village church through bonds and interest.[33]

The examples serve to illustrate the continuous presence of rural lower classes over the course of the late Middle Ages. Thus, it seems problematic to interpret the emergence and expansion of these groups primarily as a consequence of demographic growth and to ignore economic circumstances, as was done by Hermann Wopfner und Herbert Klein. Arguing against a purely demographic explanation is, for instance, the fact that the abandoned settlements (*Ortswüstungen*) obviously did not lead to the abandonment of the entire estate. In the Alpine area especially, the number of abandoned settlements cannot be equated to a decrease in population, since this was the consequence of a concentration of settlement, often the result of varying population density, that led to abandonment throughout the Middle Ages and not only in the later period. Also, the range of abandonment varied greatly regionally, due to the late medieval crises in the eastern Alpine region. For instance, it is assumed that those in Lower Austria occupied between 15 and 45 percent of cultivated land, depending on the region, and in Styria and Carinthia an above-average number of abandoned settlements appears to have existed. In Salzburg, it has been determined for some regions in Pongau that, after the plague of 1348/49, up to 40 percent of the farms were left uninhabited and two-thirds of the population had died. But these were extreme numbers quite unlike others in the country. And the region must have recovered again soon, for two decades later we no longer see any abandoned settlements, indicating that none had been permanently abandoned. Further, differentiation is required between those regions hit by one of the early waves of the plague, and those where political events in the fifteenth century slowed down recovery – such as in eastern Austria, Styria, and Carinthia. Processes of abandonment coincide with ones of expansion. Although in Tyrol wage-rulings were handed down by the territorial rulers after the plague in the mid-fourteenth century, the quick recovery was most likely due to a boom in the mining industry.[34] In different regions of

33 Fried, *Herrschaftsgeschichte*, 186, 195–99.

34 Roman Sandgruber, *Ökonomie und Politik*, Österreichische Geschichte, 12 (Vienna: Uberreiter, 1995), 51f.; see also Heinz Dopsch, 'Wandlungen und Konstanz der spätmittelalterlichen Grundherrschaft im Erzstift Salzburg', in Hans Patze (ed.), *Die Grundherrschaft im späten Mittelalter*, Vorträge und Forschungen, 27, 2 vols (Sigmaringen, 1983), ii, 229–75, esp. 245f., 252; Helmuth Feigl and Andreas Kusternig (ed.), *Mittelalterliche Wüstungen in Niederösterreich* (Vienna: NÖ Inst. Für Landeskunde, 1983); Walther Fresacher, 'Die Pest in Kärnten im 14. Jahrhundert', *Carinthia*, 153 (1963), 349–78; Herbert Klein, 'Das große

Austria, there were a growing number of newly cleared woodland areas throughout the fifteenth century. In the woodlands of Lower Austria, the large distribution of such new clearings (called *Reuter*) – detectable especially in the fifteenth century in the *urbaria* of the territorial rulers – stands in clear contrast to the simultaneous peak in the abandoning of settlements.[35] These activities can be seen in Salzburg, for instance, with peculiar intensity, where cleared woodland was used mainly to add to the land of existing farms.[36]

The evidence contradicts another traditional view, since *Inwohner* can also be documented for rural areas as early as the late medieval period.[37] At the beginning of the sixteenth century, one-quarter of the population of Piber in Styria were *Inleute* and servants. In the territories of Kammerstein and Ehrnau, there were simultaneously 83 *Inleute* in 265 households, active both in the peasant economy and in the local metal industry. And in some districts (*Ämter*) of the territory of Admont, 166 *Inleute* and servants could be found in 80 households.[38]

Rural lower classes experienced an upsurge in growth in the early modern period under economic influences such as the mining industry. Here is not the place to give a detailed depiction of rural social structure in all the different regions of the eastern Alpine region; it is sufficient to say that in numerous communities of the seventeenth and eighteenth centuries, sub-peasant households made up the majority.[39] In Dachau and Kranzberg, Fried found that after the first quarter of the eighteenth century, there was a significant acceleration in the growth of the sub-peasant strata.[40] This is widely emphasized for Austria in general.[41] In this context, it may be relevant that the proportion of the completely landless population increased as well. By 1782 in Defereggental in

Sterben von 1348/49 und seine Auswirkungen auf die Besiedlung der Ostalpenländer', *Mitteilungen der Gesellschaft für Salzburger Landeskunde*, 100 (1960), 91–170; Klein, *Daten*, 26, 32, 72f., 103.

35 In more detail: Markus Cerman, 'Mittelalterliche Grundlagen: wirtschaftlicher und gesellschaftlicher Wandel im Waldviertel bis zum frühen 16. Jahrhundert', in Herbert Knittler (ed.), *Wirtschaftsgeschichte des Waldviertels* (Horn: Waldviertler Heimatbund, 2006), 1–76, esp. pp. 11–14, 24.

36 Dopsch, 'Wandlungen', 253.

37 See Fresacher, *Bauer*, 125.

38 Gänser, 'Strukturveränderungen', 25.

39 See Wopfner, *Bergbauernbuch*, i, 150–54; Mitterauer, 'Lebensformen', 324f.; Franz Mathis, 'Bauern – Bergbau – Industrie', esp. pp. 103, 105f.

40 Fried, *Herrschaftsgeschichte*, 190f.

41 Mitterauer, 'Lebensformen', 323–27. See also Mitterauer, 'Lebensformen', 321f. and Wopfner, *Bergbauernbuch*, i, 359.

eastern Tyrol, in addition to 127 households with very little land, forty-five had no arable land at all.[42]

Sub-peasant households could certainly acquire land through tenancy or in other ways manage farmland of variable size. Sometimes the relevant sources, such as rent rolls or tax cadastres, can give the wrong impression of complete landlessness, because the property was only held in tenancy. In the sources, the land is then ascribed to the owner and not the tenant. The wide distribution of such practices is illustrated by rules such as those in Telfs, where in the seventeenth century peasants were explicitly forbidden from letting land to *Söldner*.[43] In contemporary documents, sub-peasant households were sometimes described with and sometimes without land. The estates could reach sizes of up to a *Viertelhof* (a quarter of a *Hufe*), so the property size of a smallholding. One Tyrolean *Weisthum* talks about 'herrschaftliche kleinhäusler so kain haus und äcker [haben]' and mentions these in the same sentence as the *Inwohner*.[44] Detailed information in the Carinthian land registers of the sixteenth and seventeenth centuries describe *Keuschen* that, besides pasturage, also contain arable land between about an eighth or half of a *Hufe*. The ownership of livestock was sometimes remarkable, with up to three cows, a calf, and pigs. However, such *Keuschen* characteristically did not own any draft cattle.[45] For a *Keusche* with slightly less than half a *Hufe* of arable land 1692, it is documented that it was possible to achieve self-sufficiency in normal years.[46] Particularly when it came to land ownership, the boundaries between the lower-peasant and peasant strata were blurred. This was especially the case in relation to *Keuschen* that emerged in the late Middle Ages or in the sixteenth century, whereas for later households the property size was smaller.[47]

42 Heinz Kröll and Gert Stemberger, *Defereggen: Eine Landschaft in Tirol* (Vienna: Schendl Verlag, 1985), 169.

43 Ignaz V. Zingerle and Karl Theodor von Inama-Sternegg (eds), *Die Tirolischen Weisthümer*, ii: *Oberinntal*, Österreichische Weisthümer, 3 (Vienna: Braumeuller, 1877), 10, line 24ff.

44 '*kleinhäusler* with neither house nor land'. Wießner, *Beiträge*, 44. *Weisthümer* differentiate between peasant groups and rural lower classes (see below) and reflect the differences felt in contemporary rural communities. For this and the structure of *Weisthümer* as source material, see, for instance, with a Swiss example, Simon Teuscher, *Erzähltes Recht: Lokale Herrschaft, Verschriftlichung und Traditionsbildung im Spätmittelalter*, Campus Historische Studien, 44 (Frankfurt, 2007), esp. 206–55.

45 But even this seems not to be a general rule. Thus, one Styrian *Weisthum* forbids the pasture of more than one horse (*ain roß*); Ferdinand Bischoff and Anton Schönbach (eds), *Steirische und Kärnthische Taidinge*, Österreichische Weisthümer, 6 (Vienna, 1881), 292, ll. 15–17. One Tyrolean *Weisthum* talks about 'söllmann, oder welcher ain viertel guet hat'; Zingerle and Inama-Sternegg (eds), *Die Tirolischen Weisthümer*, ii, 42, line 47.

46 Dinklage, *Geschichte*, 104, 108. See also Fresacher, *Bauer*, 26, 48.

47 Dinklage, *Geschichte*, 108.

Some specific plots of land were available for long-term acquisition, but this was rarely land belonging to specific farmsteads. These plots could be called '*walzende Gründe*', land that was not originally seen as an integral part of a farm. This could include, for example, land freed through woodland clearance, for instance, in Auen in Tyrol or earlier common land. It was especially possible to gain a substantial amount of land through woodland clearance or the conversion of extensively tilled plots into crop fields in earlier periods, which then could be used for sub-peasant estates.[48] The importance of such '*walzende Gründe*' is also emphasized for *Söldenansiedlungen,* settlements of sub-peasant inhabitants, in Bavaria.[49] Another important source of land were the commons. In villages with communal land, a successive reduction or distribution of the commons began in the late Middle Ages in order to make room for sub-peasant farms. This process continued into the modern period.[50] In Tyrol, the rulings of territorial lords as early as 1511 and repeatedly in the sixteenth century restricted communities in their practice of adding communal land to single estates or making it available for new building projects. This first needed the consent of both the community and the authorities.[51]

As far as it is possible to deduce from the *Weisthümer* still existent in Austria, the sub-peasant strata were often disadvantaged when it came to the right to the common land.[52] There were plenty of restrictions to pasture, and they could be rigorous. In this region, it was most likely that the growth of the rural lower classes came into conflict with the economic requirements of the peasant group, out of which conflict could easily have developed in the village. In the area of Lower Austria, there were regulations in the *Weisthümer* discriminating against the sub-peasant strata, especially the *Inwohner*. They were restricted in their upkeep of livestock and were only permitted to use the common land with consent of the community, the number of animals was restricted (in this case to two pigs and one milk cow, in another case to hens), or they were forbidden completely from keeping livestock or poultry.[53] For *Söllner*, the

48 Wopfner, *Bergbauernbuch*, i, 149f., 152, 157, 197.

49 Fried, *Herrschaftsgeschichte*, 199.

50 Walter Brunner, 'Die Gmein im steirischen Altsiedelland', in Gerhard Pferschy (ed.), *Siedlung, Macht und Wirtschaft: Festschrift Fritz Posch zum 70. Geburtstag* (Graz: Steiermärchischen Landesarchiv, 1981), 45–50, esp. p. 45f.; Posch, 'Grundlagen', 71f.; Wießner, *Beiträge*, 58.

51 Beimrohr, 'Besitzrechte', 100f.

52 Wießner, *Beiträge*, 60.

53 Helleiner, 'Mindervolk', 20; Ignaz V. Zingerle and K. Theodor von Inama-Sternegg (eds), *Die Tirolischen Weisthümer*, i: *Unterinntal*, Österreichische Weisthümer, 2 (Vienna: Braumeuller, 1875), 164, ll. 12–13; 167, l. 7.

livestock was limited to one cow.[54] Another form of restriction was the demand of payment from sub-peasant households in exchange for the right of pasture.[55]

Taking livestock of non-residents or citizens of nearby towns to the village green was closely connected to these restrictions. By 1371, the *Weisthum* of Partschins in Tyrol said that: 'niemant soll kain fremdes viech einnehmen'.[56] A corresponding ban on the movement of cattle can also be found in Styrian *Weisthümer*.[57] But where there was considerable alpine pasture, the opposite would be the case and people would try to use the resources exhaustively by taking up livestock from non-residents.[58] Grazing foreign livestock on the common or alpine pasture in exchange for money may have seemed an attractive way of creating additional income for the social strata with little or no land, and as such, they would be especially affected by the restrictions. Similar restrictions applied to the use of the streams (for fishing or catching crayfish)[59] or the common forest.[60] In some regulations, *Söldner* were allotted less wood than *Lehner* (farm owners), or were forbidden it completely.[61]

These disadvantages could be traced back to the fact that the sub-peasant strata did not entirely belong to the village community. In this respect, it would again be right to assume regional differences. A general interpretation, according to which the sub-peasant strata should not be considered as neighbours and members of the community, is probably not maintainable. For example, the village ordinances of Wiesing in 1676 were explicitly addressed to 'ain ersambe nachperson und söldner' (an honourable neighbour and *söldner*), and the individual rulings applied to *lechensäß* (farm owners) or *söldner*.[62]

---

54 Zingerle and Inama-Sternegg (eds), *Die Tirolischen Weisthümer*, i, 151.

55 Wießner, *Beiträge*, 63.

56 'Nobody shall take foreign livestock with them'. Bischoff and Schönbach (eds), *Steirische und Kärnthische Taidinge*, 536, ll. 31–33; Zingerle and Inama-Sternegg (eds), *Die Tirolischen Weisthümer*, ii, 27, ll. 27ff., and see Wießner, *Beiträge*, 54.

57 Bischoff and Schönbach (eds), *Steirische und Kärnthische Taidinge*, 224, ll. 14–16.

58 For this *Lehnvieh*, see Nikolaus Grass, *Beiträge zur Rechtsgeschichte der Alpwirtschaft* (Innsbruck, 1948), 34–62.

59 Compare Helleiner, 'Mindervolk', 20.

60 Zingerle and Inama-Sternegg (eds), *Die Tirolischen Weisthümer*, i, 220, ll. 37–38, 262, ll. 45–46, 283, ll. 7–8.

61 Zingerle and Inama-Sternegg (eds), *Die Tirolischen Weisthümer*, ii, 11, ll. 9–12, 52, ll. 33–34.

62 Zingerle and Inama-Sternegg (eds), *Die Tirolischen Weisthümer*, i, 157. From a comment in a further Tyrolean *Weisthum*, it seems that the presence of *Söldner* and *Inleuten* was expected. See Zingerle and Inama-Sternegg (eds), *Die Tirolischen Weisthümer*, i, 131, ll. 32–37.

However, there are indeed indications that they had no right to neighbourhood at all, or only with certain restrictions. Thus, one *Weisthum* required that only neighbours with *gehöfft* (farm) and *wierts namen* were allowed to take part in the *Taiding* (yearly legislative assembly). This was also the case in some areas for the holding of commissions.[63] In another Tyrolean *Weisthum*, *unangesessene* (non-resident) *söldner* are mentioned.[64] It is to be assumed that the potential for conflict within the village community existed, which in this case developed along the social boundaries of peasant and sub-peasant groups.[65]

Regional differences in community rights are perhaps explicable through the settlement history. Thus, it is assumed for Styria that, in the *Altsiedelland* ('old-settlement' land, which had been acquired and settled between the fifth and eighth century), both farmhouses and sub-peasant *Keusche* could use the common land proportionally. In the colonization and settlement villages of eastern Styria, however, the *Keuschler* were excluded from its use.[66]

The question of community rights may point to differences in the original local evolutionary context of the rural lower classes. For instance, in the late Middle Ages, Bavarian farmhouses were permitted to erect additional farmsteads belonging to the farm as long as they had the consent of the village community; however, as opposed to the simultaneously erected *Sölden* of the landlords, these were not counted as proper households (*Ehofstätte*) and thus did not hold communal rights (and vanished again in the early modern period).[67] In a Tyrolean *Weisthum* of the seventeenth century, a regulation says that *söl-leut und klain trager* were to pay taxes in the future in the same way as the owners of *steuerbare güter* (goods that were taxable).[68] Thus, it seems as though sub-peasant households sometimes were not counted as taxable houses.

It seems possible that the group of community members with full rights could allow, restrict, or prohibit access to the village resources. At least in some Austrian *Weisthümer*, the village community praised itself for the right of

63 Wießner, *Beiträge*, 61; Fried, *Herrschaftsgeschichte*, 224.

64 Ignaz V. Zingerle and Josef Egger (eds), *Die Tirolischen Weisthümer*, iv: *Burgrafenamt und Etschland*, Österreichische Weisthümer, 5 (Vienna: Braumeuller, 1888), 339, ll. 8–9.

65 Beimrohr, 'Besitzrechte', 100. See Wießner, *Beiträge*, 60; for Bavaria, see Fried, *Herrschaftsgeschichte*, 195; for Swabia, see Grees, *Unterschichten*.

66 Brunner, 'Gmein', 47.

67 Fried, *Herrschaftsgeschichte*, 197, 205. Details to the question of the community rights of *Sölden* in Swabia: Grees, *Unterschichten*, 15, 24ff.

68 Zingerle and Inama-Sternegg (eds), *Die Tirolischen Weisthümer*, i, 71, ll. 10–17.

regulating village community life and especially the usage of community resources.[69]

The exclusion of specific groups from full membership of the community was not a constant throughout history. Karl F. Helleiner refers to *Weisthümer* of the fifteenth or eighteenth century, in which the owners of newly built houses immediately gained the same rights as those of the original estates. Thus, in 1434, the abbot of Melk declared for the Lower Austrian village of Rohrendorf that: 'Wer hewslich pawt zu sitzn auf unserm purkfrid und gründt, es sei auf wismat, paungarten, weingarten oder acker, der sol haben all di rechtn di ainer hat, der vor hundert jarn auf dem aigen gesessen ist'.[70]

For Bavaria, it has been proven that the use of common land was bound to whether the respective household owned land – even if only on a small scale. Only people completely without land, such as *Häusler* with no land or *Inwohner*, would have been excluded.[71] We can frequently see in the *Weisthümer* of Tyrol, Carinthia, or Styria that there were rules about the usage of common pasture or forest for all village members, peasants and rural lower classes, graded according to the size of the estate.[72] In late medieval Tyrol, the sub-peasant strata was directly involved: 'als vil ein höfer schlecht, als viel sollen zween halbhöfer schlachen; als vil ain halbhöfer schlecht, als vil sollen zween saltner schlachen'.[73] This applied not only in the villages but also in places with market rights, where there was a differentiation between citizens and *Keuschler*.[74] One case appears especially interesting, in which two *Keuschler* were explicitly counted as belonging to the community, but were only allocated half as much wood as the other households, since they were only *Keuschen* and did not have

69 Compare Wießner, *Beiträge*, 53, 55, 57. For the role of the community in Tyrol, see Beimrohr, 'Besitzreche', 97.

70 'Anyone who builds a house and settles here with meadows, orchards, vineyards, or fields should have the same rights as one who has had his own property here for a hundred years'. Zingerle and Inama-Sternegg (eds), *Die Tirolischen Weisthümer*, i, 871, line 39ff.; compare Helleiner, 'Mindervolk', 28f.; Fried, *Herrschaftsgeschichte*, 205f., 226f.; according to K. Bader, this also refers to long-term conflicts within the village about access to the communal resources. Karl Siegfried Bader, *Studien zur Rechtsgeschichte des mittelalterlichen Dorfes*, i (Weimar: Böhlau, 1957). This might explain the different regional structures.

71 Fried, *Herrschaftsgeschichte*, 205.

72 Compare Hermann Wießner, *Sachinhalt und wirtschaftliche Bedeutung der Weisthümer im deutschen Kulturgebiet* (Baden: Verlag Rudolf M. Rohrer, 1934), 259–61. For Bavaria, see also Fried, *Herrschaftsgeschichte*, 206.

73 'A *halbhöfner* may fell half as much wood as a *höfner* and a *söldner* may fell half as much as a *halbhöfner*'. Zingerle and Egger (eds), *Die Tirolischen Weisthümer*, iv, 168, ll. 34–35. See Wießner, *Beiträge*, 63.

74 Bischoff and Schönbach (eds), *Steirische und Kärnthische Taidinge*, 258, ll. 1–3.

to pay socage: 'weilen (…) keine hueben sondern nur keuschen und kein robath zu verrichten haben'.[75] Here, it appears that next to the size of the land, the lack of feudal duties needing to be paid was also a factor. Thus, one must rethink the role of the members of the community with this in mind; it also lends weight the view that the rule not only made a difference between peasant and sub-peasant strata but also regulated usage within the peasant group according to property size. A Carinthian *Almbrief* (a document regulating the use of alpine pasture) from the early seventeenth century ruled that farmers with one whole *Hufe* of land (*Ganzhufner*) were allowed to graze up to six cows on the alpine pasture, and those with only half a *Hufe* of land (*Halbhufner*) were only allowed four.[76] A similar difference was made in one Tyrolean example between those 'with half a fief' and those 'with quarter of a fief' (*Halblehner* and *Viertellehner*).[77] In numerous cases, the rural lower classes were simply included as one further group of villagers with usage rights according to property and thus not really subject to a separate ruling.

In a *Weisthum* from Tyrol, not only the use of pasture but the entire keeping of livestock was prescribed according to property sizes. While the normal farmer (*pauer oder ganzlechner*) was allowed to keep and graze six dairy cows, three horses, and six heifers, those with no house and land (*kleinhäusler so kain haus und äcker und denen inwonern*) were only permitted one dairy cow.[78] Another *Weisthum* allowed a farmhouse two horses, two cows, and two calves for grazing, and a *halblechner* was still allowed one of each, while the *söllner* was permitted one cow, but only as long as the household could feed it during the wintertime.[79] The amount of wood one was permitted from the communal forest or at clearances was often connected to property size and counted alike for peasant and sub-peasant groups.[80]

But the rural lower classes were not everywhere dependent solely on the commons in order to feed their livestock. The ready availability of surplus

---

75 Bischoff and Schönbach (eds), *Steirische und Kärnthische Taidinge*, 523, ll. 25–29.

76 Bischoff and Schönbach (eds), *Steirische und Kärnthische Taidinge*, 470, l. 13.

77 Zingerle and Inama-Sternegg (eds), *Die Tirolischen Weisthümer*, i, 64, ll. 36–38. For Swiss rulings in the *Alpbriefe*, see Stefan Sonderegger, 'Alpwirtschaft im Toggenburg, Werdenberg und Sarganserland', in Wissenschaftliche Kommission der Sankt-Galler Kantonsgeschichte, Silvio Bucher, Max Baumann, et al. (eds), *Sankt-Galler Geschichte*, iii (St Gallen: Amt für Kultur des Kantons St. Gallen, 2003), 245–60.

78 Wießner, *Beiträge*, 44.

79 Zingerle and Inama-Sternegg (eds), *Die Tirolischen Weisthümer*, i, 151, ll. 21–24. See Wießner, *Beiträge*, 44f., also p. 61.

80 Zingerle and Egger (eds), *Die Tirolischen Weisthümer*, iv, 174, ll. 20–26; Bischoff and Schönbach (eds), *Steirische und Kärnthische Taidinge*, 437, ll. 21–25, and 438, ll. 12–15. See Wießner, *Beiträge*, 61.

labour created an opportunity in these households (but also for farms that made use of the labour), to pursue labour-intensive occupations or to raise the productivity of the surface area in the alpine economy through additional labour.[81] For instance, in Tyrol, next to the normal labour-intensive mowing of the alpine pasture, it was also possible to gather grass in other, normally less accessible places. Of course, grass gathering was also done on the commons, but it was by no means limited to it. In connection with this, the *Weisthümer* sometimes imposed bans, such as in a Styrian example from the early seventeenth century.[82]

This introductory overview as well as the discussion about property and community rights of the sub-peasant strata indicates that it is not possible to identify clear general distinctions in the eastern Alpine region. Where the sources suggest legally differentiated categories, as in the *Weisthümer*, it is not always the case that there was a corresponding *de facto* economic discrimination of the sub-peasant strata. Helleiner assumes that there was subordination of sub-peasant strata, servants, and *Inwohner* to the labour demand of the peasant groups that, in his opinion, are seen clearly in the *Weisthümer* of Lower Austria (see below). The traditional historiography has occasionally referred to the legal dependency of *Inwohner* and their families on the head of the estate. Even though newer research shows existing dependencies,[83] this is a subject that could profit from deeper research, at least for the area of the eastern Alps. *Inwohner* probably cannot simply be ascribed to this subordinate category across the board, as becomes especially apparent when we think of retired peasants who were granted an annuity.

As cited, some evidence indicates that *Inwohner* did not have to pay duties and taxes (or rather, these had to be paid by the households that accommodated them), or that they were considered as non-resident (*unangesessen*) or without community rights. But again, there can be no generalization for the rural lower classes. As a rule, independent households such as *Häusler* paid duties to their lords and the state and were thus not really distinguishable from peasant groups.

---

81 See, for instance, Wopfner, *Bergbauernbuch*, iii, 19f., 143f. For examples of such labour in alpine agriculture, see Kröll and Stemberger, *Defereggen*, 168.

82 Bischoff and Schönbach (eds), *Steirische und Kärnthische Taidinge*, 291, ll. 22–28. See Wopfner, *Bergbauernbuch*, i, 352f.; Grass, *Beiträge*, 159ff.; Kröll and Stemberger, *Defereggen*, 172.

83 See, for example, Jürgen Schlumbohm, *Lebensläufe, Familien, Höfe: Die Bauern und Heuerleute des osnabrückischen Kirchspiels Belm in proto-industrieller Zeit, 1650–1860* (Göttingen: Vandenhoeck und Ruprecht, 1994).

2 Craftsmanship, Mixed Employment, Itinerant Trade: Forms of Income in the Eastern Alpine Region

The rural cottage industry, a frequent source of income for rural lower classes in the eastern Alpine region, has long stood in the shadow of commercial types of cottage and proto-industry. This has been the case, even though the concentration of (manufacturing) trade has been highlighted in particular for alpine regions like Tyrol and has been at least partially explained through economic necessity due to minimal agricultural property sizes (smallholder structure), geographical isolation,[84] or the strong formation of the lower classes.

Perhaps it would be more correct, taking the situation in Tyrol, eastern Tyrol, or Vorarlberg into account, to distinguish between two causalities. The first opinion, which is generally accepted in scholarship, would be that the formation of the lower classes leads to more people taking up types of mixed occupation and trade. This could be the result of agricultural change, or in the alpine region the result of a structural change in the economy as well. Here, the decline of the mining industry probably played a great part, since a group of people who were no longer rooted in agriculture then had to take up different, in some cases non-agrarian, professions. Thus, it was the loss of work under the mountains that made it necessary for people to reorientate themselves.[85] The second opinion is that a supra-regional demand for specialized services or produce existed, which contributed to the growth of the lower classes and their commercial orientation.

In the same way as the *Saumhandel* (the trading of goods across the Alps on foot and with pack-animals), which was at a high point at the transition of the late medieval to the early modern period, the mining industry also brought with it an intensification of contact with the outside world, geographical mobility, and economic integration for the miners. In a way, mining could make spaces accessible, just as the trading routes across the Alps created a demand for trade and services along those routes which were embedded in the peasant

---

84 See, for instance, Beimrohr, 'Besitzrechte', 100; John W. Cole and Eric R. Wolf, *Die unsichtbare Grenze. Ethnizität und Ökologie in einem Alpental* (Vienna: Folio Verlag, 1995), 212; Dinklage, *Geschichte*, 128; Wopfner, *Bergbauernbuch*, i, 148; for Styria, see Posch, 'Grundlagen', 73.

85 Wopfner, *Bergbauernbuch*, i, 150; Beimrohr, 'Besitzrechte', 100f.; Mitterauer, 'Lebensformen', 324; Cole and Wolf, *Grenze*, 113; Dinklage, *Geschichte*, 108f. As an especially impressive example, see the mining industry and trade in Absam in Mathis, 'Bauern', 114–21.

trade. *Saumhandel* and later forms of itinerant trade (see below) are also connected.[86]

However, it is also imperative that the demands of a labour-intensive agricultural economy, such as the alpine and high alpine forms of agriculture, are not disregarded. In some instances, the decline of mining can lead to a re-agrarianization on the basis of smallholder existence. The exchange of labour between sub-, small, and large peasant households is a central factor and can reach far beyond the local context, as in the case of seasonal agricultural labourers who relocate along with the harvest.[87]

Based on a detailed analysis of the *Weisthümer*, Karl F. Helleiner questions the free labour of *Inwohner* on the farms in the general context of the regulation of the rural labour market with regard to the interests of the farmowners. *Inwohner* not only served as labourers for those providing them with accommodation, but basically for all farms in the village.[88] The *Weisthum* of Flaurling in the Upper Inn Valley dating from the fifteenth century says that all *Selleut* should mainly work for their pay (*umb unsern lon*) on the local estates.[89] The creation of small *Zugüter* (additional land), the acceptance of *Inwohner*, the high number of servants, all of this could also be interpreted as forms of 'labour hording', the long-term binding of manpower to the local economy in order to secure enough manpower during the seasonal high points.[90]

As implied, forms of mixed employment were especially common amongst the rural lower classes of the eastern Alpine region. In the relevant sources, one can often find combinations such as 'smith and grocer', 'bricklayer and weaver', 'smith and wagoner', 'weaver and trader', etc.[91] Different trades and services were bound by seasonal opportunity. Builders, bricklayers, and carpenters could hardly work during the winter months. The combination of 'bricklayer and weaver' thus signals combined sources of income that were characteristic. During the winter, many were employed in the typically indoor trade of weaving. For instance, we know that in the western regions of Tyrol thousands of men moved away in the spring to work as bricklayers or carpenters in

86 Cole and Wolf, *Grenze*, 113; Kröll and Stemberger, *Defereggen*, 198, 204; Wopfner, *Bergbauernbuch*, i, 149f.

87 Cole and Wolf, *Grenze*, 222–25.

88 Helleiner, 'Mindervolk', 14–15, 23.

89 Zingerle and Inama-Sternegg (eds), *Die Tirolischen Weisthümer*, ii, 25, ll. 40–41.

90 Compare George Grantham, 'Economic History and the History of the Labour Markets', in George Grantham and Mary MacKinnon (eds), *Labour Market Evolution* (London: Routledge, 1994), 1–26, esp. p. 16.

91 Mitterauer, 'Lebensformen', 331. For mixed employment and trade, see Mathis, 'Wirtschaft', 95–108.

Switzerland, in southern Germany, in the Rhineland, in Saxony, Thuringia, or Westphalia. In the eighteenth century, this itinerant employment was at a peak. What caused seasonal emigration in Tyrol was, for other regions, just a seasonal change of job for the rural lower classes. Both forestry and the transport industry continued to be very seasonal occupations. Both employed a significant circle of persons that can be seen as belonging mainly to the sub-peasant population. As a rule, we can probably assume that the income of the rural lower classes depended on various forms of mixed employment.

One result of this characteristic mixed employment was the seasonal itinerancy. Seasonal peaks in the demand for agricultural labourers, such as during the grape or crop harvests, provided a strong attraction for the members of rural lower classes and often resulted in long-range travelling. But trade and industrial employment opportunities could also cause seasonal movement, as was the case with the bricklayers and carpenters of western Tyrol. Since the early modern period, itinerant trade has been a feature of the western parts of Austria in particular. The yearly seasonal work in the building trade in Germany and Austria was a widespread phenomenon in the villages of Tyrol and Vorarlberg and represented one of the main opportunities for additional employment for sub-peasant classes or smallholders. For children and teenagers, too, there was strong seasonal movement, but usually with different destinations and different employment (*Schwabenkinder*).[92] In Tyrol, entire families, who travelled together after spending the winter in the country, were called 'Laininger', 'Dörcher', and 'Karner'. These were landless itinerant traders.[93]

The itinerant trader is a characteristic type of the mobile rural lower class, to be differentiated from the seasonal worker because he is forced to travel in quite a different way. People travelled as pedlars in Tyrol, for example, in the Zillertal – a region that was shaped by the heavy decline of the mining industry, so that people were forced to seek new employment. The itinerant trade of the Zillertal people led them through the whole of Europe and in some cases even further. Later, they would have their own trading stations in places like Amsterdam and Hamburg. A catchment area of that size is of course not typical for the kind of trade common among the rural lower classes. Often, they sold the products produced in their home regions, such as metalwork from the Stubai valley, or whittle work from Gröden. The itinerant bird-dealers from Tyrol in particular grew to be very well known. But it was not exclusively products

92 For seasonal employment migration in Vorarlberg, see Arno Fitz, *Die Frühindustrialisierung Vorarlbergs und ihre Auswirkungen auf die Familienstruktur* (Dornbirn: Vorarlberger Verl.-Anst., 1985), 30–33; for Tyrol, see Wopfner, *Bergbauernbuch*, i, 384–402.

93 Wopfner, *Bergbauernbuch*, i, 399.

from the hometowns that were sold in long-distance trade. Tyrolean traders from the Paznaun, Ziller, and Defereggen valley sold goods that had been bought elsewhere – livestock, grains, wine, silks, gloves, fruit, woollen carpets, etc. – with a great turnover. The carpet trade from Deferegger reached even as far as Russia.[94] Such trade increased opportunities for upward social mobility. Itinerant trade and employment in the building trade were important factors in cultural transfer. Often, individual trade (*Kraxnträger*) developed into veritable haulage businesses and trading companies (for instance, in the Deferegger valley).[95]

The itinerant trade was, of course, not a form of employment open only to the rural lower classes; it also provided additional income for peasants. As a result, it did not absorb an already existing stratum of already existing people with little or no land – possibly because they were originally employed in the now-defunct mining industry – but actually caused an increasing partitioning of houses and land.[96] Thus, it represented a second way in which lower classes developed that was different from the way in which earlier rural lower classes that had grown out of other circumstances were provided a new economic basis.

Numerous rural craftsmen did not work in their own workshop but moved from farm to farm and received their wages partially in kind and through boarding. This is another, locally limited type of itinerant work, and those craftsmen are different from those itinerant traders who travelled long distances. This type made it possible for rural craftsmen to live as *Inwohner* without their own house. The execution of craftwork in the farmhouse was possible, especially when, at that time, the tools needed were easily transportable. But even weavers, whose working conditions rather forced them to settle, sometimes travelled from farm to farm, processing the farmers' spun flax on site. Separating home and workplace was something that was characteristic of many lines of business carried out by mobile rural lower classes; it was also characteristic of charcoal burners and miners. The charcoal burners were not allowed to leave their kilns for six weeks at a time, and thus were forced to stay away from their families for long periods of time.[97]

---

94 For the itinerant trade, see Wopfner, *Bergbauernbuch*, i, 391–95; Kröll and Stemberger, *Defereggen*, 202–14.

95 Kröll and Stemberger, *Defereggen*, 214–23.

96 For the Defereggental, see Kröll and Stemberger, *Defereggen*, 131.

97 Kröll and Stemberger, *Defereggen*, 189, 191. For charcoal burning, see Dinklage, *Geschichte*, 84; Gänser, 'Siedlungs- und Bevölkerungsentwicklung', 124; Gänser, 'Strukturveränderungen', 26, 28.

A special branch of itinerant work in Tyrol was that of forestry workers, who travelled to various places in Europe. Like bricklayers in the building trade, they were highly sought-out specialists for woodwork or for the transportation of tree trunks. In combination with mining (for instance, at the salt works), supplying wood for towns or the export of wood to Italy, opportunities for employment and stable settlement in the eastern Alpine region also existed. During the period in particular when mining was in its prime in Tyrol, forestry was in high demand.[98]

Similar to the seasonal itinerancy in the building trade, craftsmanship, too, was sometimes seasonal. The isolation of the individual farms certainly encouraged the necessity of learning some kind of craft or trade. 'Der Sattler kam im Winter auf die Stör' (the saddler visited in winter), Anna Starzer noted down. She also speaks of the shoemaker, who visited the farm for a week in winter after the slaughter of a calf, while the seamstress usually came twice a year, worked in the living rooms, and even brought an apprentice with her. Rural craftsmanship, be it settled or carried out as seasonal employment, was without a doubt an important branch of employment and additional income for those households who did not possess enough land. Amongst the numerous services that were regularly made use of by the farms, Starzer mentions smiths, wagoners, bricklayers, carpenters, coopers, thatchers, weavers, rope makers, and fountain builders.[99]

For Tyrol, the connection between agriculture and craft or trade has been noted as a special feature.[100] The lack of significance of possible restrictions on entering a town was certainly very positive for the dissemination of rural craft. Formal acceptance can also be seen in the existence of rural craft guilds. The connection between smallholders and the sub-peasant strata becomes especially apparent here. And in regard to the itinerant work in the building trade mentioned above, it is worth mentioning that in 1699 there were 644 bricklayers solely from the Lechtal who went abroad. In 1695, a main trade centre (*Hauptlade*) of the bricklayers, stonemasons, and carpenters had been established in Imst.[101] In the alpine region, the cottage or proto-industrial trade that was focused either on local or supra-regional sales offered a great number of employment opportunities. Above all, the textile production has been studied

98 Wopfner, *Bergbauernbuch*, i, 386, 569f., 575f., 614–16; Kröll and Stemberger, *Defereggen*, 184f.

99 Anna Starzer, *Die gute alte Zeit auf dem Bauernhof: Aufzeichnungen einer Bäuerin* (Naarn, 1990), 44–56.

100 Kröll and Stemberger, *Defereggen*, 189.

101 Wopfner, *Bergbauernbuch*, i, 356–61.

in this context.[102] Less well known is the production of blankets and rugs (in the Tyrolean Pustertal), the production of felt hats (in Hochtal Sexten, which already had a relevant guild at the beginning of the seventeenth century), knitting (in Paznautal), bobbing (in Gröden and the upper Inn valley), the production of straw hats (in Brixental), or other weaving work.[103] The metal trade was one of the main sectors of proto-industrialization in the eastern Alps, with a concentration in the pre-Alpine region of lower southwestern Austria, upper Austria, upper Styria, the upper Steiermark, Carinthia, and also in Tyrol, especially in the Stubai valley. Connected hereto were all the charcoal burners and forestry workers. The production of all sorts of wooden objects, such as tableware or toys, carved figures or the production of pipes, was certainly of great importance in the alpine region, though often ignored in studies of 'classic proto-industrialization'.[104]

3 Conclusion

Sub-peasant strata or rural lower classes existed in various forms in the eastern Alpine region in the late Middle Ages and the early modern period. This necessitates questions about the affiliation, social boundaries, and internal differentiations of these social groups. Possession of land and livestock is often, but not always, a useful criterion, and can lead to the much discussed problem of the fluid boundaries with the peasant classes. One approach, focusing on the type of landownership (for example, common land or land that was not originally seen as an integral part of a farm, so called *walzende Gründe*) can be useful in some places. Using house and landownership, it is also possible to trace important differences in the sub-peasant groups, for instance, between *Häusler* and entirely landless *Inwohner*. With *Inwohner* and servants in particular, it is not possible to talk about rural lower classes in a general way, due to different affiliations according to their life stage, occupation and social standing. When it comes to the economic foundations of the sub-peasant social groups, apart from the option of an occupation in labour-intensive agriculture, modes of

102 For Tyrol, see Wopfner, *Bergbauernbuch*, i, 361ff.; for Vorarlberg, see Fitz, *Die Frühindustrialisierung Vorarlbergs*; for an overview, see Markus Cerman, 'Proto-industrielle Entwicklung in Österreich', in Markus Cerman and Sheilagh C. Ogilvie (eds), *Proto-Industrialisierung in Europa: Industrielles Gewerbe vor dem Fabrikzeitalter* (Vienna: Verlag für Gesellschaftskritik, 1994), 161–75.

103 Wopfner, *Bergbauernbuch*, i, 366–75.

104 Wopfner, *Bergbauernbuch*, i, 376–80.

employment were available that can be connected with two types of lower-class formation. On the one hand, the lower classes that had emerged due to agricultural differentiation but mainly also due to the decline in mining industry took up employment in local or itinerant trade. On the other hand, mixed employment or employment in itinerant trade enabled the growing partitioning of land and was one reason for the move away from a mainly agricultural rural economy. In the regions of western Austria in particular, the *Saumhandel* and the flow of trade across the Alps, together with the decline in mining, created the foundation for a reorientation towards trade and itinerancy. We must therefore distinguish between regional and supra-regional factors of influence on the emergence of rural lower classes. Forms of itinerant trade and labour migration could sometimes lead to added growth in a region, irrespective of its economic circumstances. In the shadow of commercial proto-industrialization, economic and social history has studied the manifold branches of the rural cottage industry, the itinerant trade, and forms of mixed employment in comparatively little detail. When it comes to the position of the sub-peasant strata in the late medieval and early modern alpine region, this essay has been able to identify clear research lacunae.

Active Manorial Lords and Peasant Farmers in the Economic Life of the Late Middle Ages: Results from New Swiss and German Research

Stefan Sonderegger

In German medieval historiography, the model idea that there had been a gradual change from the manorial system, from the high to late medieval period, is widespread.[1] It is understood mainly as the process in which manorial demesne farming was replaced by the lease of land in exchange for duties as well as that of the manorial lords' gradual pulling back from agricultural production. The manorial system of the late medieval period is characterized as *Rentengrundherrschaft*.[2] Newer empirical studies of the fourteenth, fifteenth, and sixteenth centuries, however, point in a different direction: regional studies analysing pragmatic written sources, such as interest ledgers and account books, show that many manorial lords were now more than ever taking an interest in their farmers' agricultural business, without completely giving up

1 One basic difficulty in describing the Swiss and German circumstances in English is the translation of the key terms. In the present text the following terms are used: the German word '*Grundherrschaft*' is described as 'manorial system' or 'manorial lordship', '*Grundherr*' as 'manorial lord' or 'landlord'. 'Manorial demesne' in this paper is used to refer to such land as the manorial lord farmed for himself instead of parcelling out the land in leasehold in return for payment in duties; this is equivalent to the German term '*grundherrliche Eigenwirtschaft*'. To avoid misunderstandings, it is also necessary to define what is meant here by 'lease/leasehold'. The literal translation into German as '*verpachten/Pacht*' is not applicable, as a modern lease is free of manorial ties, which is not the case for the late medieval circumstances in the region of northwestern Switzerland and southeastern Germany described in this section. In these circumstances, 'lease' is translated as '*belehnen*' or '*verleihen*' in return for duties and other obligations. The land leased to farmers by manorial lords (*Grundherren*) to be tilled are 'peasant fiefs' ('*Bauernlehen*') within the manorial system. This means that land was leased out in tenure to tenant farmers, who paid the manorial lord (*Grundherr*) various duties, at times connected to personal obligations.

2 In older scholarship, notably Friedrich Lütge, *Geschichte der deutschen Agrarverfassung vom frühen Mittelalter bis zum 19. Jahrhundert*, 2nd edn, Deutsche Agrargeschichte, 3 (Stuttgart: E. Ulmer, 1967), 56. In the late Middle Ages, feudal lords had detached themselves more and more from agricultural production, producing a *reine* (*absolute*) *Renten-Grundherrschaft*. Newer scholarship is more differentiated, seeing a tendency to disengage from the peasant economy. Werner Rösener, *Grundherrschaft im Wandel. Untersuchungen zur Entwicklung geistlicher Grundherrschaften im südwestdeutschen Raum vom 9. bis 14. Jahrhundert*, Veröffentlichungen des Max-Planck-Instituts für Geschichte, 102 (Göttingen, 1991), 563.

 | DOI:10.1163/9789004433458_012

demesne farming (*Eigenwirtschaft*). It seems, then, as if two oppositional interpretations of late medieval manorialism were in place. How is this to be explained?

The aim of the present article is to show how many late medieval manorial lords were highly engaged and were able to adapt to ever-changing situations.[3] For this reason, everyday relations have been studied, mainly of an economic nature between peasant farmers and their lords, and thus, the still-widespread idea of a solidified[4] manorial system in the later Middle Ages has been put into perspective. To do this, an open approach has been used: the late medieval manorial system is seen as sphere of action, in which the interests of landlord and peasant farmer were repeatedly negotiated.[5]

Manorial lords and peasant farmers of the late Middle Ages and the early modern period came into contact mainly over economic resources. In this, many forms of cooperation between the two parties existed. This article looks at the collaboration in agricultural practice and the associated rural manual labour, as well as the exchange of goods; it shall be shown that special forms of exchange existed alongside the official markets, organized by the lords.

The results presented here are based on studies of German-speaking Switzerland[6] and the neighbouring regions of southern Germany and Austria. This

---

3 Hans-Jörg Gilomen, *Die Grundherrschaft des Basler Cluniazenser-Priorates St.Alban im Mittelalter: Ein Beitrag zur Wirtschaftsgeschichte am Oberrhein*, Quellen und Forschungen zur Basler Geschichte, 9 (Basel: F. Reinhardt, 1977), 194–95.

4 Lütge, *Geschichte der deutschen Agrarverfassung*, 193, even mentions, in relation to the southwestern part of the territory, a *Versteinerung* (*petrifaction*) of manorialism.

5 The scholarship and discussion of manorialism are lengthy and not easy to digest at a glance. The approach used here orientates itself mainly through the regional studies on rural society in Switzerland that are mentioned. See also Heide Wunder, *Die bäuerliche Gemeinde in Deutschland*, Kleine Vandenhoeck-Reihe 1483 (Göttingen 1986), who coined the phrase 'Herrschaft mit Bauern' (rule with peasants) for the late Middle Ages. Furthermore, the detailed study of the monastery of Salem by Katherine Brun, *The Abbot and His Peasants: Territorial Formation in Salem from the Later Middle Ages to the Thirty Years War*, Quellen und Forschungen zur Agrargeschichte, 56 (Stuttgart: Lucius & Lucius, 2013), which summarizes the relationship between abbey and vassals in the following terms on p. 415: 'It was a multidirectional bargaining process that involved shifting alliances, unequal partnerships, reciprocity, compromise, and even cooperation among various groups'. From the perspective of legal history, see Sigrid Hirbodian, 'Recht und Ordnung im Dorf. Zur Bedeutung von Weistümern und Dorfordnungen in Spätmittelalter und Frühneuzeit', in Kurt Andermann and Oliver Auge (eds), *Dorf und Gemeinde. Grundstrukturen der ländlichen Gesellschaft in Spätmittelalter und Frühneuzeit*, Kraichtaler Kolloquien, 8 (Epfendorf, 2012), 45–63, at p. 63.

6 In Switzerland, manorialism and rural society has been studied mainly by the Zurich professors Roger Sablonier and Hans-Jörg Gilomen, and their students. An overview of the work produced under Sablonier is given by Thomas Meier and Roger Sablonier (eds), *Wirtschaft und Herrschaft: Beiträge zur ländlichen Gesellschaft in der östlichen Schweiz (1200–1800)* (Zurich: Chronos, 1999). Taking as a starting point a single secular or ecclesiastical manor, these

region is ideal for a research paper for a variety of reasons. Here, ever since the High Middle Ages, one can find significant manorial lords of various types – ecclesiastical and aristocratic, as well as lay-urban.[7] The main ecclesiastical lord was the Abbey of St Gall, which was founded in the eighth century and was an important imperial monastery with extended property on both sides of Lake Constance. During the fifteenth and sixteenth centuries, the abbey expanded its manorial lordship into a territorial lordship in eastern Switzerland. Until the abolition of the monastery in 1803, the prince-abbot of St Gall owned one of the largest territories in the Swiss confederation. Newer studies have been conducted on this ancient Benedictine monastery, situated in the town of St Gallen,[8] and on the Fraumünster in Zurich.[9] More recent studies have also examined the newer institutions of the High and late Middle Ages, such as the Dominican priory St Katharinental in Diessenhofen in the Thurgau,[10] the

studies examined not only the organization of lordships but especially the relations between representatives of the manorial lord and the peasant farmers. Thus, the relevant findings for the study of the history of rural society in pre-modern times were formulated. Cf. Julien Demade, 'The Medieval Countryside in German-language Historiography since the 1930s', in Isabel Alfonso Antón (ed.), *The Rural History of Medieval European Societies: Trends and Perspectives*, The Medieval Countryside, 1 (Turnhout: Brepols, 2007), 173–252, at pp. 233–36. A bibliography of the newer literature about rural society in German-speaking Switzerland can be found in Katja Hürlimann and Stefan Sonderegger, 'Ländliche Gesellschaft im Mittelalter', *Traverse*, 18/1 (2011), 48–76.

7 For the characterization of different types of manorial lords in the region, see Dorothee Rippmann, 'Wirtschaft und Sozialstruktur auf dem Land im Spätmittelalter', in Kanton Basel-Land (ed.) *Nah dran, weit weg: Geschichte des Kantons Basel-Landschaft* 2 (Liestal, 2001), 139–64, at pp. 140–46.

8 Johannes Duft, Anton Gössi and Werner Vogler, *Die Abtei St. Gallen: Abriss der Geschichte, Kurzbiographien der Äbte, das stift-sanktgallische Offizialat* (St Gallen, 1986). Philip Robinson, *Die Fürstabtei St.Gallen und ihr Territorium 1463–1529: Eine Studie zur Entwicklung territorialer Staatlichkeit*, Sankt Galler Kultur und Geschichte, 24 (St Gallen, 1995). Philipp Lenz, *Reichsabtei und Klosterreform: Das Kloster St. Gallen unter dem Pfleger und Abt Ulrich Rösch (1457–1491)*, Monasterium Sancti Galli, 6 (St Gallen: Verlag am Klosterhof, 2014).

9 Christa Köppel, Von der Äbtissin zu den gnädigen Herren: Untersuchungen zu Wirtschaft und Verwaltung der Fraumünsterabtei und des späteren Fraumünsteramts in Zürich, 1418–1549 (Zurich: Chronos, 1991).

10 Erwin Eugster and Verena Baumer-Müller, 'St. Katharinenthal', in *Helvetia Sacra. Abteilung IV, Die Orden mit Augustinerregel*, v, no. 2: *Die Dominikaner und Dominikanerinnen in der Schweiz* (Basel, 1999), 780–840; Albert Knöpfli, *Das Kloster Sankt Katharinenthal*, die Kunstdenkmäler des Kantons Thurgau, 4 (Basel: Wiese, 1989). Peter Erni, 'Geschriebene Landschaft. Der Wandel von Kulturlandschaft und Güterstruktur in Basadingen nach dem Schriftgut des Klosters St. Katharinental (14.-18.Jh.)', *Thurgauer Beiträge zur Geschichte*, 137 (2000), 1–231.

Cistercian Abbey Magdenau[11] to the west of St Gallen, the Dominican women's priory St Catherine in the town of St Gallen,[12] and the Premonstratensian abbey Rüti in Zurich,[13] which I shall make use of here, as well as those of the Cistercian abbey of Salem[14] and the Benedictine monasteries of Reichenau,[15] Ellwangen, and Scheyern in southern Germany.[16]

The current state of research is fruitful in relation to the urban institutions that act as manorial lords. Here, one can mention the Heiliggeist hospital in St Gallen,[17] which was founded in 1228, as well as St Gallen's leprosarium, which

---

11 Christian Schäfli, 'Herrschaft und Wirtschaft des Klosters Magdenau im ausgehenden Mittelalter: Edition und Analyse des Lehenbuches des Zisterzienserinnenklosters Magdenau', Master's thesis, University of Zurich, Zurich, 2008.

12 Rezia Krauer, Stefan Sonderegger, Claudia Sutter and Monika Michel-Rüegg, 'Klosterfrauen wirtschaften', in Katrin Eberhard and Ursula Hasler (eds), *St. Katharinen. Frauenkloster, Bibliothek, Bildungsstätte – Gestern und Heute* (Herisau: Appenzeller Verlag, 2013), 112–76; Simone Mengis, *Schreibende Frauen um 1500. Scriptorium und Bibliothek des Dominikanerinnenklosters St. Katharina St. Gallen*, Scrinium Friburgense, 28 (Berlin, 2013).

13 Alfred Zangger, *Grundherrschaft und Bauern: Eine wirtschafts- und sozialgeschichtliche Untersuchung der Grundherrschaft der Prämonstratenserabtei Rüti (ZH) im Spätmittelalter* (Zurich, 1991).

14 Brun, *The Abbot and His Peasants*.

15 Harald Derschka (ed.), *Die Reichenauer Lehenbücher der Äbte Friedrich von Zollern (1402–1427) und Friedrich von Wartenberg (1428–1453)*, Veröffentlichungen der Kommission für geschichtliche Landeskunde in Baden-Württemberg, Reihe A/Quellen, 61 (Stuttgart, 2018).

16 Shami Ghosh, 'The Imperial Abbey of Ellwangen and Its Tenants: A Study of the Polyptych of 1337', *Agricultural History Review*, 62/2 (2014), 187–209. The author is of the opinion that – in opposition to the general opinion of current scholarship – the strong commercialization of English agriculture was not an exception. Similarly, strong tendencies to commercialism are visible in the region of southern Germany-eastern Switzerland-Austria at the same time. For this in greater detail, and a comprehensive knowledge of the literature, see Shami Ghosh, 'Rural Commercialisation in Fourteenth-century Bavaria: The Evidence from Scheyern Abbey', *Vierteljahresschrift für Sozial- und Wirtschaftsgeschichte*, 2017/1 (2017), 52–77. From my own research and knowledge of the literature, I must agree with Ghosh. That England is seen as an exception by scholars has to do with the fact that much of the pertinent literature dealing with Germany, Austria, and Switzerland is in German and comprises regional studies that have not been received widely enough outside the German-speaking regions. See also Govind P. Sreenivasan, 'Beyond the Village: Recent Approaches to the Social History of the Early German Peasantry', *History Compass*, 11/1 (2013), 47–64.

17 Stefan Sonderegger, *Landwirtschaftliche Entwicklung in der spätmittelalterlichen Nordostschweiz: Eine Untersuchung ausgehend von den wirtschaftlichen Aktivitäten des Heiliggeist-Spitals St. Gallen*, St Galler Kultur und Geschichte, 22, published dissertations, University of Zurich (St Gallen: Buchhandlung am Rössliter, 1994); Stefan Sonderegger, 'The Financing Strategy of a Major Urban Hospital in the Late Middle Ages (St Gallen fifteenth

is first mentioned in 1225.[18] Additional information comes from the studies of hospitals in Lucerne[19] and Zurich,[20] as well as of the monastery of St Albans,[21] of the hospital in Basel,[22] and of hospitals in the regions north of Lake Constance.[23] There are also some very interesting studies concerning the region

century)', in Francesco Ammannati (ed.), *Assistenza e solidarietà in Europa, secc. XIII–XVIII, atti della 'Quarantaquattresima Settimana di Studi', 22–26 aprile 2012* (Social Assistance and Solidarity in Europe from the Thirteenth to the Eighteenth Centuries), Istituto internazionale di storia economica F. Datini, 2 (Florence: Florence University Press, 2013), 209–26.

18 Pascale Sutter, *'Arme Siechen': Das St.Galler Siechenhaus Linsebühl im Spätmittelalter und in der frühen Neuzeit*, St Galler Kultur und Geschichte, 26 (St Gallen, 1996).

19 Stefan Jäggi, 'Die Rechnung des Heilig-Geist-Spitals von Luzern für die Jahre 1502–1507', *Der Geschichtsfreund. Mitteilungen des Historischen Vereins der Zentralschweiz*, 143 (1990), 5–69.

20 Daniela Schwab, 'Das Urbar des Zürcher Heiliggeistspitals aus dem 15. Jahrhundert: Edition und Kommentar', Master's thesis, University of Zurich, Zurich, 2013.

21 Gilomen, *Die Grundherrschaft des Basler Cluniazenser-Priorates*.

22 Michaela von Tscharner-Aue, *Die Wirtschaftsführung des Basler Spitals bis zum Jahre 1500: Ein Beitrag zur Geschichte der Löhne und Preise*, Quellen und Forschungen zur Basler Geschichte, 12 (Basel, 1983).

23 Christian Heimpel, *Die Entwicklung der Einnahmen und Ausgaben des Heiliggeistspitals zu Biberach an der Riss von 1500 bis 1630*, Quellen und Forschungen zur Agrargeschichte, 15 (Stuttgart, 1966); Bernhard Zeller, *Das Heilig-Geist-Spital zu Lindau im Bodensee, von seinen Anfängen bis zum Ausgang des 16. Jahrhunderts*, Schwäbische Geschichtsquellen und Forschungen, 4 (Lindau, 1952); Alfons Semler, *Geschichte des Heilig-Geist-Spitals in Überlingen am Bodensee* (Überlingen, 1957); Klaus Militzer, *Das Markgröninger Heilig-Geist-Spital im Mittelalter: Ein Beitrag zur Wirtschaftsgeschichte des 15. Jahrhunderts*, VuF Sonderband, 19 (Sigmaringen, 1975). Ulrich Knefelkamp, *Das Heilig-Geist-Spital in Nürnberg vom 14.–17. Jahrhundert. Geschichte, Struktur, Alltag*, Nürnberger Forschungen, 26 (Nuremberg: Verein für Geschichte der Stadt Nürnberg, 1989). Cf. general research for the hospitals from an economic perspective: Holger R. Stunz, 'Hospitäler im deutschsprachigen Raum im Spätmittelalter als Unternehmen für die "caritas": Typen und Phasen der Finanzierung', in Michael Matheus (ed.), *Funktions- und Strukturwandel spätmittelalterlicher Hospitäler im europäischen Vergleich*, Geschichtliche Landeskunde, 56 (Stuttgart, 2005), 129–59; see further Michel Pauly, 'Von der Fremdenherberge zum Seniorenheim: Funktionswandel in mittelalterlichen Hospitälern an ausgewählten Beispielen aus dem Maas-Mosel-Rhein-Raum', in Michael Matheus (ed.), *Funktions- und Strukturwandel spätmittelalterlicher Hospitäler im europäischen Vergleich*, Geschichtliche Landeskunde, 56 (Stuttgart, 2005), 101–16. Cf. Oliver Landolt, 'Finanzielle und wirtschaftliche Aspekte der Sozialpolitik spätmittelalterlicher Spitäler', in Neithard Bulst and Karl-Heinz Spiess (eds), *Sozialgeschichte mittelalterlicher Hospitäler*, VuF, 65 (Ostfildern: Jan Thorbecke, 2007), 273–99; Martin Scheutz, Andrea Sommerlechner, Herwig Weigl, and Alfred Stefan Weiss (eds), *Quellen zur europäischen Spitalgeschichte in Mittelalter und Früher Neuzeit*, Quelleneditionen des Instituts für Österreichische Geschichtsforschung, 5 (Vienna, 2010). Lies Vervaet, 'Goederenbeheer in een veranderende samenleving Het Sint-Janshospitaal van Brugge ca. 1275–ca. 1575', PhD thesis, University of Ghent, Ghent, 2014. Lies Vervaet, 'Het

around Basel that have been undertaken from an economic and socio-historical viewpoint.[24]

This research indicates that there are various types of manorial lords represented in a relatively small region. Amongst these, we find one very old, very large monastery, and new ones that were only founded at the beginning of the late medieval period; besides these ecclesiastical institutions, there are also secular ones. Due to these differences, we must pose the question of whether there were specific forms of relationships between the different lords and their peasant farmers. For example, it is probable that great differences existed between an old Benedictine monastery like that of St Gall and a secular institution like a communal hospital which was only founded in the transition to the late medieval period, differences in the way they were organized, managed their economy, and interacted with their peasant farmers.

1 De facto Manorial Lords

Economic relations between lords and peasant farmers in the late medieval and early modern period were largely bound to the land, the management of which was essential in order to safeguard the livelihood of both lords and peasant farmers. The lords gave their land to the peasant in return for duties; the tenure was based on a *quid pro quo* contract. The contribution of the lord was his giving the land in tenure to those willing to work it, theirs was to pay duties in the form of interest, paid in natural produce and money, tithes, and possibly manual labour. These economic, legal, and manorial bonds created the relationship between lord and peasant farmer that governed their daily life.

But the relationship between them was not simply a dual one. In reality, there were various participants, as a look at the situation in the eastern part of Switzerland in the late Middle Ages shows. During my editorial work for the

Brugse Sint-Janshospitaal en zijn grote hoevepachters in de 15e en 16e eeuw: wederkerigheid en continuïteit in functie van voedselzekerheid', *Revue Belge de Philologie et d'Histoire / Belgisch Tijdschrift voor Filologie en Geschiedenis* 90/4 (2012), 1121–54.

24 Mireille Othenin-Girard, *Ländliche Lebensweise und Lebensformen im Spätmittelalter: Eine wirtschafts- und sozialgeschichtliche Untersuchung der Herrschaft Farnsburg*, Quellen und Forschungen zur Geschichte und Landeskunde des Kantons Basel-Landschaft, 48 (Liestal, 1994). Dorothee Rippmann, *Bauern und Städter. Stadt-Land-Beziehungen im 15. Jahrhundert: das Beispiel Basel, unter besonderer Berücksichtigung der Nahmarktbeziehungen und der sozialen Verhältnisse im Umland*, Basler Beiträge zur Geschichtswissenschaft, 159 (Basel, 1990).

Chartularium Sangallense,[25] I was able to view the entire inventory of documents of northeastern Switzerland up to 1411. In this new edition, many previously unknown documents which provide information about legal and economic history have been included. It is noticeable that alongside the monastery of St Gall, there were many other actors who could be consider manorial lords, according to the role they played with regard to the peasant farmers. This makes it vital to first clarify the legal position of the lords who came into contact with peasant farmers. It is my opinion that until now studies of rural society have not sufficiently taken the actual ownership and lordship situation into account. By looking at the now fully edited and extensive archival material of the imperial monastery and town of St Gallen, it is possible to show what I mean by this and what conclusions can be drawn from it.[26]

In the east of Switzerland, the Benedictine abbey of St Gall held the overlordship (*dominium directum / Obereigentum*) over most of the land. The abbey rarely cultivated the land itself, but leased it to, among others, townspeople and urban institutions such as the communal hospital, the leprosorium, or new urban monasteries. The old abbey of St Gall thus continued to hold the overlordship, *the dominium directum*, over the land. Citizens and communal institutions were the abbey's tenants with all the associated rights, that is, the holders of the *dominium indirectum / Untereigentum*.[27] However, these urban actors rarely worked the land themselves; instead, they subleased it to peasant farmers in the region in return for duties in natural produce and money, as well

---

25 This is a new edition of the deed books of the abbey of St Gall in the project Chartularium Sangallense by Otto P. Clavadetscher (vols iii-vii) and Stefan Sonderegger (vols viii-xiii). The new edition contains around 40 percent more documents than the old deed book. Cf. Stefan Sonderegger, 'Vom Nutzen der Neubearbeitung einer regionalen Urkundenedition. Dargestellt am Chartularium Sangallense', in Theo Kölzer, Willibald Rosner, and Roman Zehetmayer (eds), *Regionale Urkundenbücher: Die Vorträge der 12. Tagung der Commission Internationale de Diplomatique*, Nöla, 14 (St Pölten: Niederösterreichisches Institut für Landeskunde, 2010), 86–116.

26 The graphic models used here in the discussion are based on the studies of subleasing / subtenures carried out in the dissertation completed under my supervision by Rezia Krauer, 'Die Beteiligung städtischer Akteure am ländlichen Bodenmarkt: Die Region St. Gallen im 13. und 14. Jahrhundert', PhD thesis, University of Zurich, Zurich, 2018 (currently in press). For sub-leasehold in Switzerland, see also Gilomen, *Die Grundherrschaft des Basler Cluniazenser-Priorates*, 209. Subtenure is a subject that has not yet been studied thoroughly enough in German research.

27 The amount first tenants (the holders of the *dominium indirectum / Untereigentum*) had to pay in rent to the holder of the overlordship (*Rekognitionszins*) is not recorded, when the act of paying rent is recorded at all, but, in any case, this is not the subject studied here. For the income of the monastery of St Gall, see Robinson, *Die Fürstabtei St. Gallen*, 160–67.

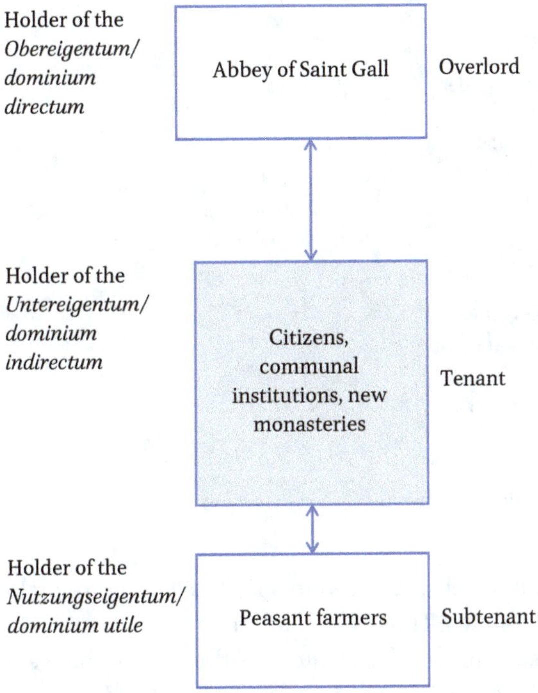

FIGURE 11.1 Visual representation of subtenure

as to others, partially bound to serfdom.[28] These subtenants – the peasant farmers – were the ones who used the territory for agricultural use; they were the holders of the *dominium utile / Nutzungseigentum*.[29] In this way, the holders of the *dominium indirectum*, that is, the citizens, urban institutions, and new monasteries, were in fact made into manorial lords themselves, who received duties from their subtenants who actually cultivated the land.

28 An example of this were the so-called '*Fasnachtshühner*' (Carneval chickens), which the wine farmers of the urban hospital of St Gallen were obliged to pay in the mid-fifteenth century. StadtASG SpA, C, 2, fol. 31v and 32r.

29 Gilomen, *Die Grundherrschaft des Basler Cluniazenser-Priorates*, 209–11. The peasants in subtenure could themselves sublease parts of their land, as in theory the system of subtenure was open to the bottom, but this is difficult to find sources for. For leases of land between farmers, see Tim Soens and Erik Thoen, 'The Origins of Leasehold in the Former County of Flanders', 31–55, at p. 47; further, for England, see Jane Whittle, 'Leasehold Tenure in England *c.* 1300–*c.* 1600: Its Form and Incidence', 139–54, and Miriam Müller, 'Peasants, Lords and Developments in Leasing in Later Medieval England', 155–78, all three in Bas J.P. van Bavel and Philipp R. Schofield (eds), *The Development of Leasehold in Northwestern Europe, c. 1200–1600*, (Turnhout: Brepols, 2008).

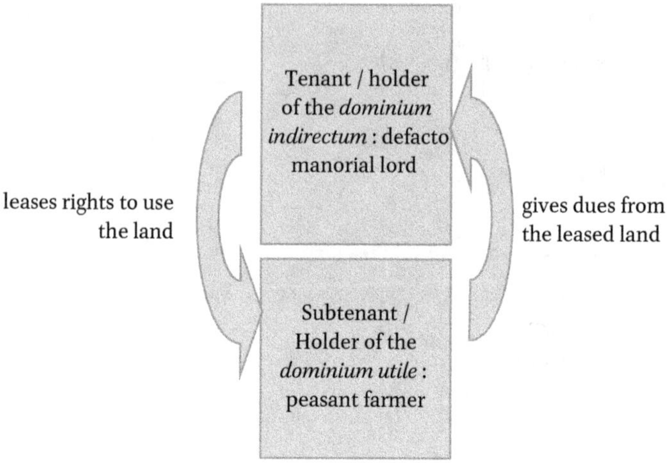

FIGURE 11.2 Visual representation of de facto lordship

The results that I present in this article are based to a large extent on the relations between tenants and subtenants. Thus, the relationships are examined at the level of subleasing. It was at this level that most of the contact between lords and peasant farmers took place, since the farmers were not in direct contact with the overlord (the holder of the *dominium directum*), but with some of his tenants (the holders of *dominium indirectum*); the latter took the de facto position of the manorial lord, not only acting as representative of the overlord, but widely independent of him and with his own distinct interests.[30]

2 Peasant Agriculture – Cooperation and Dependencies

Peasant agriculture was connected intimately with their lords. Swiss studies on the history of rural society in the late Middle Ages based on the example of different manorial systems reach the same conclusion on one important point: between landlord and peasant farmer there was not simply a bond of duties but instead a complex relationship based on exchange. The following will show peasant agriculture in the interplay of cooperation and dependence between manorial lord and tenant. Those called 'tenants' in the following are generally 'subtenants / peasant farmers' according to the model above.

30 Therefore, the common term of '*Herrschaftsdelegation*' (delegation of lordship) is not applicable here.

2.1 *Constancy in the Relationship with the Manorial Lord*

The quality of the relationship between peasants and lords depended greatly on the conditions on which the lords gave their land to the peasant farmers in tenure. In the north of Switzerland, there are two contrasting legal forms in the late Middle Ages: the temporary (Zeitleihe) and the hereditary tenure (*Erbleihe*).[31]

The *Zeitleihe* is a non-hereditary, time limited right of use of the land.[32] The specified period of lease could be from one year to twenty-five years. In the female Cistercian monastery in Magdenau in the canton of St Gallen, where the *Zeitleihe* was the most common type of lease on the brink of the sixteenth century, fifteen years was the most common time period.[33] In the Premonstratensian monastery of Rüti in Zurich, lease periods of one, two, three, five, seven, eight, ten, twelve, and twenty-five years are known, though the three-year period was by far the most common. This may well have to do with the three-year cycle of crop rotation.[34] The three-year, short-term lease could have been a kind of trial period, where after the so-called '*Umschnitt*', the three-year contract was either dissolved or replaced by a contract that was more profitable for the tenant. This could have been beneficial for both parties; it allowed the monastery to judge the capabilities of the tenant farmer, and the latter to judge the quality of the land, its productivity, and yield. Regarded in this light, the short-term lease can be seen as the normal precursor to a longer, fixed-term lease or even to a hereditary tenure.[35] Despite its benefits, the short-term lease would have been a risky type of lease, not conducive to furthering the initiative of the tenant in working and managing the farm.[36]

The high legal and economic availability of the land given as leasehold, that evolved from the long-term use, is the most important criterion distinguishing

31 As a comparison to the situation in northwestern Europe, see Bas J.P. van Bavel and Philipp R. Schofield (eds), *The Development of Leasehold in Northwestern Europe, c. 1200–1600* (Turnhout: Brepols, 2008).

32 Karl Otto Scherner, 'Art. Zeitpacht', in Albrecht Cordes, Bernd Kannowski, Hans-Peter Haferkamp, et al. (eds), *Handwörterbuch zur deutschen Rechtsgeschichte*, v (Berlin, 1998), para. 1645–46.

33 Schäfli, 'Herrschaft und Wirtschaft', 39.

34 Zangger, *Grundherrschaft und Bauern*, 392.

35 Temporary leases could, as shown by Rippmann, be dependent on location. Leases close to the town in Basel were always for a short period only. The urban workspaces were allotted at a high rate in the period before the fifteenth century. Thus, the type of *Zeitleihe* there had to do with the high rentability of the territory. Rippmann, *Bauern und Städter*, 240–301.

36 Rippmann, *Bauern und Städter*, 397, esp. 129.

the hereditary tenure from the temporary lease. A farm could, in theory, be managed over many generations by the same family. The holders of hereditary tenure had great control over the land they held in lease. They could sell,[37] sublease, or mortgage either parts of the fief, or rights of use of the land held in hereditary tenure. In theory, the consent of the overlord was necessary, which can be seen in documents where sellers ask their lord to agree to a sale of land to a new tenant or to take on a new subtenant. Conflicts between lord and tenant that ensued after the latter had sold their land or the rights to it without the consent of their lords show that in fact the holders of an hereditary tenure did view themselves as owners.[38] Hereditary tenures could be dangerous for the landlord, as it resulted in the slow but continuous estrangement from legal claims.[39] On the other hand, and this is a relevant difference from short-term

37 The possibility of a sale allows for the conclusion that within the rural community there was a market for lands and rights connected to land that has not yet been sufficiently studied. Exceptions to this are Rippmann, *Bauern und Städter*, and recently decisively Krauer, 'Die Beteiligung städtischer'. For this subject in general, see Markus Cerman, 'Bodenmärkte und ländliche Wirtschaft in vergleichender Sicht: England und das östliche Mitteleuropa im Spätmittelalter', *Jahrbuch für Wirtschaftsgeschichte*, 2 (2004), 125–50; Markus Cerman, 'Social Structure and Land Markets in Late Medieval Central and East-central Europe', *Continuity and Change*, 23/1 (2008), 55–100; Bas J.P. van Bavel, 'The Organization and Rise of Land and Lease Markets in Northwestern Europe and Italy, *c.* 1000–1800', *Continuity and Change*, 23/1 (2008), 13–54; Volker Stamm, 'Kauf und Verkauf von Land und Grundrenten im hohen und späten Mittelalter: Eine Untersuchung zur historischen Wirtschaftsanthropologie', *Vierteljahresschrift für Sozial- und Wirtschaftsgeschichte*, 2009/1 (2009), 33–43.

38 Cf. Peter Liver, 'Zur Entstehung des freien bäuerlichen Grundeigentums', *Zeitschrift für Schweizerisches Recht*, 65 (1946), 329–60; Otto P. Clavadetscher, 'Die Annäherung der spätmittelalterlichen Erbleihe im nordalpinen Graubünden an das freie Grundeigentum', in Ludwig Petry (ed.), *Festschrift für Johannes Bärmann*, part 1, Geschichtliche Landeskunde, 3 (Wiesbaden: F. Steiner, 1966), 27–44; Martin Salzmann, 'Heimfall eines verwirkten Lehens. Motive und Hintergründe zu einem Prozess aus dem Thurgau des 16. Jahrhunderts', in Clausdieter Schott and Eva Petrig Schuler (eds), *Festschrift für Claudio Soliva zum 65. Geburtstag* (Zurich, 1994), 233–52.

39 For examples of conflicts between lords and farmers concerning claims of ownership, see Stefan Sonderegger, 'Das erste Zinsbuch: Spiegel von Wirtschaft und Gesellschaft im Spätmittelalter', in Katrin Eberhard and Ursula Hasler (eds), *St. Katharinen: Frauenkloster, Bibliothek, Bildungsstätte – Gestern und Heute* (Herisau, 2013), 134–37. See also Claudia Sutter, 'Frankrüti, Berg SG: Wirtschafts- und Konfliktgeschichte eines spätmittelalterlichen Hofes unter dem Kloster St. Katharinen St. Gallen', Master's thesis, University of Zurich, Zurich, 2012; Walter Müller, 'Gelehrte, Juristen und bäuerliche Urteilsfinder in einem sanktgallischen Lehenprozess', in W. Lendi (ed.), *Festgabe für Paul Staerkle zu seinem 80. Geburtstag am 26. März 1972*, St Galler Kultur und Geschichte, 2 (St Gallen, 1972), 64–75. Compare also Salzmann, 'Heimfall eines verwirkten Lehens'.

leases, the larger scope for action and the possibility of passing on the land to one's family motivated those with an hereditary tenure to a far greater extent to apply their own initiative. This was largely encouraged, for instance, by urban and secular manorial lords.

The type of lease used most often by the Heiliggeist hospital in the town of St Gallen when giving land in leasehold to peasant farmers from the region was hereditary tenure. This indicates that it was important to the manorial lords to maintain good relations with the tenant over the years. The hereditary tenure favoured continuity in the agricultural management of the land. Farms were in the same hands for decades. Thus, the environment changed only marginally, and the contacts on both sides remained the same for a long period of time, only altering over the generations. The parties knew each other, and a trusting relationship between manorial lord and tenant farmer could be built up. Both sides could profit from the fact that the land remained in the family over generations: if a son inherited from his father, he would be familiar with the land from the beginning and would know exactly what to look out for and how to work it,[40] quite different from when a family newly took over a farm and first needed to familiarize themselves with its running.[41]

One method used by the landlords to keep their tenants on the farm was to allow and encourage ways of generating additional income, for example, through the transport of grain, wine, empty barrels of wine, straw, or especially wood. Sometimes tenant farmers would also carry out building work for their lords.[42]

2.2 *Labour and Agricultural Cooperation between Farmers and Lords*

Further opportunities for additional income for the families of peasant farmers came through cooperation of manorial lord and tenant when it came to structural investment on the farm. In the case of the most important secular

---

40 Michael Mitterauer, 'Mittelalter', in Andreas Gestrich, Jens-Uwe Krause, and Michael Mitterauer (eds), *Geschichte der Familie* (Stuttgart, 2003), 160–363, at p. 300.

41 Adrian Zwahlen, *Die wirtschaftliche Entwicklung der Schoretshueb: Eine Mikrogeschichte zur spätmittelalterlichen Getreideproduktion in der spezialisierten Landwirtschaft der Nordostschweiz* (Zurich, 2012), 105–06, Table 3. The farm Schoretshueb of the St Gallen hospital is a model example of the constancy enabled through hereditary tenure in the relations between landlord and tenant farmer, looked at by Schwab, 'Das Urbar des Zürcher Heiliggeistspitals'. The constancy is expressed in the long period of time that the farm remained in the same family – more than a hundred years. The inheritance of the sons of the following generation was a longstanding tradition in this instance.

42 Schwab, 'Das Urbar des Zürcher Heiliggeistspitals', 87–93.

manorial lord in the town of St Gallen – the communal hospital, which was an active participant in the rural economy due to commercial interests – this is very well documented in the administrative archival records. As opposed to the usual maintenance of the farm, which was the duty of the tenant, renovations and new buildings were financially subsidized by the hospital as landlord, by allowing the tenants a reduction of the duties undertaken as manual labour and its associated expenses. These renovations and new building works presented an opportunity for the tenant to pay his duties not only with agricultural produce but also through different services. Alongside those times in the annual cycle when the farmer was fully occupied with agricultural duties, there were other times in which diverse work was possible that provided the family additional income. Such work is well documented when it comes to woodcraft, for instance, in the reduction of duties for the manufacturing of wooden shingles,[43] or for cutting, preparing, and delivering of wood.[44] New buildings or renovations on the farms were usually carried out by lords and tenant farmers together; both had a vested interest in them. Special initiatives of the tenant were supported financially by the lords because they served to preserve or increase the value of the farm. Similar work undertaken autonomously by the tenant was 'pre-financed' by him and compensated for by the lord in the case of his departure from the leasehold.[45]

Since, according to legal practice, wooden buildings and especially such buildings as stables or granaries were counted as movable goods, the tenant could be return on such investments even after having left the leasehold. Such chattel did not belong to the manorial lord, but to the tenant.[46] Peasant families who moved were able to dismantle such buildings and rebuild on the new site.

43 Stadtarchiv St Gallen, Spitalarchiv, vol. A, 3, fol. 63r.

44 Stefan Sonderegger, 'Gaiserwald im Mittelalter', in Ernst Ziegler (ed.), *Gaiserwald: Abtwil, St. Josefen, Engelburg* (Gaiserwald, 2004), 11–36, at pp. 24–28. For the history of Swiss forest use, see Katja Hürlimann, 'Worum geht es in der Wald- und Forstgeschichte?', *Schweizerisches Zeitschrift für Forstwesen*, 154 (2003), 322–27.

45 Stadtarchiv St.Gallen, Spitalarchiv, vol. A, 3, fol. 67r.

46 Werner Meyer, *Hirsebrei und Hellebarde: Auf den Spuren des mittelalterlichen Lebens in der Schweiz* (Olten, 1985), 86. This is still applicable in modern law; see Article 677 in Schweizerische Eidgenossenschaft, *Schweizerisches Zivilgesetzbuch* (ZGB) [Swiss Civil Code], Art. 677.A.III.5.1, https://www.admin.ch/opc/de/classified-compilation/19070042/index.html #a677: 'Hütten, Buden, Baracken u. dgl. behalten, wenn sie ohne Absicht bleibender Verbindung auf fremdem Boden aufgerichtet sind, ihren besonderen Eigentümer'. ('Sheds, huts, shacks, cabins and the like retain their separate owner if they are constructed on land belonging to another person without the intention of becoming a permanent fixture'.) Cf. Otto P. Clavadetscher, 'Kontinuität und Wandel im Recht und in den Lebensverhältnissen', *Neujahrsblatt, e. by Historischen Verein des Kantons St. Gallen*, 132 (1992),

The opportunity to transfer such buildings when moving away from a farm is well documented in the eastern Swiss sources. One example: in 1453, the monastery of Magdenau to the west of St Gallen gave a farm with a granary and a barn to one Ueli Schnätzer and his wife in leasehold. One can assume this granary and barn to have been separate buildings next to the farm. Schnätzer had probably built these on his own initiative, possibly with financial assistance from the monastery. As owner he was free to do with these as he liked, since in his contract it says: 'if he does not wish to be there any longer, he shall be free to take barn and granary with him'.[47] Another option upon moving away was to sell the buildings, which had apparently been built without much assistance from the manorial lord by the tenant farmer, in which case the lord would have first refusal. These legal details were in every case noted in the contract.[48] It is apparent from such contracts that, amongst other things, all other real property on the land belonged entirely to the landlord, and the tenant had the duty of maintenance. This was common practice.

Besides the legal information, the contracts also hint at the division of costs. The contribution of the lord comprised the supply of materials, and the providing of money, grain payments, and infrastructure for transport. Grain payments in the German-speaking part of Switzerland often consisted of spelt and oats, the usual winter and summer grains in the Swiss midlands. To a great extent, money and spelt served as salary and meals for the men working on the building site, as well as for their families.[49] Such payments are rarely mentioned in the sources, but we can assume that next to skilled labourers and wagoners, there were also helpers from local peasant families.[50] Thus, such renovations and rebuilding work carried out in cooperation aided the income of the farming families. The prerequisite for such cooperation was the active participation of the lords in the peasant farmer's economy, as was typical in the newer manorial lordships that only emerged in the later Middle Ages.

7–28, at pp. 22–23; Alfred Zangger, 'Wirtschaft und Leben im Zürcher Oberland im 15. Jahrhundert', *Jahrheft der Ritterhausgesellschaft Bubikon*, 61 (1997), 14–35, at p. 26.

47 Archiv des Zisterzienserinnenklosters Magdenau, Bd. XLI, fol. 31r.

48 Archiv des Zisterzienserinnenklosters Magdenau, Bd. XLI, fol. 75r.

49 Dorothee Rippmann, '"Sein Brot verdienen": Die Verköstigung von Arbeitskräften im Spätmittelalter', *Medium Aevum Quotidianum*, 34 (1996), 91–114.

50 Alfred Zangger, 'Alltagsbeziehungen zwischen Klosterherrschaft und Bauern am Beispiel des Prämonstratenserklosters Rüti im 15. Jahrhundert', in Thomas Meier and Roger Sablonier (eds), *Wirtschaft und Herrschaft: Beiträge zur ländlichen Gesellschaft in der östlichen Schweiz (1200–1800)* (Zurich, 1999), 295–309, at p. 303; Sonderegger, *Landwirtschaftliche Entwicklung*, 103–13.

A close cooperation between manorial lord and tenants existed not only in connection with the maintenance of the farm buildings but also in connection with agricultural production. Grain and wine production were more labour-intensive than livestock farming. The latter freed workers, who, at certain times, could then gain employment as hired hands on farms committed to arable farming or wine production; for the vineyards around Lake Zurich as well in the St Gallen Rhine valley, this phenomenon is well documented.[51] For wine production, the cost and returns, and thus also the risks, were noted in the contracts between manorial lords and wine producers.[52] Part-contracts were common, usually in the form of so-called '*Halbpacht*', meaning that half of the yield was given to the lords by the farmers. The payment of material for the maintenance of the vines (vine stakes, fertilizer) and of the workers' salaries for the work in the vineyards, during the vintage and for the transport, was divided between lord and tenant. The burden of work and cost was, on the whole, evenly shared. In years where the yield was poor, manorial lords could forego a part or the whole of the wine due to them, and they would then in good years claim a greater part. With this kind of cooperation, both parties contributed to the upkeep and the intensification – well documented for eastern Switzerland since the fifteenth century – of the market-orientated viticulture.[53]

2.3 *Dealing with One Another*

The agricultural labour documented in the interest ledgers provides a good insight into the daily relations between manorial lords and their tenants. As opposed to deeds and urbaria, which only record the claims for duties that the lords made, the interest ledgers (*Zinsbücher*) and account books (*Rechnungsbücher*), that are kept in series, record the duties actually paid by the tenant

51 Zangger, 'Wirtschaft und Leben', 21–22; Stefan Sonderegger, 'Der Rebbrief von 1471 – eine wichtige Quelle zum Weinbau im St. Galler Rheintal. Kommentar und Neuedition', in Thomas Meier and Roger Sablonier (eds), *Wirtschaft und Herrschaft: Beiträge zur ländlichen Gesellschaft in der östlichen Schweiz (1200–1800)* (Zurich, 1999), 43–53.

52 The legal form of lease (*Halbpacht*) in viticulture shows similarities to the *mezzadria* in Tuscany, cf. Steven A. Epstein, *An Economic and Social History of Later Medieval Europe, 1000–1500* (Cambridge, 2009), 59–60.

53 Stefan Sonderegger, 'Landwirtschaftliche Spezialisierung in der spätmittelalterlichen Nordostschweiz', in Markus Cerman and Erich Landsteiner (eds), *Zwischen Land und Stadt: Wirtschaftsverflechtungen von ländlichen und städtischen Räumen in Europa 1300–1600* (Innsbruck, 2010), 139–60.

farmers. Thus, the portrayal of agriculture as recorded on paper or parchment by the lords could diverge widely from the actual practice of peasant farming. Grain duties were paid in cash or different agricultural produce. Feudal claims to natural produce and cash duties were paid in manual labour.[54] As is apparent from the interest registers and bills, daily labourers were tallied together with the feudal claims of duties, meaning that they were deducted from the claims for natural produce or cash. Books kept serially dealing with the management of these lands give the impression that lords and tenants often looked for the best possible solution for both parties with a large amount of flexibility on both sides. Tithes in grain were, in theory, duties that were paid in proportion to the yield.[55] But the information gained from Swiss sources from the fifteenth century show a different picture. Similar to the procedure with interest duties, an amount was fixed, but there was space for leniency on both sides of the mark. This is apparent in formulations such as 'the tithe is usually given' or that the tithe is at one point greater and at another time less.[56] The payment owed fixed by written contract seems to have been more of an approximation,[57] especially in the case of the tithes. The actual duties were often only specified after a personal meeting between the lord and tenant, in which they discussed how much of the land was going to be tilled and how good or bad the yield was likely to be, or already had been. Both sides argued and took positions. It could happen that a farmer 'says he ought not to give it'.[58] This should not be seen in general as a refusal to pay, but rather an understanding on the part of the lord that the position of the tenant farmers that they should be allowed to deviate from the fixed amount was legitimate. The reasons for this could be manifold. One reason often given by the peasant farmers was that one part of the land had not been used,[59] something that was obviously for them to decide and was accepted by the lords. That the exact amount of annual duties was negotiated between both parties on the basis of experience and taking into account the current situation indicates that in general relations were good. Prerequisite for these negotiations was a strong presence of the manorial lord in the living environment of the peasant farmer. Specifically, this means that the manorial

54 However, this did not make it compulsory labour classed as *Fronarbeit*.

55 For the tithes, cf. the work of Köppel, *Von der Äbtissin*.

56 Stadtarchiv St.Gallen, Spitalarchiv, vol. A, 3, fol. 27r.

57 Stadtarchiv St.Gallen, Spitalarchiv, vol. A, 3, fol. 32v, 'git ettwenn' (= gibt etwa, gives roughly).

58 Stadtarchiv St.Gallen, Spitalarchiv, vol. A, 3, fol. 105r.

59 Stadtarchiv St. Gallen, Spitalarchiv, vol. A, 3, fol. 32r ('Der Zehend uff Voelis Huob git de anno 1443 nit me denn 10 Mut Korn, won (= weil) es was ain tail nit gebuwen'.) and fol. 105r ('Er spricht, er soell es nit gen, in der Brach'.). Cf. also Erni, 'Geschriebene Landschaft', 83.

lords were present through *Amtshäuser* (administrative buildings) and their officials in urban surroundings or in the towns.[60] These were often central locations of manorial administration, which served to supply the rural community with produce that it did not have itself. Further, in such places, the peasant farmers' payments could be collected and the commercial relationships between tenants organized and taken note of. In summary, one can say that late medieval landlords took on the market-like role of provider and a hub for more or less direct exchange between the peasant farmers.[61]

The impression of a consensus between manorial lord and tenant farmer is shown in exceptional situations, too. In Europe, the years of 1442 and 1444 were difficult ones for agriculture; in the interest ledgers there is a markedly higher amount of exemptions from duties than usual.[62] The reasons for this are most likely to be found in failed yield due to adverse weather conditions, which would be especially detrimental for the grain fields, and there are many comments about exemptions from duties due to damage caused by bad weather.

The consequences for agriculture and thus for the community were grave. Hail, or storms described with hail to show their severity, destroyed the forthcoming harvest. Destructive storms radically changed the conditions. Instead of being able to provide for themselves from their own agricultural produce and being able to generate a small amount of income through sales, farmers had to buy in more grain for their own provision. Added to this, the tenant farmer had not only lost the basis of his food supply for the next or possibly the

60 For delegation of feudal obligations to officials, see, for instance, Teuscher, *Erzähltes Recht*, 114–16.

61 Zangger, 'Alltagsbeziehungen', 300. For the exchange between Glarus and Zurich, see Rolf Kamm, *Glarus zwischen Habsburg und Zürich: Die Entstehung des Landes im Spätmittelalter* (Baden: Hier & Jetzt, 2010). For the administration of the hospital of St Gallen in the region with viticulture, see Sonderegger, *Landwirtschaftliche Entwicklung*, 302 and 363–70.

62 Stefan Sonderegger, '"*...der Zins ist abgelon...*": Aushandeln von Schadensteilungen zwischen Grundherren und Bauern in schwierigen Zeiten der Landwirtschaft', in Rolf Kiessling, Wolfgang Scheffknecht (eds), *Umweltgeschichte in der Region*, Forum Suevicum: Beiträge zur Geschichte Ostschwabens und der benachbarten Regionen, 9 (Konstanz, 2012), 139–57. See also Christian Jörg, *'Teure, Hunger, Grosses Sterben': Hungersnöte und Versorgungskrisen in den Städten des Reiches während des 15. Jahrhunderts*, Monographien zur Geschichte des Mittelalters, 55 (Stuttgart, 2008); Horst Buszello, 'Teuerung und Hungersnot am Ober- und Hochrhein im Spätmittelalter und in der Frühen Neuzeit (circa 1300–1800)', in Ursula Huggle (ed.), *Kriege, Krisen und Katastrophen am Oberrhein vom Mittelalter bis zur Frühen Neuzeit, Tagung des Historischen Seminars Abteilung Landesgeschichte an der Universität Freiburg und der Stadt Neuenburg am Rhein 13. und 14.10.2006*, Das Markgräflerland, 2 (Schopfheim: Geschichtsverein Markgräflerland, 2007), 32–71.

next few years, he also faced the difficulty of only partly, or in the worst case, not being at all able to pay his duties to his lord.

If the harvest was ruined through no fault of the farmer, tenants were often exempted from part of the duties. This fact shows the following: this stance – the reduction or waiving of peasant farmers' duties by the lord, as is often documented for loss of yield due to poor weather – is a concession on the side of the landlords. The reasons for this are primarily rational; just like their lords, peasant farmers live off the management of the land. If there was no reason to assume a fault of the tenant, negligent management of the land, or embezzlement, then it was more important to show consideration for bad harvests and allow continuity on the farm, than to provoke the peasant farmers into leaving by insisting on payment. Land that was not worked did neither party any good; it was vital, especially in precarious situations, for the tenant farmer to be able to count on constructive engagement of the landlord to find a solution.

3 Credit and Debt of Peasant Farmers

But since the concessions made by the lords were usually only a reduction and not total exemption from duties, the consequences of a bad harvest could still weigh on the family for a considerable time: in order to pay for missing yield, the tenant often had to take out loans with their lords or other credit lenders. When discussing the lords' loans to their tenant farmers, one must also consider the negatives, namely, the wide-spread indebtedness of peasant farmers. This led to a high level of economic dependency within the rural community, which manifested itself differently depending on agricultural structure. The form of indebtedness that was probably most common among peasant farmers was the need to take out a loan to tide themselves over during the low times in the fluctuating yield from year to year.[63] Debt was incurred for various different reasons. In cases like those mentioned – of failed harvests, in which case a loan was needed alongside the reduction of duties, and possibly even loans in the form of grain from the possession of the feudal lord – the reason is obvious. But there were other forms, too, not always clear from the sources. It could be that large sums of money were paid in order to buy added land, or to pay off inheriting siblings, as well as higher maintenance costs and duties after having

63 Hans-Jörg Gilomen, 'Das Motiv der bäuerlichen Verschuldung in den Bauernunruhen an der Wende zur Neuzeit', in Susanna Burghartz, Hans-Jörg Gilomen, and Guy Paul Marchal (eds), *Spannungen und Widersprüche*, Gedenkschrift für Frantisek Graus (Sigmaringen, 1992), 173–89.

acquired more land. In such cases, the debt could make up a multiple of the annual interest, and the reduction of such debt could have lasted a generation or perhaps was not possible at all, so that it was impossible to avert the need to give up the farm – in fact an insolvency.[64]

In commercial agriculture, influenced by urban requirements, the indebtedness of peasant farmers was part of the structure of the relations between farmers and lords. This financial obligation allowed the lords to participate even more actively in the economy of their tenant farmers. Studies of agricultural specialization of cattle farming and viticulture of the late Middle Ages in the eastern parts of modern-day Switzerland testify to this. The driving force was the economic interest of the regional centre, the imperial city of St Gallen, which greatly influenced the rural economy through manorial urban institutions and citizens who owned territory in the countryside. In the foreground stood the securing of subsistence; then, there were commercial interests, which furthered cattle farming and viticulture through the sale of beef cattle, whey products, and wine in the town and in the countryside. As a result, three specialized agricultural zones emerged around the town that were dependent upon one another, with a focus on grain, cattle, and wine. This model resulted in a spatial network with zones of different agricultural structure that stand in a complementary relationship to each other. Seemingly, at the central point, there was the town of St Gallen as regional centre and intermediary between the three zones.[65] Such agricultural specialization led to risky financial ties and dependencies of many peasant families. In commercial cattle farming orientated along urban demand, and similarly with viticulture, this is well documented, as the following shall show.

In so-called '*Viehgemeinschaften*' (livestock collectives), urban investors – butchers, merchants, and hospitals – participated in the farming of livestock of the regional farmers.[66] In this widespread form of shared capital, the creditor

64 Alfred Zangger, 'Wittenbach im Mittelalter', in Edgar Krayss, et al. (eds), *Wittenbach. Landschaft und Menschen im Wandel der Zeit* (Wittenbach, 2004), 47–146, at pp. 125–32, has proven that some debts consisted of five times as much as the annual interest.

65 Sonderegger, 'Landwirtschaftliche Spezialisierung'. However, it is to be noted that such specialization should not be seen as a closed system. Exchange existed not only between the different zones of one region, but also with regions outside of these. For eastern Switzerland, we already have proof of grain import from Swabia. Studies from similar regions would be desirable for comparison.

66 Cf. the examples in Stefan Sonderegger and Matthias Weishaupt, 'Spätmittelalterliche Landwirtschaft in der Nordostschweiz', *Appenzellische Jahrbücher*, 1987 (1988), 29–71; Rippmann, *Bauern und Städter*, 204–30; Matthias Steinbrink, *Ulrich Meltinger: Ein Basler Kaufmann am Ende des 15. Jahrhunderts*, VSWG Beiheft, 197 (Stuttgart: Steiner, 2007), 169–72.

lent money for the livestock to the farmer, who had to pay for the buying, stabling, care, and feeding of the animals. For this expenditure, the farmer received milk and manure in return and could use the animal for its strength. The common profit lay in the increase of value and in the offspring, which could be shared, depending on the investment of the creditor. Such livestock sharing clearly shows how strongly the peasant's indebtedness was linked to urban investment of capital in the rural economy. Often the peasant farmer would add to his debts, for instance, taking on further loans in order to buy feed, to buy more livestock, or other things. With these loans one can assume, just by looking at the size of the *Viehgemeinschaften* – there were ones with over thirty cattle[67] – that the sums were high. To lessen the risk, creditors demanded that the farmers stake their property as pledge for the loan. Difficulties in repayment ended in worst-case scenarios with the auctioning off of the farm and movable property of indebted families.

A different type of debt can be seen resulting from urban influence on agriculture in the case of viticulture. In zones where the specialization of viticulture was so far progressed that it resembled monocultures, to a large extent staple foods had to be bought in. Urban manorial lords in particular are known to have exchanged wine with their peasant farmers for necessary items, such as grain, meat, and even cash.[68] Such a credit-based service served the everyday needs of the consumer – in this case the wine farmer – and made cashless trade relations possible.[69] This tied the tenant farmers very strongly through commitments to the lords and their economic interests. In addition to the feudal duties in the form of interests, tithes, and manual labour, continuous long-term debts bound the tenants to their manorial lords.[70] The question is, whether the manorial lords actually encouraged this kind of debt in order to strengthen the foundation for their claims to power and/or to safeguard their material interests.[71]

67 Stadtarchiv St. Gallen, Spitalarchiv, G, 9, fol. 35v.

68 Sonderegger, *Landwirtschaftliche Entwicklung*, 363–78; Bruno Meier and Dominik Sauerländer, *Das Surbtal im Spätmittelalter: Kulturlandschaft und Gesellschaft einer ländlichen Region (1250–1550)*, Beiträge zur Aargauergeschichte, 6 (Aarau, 1995), 145.

69 Hans-Jörg Gilomen, 'Die ökonomischen Grundlagen des Kredits und die christlich-jüdische Konkurrenz im Spätmittelalter', in Eveline Brugger and Birgit Wiedl (eds), *Ein Thema – zwei Perspektiven: Juden und Christen in Mittelalter und Frühneuzeit* (Innsbruck, 2007), 139–69, at p. 146.

70 See the examples concerning viticulture in Sonderegger, *Landwirtschaftliche Entwicklung*, 378–93.

71 Stefan Sonderegger, 'Wirtschaftliche Regionalisierung in der spätmittelalterlichen Nordostschweiz. Am Beispiel der Wirtschaftsführung des Heiliggeistspitals St. Gallen', *Schriften des Vereins für Geschichte des Bodensees und seiner Umgebung*, 105 (1987), 19–37. With

4 Written Rules and Controls

Risk and profit sharing, investment sharing and help, loans, exemption from duties and more document the predominantly cooperative side of the active engagement of the lords with the peasant farmer's economy. But legal dependencies – as shown in the case of commercial and specialized cattle farming – were also superimposed on the relationship between lord and tenant by financial obligations from loans. Here we are dealing with a complex situation of dependencies. Peasant farmers were bound by feudal rights to lords, and economically they were dependent on their lord in various ways – for production, their subsistence, and even for the sale of the end product.

These dependencies were actively controlled and managed. On the one hand, this was done through the presence of feudal bailiffs and *Amtshäuser* in the countryside, and on the other, through legal and administrative documents. Writing was used specifically for economic administration. This can be seen on two levels: legal and administrative. Regarding the legal level, on the leasing of land, the connected rights and duties of the tenants were documented in great detail in writing. The duty of annual payment of dues and the tax duty when the property changed hands in a sale (*Erschatz*) of the land were specifically mentioned. Further, particulars could be found on arbitration procedures in case of conflict, and on sanctions in the case of the farmer failing to pay taxes or in a case of bad management. Even risk and damage sharing between the hospital and the tenant farmers in case of a failed harvest has been documented since the middle of the fourteenth century. But here, too, it depends on the type of landlord. New, urban lordships differed from the old, ecclesiastical lordships in the same region in the fifteenth century. The level of detail illustrated above is inherent in the urban context, meaning in urban hospitals and new urban monasteries founded in the thirteenth century. In comparison, leasehold contracts from the old Benedictine monastery of St Gall, that were issued at the same time, have far less detail.[72] The monastic contracts do not regulate the management of the farm; they only document the relationship of the feudal overlord to his tenants and not to the subtenants, who were the peasant farmers.

In addition to this legal level, there is the administrative one. Alongside thousands of deeds, the hospital of St Gallen possessed an extensive collection

a focus on lordship, see recently Julien Demade, 'Grundrente, Jahreszyklus und monetarisierte Zirkulation: Zur Funktionsweise des spätmittelalterlichen Feudalismus', *Historische Anthropologie*, 17/2 (2009), 222–44.

72 Cf. Sonderegger, 'Vom Nutzen', 86–116.

of administrative documents. Administrative records, interest ledgers, annual financial statements, and debt registers served to control the enforcement of that which was legally agreed to in the deeds, as well as to control the payments and debts of the farmers.[73] In this area, too, there were great differences, for a collection of administrative writing like this did not exist in the old Benedictine monastery of St Gall, or at least it hardly approached the quantity of that produced elsewhere.[74] Here is a concrete example showing how the extension of the use of written text occurred in pragmatic connection with and in the context of urban economic life, in the north Alpine region.[75] Urban hospitals embodied the new 'category' of lords,[76] for whom economic interest was a high priority. This can be explained by the hospitals' function. Alongside their social role, they also had an economic role to fulfil. With their territory in the urban surroundings, they not only secured food for their inhabitants, but through the agricultural produce trade they also ensured the provision of the inhabitants of the town and its surroundings. It is within this context that the active participation of manorial lords such as these in the economy of their tenant farmers must be seen. In urban institutions in particular, there are many examples that show how late medieval manorial lords acted in an economically dynamic and innovative way. Late medieval manorial lordship was diverse; the generalizing idea of a withdrawal of the lord from the peasant farmer's economy does not do it justice.

73 Cf. the collection of records in the Stadtarchiv der Ortsbürgergemeinde St. Gallen: Stadtarchiv St. Gallen, SpA, vol. A, 3 -A, 204 (Pfennigzinsbücher des Spitals von 14442 bis 1872); SpA, vol. B, 1 – B, 370 (Jahrrechnungen des Spitals von 1444 bis 1849), SpA, vol. C, 1 – C, 97 (Schuldbücher des Spitals von 1434 bis 1869).

74 Roger Sablonier and Alfred Zangger, *Inventar spätmittelalterlicher Wirtschafts- und Verwaltungsquellen im Stiftsarchiv Einsiedeln*, Stiftsarchiv St. Gallen, Staatsarchiv des Kantons Schaffhausen, Staatsarchiv des Kantons Thurgau, (Zurich, 1989). According to Robinson, *Die Fürstabtei*, 202, the recordkeeping at the monastery of St Gall was not very extensive, if compared to the records kept by other ruling institutions, for instance, those of towns.

75 Hagen Keller, 'Die Entwicklung der europäischen Schriftkultur im Spiegel der mittelalterlichen Überlieferung: Beobachtungen und Überlegungen', in Karl Leidinger and Dieter Metzler (eds), *Geschichte und Geschichtsbewusstsein, Festschrift für Karl-Ernst Jeismann zum 65. Geburtstag* (Munster, 1990), 171–204. See also Dorothee Rippmann, 'Leben, Arbeit und materielle Kultur im Lichte pragmatischer Schriftlichkeit in der Schweiz', in Gudrun Gleba and Niels Petersen (eds), *Wirtschafts- und Rechnungsbücher des Mittelalters und der Frühen Neuzeit: Formen und Methoden der Rechnungslegung: Städte, Klöster und Kaufleute* (Göttingen, 2015), 209–53.

76 Ludolf Kuchenbuch, 'Vom Dienst zum Zins? Bemerkungen über agrarische Transformationen in Europa vom späteren 11. zum beginnenden 14. Jahrhundert', *Zeitschrift für Agrargeschichte und Agrarsoziologie*, 51 (2003), 11–29, at p. 16.

5 Conclusion

The present article has looked at relations between lords and farmers in the day-to-day economy of the late Middle Ages. The basis for this has been recent study of the late medieval rural community, with a focus on the German-speaking part of Switzerland and southern Germany. As an initial result, it has become clear that there is a need to differentiate the typical narrative of literature on the topic, which depicts the shift from manorialism / *Grundherrschaft* to the so-called rental-based manorial system / *Rentengrundherrschaft* in the course of the high and late medieval period. Traditional features of a *Rentengrundherrschaft* include the extensive relinquishing of the manorial demesne in favour of parcelling out land in leasehold in return for payment in duties, and the general tendency of the proprietor of the land to disengage from agricultural production. However, newer regional studies of the fourteenth, fifteenth, and sixteenth centuries point in another direction. They show that many manorial lords participated more actively than before in the economy of their tenant farmers, and that they were very active. Thus, one late medieval lordship system does not exist. Or, to put it in highly simplified terms: at the two ends of a wide spectrum of different manorial lordship, both of these types of lord could be found; at one end was the lord who engaged more than ever in the farming economy whilst at the same time continuing to work his own demesne, and at the other end the type of lord who was himself hardly active at all any longer in agriculture and only collected payments due.

This is the conclusion arrived at when asking the question of which manorial lords the peasant farmer had a relationship with his day-to-day activities. Connected to this question is that of actual ownership and lordship. These are questions that, in my opinion, have as yet not been asked enough when studying rural society. Answering them will help to gain a differentiated picture of the late medieval manorial system. Using the example of the imperial abbey of St Gall, it is possible to show what is meant by this. With many territories in eastern Switzerland, the ancient Benedictine monastery of St Gall, founded in the early Middle Ages, had the overlordship – the *dominium directum / Obereigentum* – but did not work the land itself, rather leasing it to urban citizens or urban institutions, lay or ecclesiastical, that were founded in the late Middle Ages. The old abbey of St Gall thus still held the overlordship, *the dominium directum*, over the land; citizens and communal institutions were thus their tenants with all the associated rights, that is, they were the holders of the *dominium indirectum / Untereigentum*. Like the monastery, these urban actors usually did not work the land themselves, but subleased it to peasant families in the region. These subtenants – peasant farmers – were those who used the territory for agricultural purposes; they held the *dominium utile / Nutzungseigentum*, the right to use the land, which they paid for in natural produce, money, and other obligations. Thus, the holders of the *dominium indirectum* – citizens, communal institutions, and new monasteries – in practice turned into manorial lords themselves, over their subtenants, that is, over the peasant farmers. Whilst the overlord had mostly withdrawn from the agricultural economy, the new de facto manorial lords were participating more than ever, and with their own, mainly commercial interests in the farming economy.

These new lords of the late Middle Ages and the early modern period were in close contact with their peasant farmers. Daily economic relations can be summed up as ambivalent. One the one hand, in many regions there was intense cooperation that encouraged consensual agreement. On the other hand, strong economic and financial ties caused great dependencies. With the active engagement of these new manorial landlords in the rural economy, the duties of the peasant farmers towards their landlords were strengthened. Added to the traditional dependencies, more and more economic ones came into existence. The peasant families were still bound legally – manorial – to their landlord, and new dependencies were created economically, from the production to the commercialization. The relationship between lord and peasant farmer, which up until then had been of a strongly feudalistic nature, was increasingly superimposed with capitalist[77] momentum.

6 Prospect

The question remains whether the results offered here for the regions of northern Switzerland and the region around Lake Constance are also representative of the Alpine regions of Tyrol and Bavaria, which are the focus of this collection of essays. Current research only allows an indication, not a conclusive answer. With the following comments, I would like to encourage further regional studies, on the basis of which it may in future be possible to make general statements about the relations between manorial lords and peasant farmers in the transition period from the late Middle Ages to the early modern period.

77 Capitalist is here (based on the results of this research and in the context of the agriculture) understood to mean that the following criteria were of great importance: free disposition of the proprietors over the various categories of property; great freedom of decision for the actors as well as freedom of action; agriculture focused on profit and a high importance of loans. For the discussion of the term in general, see Jürgen Kocka, 'Writing the History of Capitalism', *Bulletin of the German Historical Institute*, 47 (2010), 7–24.

One argument in favour of the result presented here being in part representative is based on the following line of thought: work on the development of the manorial system relies mainly on edited sources. This can be shown by the region of St Gallen, which is the focus of my research. The monastery of St Gall is cited – as shown above – as a model case for the development of an important ecclesiastical lordship into a *Rentengrundherrschaft*. But the sources used to defend this view are taken from the old edition of charters (*Urkundenbuch*) of the abbey of St Gall.[78] This is – the name gives it away – an institutional collection, that mainly indexes only those charters and urbaria up to 1463 that are connected to the monastery of St Gall. However, this choice means that nearly half of the existing regional documents are ignored. Many older editions take this stance and only publish the sources of one single landlord. Thus, they only give us an insight into a very narrow section of the relations between manorial lord and peasant farmer. Current editions from the region studied here that take a regional approach[79] have a view to a more encompassing collection. They try to collect as many of the pertinent sources of a region as possible. Thus, they publish a mass of hitherto unpublished private documents, amongst which there are many leasehold contracts with details of the relationship between lord and lessee.

It is precisely these private documents, formerly unknown, which show that manorialism was not a dual relationship solely between one manorial lord and peasant farmer, but that there were different actors in-between, that de facto carried out the practice of the lordship. In a multi-layered complex of the manorial system, we are suddenly presented with very active lords and farmers, who entertain tight economic contact with one another. As soon as the mass of as yet unedited sources can be used for other regions too, we are likely to see that there, too, the relationships between lords and farmers were manifold and dynamic. This can also be taken without hesitation as an appeal for new editions from the late medieval – early modern period. The recently completed dissertation by Rezia Krauer on the land market in the region of St Gallen in the fourteenth century, which to a great extent relies on newly edited sources, clearly shows the potential of basic registering of sources for historical research. Her results are confirmed by the studies of Volker Stamm for Tyrol,[80] who – again on the basis of charters – comes to the conclusion that the

78 Hermann Wartmann, Traugott Schiess, Placid Bütler, and Paul Staerkle (eds), *Urkundenbuch der Abtei Sanct Gallen*, 6 vols (Zurich, 1863–1970).

79 Reworked edition of the St. Galler Urkundenbuch (Chartularium Sangallense), the Bündner Urkundenbuch and the Urkundenbuch Fürstentum Liechtenstein digital.

80 Stamm, 'Kauf und Verkauf', 42.

apparently rigid construct of an overlordship concentrated on a handful of territorial lords hides from view the widespread opportunities for economic action of many actors.

But it would be going too far to solely explain away gaps in the research due to missing source editions. This is because the material that provides most insight into the relationship between lords and peasant farmers are urbaria, tax books, interest ledgers, and notes kept by chance. These kinds of records of everyday life only start at the transition from the fourteenth to the fifteenth century, but quickly turn into a mass that is hard to view comprehensively and also not available in editions. The regional studies quoted above are based on such archival matter; Switzerland can fall back on a research tradition of four decades. In the questions and methods, similar studies for Vorarlberg, Tyrol, and Bavaria arrive at comparable results. Peasant farmers are not just seen as passive objects of the lords, (see hereto the chapter 'Peasant Participation', pp. 121–124 and the literature mentioned there); their freedom to dispose of the land they held in lease from manorial lords seems to have been similarly great as in the regions of northern Switzerland and Lake Constance. So, we can assume that in the whole of the eastern Alpine region, in relation to land use, there was the possibility for the peasant farmer to negotiate with the landlord.

Finally, I would like to mention that the present sketch is mainly confined to economic relations between manorial landlord and tenant. However, contact between lords and peasants occurred in all sectors and at all social levels. In northern Switzerland and the region around Lake Constance, as well as in Tyrol and Bavaria, one can assume a strong social differentiation in rural society. Certain new studies of Tyrol and Vorarlberg[81] show the detailed position of some heads of a village between lordship and village community. These so-called '*Ammänner*' (mayors), who had legal and political functions, blur the distinctions between belonging to the official nobility or the village community, especially as social climbing and falling was continuous. In any case, villages are central to the exploration of the relations between lords and peasants. It might at first glance be surprising that the rise of communal autonomy that shows itself in the development of village and church communities, of alpine cooperatives and other user communities should strengthen the bonds

81 Matthias Moosbrugger, 'Der hintere Bregenzerwald – eine Bauernrepublik? Neue Untersuchungen zu seiner Verfassungs- und Strukturgeschichte im Spätmittelalter', Forschungen zur Geschichte Vorarlbergs, 9, dissertation, University of Innsbruck, Konstanz, 2009; Alois Niederstätter, *Geschichte Vorarlbergs*, i: *Vorarlberg im Mittelalter* (Innsbruck, 2014), 119–46.

between lords and peasants. But it is clear from village regulations (*Weistum / Dorfoffnung*) that the regulation of the neighbouring field, forest, and meadow use, as well as the justice system, was in the interest of the lords as well as the peasants. A good relationship between landlords and peasant farmers was dependent on structures that served to regulate conflict and thus also served the development and maintenance of a certain level of consensus amongst each other. Both – conflict and consensus between manorial lord and tenants – belonged to daily life. The theme of the relations between lords and peasant farmers in Scandinavia and the Alps continues to present a wide field of research.

Acknowledgements

I would like to thank Dorothee Guggenheimer, Rezia Krauer and Nicole Stadelmann for their critical reading, as well as Maria Tranter for translating this article into English.

Glossary

Abgabengrundherrschaft rent providing manorial system
Allmende, Gmain common (meadows, woods, wastes, or pasturage)
Alm alpine pasture
Amman leader in a Hofmark, elected by peasants and confirmed by the manorial lord
Ármaðr (old Norwegian) bailiff
Bauding, Bautaiding manorial meeting/court
Ding, Taiding, Ehafttaiding thing, court, assembly
Dominium directum direct ownership
Dominium utile proprietal possession
Dómr (Old Norwegian) ad hoc legal commission
Dorfgemeinde village community
Dorfmeister (see also Danish Oldermann) elected or appointed village leader
Dorfordnung village law
Eigenleute, Leibeigene serfs, bondsmen
Eigentum property
Erbrecht hereditary tenancy
Foged (Denmark) district judge
Freistift tenancy at will
Freizügigkeit freedom to leave at will
Frondienst labour service, labour obligation
Fut/fogd (Norway) royal bailiff
Gemeinde community, commune
Genossenschaft community
Gerichtsbarkeit jurisdiction, judicial power
Gerichtsgemeinde legal community
Gerichtsherrschaft judicial authority/legal dominion
Gmain an association of inhabitants holding a plot of land in a village with the right to use common land belonging to this village
Grundherr lord of the manor
Grundherrschaft (see also Rentengrundherrschaft) manorial system
Häusler, Kötter, Söldner, Söllleute cottar
Herredsting (Denmark) local thing
Herrschaft dominion
Hof peasant holding, farm
Hofmark territory with manorial jurisdiction
Hofmarksgericht seignorial court
Kopfzins personal tax

 DOI:10.1163/9789004433458_013

Lagrettemenn (Norway) co-judges, jurors, court witnesses
Landgericht territorial court
Landrecht territorial law
Landsgemeinde cantonal assembly
Landtag territorial diet
Leibeigenschaft serfdom, personal bondage
Leibherrschaft dominion over people
Leibrecht lifelong tenure
Lensmann (Norway) district sheriff
Lögmaðr (ON), lagmann lawman
Meier steward, bailiff
Ministerialen Legally unfree officials of high status in the Middle Ages.
Nachbarschaft neighbourhood community
Odelsrett (Norway) pre-emption to inherited land
Oldermand (Denmark) appointed or elected village leader
Pfleger local territorial administrator, sheriff
Rentengrundherrschaft rent providing manorial system without tenant labour service
Retterting (Denmark) manorial *thing*
Richter judge
Schwaighof pastoral farm, dairy farm
Sorenskrivar (Norway) district judge
Talgemeinde vally community
Todfallabgabe mortuary fee
Unfreie; Hörige, Knechte, Sklaven, Servi unfree persons; servi, villeins, thralls, bondmen
Vierer panel of village or Hofmark officials
Villikation binate manorial system
Villikationsverfassung manorial organization
Vogt (ecclesiastical) advocate, bailiff
Zensualen people between unfree and fully free status

Bibliography

Archival Documentation

Archiv des Zisterzienserinnenklosters Magdenau:

Bd. XLI.

Bergen State Archive, Bergen:

Sorenskrivaren i Nordhordland, tingbok 20, 1681, folio 24a.

thing protocol for Nordhordland No. 33, 1712–15, folios 67a, 68b, 70b, 71a-b, 72b, 74a, 75b, 76b, 77a-b, 79b, 80a.

Deutsche Nationalbibliothek, Leipzig and Frankfurt am Main:

Stenographische Berichte des Tiroler Landtages, Tirol Langtag.

Schweizerische Eidgenossenschaft, *Schweizerisches Zivilgesetzbuch* (*ZGB*) [Swiss Civil Code], https://www.admin.ch/opc/en/classified-compilation/19070042/index.html.

Stadtarchiv der Ortsbürgergemeonde St Gallen, St Gallen:

Stadtarchiv SpA, C, 2.

Spitalarchiv, A, 3.

Spitalarchiv, G, 9.

SpA, A, 3 bis A, 204 (Pfennigzinsbücher des Spitals von 14442 bis 1872).

SpA, B, 1 bis b, 370 (Jahrrechnungen des Spitals von 1444 bis 1849).

SpA, C, 1 bis C, 97 (Schuldbücher des Spitals von 1434 bis 1869).

Tiroler Landesarchiv, Innsbruck:

Protocols of the Tiroler Landtag, signature 6579.

Primary Sources

Ágrip af Nóregskonunga sögum. Fargskinna, Nóregs konunga tal, ed. Bjarni Einarsson. Íslenzk fornrit, 29 (Reykjavík: Hið Íslenzka fornritafélag, 1985).

Baglersoger, trans. Gunnar Pedersen, in Halvdan Koht, Gunnar Pedersen and Karl Jónsson (eds), *Kongesoger*, Den norrøne litteraturen, 4 (Oslo: Det norske Samlaget, 1962), 201–86.

Böglunga sögur in *Fornmanna sögur*, 10 (Copenhagen, 1835).

Borgfirðingar sögur, ed. Guðni Jónsson, Íslenzk fornrit, 3 (Reykjavík: Hið Íslenzka fornritafélag, 1938).

Brennu-Njáls saga, ed. Einar Ól. Sveinsson, Íslenzk fornrit, 12 (Reykjavík: Hið Íslenzka fornritafélag, 1954).

Chartularium Sangallense, Otto P. Clavadetscher and Stefan Sonderegger (eds), 13 vols (St Gallen: Herausgeber- und Verlags- Gemeinschaft Chartularium Sangallense / Thorbecke, 1983).

Danmarks gamle Love paa Nutidsdansk, ed. E. Kroman and S. Iuul, Danske Sprog- og Litteraturselskab, 3 vols (Copenhagen: G.E.C Gad, 1945–48).

Die Rechtsquellen der Kantone Appenzell, i: *Appenzeller Landbücher*, Nathalie Büsser and Margrit Meyer Kälin (eds), Sammlung Schweizerischer Rechtsquellen, Abt. 13 (Basel: Schwabe, 2009).

Diplomatarium Norvegicum: Oldbreve til Kundskab om Norges indre og ydre Forhold, Sprog, Slægter, sæder, Lovgivning og Rettergang i Middelalderen, ed. Chr. C.A. Lange, C.R. Unger, et al., 23 vols (Christiania: P.T. Mallings Forlagshandel, 1847–2011).

Diplomatarium Suecanum, ed. Johan Gustaf Liljegren, Emil Hildebrand, et al., utgivet av Kungl. Vitterhets historie och antikvitetsakademien och Riksarkivet, 11 vols (Stockholm: Nordstedt, 1842–[2014]).

The Earliest Norwegian Laws: Being the Gulathing Law and the Frostathing law, ed. and trans. Laurence M. Larson, Records of Civilizations, 20 (New York: Columbia University Press, 1935).

Egils saga, ed. Sigurður Nordal, Íslenzk fornrit, 2 (Reykjavík: Hið Íslenzka fornritafélag, 1933).

Eyrbyggja saga, ed. Einar Ól. Sveinsson, Íslenzk fornrit, 4 (Reykjavík: Hið Íslenzka fornritafélag, 1935).

Fagrskinna. See *Ágrip af Nóregskonunga sögum*.

Frostatingslova, trans. Jørn Sandnes and Jan Ragnar Hagland (Oslo: Det norske samlaget, 1994).

Frostatingsloven, in Rudolf Keyser, P.A. Munch, Gustav Storm and Ebbe Hertzberg (eds), *Norges gamle Love indtil 1387*, 5 vols (Christiania: Chr. Grøndahl, 1846–95), i, 119–258.

Grettis saga, ed. Guðni Jónsson, Íslenzk fornrit, 7 (Reykjavík: Hið Íslenzka fornritafélag, 1936).

Gulathing, in Ari Þorgilsson, *Íslendingabók*, ed. Anne Holtsmark, Nordisk filologi: Tekster og Lærebøker til universitetsbruk, Serie A, 5 (Oslo: Dreyer, 1967).

Gulatingsloven, in Rudolf Keyser, P.A. Munch, Gustav Storm and Ebbe Hertzberg (eds), *Norges gamle Love indtil 1387*, 5 vols (Christiania: Chr. Grøndahl, 1846–95), i, 1–118.

Gulatingslovi. Umsett frå gamalnorsk av Knut Robberstad, trans Knut Robberstad, Norrøne bokverk 33, 3rd end (Oslo: Det norske samlaget, 1969).

Heimskringla. See Snorri Sturluson.

Íslendingabók. Landnámabók, ed. Jakob Benediktsson, Íslenzk Fornrit, 1 (Reykjavík: Hið Íslenzka fornritafélag, 1968).

King Christian IV, *Kong Christian den Fjerdes norske Lovbog af 1604*, ed. and trans. Frederik Hallager and Frederik Peter Brandt (Christiania: Feilberg and Landmark, 1855;

repr. Oslo: Norsk historisk kjeldeskrift-institutt, Den rettshistoriske kommisjon, 1981).

King Christian v, *Kong Christian den Femtes Norske Lov af 15de April 1687*, ed. Otto Mejlænder (Christiania: P.T. Malling, 1883; repr. 1892).

Kjalnesinga saga, ed. Jóhannes Halldórsson, Íslenzk fornrit, 14 (Reykjavík: Hið Íslenzka fornritafélag, 1959).

Landrecht des Königs Magnus Hakonarson, trans. Rudolf Meissner (Weimar: Böhlau, 1941).

The Law of the Realm 1274, in Rudolf Keyser, P.A. Munch, Gustav Storm and Ebbe Hertzberg (eds), *Norges gamle Love indtil 1387*, 5 vols (Christiania: Chr. Grøndahl, 1846–95), ii, 7–178.

Laxdæla saga, ed. Einar Ól. Sveinsson, Íslenzk fornrit, 5 (Reykjavík: Hið Íslenzka fornritafélag, 1934).

'Lex Baiuvariorum', in Karl August Eckhardt (ed.), *Germanenrechte, Texte und Übersetzungen*, ii: *Die Gesetze des Karolingerreiches 714–911* (Weimar: H. Bohlau, 1934), 74–187.

Lex Uplandiae: Upplandslagen, E codice membr. Bibl. Univ. Upsal. xii, ed. Dag Strömbäck, Corpus codicum Suecicorum medii aevi Hafniae, 15 (Hafniae: Munksgaard, 1960).

Ljósvetninga saga, ed. Björn Sigfússon, Íslenzk fornrit, 10 (Reykjavík: Hið Íslenzka fornritafélag, 1940).

Monumenta Boica, ed. Franz Lorenz Richter, Johann Paul Voetter, Johann Nepomuk Fritz and Anton Franz, Königliche Akademie der Wissenschaften, 18 vols (Munich: Monachii, Typis Academicis, 1763–1808).

Morkinskinna, ed. C.R. Unger (Christiania, 1867).

NgL = *Norges gamle Love.*

Norges gamle Love indtil 1387, ed. Rudolf Keyser, P.A. Munch, Gustav Storm and Ebbe Hertzberg, 5 vols (Christiania: Chr. Grøndahl, 1846–95).

Norwegisches Recht: Das Rechtsbuch des Gulathings, ed. Rudolf Meissner, Germanenrechte, 6 (Weimar: Böhlau, 1935).

Norwegisches Recht: Das Rechtsbuch des Frostothings, Germanenrechte, 4 (Weimar: Böhlau, 1939).

The Older Law of the Frostathing, in Laurence M. Larson (ed. and trans.), *The Earliest Norwegian Laws: Being the Gulathing Law and the Frostathing law*, Records of Civilization, 20 (New York: Columbia University Press, 1935), 214–409.

The Older Law of the Gulathing, in Laurence M. Larson (ed. and trans.), *The Earliest Norwegian Laws: Being the Gulathing Law and the Frostathing law*, Records of Civilization, 20 (New York: Columbia University Press, 1935), 35–213.

Der Schwabenspiegel: übertragen in heutiges Deutsch mit Illustrationen aus alten Handschriften, ed. Harald Rainer Derschka (Munich: Beck, 2002).

Snorri Sturluson, *Heimskringla: Nóregs konunga sögur*, ed. Finnur Jónsson (Copenhagen: Gad, 1911).

Snorri Sturluson, *Heimskringla: History of the Kings of Norway*, trans. Lee M. Hollander (Austin: University of Texas, 1964).

Svenska landskapslagar, tolkade och forklarade för nutidens svenskar, ed. and trans. Ake Holmbäck and Elias Wessén, 5 vols (Stockholm: Hugo Gebers, 1933–46).

Sverre-soga, trans. Halvdan Koht, in Halvdan Koht, Gunnar Pedersen and Karl Jónsson (eds), *Kongesoger*, Den Norrøne litteraturen, 4 (Oslo: Norske Samlaget, 1962), 201–86.

Sverris saga. Böglunga sögur, in Gudni Jónsson (ed.), *Konunga sögur II* (Reykjavík: Íslendingasagnaútgáfan, 1957).

Sverris saga: etter cod. AM 327 4to, ed. Gustav Indrebø and Karl Jónsson (Kristiania: Dybwad, 1920).

Tacitus, *Germania*, ed. Alfons Dopsch, et al. (Leipzig: Teubner, 1930).

'Valdemars sjællandske lov: Eldre og yngre redaktion samt sjællandske kirkelov', in Erik Kroman (ed.), *Danmarks gamle Landskabslove med Kirkelovene*, viii: *Valdemars sjællandske lov* (Copenhagen: Gyldendal, 1941).

Vatnsdœla saga, ed. Einar Ól. Sveinsson, Íslenzk fornrit, 8 (Reykjavík: Hið Íslenzka fornritafélag, 1939).

Vestfirðinga saga, ed. Einar Ól. Sveinsson, Íslenzk fornrit, 6 (Reykjavík: Hið Íslenzka fornritafélag, 1943).

Secondary Literature

Aakjær, Svend, 'Om det olddanske Herred og Sogn', in P. Nørlund (ed.), *Festskrift til Kristian Erslev: den 28. Decbr. 1927 fra danske historikere* (Copenhagen: H. Hagerups boghandel, 1927), 1–30.

Abel, Wilhelm, *Die Wüstungen des ausgehenden Mittelalters*, 2nd edn (Stuttgart: Gustav Fischer Verlag, 1955).

Abel, Wilhelm, Geschichte der deutschen Landwirtschaft vom frühen Mittelalter bis zum 19. Jahrhundert (Stuttgart: E. Ulmer, 1962).

Achrainer, Martin, and Niko Hofinger, 'Politik nach "Tiroler Art – ein Dreiklang aus Fleiß, Tüchtigkeit und Zukunftsglauben". Anmerkungen, Anekdoten und Analysen zum politischen System Tirols 1945–1999', in Michael Gehler (ed.), *Tirol. 'Land im Gebirge': Zwischen Tradition und Moderne*, Geschichte der österreichischen Bundesländer seit 1945, 3 and Schriftenreihe des Forschungsinstituts für politisch-historische Studien der Dr.-Wilfried-Haslauer-Bibliothek, 6 (Vienna: Böhlau, 1999), 27–136.

Almås, Reidar, and Brynjulv Gjerdåker (eds), *Norwegian Agricultural History* (Trondheim: Tapir Academic Press, 2004).

Andergassen, Leo, and Julia Hörmann-Thurn und Taxis (eds), *Margarete Gräfin von Tirol – Margareta contessa del Tirolo* (Innsbruck: Studienverlag, 2007).

Andersen, Per, *Rex imperator in regno suo, Dansk Kongemagt og rigslovgivning i 1200-tallets Europa* (Odense: Syddansk universitetsforlag, 2005).

Andersen, Per, *Studier i dansk processhistorie. Tiden indtil Danske Lov 1683* (Copenhagen: Jurist- og Økonomforbundets forlag, 2010).

Andersen, Per Sveaas, *Samlingen av Norge og kristningen av landet 800–1130*, Handbok i Norges historie, 2 (Bergen: Universitetsforlaget, 1977).

Andrén, Anders, 'Städer och kungemakt – en studie i Danmarks politiske geografi före 1230', *Scandia*, 49/1 (1983), 31–76.

'Appenzeller Kriege', in Marco Jorio (ed.), *Historisches Lexikon der Schweiz*, 13 vols (Basel: Schwabe, 2002–2014), http://www.hls-dhs-dss.ch/textes/d/D8951.php.

Aschehoug, T.H., *Statsforfatningen i Norge og Danmark indtil 1814*, Norges offentlige ret, (Christiania: i commission hos Feilberg & Landmark, 1866).

Bader, Karl Siegfried, *Das mittelalterliche Dorf als Friedens- und Rechtsbereich*, Studien zur Rechtsgeschichte des mittelalterlichen Dorfes, 1 (Weimar: Böhlau, 1957).

Bader, Karl Siegfried, *Studien zur Rechtsgeschichte des mittelalterlichen Dorfes*, i (Weimar: Böhlau, 1957).

Bader, Karl Siegfreid, *Dorfgenossenschaft und Dorfgemeinde*, Studien zur Rechtsgeschichte des mittelalterlichen Dorfes, 2 (Weimar: H. Böhlaus, 1962).

Bader, Karl Siegfried, *Rechtsformen und Schichten der Liegeschaftsnutzung im mittelalterlichen Dorf*, Studien zur Rechtsgeschichte des mittelalterlichen Dorfes, 3 (Vienna: Böhlau, 1973).

Bagge, Sverre, 'Fantes det en norsk nasjonal identitet i middelalderen?', in May-Brith Ohman Nielsen (ed.), *Nasjonal identitet og nasjonalisme: Innlegg på HiFo-seminaret i Farsund* (Oslo: Den norske historiske forening, 1994), 7–21.

Bately, Janet, and Anton Englert (eds), *Ohthere's Voyages: A Late 9th Century Account of Voyages along the Coasts of Norway and Denmark and its Cultural Context* (Roskilde: Viking Ship Museum, 2007).

Battenberg, F., 'Schöffen, Schöffengericht', in Adalbert Erler, et al. (eds), *Handwörterbuch zur deutschen Rechtsgeschichte*, 5 vols (Berlin: Schmidt, 1964–1991), iv, 1436–69.

'Bauer, Bauerntum', in Robert-Henri Bautier, et al. (eds), *Lexikon des Mittelalters*, 9 vols (Munich and Zurich: Artemis [vols 1–6] and LexMA-Verlag [vols 7–9], 1977–1999), i, 1563–70, 1574–76, (W. Rösener) 1586–89.

'Bauernstaaten' in Robert-Henri Bautier, et al. (eds), *Lexikon des Mittelalters*, 9 vols (Munich and Zurich: Artemis [vols 1–6] and LexMA-Verlag [vols 7–9], 1977–1999), i, 1622f.

Bavel, Bas J.P. van, 'The Organization and Rise of Land and Lease Markets in Northwestern Europe and Italy, *c.* 1000–1800', *Continuity and Change*, 23/1 (2008), 13–54.

Bavel, Bas J.P. van, and Philipp R. Schofield (eds), *The Development of Leasehold in Northwestern Europe, c. 1200–1600* (Turnhout: Brepols, 2008).

Beck, Heinrich, 'Philologische Bemerkungen zu "Bauer" im Germanischen', in R. Wenskus, H. Jankuhn, K. Grinda (eds), *Wort und Begriff 'Bauer': Zusammenfassende Bericht über die Kolloquien der Kommision für die Altertumskunde Mittel- und Nordeuropas* (Göttingen: Abhandlungen der Akademie der Wissenschaften in Göttingen, 1975), 58–72.

Beimrohr, Wilfried, *Mit Brief und Siegel. Die Gerichte Tirols und ihr älteres Schriftgut im Tiroler Landesarchiv*, Tiroler Geschichtsquellen, 34 (Innsbruck: Tiroler Landesarchiv, 1994).

Beimrohr, Wilfried, 'Bauerliche Besitzrechte und die landliche Gemeinde in Tirol', in Tore Iversen, John Ragnar Myking, and Gertrud Thoma (eds), *Bauern zwischen Herrschaft und Genossenschaft: Peasant Relations to Lords and Government. Scandinavia and the Alpine Region 1000–1750* (Trondheim: Tapir Akademisk Forlag, 2007), 85–108.

Beimrohr, Wilfried, 'Die ländliche Gemeinde in Tirol aus rechtsgeschichtlicher Perspektive', *Tiroler Heimat. Jahrbuch für Geschichte und Volkskunde Nord-, Ost- und Südtirols*, 72 (2008), 161–78.

Benediktsson, Jakob. See Jakob Benediktsson.

Berg, Johan, *Gods och Landskap: Jordägand, begyggelse och samhälle i Östergötland 1000–1562* (Stockholm: Kulturgeografiska institutionen, Stockholms universitet, 2003).

Bergdolt, Klaus, *Die Pest: Geschichte des Schwarzen Todes* (Munich: C.H. Beck, 2006).

'Bern (Kanton)', in Marco Jorio (ed.), *Historisches Lexikon der Schweiz*, 13 vols (Basel: Schwabe, 2002–2014), ii, 258–66.

Bierbrauer, Peter, *Freiheit und Gemeinde im Berner Oberland 1300–1700*, Archiv des Historischen Vereins des Kantons Bern, 74 (Bern: Historischer Verein des Kantons Bern, 1991).

Bierbrauer, Peter, 'Ländliche Gemeinde in oberdeutschen-schweizerischen Raum', in Peter Blickle (ed.), *Landgemeinde und Stadtgemeinde in Mitteleuropa. Ein struktureller Vergleich*, Historische Zeitschrift, 13 (Munich, 1991), 169–90.

'Birk' in Rolf Fladby, Steinar Imsen and Harald Winge, *Norsk historisk Leksikon* (Oslo: Cappelen, 1974).

Bischoff, Ferdinand, and Anton Schönbach (eds), *Steirische und Kärnthische Taidinge*, Österreichische Weisthümer, 6 (Vienna, 1881).

Bitterauf, Theodor (ed.), *Die Traditionen des Hochstifts Freising (744–1284)*, 2 vols (Munich: Rieger, 1905–09).

Bjørkvik, Halvard, 'Jordejendom – Norge', in John Granlund (ed.), *Kulturhistoriskt lexicon för nordisk medeltid – från vikingatid till reformationstid*, 22 vols (Malmö: Allhem, 1956–78), vii, 667.

Bjørkvik, Halvard, 'Skipreide', in John Granlund (ed.), *Kulturhistoriskt lexicon för nordisk medeltid – från vikingatid till reformationstid*, 22 vols (Malmö: Allhem, 1956–78), xv, 546–51.

Bjørkvik, Halvard, 'Det norske krongodset i mellomalderen', *Historisk Tidsskrift* (*norsk*), 40 (1960/61), 201–31.

Blickle, Peter, *Die Revolution von 1525* (Munich: Oldenbourg, 1977).

Blickle, Peter, 'Bäuerliche Rebellion im Fürststift St. Galle', in Peter Blickle (ed.), *Aufruhr und Empörung? Studien zum bäuerlichen Widerstand im Alten Reich*, (Munich: Beck, 1980), 215–295.

Blickle, Peter, 'Der Kommunalismus als Gestaltungsprinzip zwischen Mittelalter und Moderne', in Nicolai Bernard and Quirinius Reichen (eds), *Gesellschaft und Gesellschaften. Festschrift Ulrich Im Hof* (Bern: Wyss-Verlag, 1982), 95–113.

Blickle, Peter, Studien zur geschichtlichen Bedeutung des deutschen Bauernstandes (Stuttgart/New York: de Gruyter 1989).

Blickle, Peter, 'Friede und Verfassung. Voraussetzungen und Folgen der Eidgenossenschaft von 1291', in *Innerschweiz und frühe Eidgenossenschaft. Jubiläumsschrift 700 Jahre Eidgenossenschaft*, i: *Verfassung-Kirche-Kunst* (Olten: Walter, 1990).

Blickle, Peter, 'Conclusion', in Peter Blickle (ed.), *Resistance, Representation and Community* (Oxford: Clarendon Press, 1997).

Blickle, Peter, 'Deutsche Agrargeschichte in der zweiten Hälfte des 20. Jahrhunderts', in Werner Troßbach and Clemens Zimmermann (eds), *Agrargeschichte. Positionen und Perspektiven* (Stuttgart: Lucius und Lucius, 1998), 7–32.

Blickle, Peter, *Von der Leibeigenschaft zu den Menschenrechten: Eine Geschichte der Freiheit in Deutschland* (Munich: C.H. Beck, 2003).

Blickle, Peter (ed.), *Revolte und Revolution in Europa* (Munich: Oldenbourg, 1975).

Blickle, Peter, et al. (ed.), Aufruhr und Empörung? Studien zum bäuerlichen Widerstand im Alten Reich (Munich: Beck, 1980).

Blickle, Renate, 'Agrarische Konflikte und Eigentumsordnung in Altbayern 1400–1800', in Winfred Schulze (ed.), *Aufstände, Revolten, Prozesse: Beiträge zu bäuerlichen Widerstandsbewegungen im frühneuzeitlichen Europa*, Geschichte und Gesellschaft: Buchumer Historische Studien, 27 (Stuttgart: Clett-Cotta, 1983), 166–87.

Bloch, Marc, *Les caractères originaux de l'histoire rurale francaise*, Instituttet for sammenlignende kulturforskning Serie B, 19 (Oslo: Aschehoug, 1931); Engl. trans. Janet Sandheimer with foreward by Bryce Lyon as *French Rural History: An Essay on Its Basic Characteristics* (London: Routledge & Kegan Paul, 1966).

Bloch, Marc, *Les caractères originaux de l'histoire rurale francaise*, ii: *Supplément établi daprès de "auteur (1931–1944)"*, ed. Robert Dauvergne (Paris: A. Colin, 1952–56).

Bloch, Marc, 'A Contribution towards a Comparative History of European Society', in *Land and Work in Medieval Europe. Selected papers by Marc Bloch*, trans. J.E. Anderson (Berkely: University of California Press, 1967), 44–81.

Bloch, Marc, *Slavery and Serfdom in the Middle Ages: Selected Essays*, trans. William R. Beer (Berkeley: University of California Press, 1975).

Bø, Arne, 'Hauld', in John Granlund (ed.), *Kulturhistoriskt lexikon för nordisk medeltid – från vikingatid till reformationstid*, 22 vols (Malmö: Allhem, 1956–78), vi, 251–54.

Bø, Arne, 'Lagting', in John Granlund (ed.), *Kulturhistoriskt lexikon för nordisk medeltid – från vikingatid till reformationstid*, 22 vols (Malmö: Allhem, 1956–78), x, 216–24.

Bøgh, Anders, 'Magten i middelalderen. En skitse af statsmagtens etablering og udviklingen af dommer-funksjoner', in *Individ, slægt og magt i dansk middelalder*, Den Jyske historiker, 42 (Aarhus: Aarhus Universitetsforlag, 1987).

Bøgh, Anders, and Brigit Løgstrup, 'Hoveri', http://danmarkshistorien.dk/leksikon-og-kilder/vis/materiale/hoveri/.

Boldt, Hans, 'Otto von Gierke', in Hans-Ulrich Wehler (ed.), *Deutsche Historiker*, 8 (Göttingen: Vandenhoeck und Ruprecht, 1982), 7–23.

'Bonde' (articles for Danmark, Norge, Island, Sverige), in John Granlund (ed.), *Kulturhistoriskt lexicon för nordisk medeltid – från vikingatid till reformationstid*, 22 vols (Malmö: Allhem, 1956–78), ii, 84–99.

'Borgrätt', in *Nordisk familjebok*, iii: *Bergsvalan-Branstad*, 2nd edn (Stockholm, 1905), 1192–93.

Bosl, Karl, *Die Reichsministerialität der Salier und Staufer 1–2*, Schriften der Monumenta Germaniae Historica, 10, 1–2 (Stuttgart: Hiersemann, 1950/51).

Brady, Thomas, *Turning Swiss. Cities and Empire, 1450–1550*, Cambridge Studies in Early Modern History (Cambridge: Cambridge University Press, 1985).

Brakensiek, Stefan, 'Regionalgeschichte als Sozialgeschichte. Studien zur ländlichen Gesellschaft im deutschsprachigen Raum', in Stefan Brakensiek and Alex Flügel (eds), *Regionalgeschichte in Europa. Methoden und Erträge der Forschung zum 16. bis 19. Jahrhundert*, Forschungen zur Regionalgeschichte, 34 (Paderborn: Schöningh, 2000), 197–251.

Brändle, Fabian, *Demokratie und Charisma. Fünf Landsgemeindekonflikte im 18. Jahrhundert*, published dissertation, University of Basel, 2002 (Zurich: Chronos, 2005).

Brandt, Frederik, *Tingsretten, fremstillet efter den norske Lovgivning* (Kristiania: Damm, 1878).

Bretholz, Berthold (ed.), Das Urbar der Liechtensteinischen Herrschaften Nikolsburg, Dürnholz, Lundenburg, Falkenstein, Feldsberg, Rabensburg, Mistelbach, Hagenberg und Gnadendorf aus dem Jahre 1414, Sudetendeutsche Geschichtsquellen, 3 (Liberec/Chomutov, 1930).

Brink, Stefan, 'Slavery in Scandinavia, as Reflected in Names, Runes and Sagas', in Per O. Hernæs and Tore Iversen (eds), *Slavery Across Time and Space: Studies in Slavery in Medieval Europe and Africa*, Trondheim Studies in History, 38 (Trondheim: Norwegian University of Science and Technology, 2002), 107–29.

Bruckmüller, Ernst, 'Täler und Gerichte', in Ernst Bruckmüller, Helmuth Stradal and Michael Mitterauer (eds), *Herrschaftsstruktur und Ständebildung. Beiträge zur Typologie der österreichischen Länder aus ihren mittelalterlichen Grundlagen*, 3 (Munich: De Gruyter Oldenbourg, 1973).

Bruckmüller, Ernst, *Österreichische Sozialgeschichte* (Vienna: Herold-Verlold, 1985).

Brückner, Th., 'Widerstandsrecht', in in Robert-Henri Bautier, et al. (eds), *Lexikon des Mittelalters*, 9 vols (Munich and Zurich: Artemis [vols 1–6] and LexMA-Verlag [vols 7–9], 1977–1999), ix, 64–66.

Buckland, William Warwick, *The Roman Law of Slavery* (Cambridge: CUP, 1908), 131–238.

Brun, Katherine, The Abbot and His Peasants: Territorial Formation in Salem from the Later Middle Ages to the Thirty Years War, Quellen und Forschungen zur Agrargeschichte, 56 (Stuttgart: Lucius & Lucius, 2013).

Brunner, Otto, *Adeliges Landleben und europäischer Geist. Leben und Werk Wolf Helmhards von Hohberg 1612–1688* (Salzburg: O. Müller, 1949).

Brunner, Otto, *Land und Herrschaft*, 5th edn (Vienna: Rohrer, 1965).

Brunner, Otto, 'Das "ganze Haus" und die alteuropäische "Ökonomik"', in *Neue Wege der Verfassungs- und Sozialgeschichte* (Göttingen: Vandenhoeck und Ruprecht, 1968), 103–27.

Brunner, Walter, 'Die Gmein im steirischen Altsiedelland', in Gerhard Pferschy (ed.), *Siedlung, Macht und Wirtschaft: Festschrift Fritz Posch zum 70. Geburtstag*(Graz: Steiermärchischen Landesarchiv, 1981), 45–50.

Bull, Edvard, *Sammenlignende studier over bondesamfundets kulturforhold: Et arbeidsprogram*, Institutt for sammenlignende kulturforskning Serie C, 2.2 (Oslo: Institutt for sammenlignende kulturforskning, 1929).

Bull, Edvard, *Det norske folks liv og historie*, ii (Oslo: Aschehoug, 1935).

Buszello, Horst, 'Teuerung und Hungersnot am Ober- und Hochrhein im Spätmittelalter und in der Frühen Neuzeit (circa 1300–1800)', in Ursula Huggle (ed.), *Kriege, Krisen und Katastrophen am Oberrhein vom Mittelalter bis zur Frühen Neuzeit, Tagung des Historischen Seminars Abteilung Landesgeschichte an der Universität Freiburg und der Stadt Neuenburg am Rhein 13. und 14.10.2006*, Das Markgräflerland, 2 (Schopfheim: Geschichtsverein Markgräflerland, 2007), 32–71.

Carlie, Anne, 'Magnate Estates along the Road: Viking Age Settlements, Communication and Contacts in South-West Scania, Sweden', *Acta Archaeologica*, 79 (2008), 110–744.

Cerman, Markus, 'Proto-industrielle Entwicklung in Österreich', in Markus Cerman and Sheilagh C. Ogilvie (eds), *Proto-Industrialisierung in Europa: Industrielles Gewerbe vor dem Fabrikzeitalter* (Vienna: Verlag für Gesellschaftskritik, 1994), 161–75.

Cerman, Markus, 'Bodenmärkte und ländliche Wirtschaft in vergleichender Sicht: England und das östliche Mitteleuropa im Spätmittelalter', *Jahrbuch für Wirtschaftsgeschichte*, 2 (2004), 125–50.

Cerman, Markus, 'Mittelalterliche Ursprünge der unterbäuerlichen Schichten', in Markus Cerman and Robert Luft (eds), *Untertanen, Herrschaft und Staat in Böhmen und im 'Alten Reich'*, Sozialgeschichtliche Perspektiven (Munich: Oldenbourg, 2005), 323–50.

Cerman, Markus, 'Unterbäuerliche Schichten in ländlichen Gesellschaften des spätmittelalterlichen östlichen Mitteleuropa', *Bohemia: Zeitschrift für Geschichte und Kultur der Böhmischen Länder*, 46 (2005), 373–401.

Cerman, Markus, 'Mittelalterliche Grundlagen: wirtschaftlicher und gesellschaftlicher Wandel im Waldviertel bis zum frühen 16. Jahrhundert', in Herbert Knittler (ed.), *Wirtschaftsgeschichte des Waldviertels* (Horn: Waldviertler Heimatbund, 2006), 1–76.

Cerman, Markus, 'Social Structure and Land Markets in Late Medieval Central and East-central Europe', *Continuity and Change*, 23/1 (2008), 55–100.

Chirot, Daniel, 'The Social and Historical Landscape of Marc Bloch', in Theda Skocpol (ed.), *Vision and Method in Historical Sociology* (Cambridge: CUP, 1984), 22–46.

Christensen, Aksel E., in Inge Skovgaard-Petersen, Aksel E. Christensen, Helge Paludan (eds), *Danmarks historie*, v, Part 1 (Copenhagen: Gyldendal, 1977), 102–03, 106–08.

Christensen, Aksel E., *Ret og magt i dansk middelalder: forelæsinger* (Copenhagen: Gyldendal, 1978).

Clavadetscher, Otto P., 'Die Annäherung der spätmittelalterlichen Erbleihe im nordalpinen Graubünden an das freie Grundeigentum', in Ludwig Petry (ed.), *Festschrift für Johannes Bärmann*, Part 1, Geschichtliche Landeskunde, 3 (Wiesbaden: F. Steiner, 1966), 27–44.

Clavadetscher, Otto P., 'Kontinuität und Wandel im Recht und in den Lebensverhältnissen', *Neujahrsblatt, ed. by Historischen Verein des Kantons St. Gallen*, 132 (1992), 7–28.

Clavadetscher, Otto P., 'Die ältesten Appenzeller Siegel als Quellen zur Verfassungsgeschichte', *Archiv für Diplomatik, Schriftgeschichte, Siegel- und Wappenkunde*, 54 (2008), 85–98.

Coing, Helmut, *Europäisches Privatrecht*, i: *Älteres Gemeines Recht (1500 bis 1800)* (Munich: C.H. Beck, 1985).

Cole, John W., and Eric R. Wolf, *Die unsichtbare Grenze. Ethnizität und Ökologie in einem Alpental* (Vienna: Folio Verlag, 1995).

Conze, Werner, 'Bauern, Bauernstand und Bauerntum', in *Geschichtliche Grundbegriffe* (Stuttgart: Klett-Cotta 1972), i, 407–39.

Corni, Gustavo, and Horst Gies, *'Blut und Boden'. Rassenideologie und Agrarpolitik im Staat Hitlers* (Idstein: Schulz-Kirchner, 1994).

Crawford, Barbara E., *Scandinavian Scotland* (Leicester: Leicester University Press, 1987).

Dahl, Ottar, *Norsk historieforskning i 19. og 20. århundre* (Oslo: Universitetsforlaget, 1970).

Dahlerup, Troels, 'Syssel', in John Granlund (ed.), *Kulturhistoriskt lexikon för nordisk medeltid – från vikingatid till reformationstid*, 22 vols (Malmö: Allhem, 1956–78), xvii, 649–50.

Dannenbauer, Heinrich, 'Adel, Burg und Herrschaft bei den Germanen', in Hellmut Kämpf (ed.), *Herrschaft und Staat im Mittelalter* (Darmstadt: Wissenschaftliche Buchgesellschaft, 1964), 66–134.

Darré, Richard Walther, Das Bauerntum als Lebensquell der Nordischen Rasse (Munich, 1928).

Degen, Bernhard, Fridolin Kurmann, André Schluchter, et al. (eds), *Fenster zur Geschichte. 20 Quellen, 20 Interpretationen. Festschrift für Markus Mattmüller* (Basel, Frankfurt a.M.: Helbing und Lichtenhahn, 1992).

Demade, Julien, 'The Medieval Countryside in German-Language Historiography since the 1930s', in Isabel Alfonso Antón (ed.), *The Rural History of Medieval European Societies: Trends and Perspectives* (Turnhout: Brepols, 2007), 173–252.

Demade, Julien, 'Grundrente, Jahreszyklus und monetarisierte Zirkulation: Zur Funktionsweise des spätmittelalterlichen Feudalismus', *Historische Anthropologie*, 17/2 (2009), 222–44.

Derschka, Harald, (ed.), *Die Reichenauer Lehenbücher der Äbte Friedrich von Zollern (1402–1427) und Friedrich von Wartenberg (1428–1453)*, Veröffentlichungen der Kommission für geschichtliche Landeskunde in Baden-Württemberg, Reihe A/Quellen, 61 (Stuttgart, 2018).

Dilcher, G., 'Widerstandsrecht', in Adalbert Erler, et al. (eds), *Handwörterbuch zur deutschen Rechtsgeschichte*, 5 vols (Berlin: Schmidt, 1964–1991), v, 1351–64.

Dinklage, Karl, *Geschichte der Kärntner Landwirtschaft* (Klagenfurt: Heyn, 1966).

Dipper, Christof, *Die Bauernbefreiung in Deutschland 1790–1850* (Stuttgart: Kohlhammer, 1980).

Dipper, Christof, 'Bauern als Gegenstand der Sozialgeschichte', in Wolfgang Schieder and Volker Sellin (eds), Sozialgeschichte in Deutschland. Entwicklungen und Perspektiven im internationalen Zusammenhang, iv: Soziale Gruppen in der Geschichte (Göttingen: Vandenhoeck und Ruprecht, 1987), 9–33.

DN = *Diplomatarium Norvegicum*, under 'Primary Sources'.

Dollinger, Philippe, *Der bayerische Bauernstand vom 9. Bis zum 13. Jahrhundert* (Munich: C.H. Beck, 1982).

Dopsch, Alfons, *Die ältere Wirtschafts- und Sozialgeschichte der Bauern in den Alpenländern Österreichs*, Instituttet for sammenlignende kulturforskning Serie A, 11 (Oslo: Aschehoug, 1930).

Dopsch, Alfons, Herrschaft und Bauer in der deutschen Kaiserzeit: Untersuchungen zur Agrar- und Sozialgeschichte des hohen Mittelalters mit besonderer Berücksichtigung des südostdeutschen Raumes (Jena: Gustav Fischer, 1939).

Dopsch, Alfons (ed.), *Die landesfürstlichen Urbare Nieder- und Oberösterreichs aus dem 13. und 14. Jahrhundert*, Österreichische Urbare Abt. 1, 1 (Vienna: W. Bramüller, 1904).

Dopsch, Heinz, 'Wandlungen und Konstanz der spätmittelalterlichen Grundherrschaft im Erzstift Salzburg', in Hans Patze (ed.), *Die Grundherrschaft im späten Mittelalter*, Vorträge und Forschungen, 27, 2 vols (Sigmaringen, 1983).

Dopsch, Heinz, 'Neue Leibeigenschaft oder alte Hörigkeit? Zu den Beschwerden und Forderungen aufständischer Bauern im Ostalpenraum an der Wende zur Neuzeit', in Paul Freedman and Monique Bourin (eds), *Forms of Servitude in Northern and Central Europe* (Turnhout: Brepols, 2005), 313–40.

Dopsch, Heinz, 'Zur entwicklung des bäuerlichen Bestizrechts im Ostlpenraum' in Tore Iversen and John Ragnar Myking (eds), *Land, Lords and Peasants: Peasants' Right to Control Land in the Middle Ages and the Early Modern Period – Norway, Scandinavia and the Alpine Region*, Trondheim Studies in History, 52 (Trondheim: NTNU, 2005), 63–80.

Dopsch, Heinz, 'Zwischen Herrschaft und Genossenschaft. Grundstrukturen bäuerlichen Lebens im Ostalmpenraum', in Tore Iversen, John Ragnar Myking, and Gertrud Thoma (eds), *Bauern zwischen Herrschaft und Genossenschaft: Peasant Relations to Lords and Government. Scandinavia and the Alpine Region 1000–1750* (Trondheim: Tapir Akademisk Forlag, 2007), 65–83.

Dopsch, Heinz, and Hans Spatzenegger, *Geschicte Salzburs: Stadt und Land*, 2 vols, 8 sections (Salzburg: Universitätsverlag A. Pustet, 1981–1991).

Dornheim, Andreas, 'Die deutsche Agrargeschichte in der NS-Zeit und die Lehrstuhl-Berufungen nach 1945 in Westdeutschland', *Zeitschrift für Agrargeschichte und Agrarsoziologie*, 53/2 (2005), 39–55.

Dørum, Knut, *Oppløsningen av skyldeiesystemet. En studie av eiendomsformer og eierinteresser knyttet til jord i Norge ca. 1600–1800* (Oslo: Tingbokprosjektet, 1996).

Døssland, Atle, *Strilesoga. Nord- og Midhordland gjennom tidene*, iii: *Frå 1650 til 1800* (Bergen: Eide, 1998).

Drüppel, H. 'Gericht, Gerichtbarkeit', in Robert-Henri Bautier, et al. (eds), *Lexikon des Mittelalters*, 9 vols (Munich and Zurich: Artemis [vols 1–6] and LexMA-Verlag [vols 7–9], 1977–1999), iv, 1322–24.

Drüppel, H. 'Landgericht', in Robert-Henri Bautier, et al. (eds), *Lexikon des Mittelalters*, 9 vols (Munich and Zurich: Artemis [vols 1–6] and LexMA-Verlag [vols 7–9], 1977–1999), v, 1660–61.

Dubach, Philipp, *Gesetz und Verfassung. Die Anfänge der territorialen Gesetzgebung im Allgäu und im Appenzell im 15. und 16. Jahrhundert*, Oberschwaben – Geschichte und Kultur, 6 (Tübingen: Bibliotheca Academica, 2001).

Duft, Johannes, Anton Gössi and Werner Vogler, *Die Abtei St.Gallen: Abriss der Geschichte, Kurzbiographien der Äbte, das stift-sanktgallische Offizialat* (St Gallen, 1986).

Dyngen, Harald Unneland, *Leilendingenes vilkår i Norge – økonomisk og rettslig fram til ca. 1350*, Master's thesis, University of Bergen, Bergen, 1986.

Dyrvik, Ståle: 'Overgangen til sjølveige i Norge: Nokre nye data for 1700-talet', *Historisk tidsskrift*, 56 (1977), 1–18.

Ebel, Johann Gottfried, *Schilderung der Gebirgsvölker der Schweitz*, i (Leipzig, 1798).

Engeler, Urs Paul, 'Der Tanz ums Kalb. Hirte, Held und Heimatschützer – der Schweizer bleibt in seinem Herzen, was er nie war: ein Bauer aus dem Bilderbuch', *Bauern, was nun? NZZ Folio*, (9/1994), 40–45.

Engels, Friedrich, 'Die Mark', in Ludolf Kuchenbuch and Bernd Michael (eds), *Feudalismus – Materialien zur Theorie und Geschichte* (Frankfurt a.M.: Ullstein, 1977), 319–33.

Epstein, Steven A., An Economic and Social History of Later Medieval Europe, 1000–1500 (Cambridge, 2009).

Erhard, Benedikt, *Bauernstand und Politik. Zur Geschichte des Tiroler Bauernbundes*, Schriftenreihe der Michael Gaismair Gesellschaft, 1 (Vienna: Jugen und Volk, 1981).

Erni, Peter, 'Geschriebene Landschaft. Der Wandel von Kulturlandschaft und Güterstruktur in Basadingen nach dem Schriftgut des Klosters St. Katharinental (14.-18. Jh.)', *Thurgauer Beiträge zur Geschichte*, 137 (2000), 1–231.

Eugster, Erwin, and Verena Baumer-Müller, 'St. Katharinenthal', in Helvetia Sacra. Abteilung IV, Die Orden mit Augustinerregel, v, no. 2: Die Dominikaner und Dominikanerinnen in der Schweiz (Basel, 1999), 780–840.

Faith, Rosamond, *The English Peasantry and the Growth of Lordship* (Leicester: Leicester University Press, 1997).

Feigl, Helmuth, 'Zur Rechtslage der unterbäuerlichen Schichten im 15., 16. und 17. Jahrhundert', in Herbert Knittler (ed.), *Wirtschafts- und sozialhistorische Beiträge. Festschrift für Alfred Hoffmann*, (Vienna: Verlag für Geschichte und Politik, 1979), 247–71.

Feigl, Helmuth, and Andreas Kusternig (ed.), *Mittelalterliche Wüstungen in Niederösterreich* (Vienna: NÖ Inst. Für Landeskunde, 1983).

Fitz, Arno, *Die Frühindustrialisierung Vorarlbergs und ihre Auswirkungen auf die Familienstruktur* (Dornbirn: Vorarlberger Verl.-Anst., 1985).

Fladby, Rolf, 'Lensmenn', in John Granlund (ed.), *Kulturhistoriskt lexikon för nordisk medeltid – från vikingatid till reformationstid*, 22 vols (Malmö: Allhem, 1956–78), x, 505–06.

Fladby, Rolf, *Fra lensmannstjener til Kongelig Majestets Foged* (Oslo: Universitetsforlaget, 1963).

Fontana, Josef, et al. (eds), *Geschichte des Landes Tirol*, i (Bozen / Vienna: Verlagsanstalt Athesia, 1985).

Frandsen, Karl-Erik, *Vang og tægt. Studier over dyrkningssystemer og agrarstrukturer i Danmarks landsbyer 1682–83* (Esbjerg: Bygd, 1983).

Franz, Günther, *Der deutsche Bauernkrieg* (Munich: Oldenbourg, 1933. [reprint, Darmstadt: Wissenschaftliche Buchgesellschaft, 1984]).

Franz, Günther, 'Wozu Bauerngeschichte?', *Übersicht. Monatsschrift für das deutsche Landvolk*, 3 (1952), 12–14.

Franz, Günther, Geschichte des deutschen Bauernstandes vom frühen Mittelalter bis zum 19. Jahrhundert (Stuttgart: E. Ulmer, 1970).

Freedman, Paul and Monique Bourin, 'Introduction', in Paul Freedman and Monique Bourin (eds), *Forms of Servitude in Northern and Central Europe: Decline, Resistance, and Expansion* (Turnhout: Brepols, 2005), 1–15.

Fresacher, Walther, *Der Bauer in Kärnten*, i: *Die persönliche Stellung des Bauers in Kärnten* (Klagenfurt, 1950).

Fresacher, Walther, 'Die Pest in Kärnten im 14. Jahrhundert', *Carinthia*, 153 (1963), 349–78.

Fried, Pankraz, *Herrschaftsgeschichte der altbayerischen Landgerichte Dachau und Kranzberg im Hoch- und Spätmittelalter sowie in der frühen Neuzeit* (Munich: Kommision für Byerisches Landesgeschichte, 1962).

Fried, Pankraz, 'Zur Geschichte der bayerischen Landgemeinde', in Theodor Mayer (ed.), *Die Anfänge der Landgemeinde und ihr Wesen*, 2 vols, Vorträge und Forschungen, 7, (Stuttgart: Jan Thorbecke, 1964), i, 79–106.

Fried, Pankraz, 'Grundherrschaft und Dorfgericht im spätmittelalterlichen Herzogtum Bayern', in Hans Patze (ed.), *Grundherrschaft im späten Mittelalter*, 2 vols, Vorträge und Forschungen, 27 (Sigmaringen: Thorbecke, 1983), ii, 277–312.

Fröhlich, Roberto, 'Die Eigenleute des Johanniterhauses Bubikon. Eigenschaft und Leibherrschaft im Herrschaftsbereich der Johanniterkomturei Bubikon 1192–1789', dissertation, University of Zurich, Zurich, 1993.

Gadd, Carl-Johan, *Den agrara revolutionen 1700–1870*, Det svenska jordbrukets historia, 3 (Borås: Natur og Kultur/LTs förlag, 2000).

Gänser, Gerald, 'Zur mittelalterlichen Siedlungs- und Bevölkerungsentwicklung im Bezirk Voitsberg', in Gerhard Pferschy (ed.), *Siedlung, Macht und Wirtschaft. Festschrift Fritz Posch zum 70. Geburtstag* (Graz: Steiermärchicher Landesarchiv, 1981), 117–27.

Gänser, Gerald, 'Strukturveränderungen im agrarischen Bereich während des 15. Jahrhunderts', *Zeitschrift des historischen Vereins für Steiermark*, 75 (1984), 23–30.

Geary, Patrick J., 'Vergleichende Geschichte und sozialwissenschaftliche Theorie', in M. Borgolte (ed.), *Das europäische Mittelalter im Spannungsbogen des Vergleichs* (Berlin: Akademie Verlag, 2002), 29–39.

Gehler, Michael (ed.), *Tirol. 'Land im Gebirge': Zwischen Tradition und Moderne*, Geschichte der österreichischen Bundesländer seit 1945, 3 and Schriftenreihe des Forschungsinstituts für politisch-historische Studien der Dr.-Wilfried-Haslauer-Bibliothek, 6 (Vienna: Böhlau, 1999).

Gelting, Michael H., 'Legal Reforms and Development of Peasant Dependence' in *Forms of Servitude in Northern and Central Europe: Decline, Resistance, and Expansion*, Medieval Texts and Cultures of Northern Europe, 9 (Turnhout: Brepols, 2005), 343–67.

Ghosh, Shami, 'The Imperial Abbey of Ellwangen and Its Tenants: A Study of the Polyptych of 1337', *Agricultural History Review*, 62/2 (2014), 187–209.

Ghosh, Shami, 'Rural Commercialisation in Fourteenth-century Bavaria: The Evidence from Scheyern Abbey', *Vierteljahresschrift für Sozial- und Wirtschaftsgeschichte*, 2017/1 (2017), 52–77.

Gierke, Otto von, Das deutsche Genossenschaftsrecht, i: Rechtsgeschichte der deutschen Genossenschaft (Berlin: Weidmann, 1868).

Gilomen, Hans-Jörg, Die Grundherrschaft des Basler Cluniazenser-Priorates St. Alban im Mittelalter: Ein Beitrag zur Wirtschaftsgeschichte am Oberrhein, Quellen und Forschungen zur Basler Geschichte, 9 (Basel: F. Reinhardt, 1977).

Gilomen, Hans-Jörg, 'Sozial- und Wirtschaftsgeschichte der Schweiz im Spätmittelalter', *Schweizerische Zeitschrift für Geschichte*, 41 (1991), 41–66.

Gilomen, Hans-Jörg, 'Das Motiv der bäuerlichen Verschuldung in den Bauernunruhen an der Wende zur Neuzeit', in Susanna Burghartz, Hans-Jörg Gilomen, and Guy Paul Marchal (eds), *Spannungen und Widersprüche*, Gedenkschrift für Frantisek Graus (Sigmaringen, 1992), 173–89.

Gilomen, Hans-Jörg, 'Die ökonomischen Grundlagen des Kredits und die christlich-jüdische Konkurrenz im Spätmittelalter', in Eveline Brugger and Birgit Wiedl (eds), *Ein Thema – zwei Perspektiven: Juden und Christen in Mittelalter und Frühneuzeit* (Innsbruck, 2007), 139–69.

Gissel, Svend, et al. (eds), *Desertion and Land Colonization in the Nordic Countries c. 1300–1600*, (Stockholm: Almquist and Wiksell, 1981).

Glaser, Hubert (ed.), *Wittelsbach und Bayern*, i: *Die Zeit der frühen Herzöge – von Otto I. zu Ludwig dem Bayer* (Munich: Hirmer, 1980).

Glete, Jan, War and the State in Early Modern Europe: Spain, The Dutch Republic and Sweden as Fiscal-military States 1500–1660 (London: Routledge, 2002).

Goetz, Hans-Warner, *Beobachtungen Zur Grundherrschaftsentwicklung der Abtei St Gallen* (Göttingen: Vandenhoeck und Ruprecht, 1989).

Goetz, Hans-Werner, 'Serfdom and the Beginnings of a "Seigneurial System" in the Carolingian Period: A Survey and the Evidence', *Early Medieval Europe*, 2/1 (1993), 29–51.

Goetz, Hans-Werner, 'Frühmittelalterliche Grundherrschaften und ihre Erforschung im europäischen Vergleich', in Michael Borgolte (ed.), *Das europäische Mittelalter im Spannungsbogen des Vergleichs* (Berlin: Akademie Verlag, 2001), 75–87.

Granlund, John (ed.), *Kulturhistoriskt lexikon för nordisk medeltid – från vikingatid till reformationstid*, 22 vols (Malmö: Allhem, 1956–78).

Grantham, George, 'Economic History and the History of the Labour Markets', in George Grantham and Mary MacKinnon (eds), *Labour Market Evolution* (London, 1994), 1–26.

Grass, Nikolaus, *Beiträge zur Rechtsgeschichte der Alpwirtschaft* (Innsbruck, 1948).

Grass, Nikolaus, 'Aus der Frühzeit des ländlichen Gemeinde in Deutschtirol', in Alois Stadler (ed.), *Die ländliche Gemeinde: Historietagung in Bad Ragaz* (Bozen: Athesia, 1988).

Grees, Hermann, *Ländliche Unterschichten und ländliche Siedlung in Ostschwaben*, Tübinger geographische Studien, 58 (Tübingen, 1975).

Gunnes, Erik, Kongens ære: Kongemakt og kirke i 'En tale mot biskopene' (Oslo: Gyldendal 1971).

Günther, Hans F.K., *Das Bauerntum als Lebens- und Gemeinschaftsform* (Leipzig: B.G. Teubner, 1939).

Gutmann, Franz, Die soziale Gliederung der Bayern zur Zeit des Volksrechtes (Straßburg: K.J. Trübner, 1906).

Hagemann, Hans-Rudolf, 'Eigentum' in Adalbert Erler, et al. (eds), *Handwörterbuch zur Deutschen Rechtsgeschichte*, 5 vols (Berlin: Schmidt, 1964–1991), vol. 1.

Halvorsen, Eyvind Fjeld, 'Domr', in John Granlund (ed.), *Kulturhistoriskt lexikon för nordisk medeltid – från vikingatid till reformationstid*, 22 vols (Malmö: Allhem, 1956–78), iii, 214–18.

Hammer, Carl I., 'Family and Familia in Early Medieval Bavaria', in Richard Wall, Jean Robin and Peter Laslett (eds), *Family Forms in Historic Europe* (Cambridge: CUP, 1983), 217–49.

Hammer, Carl I., A Large-Scale Slave Society of the Early Middle Ages: Slaves and Their Families in Early Medieval Bavaria (Aldershot: Ashgate, 2002).

Hamre, Lars, 'Rettarting', in John Granlund (ed.), *Kulturhistoriskt lexikon för nordisk medeltid – från vikingatid till reformationstid*, 22 vols (Malmö: Allhem, 1956–78), xiv, 101–08.

Hansen, Lars Ivar: 'Peasants, Land and Inheritance: Peasant Property and Rent Ownership in the Parish of Fyresdal, Southern Norway', in Tore Iversen and John Ragnar Myking (eds), *Land, Lords and Peasants: Peasants' Right to Control Land in the Middle Ages and the Early Modern Period – Norway, Scandinavia and the Alpine Region*, Trondheim Studies in History, 52 (Trondheim: NTNU, 2005), 181–98.

Hasund, Sigvald, Ikring mannedauden: Ei liti sogestudie (Kristiania, 1920).

Heimskringla. See Snorri Sturluson.

Heimpel, Christian, Die Entwicklung der Einnahmen und Ausgaben des Heiliggeistspitals zu Biberach an der Riss von 1500 bis 1630, Quellen und Forschungen zur Agrargeschichte, 15 (Stuttgart, 1966).

Heitz, Gerhard, 'Landwirtschaft – Agrarverfassung – Bauernstand. Überlegungen zu fünf Bänden', *Jahrbuch für Wirtschaftsgeschichte*, 1 (1977), 183–207.

Helle, Knut, 'Riksmøter', in John Granlund (ed.), *Kulturhistoriskt lexikon för nordisk medeltid – från vikingatid till reformationstid*, 22 vols (Malmö: Allhem, 1956–78), xiv, 252–57.

Helle, Knut, *Norge blir en stat: 1130–1319*, Handbok i Norges historie, 3 (Oslo: Universitetsforlaget, 1964).

Helle, Knut, 'Tendenser i nyere norsk høymiddelalderforskning', *Nytt fra norsk middelalder*, 2 (Oslo: Cappelen, 1970), 384–410.

Helle, Knut, *Konge og gode menn i norsk riksstyring ca. 1150–1319*. (Oslo: Universitetsforlaget, 1972).

Helle, Knut, *Gulatinget og Gulatingslova* (Leikanger: Skald, 2001).

Helle, Knut, 'Comments on the Presentations of Ulsig, Iversen and Myking', in Tore Iversen and John Ragnar Myking (eds), *Land, Lords and Peasants: Peasants' Right To Control Land in the Middle Ages and the Early Modern Period – Norway, Scandinavia and the Alpine Region*, Trondheim Studies in History, 52 (Trondheim: NTNU, 2005), 39–45.

Helleiner, Karl F., 'Ländliches Mindervolk in niederösterreichischen Weisthümern', *Zeitschrift für Agrargeschichte und Agrarsoziologie*, 25 (1977), 12–34.

Hiereth, Sebastian, *Die bayerische Gerichts- und Verwaltungsorganisation vom 13. Bis 19. Jahrhundert*, Historischer Atlas von Bayern, Teil Altbayern, 1 (Munich: Komm. für Bayer, Landegeschichte, 1950).

Hirbodian, Sigrid, 'Ländliche Rechtsquellen und die politische Kultur in Spätmittelalter und Früher Neuzeit', in Carola Fey and Steffen Krieb (eds), *Adel und Bauern in der Gesellschaft des Mittelalters. Internationales Kolloquium zum 65. Geburtstag von Werner Rösener*, Studien und Texte zur Geistes- und Sozialgeschichte des Mittelalters, 6 (Affalterbach: Didymos-Verlag, 2012), 165–76.

Hirbodian, Sigrid, 'Recht und Ordnung im Dorf. Zur Bedeutung von Weistümern und Dorfordnungen in Spätmittelalter und Frühneuzeit', in Kurt Andermann and Oliver Auge (eds), *Dorf und Gemeinde. Grundstrukturen der ländlichen Gesellschaft in Spätmittelalter und Frühneuzeit*, Kraichtaler Kolloquien, 8 (Epfendorf, 2012), 45–63.

Hitz, Florian, 'Gesellschaft und Wirtschaft im Spätmittelalter (Mitte 14. bis Ende 15. Jahrhundert)', in *Handbuch der Bündner Geschichte*, i: *Frühzeit bis Mittelalter* (Chur, 2000), 215–43.

Holm, Poul. 'The Slave Trade of Dublin', *Peritia*, 5 (Turnhout: Brepols, 1986), 317–45.

Holmsen, Andreas, *Norges historie: Fra de eldste tider til 1660* (Oslo: Gyldendal, 1939; repr. 1949, 1961).

Holmsen, Andreas, 'Problemer i norsk jordeiendomshistorie', in *Historisk tidsskrift* (*norsk*), 34 (1946–48), 220–55.

Holmsen, Andreas, *Nye studier i gammel historie* (Oslo: Universitetsforlaget, 1976).

Holmsen, Andreas, 'Det norske "skyldeie"', in Jørn Sandnes, Arnfinn Kjelland, and Claus Krag (eds), *Norske historikere i utvalg*, v: *Nye middelalderstudier* (Oslo: Universitetsforlaget, 1981), 178–81.

Hölzl, Sebastian, 'Die Freiheitsbriefe der Wittelsbacher für Tirol (1342). Eine kritische Untersuchung der 'Magna Charta Tirols'. Mit einem Exkurs: Zur Kanzlei- und Archivgeschichte der Tiroler Freiheitsbriefe vom 28. Januar 1342 von Peter Moser', *Tiroler Heimat*, 46/47 (1982/83), 5–52.

Hørby, Kaj, 'Middelalderen', in *Samfundet i vikingetid og middelalder 800–1500*, Dansk social historie, 2 (Copenhagen: Gyldendal, 1980), 77–314.

Hörmann-Thurn und Taxis, Julia (ed.), *Margarete 'Maultasch'. Zur Lebenswelt einer Landesfürstin und anderer Tiroler Frauen des Mittelalters*, Schlern-Schriften, 339 (Innsbruck: Universitätsverlag Wagner, 2007).

Hürlimann, Katja, 'Worum geht es in der Wald- und Forstgeschichte?', *Schweizerisches Zeitschrift für Forstwesen*, 154 (2003), 322–27.

Hürlimann, Katja, and Stefan Sonderegger, 'Ländliche Gesellschaft im Mittelalter', *Traverse: Zeitschrift für Geschichte*, 18/1 (2011), 48–76.

Huter, Franz, 'Zur Frage der Gemeindebildung in Tirol' in Theodor Mayer (ed.), *Die Anfänge der Landgemeinde und ihr Wesen*, 2 vols, Vorträge und Forschungen, 7 (Stuttgart: Jan Thorbecke, 1964), i, 223–35.

Hybel, Niels, and Bjørn Poulsen, *The Danish Resources c. 1000–1550: Growth and Recession*, The Northern World, 34 (Leiden: Brill, 2007).

Hybel, Niels, 'The Rise and Fall of Leasehold in Denmark c. 1100–1550', in Bas J.P. van Bavel and Phillipp R. Schofield (eds), *The Development of Leasehold in Northwestern Europe c. 1200–1600*, Comparative Rural History of the North Sea Area, 10 (Turnhout: Brepols, 2008), 99–111.

Hybel, Niels, 'The Roman Catholic Institutions', in Bjørn Paulsen and Søren Michael Sindbæk (eds), *Settlement and Lordship in Viking and Early Medieval Scandinavia*, The Medieval Countryside, 9 (Turnhout: Brepols, 2011), 223–38.

Imsen, Steiner, *Norsk bondekommunalisme fra Magnus Lagabøte til Kristian Kvart*, i: *Middelalderen* (Trondheim: Tapir forlag, 1990).

Imsen, Steinar, *Norsk bondekommunalisme fra Magnus Lagabøte til Kristian Kvart*, ii: *Lydriketiden*, Skriftserie fra Historisk institutt, 7 (Trondheim: Tapir forlag, 1994).

Imsen, Steinar, and Günter Vogler: 'Communal Autonomy and Peasant Resistance', in Peter Blickle (ed.), *Resistance, Representation and Community* (Oxford: Clarendon Press, 1997).

Indrelid, Svein, Strilesoga: Nord- og Midhordland gjennom tidene, i: Frå steinalder til vikingtid (Bergen: Eide, 1997).

Ipsen, Gunther, 'Das Dorf in der deutschen Gegenwart', *Archiv für angewandte Soziologie*, 2 1930, 172–184, 228–24.

Ipsen, Gunther, *Das Landvolk: ein soziologischer Versuch* (Hamburg: Hanseatische Verlagsanstalt, 1933).

Iversen, Frode, *Var middelalderens lendmannsgårder kjerner i eldre godssamlinger*, Arkeologiske avhandlingar og rapporter frå Universitetet i Bergen, 4 (Bergen: Arkeologisk Institutt, 1999).

Iversen, Frode, 'Eiendom, makt og statsdannelse: Kongsgårder og gods i Hordaland i yngre jernalder og midelalder', PhD thesis, University of Bergen, Bergen, 2004.

Iversen, Frode 'Den nyere norske forskningen om jordegods i vikingtid og tidlig middelalder: En sammenligning med undersøkelsene av manor- og Grundherrschaftsystemer i Vest-Europa', *Varia*, 71 (2009), 59–70. http://urn.nb.no/URN:NBN:no-30052 (permanent link).

Iversen, Tore, 'Trelldommen: Norsk slaveri i middelalderen', dr.art. thesis, University of Bergen, Bergen, 1994.

Iversen, Tore, 'Fremveksten av det norske leiglendingsvesenet i middelaldren: en forklaringsskisse', *Heimen*, 32 (1995), 169–80.

Iversen, Tore, 'Landskapslovene og kanoniske rett', in Audun Dybdahl and Jørn Sandnes (eds), *Nordiske middelalderlover. Tekst og kontekst. Rapport fra seminar ved Senter for middelalderstudier 29.-30. nov 1996*, Skrifter fra Senter for middelalderstudier, 5 (Trondheim: Tapir, 1997), 69–84.

Iversen, Tore, *Trelldommen: norsk slaveri i middelalderen*, Universitetet i Bergen Skrifter, 1 (Bergen: Historisk institutt, 1997) [published in German as: *Knechtschaft im mittelalterlichen Norwegen,* trans. Katharina Freche in collaboration with Angelika Landau, Abhandlungen zur rechtswissenschaftlichen Grundlagenforschung, 94 (Ebelsbach: Aktiv, 2004)].

Iversen, Tore, *Jordeie og jordleie – Eiendomsbegrepet i norske middelalderlover, Collegium Medievale*, 14 (2001), 79–114.

Iversen, Tore, *Knechtschaft im mittelalterlichen Norwegen*, trans. Katharina Freche in collaboration with Angelika Landau, Münchener Universitätsschriften, Juristische Fakultät, Abhandlungen zur rechtswissenschaftlichen Grundlagenforschung, 94 (Ebelsbach: Aktiv, 2004).

Iversen, Tore, 'Bauern zwischen Herrschaft uns Genossenschaft – Einleitung' in Tore Iversen, John Ragnar Myking and Gertrud Thoma (eds), *Bauern zwischen Herrschaft und Genossenschaft: Peasant Relations to Lords and Government. Scandinavia and the Alpine Region 1000–1750*, (Trondheim: Tapir Akademisk Forlag, 2007), 1–9.

Iversen, Tore, 'Die frühe norwegischer Dingordnung zwischen Herrschaft und Genossenschaf', in Tore Iversen, John Ragnar Myking, and Gertrud Thoma (eds), *Bauern zwischen Herrschaft und Genossenschaft: Peasant Relations to Lords and Government. Scandinavia and the Alpine Region 1000–1750,* (Trondheim: Tapir Akademisk Forlag, 2007), 167–86.

Iversen, Tore, 'Property and Land Tenancy in Norwegian Medieval Laws and the European Learned Law', in Per Andersen, Ditlev Tamm, and Helle Vogt (eds), *How Nordic Are the Nordic Medieval Laws? Proceedings from the First Carlsberg Conference on Medieval Legal History*, 2nd edn (Copenhagen: University of Copenhagen, 2011, [1st edn 2005]), 135–76.

Iversen, Tore, and John Ragnar Myking (eds), *Land, Lords and Peasants: Peasants' Right to Control Land in the Middle Ages and the Early Modern Period – Norway, Scandinavia and the Alpine Region*, Trondheim Studies in History, 52 (Trondheim: NTNU, 2005).

Iversen, Tore, and John Ragnar Myking, 'Changes in the Nordic Elites' Way of Extracting a Surplus from Landed Resources', in Bjørn Poulsen, Jon Vidar Sigurdsson, and Helle Vogt (eds), *Nordic Elites in Transformation 1050–1250*, i: *Material Resources*, (NY: Routledge, 2019), 32–59.

Iversen, Tore, John Ragnar Myking, and Gertrud Thoma (eds), *Bauern zwischen Herrschaft und Genossenschaft: Peasant Relations to Lords and Government. Scandinavia and the Alpine Region 1000–1750* (Trondheim: Tapir Akademisk Forlag, 2007).

Jakob Benediktsson, 'Thing, Island', in *Kulturhistorisk leksikon for nordisk middelalder*, 22 vols (Malmö: Allhem, 1956–78), xviii, 359–60.

Jäger, Georg, 'Siedlungsausbau und soziale Differenzierung der ländlichen Bevölkerung in Nordtirol wärend der frühen Neuzeit', *Tiroler Heimat*, 60 (1996).

Jäggi, Stefan, 'Die Rechnung des Heilig-Geist-Spitals von Luzern für die Jahre 1502–1507', *Der Geschichtsfreund. Mitteilungen des Historischen Vereins der Zentralschweiz*, 143 (1990), 5–69.

Jakobsen, Michael Nobel, 'Det verdslige juridiske system før 1660' (edited 28 May 2014), in *Danmarkshistoriken.dk* http://danmarkshistorien.dk/leksikon-og-kilder/vis/materiale/det-verdslige-juridiske-system-foer-1660/.

Johansson, Kenneth, 'Herrar og bönder: Om jurisdiktionen i några småländske friherrskap på 1600-talet', *Scandia*, 2 (1990), 161–82.

Johnsen, Arne Odd, *Fra ættesamfunn til statssamfunn* (Oslo: Aschehoug, 1948).

Jón Viðar Sigurðsson, 'Goder og maktforhold på Island i fristattiden', PhD thesis, University of Bergen, Bergen, 1993.

Jón Viðar Sigurðsson, 'The Icelandic Aristocracy after the Fall of the Free State', *Scandinavian Journal of History*, 3 (1995), 153–66.

Jones, Granville R.J., 'Multiple Estates and Early Settlement', in P.H. Sawyer (ed.), *Medieval Settlement – Continuity and Change* (London: Edward Arnold, 1976), 15–40.

Jordan, William Chester, *The Great Famine: Northern Europe in the Early Fourteenth Century* (Princeton: Princeton University Press, 1996).

Jörg, Christian, *'Teure, Hunger, Grosses Sterben': Hungersnöte und Versorgungskrisen in den Städten des Reiches während des 15. Jahrhunderts*, Monographien zur Geschichte des Mittelalters, 55 (Stuttgart, 2008).

Jørgensen, Jens Ulf, 'Herred', in Jørn Lund (ed.), *Den store danske encyklopædi*, vol. 8 (Copenhagen: Danmarks Nationalleksikon, 1994–2002).

Jørgensen, Lars, 'Manor, Cult and Markets at Lake Tissø', in Stefan Brink and Neil Price (eds), *The Viking World* (London: Routledge, 2008).

Jørgensen, Lars, 'From Tribute to the Estate System, 3th -12th Century: A Proposal for the Economic Development of the Magnate's Residence in Scandinavia Based on Settlement Structure from Gudme, Tissø and Lejre in Denmark', in B. Arrhenius (ed.), *Kingdoms and Regionality: Transactions from the 49th symposium 1998 in Uppsala* (Stockholm: Archaeological Research Laboratory, Stockholm University, 2001).

Jørgensen, P.J., 'Herredsfoged', in Isac Salmonsen, *Salmonsens Konversationsleksikon*, 11, ed. Christian Blangstrup (Copenhagen: Schultz, 1921).

Kamm, Rolf, *Glarus zwischen Habsburg und Zürich. Die Entstehung des Landes im Spätmittelalter*, published dissertation, University of Zurich, 2009 (Baden: Hier & Jetzt, 2010).

Kamm, Rolf, 'Die Schlacht bei Näfels 1388 – Kampf gegen den Erzfeind?', in Hans Rudolf Fuhrer (ed.), *Geschichte der Schweiz. Fenster in die Vergangenheit* i, Publikationen der Schweizerischen Gesellschaft für Militärhistorische Studienreisen, 32 (Wettingen: Schweizerischen Gesellschaft für Militärhistorische Studienreisen GMS, 2011).

Kämpf, Hellmut (ed.), *Herrschaft und Staat i Mittelalter m*(Darmstadt: Wissenschaftliche Buchgesellschaft, 1964).

Karras, Ruth Mazo, *Slavery and Society in Medieval Scandinavia* (New Haven: Yale University Press, 1988).

Karsvall, Olof, and Kristofer Jupiter (eds), *Medeltida storgårdar: 15 uppsatser om ett tvärvetenskapligt forskningsproblem* (Uppsala: Gustav Adolfs akademien Acta Academiae Regiae Gustavi Adolphi, 2014).

Katjala, Kimmo, *Northern Revolts: Medieval and Early Modern Peasant Unrest in the Nordic Countries*, Studia Fennica, Historica, 8 (Helsinki: Finnish Literature Society, 2004).

Kellenbenz, Hermann, et al. (eds), *Handbuch der europäischen Wirtscahfts- und Sozialgeschichte*, ii: *Europäische Wirtschafts- und Sozialgeschichte im Mittelalter* (Stuttgart: Clett-Kotta, 1980).

Keller, Hagen, 'Die Entwicklung der europäischen Schriftkultur im Spiegel der mittelalterlichen Überlieferung: Beobachtungen und Überlegungen', in Karl Leidinger and Dieter Metzler (eds), *Geschichte und Geschichtsbewusstsein, Festschrift für Karl-Ernst Jeismann zum 65. Geburtstag* (Munster, 1990), 171–204.

Klebel, Ernst, 'Freies Eigen und Beutellehen in Ober- und Niederbayern', *Zeitschrift für Bayerische Landesgeschichte*, 11 (1938), 45–85.

Klee, Doris, *Konflikte kommunizieren: Die Briefe des Grüninger Landvogts Jörg Berger an den Zürcher Rat (1514–1529)* (Zurich: Chronos, 2006).

Klein, Herbert, 'Das Grosse Sterben von 1348/49 und seine Auswirkung auf die Besiedlung der Ostalpenländer', in *Festschrift zum 65. Geburtstag von Herberg Klein*, Gesellschaft für Salzburger Landeskunde (Salzburg: Sesellschaft für Salzburger Landeskunde, 1965), 33–113 [First published in *Mitteilungen der Gesellschaft für Salzburger Landeskunde*, 100 (1960), 91–170].

Klein, Herbert, 'Die Salzburger Freisassen', in *Beiträge zur Siedlungs-, Verfassungs- und Wirtschaftsgeschicte von Salzburg: Festschrift zum 65. von Herbert Klein,* Mitteilungen der Gescellschaft für Salzburger Landeskunde, Ergänzungsband, 5 (Salzburg: Selbstverlag der Gesellschaft für Salzburger Landeskunde, 1965).

Klein, Herbert, 'Ritterlehen und Beutellehen in Salzburg', in *Beitrage zur Siedlungs- Verfassungs- und Wirtschaftsgeschicte von Salzburg: Festschrift zum 65. von Herbert Klein*, Mitteilungen der Gescellschaft für Salzburger Landeskunde, Ergänzungsband, 5 (Salzburg: Selbstverlag der Gesellschaft für Salzburger Landeskunde, 1965), 325–65.

Klein, Kurt, *Daten zur Siedlungsgeschichte der österreichischen Länder bis zum 16. Jahrhunder* (Vienna, 1980).

KLNM. See Granlund, John (ed.).

Knefelkamp, Ulrich, *Das Heilig-Geist-Spital in Nürnberg vom 14.–17. Jahrhundert. Geschichte, Struktur, Alltag*, Nürnberger Forschungen, 26 (Nuremberg: Verein für Geschichte der Stadt Nürnberg, 1989).

Knöpfli, Albert, *Das Kloster Sankt Katharinenthal,* die Kunstdenkmäler des Kantons Thurgau 4, (Basel: Wiese, 1989).

Kocka, Jürgen, 'Writing the History of Capitalism', *Bulletin of the German Historical Institute*, 47 (2010), 7–24.

Köfler, Werner, *Land-Landschaft-Landtag: Geschichte der Tiroler Landtage von den Anfängen bis zur Aufhebung der landständischen Verfassung 1808.* Veröffentlichungen des Tiroler Landesarchivs, 3 (Innsbruck: Universiätsverlag Wagner, 1985).

Koht, Halvdan, 'Sagaernes opfatning av vor gamle historie', *Historisk tidsskrift* (*norsk*), 5th ser., 2 (1914), 379–96.

Koht, Halvdan, *Den amerikanske nasjonen i upphav og reising* (Kristiania [Oslo]: Aschehoug, 1920).

Koht, Halvdan, *Norsk bondereising: Fyrebuing til bondepolitikken* (Oslo: Aschehoug, 1926). [French edition 1929.]

Koht, Halvdan, 'The Dawn of Nationalism in Europe', *The American Historical Review*, 52 (1947), 265–80.

Köppel, Christa, *Von der Äbtissin zu den gnädigen Herren: Untersuchungen zu Wirtschaft und Verwaltung der Fraumünsterabtei und des späteren Fraumünsteramts in Zürich, 1418–1549* (Zurich: Chronos, 1991).

Krauer, Rezia, 'Der Erwerb von Besitzrechten im Umland der Stadt St. Gallen durch St. Galler Bürger von 1370 bis 1389', Licentiate, University of Zurich, Zurich, 2009.

Krauer, Rezia, 'Die Beteiligung städtischer Akteure am ländlichen Bodenmarkt: Die Region St. Gallen im 13. und 14. Jahrhundert', PhD thesis, University of Zurich, Zurich, 2018 (currently in press).

Krauer, Rezia, Stefan Sonderegger, Claudia Sutter and Monika Michel-Rüegg, 'Klosterfrauen wirtschaften', in Katrin Eberhard and Ursula Hasler (eds), *St. Katharinen: Frauenkloster, Bibliothek, Bildungsstätte – Gestern und Heute* (Herisau: Appenzeller Verlag, 2013), 112–76.

Kreis, Georg, 'Jubiläen und Schlachtgedenken. Zivile Überlegungen zur militärischen Erinnerungskultur der Schweiz', *Appenzellische Jahrbücher* (2004), 13–27.

Kreis, Georg, 'Geschichten zur Gründungsgeschichte', in Erika Hebeisen, Pia Schubiger and Denise Tonella (eds), *Entstehung Schweiz. Unterwegs vom 12. ins 14. Jahrhundert* (Baden: Hier & Jetzt, 2011), 170–75.

Kroeschell, Karl, 'Dorf' in Adalbert Erler, et al. (eds), *Handwörterbuch zur deutschen Rechtsgeschichte*, 5 vols (Berlin: Schmidt, 1964–1991), vol. 1.

Kroeschell, Karl, 'Zur Lehre vom "germanischen Eigentumsbegriff"', in Hans Thieme, *Rechtshistorische Studien. Hans Thieme zum 70. Geburtstag zugeeignet von seinen Schülern* (Cologne: Böhlau, 1977), 34–71.

Kröll, Heinz, and Gert Stemberger, *Defereggen: Eine Landschaft in Tirol* (Vienna: A. Schendl Verlag, 1985).

Kuchenbuch, Ludolf, 'Potestas und Utilitas', *Historische Zeitschrift*, 265/1 (1997), 117–46.

Kuchenbuch, Ludolf, 'Vom Dienst zum Zins? Bemerkungen über agrarische Transformationen in Europa vom späteren 11. zum beginnenden 14. Jahrhundert', *Zeitschrift für Agrargeschichte und Agrarsoziologie*, 51 (2003), 11–29.

Kurz, Hans Rudolf, *Schweizerschlachten* (Bern: Francke, 1977).

Küster, Hanörg, *Geschichte der Landschaft in Mitteleuropa – von der Eiszeit bis zur Gegenwart* (Munich: Beck, 1996).

Landau, Peter, *Die Lex Baiuvariorum. Entstehungszeit, Entstehungsort und Charakter von Bayerns ältester Rechts- und Geschichtsquelle*, Sitzungsberichte: Bayerische Akademie der Wissenschaften, Phil- Hist. Klasse, 3 (Munich: Beck, 2004).

'Landfrieden' in Marco Jorio (ed.), *Historisches Lexikon der Schweiz*, 13 vols (Basel: Schwabe, 2002–2014), http://www.hls-dhs-dss.ch/textes/d/D8951.php.

Landolt, Oliver, 'Finanzielle und wirtschaftliche Aspekte der Sozialpolitik spätmittelalterlicher Spitäler', in Neithard Bulst and Karl-Heinz Spiess (eds), *Sozialgeschichte mittelalterlicher Hospitäler*, VuF, 65 (Ostfildern: Jan Thorbecke, 2007), 273–99.

Lang, Eberhard, 'Der Landtag in der Zweiten Republik (1945–1982)', in Richard Schober, *Geschichte des Tiroler Landtags im 19. und 20. Jahrhundert*, Veröffentlichungen des Tiroler Landesarchivs, 4 (Innsbruck: Universitätsverlag Wagner, 1984), 473–506.

Larsson, Mats G., *Från stormannagård till bondby. En studie av mellansvensk bebyggelseutveckling från äldre järnårder till medeltid*, Acta Archaeologica Lundensia, series 8, 26 (Stockholm: Almqvist and Wiksell, 1997).

Lárusson, Magnús Már. See Magnús Már Lárusson.

Lenz, Philipp, *Reichsabtei und Klosterreform: Das Kloster St. Gallen unter dem Pfleger und Abt Ulrich Rösch (1457–1491)*, Monasterium Sancti Galli, 6 (St Gallen: Verlag am Klosterhof, 2014).

Lerdam, Henrik, *Kongen og tinget. Det senmiddelalderlige retsvæsen 1340–1448* (Copenhagen: Museum Tusculanums Forlag, 2001).

Lerdam, Henrik, *Birk Lov og Ret. Birkeretens historie i Danmark indtil 1600* (Copenhagen: Museum Tusculanums Forlag, 2004).

Lieberich, Heinz, 'Zur Feudalisierung der Gerichtsbarkeit in Bayern' *Zeitschrift der Savigny-Stiftung für Rechtsgeschichte germ. Abt.* (1954).

Linder, Konrad, 'Beiträge zur Geschichte der Klostergrundherrschaft Stams unter besonderer Berücksichtigung der Leiheformen', in Nikolaus Grass (ed.), *Beiträge zur Wirtschafts- und Kulturgeschichte des Zisterzienserstiftes Stams in Tirol* (Innsbruck: Wagner, 1959), 1–199.

Lindkvist, Thomas, *Landborna i Norden under äldre medeltid*, published thesis, Studia Historica Upsaliensia, 110 (Uppsala: Almkvist & Wiksell, 1979).

Lindkvist, Thomas, 'Social and Political Power in Sweden 1000–1300: Predatory Incursions, Royal Taxation, and the Formation of a Feudal State', in Ross Samson (ed.), *Social Approaches to Viking Studies* (Glasgow: Cruithne Press, 1991), 137–45.

Lindkvist, Thomas, and Janken Myrdal, *Trälar. Ofria i agrarsamhället från vikingatid till medeltid*, Skrifter om skog- och lantbrukshistoria, 17 (Stockholm: Nordiska museet, 2003).

Liver, Peter, 'Zur Entstehung des freien bäuerlichen Grundeigentums', *Zeitschrift für Schweizerisches Recht*, 65 (1946), 329–60.

Løgstrup, Birgit, *Jorddrot og offentlig administrator: Godsejerstyret inden for skatte- og udskrivningsvæsenet i det 18. århundrede* (Copenhagen: Gad, 1983).

Løgstrup, Birgit, 'Den bortforpagtede statsmagt: Godsejeren som offentlig administrator i det 18. århundrede', *Bol og by: Landbohistorisk Tidsskrift*, 1 (1985), 21–58.

Lund, Niels, *Lið, leding og landeværn, Hær og samfund i Danmark i ældre middelalder* (Roskilde: Vikingeskibshallen, 1996).

Lunden, Kåre, 'Om årsakene til den norske bondefridomen: Ein økonomisk-historisk forklåringsmåte', *Heimen*, 15 (1971), 213–22.

Lunden, Kåre, Norsk Grålysning: Norsk nasjonalisme på allmenn bakgrunn (Oslo: Samlaget, 1992).

Lunden, Kåre, 'Kollektiv identitet', in *Nasjon eller union* (Oslo: Samlaget, 1993), 17–25.

Lunden, Kåre, 'Fanst det ein norsk nasjonal identitet i mellomalderen?', in May-Brith Ohman Nielsen (ed.), *Nasjonal identitet og nasjonalisme: Innlegg på HiFo-seminaret i Farsund* (Oslo: Den norske historiske forening, 1994), 22–39.

Lundh, Christer, and Mats Olsson, 'Tenancy Contracts in Scania from the Middle Ages to the Nineteenth Century', in Bas J.P. van Bavel and Phillipp Schofield (eds), *The Development of Leasehold in Northwestern Europe, c. 1200–1600*, Comparative Rural History of the North Sea Area, 10 (Turnhout: Brepols, 2008), 113–37.

Lütge, Friedrich, Geschichte der deutschen Agrarverfassung vom frühen Mittelalter bis zum 19. Jahrhundert, 2nd edn, Deutsche Agrargeschichte, 3 (Stuttgart: E. Ulmer, 1967).

Lyngholm, Dorte Kook, *Godsejerens ret. Adelens retshåndhævelse i 1700-tallet – lov og praksis ved Clausholm birkeret* (Auning: Dansk Center for Herregårdsforskning og Landbohistorisk Selskab, 2013).

Magnús Már Lárusson, 'Hreppr', in *Kulturhistorisk leksikon for nordisk middelalder*, 22 vols (Malmö: Allhem, 1956–78), vii, 18–22.

Maissen, Thomas, *Geschichte der Schweiz* (Baden: Hier & Jetzt, 2010).

Mathieu, Jon, *Eine Agrargeschichte der inneren Alpen. Graubünden, Tessin, Wallis 1500–1800* (Zurich: Chronos Verlag, 1992).

Mathieu, Jon, *Die Alpen: Raum–Kultur–Geschichte* (Stuttgart: Reclam, 2015).

Mathis, Franz, 'Wirtschaft im Wandel der Zeit', in Klemens Betz, Heinz Moser and Anton Zimmermann (eds), *Axams*, (Axams, 2005), 87–124.

Mathis, Franz, 'Bauern – Bergbau – Industrie: Die Absamer Wirtschaft vom Mittelalter bis zur Gegenwart', in Michael Laimgruber, Heinz Moser and Peter Steindl (eds), *Absam*, (Absam, 2008), 97–138.

Mattmüller, Markus, Fridolin Kurmann and André Schluchter, *Bevölkerungsgeschichte der Schweiz*, Basler Beiträge zur Geschichtswissenschaft, 154, 2 vols (Basel: Helbing und Lichtenhahn, 1987).

Maurer, Georg Ludwig von, *Geschichte der Markenverfassung in Deutschland* (Erlangen: F. Enke, 1856).

Maurer, Georg Ludwig von, Einleitung zur Geschichte der Mark-, Hof-, Dorf- und Stadtverfassung und der öffentlichen Gewalt, 3rd edn (Aalen: Scientia Verlag, 1966).

Mayer, Theodor, *Adel und Bauern im deutschen Staat des Mittelalters* (Leipzig: Koehler and Amelang, 1943 [unchanged reprint, Darmstadt: Wissenschafliche Buchgesellschaft, 1976]).

Mazo Karras, Ruth. See Karras, Ruth Mazo.

Meier, Bruno, and Dominik Sauerländer, Das Surbtal im Spätmittelalter: Kulturlandschaft und Gesellschaft einer ländlichen Region (1250–1550), Beiträge zur Aargauergeschichte, 6 (Aarau, 1995).

Meier, Thomas, and Regula Schmid, 'Roger Sablonier, 16. April 1941 – 8. Juni 2010', *Schweizerische Zeitschrift für Geschichte*, 60 (2010), 494–97.

Meier, Thomas, and Roger Sablonier (eds), *Wirtschaft und Herrschaft, Beiträge zur ländlichen Gesellschaft in der östlichen Schweiz (1200–1800)* (Zurich: Chronos, 1999).

Meiners, Uwe, and Werner Rösener, *Allmenden und Marken vom Mittelalter bis zum Neuzeit* (Cloppenburg: Schriften des Museumsdorfs Cloppenburg, 2004).

Mengis, Simone, *Schreibende Frauen um 1500. Scriptorium und Bibliothek des Dominikanerinnenklosters St. Katharina St. Gallen*, Scrinium Friburgense, 28 (Berlin, 2013).

Meyer, Poul, *Danske bylag* (Copenhagen: Nyt nordisk forlag, 1949).

Meyer, Poul, 'Landbirker', in John Granlund (ed.), *Kulturhistoriskt lexikon för nordisk medeltid – från vikingatid till reformationstid*, 22 vols (Malmö: Allhem, 1956–78), i, 659–61.

Meyer, Werner, *Hirsebrei und Hellebarde: Auf den Spuren des mittelalterlichen Lebens in der Schweiz* (Olten, 1985).

Meyer, Werner, and Heinz Dieter Finck, *1291 – Die Geschichte: die Anfänge der Eidgenossenschaft*, 4th edn (Zurich: Silva-Verlag, 1991).

Militzer, Klaus, *Das Markgröninger Heilig-Geist-Spital im Mittelalter: Ein Beitrag zur Wirtschaftsgeschichte des 15. Jahrhunderts*, VuF Sonderband, 19 (Sigmaringen, 1975).

Mitterauer, Michael, 'Lebensformen und Lebensverhältnisse ländlicher Unterschichten', in Herbert Matis (ed.), *Von der Glückseligkeit des Staates* (Berlin: Dunker and Humbolt, 1981), 315–38.

Mitterauer, Michael, 'Mittelalter', in Andreas Gestrich, Jens-Uwe Krause, and Michael Mitterauer (eds), *Geschichte der Familie* (Stuttgart, 2003), 160–363.

Moosbrugger, Matthias, 'Der hintere Bregenzerwald – eine Bauernrepublik? Neue Untersuchungen zu seiner Verfassungs- und Strukturgeschichte im Spätmittelalter', Forschungen zur Geschichte Vorarlbergs, 9, dissertation, University of Innsbruck, Konstanz, 2009.

Morel, Andreas F.A., Andreas Moosbrugger and Peter Anton Moosbrugger, *Zur Stuckdekoration des Rokoko in der Schweiz*, Beiträge zur Kunstgeschichte der Schweiz, 2 (Bern: Gesellschaft für schweizerische Kunstgeschichte, 1973).

Müller, Johannes von, *Der Geschichten Schweizerischer Eidgenossenschaft, neue verbesserte und vermehrte Auflage*, 1st to 4th part (Leipzig, 1825/26).

Müller, Miriam, 'Peasants, Lords and Developments in Leasing in Later Medieval England', in Bas J.P. van Bavel and Philipp R. Schofield (eds), *The Development of Leasehold in Northwestern Europe, c. 1200–1600*, (Turnhout: Brepols, 2008), 155–78.

Müller, Walter, 'Gelehrte, Juristen und bäuerliche Urteilsfinder in einem sanktgallischen Lehenprozess', in W. Lendi (ed.), *Festgabe für Paul Staerkle zu seinem 80. Geburtstag am 26. März 1972*, St. Galler Kultur und Geschichte, 2 (St Gallen, 1972), 64–75.

Myhre, Bjørn, 'Boathouses and Naval Organization', in Anne Nørgård Jørgensen and Birthe L. Clausen (eds), *Military Aspects of Scandinavian Society in a European perspective, AD 1–1300* (Copenhagen: Nationalmuseet, 1997), 169–83.

Myhre, Bjørn, "Boathouses as Indicators of Political Organization", *Norwegian Archaeological Review*, 18 (1985), 37–60.

Myhre, Bjørn, and Ingvild Øye (eds), *Jorda blir levevei 4000 f.Kr. – 1350 e.Kr.*, i: Bjørn Myhre, Åsta Brenna, Ingvild Øye, and Reidar Almås (eds), *Norges landbrukshistorie* (Oslo: Samlaget, 2002).

Myking, John Ragnar, 'Lagrettemenn og bygdeelite ca. 1650–1750', *Heimen*, 33 (1996), 159–83.

Myking, John Ragnar, 'Attractive Marriage Partners? Tenant Widows and Remarriages in Western Norway in the Seventeenth and Eighteenth Century', *Scandinavian Journal of History*, 24 (2004), 225–39.

Myking, John Ragnar, *Herre over andre si jord? Norske leiglendingsvilkår i europeisk lys 1500–1800*, Studia Humanitatis Bergensia, 21 (Kristiansand: Høyskoleforlaget, 2005).

Myking, John Ragnar, 'Peasant Participation in Local Thing and Conflict Handling Institutions in Norway', in Tore Iversen, John Ragnar Myking and Gertrud Thoma (eds), *Bauern zwischen Herrschaft und Genossenschaft: Peasant Relations to Lords and Government. Scandinavia and the Alpine Region 1000–1750* (Trondheim: Tapir Akademisk Forlag, 2007), 187–203.

Myking, John Ragnar, 'Førebuing til 1814? Bøndene si deltaking i formelle lokale institusjonar før 1814', in Anne Hilde Nagel and Ståle Dyrvik (eds), *Folkestyre? Kritisk lys på 1814-demokratiet* (Bergen: Bodoni forlag, 2014), 13–22.

Myking, John Ragnar, 'Changes in the Nordic Elites' Way of Extracting a Surplus from Landed Resources', in Bjørn Poulsen, Jon Vidar Sigurdsson and Helle Vogt (eds), *Nordic Elites in Transformation 1050–1250*, i: *Material Resources* (New York: Routledge, 2019).

Myking, John Ragnar, and Carsten Porskrog Rasmussen, 'Scandinavia, 1000–1750', in Bas J.P. van Bavel and Richard. W. Hoyle (eds), *Social Relations: Property and Power*, Rural Economy and Society in North-western Europe, 500–2000, 1 (Turnhout: Brepols, 2010), 287–314.

Myrdal, Janken, *Jordbruket under feodalismen 1000–1700*, Det svenska jordbrukets historia, 2 (Stockholm: Natur og Kultur, 1999; Borås: LTs förlag, 2000).

Myrdal, Janken, and Mats Morell, *The Agrarian History of Sweden 4000 BC to AD 2000* (Lund: Nordic Academic Press, 2011).

Myrdal, Janken, and Clas Tollin, 'Brytar och tidigmedeltida huvudgårdar', in Thomas Lindkvist and Janken Myrdal (eds), *Trälar. Ofria i agrarsamhället från vikingatid till medeltid*, Skrifter om skog- och lantbrukshistoria, 17 (Stockholm: Nordiska museet, 2003), 133–69.

Nehlsen, Hermann, *Sklavenrecht zwischen Antike und Mittelalter*, i: *Ostgoten, Westgoten, Franken, Langobarden: Germanisches und römisches Recht in den germanischen Rechtsaufzeichnungen*, Göttinger Studier zur Rechtsgeschichte, 7 (Göttingen: Musterschmidt, 1972).

Nehlsen, Hermann, 'Entstehung des Strafrechts bei den germanischen Stämmen', in Karl Kroeschell (ed.), *Gerichtslauben-Vorträge. Freiburger Festkolloquium zum 75. Geburtstag von Hans Thieme* (Sigmaringen: Thorbecke, 1983), 7–12.

Nehlsen, Hermann, 'Die servi, ancillae und mancipia der Lex Baiuvariorum. Ein Beitrag zur Geschichte der Sklaverei in Bayern', in Heinz Bellen and Heinz Heinen (eds), *Fünfzig Jahre Forschungen zur antiken Sklaverei an der Mainzer Akademie 1950–2000* (Stuttgart: Steiner, 2001), 505–21.

Nehlsen, Hermann, 'Mancipia', in Adalbert Erler, et al. (eds), *Handwörterbuch zur deutschen Rechtsgeschichte*, 5 vols (Berlin: Schmidt, 1964–1991), iii, 219–30.

Nehlsen, Hermann, 'Unfreie', in Adalbert Erler, et al. (eds), *Handwörterbuch zur deutschen Rechtsgeschichte*, 5 vols (Berlin: Schmidt, 1964–1991), iv, 464–75.

Nehlsen-von Stryk, K., 'Schwabenspiegel', in Robert-Henri Bautier, et al. (eds), *Lexikon des Mittelalters*, 9 vols (Munich and Zurich: Artemis [vols 1–6] and LexMA-Verlag [vols 7–9], 1977–1999), vii, 1603–05.

Netterstrøm, Jeppe Büchert, *At forsvare til rette. Værnsforholdet og bøndernes retslige stilling i Danmarks senmiddelalder 1400–1513* (Kerteminde: Landbohistorisk Selskab, 2003).

Netterstrøm, Jeppe Büchert, 'Freud, Protection, and Serfdom in Late Medieval and Early modern Denmark (c.1400–1600)', in Paul H. Freedman and Monique Bourin (eds), *Forms of Servitude in Northern and Central Europe: Decline, Resistance, and Expansion*, Medieval Texts and Cultures of Northern Europe, 9 (Turnhout: Brepols, 2005), 370–84.

Netterstrøm, Jeppe Büchert, and Michael Nobel Jakobsen, 'Hals og håndsret 1400–1660', in *Danmarkshistorien.dk*. http://danmarkshistorien.dk/leksikon-og-kilder/vis/materiale/hals-og-haandsret-1400-1660/?no_cache=1, last edited 06.07.2012, last accessed 03 August 2016.

Nevéus, Clara, *Trälarna i landskapslagarnas samhälle. Danmark och Sverige*, Studia historica Upsaliensia, 58, published dissertation, University of Uppsala, 1974 (Uppsala: Almkvist och Wiksell, 1974).

Niederstätter, Alois, *Geschichte Vorarlbergs*, i: *Vorarlberg im Mittelalter* (Innsbruck, 2014).

Nielsen, Herluf, 'Justitiar', in John Granlund (ed.), *Kulturhistoriskt lexikon för nordisk medeltid – från vikingatid till reformationstid*, 22 vols (Malmö: Allhem, 1956–78), viii, 47–49.

Nielsen, Herluf, 'Landskap', in John Granlund (ed.), *Kulturhistoriskt lexikon för nordisk medeltid – från vikingatid till reformationstid*, 22 vols (Malmö: Allhem, 1956–78), x, 235–36.

Nielsen, Yngvar, *Af Norges Historie* (Stockholm: Ljus 1904).

Nisple, Agathe, *Appenzell. Ein Dorf- und Kulturführer* (Herisau: Appezeller Verlag, 2001).

Njåstad, Magne, 'Resistance in the Name of the Law', in Kimmo Katjala, *Northern Revolts: Medieval and Early Modern Peasant Unrest in the Nordic Countries*, Studia Fennica, Historica, 8 (Helsinki: Finnish Literature Society, 2004), 90–117.

Norborg, Lars-Arne, 'Landbo', in John Granlund (ed.), *Kulturhistoriskt lexikon för nordisk medeltid – från vikingatid till reformationstid*, 22 vols (Malmö: Allhem, 1956–78), x, 202.

Norseng, Per G., 'Odelsrett – The Norwegiqn retrait lignager', in Tore Iversen and John Ragnar Myking (eds), *Land, Lords and Peasants: Peasants' Right to Control Land in the Middle Ages and the Early Modern Period – Norway, Scandinavia and the Alpine Region*, Trondheim Studies in History, 52 (Trondheim: NTNU, 2005), 199–218.

Oberkrome, Willi, Volksgeschichte. Methodische Innovation und völkische Ideologisierung in der deutschen Geschichtswissenschaft 1918–1945 (Göttingen: Vandenhoeck und Ruprecht, 1993).

Ofer, Monika, 'Leibeigenschaft am westbayerischen Alpenrand', unpublished paper, 2005.

Ofer, Monika, 'Nachbarschaft und Gemeinde – Zur dörflichen Selbstverwaltung im westlichen Oberbayern im 16. und beginnenden 17. Jahrhundert', in Tore Iversen, John Ragnar Myking and Gertrud Thoma (eds), *Bauern zwischen Herrschaft und Genossenschaft: Peasant Relations to Lords and Government. Scandinavia and the Alpine Region 1000–1750* (Tronheim: Tapir Akademisk Forlag, 2007), 41–57.

Olberg, G. von, 'Gerichtsverfassung', in Johannes Hoops and Heinreich Beck (eds), *Real-enzyklopädie der germanischen Altertumskunde* (Berlin, 1973–2015) xi, 171–81.

Olsen, Asle Buen, 'Courtyard Sites in Western Norway: Central Assembly Places and Juridical Institutions in the Late Iron Age', in Marianne Hem Eriksen, Unn Pedersen, Bert Rundberget, Irmelin Axelsen and Heidi Lund Berg (eds), *Viking Worlds: Things, Spaces and Movement* (Oxford: Oxbow, 2015), 43–55.

Olsen, Gunnar, *Hovedgård og bondegård: Studier over stordriftens udvikling i Danmark i tiden 1525–1774*, Landbohistoriske skrifter, 1 (Copenhagen: Landbohistorisk Selskab, 1975).

Olsson, Mats, *Storgodsdrift: Godsekonomi och arbetsorganisation i Skåne från dansk tid till mitten av 1800-talet* (Lund: Almquist & Wiksell International, 2002).

Olsson, Mats, *Skatta dig lycklig: Jordränta och jordbruk i Skåne 1660–1900* (Södertälje: Gidlunds förlag, 2005).

Opitz, Claudia, 'Neue Wege der Sozialgeschichte? Ein kritischer Blick auf Otto Brunners Konzept des "ganzen Hauses"', *Geschichte und Gesellschaft*, 20 (1994), 88–98.

Østerberg, Eva, and Sølvi Bauge Sogner, (eds), *People Meet the Law: Control and Conflict-Handling in the Courts* (Oslo: Universitetsforlaget, 2000).

Othenin-Girard, Mireille, *Ländliche Lebensweise und Lebensformen im Spätmittelalter: Eine wirtschafts- und sozialgeschichtliche Untersuchung der Herrschaft Farnsburg*, Quellen und Forschungen zur Geschichte und Landeskunde des Kantons Basel-Landschaft, 48 (Liestal 1994).

Palme, Rudolf, 'Frühe Neuzeit (1480–1665)', in Josef Fontana, et al. (eds), *Geschichte des Landes Tirol*, ii (Bozen / Vienna: Verlagsanstalt Athesia, 1986).

Patterson, Orlando, *Slavery and Social Death: A Comparative Study* (Cambridge, MA: Harvard University Press, 1982).

Pauly, Michel, 'Von der Fremdenherberge zum Seniorenheim: Funktionswandel in mittelalterlichen Hospitälern an ausgewählten Beispielen aus dem Maas-Mosel-Rhein-Raum', in Michael Matheus (ed.), *Funktions- und Strukturwandel spätmittelalterlicher Hospitäler im europäischen Vergleich*, Geschichtliche Landeskunde, 56 (Stuttgart, 2005), 101–16.

Pedersen, Frank, *Vornedskabets gennemførelse* (Odense: Landbohistorisk selskab, 1984).

Pelteret, David A.E., *Slavery in Early Medieval England* (Woodbridge: Boydell, 1995).

Pickl, Othmar, 'Das Dorf "Sedin" des Klosters Reun. Ein Beitrag zur Wüstungsforschung', in *Blätter für Heimatkunde*, 32 (1958), 111–23.

Porsmose, Erland, 'Middelalder O. 1000–1536', in Claus Bjørn, et al. (eds), *Det danske landbrugs historie*, i: *Oldtid og middelalder* (Odense: Landbohistorisk selskab, 1988).

Posch, Fritz, 'Die sozialen, rechtlichen und wirtschaftlichen Grundlagen der neuzeitlichen bäuerlichen Siedlung und die Entstehung des Kleinbauerntums', in Hanns Leo Mikoletzky (ed.), *Bericht über den 3. österreichischen Historikertag*, Veröffentlichungen des Verbandes österreichischer Geschichtsvereine 4 (Vienna, 1954), 71–75.

Posch, Fritz, 'Bauer und Keuschler', in Fritz Posch (ed.), *Das Bauerntum in der Steiermark*, Zeitschrift des historischen Vereins für Steiermark, Sonderband 7, (Graz, 1963), 68–72.

Poulsen, Bjørn, 'A Classical Manor in Viking Age and Early Medieval Denmark?', in Yoshiki Morimoto, Jean-Pierre Devroey, and Alexis Wilkin (eds), *Autour de Yoshiki Morimoto: Les Structures Agricoles en Dehors du Monde Carolingien: Formes et genèse: Actes des journées d'études organisées à l'Université Libre de Bruxelles les 6, 7 et 8 mai 2010* (Brussles: Le Livre Timperman, 2012), 451–65.

Poulsen, Bjørn, 'Den danske konges indtægter i middelalderen', in Sverre Bagge, et al. (eds), *Statsutvikling i Skandinavia i middelalderen* (Oslo: Dreyer, 2012), 55–61.

Poulsen, Bjørn, and Søren M. Sindbæk (eds), *Settlement and Lordship in Viking and Early Medieval Scandinavia* (Turnhout: Brepols, 2011).

Rankl, Helmut, *Landvolk und Frühmoderner Staat in Bayern 1400–1800*, Studien zur Bayerischen Verfassungs- und Sozialgeschichte, 17 (Munich: Kommision für Bayerische Landesgeschichte, 1999).

Rasumssen, Carsten Porskrog, *Rentegods og hovedgårsdrift: Godsstruktur og godsøkonomi i hertugdømmet Slesvig 1524–1770*, 2 vols (Aabenraa: Institut for grænseregionsforskning, 2003).

Rasmussen, Carsten Porskrog, 'Gård og gods', in John Erichsen and Mikkel Venborg Pedersen (eds), *Herregården: Menneske – samfund – landskab – bygninger*, i (Copenhagen: Nationalmuseet, 2004), 201–06.

Rasmussen, Carsten Porskrog, 'Manors and States: The Distribution and Structure of Private Manors in Early Modern Scandinavia and Their Relation to State Policies', *Scandinavian Economic History Review*, 66/2 (2018), 201–18.

Rasmussen, Carsten Porskrog, et al. (eds), *Det danske godssystem – udvikling og afvikling 1500–1919* (Århus: Historia, 1987).

Rasmussen, Poul, 'Herred', in John Granlund (ed.), *Kulturhistoriskt lexikon för nordisk medeltid – från vikingatid till reformationstid*, 22 vols (Malmö: Allhem, 1956–78), vi, 488–91.

Redlich, Oswald, 'Ueber bairische Traditionsbücher und Traditionen', *Mitteilungen des Instituts für Österreichische Geschichtsforschung*, 5 (1884), 1–82.

Reinton, Lars, *Sæterbruket i Noreg i-iii* (Oslo: Institutt for sammenlignende kulturforskning, 1955, 1959, 1961).

Reynolds, Susan, *Kingdoms and Communities in Western Europe 900–1300*, (Oxford: Clarendon Press, 1997).

Riedmann, Josef, 'Tirol', in Robert-Henri Bautier, et al. (eds), *Lexikon des Mittelalters*, 9 vols (Munich and Zurich: Artemis [vols 1–6] and LexMA-Verlag [vols 7–9], 1977–1999), viii, 803.

Riedmann, Josef, 'Mittelalter', in Josef Fontana, et al. (eds), *Geschichte des Landes Tirol*, i (Bozen: Verlagsanstalt Athesia, 1985 [2nd edn 1990]), 291–698.

Riedmann, Josef, *Geschichte Tirols* (Vienna: Verlag für Geschichte und Politikk, 1988).

Riedmann, Josef, 'Geschichtsschreibung und Geschichtsbewußtsein in Tirol, vornehmlich in der 1. Hälfte des 20. Jahrhunderts', *Tiroler Heimat*, 57 (1993), 291–304.

Riedmann, Josef, and Guiseppe Albertoni (eds), *Eines Fürsten Traum. Meinhard II. – Das Werden Tirols. Tiroler Landesausstellung 1995*, Schloss Tirol, Stift Stams (Dorf Tirol: Südtiroler Landesmuseum Schloß Tirol, 1995).

Riehls, Wilhelm Heinrich, *Naturgeschichte des deutschen Volkes*, Gunther Ipsen (ed.) (Leipzig: Kröner, 1935).

Riehl, Wilhelm Heinrich, *Die bürgerliche Gesellschaft*, Peter Steinbach (ed.) (Frankfurt: Ullstein, 1976).

Riis, Thomas, 'Villici og coloni indtil 1340. Et forsøk på en begrepsanalyse', in Svend Gissel (ed.), *Landbrugshistoriske studier tilegnede Fridlev Skrubbeltrang på halvfjerdsårsdagen*, Landbohistorisk Selskab, 4 (Copenhagen, 1970).

Rippmann, Dorothee, *Bauern und Städter: Stadt-Land-Beziehungen im 15. Jahrhundert: das Beispiel Basel, unter besonderer Berücksichtigung der Nahmarktbeziehungen und der sozialen Verhältnisse im Umland*, Basler Beiträge zur Geschichtswissenschaft, 159 (Basel, 1990).

Rippmann, Dorothee, '"Sein Brot verdienen": Die Verköstigung von Arbeitskräften im Spätmittelalter', *Medium Aevum Quotidianum*, 34 (1996), 91–114.

Rippmann, Dorothee, 'Wirtschaft und Sozialstruktur auf dem Land im Spätmittelalter', in Kanton Basel-Land (ed.), *Nah dran, weit weg: Geschichte des Kantons Basel-Landschaft 2* (Liestal, 2001), 139–64.

Rippmann, Dorothee, 'Leben, Arbeit und materielle Kultur im Lichte pragmatischer Schriftlichkeit in der Schweiz', in Gudrun Gleba and Niels Petersen (eds), *Wirtschafts-*

und Rechnungsbücher des Mittelalters und der Frühen Neuzeit: Formen und Methoden der Rechnungslegung: Städte, Klöster und Kaufleute (Göttingen, 2015), 209–53.

Rivers, Theodore John, 'Seigneurial obligations and "Lex baiuvariorum" i.13', *Traditio,* 31 (1975), 336–43.

Robinson, Philip, *Die Fürstabtei St. Gallen und ihr Territorium 1463–1529: eine Studie zur Entwicklung territorialer Staatlichkeit,* St Galler Kultur und Geschichte, 24 (St Gallen: Staatsarchiv und Stiftsarchiv, 1995).

Rockinger, Ludwig von, *Kaiser Ludwigs erstes oberbaierisches Land- und Lehenrecht,* Abhandlungen der historischen Klasse der Königlich Bayerische Akademie der Wissenschaften, Phil- Hist. Klasse, 24/3 (Munich: Verlag der K.B. Akademie der Wissenschaften, 1909).

Rosenberg, Hans, 'Deutsche Agrargeschichte in alter und neuer Sicht', in *Machteliten und Wirtschaftskonjunkturen. Studien zur neueren deutschen Sozial- und Wirtschaftsgeschichte* (Göttingen: Vandenhoeck und Ruprecht, 1978), 118–219.

Rösener, Werner, 'Grundherrschaft', in Robert-Henri Bautier, et al. (eds), *Lexikon des Mittelalters,* 9 vols (Munich and Zurich: Artemis [vols 1–6] and LexMA-Verlag [vols 7–9], 1977–1999), iv, 1746ff.

Rösener, Werner, 'Landesausbau und Kolonisation', in Robert-Henri Bautier, et al. (eds), *Lexikon des Mittelalters,* 9 vols (Munich and Zurich: Artemis [vols 1–6] and LexMA-Verlag [vols 7–9], 1977–1999), v, 1643–45.

Rösener, Werner, 'Villikationen', in Robert-Henri Bautier, et al. (eds), *Lexikon des Mittelalters,* 9 vols (Munich and Zurich: Artemis [vols 1–6] and LexMA-Verlag [vols 7–9], 1977–1999), viii, 1694–95.

Rösener, Werner, 'Die Erforschung der Grundherrschaft', in Peter Classen, et al. (eds), *Mittelalterforschung* (Berlin: Colloquium Verlag, 1981), 57–65.

Rösener, Werner, *Bauern im Mittelalter* (Munich: C.H. Beck, 1985); Engl. trans. as *Peasants in the Middle Ages* (Cambridge: Polity Press, 1992).

Rösener, Werner, *Grundherrschaft im Wandel: Untersuchungen zur Entwicklung geistlicher Grundherrschaften im südwestdeutschen Raum vom 9. bis 14. Jahrhundert* (Göttingen: Vandenhoeck und Ruprecht, 1991).

Rösener, Werner, 'Agrarwirtschaft, Agrarverfassung und ländliche Gesellschaft im Mittelalter', in Lothar Gall, et al. (eds), *Enzyklopädie deutsche Geschichte,* xiii (Munich: R. Oldenbourg, 1992).

Rösener, *Peasants in the Middle Ages.* See Rösener, *Bauern im Mittelalter,* 1985.

Rösener, Werner, Die Bauern in der europäischen Geschichte (Munich: Beck, 1993).

Rösener, Werner, *Grundherrschaft und baüerliche Gesellschaft im Hochmittelalter* (Göttingen: Vandenhoeck und Ruprecht, 1995).

Rösener, Werner, 'Agrargeschichte an den deutschen Universitäten', *Zeitschrift für Agrargeschichte und Agrarsoziologie,* 47 (1999), 111–122.

Rösener, Werner, 'Die Entstehung der Markgenossenschaften des Mittelalters in Theorie und Realität', in Uwe Meiners and Werner Rösener (eds), *Allmenden und Marken vom Mittelalter bis zur Neuzeit* (Cloppenburg: Schriften des Museumsdorfs Cloppenburg, 2004), 17–30.

Rösener, Werner, 'Das Verfügungsrecht der Bauern über Land im südwestlichen Deutschland', in Tore Iversen and John Ragnar Myking (eds), *Land, Lords and Peasants: Peasants' Right to Control Land in the Middle Ages and the Early Modern Period – Norway, Scandinavia and the Alpine Region*, Trondheim Studies in History, 52 (Trondheim: NTNU, 2005), 47–62.

Rösener, Werner, 'Vom Sklaven zum Bauern. Zur Stellung der Hörigen in der frühmittelalterlichen Grundherrschaft', in Brigitte Kasten and Dieter Hägermann (eds), *Tätigkeitsfelder und Erfahrungshorizonte des ländlichen Menschen der frühmittelalterlichen Grundherrschaft*, (Stuttgart: Steiner, 2006).

Rösener, Werner, 'Bauern zwischen Herrschaft und Genossenschaft in Deutschland – Ein Überblick', in Tore Iversen, John Ragnar Myking and Gertrud Thoma (eds), *Bauern zwischen Herrschaft und Genossenschaft: Peasant Relation to Lords and Government. Scandinavia and the Alpine Region 1000–1750* (Trondheim: Tapir Akademisk Forlag, 2007), 9–24.

Røskaft, Merete, *Maktens landskap. Sentralgårder i Trøndelag ca. 800–1200*, Skriftserie fra Historisk institutt, 39 (Trondheim: Norges teknisk-naturvitenskapelige universitet, 2003).

Rückert, 'Wüstungen (Spätmittelalter)', in *Historisches Lexikon Bayerns*. URL: http://www.historisches-lexikon-bayerns.de/artikel/artikel_45701.

Sablonier, Roger, 'Das Dorf im Übergang vom Hochmittelalter zum Spätmittelalter, Untersuchungen zum Wandel ländlicher Gemeinschaftsformen im ostschweizerischen Raum', in Lutz Fenske, Werner Rösener, and Thomas Zotz (eds), *Institutionen, Kultur und Gesellschaft im Mittelalter: Festschrift für Josef Fleckenstein* (Sigmaringen: Thorbecke, 1984), 120–34.

Sablonier, Roger, 'Schweizer Eidgenossenschaft im 15. Jahrhundert: Staatlichkeit, Politik und Selbstverständnis', in Josef Wiget (ed.), *Die Entstehung der Schweiz. Vom Bundesbrief 1291 zur nationalen Geschichtskultur des 20. Jahrhunderts* (Schwyz: Historischer Verein des Katons Schwyz, 1999).

Sablonier, Roger, 'Politik und Staatlichkeit im spätmittelalterlichen Rätien', in *Handbuch der Bündner Geschichte*, i: *Frühzeit bis Mittelalter* (Chur, 2000), 245–94.

Sablonier, Roger, *Gründungszeit ohne Eidgenossen. Politik und Gesellschaft in der Innerschweiz um 1300* 2nd edn (Baden: Hier & Jetzt, 2009).

Sablonier, Roger, and Alfred Zangger, *Inventar spätmittelalterlicher Wirtschafts- und Verwaltungsquellen im Stiftsarchiv Einsiedeln*, Stiftsarchiv St. Gallen, Staatsarchiv des Kantons Schaffhausen, Staatsarchiv des Kantons Thurgau, (Zurich, 1989).

Sablonier, Roger, and Mattias Weishaupt, *Die alte Schweiz als 'Bauernstaat'*, Reihe Kurzfassungen der Projekte (Basel: Nationales Forschungsprogramm 21: Kulturelle Vielfalt und nationale Identität, 1991).

Sack, Robert Davis, Human Territorality: Its Theory and History (Cambridge: Cambridge Unversity Press, 1986).

Sagestetter, Maria Rita, *Hoch- und Niedergerichtsbarkeit im Spätmittelalterlichen Herzogtum Bayern* (Munich: Beck'sche Verlagsbuchhandlung, 2000).

'St Gallen (Gemeinde)' in Marco Jorio (ed.), *Historisches Lexikon der Schweiz*, 13 vols (Basel: Schwabe, 2002–2014), http://www.hls-dhs-dss.ch/textes/d/D1321.php.

Salvesen, Helge, 'The Strength of Tradition: A Historiographical Analysis of Research into Norwegian Agrarian Hinstory during the Late Middle Ages and the Early Modern Period', *Scandinavian Journal of History*, 7 (1982), 75–133.

Salvesen, Helge, and Jørn Sandnes, *Ødegårdstid i Norge. Det nordiske ødegårdsprosjekts norske undersøkelser* (Oslo: Universitetsforlaget, 1978).

Salzmann, Matin, 'Heimfall eines verwirkten Lehens. Motive und Hintergründe zu einem Prozess aus dem Thurgau des 16. Jahrhunderts', in Clausdieter Schott and Eva Petrig Schuler (eds), *Festschrift für Claudio Soliva zum 65. Geburtstag* (Zurich, 1994), 233–52.

Sandgruber, Roman *Ökonomie und Politik*, Österreichische Geschichte, 12 (Vienna: Uberreiter, 1995).

Sandnes, Jørn, 'Reitar. En namegruppe som agrarhistorisk kilde', *Heimen*, 14 (1968), 388–95.

Sandnes, Jørn, Ødetid og gjenreisning. Trøndsk busetningshistorie ca.1200–1660 (Oslo: Universitetsforlaget, 1971).

Sandnes, Jørn, 'Bondesamfunnet', in Nina Karin Monsen and Ingrid Semmingsen (eds), *Norges kulturhistorie*, i: *Vår fjerne fortid* (Oslo: Aschehoug, 1979), 50.

Sandnes, Jørn, 'Tolv kyr, to hester og tre træler', *Historisk Tidsskrift (norsk)*, 62 (1983), 79–82.

Sandnes, Jørn, 'Trøndelags eldste politiske historie', in Claus Krag and Jørn Sandnes (eds), *Nye middelalderstudier – Kongedømme, kirke, stat.* Norske historikere i utvalg, 6 (Oslo: Universitetsforlaget, 1983), 39–50.

Sandvik, Gudmund, *Prestegård og prestelønn* (Oslo: Universitetsforlaget, 1965).

Sanmark, Alexandra, 'The Communal Nature of the Judicial Systems in Early Medieval Norway', *Collegium Medievale*, 19 (2006), 31–64.

Sanmark, Alexandra 'Administrative Organisation and State Formation: A Case Study of Assembly Sites in Södermanland, Sweden', *Medieval Archaeology*, 53 (2009), 205–40.

Sawyer, Peter H., *Medieval Settlement: Continuity and Change* (London: Edward Arnold, 1976).

Sawyer, Birgit, and Peter Sawyer, *Medieval Scandinavia: From Conversion to Reformation circa 800–1500* (Minneapolis: University of Minnesota Press, 1996).

Schäfli, Christian, 'Herrschaft und Wirtschaft des Klosters Magdenau im ausgehenden Mittelalter: Edition und Analyse des Lehenbuches des Zisterzienserinnenklosters Magdenau', Master's thesis, University of Zurich, Zurich, 2008.

Schennach, Martin P., *Ritter, Landsknecht, Aufgebot. Quellen zum Tiroler Kriegswesen. 14.-17. Jahrhundert*, Tiroler Geschichtsquellen, 49 (Innsbruck: Tiroler Landesarchiv, 2004).

Schennach, Martin P., *Gesetze und Herrschaft. Die Entstehung des Gesetzgebungsstaates am Beispiel Tirols*, Forschung zur deutschen Rechtsgeschichte, 28 (Cologne: Böhlau, 2010).

Scherner, Karl Otto, 'Art. Zeitpacht', in Albrecht Cordes, Bernd Kannowski, Hans-Peter Haferkamp, et al. (eds), *Handwörterbuch zur deutschen Rechtsgeschichte*, v (Berlin, 1998), para. 1645–46.

Scheutz, Martin, Andrea Sommerlechner, Herwig Weigl, and Alfred Stefan Weiss (eds), *Quellen zur europäischen Spitalgeschichte in Mittelalter und Früher Neuzeit*, Quelleneditionen des Instituts für Österreichische Geschichtsforschung, 5 (Vienna, 2010).

Schläpfer, Walter, 'Demokratie und Aristokratie in der Appenzellergeschichte des 17. und 18. Jahrhunderts', *Appenzellische Jahrbücher* (1948), 3–26.

Schlesinger, Walter, 'Herrschaft und Gefolgschaft in der germanisch-deutschen Verfassungsgeschichte', in Hellmut Kämpf (ed.), *Herrschaft und Staat im Mittelalter* (Darmstadt: Wissenschaftliche Buchgesellschaft, 1964), 135–90.

Schlumbohm, Jürgen, *Lebensläufe, Familien, Höfe: Die Bauern und Heuerleute des osnabrückischen Kirchspiels Belm in proto-industrieller Zeit, 1650–1860* (Göttingen: VAndenhoeck und Ruprecht, 1994).

Schmugge, Ludwig, 'Mobilität und Freiheit im Mittelalter', in Johannes Fried (ed.), *Die abendländische Freiheit vom 10. bis zum 14. Jahrhundert*, Vorträge und Forschunge: Konstanzer Arbeitskreis für mittelalterliche Geschichte, 49 (Sigmaringen: Jan Thorbecke, 1991), 312–14.

Schnelbögl, Wolfgang, *Die innere Entwicklung der bayerischen Landfrieden des 13. Jahrhunderts*, Deutschrechtliche Beiträge, 13/2 (Heidelberg: C. Winter, 1932).

Schott, C, and H. Romer, 'Immunität', in Robert-Henri Bautier, et al. (eds), *Lexikon des Mittelalters*, 9 vols (Munich and Zurich: Artemis [vols 1–6] and LexMA-Verlag [vols 7–9], 1977–1999), v, 390–92.

Schreiner, Klaus, '"Grundherrschaft". Entstehung und Bedeutungswandel eines geschichtswissenschaftlichen Ordnungs- und Erklärungsbegriffs', in Hans Patze (ed.), *Die Grundherrschaft im späten Mittelalter*, 1, Vorträge und Forschungen, 27/1 (Sigmaringen: Thorbecke, 1983).

Schröder, K.H., and G. Schwarz, *Die ländlichen Siedlungsformen in Mitteleuropa*, Forschung zur deutschen Landeskunde, 175 (Trier: Univeristy of Trier, 1978).

Schulze, Hans Kurt, 'Grundherrschaft', in Adalbert Erler, et al. (eds), *Handwörterbuch zur deutschen Rechtsgeschichte*, 5 vols (Berlin: Schmidt, 1964–1991), i, 1824–42.

Schulze, Hans Kurt, *Grundstrukturen der Verfassung im Mittelalter*, i (Stuttgart: Kohlhammer, 1985).

Schultz, Knut, 'Hofrecht', in Robert-Henri Bautier, et al. (eds), *Lexikon des Mittelalters*, 9 vols (Munich and Zurich: Artemis [vols 1–6] and LexMA-Verlag [vols 7–9], 1977–1999), v, 77–78.

Schultz, Knut, 'Zensualen, Zinsleute, Zensualität', in Robert-Henri Bautier, et al. (eds), *Lexikon des Mittelalters*, 9 vols (Munich and Zurich: Artemis [vols 1–6] and LexMA-Verlag [vols 7–9], 1977–1999), ix, 530–33.

Schwab, Daniela, 'Das Urbar des Zürcher Heiliggeistspitals aus dem 15. Jahrhundert: Edition und Kommentar', Master's thesis, University of Zurich, Zurich, 2013.

Schwind, Ernst Freiherr von, and Alfons Dopsch, Ausgewählte Urkunden zur Verfassungsgeschichte der deutsch-österreichischen Erblande im Mittelalter (Innsbruck: Wagner, 1894).

Seip, Jens Arup, 'Problemer og metode i norsk høymiddelalderforskning', *Historisk tidsskrift (norsk)*, 32 (1940), 49–131.

Seland, Bjørg, *Gardtinget. En norsk landsbyorganisasjon*, ADH-serien, 75 (Kristiansand: Agder distriktshøgskole, 1994).

Semler, Alfons, *Geschichte des Heilig-Geist-Spitals in Überlingen am Bodensee* (Überlingen, 1957).

Sieder, Reinhard, and Michael Mitterauer, 'The Reconstruction of the Family Life Course: Theoretical Problems and Empirical Results', in Richard Wall, Jean Robin and Peter Laslett (eds), *Family Forms in Historic Europe* (Cambridge: CUP, 1983), 309–45.

Siems, H., 'Lex Baiuvariorum', in Adalbert Erler, et al. (eds), *Handwörterbuch zur deutschen Rechtsgeschichte*, 5 vols (Berlin: Schmidt, 1964–1991), ii, 1887–1901.

Simek, Rudolph, and Hermann Pálsson, *Lexikon der altnordischen Literatur: die mittelalteriche Literatur Norwegens und Islands* (Stuttgart: Kröner, 2007).

Sjøholm, Else, 'Rättshistorisk metod och teoribildning', *Scandia*, 44 (1978), 229–56.

Sjøholm, Else, 'Medeltids-lagarna som historiske källor', in Hedda Gunneng and Birgit Strand (eds), *Kvinnans ekonomiska ställning under Nordisk medeltid* (Upsatser framlagda vid ett kvinnohistorisk symposium i Kungälv 8.-12.oktober 1979), Kvinnohistoriskt arkiv, 19 (Stockholm: Kompendiet, Lindome, 1981), 74–81.

Skevik, Olav, *Folk og fylker i fjerne tider. Inntrøndelags historie før 1600* (Stjørdal: Nord-Trøndelag fylkeskommune, 1997).

Skocpol, Theda, and Margaret Somers, 'The Uses of Comparative History in Macro-social Inquiry', *Comparative Studies in Society and History*, 22/1 (1980), 174–97.

Skre, Dagfinn, *Herredømme, bosetning og besittelse på Romerike 200–1350 e. Kr.*, published PhD thesis, Acta humaniora 32 (Oslo: Universitetsforlaget, 1998).

Skrubbeltrang, Friedlev, 'Bonde', in John Granlund (ed.), *Kulturhistoriskt lexikon för nordisk medeltid – från vikingatid till reformationstid*, 22 vols (Malmö: Allhem, 1956–78), ii, 87.

Skrubbeltrang, Friedlev, *Det danske landbosamfund 1500–1800* (Odense: Den danske historiske forening, 1978).

Skyum-Nielsen, Nils, *Kvinde og slave* (Copenhagen: Munksgaard, 1971).

Slagstad, Rune, *De nasjonale strateger* (Oslo: Pax, 1998).

Snorri Sturluson. See Snorri Sturluson under 'Primary Sources'.

Soens, Tim, and Erik Thoen, 'The Origins of Leasehold in the Former County of Flanders', in Bas J.P. van Bavel and Philipp R. Schofield (eds), *The Development of Leasehold in Northwestern Europe, c. 1200–1600*, (Turnhout: Brepols, 2008), 31–55.

Solem, Jon, 'Den norske almenningsinstitusjonen i middelalderen', *Heimen*, 4 (2003), 243–65.

Sonderegger, Stefan, 'Landesausbau und Kolonisation', in Robert-Henri Bautier, et al. (eds), *Lexikon des Mittelalters*, 9 vols (Munich and Zurich: Artemis [vols 1–6] and LexMA-Verlag [vols 7–9], 1977–1999), v, 1643–45.

Sonderegger, Stefan, 'Wirtschaftliche Regionalisierung in der spätmittelalterlichen Nordostschweiz. Am Beispiel der Wirtschaftsführung des Heiliggeistspitals St. Gallen', *Schriften des Vereins für Geschichte des Bodensees und seiner Umgebung*, 105 (1987), 19–37.

Sonderegger, Stefan, *Landwirtschaftliche Entwicklung in der Nordostschweiz. Eine Untersuchung ausgehend von den wirtschaftlichen Aktivitäten des Heiliggeist-Spitals St. Gallen*, St Galler Kultur und Geschichte, 22, published dissertation, University of Zurich, 1993 (St Gallen: Buchhandlung am Rössliter, 1994).

Sonderegger, Stefan, 'Die Aufnahme der Appenzeller "lendlin" in den Schwäbischen Städtebund', in Peter Blickle and Peter Witschi (eds), *Appenzell-Oberschwaben* (Konstanz: Konstanzer Universitätsverlag, 1997).

Sonderegger, Stefan, 'Der Rebbrief von 1471 – eine wichtige Quelle zum Weinbau im St. Galler Rheintal. Kommentar und Neuedition', in Thomas Meier and Roger Sablonier (eds), *Wirtschaft und Herrschaft: Beiträge zur ländlichen Gesellschaft in der östlichen Schweiz (1200–1800)* (Zurich: Chronos, 1999), 43–53.

Sonderegger, Stefan, 'Alpwirtschaft im Toggenburg, Werdenberg und Sarganserland', in Wissenschaftliche Kommission der Sankt-Galler Kantonsgeschichte, Silvio Bucher, Max Baumann, et al. (eds), *Sankt-Galler Geschichte*, iii (St Gallen: Amt für Kultur des Kantons St. Gallen, 2003), 245–60.

Sonderegger, Stefan, 'Gaiserwald im Mittelalter', in Ernst Ziegler (ed.), *Gaiserwald: Abtwil, St. Josefen, Engelburg* (Gaiserwald, 2004), 11–36.

Sonderegger, Stefan, 'Ein beinahe vergessener Beitrag der St. Galler zu den Appenzellerkriegen', in Peter Niederhäuser and Alois Niederstätter (eds), *Die Appenzellerkriege – eine Krisenzeit am Bodensee?*, Forschungen zur Geschichte Vorarlbergs, Neue Folge, 7 (Konstanz: UVK Verlagsgesellschaft, 2006), 117–28.

Sonderegger, Stefan, 'Landwirtschaftliche Spezialisierung in der spätmittelalterlichen Nordostschweiz', in Markus Cerman and Erich Landsteiner (eds), *Zwischen Land und Stadt: Wirtschaftsverflechtungen von ländlichen und städtischen Räumen in Europa 1300–1600*, Jahrbuch für Geschichte des ländlichen Raumes, 2009 (Innsbruck: Studien Verlag, 2010), 139–60.

Sonderegger, Stefan, 'Vom Nutzen der Bearbeitung einer regionalen Urkundenedition. Dargestellt am Chartularium Sangallense', in Theo Kölzer, Willibald Rosner and Roman Zehetmayer (eds), *Regionale Urkundenbücher. Die Vorträge der 12. Tagung der Commission Internationale de Diplomatique*, Nöla, 14 (St Pölten: Niederösterreichisches Institut für Landeskunde, 2010), 86–116.

Sonderegger, Stefan, 'Getreide, Fleisch und Geld gegen Wein. Stadt-Umland-Beziehungen im spätmittel-alterlichen St Gallen', in Frank Konersmann and Klaus-Joachim Lorenzen-Schmidt (eds), *Bauern als Händler. Ökonomische Diversifizierung und soziale Differenzierung bäuerlicher Agrarproduzenten (15.–19. Jahr-hundert)*, Quellen und Forschungen zur Agrargeschichte, 52 (Stuttgart: Lucius & Lucius, 2011), 17–33.

Sonderegger, Stefan, 'Bauernfamilien und ihre Landwirtschaft im Spätmittelalter. Beispiele aus Untersuchungen zur ländlichen Gesellschaft der Nordschweiz', *Zeitschrift für Agrargeschichte und Agrarsoziologie*, 60/2 (2012), 35–57.

Sonderegger, Stefan, 'Landwirtschaft auf dem Papier und in der Praxis', in Carola Fey and Steffen Krieb (eds), *Adel und Bauern in der Gesellschaft des Mittelalters. Internationales Kolloquium zum 65. Geburtstag von Werner Rösener*, Studien und Texte zur Geistes- und Sozialgeschichte des Mittelalters, 6 (Korb: Didymos, 2012), 249–70.

Sonderegger, Stefan, '"*...der Zins ist abgelon...*": Aushandeln von Schadensteilungen zwischen Grundherren und Bauern in schwierigen Zeiten der Landwirtschaft', in Rolf Kiessling, Wolfgang Scheffknecht (eds), *Umweltgeschichte in der Region,* Forum Suevicum: Beiträge zur Geschichte Ostschwabens und der benachbarten Regionen, 9 (Konstanz, 2012), 139–57.

Sonderegger, Stefan, 'Das erste Zinsbuch: Spiegel von Wirtschaft und Gesellschaft im Spätmittelalter', in Katrin Eberhard and Ursula Hasler (eds), *St. Katharinen: Frauenkloster, Bibliothek, Bildungsstätte – Gestern und Heute* (Herisau, 2013), 134–37.

Sonderegger, Stefan, 'The Financing Strategy of a Major Urban Hospital in the Late Middle Ages (St Gallen 15th Century)', in Francesco Ammannati (ed.), *Assistenza e solidarietà in Europa Secc. XIII–XVIII / Social Assistance and Solidarity in Europe from the 13th to the 18th Centuries: atti della "Quarantaquattresima Settimana di Studi", 22–26 aprile 2012*, Atti delle Settimane di Studi e altri Convegni, 44 (Florence: Florence University Press, 2013), 209–26.

Sonderegger, Stefan, *Aktive Grundherren und Bauern: Beziehungen zwischen Herren und Bauern im wirtschaftlichen Alltag im 14. bis 16. Jahrhundert*, forthcoming.

Sonderegger, Stefan, and Matthias Weishaupt, 'Spätmittelalterliche Landwirtschaft in der Nordostschweiz', *Appenzellische Jahrbücher*, 1987 (1988), 29–71.

'Sorenskriver', in Rolf Fladby, Steinar Imsen and Harald Winge (eds), *Norsk historisk Leksikon* (Oslo: Cappelen, 1974), 312–25.

Spindler, Max, 'Die Auseinandersetzungen mit Landeladel, Epiropat und Königtum unter den drei ersten wittelsbachischen Herzögen (1180–1253)', in Max Spindler (ed.), *Handbuch der bayerischen Geschichte* (Munich: C.H. Beck, 1966), ii, 11–72.

Sreenivasan, Govind P., 'Beyond the Village: Recent Approaches to the Social History of the Early German Peasantry', *History Compass*, 11/1 (2013), 47–64.

Stadler, Hans, 'Talschaft', in *Historischen Lexikon der Schweitz*. http://www.hls-dhs-dss.ch/textes/d/D26442.php.

Stamm, Volker, 'Kauf und Verkauf von Land und Grundrenten im hohen und späten Mittelalter: Eine Untersuchung zur historischen Wirtschaftsanthropologie', *VSWG*, 2009/1 (2009), 33–43.

Starzer, Anna, *Die gute alte Zeit auf dem Bauernhof: Aufzeichnungen einer Bäuerin* (Naarn, 1990).

'Stavnsbånd 1733–1800', in *Danmarkshistoriendk*. URL: http://danmarkshistorien.dk/leksikon-og-kilder/vis/materiale/stavnsbaand-1733-1800.

Štefanová, Dana, *Erbschaftspraxis, Besitz und Handlungsspielräume von Untertanen in der Gutsherrschaft* (Vienna: Oldenbourg, 2009).

Steinbrink, Matthias, *Ulrich Meltinger: Ein Basler Kaufmann am Ende des 15. Jahrhunderts*, VSWG Beiheft, 197 (Stuttgart: Steiner, 2007).

Steinnes, Asgaut, 'Kor gammal er den norske leidangsskipnaden?', *Syn og Segn*, 35 (1929), 49–65.

Stene, Erna, 'Økonomi og samfunn i Inntrøndelag i jernalderen. Storgårder og kirkesteder', *Årbok for Nord-Trøndelag Historielag* (1992).

Stenvik, Lars F., 'Skei – et maktsenter fram fra skyggen', *VITARK*, 2 (Trondheim: Vitenskapmuseet, NTNU, 2001).

Stettler, Bernhard, *Die Eidgenossenschaft im 15. Jahrhundert. Die Suche nach einem gemeinsamen Nenner* (Zurich: Widmar-Dean, 2004).

Stolz, Otto, *Geschichte der Gerichte Deutschtirol, Abhandlungen zum historischen Atlas der Österreichischen Alpenländer*, special print (Sonderdruck), Archiv für österreichische Geschichte, 102 (Vienna: Hölder, 1913).

Stolz, Otto, *Die Schwaighöfe in Tirol: Ein Beitrag zur Siedlungs- und Wirtschaftsgeschichte der Hochalpentäler*, Deutscher und Österreichischer Alpenverein, Wissenschaftliche Veröfentlichungen, 5 (1930).

Stolz, Otto, *Rechtsgeschichte des Bauernstandes und der Landwirtschaft in Tirol und Voralberg* (Bozen: Ferrari-Auer, 1949; repr. Hildesheim: Georg Olms Verlag, 1985).

Storli, Inger, '"Barbarians" of the North: Reflections on the Establishment of Courtyard Sites in North Norway', *Norwegian Archaeological Review*, 33/2 (2000), 98–100.

Storli, Inger, *Hålogaland før rikssamlingen: Politiske prosesser i perioden 200–900 e.Kr.*, Institutt for Sammenlignende Kulturforskning, Serie B, Skrifter, 123 (Oslo: Novus forlag, 2006).

Störmer, Wilhelm, 'Frümittelalterliche Grundherrschaft bayerischer Kirchen (8. – 10. Jahrhundert)', in Werner Rösener (ed.), *Strukturen der Grundherrschaft im frühen Mittelalter* (Göttingen: Vandenhoeck und Ruprecht, 1993), 377–88.

Störmer, Wilhelm, 'Grundherrschaften frühmittelalterlicher Klöster und Stifte im Wandel des Hochmittelalter', in Werner Rösener (ed.), *Grundherrschaft und bäuerliche Gesellschaft im Hochmittelalter* (Göttingen: Vandenhoeck und Ruprecht, 1995), 184–214.

Stunz, Holger R., 'Hospitäler im deutschsprachigen Raum im Spätmittelalter als Unternehmen für die "caritas": Typen und Phasen der Finanzierung', in Michael Matheus (ed.), *Funktions- und Strukturwandel spätmittelalterlicher Hospitäler im europäischen Vergleich*, Geschichtliche Landeskunde, 56 (Stuttgart, 2005), 129–59.

Sturluson, Snorri. See Snorri Sturluson under 'Primary Sources'.

Sunde, Jørn Øyrehagen, '"Fornuft og Erfarenhed". Framveksten av metodisk medvit i dansknorsk rett på 1700-talet', Dr. juris. dissertation, University of Bergen, Bergen, 2006.

Sutter, Andreas, 'Die Genese der direkten Demokratie – Aktuelle Debatten und wissenschaftliche Ergebnisse (part 1)', *Schweizerische Zeitschrift für Geschichte*, 62/3 (2012), 456–73.

Sutter, Claudia, 'Frankrüti, Berg SG: Wirtschafts- und Konfliktgeschichte eines spätmittelalterlichen Hofes unter dem Kloster St. Katharinen St. Gallen', Master's thesis, University of Zurich, Zurich, 2012.

Sutter, Pascale, *'Arme Siechen': Das St.Galler Siechenhaus Linsebühl im Spätmittelalter und in der frühen Neuzeit*, St Galler Kultur und Geschichte, 26 (St Gallen, 1996).

Tamm, Ditlev, et al., 'The Law and the Judicial System', in Eva Österberg and Sølvi Bauge Sogner (eds), *People Meet the Law: Control and Conflict-handling in the Courts* (Oslo: Universitetsforlaget 2000), 27–56.

Tanner, Albert, *Spulen – Weben – Sticken. Die Industrialisierung in Appenzell Ausserrhoden* (Zurich: Juris Druck, 1982).

Taranger, Absalon, 'De norske folkelovbøker', *Tidsskrift for Retsvidenskab*, 39, 41 (1926, 1928), 183–211, 1–68.

Tscharner-Aue, Michaela Von, *Die Wirtschaftsführung des Basler Spitals bis zum Jahre 1500: Ein Beitrag zur Geschichte der Löhne und Preise*, Quellen und Forschungen zur Basler Geschichte, 12 (Basel, 1983).

Tellenbach, Gerd, Königtum und Stämme in der Werdezeit des Deutschen Reiches (Weimar, 1939).

Teuscher, Simon, Erzähltes Recht: Lokale Herrschaft, Verschriftlichung und Traditionsbildung im Spätmittelalter, Campus Historische Studien, 44 (Frankfurt, 2007).

Thoma, Gertrud, 'Klosterbauern in Bayern und Tirol im Spätmittelalter', in Tore Iversen and John Ragnar Myking (eds), *Land, Lords and Peasants: Peasants' Right to Control Land in the Middle Ages and the Early Modern Period – Norway, Scandinavia and the Alpine Region*, Trondheim Studies in History, 52 (Trondheim: NTNU, 2005), 106–115.

Thoma, Gertrud, 'Klosterbauern zwischen Herrschaft und Genossenschaft – Die Hofmarkordnung von Seebruck auf dem Hintergrund der Gemeindeentwicklung in Bayern im Spätmittelalter', in Tore Iversen, John Ragnar Myking and Gertrud Thoma (eds), *Bauern zwischen Herrschaft und Genossenschaft: Peasant Relations to Lords and Government. Scandinavia and the Alpine Region 1000–1750* (Trondheim: Tapir Akademisk Forlag, 2007), 25–39.

Thommen, Heinrich, 'Uli Rotach im Kampf gegen zwölf Feinde. Ludwig Vogels Historiengemälde von 1829', *Appenzellische Jahrbücher* (2004), 59–75.

Tilly, Charles, 'Reflections on the History of European State-Making', in Charles Tilly (ed.), *The Formation of National States in Western Europe* (Princeton: Princeton University Press, 1975).

Tretvik, Aud Mikkelsen, "'... med mig tiltagne 2de edsvorne Lagrettemænd...'. Om bønders deltakelse i lokalforvaltningen på 1700-tallet", *Heimen*, 33 (1996), 189–200.

Trossbach, Werner, and Clemens Zimmermann, *Die Geschichte des Dorfes – von den Anfängen im Frankenreich zur bundesdeutschen Gegenwart* (Stuttgart: UTB, 2006).

Ulsig, Erik, 'Hoveri', in John Granlund (ed.), *Kulturhistoriskt lexikon för nordisk medeltid – från vikingatid till reformationstid*, 22 vols (Malmö: Allhem, 1956–78), vol. 21.

Ulsig, Erik, 'Landboer og bryder, skat og landgilde', in Karsten Fledelius, Niels Lund, and Herluf Nielsen (eds), *Middelalder, metode og medier: Festskrift til Niels Skyum-Nielsen* (Copenhagen: Museum Tusculanum, 1981).

Ulsig, Erik, 'Peasants Right To Control Land in Denmark', in Tore Iversen and John Ragnar Myking (eds), Land, Lords and Peasants: Peasants' Right To Control Land in the Middle Ages and the Early Modern Period – Norway, Scandinavia and the Alpine Region, Trondheim Studies in History, 52 (Trondheim: NTNU, 2005), 29–37.

Verhulst, Adriaan, 'Die Grundherrschaftsentwicklung im ostfränkischen Raum vom 8. Bis 10. Jahrhundert. Grundzüge und Fragen aus westfränkischer Sicht', in Werner Rösener (ed.), *Strukturen der Grundherrschaft im frühen Mittelalter* (Göttingen: Vandenhoeck und Ruprecht, 1989), 29–46.

Verhulst, Adriaan, 'Aspekte der Grundherrschaftsentwicklung des Hochmittelalters aus westeuropäischer Perspektiv', in Werner Rösener (ed.), *Grundherrschaft und bäuerliche Gesellsahft im Hochmittelalter* (Göttingen: Vandenhoeck und Ruprecht, 1995), 16–30.

Verlinden, Charles, 'Medieval Slavery in Europe and Colonial Slavery in America', in *The Beginnings of Modern Colonization: Eleven Essays with an Introduction* (Ithaca: Cornell University Press, 1970).

Verlinden, Charles, 'Wo und warum gab es einen Großhandel mit Sklaven im Mittelalter', *Vierteljahrschrift für Sozial- und Wirtschaftsgeschichte*, 66 (1979), 153–73.

Vervaet, Lies, 'Het Brugse Sint-Janshospitaal en zijn grote hoevepachters in de 15e en 16e eeuw: wederkerigheid en continuïteit in functie van voedselzekerheid', *Revue Belge de Philologie et d'Histoire / Belgisch Tijdschrift voor Filologie en Geschiedenis* 90/4 (2012), 1121–54.

Vervaet, Lies, 'Goederenbeheer in een veranderende samenleving Het Sint-Janshospitaal van Brugge ca. 1275–ca. 1575', PhD thesis, University of Ghent, Ghent, 2014.

'Vornedskab', *Den store danske*: Gyldendals åbne encyklopædi, http://www.denstoredanske.dk/Danmarks_geografi_og_historie/Danmarks_historie/Landbohistorie/vornedskap.

Walliser, Peter, 'Allod', in Marco Jorio (ed.), *Historisches Lexikon der Schweiz*, 13 vols (Basel: Schwabe, 2002–2014), https://hls-dhs-dss.ch/de/articles/008978/2002-06-04/.

Wallnöfer, Adelina, 'Die Bauern in der tiroler "Landschaft" vor 1500. Politische Aktivität der Gerichte und deren Repräsentanten auf den Landtagen', PhD dissertation, University of Innsbruck, Innsbruck, 1984.

Wallnöfer, Adelina, *Die politische Repräsentation des gemeinen Mannes in Tirol. Die Gerichte und ihre Vertreter auf den Landtagen vor 1500*, Veröffentlichungen des Südtiroler Landesarchivs – Pubblicazioni dell'Archivio provinciale di Bolzano, 41 (Innsbruck: Universitätsverlag Wagner, 2017.

Wartmann, Hermann, Traugott Schiess, Placid Bütler, and Paul Staerkle (eds), *Urkundenbuch der Abtei Sanct Gallen*, 6 vols (Zurich, 1863–1970).

Weishaupt, Matthias, *Bauern, Hirten und 'frume edle puren': Bauern und Bauernstaatsideologie in der spätmittelalterlichen Eidgenossenschaft und der nationalen Geschichtsschreibung der Schweiz* (Basel, Frankfurt am Main: Helbing & Lichtenhahn, 1992).

Weishaupt, Matthias, 'Hirten, "Bauern & Bürger" und Bauernsoldaten. Die ideologische Vereinnahmung der mittelalterlichen Bauern in der nationalen Geschichtsschreibung der Schweiz', in Albert Tanner and Anne-Lise Head-König (eds), *Die Bauern in der Geschichte der Schweiz*, Schweizerische Gesellschaft für Wirtschafts- und Sozialgeschichte, 10 (Zurich: Chronos, 1992), 23–39.

Weishaupt, Matthias, 'Uli Rotach. Faktum oder Fiktion?', in Peter Niederhäuser and Alois Niederstätter (eds), *Die Appenzellerkriege – eine Krisenzeit am Bodensee?*,

Forschungen zur Geschichte Vorarlbergs, Neue Folge, 7 (Konstanz: UVK Verlagsgesellschaft, 2006), 175–79.

Weitzel, Jürgen, 'Gericht', in Robert-Henri Bautier, et al. (eds), *Lexikon des Mittelalters*, 9 vols (Munich and Zurich: Artemis [vols 1–6] and LexMA-Verlag [vols 7–9], 1977–1999), iii, 1058.

Weitzel, Jürgen, 'Iudex', in Robert-Henri Bautier, et al. (eds), *Lexikon des Mittelalters*, 9 vols (Munich and Zurich: Artemis [vols 1–6] and LexMA-Verlag [vols 7–9], 1977–1999), v, 793–94.

Weitzel, Jürgen, 'Schöffe, -ngericht, -nbank', in Robert-Henri Bautier, et al. (eds), *Lexikon des Mittelalters*, 9 vols (Munich and Zurich: Artemis [vols 1–6] and LexMA-Verlag [vols 7–9], 1977–1999), vii, 1514–16.

Weitzel, Jürgen, *Dinggenossenschaft und Recht*, i: *Untersuchungen zum Rechtsverständnis im fränkisch-deutschen Mittelalter* (Cologne: Böhlau Verlag, 1985).

Weitzel, Jürgen, 'Schöffen', in Johannes Hoops and Heinreich Beck (eds), *Real-enzyklopädie der germanischen Altertumskunde* (Berlin, 1973–2015), xxvii, 233–36.

Wenskus, R., 'Ding', in Johannes Hoops and Heinreich Beck (eds), *Real-enzyklopädie der germanischen Altertumskunde* (Berlin, 1973–2015) v, 443–55.

Whittle, Jane, 'Leasehold Tenure in England *c.* 1300-*c.* 1600: Its Form and Incidence', in Bas J.P. van Bavel and Philipp R. Schofield (eds), *The Development of Leasehold in Northwestern Europe, c. 1200–1600*, (Turnhout: Brepols, 2008), 139–54.

Wickham, Chris, *Farming the Early Middle Ages: Europe and the Mediterranean 400–800* (Oxford: Oxford University Press, 2005).

Widgren, Mats, 'Hur drevs den vikingtida-medeltida storgården?: några frågor från Lägerbovada, Ydre' in Olof Karsvall and Kristofer Jupiter (eds), *Medeltida storgårdar: 15 uppsatser om ett tvärvetenskapligt forskningsproblem* (Uppsala: Gustav Adolfs akademien Acta Academiae Regiae Gustavi Adolphi, 2014), 59–72.

Wiesflecker, Hermann, *Meinhard der Zweite. Tirol, Kärnten und ihre Nachbarländer am Ende des 13. Jahrhunderts*, Schlern-Schriften, 124 (Innsbruck: Wagner, 1955 [unchanged reprint 1995]).

Wießner, Hermann, *Sachinhalt und wirtschaftliche Bedeutung der Weisthümer im deutschen Kulturgebiet* (Baden: Verlag Rudolf M. Rohrer, 1934), 259–61.

Wießner, Hermann, *Beiträge zur Geschichte des Dorfes und der Dorfgemeinde in Österreich*, (Klagenfurt: Kleinmyr, 1946).

Wohlhaupter, Eugen, *Hoch- und Niedergerichts in der mittelalterlichen Gerichtsverfassung Bayerns*, Deutschrechtliche Beiträge, 12/2 (Heidelberg: C. Winter, 1929).

Wolfram, Richard, *Studien zur älteren Schweizer Volkskultur – Mythos, Sozialordnung, Brauchbewusstsein*, Österreichische Akademie der Wissenschaften, Philos.-hist. Klasse, 362 (Vienna: Verlag de Akademie, 1980).

Wopfner, Hermann, *Von der Ehre und Freiheit des Tiroler Bauernstandes*, i: Von der Freiheit des Landes Tirol (Innsbruck, 1934).

Wopfner, Hermann, *Bergbauernbuch: von arbeit und leben des Tiroler Bergbauern in Vergangenheit und Gegenwart*, ed. Nikolaus Grass, Tiroler Wirtschaftsstudien, 47–49, 3 vols (Innsbruck: Wagner, 1995–97).

Wopfner, Hermann, *Tiroler Bauer und Tiroler Landesfreiheit*, Tiroler Heimatschriften, 1 (Innsbruck, n.d.).

Wretschko, Alfred, 'Über Eigenleute und Eigenleuteteilungen in Tirol', *Zeitschrift der Savigny-Stiftung für Rechtsgeschichte: Germanistische Abteilung*, 46 (1926), 366–74.

Wunder, Heide, *Die bäuerliche Gemeinde in Deutschland*, Kleine Vandenhoeck-Reihe 1483 (Göttingen: Vandenhoek und Ruprecht, 1986).

Zangger, Alfred, *Grundherrschaft und Bauern: Eine wirtschafts- und sozialgeschichtliche Untersuchung der Grundherrschaft der Prämonstratenserabtei Rüti (ZH) im Spätmittelalter* (Zurich, 1991).

Zangger, Alfred, 'Wirtschaft und Leben im Zürcher Oberland im 15. Jahrhundert', *Jahrheft der Ritterhausgesellschaft Bubikon*, 61 (1997), 14–35.

Zangger, Alfred, 'Alltagsbeziehungen zwischen Klosterherrschaft und Bauern am Beispiel des Prämonstratenserklosters Rüti im 15. Jahrhundert', in Thomas Meier and Roger Sablonier (eds), *Wirtschaft und Herrschaft. Beiträge zur ländlichen Gesellschaft in der östlichen Schweiz (1200–1800)*, (Zurich: Chronos, 1999), 295–309.

Zangger, Alfred, 'Wittenbach im Mittelalter', in Edgar Krayss, et al. (eds), *Wittenbach. Landschaft und Menschen im Wandel der Zeit* (Wittenbach, 2004), 47–146.

Zehetmayer, Roman, *Das Urbar des Grafen Burkhard III. von Maidburg-Hardegg aus dem Jahre 1363*, Fontes rerum Austriacarum, Abteilung 3, Fontes iuris 15 (Vienna: Böhlau, 2001).

Zeller, Bernhard, *Das Heilig-Geist-Spital zu Lindau im Bodensee, von seinen Anfängen bis zum Ausgang des 16. Jahrhunderts*, Schwäbische Geschichtsquellen und Forschungen, 4 (Lindau, 1952).

Zingerle, Ignaz V., K. Theodor von Inama-Sternegg, and Josef Egger (eds), *Die Tirolischen Weisthümer*, Österreichische Weisthümer, 4 vols (Vienna: Braumeuller, 1875–91).

'Zurich (Kanton)', in Marco Jorio (ed.), *Historisches Lexikon der Schweiz*, 13 vols (Basel: Schwabe, 2002–2014), xiii, 848–56.

Zwahlen, Adrian, *Die wirtschaftliche Entwicklung der Schoretshueb: Eine Mikrogeschichte zur spätmittelalterlichen Getreideproduktion in der spezialisierten Landwirtschaft der Nordostschweiz* (Zurich, 2012).

Index

www.ingramcontent.com/pod-product-compliance
Lightning Source LLC
LaVergne TN
LVHW010639300926
849161LV00005B/989